A Witches' Bible
The Complete Witches' Handbook

A Witches' Bible
The Complete Witches' Handbook

Janet and Stewart Farrar

ROBERT HALE

First published in 1981

This edition first published in Great Britain in 1997 by Robert Hale, an imprint of The Crowood Press Ltd, Ramsbury, Marlborough Wiltshire SN8 2HR

www. crowood.com

www.halebooks.com

This impression 2016

British Library Cataloguing-in-Publication Data
A catalogue record for this book is available from the British Library.

ISBN 978 0 7090 7227 0

The right of Janet and Stewart Farrar to be identified as authors of this work has been asserted by them in accordance with the Copyright, Designs and Patents Act 1988.

Printed and bound in India by Replika Press Pvt Ltd

Part 1

The Sabbats
and Rites for Birth, Marriage
and Death

also published separately as *Eight Sabbats for Witches*

with line illustrations by Stewart Farrar
and photographs by Ian David & Stewart Farrar

To our dear friend
KATH D'EATH, née CARTER
(1905–76)

"And ye shall meet, and know,
and remember,
and love them again."

"I wish there were some way of reconciling formal education and natural knowing. Our inability to do this is a terrible waste of one of our most valuable resources. There is a fund of knowledge, a different kind of information, common to all people everywhere. It is embodied in folklore and superstition, in mythology and old wives' tales. It has been allowed to persist simply because it is seldom taken seriously and has never been seen to be a threat to organized science or religion. It is a threat, because inherent in the natural way of knowing is a sense of rightness that in this time of transition and indecision could serve us very well."

Lyall Watson, *Gifts of Unknown Things*

"If we are to get out of the mess to which civilized ignorance has brought us, we must prepare ourselves, in some ways at least, for the return of paganism."

Tom Graves, *Needles of Stone*

Contents

Acknowledgements

We would like to thank Doreen Valiente for her invaluable help in providing information, for permission to reproduce several ritual passages which she herself wrote for Gardner's Book of Shadows, and for reading our manuscript before publication.

We are grateful to Messrs. Faber & Faber for permission to quote extensively from Robert Graves' *The White Goddess*.

We are also grateful to the Society of the Inner Light for permission to use passages from Dion Fortune's *The Sea Priestess* as part of our Handfasting Ritual.

Illustrations

PICTURE CREDITS

All photographs are by Ian David, with the
exception of Numbers 11 and 15, which are
by Stewart Farrar.

Introduction

Modern witchcraft, in Europe and America, is a fact. It is no longer an underground relic of which the scale, and even the existence, is hotly disputed by anthropologists. It is no longer the bizarre hobby of a handful of cranks. It is the active religious practice of a substantial number of people. Just how large a number is not certain, because Wicca, beyond the individual coven, is not a hierarchically organized religion. Where formal organizations do exist, as in the United States, this is for legal and tax reasons, not for dogmatic uniformity or the numbering of members. But the numbers are, for example, enough to support a variety of lively periodicals and to justify the publication of an ever-growing body of literature, on both sides of the Atlantic; so a reasonable estimate would be that the active adherents of Wicca now number tens of thousands, at the very least. And all the evidence suggests that the number is growing steadily.

Wicca is both a religion and a Craft—aspects which Margaret Murray has distinguished as "ritual witchcraft" and "operative witchcraft". As a religion—like any other religion, its purpose is to put the individual and the group in harmony with the Divine creative principle of the Cosmos, and its manifestations, at all levels. As a Craft, its purpose is to achieve practical ends by psychic means, for good, useful and healing purposes. In both aspects, the distinguishing characteristics of Wicca are its Nature-based attitude, its small-group autonomy with no gulf between priesthood and 'congregation', and its philosophy of creative polarity at all levels, from Goddess and God to Priestess and Priest.

This book is concerned with the first aspect—Wicca as a religion, ritually expressed.

Witches, on the whole, enjoy ritual—and they are naturally joyous people. Like worshippers of other religions, they find that appropriate ritual uplifts and enriches them. But their rituals tend to be more varied than other faiths', ranging from the formal to the spontaneous and differing also from coven to coven, according to their individual preferences and the schools of thought (Gardnerian, Alexandrian, 'Traditional', Celtic, Dianic, Saxon and so on) on which they have based themselves.

But as the twentieth-century Wiccan revival matures (and in many covens passes into its second generation), the inter-school acrimony which marred its early years has considerably diminished. Dogmatists still slang each other in the period- icals—but increasingly their dogmatism is condemned by other correspondents as pointlessly disruptive; and most ordinary covens are simply bored by it. The years have taught them that their own path works—and if (like our own coven) they have friends of other paths, they have also come to understand that *those* paths work too.

Out of this greater mutual tolerance has grown an increased awareness of Wicca's common basis, its essential spirit which has little to do with the details of form. Also, with the exchange of ideas both through the printed word and through more open personal contact, there is a growing body of shared tradition on which everyone may draw.

It is as a contribution to this growth that we offer our present book. To be valid, and useful, any such contribution must be a branch arising healthily out of the parent trunk of our racial history, as well as the specific forms of Wiccan practice as it now stands (in our case, the Gardnerian/Alexandrian forms); and this is what we have worked to achieve.

Fortunately, a framework exists which is common to all Wiccan paths, and indeed to many others: the Eight Festivals.

The modern witches' calendar (whatever their 'school') is rooted, like that of their predecessors through untold centuries, in Sabbats, seasonal festivals which mark key points in the natural year, for Wicca, as we have stressed, is a Nature-oriented religion and Craft. And since, for witches, Nature is a many-levelled reality, their 'natural year' includes many aspects—agricultural, pastoral, wildlife, botanical, solar, lunar, planetary, psychic—the tides and cycles of which all affect or reflect each other. The Sabbats are the witches' way of celebrating, and putting themselves in tune with, these tides and cycles. For men and women are also a part of many-levelled Nature; and witches strive, consciously and constantly, to express that unity.

The witches' Sabbats are eight:

IMBOLG, 2nd February (also called Candlemas, Oimelc, Imbolc).

SPRING EQUINOX, 21st March (Alban Eilir).

BEALTAINE, 30th April (Beltane, May Eve, Walpurgis Night, Cyntefyn, Roodmass).

MIDSUMMER, 22nd June (Summer Solstice, Alban Hefin; also sometimes called Beltane).

LUGHNASADH, 31st July (August Eve, Lammas Eve, Lady Day Eve).

AUTUMN EQUINOX, 21st September (Alban Elfed).

SAMHAIN, 31st October (Hallowe'en, All Hallows Eve, Calan Gaeaf).

YULE, 22nd December (Winter Solstice, Alban Arthan).

Of these, Imbolg, Bealtaine, Lughnasadh and Samhain are the 'Greater Sabbats'; the Equinoxes and Solstices are the 'Lesser Sabbats'. (The actual dates of Equinoxes and Solstices may vary by a day or two in traditional usage, and also from year to year in astronomical fact, while the Greater Sabbats tend to involve both the 'Eve' and the following 'Day'.) The solar-astronomical Lesser Sabbats are both older and newer than the natural-fertility Greater Sabbats—older, in that they were the highly sophisticated preoccupation of the mysterious Mega-lithic peoples who pre-dated Celt, Roman and Saxon on Europe's Atlantic fringe by thousands of years; newer, in that the Celts—perhaps the biggest single influence in giving to the Old Religion the actual ritual shape in which it has survived in the West—were not solar-oriented and celebrated only the Greater Sabbats, until what Margaret Murray has called the "solstitial invaders" (the Saxon and other peoples who swept westward with the decay of the Roman Empire) met and interacted with the Celtic tradition. And even they brought only the Solstices: "The Equinoxes," says Murray, "were never observed in Britain." (For some thoughts on how they subsequently entered British folklore, see page 72—and remember that, since Murray, more has been learned about Megalithic astronomy, which may well have left buried folk-memories to be revived later.)

All this is reflected in the fact that it is the Greater Sabbats which have Gaelic names. Of the various forms which witches use, we have chosen the Irish Gaelic ones, for personal and historical reasons—personal, because we live in Ireland, where those forms have living meanings; historical, because Ireland was the only Celtic country never to be absorbed by the Roman Empire, and so it is in Ireland's mythology and in her ancient language that the lineaments of the Old Religion can often be most clearly discerned.[1] Even the Celtic Church remained stubbornly independent of the Vatican for many centuries.[2]

---

1. Ireland virtually escaped the horrors of the witchcraft persecution. From the fourteenth to the eighteenth century only a handful of trials for witchcraft are recorded. "In England and Scotland during the mediaeval and later periods of its existence, witchcraft was an offence against the laws of God and man; in Celtic Ireland dealings with the unseen were not regarded with such abhorrence, and indeed had the sanction of custom and antiquity" (St John D. Seymour, *Irish Witchcraft and Demonology*, p. 4—and Seymour was a Christian theologian writing in 1913). Nor is there any evidence of torture being used to extract evidence in the few Irish witchcraft trials, except for the flogging in 1324 of Petronilla of Meath, Dame Alice Kyteler's servant, on the orders of the Bishop of Ossory, and that "seems to have been carried out in what may be termed a purely unofficial manner" (*ibid.*, pp. 18–19).

Moreover, Ireland is still predominantly agricultural and a community of human dimensions, where folk-memories still flourish that have elsewhere died in the concrete jungle. Scratch the topsoil of Irish Christianity, and you come at once to the bedrock of paganism. But the use of Irish Gaelic forms is only *our* choice, and we would not wish to impose it on anyone else.

Why have we written this book, with its detailed suggestions for Sabbat rituals, if we do not wish to 'impose' patterns upon other witches—which we most certainly do not?

We have written it because eight years of running our own coven has convinced us that some such attempt is needed. And we think it is needed because the Book of Shadows, Gerald Gardner's anthology of inherited rituals which—with Doreen Valiente's help—he linked together with modern elements to fill in the gaps and make a workable whole, is surprisingly inadequate in one aspect: the Eight Sabbats.

The modern Wiccan revival, so rapidly expanding, owes a tremendous debt to Gerald Gardner, however much he may have been criticized in certain respects. His Book of Shadows is the foundation-stone of the Gardnerian form of modern Wicca, and also of its Alexandrian offshoot; and it has had considerable influence on many Traditional covens. Doreen Valiente, too, deserves every witch's gratitude; some of her contributions to the Book of Shadows have become its best-loved passages—the Charge, for instance, the unique and definitive statement of Wiccan philosophy. But for some reason, the rituals which the Book lays down for the Eight Sabbats are very sketchy indeed—nothing like as full and satisfying as the rest. The summary which Stewart gave to them in Chapter 7 of *What Witches Do* (see Bibliography) would seem to include everything which Gardner had to say on them. Anything else was left to the covens' imagination and inventiveness.

Some witches may feel that this is enough. Wicca is, after all,

---

2. There is a tiny Russian Orthodox community in Ireland, based on exiles from Russia; interestingly, "it has attracted quite a number of Irish converts, some of whom regard it as the Irish Church which existed from before the arrival of St Patrick to the years following Henry's invasion and the establishment of the links with Rome" (*Sunday Press*, Dublin, 12th March 1978).

a natural and spontaneous religion, in which every coven is a law to itself, and rigid forms are avoided. Nothing is quite the same for two Circles running—and quite right too, or Wicca would fossilize. So why not leave these sketchy Sabbat rituals as they are, use them as a starting-point and let each Sabbat take its own course? Everyone knows the 'feel' of the seasons . . .

We feel that there are two reasons why this is *not* enough. First, the other basic rituals—casting the Circle, Drawing Down the Moon, the Charge, the Legend of the Descent of the Goddess, and so on—*are* all substantial, and newcomers and old hands alike find them moving and satisfying. The flexibility which a good High Priestess and High Priest bring to them, and the planned or spontaneous embellishments which they add, merely enhance the basic rituals and keep them vivid and alive. If they had been sketchy to begin with, would ordinary people have been able to make so much of them?

Second, in our urban civilization it is unfortunately not true that everyone knows the 'feel' of the seasons, except very superficially. Even many country-dwellers, with their cars and electricity and television and standardized market-town (or even village) supermarkets, are remarkably well insulated from the gut-feeling of Nature. The archetypal knowledge of the physical and psychic tides of the year, which made such concepts as the fraternal rivalry of the Oak King and Holly King and their sacrificial mating with the Great Mother (to take just one example) perfectly comprehensible to our ancestors— concepts which, together with their symbolism, are so astonishingly widespread in time and space that they *must* be archetypal: this knowledge is virtually lost to modern consciousness.

Archetypes cannot be eradicated, any more than bones or nerves can; they are as much part of us. But they can become so deeply buried that it takes deliberate effort to re-establish healthy and fruitful communication with them.

Most people's awareness of the seasonal rhythms today is limited to such surface manifestations as Christmas cards, Easter eggs, sunbathing, autumn leaves and overcoats. And to be honest, the Book of Shadows' Sabbat rituals go very little deeper.

To return to ourselves. Ours is an Alexandrian coven—if we

must tie a label round our necks, for we are unsectarian by temperament and principle and prefer simply to call ourselves 'witches'. We have many Gardnerian and Traditional friends and regard their ways as just as valid as ours. We were initiated and trained by Alex and Maxine Sanders, founded our own coven in London at Yule 1970 and thereafter followed our own judgement (at one stage defying an order to disband the coven and return to Alex for 'further instruction'). We have seen ourselves referred to as 'reformed' Alexandrians—which has some truth, in that we have learned to sort out the undeniable wheat from the regrettable chaff. Other covens, and solo witches, have hived off from ours in the normal process of growth, and since we moved from crowded London to the fields and mountains of Ireland in April 1976 we have built up yet others; so our experience has been varied.

Our coven is organized on the customary Gardnerian/ Alexandrian lines; namely, it is based on the polarity of psychic femaleness and maleness. It consists, as far as possible, of 'working partnerships', each of one female and one male witch. Working partners may be a married couple, lovers, friends, brother and sister, parent and child; it does not matter whether or not their relationship is a sexual one. What matters is their psychic *gender*, so that in magical working they are two poles of a battery. The senior working partnership is, of course, that of the High Priestess and High Priest. She is *prima inter pares*, first among equals; the High Priest is her complementary equal (otherwise their 'battery' would produce no power), but she is the leader of the coven and he the 'Prince Consort'.

This question of the matriarchal emphasis in Wicca has been the cause of considerable argument, even among witches—with everything from cave paintings to Margaret Murray being used as ammunition in attempts to prove what used to be done, what is the 'true' tradition. Such evidence, honestly examined, is of course important—but we feel it is not the whole answer. More attention should be paid to the role of the Old Religion in today's conditions; in short, to what works best *now*, as well as to those factors which are timeless. And as we see it, the matriarchal emphasis is justified on both these counts.

First, the timeless aspect. Wicca, by its very nature, is concerned especially with the development and use of 'the gift of the Goddess'—the psychic and intuitive faculties—and to a rather lesser degree with 'the gift of the God'—the linear-logical, conscious faculties. Neither can function without the other, and the gift of the Goddess must be developed and exercised in both male and female witches. But the fact remains that, *on the whole*, woman has a flying start with the gift of the Goddess, just as man *on the whole* has a flying start with muscle. And within the Circle the High Priestess (though she calls upon her High Priest to invoke it) is the channel and representative of the Goddess.

This is not just Wiccan custom, it is a fact of Nature. "A woman," says Carl Jung, "can identify directly with the Earth Mother, but a man cannot (except in psychotic cases)." (*Collected Works, volume IX, part 1*, 2nd edition, para. 193.) On this point, Wiccan experience fully supports that of clinical psychology. If Wiccan emphasis is on the gift of the Goddess (supported and energized by the gift of the God), then in practice it must also be on the Priestess (supported and ener-gized by the Priest). (For a deeper study of this magical rela-tionship, read any of Dion Fortune's novels—especially *The Sea Priestess* and *Moon Magic*.)

Second, the 'now' aspect—the requirements of our present stage of evolution. A whole book could be written on this; here, we can only over-simplify history considerably—but without, we believe, distorting its basic truth. By and large, until three or four thousand years ago the human race lived (like other animals though at a much complex level) by 'the gift of the Goddess'; in psychological terms, human activity was domin-ated by the promptings of the subconscious mind, conscious-ness being still on the whole secondary. Society was generally matrilinear (acknowledging descent through the mother) and often also matriarchal (woman-governed), with the emphasis on the Goddess, the Priestess, the Queen, the Mother.[3] "Before

---

3. Ancient Egypt was a copybook example of the transition stage; it was matrilinear but patriarchal, both royalty and property passing strictly through the female line. All the male Pharaohs held the throne *because they were married to the heiress*: "The queen was queen by right of birth, the king was king by right of marriage" (Margaret Murray, *The Splendour that was Egypt*, p. 70), hence the Pharaonic habit of marrying sisters and daughters to retain the right to the throne. Matrilinear inheritance was the rule at all levels of society and

civilization sets in, the earth is one universal deity . . . a living
creature; a female, because it receives the power of the sun, is
animated thereby and made fertile. . . . The oldest and deepest
element in any religion is the cult of the earth spirit in her many
aspects." (John Michell, *The Earth Spirit*, p. 4.) To this should
be added—certainly as mankind's awareness increased—the
Queen of Heaven aspect too; for, to humanity in this phase, the
Great Mother was the womb and nourisher of the whole
cosmos, matter and spirit alike. [1]

We must emphasize that this interpretation is *not* a backstairs
way of introducing any idea of 'female intellectual inferiority'.
On the contrary, as Merlin Stone points out (*The Paradise
Papers*, p. 210), the Goddess-worshipping cultures produced
"inventions in methods of agriculture, medicine, architecture,
metallurgy, wheeled vehicles, ceramics, textiles and written
language"—in which women played a full part (sometimes, as
with the introduction of agriculture, the leading one). It would
be truer to say that the developing intellect was a tool for making
the most of what was natural, instead of (as it became later) all
too often for distorting or crushing it.

But the long climb to consciousness was accelerating—and
suddenly (in terms of the evolutionary time-scale) the conscious
mind was launched on its meteoric rise to dictatorship over
mankind's affairs and environment. Inevitably, this was
expressed in patriarchal monotheism—the rule of the God, the
Priest, the King, the Father. (In the Mediterranean cradle of
civilization, the carriers of this new outlook were the patri-

---

persisted to the very end; that was why first Julius Caesar and then Antony
married Cleopatra, the last Pharaoh—it was the only way they could be
acknowledged as rulers of Egypt. Octavius (Augustus Caesar) offered to
marry her too, after Antony's defeat and death, but she preferred suicide
(*ibid.*, pp. 70–71). Rome confronted the same principle a century later at the
other end of its Empire, in Britain, when Roman flouting of it (whether
clumsy or deliberate) provoked the furious revolt of the Celtic Iceni under
Boudicca (Boadicea). (See Lethbridge's *Witches*, pp. 79–80.)
4. Kalderash Gypsies (one of the three main Romany groups) maintain that *O
Del*, The (masculine) God, did not create the world. "The earth (*phu*), that is,
the universe, existed before him; it always existed. 'It is the mother of all of us'
(*amari De*) and is called *De Develeski*, the Divine Mother. In this one recognizes a trace of the primitive matriarchy." (Jean-Paul Clébert, *The Gypsies*, p.
134.)

linear, God-worshipping Indo-European peoples who conquered or infiltrated the indigenous matrilinear, Goddess-
worshipping cultures; for the history of the take-over, and its
effect on religion and the subsequent relationship between the
sexes, Ms Stone's *Paradise Papers*, quoted above, is well worth
reading.) It was a necessary, if bloodily tragic, stage in
mankind's evolution; and it involved, equally inevitably, a
certain shelving—often a vigorous Establishment suppression—of the free exercise of the gift of the Goddess.

This is over-simplification enough to make a historian's hair
stand on end, but food for thought. And here is more. That
stage of evolution is over. The development of the conscious
mind (certainly in the best examples available to mankind) has
reached its peak. Our next evolutionary task is to revive the gift
of the Goddess at full strength *and combine the two*—with
unimaginable prospects for the human race and the planet we
live on. God is not dead; he is a grass-widower, awaiting the
readmission of his exiled Consort. And if Wicca is to play its
part in this, a special emphasis *on that which is to be reawakened* is
a practical necessity, in order to restore the balance between the
two Gifts.[5]

For balance it is, and must be, which is why we emphasize
both the essential equality of man and woman in a Wiccan
working partnership *and* the advisability of the High Priestess's
being recognized as 'first among equals' in her own relationship with her High Priest and the coven—a delicate balance
with some partnerships, but our own experience (and our
observation of other covens) convinces us that it is worth
pursuing.

One might also point out that in this time of spiritual turmoil
and wide-spread religious re-assessment, Catholicism,

---

5. As this book was going to press, we read Annie Wilson's newly published
book *The Wise Virgin*. In her Section Four, "The Heart of the Matter", she
deals in depth with this question of the evolution of consciousness and has
some very perceptive things to say about its psychological, spiritual and sexual
(in the widest sense) implications. She, too, concludes that a new synthesis, of
excitingly creative potential, is not only possible but urgently necessary if we
in the West "are to balance our acute lopsidedness". This is very helpful
reading for a deeper understanding of the nature, function and relationship of
male and female.

Judaism, Islam and much of Protestanism still stubbornly cling to the male monopoly of priesthood as 'divinely ordained'; the Priestess is still banned, to the great spiritual impoverishment of mankind. This balance, too, Wicca can help to redress. And every active Wiccan Priestess knows from her own experience how great is the vacuum to be filled—indeed, there are times when it is difficult not to be overwhelmed by it (even, let it be whispered, times when priests and ministers of other religions come to her unofficially for help, frustrated by their own lack of female colleagues).

After that necessary digression—back to the structure of the coven.

The ideal of a coven consisting entirely of working partnerships is, of course, seldom achieved; there will always be one or two unpartnered members.

One woman member is appointed as the Maiden; she is in effect an assistant High Priestess for ritual purposes—though not necessarily in the sphere of leadership and authority. The role of the Maiden varies from coven to coven, but most find it useful to have one, to play a particular role in the rituals. (The Maiden usually—in our coven, anyway—has her own working partner just like any other coven member.)

In this book, we have assumed the above structure—High Priestess, High Priest, Maiden, some working partnerships and one or two unpartnered members.

As for the Sabbats—in our own coven we began, as one might expect, by taking the Book of Shadows as each one came up, applying a little on-the-spot inventiveness to the limited material it gave and letting it develop into a coven party. (Let us be quite clear about that, lest all this serious analysis mislead anybody: every Sabbat *should* develop into a party.) But over the years we began to find this inadequate. Eight good parties, each starting off with a bit of partly inherited and partly spontaneous ritual, were not enough to express the joy, mystery and magic of the turning year, or the ebb and flow of the psychic tides which underlie it. They were like eight little tunes, pleasant but separate, when what we really wanted was eight movements of one symphony.

So we began to delve and study, to seek out seasonal clues in everything from Robert Graves's *White Goddess* to Ovid's *Fasti*, from books on folklore customs to theories about stone circles, from Jungian psychology to weather lore. Archaeological holidays in Greece and Egypt, and fortunate professional visits to the Continent, helped to widen our horizons. Above all, perhaps, moving into the country, surrounded by plants, trees, crops, animals and weather of practical concern to us, brought us face-to-face with manifested Nature in our daily lives; her rhythms began to be truly our rhythms.

We tried to discover the yearly pattern behind all this and to apply what we learned to our Sabbat rituals. And as we did so, the Sabbats began to come to life for us.

We tried always to *extract* a pattern, not to *impose* one; and extracting it is not easy. It is a complex task, because Wicca[6] is an integral part of the Western pagan tradition; and the roots of that tradition spread wide, from the Norse lands to the Middle East and Egypt, from the steppes to the Atlantic seaboard. To emphasize one strand of the web (say the Celtic, the Norse or the Greek) and to use its particular forms and symbols, because you are in tune with them, is reasonable and even desirable; but to *isolate* that one strand, to attempt to reject the others as alien to it, is as unrealistic and doomed to failure as trying to

---

6. Like most modern witches, we call the Craft 'Wicca'. This has become a well-established, and much-loved, usage, and there is every reason why it should continue—but we might as well be honest and admit that it is in effect a *new* word, mistakenly derived. The Old English for 'witchcraft' was *wicca-craeft*, not *wicca*. *Wicca* meant 'a male witch' (feminine *wicce*, plural *wiccan*), from the verb *wiccian*, 'to bewitch, to practise witchcraft', which the *Oxford English Dictionary* says is "of obscure origin". For the OED, the trail seems to stop there; but Gardner's assertion that Wicca (or, as he spells it, Wica) means "the Craft of the Wise" is supported by Margaret Murray, who wrote the *Encyclopaedia Britannica* (1957) entry on Witchcraft. "The actual meaning of this word 'witch' is allied with 'wit', *to know*." Robert Graves (*The White Goddess*, p. 173), discussing the willow which in Greece was sacred to Hecate, says: "Its connexion with witches is so strong in Northern Europe that the words 'witch' and 'wicked' are derived from the same ancient word for willow, which also yields 'wicker'." To complete the picture, 'wizard' did mean 'a wise one', being derived from the Late Middle English *wys* or *wis*, 'wise'. But 'warlock', in the sense of 'a male witch', is Scottish Late Middle English and entirely derogatory; its root means 'traitor, enemy, devil'; and if the very few modern male witches who call themselves warlocks realized its origin, they would join the majority and share the title 'witch' with their sisters.

unscramble one parent's genes from a living offspring. The Old Religion, too, is a living organism. Its spirit is timeless, and the sap that runs in its veins does not change—but at any one time and place, it is at a particular stage of growth. You can put yourself in tune with that growth, encourage and contribute to it and influence its future; but you are asking for trouble and disappointment if you distort or misrepresent it.

We have already pointed out that the Eight Sabbats reflect two distinct themes, with different though interacting historical roots: the solar theme and the natural-fertility theme. They are no longer separable, but each must be understood if both are to be fitted into our 'symphony'.

It seemed to us that a key to this understanding was to recognize that two concepts of the God-figure were involved. The Goddess is always there; she changes her aspect (both in her fecundity cycle as the Earth Mother and in her lunar phases as the Queen of Heaven), but she is ever-present. But the God, in both concepts, dies and is reborn.

This is fundamental. The concept of a sacrificed and resurrected God is found everywhere, back to the dimmest hints of prehistory; Osiris, Tammuz, Dionysos, Balder and Christ are only some of his later forms. But you will search in vain throughout the history of religion for a sacrificed and resurrected Goddess—seasonally lost to view, perhaps, like Persephone, but sacrificed, never. Such a concept would be religiously, psychologically and naturally unthinkable.[7]

Let us look, then, at these two God-themes.

The Sun-God figure, which dominates the Lesser Sabbats of solstices and equinoxes, is comparatively simple; his cycle can be observed even through the window of a high-rise flat. He dies and is reborn at Yule; begins to make his young maturity felt, and to impregnate Mother Earth with it, around the Spring

---

7. We have come across only one apparent exception to this rule. On p. 468 of *The Golden Bough* Frazer says: "In Greece the great goddess Artemis herself appears to have been annually hanged in effigy in her sacred grove of Condylea among the Arcadian hills, and there accordingly she went by the name of the Hanged One." But Frazer missed the point. 'Hanged Artemis' is no sacrifice—she is an aspect of the Spider Goddess Arachne/Ariadne/Arianrhod/ (Aradia?), who descends to aid us on her magic thread, and whose spiral web is the key to rebirth. (See James Vogh, *The Thirteenth Zodiac*.)

Equinox; blazes at the peak of his glory at Midsummer; resigns himself to waning power, and waning influence on the Great Mother, around the Autumn Equinox; and again faces Yuletide death and rebirth.

The natural-fertility theme is more complex; it involves *two* God-figures—the God of the Waxing Year (who appears time and again in mythology as the Oak King)[8] and the God of the Waning Year (the Holly King). They are the light and dark twins, each the other's 'other self', eternal rivals eternally conquering and succeeding each other. They compete eternally for the favour of the Great Mother; and each, at the peak of his half-yearly reign, is sacrificially mated with her, dies in her embrace and is resurrected to complete his reign.

'Light and dark' do not mean 'good and evil'; they mean the expansive and contractive phases of the yearly cycle, each as necessary as the other. From the creative tension between the two of them, and between them on the one hand and the Goddess on the other, life is generated.

This theme in fact overflows into the Lesser Sabbats of Yule and Midsummer. At Yule the Holly King ends his reign and falls to the Oak King; at Midsummer the Oak King in turn is ousted by the Holly King.

This is a book of suggested rituals, not a work of detailed historical analysis; so it is not the place to explain in depth just how we extracted the above pattern. But we believe that anyone who studies Western mythology with an open mind will inevitably reach the same general conclusions; and most witches will probably recognize the pattern already.

(Some of them may quite reasonably ask: "Where does our Horned God fit into this?" The Horned God is a natural-fertility figure; the roots of his symbolism go back to totemic and hunting epochs. He is Oak King *and* Holly King, the complementary twins seen as one complete entity. We would suggest that Oak King and Holly King are a subtlety which developed in amplification of the Horned God concept as vegetation became more important to man. They did not abolish him—they merely increased our understanding of him.)

---

8. Also doubtless relatable to the Green Man or Foliate Mask whose carved features appear in so many old churches.

At the beginning of each Section of this book, we give more details of the background to each Sabbat and explain how we have used it to devise our ritual.

But to help to make the overall pattern clearer, we have tried to summarize it in the diagram on p. 26. It *is* only a summary, but we have found it helpful, and we hope that other people will too.

One or two comments on it are necessary. First, the 'aspects of the Goddess'—Birth, Initiation, Consummation, Repose and Death—are those suggested in Graves's *White Goddess*. (Robert Graves's writings, and those of Doreen Valiente, have been of more help to us in our research than perhaps any others.) It should be emphasized again that these do not mean the birth and death of the Goddess herself (an unthinkable concept, as we have pointed out) but the face which she shows to the God and to her worshippers as the year turns. She does not *undergo* the experiences so much as *preside* over them.

Second, the placing of the sacrificial mating and rebirth of Oak King and Holly King, at Bealtaine and Lughnasadh respectively, may seem a little arbitrary. Because this cycle is a fertility one, the actual spacing of its rhythm varies from region to region; naturally so, because the calendars of a Scottish Highland croft and an Italian vineyard (for example) do not keep exact step with each other. The two sacrifices appear at various times in the Spring and Autumn; so in devising a coherent cycle of Sabbats, a choice had to be made. Bealtaine seemed the obvious choice for the Oak King's mating; but the Holly King's (even confining ourselves to the Greater Sabbats, as seemed fitting) could be either Lughnasadh or Samhain—at both of which traces of it are to be found. One reason why we settled for Lughnasadh was that Samhain (Hallowe'en) is already so charged with meaning and tradition that to incorporate the Holly King's sacrifice, mating and rebirth in its ritual would overload it to the point of confusion. Each Sabbat, however complex its overtones, should have a central theme and a clear message. Again, the Holly King's sacrifice is also that of the Corn King—a stubbornly indestructible folk-theme, as many symbolic customs indicate;[9] and Lughnasadh, not

9. Read *Harvest Home* by Thomas Tryon—a terrifying but discerning novel, now made into a very good film.

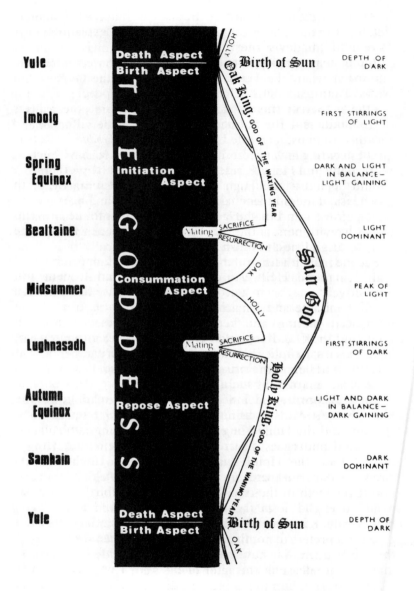

Samhain, marks the harvest. Finally, we have tried wherever possible to include in our suggested rituals the essentials of the Book of Shadows rites; and that for Lughnasadh, cryptic though it is, does point to this interpretation. It is the only occasion when the High Priestess invokes the Goddess into herself, instead of the High Priest doing it for her, a hint perhaps that at this Sabbat she is even more powerfully in command, and the Sacrificial God even more vulnerable? It seemed so to us.

In deciding how to cast male witches for the roles of Sun God, Oak King and Holly King, we were governed by two considerations: (1) that the High Priestess, as representative of the Goddess, has only one 'consort'—her working partner, the High Priest—and that any ritual which symbolizes her mating must be with him; and (2) that it is not practicable or desirable for the High Priest to finish any ritual symbolically 'dead', since he is the male leader of the coven under the High Priestess and must, so to speak, be restored to availability in the course of the ritual.

At Bealtaine and Lughnasadh, therefore—the two rites of sacrificial mating and rebirth—we have the High Priest enacting the Oak King and Holly King, respectively. In each case the ritual implies his mating with the Great Mother, and his 'death'; and before the ritual drama ends, he is reborn. The Sun God is not enacted, as such, at these Sabbats.

At Midsummer and Yule, however, all three God-aspects are involved. At Midsummer, the Sun God is at the peak of his power, and the Holly King 'slays' the Oak King. At Yule, the Sun God undergoes death and rebirth, and the Oak King in turn 'slays' the Holly King. On these two occasions, the Goddess does not mate, she presides; and at Yule, in addition, she gives birth to the renewed Sun God. So for these two, we have the High Priest enacting the Sun God, while the Oak King and Holly King are ritually chosen by lot (unless the High Priestess prefers to nominate them) and crowned for their roles by the Maiden. We have been careful to include in each ritual the formal release of the actor of the slain King from his role (thus restoring him to his place in the coven for the rest of the Sabbat), and also an explanation of what happens to the spirit of the slain King during his coming half-year of eclipse.

This book is about the Sabbats. But Esbats (non-Festival meetings) and Sabbats have one thing in common: they are all held within a Magic Circle, which is ritually set up, or 'cast', at the beginning of the meeting and ritually dispersed, or 'banished', at the end. These opening and closing rituals, even within the Gardnerian/Alexandrian tradition, tend to vary in detail from coven to coven and may also vary from occasion to occasion in the same coven, according to the work to be done and the High Priestess's intuitive or conscious decision. Nevertheless, each coven has its basic opening and closing rituals, however flexible; and it will use these at Esbats and Sabbats alike. Usually the opening ritual includes, in addition to the actual casting of the Circle, 'Drawing Down the Moon' (invocation of the spirit of the Goddess into the High Priestess by the High Priest) and the recital of the Charge (the traditional address of the Goddess to her followers).

Another common feature of all eight Sabbats, as laid down by the Book of Shadows, is the Great Rite, the ritual of male-female polarity enacted by the High Priestess and High Priest.

Since this book consists of *our* detailed suggestions for the eight Sabbat rituals, it would therefore be incomplete if we did not also present *our* particular way of carrying out the Opening Ritual, the Great Rite and the Closing Ritual. So we have included them as Sections I, II and III. We do not suggest that ours are 'better' than other covens'; but they are at least in the same style as our suggested Sabbat rituals, thus putting the latter in context instead of leaving them topless and tailless. Also, we hope that some covens will find it useful to have a form for the symbolic Great Rite, which the Book of Shadows fails to give.

We hope it is no longer necessary at this late stage to defend ourselves against the charge of 'betraying secrets' by publishing our versions of the Opening, Closing and Great Rite rituals. The basic Gardnerian rituals have been 'in the public domain' for many years now; and so many versions of these particular three (some garbled, and at least one—by Peter Haining—shamelessly black) have been published, that we make no apology for offering what we feel to be coherent and workable ones.

Besides, with the publication of Doreen Valiente's *Witchcraft for Tomorrow*, the Wiccan situation has changed. On the principle that 'you have a right to be a pagan if you want to be', she has decided "to write a book which will put witchcraft within the reach of all" (and no one is better qualified to take that decision than the co-author of the Book of Shadows). *Witchcraft for Tomorrow* includes a *Liber Umbrarum*, her completely new and very simple Book of Shadows for people who want to initiate themselves and organize their own covens. Already, like Gardner before her, she is being both praised and attacked for her initiative. For ourselves, we welcome it wholeheartedly. Since Stewart published *What Witches Do*, nine years ago, we have been (and still are) flooded with letters from people asking to be put in touch with a coven in their locality. Most of them we have been unable to help, especially as they are scattered all round the world. In future we shall refer them to *Witchcraft for Tomorrow*. The need is genuine, widespread and growing; and to leave it unsatisfied for reasons of alleged 'secrecy' is negative and unrealistic.

Interestingly, what Doreen Valiente has done for Gardnerian Wicca in *Witchcraft for Tomorrow*, Raymond Buckland has also done for another tradition, Saxon Wicca, in *The Tree, The Complete Book of Saxon Witchcraft* (see Bibliography). That, too, includes a simple but comprehensive Book of Shadows and procedures for self-initiation and the founding of your own coven. We found many of the rituals in *The Tree* admirable, though we were less happy about its eight Festival rites, which are even scantier than those in the Gardnerian Book of Shadows, and amount to little more than brief spoken declamations; they are based on the idea that the Goddess rules the summer, from Bealtaine to Samhain, and the God the winter, from Samhain to Bealtaine—a concept to which we cannot attune ourselves. Persephone, who withdraws to the underworld in winter, is only one aspect of the Goddess—a fact which her legend emphasizes by making her the *daughter* of the Great Mother.

However, to each his own; it is presumptuous to be too dogmatic, from the outside, about other traditions of the Craft. What matters is that anyone who wants to follow the Wiccan path but cannot get in touch with an established coven, now has *two* valid Wiccan traditions open to him in published form. What he makes of them depends on his own sincerity and determination—but that would be equally true if he joined an established coven in the normal way.

Referring again to *What Witches Do*, there is one apology Stewart *would* like to make. When he wrote it, as a first-year witch, he included material which he then understood to be either traditional or originating from his teachers. He now knows that much of it was in fact written for Gardner by Doreen Valiente. She has been kind enough to say: "I of course accept that you did not know this when you published them; how could you?" So we are glad, this time round, to have the opportunity to put the record straight. And we are grateful to her for having read this manuscript before publication, at our request, to make sure that we have neither quoted her without acknowledgement nor misquoted her. (A similar apology, by the way, to the shade of the late Franz Bardon.)

Doreen's help has given us another reason for including the Opening, Great Rite and Closing rituals as well as the eight Festivals; it has enabled us to give definitive answers to most (we hope) of the questions that people have been asking for the past quarter-century about the sources of the various elements in the Book of Shadows (or at least those sections of it within the scope of this book) and the circumstances of its compiling. We believe it is time for this to be done. The confusion and mis-representation (sometimes innocent, sometimes deliberate) has gone on long enough, leading even such a distinguished occult historian as our friend Francis King to arrive at mistaken—if understandable—conclusions about it.

To clarify sources and origins is *not* to 'take the mystery out of the Mysteries'. The Mysteries cannot, by their nature, ever be fully described in words; they can only be experienced. But they can be invoked and activated by effective ritual. One must never confuse the words and actions of ritual with the Mystery itself. The ritual is not the Mystery—it is a way of contacting and experiencing it. To plead 'safeguarding the Mysteries' as an excuse for falsifying history and concealing plagiarism is wrong, and a disservice both to the Mysteries themselves and to those whom you teach. That includes, for example, claiming to have copied the Book of Shadows from your grandmother many years before it was in fact compiled, or dictating other teachers' work to trusting students as your own.

The rituals in this book are given as for indoor working, but they can all be easily adapted for outdoor working where this is happily possible. For example, candles can be lit in lanterns or jars, and bonfires lit where suitable and safe. (If you work skyclad—that is, naked—a bonfire helps!)

Because each of these rituals is performed only once a year, obviously no one is going to know them by heart in the way that Esbat rituals are known. So the declamations at least will be read from the script. Eyesight varies, so it is up to the person concerned whether, and when, to pick up one of the altar candles to read by—or, if he or she needs both hands, to call another witch to hold it. To save repetition, we have not referred to this except where experience has taught us it is particularly necessary; for example, when the High Priestess drapes a veil over her face (at which times, incidentally, provided the veil is long enough, she should hold the script *inside* it).

We have found it a great help, wherever possible, to have a brief rehearsal beforehand. It need take only five minutes, before the Circle is cast. No declamations are read; all that is required is for the High Priest or High Priestess to have the script in his or her hand, and to run quickly through the sequence, explaining, "Then I do this, and you do that, while she stands over there . . ." and so on, to make sure that everybody has the basic sequence and any key movements clear. This does not detract from the ritual itself; in fact, it makes it run much more smoothly when the time comes and avoids excessive 'sheepdogging' or worrying about possible mistakes.

We have added the third part of the book—"Birth, Marriage and Death"—because, again, we feel there is a need for it. Alongside the universal rhythm of the seasons, runs the rhythm of our individual lives. Every religion feels the need for a sacramental acknowledgement of the milestones in those lives—the welcoming of new children, the joining together of man and wife, the solemn valediction to dead friends. Wicca is no exception, yet the Gardnerian Book of Shadows offers no ritual for any of them. So we give our own versions of the

Wiccaning, Handfasting and Requiem, in the hope that other people may find them useful.

Postscript to 1985 Reprint

Since this book was published, our later book *The Witches' Way* has appeared (Robert Hale Ltd., 1984). As well as giving an overall survey of Craft practice, it completes the task we began here—of establishing (again with Doreen Valiente's help) the exact form and wording of Gardner's rituals, from his original manuscripts in Doreen's possession. For example, it includes his own fuller version of the Great Rite, and all the non-ritual passages of his Book of Shadows.

We hope that readers will find it a helpful complementary volume to the present one.

This book was written in Ballycroy, Co. Mayo, on Ireland's Atlantic coast. But since then, our work has required us to move closer to Dublin. We can be written to at the address below.

JANET FARRAR
STEWART FARRAR

Barfordstown Lodge,
Kells,
Co. Meath, Ireland.

Bealtaine 1985

The Frame

I   The Opening Ritual

With this basic Wiccan ritual, we set up our Temple—our place of worship and magical working. It may be in a living-room with the furniture pushed back; it may be, if we are lucky enough to have one, in a room which is set aside for the purpose and used for no other; it may be, weather and privacy permitting, in the open air. But wherever we hold our Sabbat, this (in one form or another) is its essential beginning, just as the Closing Ritual given in Section III is its essential ending.

The Opening Ritual is the same for each of the Sabbats; where there are differences of detail, or of the furnishing or decorating of the Temple, these will be indicated at the beginning of each Sabbat Section.

The Preparation

The Circle area is cleared and an altar set up at the Northern point of its circumference. (See Plate 1.) This altar may be a small table (a coffee-table is ideal) or merely a cloth laid on the floor. Arranged on the altar are:

> the pentacle in the centre
> the North candle, behind the pentacle
> a pair of altar candles, one at each side
> the chalice of red wine or of mead
> the wand
> the scourge of silken cords
> a small bowl of water
> a small bowl with a little salt in it
> the cords (red, white and blue, nine feet long each)
> the white-handled knife
> each witch's individual athame (black-handled knife)
> the incense-burner
> a small hand-bell
> a dish of cakes or biscuits
> the sword, on the floor in front of the altar, or on the altar itself.

A supply of the chosen incense, and matches or a cigarette-lighter, should be handy by the altar. (We find a taper useful for carrying flame from candle to candle.)

A candle is placed at each of the East, South and West points of the circumference of the Circle, completing the four 'elemental' candles which must burn throughout the ritual. (The elemental placings are East, Air; South, Fire; West, Water; and North, Earth.)

Music should be available. For ourselves, we have built up a small library of C-120 cassettes of suitable music, transferred from discs or other cassettes, with each piece of music repeated as often as necessary to fill the whole sixty minutes of one track. Cassettes are ideal, because they can be played on anything from stereo hi-fi, if your living-room has it, to a portable player if you are meeting elsewhere. It is a good idea to adjust the volume to suit the loudest passages *before* the ritual, otherwise you may be unexpectedly deafened and have to fiddle with it at an inappropriate moment.

Make sure the room is warm enough well in advance—especially if, like ourselves and most Gardnerian/Alexandrian covens, you normally work skyclad.

Only one place outside the Circle itself needs to be clear—the North-East quadrant, because the coven stands there to begin with, waiting for the High Priestess to admit them.

Take the phone off the hook, light the incense and the six candles, start the music, and you are ready to begin.

The Ritual

The High Priestess and High Priest kneel before the altar, with him to her right. The rest of the coven stand outside the North-East quadrant of the Circle.

The High Priestess puts the bowl of water on the pentacle, puts the point of her athame in the water (see Plate 2) and says:

"I exorcise thee, O creature of water, that thou cast out from thee all the impurities and uncleanliness of the spirits of the world of phantasm; in the names of Cernunnos and Aradia." (Or whatever God and Goddess names the coven uses.)[1]

She lays down her athame and holds up the bowl of water in both hands. The High Priest puts the bowl of salt on the pentacle, puts the tip of his athame in the salt and says:

"Blessings be upon this creature of salt; let all malignity and hindrance be cast forth hencefrom, and let all good enter herein; wherefore do I bless thee, that thou mayest aid me, in the names of Cernunnos and Aradia."[1]

He lays down his athame and pours the salt into the bowl of water which the High Priestess is holding up. They then both

---

1. Both these consecrations are very loosely based on those in *The Key of Solomon*, a mediaeval grimoire, or 'grammar', of magical practice translated and edited by MacGregor Mathers from manuscripts in the British Museum and published in 1888. (See Bibliography under Mathers.) The wording for the consecration of magical tools in Gardner's Book of Shadows also follows (and rather more closely) that in *The Key of Solomon*. That these were Gardner's own borrowings, rather than part of the traditional material he obtained from the New Forest coven which initiated him, is suggested by the fact that their English corresponds to that of Mathers, instead of deriving independently from the original Latin. There is no harm in that; like most of Gardner's borrowings, they suit their purpose admirably.

put down their bowls on the altar, and the High Priest leaves the Circle to stand with the coven.

The High Priestess draws the Circle with the sword, leaving a gateway in the North-East (by raising her sword higher than the heads of the coven as she passes them). She proceeds deosil (clockwise)[2] from North to North, saying as she goes:

"I conjure thee, O Circle of Power, that thou beest a meeting-place of love and joy and truth; a shield against all wickedness and evil; a boundary between the world of men and the realms of the Mighty Ones; a rampart and protection that shall preserve and contain the power that we shall raise within thee. Wherefore do I bless thee and consecrate thee, in the names of Cernunnos and Aradia."

She then lays down the sword and admits the High Priest to the Circle with a kiss, spinning with him deosil. The High Priest admits a woman in the same way; that woman admits a man; and so on, till all the coven are in the Circle.

The High Priestess picks up the sword and closes the gateway, by drawing that part of the Circle in the same way as she did the rest of it.[3]

---

2. All magical movements involving rotation or circling are normally made clockwise, 'the way of the Sun'. This is known as 'deosil', from the Gaelic (Irish *deiseal*, Scottish *deiseil*, both pronounced approximately 'jesh'l') meaning 'to the right' or 'to the South'. (In Irish one says *'Deiseal'*—'May it go right'—when a friend sneezes.) An anti-clockwise movement is known as 'widdershins' (Middle High German *widersinnes*, 'in a contrary direction') or 'tuathal' (Irish *tuathal* pronounced 'twa-h'l', Scottish *tuaitheal* pronounced 'twa-y'l') meaning 'to the left, to the North, in a wrong direction'. A widdershins magical movement is considered black or malevolent, *unless* it has a precise symbolic meaning such as an attempt to regress in time, or a return to the source preparatory to rebirth; in such cases it is always in due course 'unwound' by a deosil movement—much as a Scottish Highlander begins a sword dance *tuaitheal*, because it is a war-dance, and ends it *deiseil* to symbolize victory. (See pp. 118, 134 and 169 for examples in our rituals.) We would be interested to hear from witches in the southern hemisphere (where of course the Sun moves anti-clockwise) about their customs in ritual movements, orientation of the elements and placing of the altar.

3. Normally, no one leaves or enters the Circle between the casting and banishing rituals; but if it should be necessary, a gateway must be opened by a ritual widdershins (anti-clockwise) sweep of the athame and closed immediately after use by a deosil (clockwise) sweep. (Sword and athame are ritually interchangeable.) See, for example, p. 53.

The High Priestess then names three witches to strengthen the Circle (which she has already established in the Earth element) with the elements of Water, Air and Fire.

The first witch carries the bowl of consecrated water round the Circle, deosil from North to North, sprinkling the perimeter as he/she goes. Then he/she sprinkles each member of the coven in turn. If it is a man, he ends by sprinkling the High Priestess, who then sprinkles him; if it is a woman, she ends by sprinkling the High Priest, who then sprinkles her. The water-carrier then replaces the bowl on the altar.

The second witch carries the smoking incense-burner round the perimeter, deosil from North to North, and replaces it on the altar.

The third witch carries one of the altar candles round the perimeter, deosil from North to North, and replaces it on the altar.

All the coven then pick up their athames and face the East, with the High Priestess and High Priest in front (he standing to her right). The High Priestess says:

"Ye Lords of the Watchtowers of the East, ye Lords of Air; I do summon, stir and call you up, to witness our rites and to guard the Circle."

As she speaks, she draws the Invoking Pentagram of Earth with her athame in the air in front of her, thus:[4]

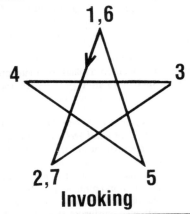

1,6
4   3
2,7   5
Invoking

---

4. This Watchtowers ritual is obviously based on the Golden Dawn's "Lesser Ritual of the Pentagram" (see Israel Regardie's *Golden Dawn*, volume I, pp.

After drawing the Pentagram, she kisses her athame blade and lays it on her heart for a second or two.

The High Priest and the rest of the coven copy all these gestures with their own athames; any who are without athames use their right forefingers.

The High Priestess and coven then face the South and repeat the summoning; this time it is to *"Ye Lords of the Watchtowers of the South, ye Lords of Fire . . .".*

They then face the West, where the summoning is to *"Ye Lords of the Watchtowers of the West, ye Lords of Water, ye Lords of Death and of Initiation . . .".*

They then face the North, where the summoning is longer; the High Priestess says:

"Ye Lords of the Watchtowers of the North, ye Lords of Earth; Boreas, thou guardian of the Northern portals; thou powerful God, thou gentle Goddess; we do summon, stir and call you up, to witness our rites and to guard the Circle."

All the coven replace their athames on the altar, and all but the High Priestess and High Priest go to the South of the Circle, where they stand facing towards the altar.

The High Priest now proceeds to 'draw down the Moon' on the High Priestess. She stands with her back to the altar, with the wand in her right hand and the scourge in her left, held against her breasts in the 'Osiris position'—the two shafts grasped in her clenched fists, her wrists crossed, and the shafts crossed again above them. (See Plate 10.) He kneels before her.

The High Priest gives the High Priestess the Fivefold Kiss, kissing her on the right foot, left foot, right knee, left knee, womb, right breast, left breast and lips. (When he reaches the womb, she opens her arms to the 'blessing position'.) As he does so, he says:

"Blessed be thy feet, that have brought thee in these ways.
Blessed be thy knees, that shall kneel at the sacred altar.
Blessed be thy womb,⁵ without which we would not be.

106–7 and, for more complex material on the Invoking and Banishing Pentagrams, volume III, pp. 9–19). Incidentally, the Golden Dawn, and many witches, end the Pentagrams by merely returning to the starting-point—i.e., omitting the sixth 'sealing' stroke. As always, it is a matter of what 'feels right' to you.

5. When a woman gives the Fivefold Kiss to a man (as at the Imbolg Sabbat) she says 'phallus' instead of 'womb', kissing him just above the pubic hair; and 'breast, formed in strength' instead of 'breasts, formed in beauty'.

Blessed be thy breasts, formed in beauty.[5]
Blessed be thy lips, that shall utter the Sacred Names."

For the kiss on the lips, they embrace, length-to-length, with their feet touching each other's.

The High Priest kneels again before the High Priestess, who resumes the 'blessing position', but with her right foot slightly forward. The High Priest invokes:

"I invoke thee and call upon thee, Mighty Mother of us all, bringer of all fruitfulness; by seed and root, by bud and stem, by leaf and flower and fruit, by life and love do I invoke thee to descend upon the body of this thy servant and priestess."

During this invocation he touches her with his right fore-finger on her right breast, left breast and womb; the same three again; and finally the right breast. Still kneeling, he then spreads his arms outwards and downwards, with the palms forward, and says:[6]

"Hail, Aradia! From the Amalthean Horn
Pour forth thy store of love; I lowly bend
Before thee, I adore thee to the end,
With loving sacrifice thy shrine adorn.
Thy foot is to my lip . . ."

He kisses her right foot and continues:

". . . my prayer upborne
Upon the rising incense-smoke; then spend
Thine ancient love, O Mighty One, descend
To aid me, who without thee am forlorn."

He then stands up and takes a pace backwards, still facing the High Priestess.

The High Priestess draws the Invoking Pentagram of Earth in the air in front of him with the wand, saying:[7]

"Of the Mother darksome and divine
Mine the scourge, and mine the kiss;

---

6. From a poem by Aleister Crowley, originally addressed to Tyche, Goddess of Fortune. Adapted for Craft use by Gardner, who was very fond of it.
7. From Doreen Valiente's rhymed version of the Charge.

The five-point star of love and bliss—
Here I charge you, in this sign."

With this, Drawing Down the Moon is complete; the next
stage is the Charge.[8] The High Priestess lays down the wand
and scourge on the altar, and she and the High Priest face the
coven, with him on her left. The High Priest says:

*"Listen to the words of the Great Mother; she who of old was also
called among men Artemis, Astarte, Athene, Dione, Melusine,
Aphrodite, Cerridwen, Dana, Arianrhod, Isis, Bride,[9] and by
many other names."* [10]

The High Priestess says:

"Whenever ye have need of any thing, once in the month, and

---

8. The history of the Charge is as follows. Gardner drafted a first version, very
similar to the one we give here down to "all in my praise" (this opening passage
being adapted from the Tuscan witches' rituals recorded in Leland's *Aradia:
the Gospel of the Witches*) followed by some voluptuously-worded extracts from
Aleister Crowley. Doreen Valiente tells us she "felt that this was not really
suitable for the Old Craft of the Wise, however beautiful the words might be
or how much one might agree with what they said; so I wrote a version of the
Charge in verse, keeping the words from *Aradia*, because these are traditional." This verse version began "Mother darksome and divine . . .", and its
first stanza is still used as the High Priestess's response to the Drawing Down
of the Moon. But most people seemed to prefer a prose Charge, so she wrote
the final prose version we give here; it still contains one or two Crowley phrases
("Keep pure your highest ideal", for example, is from his essay *The Law of
Liberty*, and "Nor do I demand (aught in) sacrifice" is from *The Book of the
Law*) but she has integrated the whole to give us the best-loved declamation in
today's Craft. It might be called a Wiccan Credo. Our version has one or two
tiny differences from Doreen's (such as "witches" for "witcheries") but we
have let them stand, with apologies to her.
9. Pronounced 'Breed'. If you have a local Goddess-name, by all means add it
to the list. While we lived in County Wexford, we used to add Carman, a
Wexford goddess (or heroine or villainess, according to your version) who
gave the county and town their Gaelic name of Loch Garman (Loch
gCarman).
10. In the Book of Shadows, another sentence follows here: "At her altars the
youth of Lacedaemon in Sparta made due sacrifice." The sentence originated
from Gardner, not Valiente. Like many covens, we omit it. The Spartan
sacrifice, though it has been variously described, was certainly a gruesome
business (see for example Robert Graves's *Greek Myths*, para 116.4) and out of
keeping with the Charge's later statement "Nor do I demand sacrifice". By the
way, the sentence is also inaccurately worded; Sparta was in Lacedaemon, not
Lacedaemon in Sparta.

better it be when the moon is full, then shall ye assemble in some secret place and adore the spirit of me, who am Queen of all witches. There shall ye assemble, ye who are fain to learn all sorcery, yet have not won its deepest secrets; to these will I teach things that are yet unknown. And ye shall be free from slavery; and as a sign that ye be really free, ye shall be naked in your rites; and ye shall dance, sing, feast, make music and love, all in my praise. For mine is the ecstasy of the spirit, and mine also is joy on earth; for my law is love unto all beings. Keep pure your highest ideal; strive ever towards it; let naught stop you or turn you aside. For mine is the secret door which opens upon the Land of Youth, and mine is the cup of the wine of life, and the Cauldron of Cerridwen, which is the Holy Grail of immortality. I am the gracious Goddess, who gives the gift of joy unto the heart of man. Upon earth, I give the knowledge of the spirit eternal; and beyond death, I give peace, and freedom, and reunion with those who have gone before. Nor do I demand sacrifice; for behold, I am the Mother of all living, and my love is poured out upon the earth."

The High Priest says:

"Hear ye the words of the Star Goddess; she in the dust of whose feet are the hosts of heaven, and whose body encircles the universe."

The High Priestess says:

"I who am the beauty of the green earth, and the white Moon among the stars, and the mystery of the waters, and the desire of the heart of man, call unto thy soul. Arise, and come unto me. For I am the soul of nature, who gives life to the universe. From me all things proceed, and unto me all things must return; and before my face, beloved of Gods and of men, let thine innermost divine self be enfolded in the rapture of the infinite. Let my worship be within the heart that rejoiceth; for behold, all acts of love and pleasure are my rituals. And therefore let there be beauty and strength, power and compassion, honour and humility, mirth and reverence within you. And thou who thinkest to seek for me, know thy seeking and yearning shall avail thee not unless thou knowest the mystery; that if that which thou seekest thou findest not within thee, thou wilt never find it without thee. For behold, I have been with thee from the beginning; and I am that which is attained at the end of desire."

This is the end of the Charge.

The High Priest, still facing the coven, raises his arms wide and says:[11]

"Bagahi laca bachahé
Lamac cahi achabahé
Karrelyos
Lamac lamec bachalyos
Cabahagi sabalyos
Baryolas
Lagozatha cabyolas
Samahac et famyolas
Harrahya!"

The High Priestess and the coven repeat "Harrahya!"

The High Priest and the High Priestess then turn to face the altar with their arms raised, their hands giving the 'Horned God' salute (forefinger and little finger straight, thumb and middle fingers folded into palm). The High Priest says:[12]

"Great God Cernunnos, return to earth again!
Come at my call and show thyself to men.
Shepherd of Goats, upon the wild hill's way,
Lead thy lost flock from darkness unto day.
Forgotten are the ways of sleep and night—
Men seek for them, whose eyes have lost the light.
Open the door, the door that hath no key,
The door of dreams, whereby men come to thee.
Shepherd of Goats, O answer unto me!"

The High Priest and High Priestess say together:[13]

"Akhera goiti—akhera beiti!"

—lowering their hands on the second phrase.

The High Priestess, followed by the High Priest, then leads the coven into the Witches' Rune—a ring dance deosil, facing inwards and holding hands (left palms upwards, right palms

---

11. This strange incantation, first known to have appeared in a thirteenth-century French play, is traditional in witchcraft. Its meaning is unknown—though Michael Harrison in *The Roots of Witchcraft* makes out an interesting case for its being a corruption of Basque, and a Samhain rallying-call.
12. This is the Invocation to Pan from Chapter XIII of *Moon Magic* by Dion Fortune, with the coven's God-name substituted for that of Pan.
13. This is an old Basque witches' incantation, meaning 'The he-goat above—the he-goat below'. We found it in Michael Harrison's *The Roots of Witchcraft*, liked it and adopted it.

downwards), men and women alternately as far as possible. The High Priestess sets the pace—and may sometimes let go of the hand of the man in front of her, and weave the coven after her, in and out like a snake. However complex her weaving, no one must let go, but all must keep moving, still hand-in-hand, till the line unravels itself. As the ring-dance proceeds, the whole coven chants:[14]

> *"Eko, Eko, Azarak,*
> *Eko, Eko, Zomelak,*
> *Eko, Eko, Cernunnos*   (repeated three times)
> *Eko, Eko, Aradia!*
> *Darksome night and shining moon,*
> *East, then South, then West, then North;*
> *Hearken to the Witches' Rune—*
> *Here we come to call ye forth!*
> *Earth and water, air and fire,*
> *Wand and pentacle and sword,*
> *Work ye unto our desire,*
> *Hearken ye unto our word!*
> *Cords and censer, scourge and knife,*
> *Powers of the witch's blade—*
> *Waken all ye into life,*
> *Come ye as the charm is made!*

14. This chant, the "Witches' Rune", was written by Doreen Valiente and Gerald Gardner together. The *"Eko, Eko"* lines (to which covens usually insert their own God and Goddess names in lines 3 and 4) were not part of their original Rune; she tells us: "We used to use them as a preface to the old chant *'Bagabi lacha bachabe'* " (to which Michael Harrison also attributes them) "but I don't think they were originally a part of this chant either, they were part of another old chant. Writing from memory, it went something like this:

> *Eko Eko Azarak*
> *Eko Eko Zomelak*
> *Zod ru koz e zod ru koo*
> *Zod ru goz e goo ru moo*
> *Eeo Eeo hoo hoo hoo!*

No, I don't know what they meant! But I think somehow that 'Azarak' and 'Zomelak' are God-names." She adds: "There's no reason why these words shouldn't be used as you have used them." We give here the version to which we, and many other covens, have become accustomed; the only differences are that the original has "I, my" instead of "we, our", and has *"East, then South and West and North"* and *"In the earth and air and sea, By the light of moon or sun"*,

Queen of heaven, Queen of hell,
Hornèd hunter of the night—
Lend your power unto the spell,
And work our will by magic rite!
By all the power of land and sea,
By all the might of moon and sun—
As we do will, so mote it be;
Chant the spell, and be it done!
Eko, Eko, Azarak,
Eko, Eko, Zomelak,
Eko, Eko, Cernunnos,   (repeated till ready)
Eko, Eko, Aradia!"

When the High Priestess decides it is time (and, if she has been weaving, has restored the coven to a plain ring), she orders:

"Down!"

The whole coven drops to the ground and sits in a ring facing inwards.

This is the end of the Opening Ritual. If the meeting were an Esbat, the High Priestess would now direct the particular work to be done. If it is a Sabbat, the appropriate ritual now begins.

One other short ritual should be set down here, to complete the picture: the Consecration of the Wine and Cakes. This takes place at every Esbat, usually after the work is over and before the coven relaxes within the Circle. At a Sabbat, both wine and cakes have to be consecrated if the Great Rite is actual (see Section II); if the Great Rite is symbolic, consecration of the wine is an integral part of it, leaving only the cakes to be consecrated by the usual ritual.

Consecration of the Wine and Cakes

A male witch kneels before a female witch in front of the altar. He holds up the chalice of wine to her; she holds her athame point downwards, and lowers the point into the wine. (See Plate 17.)

The man says:

"As the athame is to the male, so the cup is to the female; and conjoined, they become one in truth."

The woman lays down her athame on the altar and then kisses the man (who remains kneeling) and accepts the chalice from him. She sips the wine, kisses the man again and passes the chalice back to him. He sips, rises and gives it to another woman with a kiss.

The chalice is passed in this way around the whole coven, man-to-woman and woman-to-man (each time with a kiss) until everyone has sipped the wine.

If there is more work to be done, the chalice is now returned to the altar. If the coven is now ready to relax within the Circle, the chalice is placed between them as they sit on the floor, and anyone may drink from it as he or she wishes; the ritual passing-and-kissing is necessary only for the first time round. Nor, if the chalice is refilled during this relaxation, does it have to be re-consecrated.

To consecrate the cakes, the woman picks up her athame again, and the man, kneeling before her, holds up the dish of cakes. (See Plate 3.) She draws the Invoking Pentagram of Earth in the air above the cakes with her athame, while the man says:[15]

"O Queen most secret, bless this food into our bodies; bestowing health, wealth, strength, joy, and peace, and that fulfilment of love which is perfect happiness."

The woman lays down her athame on the altar, kisses the man and takes a cake from the dish. She kisses him again, and he takes a cake. He then rises and passes the dish to another woman with a kiss.

The dish is passed in this way round the whole coven, man-to-woman and woman-to-man (each time with a kiss), until everyone has taken a cake.

---

15 Adapted from Crowley's *Gnostic Mass.*

II The Great Rite

To say that the Great Rite is a ritual of male/female polarity is true but sounds a little coldly technical. To say that it is a sexual rite is also true but sounds (to the uninformed) like an orgy. In fact it is neither cold nor an orgy; so let us try to put it in proportion.

It can be enacted in either of two forms. It can be (and, we would guess, in most covens usually is) purely symbolic—in which case the whole coven is present the whole time. Or it can be 'actual'—that is to say, involving intercourse—in which case all of the coven except the man and woman concerned leave the Circle and the room, before the ritual becomes intimate, and do not return until they are summoned.

But whether it is symbolic or 'actual', witches make no apology for its sexual nature. To them, sex is holy—a manifestation of that essential polarity which pervades and activates the whole universe, from Macrocosm to Microcosm, and without which the universe would be inert and static—in other words, would not exist. The couple enacting the Great Rite are offering themselves, with reverence and joy, as expressions of the God and Goddess aspects of the Ultimate Source. "As above, so below." They are making themselves, to the best of their ability, channels for that divine polarity on *all* levels, from physical to spiritual. That is why it is called the *Great* Rite.

It is also why the 'actual' Great Rite is enacted without witnesses—not through shame but for the dignity of privacy. And it is why the Great Rite in its 'actual' form should, we feel, be enacted only by a married couple or by lovers of a marriage-like unity; because it *is* a magical rite, and a powerful one; and charged with the intensity of intercourse, by a couple whose relationship is less close, it may well activate links on levels for which they are unprepared and which may prove unbalanced and disturbing.

"Ritual sexual intercourse," says Doreen Valiente, "is a very old idea indeed—probably as old as humanity itself. Obviously, it is the very opposite of promiscuity. Intercourse for ritual purposes should be with a carefully selected partner, at the right time and in the right place. . . . It is love and only love that can give sex the spark of magic." (*Natural Magic* p. 110.)

The *symbolic* Great Rite, however, is a perfectly safe and beneficial ritual for two experienced witches at the level of friendship normal between members of the same coven. It is up to the High Priestess to decide who is suitable.

Perhaps a good way to express it would be to say that the 'actual' Great Rite is sex magic, while the symbolic Great Rite is the magic of gender.

The Great Rite invocation specifically declares that the body of the woman taking part is an altar, with her womb and generative organs as its sacred focus, and reveres it as such. It should hardly be necessary to emphasize to our readers that this has nothing to do with any 'Black Mass'—because the Black Mass itself had nothing to do with the Old Religion. The Black Mass was a *Christian* heresy, using perverted Christian forms, performed by sophisticated degenerates and unfrocked or corrupt priests, in which the living altar was used to desecrate the Christian Host. Such obscenity is of course utterly alien to the spirit and intent of the Great Rite.

In many sincere and honourable pagan religions, on the other hand, "there is one genuinely ancient figure—the naked woman upon the altar," Doreen Valiente points out, and goes on: "It would be more correct to say, the naked woman who is the altar; because this is her original role. . . . This use of a living woman's naked body as the altar where the forces of Life are worshipped and invoked goes back to before the beginnings of Christianity; back to the days of the ancient worship of the Great Goddess of Nature, in whom all things were one, under the image of Woman." (*An ABC of Witchcraft*, p. 44.)

In fact, not only the archetypal altar but every church, temple or synagogue *is* the body of the Goddess—psychologically, spiritually and in its historical evolution. The whole complex symbolism of ecclesiastical architecture bears this out beyond question, point by point; anyone who doubts it should read Lawrence Durdin-Robertson's richly documented (if confusingly presented) manual *The Symbolism of Temple Architecture*.

So Wiccan symbolism merely does vividly and naturally what other religions do obliquely and subconsciously.

At the Sabbats, the Great Rite is usually enacted by the High Priestess and High Priest. The Sabbats are special occasions, peaks of heightened awareness and significance in the witches' year; so it is fitting that at these festivals the coven leaders should take this key role upon themselves on the coven's behalf. However, rigid procedures are foreign to Wicca, and there may well be occasions when they decide that another couple should be named for the Sabbat Great Rite.

The Preparation

The only extra item needed for the Great Rite, whether symbolic or 'actual', is a veil at least a yard square. It should preferably be one of the Goddess colours—blue, green, silver or white.

The chalice should be filled with wine in readiness.

The High Priestess may also decide to change the music tape to something specially appropriate—possibly some music of personal significance to her and her partner. (For simplicity we are assuming, here and below, that it is the High Priestess and High Priest who are enacting the Rite.)

The Symbolic Ritual

If the cauldron is in the centre, it will be moved to the South of the Circle, unless the ritual indicates some other position.

The coven, except for the High Priestess and High Priest, arrange themselves around the perimeter of the Circle, man and woman alternately as far as possible, facing the centre.

The High Priestess and High Priest stand facing each other in the centre of the Circle, she with her back to the altar, he with his back to the South.

The High Priest gives the High Priestess the Fivefold Kiss.

The High Priestess then lays herself down face upwards, with her hips in the centre of the Circle, her head towards the altar, and her arms and legs outstretched to form the Pentagram.

The High Priest fetches the veil and spreads it over the High Priestess's body, covering her from breasts to knees. He then kneels facing her, with his knees between her feet. (See Plate 4.)

The High Priest calls a woman witch by name, to bring his athame from the altar. The woman witch does so and stands with the athame in her hands, a yard to the West of the High Priestess's hips and facing her.

The High Priest calls a man witch by name, to bring the chalice of wine from the altar. The man witch does so and stands with the chalice in his hands, a yard to the East of the High Priestess's hips and facing her.

The High Priest delivers the Invocation:

"Assist me to erect the ancient altar, at which in days past
all worshipped;
The great altar of all things.
For in old time, Woman was the altar.
Thus was the altar made and placed,
And the sacred place was the point within the centre of the Circle.
As we have of old been taught that the point within the centre is
the origin of all things,
Therefore should we adore it;
Therefore whom we adore we also invoke.
O Circle of Stars,
Whereof our father is but the younger brother,

Marvel beyond imagination, soul of infinite space,
Before whom time is ashamed, the mind bewildered, and the
    understanding dark,
Not unto thee may we attain unless thine image be love.
Therefore by seed and root, and stem and bud,
And leaf and flower and fruit do we invoke thee,
O Queen of Space, O Jewel of Light,
Continuous one of the heavens;
Let it be ever thus
That men speak not of thee as One, but as None;
And let them not speak of thee at all, since thou art continuous. [1]
For thou art the point within the Circle, which we adore;
The point of life, without which we would not be.
And in this way truly are erected the holy twin pillars; [2]
In beauty and in strength were they erected
To the wonder and glory of all men."

The High Priest removes the veil from the High Priestess's body, and hands it to the woman witch, from whom he takes his athame.

The High Priestess rises and kneels facing the High Priest, and takes the chalice from the man witch.

(Note that both these handings-over are done *without* the customary ritual kiss.)

The High Priest continues the Invocation:

       "Altar of mysteries manifold, [3]
       The sacred Circle's secret point—
       Thus do I sign thee as of old,
       With kisses of my lips anoint."

The High Priest kisses the High Priestess on the lips, and continues:

---

1. From *"O Circle of Stars"* down to *"since thou art continuous"*, this Book of Shadows invocation is taken from the *Gnostic Mass* in Aleister Crowley's *Magick*.
2. The "holy twin pillars" are Boaz and Jachin, which flanked the entrance to the Holy of Holies in Solomon's Temple. Boaz (coloured black) represents Severity ("strength"), and Jachin (white) Mildness ("beauty"). Cf. the Tree of Life and the High Priestess Tarot card. In the Great Rite, they are clearly symbolized by the woman-altar's legs.
3. From *"Altar of mysteries manifold"* to the end of the Invocation was written by Doreen Valiente, who also composed a fully rhyming version.

"Open for me the secret way,
The pathway of intelligence,
Beyond the gates of night and day,
Beyond the bounds of time and sense.
Behold the mystery aright—
The five true points of fellowship . . ."

The High Priestess holds up the chalice, and the High Priest lowers the point of his athame into the wine. (Both use both their hands for this—see Plate 19.) The High Priest continues:

"Here where the Lance and Grail unite,
And feet, and knees, and breast, and lip."

The High Priest hands his athame to the woman witch and then places both his hands round those of the High Priestess as she holds the chalice. He kisses her, and she sips the wine; she kisses him, and he sips the wine. Both of them keep their hands round the chalice while they do this.

The High Priest then takes the chalice from the High Priestess, and they both rise to their feet.

The High Priest hands the chalice to the woman witch with a kiss, and she sips; she passes the chalice to the man witch with a kiss, and he sips. From him, the chalice is passed man-to-woman, woman-to-man, round the coven, each time with a kiss, in the normal way.

The High Priestess and High Priest then consecrate the cakes, which are passed round in the normal way.

The 'Actual' Ritual

The 'actual' Great Rite follows the same procedure as the symbolic one above, with the following exceptions.

The woman and man witch are not summoned, and the athame and chalice remain on the altar.

When the High Priest reaches *"To the wonder and glory of all men"* in the Invocation, he stops. The Maiden then fetches her athame from the altar and ritually opens a gateway in the Circle by the door of the room. The coven file through and leave the room. The Maiden steps last out of the Circle, ritually seals the gateway behind her, lays her athame on the floor outside the Circle and leaves the room, closing the door behind her.

The High Priestess and High Priest are thus left alone in the room and the Circle.

The High Priest continues the Invocation to the end, but the actual details of enacting the Rite are now a private matter for him and the High Priestess. No member of the coven may question them on it afterwards, directly or indirectly.

When they are ready to re-admit the coven, the High Priest takes his athame from the altar, ritually opens the gateway, opens the door and summons the coven. He returns his athame to the altar.

The Maiden picks up her athame on the way in and ritually seals the gateway after the coven have re-entered the Circle. She returns her athame to the altar.

Wine and cakes are now consecrated in the normal way.

III   The Closing Ritual

A Magic Circle, once cast, must always and without exception be banished when the occasion or purpose for which it was cast is finished.[1] It would be bad manners not to thank, and bid farewell to, the entities you had invoked to guard it; bad magic to create a barrier on the astral plane and then to leave it undismantled, a stray obstacle like an upturned rake on a garden path; and bad psychology to have so little belief in its reality and effectiveness that you assume it will go away the moment you stop thinking about it.

---

1. The Rite of Hagiel, as described in Chapter XIV of *What Witches Do*, may appear to break this rule; but the special circumstances should be clear to careful readers of it. For one thing, the Lords of the Watchtowers are not summoned.

The Preparation

Strictly speaking, no preparation is needed for the ritual of banishing the Circle; but two provisions should be borne in mind, during your activities *in* the Circle, in anticipation of it.

First, if any objects have been consecrated in the Circle, they should be kept together—or at least each of them remembered—so that they can be picked up and carried by someone placed at the back of the coven during the banishing. To make the gestures of a Banishing Pentagram *towards* a newly consecrated object would have a neutralizing effect.

Second, you should see that at least one cake, or biscuit, and a little of the wine are left, so that these can be taken outside afterwards and scattered or poured as an offering to the Earth. (Living in Ireland, we follow local tradition by making this offering in a slightly different way; we leave it overnight in two little bowls, outside on a west-facing window-sill, for the *sidhe* (pronounced 'shee'), or fairy-folk. The *sidhe*, incidentally, are reputed to like a pat of butter on the cake or biscuit.)

The Ritual

The High Priestess faces the East with her athame in her hand. The High Priest stands to her right, and the rest of the coven stand behind them. All carry their athames, if they have them, except for the person carrying the newly-consecrated objects (if any) who stands right at the back. The Maiden (or someone detailed by the High Priestess for the purpose) stands near to the front, ready to blow out each candle in turn.

The High Priestess says:

"Ye Lords of the Watchtowers of the East, ye Lords of Air; we do thank you for attending our rites; and ere ye depart to your pleasant and lovely realms, we bid you hail and farewell. . . . Hail and farewell."

As she speaks, she draws the Banishing Pentagram of Earth with her athame in the air in front of her, thus:

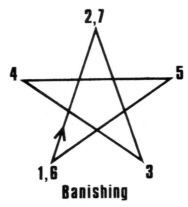

Banishing

After drawing the Pentagram, she kisses her athame blade and lays it on her heart for a second or two.

The High Priest and the rest of the coven copy all these gestures with their own athames; any who are without athames use their right forefingers. (The bearer of the consecrated objects makes no gestures.) All say the second *"Hail and farewell"* with her.

The Maiden steps forward and blows out the East candle.

The whole procedure is repeated facing South, the High Priestess saying:

"Ye Lords of the Watchtowers of the South, ye Lords of Fire; we do thank you . . ." etc.

Then to the West, the High Priestess saying:

"Ye Lords of the Watchtowers of the West, ye Lords of Water; ye Lords of Death and of Initiation; we do thank you . . ." etc.

Then to the North, the High Priestess saying:

"Ye Lords of the Watchtowers of the North, ye Lords of Earth; Boreas, thou guardian of the Northern portals; thou powerful God, thou gentle Goddess; we do thank you . . ." etc.

At the North, the Maiden merely blows out the Earth candle; for purely practical reasons, she leaves the two altar candles burning until the room lights are turned on.

The Sabbat is over.

The Sabbats

IV   Imbolg, 2nd February

We have called the four Greater Sabbats by their Celtic names for consistency, and used the Irish Gaelic forms of those names for the reasons we gave on p. 14. But Imbolg is more commonly known, even among witches, by the pretty name of Candlemas under which it was Christianized—understandably enough, because this Feast of Lights can and should be a pretty occasion.

Imbolg is *i mbolg* (pronounced 'im*mol*'g', with a slight unstressed vowel between the 'l' and the 'g') which means 'in the belly'. It is the quickening of the year, the first foetal stirrings of Spring in the womb of Mother Earth. Like all the Celtic Great Sabbats, it is a fire festival—but here the emphasis is on light rather than heat, the strengthening spark of light beginning to pierce the gloom of Winter. (Farther south, where winter is less forbiddingly dark, the emphasis may be the other way; Armenian Christians, for example, light their new sacred fire of the year on Candlemas Eve, not Easter as elsewhere.)

The Moon is the light-symbol of the Goddess, and the Moon above all stands for her threefold aspect of Maid, Mother and Crone (Enchantment, Ripeness and Wisdom). Lunar light is particularly that of inspiration. So it is fitting that Imbolg should be the feast of Brigid (Brid, Brigante), the radiant triple Muse-Goddess, who is also a fertility-bringer; for at Imbolg, when the first trumpets of Spring can be heard in the distance, the spirit is quickened as well as the body and the Earth.

Brigid (who also gave her name to Brigantia, the Celtic kingdom of the whole of the North of England above a line from the Wash to Staffordshire) is a classic example of a pagan deity Christianized with little attempt to hide the fact—or as Frazer puts it in *The Golden Bough* (p. 177),[1] she is "an old heathen goddess of fertility, disguised in a threadbare Christian cloak". St Brigid's Day, *Lá Fhéile Bríd* (pronounced approximately 'law ella breed') in Ireland, is 1st February, the eve of Imbolg. The historical St Brigid lived from about AD 453–523; but her legends, characteristics and holy places are those of the Goddess Brid, and the folk-customs of St Brigid's Day in the Celtic lands are plainly pre-Christian. It is significant that Brigid is known as "the Mary of the Gael", for like Mary she transcends the human biographical data to fill man's "Goddess-shaped yearning" (see p. 139 below). Tradition, incidentally, says that St Brigid was brought up by a wizard and that she had the power to multiply food and drink to nourish the needy—including the delightful ability to turn her bath-water into beer.

The making of St Brigid's Crosses of rush or straw (and they are still widely made in Ireland, both at home and for the handicraft shops) "is probably derived from an ancient pre-Christian ceremony connected with the preparation of the seed

---

1. Every book reference in the text, with its publisher and date, and where necessary (as here, with *The Golden Bough*) the edition to which page references are made, is listed in the Bibliography at the end—together with some of the books we have found most useful in our study of seasonal traditions and mythology.

grain for growing in the Spring" (*The Irish Times*, 1st February 1977).

In Scotland, on the eve of St Brigid's Day, the women of the house would dress up a sheaf of oats in woman's clothing and lay it in a basket called 'Brigid's bed', side by side with a phallic club. They would then call out three times: "Brid is come, Brid is welcome!" and leave candles burning by the 'bed' all night. If the impression of the club was found in the ashes of the hearth in the morning, the year would be fruitful and prosperous. The ancient meaning is clear: with the use of appropriate symbols, the women of the house prepare a place for the Goddess and make her welcome, and invite the fertilizing God to come and impregnate her. Then they discreetly withdraw—and, when the night is over, return to look for a sign of the God's visit (his footprint by the fire of the Goddess of Light?). If the sign is there, their invocation has succeeded, and the year is pregnant with the hoped-for bounty.

In the Isle of Man, a similar ritual was carried out; there, the occasion was called *Laa'l Breeshey*. In Northern England—the old Brigantia, Candlemas was known as 'the Wives' Feast Day'.

The welcoming ritual is still part of *Lá Fhéile Bríd* in many Irish homes. Philomena Rooney of Wexford, whose family live near the Leitrim-Donegal border, tells us she still goes home for it whenever she can. While her grandparents were still alive, the whole family would gather at their house on St Brigid's Eve, 31st January. Her uncle would have gathered a cartload of rushes from the farm and would bring them to the door at midnight. The ritual is always the same.

> "The person bringing the rushes to the house covers his or her head and knocks on the door. The *Bean an Tighe* (woman of the house) sends someone to open the door and says to the person entering "*Fáilte leat a Bhríd*" ("Welcome, Brigid"), to which the person entering replies "*Beannacht Dé ar daoine an tighe seo*" ("God bless the people of this house"). The holy water is sprinkled on the rushes, and everyone joins in making the crosses. When the crosses are made, the remaining rushes are buried, following which everyone joins in a meal. On 1st February last year's crosses are burned and replaced with the newly made ones."

In Philomena's family, two types were made. Her grandmother, who came from North Leitrim, made the Celtic Cross, equal-armed and enclosed in a circle. Her grandfather, who came from South Donegal, made the plain equal-armed cross. She supposes that these were local traditional styles.[2] Great importance was attached to the burning of last year's crosses. "We have this thing that you should never throw it out, you should burn it." Here again is the theme which recurs throughout the year's ritual cycle: the magical importance of fire.

In Ireland, this land of magic wells (over three thousand Irish holy wells are listed), there are probably more wells of Brigid than there are even of St Patrick—which is hardly surprising, because the lady was here first by untold centuries. There is a *tobar Bhríd* (Brigid's Well) barely a mile from our first Irish home, near Ferns in County Wexford, in a neighbouring farmer's field; it is a very ancient spring, and the locality is known to have been holy to Brigid for a good thousand years, and doubtless for a very long time before that. The farmer (regretfully, for he is sensitive to tradition) had to cover the well with a rock because it had become a danger to children. But he told us there were always bits of cloth[3] to be seen tied to nearby

---

2. Local patterns of the Brigid's Crosses do vary considerably. Philomena's 'plain' cross in fact has the four arms woven in separately with their roots off-centre, producing a swastika (fire-wheel) effect. This is also our County Mayo type, though we have also seen single and multiple diamond patterns. A County Armagh type given to us by a friend has each of the two crosspieces consisting of three bundles, interlacing with the other three at the centre, and we have seen similar ones from Counties Galway, Clare and Kerry; memory perhaps of 'the Three Brigids', the original Triple Muse Goddess? (See *The White Goddess*, pp. 101, 394 and elsewhere.) A County Derry example has five bands instead of three, and a West Donegal one has a triple vertical and a single horizontal. Such local diversity shows how deep-rooted the folk custom is. The Brigid's Cross in the fire-wheel form, with three-banded arms, is the symbol of Radio Telefís Éireann.

3. These pieces of cloth probably symbolize clothing. Gypsy women, in their famous annual pilgrimage to Saintes-Maries-de-la-Mer in southern France on 24th and 25th May, leave items of clothing, representing the absent or sick, in the crypt-shrine of their patroness Black Sara. "The ceremonial is clearly not original. The rite of hanging up garments is known among the Dravidians of northern India who 'believe in fact that the linen and clothes of a sick person become impregnated with his malady, and that the patient will be cured if his linen is purified by contact with a sacred tree'. Hence, among them are seen trees or images covered with rags of clothing which they call *Chitraiya*

bushes, put there secretly by people invoking Brid's help as they had done since time immemorial; and we could, literally, still feel the power of the place by laying our hands on the rock.

(Incidentally, if like most witches you believe in the magic of names, you should pronounce Brid or Bride as 'Breed' and *not* to rhyme with 'hide' as it has been somewhat harshly anglicized—for example in London's own *tobar Bhríd*, Bridewell.)

In ancient Rome, February was cleansing time—*Februarius mensis*, 'the month of ritual purification'. At its beginning came the Lupercalia, when the Luperci, the priests of Pan, ran through the streets naked except for a goatskin girdle and carrying goatskin thongs. With these they struck everybody who passed, and in particular married women, who were believed to be made fertile thereby. This ritual was both popular and patrician (Mark Antony is on record as having performed the Lupercus role) and survived for centuries into the Christian era. Women developed the habit of stripping themselves as well, to allow the Luperci more scope. Pope Gelasius I, who reigned AD 492–6, banned this cheerfully scandalous festival and met with such an outcry that he had to apologize. It was finally abolished at the beginning of the next century.

Lupercalia aside, the tradition of February cleansing remained strong. Doreen Valiente says in *An ABC of Witchcraft Past and Present*: "The evergreens for Yuletide decorations were holly, ivy, mistletoe, the sweet-smelling bay and rosemary, and green branches of the box tree. By Candlemas, all had to be gathered up and burnt, or hobgoblins would haunt the house. In other words, by that time a new tide of life had

---

Bhavani, 'Our Lady of the Rags'. There exists likewise a 'Tree for Tatters' (*sinderich ogateh*) among the Kirghiz of the Sea of Aral. One could probably find other examples of this magical prophylaxis." (Jean-Paul Clébert, *The Gypsies*, p. 143.) One can indeed. We wonder, for example, why Irish itinerants always seem to leave some clothing behind on the bushes by an abandoned camp-site. They are notoriously untidy, it is true, but many of these garments are by no means rubbish. One magic well near Wexford town was consecrated to no saint or deity, yet was much venerated; its cloth-laden bush, local historian Nicky Furlong records, "was chopped down by a normally well-adjusted clergyman. That ended the secret cult. (He died very suddenly afterwards, God rest him.)"

started to flow through the whole world of nature, and people had to get rid of the past and look to the future. Spring-cleaning was originally a nature ritual." In some parts of Ireland, we find, there is a tradition of leaving the Christmas tree in place (stripped of its decorations but retaining its lights) until Candlemass; if it has kept its green needles, good luck and fruitfulness are assured for the year ahead.

One other strange Candlemas belief is widespread in the British Isles, France, Germany and Spain: that fine weather on Candlemas Day means more Winter to come, but bad weather on that day means that Winter is over. Perhaps this is a kind of 'touch wood' acknowledgement of the fact that Candlemas is the natural turning-point between Winter and Spring, and so to be impatient about it is unlucky.

In the Candlemas ritual in the Book of Shadows, the High Priestess invokes the God into the High Priest, instead of him invoking the Goddess into her. Perhaps this too, like the Scottish 'Brigid's bed' tradition, is really a seasonal invitation to the God to impregnate the Earth Mother. We have kept to this procedure and retained the form of the invocation.

The Book of Shadows also mentions the (sixteenth-century) Volta Dance; but we wonder if what is really meant is the very much older traditional witches' dance in which the man and woman link arms back-to-back. We have therefore used this earlier dance.

In Christian tradition, the Crown of Lights is often worn by a very young girl, presumably to symbolize the extreme youth of the year. This is perfectly valid, of course; but we, with our Triple Goddess enactment, prefer to allot it to the Mother— because it is Mother Earth who is quickened at Imbolg.

The Preparation

The High Priestess selects two woman witches who, with herself, will represent the Triple Goddess—Maid (Enchantment), Mother (Ripeness) and Crone (Wisdom)—and allocates the three roles.

A Crown of Lights is prepared for the Mother and left on or by the altar. Traditionally, the Crown should be of candles or tapers, which are lit during the ritual; but this requires care, and some people may be wary of it. If a candle or taper Crown is made, it should be constructed firmly enough to hold them without wobbling and should incorporate a cap to protect the hair against dripping wax. (You can work wonders with kitchen foil.)

We have found that birthday-cake candles, which can be bought in packets almost anywhere, make an ideal Crown of Lights. They weigh practically nothing, hardly drip at all and burn quite long enough for the purpose of the ritual. A very simple birthday-candle crown can be made as follows. Get a roll of self-adhesive tape about three-quarters of an inch wide (the plain-coloured plastic kind is suitable) and cut off a length four or five inches longer than the circumference of the lady's head. Pin this, sticky side *upwards*, to a board. Stick the bottom ends of the candles across this, spaced about one and half inches apart, but leaving a good three inches of each end of the tape empty. Now cut a second piece of the tape of the same length as the first, hold it sticky side *downwards*, and apply it carefully to the first tape, moulding it around the base of each candle. Unpin the ends, and you now have a neat band of candles which can be wrapped round the head, the free ends being secured together by a safety-pin at the back. The candle-band should be wrapped around a kitchen-foil skull-cap which has been moulded to the head beforehand; the foil can then be trimmed to match the bottom edge of the band. You can see the finished result in use in Plate 5; in that case, it has been improved still further by fitting foil and candle-band inside an existing copper crown.

(Incidentally, that copper crown—seen closer in Plate 10— with its crescent-moon front was made for Janet by our coppersmith friend Peter Clark of Tintine, The Rower, County Kilkenny. Peter supplies beautiful ritual equipment in copper or bronze, either from stock or made to your own requirements.)

An alternative form of the Crown of Lights, avoiding the wax-dripping risk, is a handyman's job—a crown incorporating a number of flashlamp bulbs, soldered to their leads, with small batteries concealed under a Foreign-Legion-type piece of fabric falling over the neck; the 'switch' being a small crocodile-clip, or simply two bared wire-ends can be twisted together. This bulb-crown can be kept from year to year, and decorated with fresh foliage each time. (It does, however, require some experiment in the construction, both as to the distribution of the weight of the batteries and as to the components and wiring; too many bulbs in parallel will give a fine light for the first minute and then fade rapidly because of the excessive drain.) If you do not like either of these, the third possibility is a crown incorporating little mirrors—as many as possible of them, facing outwards to catch the light.

A bundle of straw a foot to eighteen inches long, with a straw crosspiece for arms, should be dressed in woman's clothing—a doll's dress will do, or simply a cloth pinned round. If you possess a corn dolly of suitable shape for dressing (a Brigid's Cross is ideal), this may be even better. (See Plate 6.) This figure is called a 'Biddy'—or, if you prefer the Gaelic, '*Brídeóg*' (pronounced 'breed-oge').

You also need a phallic wand, which can be a simple staff about the same length as the Biddy; though, since the Book of Shadows rituals frequently call for a phallic wand as distinct from the coven's 'normal' one, it is worth while making yourselves a permanent version. Ours is a piece of thin branch with a pine-cone secured to the tip, and black and white ribbons spiralling in opposite directions along the shaft. (See Plate 6).

Biddy and wand should be ready beside the altar, together with two unlit candles in candle-holders.

Also beside the altar is a small bouquet of greenery (as springlike as possible and incorporating spring flowers if you can get them) for the woman who portrays the Maid; and a dark-coloured scarf or cloak for the Crone.

The broomstick (the traditional witch's besom of twigs) is by the altar too.

The cauldron, with a candle burning inside it, is placed beside the South candle. By the cauldron are laid three or four twigs of evergreen or dried vegetation such as holly, ivy, mistletoe, bay, rosemary or box.

If, like us, you follow the tradition of keeping the Christmas Tree (without its decorations but with its lights) in the house till Candlemas, it should, if practicable, be in the room where the Circle is held, with all its lights lit.

The Ritual

The Opening Ritual is shorter for Imbolg. The High Priest does not Draw Down the Moon on the High Priestess, nor does he make the *"Great God Cernunnos"* invocation; and the Charge is not declaimed until later.

After the Witches' Rune, all the working partners (including the High Priestess and High Priest) dance back-to-back in couples, with their arms hooked through each other's elbows. Unpartnered witches dance solo, though after a while partners break up and re-combine with unpartnered ones, so that everybody can take part.

When the High Priestess decides that the dancing has gone on long enough, she stops it, and the coven arrange themselves around the Circle facing inwards. The High Priest stands with his back to the altar, and the High Priestess faces him.

The High Priest gives the High Priestess the Fivefold Kiss; then she in turn gives him the Fivefold Kiss. The High Priest takes the wand in his right hand and the scourge in his left, and assumes the Osiris Position (see p. 40).

The High Priestess, facing the High Priest as he stands before the altar, invokes:[1]

> *"Dread Lord of Death and Resurrection,*
> *Of Life, and the Giver of Life;*
> *Lord within ourselves, whose name is Mystery of Mysteries,*
> *Encourage our hearts,*
> *Let thy Light crystallize itself in our blood,*
> *Fulfilling of us resurrection;*
> *For there is no part of us that is not of the Gods.*
> *Descend, we pray thee, upon thy servant and priest."*

The High Priest draws the Invoking Pentagram of Earth in the air, towards the High Priestess, and says:

> *"Blessed be."*

The High Priest steps to one side, while the High Priestess and the women of the coven prepare 'Brigid's bed'. They lay the Biddy and the phallic wand side by side in the centre of the Circle, with the heads towards the altar. They place the

---

4. Lines 3–5 of this invocation are from Crowley's *Gnostic Mass*.

candlesticks on either side of the 'bed' and light the candles.
(See Plate 6.)

High Priestess and women stand around the 'bed' and say
together:

"*Brid is come—Brid is welcome!*" (Repeated three times.)

The High Priest lays down his wand and scourge on the altar.
The High Priestess summons the two selected women; she and
they now assume their Triple Goddess roles. (See Plate 5.) The
Mother stands with her back to the centre of the altar, and the
High Priest crowns her with the Crown of Lights; the Maid and
Crone arrange her hair becomingly, and the High Priest lights
the tapers on the Crown (or switches on the bulbs).

The Crone now stands beside the Mother, to her left, and the
High Priest and Maid drape the shawl or cloak over her
shoulders.

The Maid now stands beside the Mother, to her right, and the
High Priest puts the bouquet into her hands.

The High Priest goes to the South, where he stands facing the
three women. He declaims:

> "*Behold the Three-Formed Goddess;*
> *She who is ever Three—Maid, Mother and Crone;*
> *Yet is she ever One.*
> *For without Spring there can be no Summer,*
> *Without Summer, no Winter,*
> *Without Winter, no new Spring.*"

The High Priest then delivers the Charge in its entirety, from
"*Listen to the words of the Great Mother*" right to "*that which is
attained at the end of desire*"—but substituting "she, her, hers"
for "I, me, my, mine".

When he has finished, the Maid takes up the broomstick and
makes her way slowly deosil round the Circle, ritually sweeping
it clear of all that is old and outworn. The Mother and the Crone
walk behind her in stately procession. The Maid then replaces
the broom beside the altar, and the three women resume their
places in front of the altar.

The High Priest then turns and kneels before the cauldron.
He picks up each of the evergreen twigs in turn, sets fire to each
from the cauldron candle, blows the twig out and puts it in the
cauldron beside the candle. (This symbolic burning is all that is

advisable in a small room, because of smoke; out of doors, or in a large room, they may be burned away completely.)

As he does this, he declaims:

"Thus we banish winter,
Thus we welcome spring;
Say farewell to what is dead,
And greet each living thing.
Thus we banish winter,
Thus we welcome spring!"

The High Priest goes to the Mother, blows out or switches off the Crown of Lights and removes it from the Mother's head. On this signal, the Maid lays her bouquet, and the Crone her shawl or cloak, beside the altar, and the High Priest lays the Crown of Lights there also.

The High Priest steps aside, and the three women fetch the Biddy, the phallic wand and the candles (which they extinguish) from the centre of the Circle and lay them beside the altar.

The Great Rite is now enacted.

After the Cakes and Wine, a suitable game for Imbolg is the Candle Game. The men sit in a ring facing inwards, close enough to reach each other, and the women stand behind them. The men pass a lighted candle deosil from hand to hand, while the women (without stepping inside the ring of men) lean forward and try to blow it out. When a woman succeeds, she gives three flicks of the scourge to the man who was holding it at the time, and he gives her the Fivefold Kiss in return. The candle is then relit and the game continues.

If the custom of keeping the Christmas Tree till Candlemas has been observed, the Tree must be taken out of the house and disposed of as soon as possible after the ritual.

V   Spring Equinox, 21st March

"The Sun," as Robert Graves puts it, "arms himself at the Spring Equinox." Light and dark are in balance, but the light is mastering the darkness. It is basically a solar festival, and a newcomer to the Old Religion in Celtic and Teutonic Europe. Although Teutonic influence—Margaret Murray's "solstitial invaders"—added Yule and Midsummer to the four Great Sabbats of the pastoral Celts, the new synthesis still embraced only six Festivals. "The Equinoxes," says Murray, "were never observed in Britain" (except, as we now know, by the pre-Celtic Megalithic peoples—see p. 14).

Yet the Equinoxes are now unquestionably with us; modern pagans, almost universally, celebrate the eight Festivals, and no one suggests that the two Equinoxes are an innovation thought up by Gerald Gardner or by Druid Revival romantics. They are

72

a genuine part of pagan tradition as it exists today, even if their seeds blew in from the Mediterranean and germinated in the soil of the underground centuries, along with many other fruitful elements. (Wiccan purists who reject anything that stems from classical Greece or Rome, from Ancient Egypt, from the Hebrew Qabala or from the Tuscan *Aradia*, had better stop celebrating the Equinoxes, too.) The importing of such concepts is always a complex process. Folk-awareness of the Spring Equinox in the British Isles, for example, must have been mainly imported with the Christian Easter. But Easter brought in its luggage, so to speak, the Mediterranean pagan overtones of the Spring Equinox.

The difficulty which faces witches in deciding just how to celebrate the Spring Equinox Sabbat is not that the 'foreign' associations are in fact alien to the native ones but that they overlap with them, expressing themes that had long ago become attached to the older native Sabbats. For instance, the sacrificial mating theme in Mediterranean lands has strong links with the Spring Equinox. The grim festival of the Phrygian goddess Cybele, at which the self-castration, death and resurrection of her son/lover Attis was marked by worshippers castrating themselves to become her priests, was from 22nd to 25th March. In Rome these rites took place on the spot where St Peter's now stands in Vatican City. In fact, in places where Attis-worship was widespread, the local Christians used to celebrate the death and resurrection of Christ at the same date; and pagans and Christians used to quarrel bitterly about which of their gods was the true prototype and which the imitation. On sheer chronology, there should have been no dispute, because Attis came from Phrygia many centuries before Christ; but the Christians had the unanswerable argument that the Devil cunningly placed counterfeits ahead of the true Coming in order to deceive mankind.

Easter—Jesus's willing death, descent into Hell and resurrection—can be seen as the Christian version of the sacrificial mating theme, for 'Hell' in this sense is patriarchal monotheism's **view** of the collective unconscious, the dreaded feminine **aspect**, the Goddess, into whom the sacrificed God is plunged as the necessary prelude to rebirth. Christ's 'Harrowing of Hell', as described in the apocryphal Gospel of

Nicodemus, involved his rescuing of the souls of the just from
Adam onwards "who had fallen asleep since the beginning of
the world" and his raising of them to Heaven. Stripped of
theological dogma, this can have a positive meaning—the reintegration of the buried treasures of the unconscious ('the gift
of the Goddess') with the light of analytical consciousness ('the
gift of the God').

Spring, too, was a particular season in classical and pre-
classical times for a form of the sacrificial mating which was also
kindlier and more positive than the Attis cult—the *Hieros
gamos*, or sacred marriage. In this, woman identified herself
with the Goddess, and man sank himself into the Goddess
through her, giving of his masculinity but not destroying it, and
emerging from the experience spiritually revitalized. The Great
Rite, whether symbolic or actual, is obviously the witches'
hieros gamos; and then, as now, it shocked many people who did
not understand it.[1] (For a profound Jungian commentary on the
hieros gamos, see M. Esther Harding's *Woman's Mysteries*.)

But in the North, where Spring comes later, these aspects
really belonged to Bealtaine instead of to the unobserved

---

1. The most savage opponents of the *hieros gamos* and all it stood for were of
course the Hebrew prophets. Their tirades against "harlotry" and "whoring
after strange gods", with which the Old Testament abounds, were political,
not ethical. The Goddess-worship which surrounded them, and to which
ordinary Hebrew families still clung for centuries alongside the official
Yahweh-worship, was a direct threat to the patriarchal system they were
trying to enforce. For unless every woman was an exclusive chattel of her
husband, and a virgin on marriage, how could paternity be certain? And
unquestionable paternity was the keystone of the whole system. Hence the
Biblical death-penalty for adulteresses, for brides found to be non-virgin and
even for the victims of rape (unless they were neither married nor betrothed,
in which case they had to marry the rapist); the ruthlessness with which the
Hebrews, "according to the word of the Lord", massacred the entire population of conquered Canaanite cities, men, women and children (except for any
attractive virgins, whom "the word of the Lord" permitted them to kidnap as
wives); and even the Levitic rewriting of the Creation myth to give divine
sanction to male superiority (it is interesting that the Serpent and the Tree
were both universally recognized Goddess-symbols). From this ancient
political battle, Christianity (outdoing even Judaism and Islam) inherited the
hatred of sex, the warped asceticism and the contempt for women that has
bedevilled it from St Paul onwards and is still far from dead. (See again Merlin
Stone's *Paradise Papers*.)

Equinox; and it is at Bealtaine, as will be seen, that we have placed our corresponding 'Love Chase' ritual. It is perhaps significant that Easter (owing to the complex lunar method of dating it) reflects this overlap by falling anywhere from just after the Equinox to just before Bealtaine. Easter, by the way, is named after the Teutonic goddess Eostre, whose name is probably yet another variant of Ishtar, Astarte and Aset (the correct Egyptian name 'Isis' being the Greek form). Eostre's spring rites bore a family resemblance to those of the Babylonian Ishtar. Another piece of pagan 'luggage'!

But if in the human-fertility aspect the Spring Equinox must bow to Bealtaine, it can properly retain the vegetation-fertility aspect, even if in the North it marks a different stage of it. Round the Mediterranean, the Equinox is the time of sprouting; in the North, it is the time of sowing. As a solar festival, too, it must share with the Greater Sabbats the eternal theme of fire and light, which has survived strongly in Easter folklore. In many parts of Europe, particularly Germany, Easter bonfires are lit with fire obtained from the priest, on traditional hilltop sites often known locally as 'Easter Mountain''. (Relic of earlier, larger-scale customs—see under Bealtaine, p. 82) As far as the light shines, it is believed, the land will be fruitful and the homes secure. And, as always, people jump the dying embers, and cattle are driven over them.

The Book of Shadows says that for this festival, "the symbol of the Wheel should be placed on the Altar, flanked with burning candles, or fire in some form." So, assuming this to be one of the genuine traditional elements which Gardner was given, we can take it that British witches, in absorbing the 'non-native' Equinoxes into their calendar, used the fire-wheel symbol which also features in many midsummer folk-customs throughout Europe.

A hint that the solar fire-wheel *is* a genuine equinoctial tradition, and not merely a gap-filling choice of Gardner's, may be found in the custom of wearing shamrock on St Patrick's Day—which falls on 17th March. According to the usual explanation, the shamrock became Ireland's national emblem because St Patrick once used its three-leaved shape to illustrate the doctrine of the Trinity. But the *Oxford English Dictionary* says this tradition is 'late'; and in fact the first printed reference to it was in an eighteenth-century botanical work. And Dinneen's *Irish-English Dictionary*, defining *seamróg*, says its use as a national emblem in Ireland (and, incidentally, in Hanover, in the home territory of the "solstitial invaders") is possibly "a survival of the trignetra, a Christianized wheel or sun symbol", and adds that the four-leaved variety is "believed to bring luck, related to an early apotropaic sign enclosed in a circle (sun or wheel symbol)".

The St Patrick's Day shamrock has become standardized as the lesser yellow trefoil (*Trifolium dubius* or *minus*), but in Shakespeare's day 'shamrock' meant wood sorrel, *Oxalis acetosella*; and Dinneen defines *seamróg* as "a shamrock, trefoil, clover, a bunch of green grass". Culpeper's *Complete Herbal* says "all the Sorrels are under the dominion of Venus." So the threefold spring-green leaves in the Irishman's equinox buttonhole bring us back not only to the Sun God but also, through the modern screen of the Trinity, to the Triple Goddess. (Artemis, the Greek Triple Moon Goddess, fed her hinds on trefoil.)

And as for the lucky four-leaved variety—any Jungian psychologist (and the Lords of the Watchtowers!) will tell you that the quartered circle is an archetypal symbol of wholeness and balance. The solar fire-wheel, the Celtic cross, the four-leaved shamrock, the Magic Circle with its four cardinal candles, the Egyptian hieroglyph *niewt* meaning 'town', the Easter hot-cross bun, the Byzantine basilica—all deliver the same immemorial message, much older than Christianity.

The Easter egg, too, is pre-Christian. It is the World Egg, laid by the Goddess and split open by the heat of the Sun God; "and the hatching-out of the world was celebrated each year at the Spring festival of the Sun" (Graves, *The White Goddess*, pp. 248-9). Originally it was a snake's egg; the caduceus of Hermes portrays the coupling snakes, Goddess and God, who produced it. But under the influence of the Orphic mysteries, as Graves points out, "since the cock was the Orphic bird of resurrection, sacred to Apollo's son Aesculapius the healer, hens' eggs took the place of snakes' in the later Druidic mysteries and were coloured scarlet in the Sun's honour; and became Easter eggs." (Decorated eggs boiled in an infusion of furze blossom were rolled down hillsides in Ireland on Easter Monday.)

Stewart wrote in *What Witches Do*: "The Spring Equinox is obviously an occasion for decorating the room with daffodils and other spring blossoms, and also for honouring one of the younger women by appointing her the coven's Spring Queen and sending her home afterwards with an armful of the flowers." We have kept to this pleasant little custom.

The Preparation

A wheel symbol stands on the altar; it may be anything that feels suitable—a cut-out disc painted yellow or gold and decorated with spring flowers, a circular mirror, a round brass tray; ours is a 14-inch drumkit cymbal, highly polished and with a daffodil or primrose posy in its central hole.

The High Priest's robe (if any) and accessories should be symbolic of the Sun; any metal he wears should be gold, gilt, brass or bronze.

The altar and room should be decorated with spring flowers—particularly the yellow ones such as daffodils, primroses, gorse or forsythia. One bouquet should be ready for handing to the Spring Queen, and a chaplet of flowers for her crowning.

The cauldron is placed in the centre of the Circle, with an unlit candle inside it. A taper is ready on the altar for the Maiden to carry fire to the High Priest.

A phallic wand is ready on the altar.

Half as many cords as there are people present are ready on the altar, tied together at their centre-point in a single knot. (If there is an odd number of people, add one before dividing by two; e.g., for nine people take five cords.)

If you like, you can have a bowl of hard-boiled eggs, with painted shells (scarlet all over, or decorated as you wish), on the altar—one for each person plus one for the *sidhe* or earth-offering. These can be handed out during the feasting.

The Ritual

The Opening Ritual proceeds as usual, but without the Witches' Rune.

The High Priest stand in the East, and the High Priestess in the West, facing each other across the cauldron. The High Priestess carries the phallic wand in her right hand. The rest of the coven distribute themselves around the perimeter of the Circle.

The High Priestess says:[2]

> *"We kindle this fire today*
> *In presence of the Holy Ones,*
> *Without malice, without jealousy, without envy,*
> *Without fear of aught beneath the Sun*
> *But the High Gods.*
> *Thee we invoke, O Light of Life,*
> *Be Thou a bright flame before us,*
> *Be Thou a guiding star above us,*
> *Be Thou a smooth path beneath us;*
> *Kindle Thou within our hearts*
> *A flame of love for our neighbours,*
> *To our foes, to our friends, to our kindred all,*
> *To all men on the broad earth.*
> *O merciful Son of Cerridwen,*
> *From the lowliest thing that liveth*
> *To the Name which is highest of all."*

The High Priestess holds the phallic wand on high and walks slowly deosil round the cauldron to stand in front of the High Priest. She says:

"O Sun, be Thou armed to conquer the Dark!"

The High Priestess presents the phallic wand to the High Priest and then steps to one side.

The High Priest holds up the phallic wand in salute and replaces it on the altar.

The Maiden lights the taper from one of the altar candles and

---

2. Adapted by Doreen Valiente from two Scottish Gaelic blessings in Alexander Carmichael's *Carmina Gadelica* (see Bibliography). Carmichael, who lived 1832–1912, collected and translated a rich harvest of Gaelic prayers and blessings, handed down by word of mouth in the Highlands and Islands of Scotland. As Doreen says, "This beautiful old poetry is really sheer paganism with a thin Christian veneer." The six-volume *Carmina Gadelica*, though a treasure to own, is expensive; fortunately a selection of the English translations has been published as a recent paperback *The Sun Dances* (see Bibliography). The two sources Doreen used here will be found on pages 231 and 49 of volume I of *Carmina Gadelica*, and on pages 3 and 11 of *The Sun Dances*; Carmichael obtained them from crofters' wives in North Uist and Lochaber, respectively.

presents it to the High Priest. The Maiden then steps to one side.

The High Priest carries the taper to the cauldron and lights the cauldron candle with it. He gives the taper back to the Maiden, who blows it out and replaces it on the altar, picking up the cords instead.

The Maiden gives the cords to the High Priest.

The High Priestess arranges everybody round the cauldron, man facing woman as far as possible. The High Priest hands out the ends of the cords in accordance with her instructions, retaining one end of the final cord himself and handing the other end of it to the High Priestess. (If there is an odd number of people, with more women than men, he retains two cord-ends himself or, with more men than women, hands two cord-ends to the High Priestess; in either case, he must be linked with two women or she with two men.)

When everyone is holding a cord, they all pull the cords taut, with the central knot above the cauldron. They then start circling deosil in the Wheel Dance, to the Witches' Rune, building up speed, always keeping the cords taut and the knot over the cauldron.

The Wheel Dance continues till the High Priestess cries "*Down!*", and the coven all sit in a circle round the cauldron. The High Priest gathers up the cords (being careful not to let them drop on to the candle-flame) and replaces them on the altar.

The cauldron is then moved to beside the East candle, and the Great Rite is enacted.

After the Great Rite, the High Priest names a woman witch as the Spring Queen and stands her in front of the altar. He crowns her with the chaplet of flowers and gives her the Fivefold Kiss.

The High Priest then calls forward each man in turn to give the Spring Queen the Fivefold Kiss. When the last man has done so, the High Priest presents the Spring Queen with her bouquet.

The cauldron is replaced in the centre of the Circle, and, starting with the Spring Queen, everyone jumps the cauldron, singly or in couples—not forgetting to wish.

The cauldron-jumping over, the party begins.

VI Bealtaine, 30th April

In the Celtic tradition, the two greatest festivals of all are Bealtaine and Samhain—the beginning of Summer and the beginning of Winter. To the Celts, as to all pastoral peoples, the year had two seasons, not four; subtler divisions concerned crop-raisers rather than cattle-raisers. Beltane, the anglicized form, corresponds to the modern Irish Gaelic word *Bealtaine* (pronounced 'b'*yol*-tinnuh', approximately rhyming with 'winner'), the name of the month of May, and to the Scottish Gaelic word *Bealtuinn* (pronounced 'b'*yal*-ten', with the 'n' like 'ni' in 'onion'), meaning May Day.

The original meaning is 'Bel-fire'—the fire of the Celtic or proto-Celtic god variously known as Bel, Beli, Balar, Balor or the latinized Belenus—names traceable back to the Middle Eastern Baal, which simply means 'Lord'.[1] Some people have suggested that Bel is the British-Celtic equivalent of the Gaulish-Celtic Cernunnos; that may be true in the sense that both are archetypal male-principle deities, mates of the Great Mother, but we feel that the evidence points to their being different aspects of that principle. Cernunnos is always represented as the Horned God; he is above all a nature deity, the god of animals, the Celtic Pan. (Herne the Hunter, who haunts Windsor Great Park with his Wild Hunt, is a later English Cernunnos, as his name suggests.) He is also sometimes seen as a chthonic (underworld) deity, the Celtic Pluto. Originally, the Horned God was doubtless the tribal totem animal, whose mating with the Great Mother would have been the key fertility ritual of the totemic period. (See Lethbridge's *Witches; Investigating an Ancient Religion*, pp. 25–27.)

Bel, on the other hand, was 'the Bright One', god of light and fire. He had Sun-like qualities (classical writers equated him with Apollo) but he was not, strictly speaking, a Sun-God; as we have pointed out, the Celts were not solar-oriented. No people who worshipped the Sun as a god would give it a feminine name—and *grian* (Irish and Scottish Gaelic for 'Sun') is a feminine noun. So is *Mór*, a personalized Irish name for the Sun, as in the greeting *'Mór dhuit'*—'May the Sun bless you.' It may seem a subtle difference, but a god-symbol is not always regarded as *the same thing* as the god himself by his worshippers. Christians do not worship a lamb or a dove, nor did ancient Egyptians worship a baboon or a hawk; yet the first two are symbols of Christ and the Holy Spirit, and the second two of Thoth and Horus. To some people the Sun *was* a god, but not to the Celts with their feminine Sun, even though Bel/Balor, Oghma, Lugh and Llew had solar *attributes*. A traditional Scottish Gaelic folk-prayer (see Kenneth Jackson's *Celtic Miscellany*, item 34) addresses the Sun as "happy mother of the stars", rising "like a young queen in flower". (For further evidence that the pagan Celts' ritual calendar was oriented to the natural vegetation year and herd-raising, and not to the solar year and agriculture, see Frazer's *Golden Bough*, pp. 828–830.)

---

1. Of family interest to us: Janet's maiden name was Owen, and Owen family tradition claims descent from the Canaanite lords of Shechem, who themselves claimed to be of the seed of Baal.

Symbolically, both the Cernunnos aspect and the Bel aspect can be seen as ways of visualizing the Great Father who impregnates the Great Mother.[2] And these are the two themes which dominate the May Eve/May Day festival throughout Celtic and British folklore: fertility and fire.

The Bel-fires were lit on the hilltops to celebrate the return of life and fertility to the world. In the Scottish Highlands as late as the eighteenth century, Robert Graves tells us (*The White Goddess*, p. 416), fire was kindled by drilling an oak-plank, "but only in the kindling of the Beltane need-fire, to which miraculous virtue was ascribed. . . . It originally culminated in the sacrifice of a man representing the Oak-god." (It is interesting that in Rome the Vestal Virgins, guardians of the sacred fire, used to throw manikins made of rushes into the River Tiber at the May full moon as symbolic human sacrifices.)

In pagan Ireland no one could light a Bealtaine fire until the Ard Ri, the High King, had lit the first one on Tara Hill. In AD 433, St Patrick showed an acute understanding of symbolism when he lit a fire on Slane Hill, ten miles from Tara, *before* the High King Laoghaire lit his; he could not have made a more dramatic claim to the usurpation of spiritual leadership over the whole island. St David made a similar historic gesture in Wales in the following century.

Incidentally, much of the symbolism of Tara as the spiritual focus of ancient Ireland is immediately recognizable to anyone who has worked in a Magic Circle. Tara is in Meath (*Midhe*, 'centre') and was the seat of the High Kings; its ground-plan is still visible as great twin circular earthworks. Tara's ritual Banqueting Hall had a central hall for the High King himself, surrounded by four inward-facing halls which were allotted to the four provincial kingdoms: to the North for Ulster, to the East for Leinster, to the South for Munster, and to the West for Connacht. That is why the four provinces are traditionally

---

2. There is always overlap. The Cerne Abbas giant cut in the Dorset turf is a Baal figure, as shown by his Herculean club and phallus, and his local name, Helith, is clearly the Greek *helios* (Sun); yet 'Cerne' is equally clearly Cernunnos. And Baal Hammon of Carthage was also a true Baal or Bel (his Great Mother consort was named Tanit—cf. the Irish Dana and the Welsh Don); yet he was horned.

known as 'fifths', because of the vital Centre which completes them, as Spirit completes and integrates Earth, Air, Fire and Water. Even the elemental ritual tools are represented, in the Four Treasures of the Tuatha Dé Danann: the Stone of Fál (Destiny) which cried aloud when the rightful High King sat on it, the Sword and Spear of Lugh, and the Cauldron of the Dagda (the Father God).

All four were male symbols, as one might expect in a warrior society; but the archetypal matrilinear foundations still shone through at the inauguration of a lesser king, ruler of a *tuath* or tribe. This was "a symbolic marriage with Sovereignty, a fertility rite for which the technical term was *banais rígi* 'royal wedding'". The same used to be true of the High Kings: "The legendary Queen Medb, whose name means 'intoxication', was originally a personification of sovereignty, for we are told that she was the wife of nine kings of Ireland, and elsewhere that only one who was mated with her could be king. Of King Cormac it was said . . . 'until Medb slept with the lad, Cormac was not king of Ireland.' " (Dillon and Chadwick, *The Celtic Realms*, p. 125.)

It is easy to see, then, why Tara had to be the igniting-point for the community's regenerative Bel-fire; and the same would have been true of the corresponding spiritual foci in other lands. Ireland merely happens to be the country where the details of the tradition have been most clearly preserved.

(On the whole complex symbolism of Tara, the Reeses' *Celtic Heritage* makes fascinating reading for witches and occultists.)

A feature of the Bealtaine fire festival in many lands was jumping over the fire. (We say 'was', but in discussing seasonal folk-customs the past tense seldom proves to be entirely justified.) Young people jumped it to bring themselves husbands or wives; intending travellers to ensure a safe journey; pregnant women to ensure an easy delivery, and so on. Cattle were driven through its ashes—or between two such fires—to ensure a good milk-yield. The magical properties of the festival fire form a persistent belief, as we shall also see under Midsummer, Samhain and Yule. (Both Scottish and Irish Gaelic, incidentally, have a saying 'caught between two Bealtaine fires', meaning 'caught in a dilemma'.)

Talking of cattle—next day, 1st May, was an important one

in old Ireland. On that day the women, children and herdsmen took the cattle off to the summer pastures, or 'booleys' (*buaile* or *buailte*), until Samhain. The same thing still happens, on the same dates, in the Alps and other parts of Europe. Another Irish (and Scottish) Gaelic word for summer pasture is *áiridh*; and Doreen Valiente suggests (*Witchcraft for Tomorrow*, p. 164) that "there is just a chance that the name 'Aradia' is Celtic in origin," connected with this word. In North Italian witchcraft, which, as Leland (see Bibliography) has shown, derives from Etruscan roots, Aradia is the daughter of Diana (or, as the Etruscans themselves called her, Aritimi, a variant of the Greek Artemis). The Etruscans flourished in Tuscany from about the eighth to the fourth century BC, till the Romans conquered the last of their city-states, Volsinii, in 280 BC. From the fifth century onwards, they had much contact with the Gaulish Celts, sometimes as enemies and sometimes as allies; so it may very well be that the Celts brought Aradia there. 'Daughter', in the development of pantheons, often means 'later version'—and in the Aradia legend, Aradia learned much of her wisdom from her mother, which would tally with the undoubted fact that the brilliant Etruscan civilization was admired and envied by their Celtic neighbours. It is interesting that, in both Irish and Scottish, *áiridh* or a slight variant of it also means 'worth, merit'.

And in case anyone thinks that Aradia reached Britain only through Leland's nineteenth-century researches—in the form 'Herodias', she appears as an English witch-goddess name in the tenth-century *Canon Episcopi*.

Back to Bealtaine itself. Oak is the tree of the God of the Waxing Year; hawthorn, at this season, is a tree of the White Goddess. The strong folklore taboo on breaking hawthorn branches or bringing them into the house is traditionally lifted on May Eve, when sprigs of it may be cut for the Goddess's festival. (Irish farmers, and even earth-moving roadbuilders, are still reluctant to cut down lone hawthorns; a 'fairy' hawthorn stood by itself in the middle of a pasture of the farm we lived on at Ferns, County Wexford, and similar respected examples can be seen all over the country.)

However, if you want blossoms for your ritual (for example, as chaplets in the women witches' hair), you cannot be certain of finding hawthorn in flower as early as May Eve, and you will probably have to be content with the young leaves. Our own solution is to use blackthorn, whose flowers appear in April, ahead of the leaves. Blackthorn (sloe) is also a Goddess tree at this season—but it belongs to the Goddess in her dark, devouring aspect, as the bitterness of its autumn fruit would suggest. It used to be regarded as 'the witches' tree'—in the malevolent sense—and unlucky. But to fear the dark aspect of the Goddess is to miss the truth that she consumes only to give new birth. If the Mysteries could be summed up in one sentence, it might be this: "At the core of the Bright Mother is the Dark Mother, and at the core of the Dark Mother is the Bright Mother." The sacrifice-and-rebirth theme of our Bealtaine ritual reflects this truth, so, to symbolize the two aspects in balance, our women wear hawthorn in leaf and blackthorn in blossom, intertwined.

Another taboo lifted on May Eve was the early British one on hunting the hare. The hare, as well as being a Moon animal, has a fine reputation for randiness and fecundity; so has the goat, and both figure in the sacrificial aspect of the May Day fertility traditions. The Love Chase is a widespread form of this tradition; it underlies the Lady Godiva legend and that of the Teutonic goddess Eostre or Ostara after whom Easter is named, as well as such folk-festivals as the May Day 'Obby Oss' ceremony in Padstow, Cornwall. (On the alluring and mysterious figure of the love-chase woman "neither clothed nor unclothed, neither on foot nor on horseback, neither on water nor on dry land, neither with nor without a gift", who is "easily recognized as the May-Eve aspect of the Love-and-Death goddess," see Graves, *The White Goddess*, p. 403 onwards.)

But apart from—or rather, in amplification of—the enactment of these Goddess and God-King mysteries, Bealtaine for ordinary people was a festival of unashamed human sexuality and fertility. Maypole, nuts and 'the gown of green' were frank symbols of penis, testicles and the covering of a woman by a man. Dancing round the maypole, hunting for nuts in the woods, 'greenwood marriages' and staying up all night to watch the May sun rise, were unequivocal activities, which is why the Puritans suppressed them with such pious horror. (Parliament made maypoles illegal in 1644, but they came back with the

Restoration; in 1661 a 134-foot maypole was set up in the Strand.)

Robin Hood, Maid Marian and Little John played a big part in May Day folklore; and many people with surnames such as Hodson, Robinson, Jenkinson, Johnson and Godkin owe their ancestry to some distant May Eve in the woods.

Branches and flowers used to be brought back from the woods on May morning to decorate the village's doors and windows, and young people would carry garlands in procession, singing. The garlands were usually of intersecting hoops. Sir J. G. Frazer wrote at the beginning of this century: "It appears that a hoop wreathed with rowan and marsh marigold, and bearing suspended within it two balls, is still carried on May Day by villagers in some parts of Ireland. The balls, which are sometimes covered with gold and silver paper, are said to have originally represented the sun and moon." (*The Golden Bough*, p. 159.) Maybe—but Frazer, splendid pioneer though he was, often seemed to be (or, in the climate of his time, discreetly pretended to be) blind to sexual symbolism.

Another May morning custom in Ireland was 'skimming the wells'. You went to the well of a prosperous neighbour (presumably before he was up and about) and skimmed the surface of the water, to acquire his luck for yourself. In another variant of this custom, you skimmed your own well, to ensure a good butter-yield for the year—and also, one may guess, to forestall any neighbour who was after *your* luck.

Folk-memory survives in curious ways. A Dublin friend—a good Catholic in his fifties—tells us that when he was a boy in north County Longford, his father and mother used to take the children out at midnight on May Eve, and the whole family would dance naked in the young crops. The explanation the children were given was that this would protect them against catching colds for the next twelve months; but it would be interesting to know whether the parents themselves believed this to be the true reason or were really concerned with the fertility of the crops and were giving the children a 'respectable' explanation in case they talked—particularly in the priest's hearing. Our friend also tells us that the crops were always sown by 25th March to ensure a good harvest; and 25th March used to be regarded as the Spring Equinox (compare

25th December for Christmas instead of the astronomically exact solstice).

"One of the most widespread superstitions in England held that washing the face in May morning dew would beautify the skin," the *Encyclopaedia Britannica* says. "Pepys alludes to the practice in his *Diary*, and as late as 1791 a London newspaper reported that 'yesterday, being the first of May, a number of persons went into the fields and bathed their faces with the dew on the grass with the idea that it would render them beautiful.'" Ireland has the same tradition.

But to return to the greenwood. Today, over-population and not under-population is humanity's problem; and more enlightened attitudes to sexual relationships (though still developing unevenly) would hardly be compatible with the greenwood-orgy method of producing a new crop of Hodsons and Godkins. But both the cheerful frankness and the dark mystery can and should be expressed. That is what the Sabbats are all about.

In our Bealtaine rite, we have woven as much as we could of the traditional symbolism, short of overloading it and blunting its edge with obscurity—or, worse, taking the fun out of it. We leave it to the reader to discern the weaving. But perhaps it is worth mentioning that the High Priest's declamation, "*I am a stag of seven times*," etc., consists of those lines of the Song of Amergin which belong, according to Robert Graves's allocation, to the seven tree-months in the Oak King's cycle.

We have added one quite separate little rite which was suggested to us by reading Ovid's *Fasti*. On 1st May, the Romans paid homage to their Lares, or household gods; and it seemed appropriate for us to do the same on the night when the Bel-fire is extinguished and rekindled. All homes, to be honest, possess objects which are in effect Lares. Ours include a foot-high Venus de Milo acquired by Stewart's parents before he was born; slightly battered, twice broken in two and mended, she has come to be a much-loved Guardian of the Home and a true Lar. She now smiles Hellenistically down on our Bealtaine rites. Other witches may also feel that this little annual homage is a pleasant custom to adopt.

The Preparation

The cauldron is placed in the centre of the Circle, with a candle burning inside it; this represents the Bel-fire.

Sprigs of hawthorn and blackthorn decorate the altar, and chaplets of the two combined (with the thorns clipped off) are made for the women witches. (A shot of hair-spray on the blossoms beforehand will help to prevent the petals falling.) The hawthorn and blackthorn should be gathered on May Eve itself, and it is customary to apologize and explain to each tree as you cut it.

If oak leaves can be found at this season in your area, a chaplet of them is made for the High Priest, in his role as Oak King. (A permanent oak crown is a useful coven accessory—see under Yule, p. 145.)

A green scarf, or piece of gauze, at least a yard square, is laid by the altar.

As many wax tapers as there are people in the coven are placed close to the cauldron.

The 'cakes' for consecration on this occasion should be a bowl of nuts.

If you are including the rite for the Guardian of the House, this (or these) are placed on the edge of the Circle near the East candle, with one or two joss-sticks in a holder ready for lighting at the appropriate moment. (If your Guardian is not movable, a symbol of it may stand in its place; for example, if it is a tree in your garden, bring in a sprig of it—again with the appropriate apology and explanation.)

The Ritual

After the Witches' Rune, the coven spread themselves around the Circle area between the cauldron and the perimeter and start a soft, rhythmic clapping.

The High Priest picks up the green scarf, gathers it lengthwise like a rope and holds it with one end in each hand. He starts to move towards the High Priestess, making as though to throw the scarf over her shoulders and pull her to him; but she backs away from him, tantalizingly.

While the coven continue their rhythmic clapping, the High Priestess continues to elude the pursuing High Priest. She beckons to him and teases him but always steps back before he can capture her with the scarf. She weaves in and out of the coven, and the other women step in the High Priest's way to help her elude him.

After a while, say after two or three 'laps' of the Circle, the High Priestess allows the High Priest to capture her by throwing the scarf over her head to behind her shoulders and pulling her to him. They kiss and separate, and the High Priest hands the scarf to another man.

The other man then pursues *his* partner, who eludes him, beckons to him and teases him in exactly the same way; the clapping goes on all the time. (See Plate 12.) After a while she, too, allows herself to be captured and kissed.

The man then hands the scarf to another man, and the pursuit-game continues until every couple in the coven has taken part.

The last man hands the scarf back to the High Priest.

Once again the High Priest pursues the High Priestess; but this time the pace is much slower, almost stately, and her eluding and beckoning more solemn, as though she is tempting him into danger; and this time the others do not intervene. The pursuit continues until the High Priestess places herself between the cauldron and the altar, facing the altar and two or three paces from it. Then the High Priest halts with his back to the altar and captures her with the scarf.

They embrace solemnly but wholeheartedly; but after a few seconds of the kiss, the High Priest lets the scarf fall from his hands, and the High Priestess releases him and takes a step backwards.

The High Priest drops to his knees, sits back on his heels and lowers his head, chin on chest.

The High Priestess spreads her arms, signalling for the clapping to stop. She then calls forward two women by name and places them on each side of the High Priest, facing inwards, so that the three tower over him. The High Priestess picks up the scarf, and the three of them spread it between them over the High Priest. They lower it slowly and then release it, so that it covers his head like a shroud.

The High Priestess sends the two women back to their places and calls forward two men by name. She instructs them to extinguish the two altar candles (*not* the Earth candle), and when they have done so, she sends them back to their places.

The High Priestess then turns and kneels close to the cauldron, facing it. She gestures to the rest of the coven to kneel around the cauldron with her.

Only the High Priest stays where he is in front of the altar, kneeling but 'dead'.

When everyone is in place, the High Priestess blows out the candle in the cauldron and is silent for a moment. Then she says:

"*The Bel-fire is extinguished, and the Oak King is dead. He has embraced the Great Mother and died of his love; so has it been, year by year, since time began. Yet if the Oak King is dead—he who is the God of the Waxing Year—all is dead; the fields bear no crops, the trees bear no fruit, and the creatures of the Great Mother bear no young. What shall we do, therefore, that the Oak King may live again?*"

The coven reply:

"*Re-kindle the Bel-fire!*"

The High Priestess says:

"*So mote it be.*"

The High Priestess takes a taper, rises, goes to the altar, lights the taper from the Earth candle and kneels again at the cauldron. She relights the cauldron candle with her taper. (See Plate 7.) Then she says:

"*Take each of you a taper and light it from the Bel-fire.*"

The coven do so; and finally the High Priestess lights a second taper for herself. Summoning the original two women to accompany her, she rises and turns to face the High Priest. She gestures to the two women to lift the scarf from the High Priest's head; they do so (see Plate 8) and lay it on the floor.

The High Priestess sends the two women back to their places and summons the two men. She instructs them to relight the altar candles with their tapers. When they have done so, she sends them back to their places.

She then holds out one of her tapers to the High Priest (who so far has not moved) and says:

"*Come back to us, Oak King, that the land may be fruitful.*"

The High Priest rises, and accepts the taper. He says:

"I am a stag of seven tines;
I am a wide flood on a plain;
I am a wind on the deep waters;
I am a shining tear of the sun;
I am a hawk on a cliff;
I am fair among flowers;
I am a god who sets the head afire with smoke."

The High Priestess and High Priest lead a ring dance around the cauldron, the rest of the coven following, all carrying their tapers. The mood becomes joyous. As they dance, they chant:

"Oh, do not tell the Priest of our Art,
Or he would call it a sin;
But we shall be out in the woods all night,
A-conjuring Summer in!
And we bring you news by word of mouth
For women, cattle and corn—
Now is the Sun come up from the South
With Oak, and Ash, and Thorn!"[3]

They repeat *"With Oak, and Ash, and Thorn"* ad lib., till the High Priestess blows out her taper and lays it by the cauldron. The rest do the same. Then the entire coven link hands and circle faster and faster. Every now and then the High Priestess calls a name, or a couple's names, and whoever is called breaks away, jumps the cauldron and rejoins the ring. When all have jumped, the High Priestess cries *"Down!"* and everybody sits.

That, apart from the Great Rite, is the end of the Bealtaine ritual; but if the Guardian of the House is to be honoured, it is most suitably done while the rest of the coven are relaxing. The Guardian ritual is of course performed by the couple, or individual, in whose house the Sabbat is being held—who may or may not be the High Priestess and High Priest. If it is an

---

3. This (the only substantial item in the Book of Shadows' Bealtaine ritual) is a slightly altered version of verse 5 of Rudyard Kipling's poem *A Tree Song*, from the "Weland's Sword" story in *Puck of Pook's Hill.* It is one of Gerald Gardner's happier borrowings, and we are sure the shade of Kipling does not mind.

individual, his or her working partner will assist; if he or she is unpartnered, the High Priestess or High Priest may do so.

The couple approach the East candle, while the rest of the coven remain seated but turn to face East with them.

One of the couple lights the joss-sticks in front of the Guardian, while the other says:

"*Guardian of this House, watch over it in the year to come, till again the Bel-fire is extinguished and relit. Bless this house, and be blessed by it; let all who live here, and all friends who are welcomed here, prosper under this roof. So mote it be!*"

All say:

"*So mote it be!*"

The couple rejoin the coven.

Bealtaine and Samhain are traditional 'Mischief Nights'—what Doreen Valiente has called "the in-between times, when the year was swinging on its hinges, the doors of the Other World were open, and anything could happen". So when all is done, the Great Rite celebrated, and the wine and nuts shared, this is the night for forfeits. In imposing bizarre little tasks or ordeals, the High Priestess's inventiveness may run wild—always remembering, of course, that it is the High Priest's final privilege to devise a forfeit for *her*.

One final point; if you are holding your Bealtaine festival outdoors, the Bel-fire which is lit should be a bonfire. This should be laid ready with kindling which will catch quickly. But the *old* Bel-fire which the High Priestess extinguishes should be a candle, protected if necessary inside a lantern. It would not be practicable, unless the Sabbat were a large-scale affair, to extinguish a bonfire in the middle of the ritual.

If you live in an area where witchcraft activity is known and respected—or at least tolerated—and have the use of a hilltop, the sudden blazing up of a Bealtaine fire in the darkness may stir some interesting folk-memories.

But if you do light a bonfire—on this or any other occasion, have a fire-extinguisher ready to hand in case of emergency. Witches who start heath-fires or woodland-fires will quickly lose any local respect they may have built up; and quite right too.

VII   Midsummer, 22nd June

The Sun-God significance of the Midsummer Sabbat is, literally, as clear as day. At the Summer Solstice, he is at his highest and brightest, and his day is at its longest. Witches, naturally and rightly, greet and honour him at the peak of his annual cycle, invoking him to "put to flight the powers of darkness" and to bring fertility to the land. Midsummer is perhaps the most celebratory of the Festivals, in the sense that it rejoices in the full flood of the year's abundance, the apogee of light and warmth.

But the Sabbat cycle, even at the height of its joy, always takes into account what lies behind and before. As the ancient Greeks put it: *"Panta rhei, ouden menei"*[1]—"Everything flows,

---

1. πάντα ῥεῖ οὐδὲν μένει—Heraclitus, c.513BC.

nothing is static." Life is a process, not a state; and the witches' Sabbats are essentially a means of putting oneself in tune with that process.

So at Midsummer, the 'process' aspect is reflected in the other God-theme—that of the Oak King and Holly King. At Midsummer, the Oak King, God of the Waxing Year, falls to the Holly King, his twin, the God of the Waning Year, because the blazing peak of summer is also, by its very nature, the beginning of the Holly King's reign, with its inexorable progression to the dark nadir of midwinter, when he in turn will die at the hands of the reborn Oak King.

The Oak King's midsummer death has taken many forms in mythology. He was burned alive, or blinded with a mistletoe stake, or crucified on a T-shaped cross; and in ancient times the human enactor of the Oak King was thus sacrificed in actuality. His death was followed by a seven-day wake. But the Oak King himself, as God of the Waxing Year, withdrew to the circumpolar stars, the Corona Borealis, the Celtic Caer Arianrhod— that turning wheel of the heavens which the ancient Egyptians called *ikhem-sek*, 'not-knowing-destruction', because its stars never dipped below the horizon even at midwinter. Here he awaited his equally inevitable rebirth.

Robert Graves suggests that the biblical story of Samson (a folk-hero of the Oak King type) reflects this pattern: after being shorn of his power, he is blinded and sent to serve in a turning mill. (One might also suggest that Delilah, who presides over his downfall, represents the Goddess as Death-in-Life and that, in demoting her to villainess, Hebrew patriarchalism forgot or suppressed the sequel—that in due course, as Life-in-Death, she would be destined to preside over his restoration.)

Graves points out, further, that "since in mediaeval practice St John the Baptist, who lost his head on St John's Day" (24th June), "took over the Oak King's title and customs, it was natural to let Jesus, as John's merciful successor, take over the Holly King. . . . 'Of all the trees that are in the wood, the holly bears the crown'. . . . The identification of the pacific Jesus with the holly or holly-oak must be regretted as poetically inept, except in so far as he declared that he had come to bring not peace but the sword." (*The White Goddess*, pp. 180–1.)

Any significant Midsummer Sabbat ritual must embrace both

these God-themes, for the solstices are key points on both. But what of the Goddess? What is her role in the Midsummer drama?

Tne Goddess, as we have pointed out, is unlike the God in that she never undergoes death and rebirth. In fact, she never changes—she merely presents different faces. At the Winter Solstice she shows her Life-in-Death aspect; though her Earth-body seems cold and still, yet she gives birth to the new Sun-God and presides over the replacement of Holly King by Oak King with his promise of resurgent life. At the Summer Solstice she shows her Death-in-Life aspect; her Earth-body is exuberantly fecund and sensuous, greeting her Sun-God consort at the zenith of his powers—yet she knows it is a transient zenith, and at the same time she presides over the death of the Oak King and the enthronement of his dark (but necessary, and thus not evil) twin. At Midsummer the Goddess dances her magnificent Dance of Life; but even as she dances, she whispers to us: "*Panta rhei, ouden menei.*"

Midsummer is both a fire festival and a water festival, the fire being the God-aspect and the water the Goddess-aspect, as the ritual should make clear. Midsummer is also sometimes called Beltane, because bonfires are lit as they are on May Eve; it has been suggested that St Patrick was largely responsible for this in Ireland, because he shifted Ireland's 'bonfire night' to St John's Eve to play down the pagan implications of May Eve.[2] He may

---

2. Throughout most of Ireland, the night for the communal Midsummer fire is 23rd June, the eve of St John's Day. But in some places it is traditionally 28th June, the eve of St Peter and St Paul's Day, sometimes known as 'Little Bonfire Night'. We have been unable to pin down the reason for this curious difference, but it might possibly have something to do with the old Julian calendar. In 1582 Pope Gregory XIII wiped out ten days to make the calendar astronomically correct, and it is the Gregorian calendar which the world still uses today. (It was not adopted by England, Scotland and Wales till 1752—by which time eleven days had to be dropped—and was general in Ireland by 1782.) But it is noticeable in many parts of Europe that old folk-customs which have escaped official Christian take-over tend to be pegged to the old calendar (see, for example, p. 124). St Peter and Paul is nearer to the Midsummer Solstice than St John *if the Gregorian reform is ignored*. So perhaps a stubborn pagan custom, which did in places ignore that reform, was there merely attached to the nearest important saint's day to make it as respectable as could be managed.

indeed have shifted the emphasis, but he can hardly have shifted the name, because Bealtaine *means* May in Irish; the use of the name for Midsummer can have arisen only in non-Gaelic-speaking countries.

In any case, Midsummer was a principal fire festival throughout Europe, and even among the Arabs and Berbers of North Africa; it was lesser, and late-developing, in the Celtic countries because they were not originally or naturally solar-oriented. Many of the customs have survived into modern times and often involve the turning, or rolling downhill, of a flaming wheel as a solar symbol. As at Bealtaine and Samhain (indeed, at every Festival) the bonfire itself has always been regarded as having great magical power. We have already mentioned (under Bealtaine) the custom of jumping the fire and driving cattle through it. Ashes from it were also scattered on the fields. In Ireland a burnt sod from the St John's Eve fire was a protective charm. In flax-growing countries the height achieved in jumping the fire was believed to foretell the height to which the flax would grow. Moroccans rubbed a paste of the ashes into their hair to prevent baldness. Another custom widespread throughout Europe was to strengthen the eyes by looking at the fire through bunches of larkspur or other flowers held in the hand.

Chapter LXII of Frazer's *Golden Bough* is a mine of information on fire-festival traditions.

For modern witches, fire is a central feature of the Midsummer Sabbat as it is of Bealtaine. But since the cauldron (which on May Eve holds the Bealtaine fire) is used at Midsummer for the water with which the High Priestess sprinkles her coven—and is referred to as 'the cauldron of Cerridwen', reaffirming its Goddess symbolism—we have drawn on another long-standing tradition by suggesting twin bonfires for the Midsummer rite (or twin candles as their equivalent if the festival is indoors). Magically, passing *between* them is regarded as the same as passing *over* a single fire and, if you are driving cattle through as a spell for a good milk-yield, is obviously more practical!

Of all the Sabbats, Midsummer in temperate climates is the one to hold out of doors if facilities and privacy permit; for skyclad observance, it and Lughnasadh may prove to be the

1. The Altar

2. (*Overleaf*) The Opening Ritual: Consecrating the Water and Salt

3. (*Overleaf, right*), Consecrating the Cakes

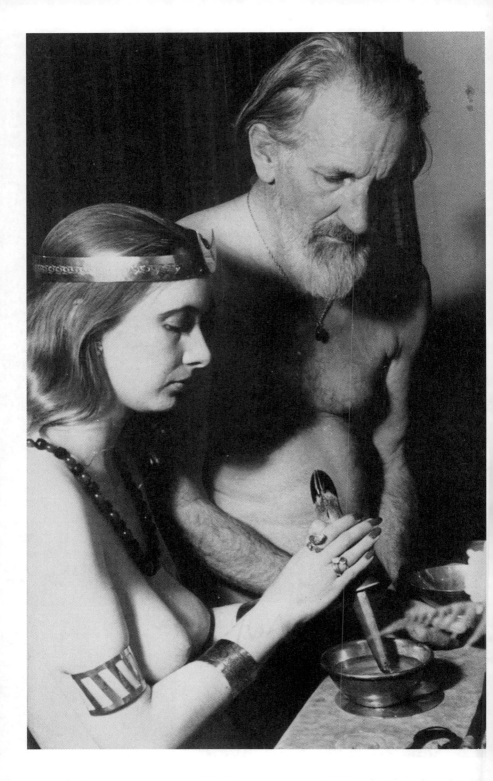

4. The Great Rite: "Assist me to erect the ancient altar"
5. Imbolg: The Triple Goddess – Maid, Mother and Crone

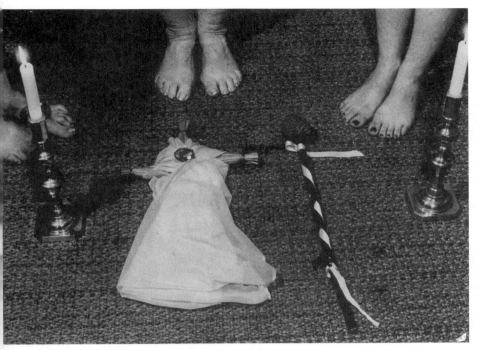

6. Imbolg: Brigid's Bed
7. Bealtaine: "Re-kindle the Bel-fire!"

8. Bealtaine: Re-birth of the Oak King

9. (*Facing*) Midsummer: The Oak King has been vanquished by the
Holly King, and the Goddess performs her Midsummer Dance to the Sun

10. The Wand and the Scourge held in the 'Osiris Position'

only ones. But as with the other Sabbats, we have described our ritual as for indoor celebration—if only because adaptation of an indoor 'script' to outdoor use is easier than the other way round.

Talking of skyclad—one Midsummer tradition may be of interest to any woman who is anxious to conceive and who owns a vegetable garden. She should walk through it naked on Midsummer Eve and also pluck some St John's Wort, if there is any. (If your vegetable garden is anything like ours, shoes might be thought a permissible modification of nakedness!) This is an intriguing mirror-image of the ancient and widespread fertility rite in which women walked naked round the fields to ensure an abundant harvest, often emphasizing their sympathetic magic by 'riding' (a discreet euphemism) phallic 'broomsticks'. (See p. 86 for a twentieth-century survival of this.)

The Preparation

The cauldron is placed immediately in front of the altar, with some water in it and decorated with flowers. A branch of heather is placed beside it, ready for the High Priestess to sprinkle water with. (Quite apart from this branch, heather is a good plant, symbolically, for Circle decorations on this night; red heather is the passionate flower of Midsummer, and white heather represents the moderating influence—will controlling or directing passion.)

Two crowns, one of oak leaves and one of holly leaves, are made and placed beside the altar. The High Priest (who represents the Sun God) should be crowned too, but from the start of the ritual; his crown should be gold-coloured, and he may add any other accessories or decorations which enhance the solar symbolism.

High Priestess and Maiden may wear chaplets of summer flowers.

The two altar candles, in their holders, may be used at the appropriate moment as the 'bonfires'; or two other candles in holders may be kept ready. Outdoors, of course, two small bonfires will be laid ready for quick lighting—one halfway between the centre of the Circle and the East candle, one halfway between the centre and the West candle. (The outdoor Circle will, of course, be much larger, leaving room to dance between and around the bonfires.)

A dark-coloured scarf is laid by the altar, ready to use as a blindfold.

A number of straws are laid on the altar—as many as there are men at the Sabbat, except for the High Priest. One of them is longer than the rest, and one shorter. (If the High Priestess, for her own reasons, decides to nominate the two Kings instead of drawing lots for them, the straws are of course not needed.)

The Ritual

After the Witches' Rune, the Maiden fetches the straws from the altar and holds them in her hand so that all the ends are protruding separately, but nobody can see which are the short and long ones. The High Priestess says:

"Let the men draw lots."

Each man (except the High Priest) draws a straw from the Maiden's hand and shows it to the High Priestess. The High Priestess points to the man who has drawn the long straw and says:

"Thou are the Oak King, God of the Waxing Year. Maiden, bring his crown!"

The Maiden places the oak-leaf crown on the head of the Oak King.

The High Priestess points to the man who has drawn the short straw and says:

"Thou art the Holly King, God of the Waning Year. Maiden, bring his crown!"

The Maiden places the holly-leaf crown on the head of the Holly King.

The High Priestess leads the Oak King to the centre of the Circle, where he stands facing West. The rest of the coven surround him, facing inwards, except for the High Priestess and High Priest, who stand with their backs to the altar on either side of the cauldron.

The High Priestess says:

"With the Sun God at the height of his power and majesty, the waxing of the year is accomplished, and the reign of the Oak King is ended. With the Sun God at the height of his splendour, the waning of the year begins; the Holly King must slay his brother the Oak King, and rule over my land until the depth of winter, when his brother shall be born again."

The Holly King moves in front of the Oak King, facing him, and places his hands on the Oak King's shoulders, pressing downwards. The Oak King falls to his knees. Meanwhile the Maiden fetches the scarf, and she and the Holly King blindfold the Oak King. The rest of the coven move back to the perimeter of the Circle and sit down, facing inwards.

The High Priestess picks up her athame and moves forward;[3] the Holly King takes her place before the altar, on the other side of the cauldron from the High Priest. The High Priestess, athame in hand, dances deosil around the kneeling Oak King (see Plate 9) while the High Priest declaims the following poem, steadily and clearly, emphasizing the beat and maintaining the rhythm:

> "*Dance, Lady, dance—on the Oak King's tomb,*
> *Where he lies half a year in thy quiet womb.*
>
> *Dance, Lady, dance—at the Holly King's birth,*
> *Who has slain his twin for the love of Earth.*
>
> *Dance, Lady, dance—to the Sun God's power*
> *And his touch of gold on field and flower.*
>
> *Dance, Lady, dance—with thy blade in hand,*
> *That shall summon the Sun to bless thy land.*
>
> *Dance, Lady, dance—in the Silver Wheel,*
> *Where the Oak King rests, his wounds to heal.*
>
> *Dance, Lady, dance—for the Holly King's reign,*
> *Till his brother the Oak shall rise again.*
>
> *Dance, Lady, dance—in the moonlit sky*
> *To the Threefold Name men know thee by.*
>
> *Dance, Lady, dance—on the turning Earth*
> *For the Birth that is Death, and the Death that is Birth.*
>
> *Dance, Lady, dance—to the Sun on high,*
> *For his burning splendour, too, must die.*
>
> *Dance, Lady, dance—to the year's long tide,*
> *For through all change must thou abide.*"

---

3. It is symbolically fitting that the High Priestess, representing the Goddess, should perform the Midsummer Dance; but if she feels that one of her other women witches is a particularly talented dancer and would do it more effectively, she may delegate the task to her.

—and now, accelerating the rhythm—

> *"Dance for the Sun in glory,*
> *Dance for the Oak King's passing,*
> *Dance for the Holly King's triumph—*
> *Dance, Lady, dance—*
> *Dance, Lady, dance—*
> *Dance, Lady, dance . . ."*

The coven join in the chant *"Dance, Lady, dance,"* to a fast insistent beat, till the High Priest signals to them to stop and also stops himself.

The High Priestess ends her dance by laying down her athame on the altar. She and the Maiden help the Oak King to rise, and they lead him, still blindfold, to kneel before the West candle.

The High Priest then says:

"The spirit of the Oak King is gone from us, to rest in Caer Arianrhod, the Castle of the Silver Wheel; until, with the turning of the year, the season shall come when he shall return to rule again. The spirit is gone; therefore let the man among us who has stood for that spirit be freed from his task."

The Maiden removes the Oak King's blindfold, and the High Priestess removes his oak-leaf crown. They lay them on each side of the West candle and then help the man rise; he turns and again becomes a part of the coven.

The High Priest says:

"Let the Midsummer fires shine forth!"

The Maiden and the Holly King fetch the two altar candles and place them on the East-West line, equidistant from the centre and four or five feet apart. Meanwhile the High Priestess rejoins the High Priest at the altar. (Outdoors, Maiden and Holly King light the two bonfires.)

The Maiden then fetches the High Priest's athame from the altar and stands beside the westerly midsummer candle, facing East. The Holly King fetches the chalice of wine and stands beside the easterly midsummer candle, facing West.

The symbolic Great Rite is then enacted by the High Priestess and High Priest—the High Priestess placing herself between the two candles, and the Maiden and Holly King handing over the athame and chalice at the appropriate moment.

After the Great Rite and the passing of the chalice, the High Priest stands before the altar with the wand in his right hand and the scourge in his left, crossed over his breast in the Osiris Position. The High Priestess faces him, and invokes joyfully:[1]

"Great One of Heaven, Power of the Sun, we invoke thee in thine ancient names—Michael, Balin, Arthur, Lugh; come again as of old into this thy land. Lift up thy shining spear of light to protect us. Put to flight the powers of darkness. Give us fair woodlands and green fields, blossoming orchards and ripening corn. Bring us to stand upon thy hill of vision and show us the path to the lovely realms of the Gods."

She then traces the Invoking Pentagram of Earth in front of the High Priest with her right forefinger. The High Priest raises both his hands high and then plunges the wand into the water in the cauldron. He then holds it up, saying:

"The Spear to the Cauldron, the Lance to the Grail, Spirit to Flesh, Man to Woman, Sun to Earth."

The High Priest lays the wand and scourge down on the altar and joins the rest of the coven. The High Priestess picks up the heather branch and stands by the cauldron. She says:

"Dance ye before the Cauldron of Cerridwen, the Goddess, and be ye blessed with the touch of this consecrated water; even as the Sun, the Lord of Life, ariseth in his strength in the sign of the Waters of Life!"

The coven, led by the High Priest, start to move deosil round the Circle, outside the two candles. As each person passes her, the High Priestess sprinkles him or her with water with her heather branch. When she has sprinkled everybody, she joins the moving ring.

The High Priestess then orders everybody in turn—singly or in couples—to pass between the midsummer candles and to wish as they go. When everyone has been through, the High Priestess and High Priest pass through together. They then turn back and pick up the two candles and return them to the altar, to leave room for the dance.

High Priestess and High Priest then lead the coven in spontaneous and joyous dancing, until the High Priestess decides it is time for the party stage of the Sabbat.

---

4. Written by Doreen Valiente, down to "Waters of Life".

VIII Lughnasadh, 31st July

Lughnasadh (pronounced '*loo*-nus-uh') means 'the commemoration of Lugh'. In its simplified spelling, *Lúnasa*, it is Irish Gaelic for the month of August. As *Lunasda* or *Lunasdal* ('*loo*-nus-duh', '-dul'), it is Scottish Gaelic for Lammas, 1st August; and the Manx equivalent is *Laa Luanys* or *Laa Lunys*. In Scotland, the period from a fortnight before Lunasda to a fortnight after is known as Iuchar, while in the Dingle Peninsula of County Kerry the second fortnight is known as *An Lughna Dubh* (the dark Lugh-festival)—suggesting "that they are echoes of a lunar reckoning whereby Lughnasa would have been celebrated in conjunction with a phase of the moon" (Máire MacNeill, *The Festival of Lughnasa*, p. 16).

Throughout the British Isles (not only in the 'Celtic fringe' but also in such places as County Durham and Yorkshire),

Lughnasadh folk-customs have attached themselves almost entirely to the Sunday before or the Sunday after 1st August—not merely through Christianization but because they involved large gatherings of people, often on mountains or high hills, which were possible only on the days of leisure which Christianity had conveniently provided.

Of the Lughnasadh survivals in these islands, Ireland supplies a veritable gold-mine, partly because, as we have already pointed out, in Ireland rural culture has been far less eroded by urban culture than elsewhere, but also for another historical reason. During the centuries when the Catholic religion was proscribed or persecuted, the Irish peasantry, deprived of their buildings of worship, clung all the more fervently to the open-air holy places which were all that was left to them. So, obeying an urge far older than Christianity, priests and people together climbed the sacred heights or sought out the magical wells, to mark those turning-points in Mother Earth's year which were too important to them to be unacknowledged merely because their churches were roofless or requisitioned by an alien creed. On such heights as Croagh Patrick, they still do; more of that later.

Máire MacNeill's book, quoted above, brings together an astonishing wealth of these survivals—seven hundred pages of customs, folklore and root-legend which should not be missed by any serious student of the Eight Festivals.

Who was Lugh? He was a fire- and light-god of the Baal/Hercules type; his name may be from the same root as the Latin *lux*, meaning light (which also gives us Lucifer, 'the light-bringer'). He is really the same god as Baal/Beli/Balor, but a later and more sophisticated version of him. In mythology, the historical replacing of one god by a later form (following invasion, for example, or a revolutionary advance in technology) is often remembered as the killing, blinding or emasculation of the older by the younger, while the essential continuity is acknowledged by making the younger into the son or grandson of the elder. (If the superseded deity is a goddess, she often reappears as the wife of the newcomer.) Thus Lugh, in Irish legend, was a leader of the Tuatha Dé Danann ('the peoples of the Goddess Dana'), the last-but-one conquerors of Ireland in the mythological cycle, while Balor was king of the

Fomors, whom the Tuatha Dé defeated; and in the battle Lugh blinded Balor. Yet according to most versions, Balor was his grandfather, and Dana/Danu was Balor's wife. (In this case, marriage demoted Balor, not Dana.)

Other versions make Lugh Balor's son. The folklore of our own village does, apparently; as Máire MacNeill (*ibid.*, p. 408) records: "From Ballycroy in Mayo comes a saying proverbial in thunder-storms:

> '*Tá gaoth Lugha Lámhfhada ag eiteall anocht san aer.*'
> '*Seadh, agus drithleógai a athar. Balor Béimeann an t-athair.*'
> ('Lugh Long-arm's wind is flying in the air tonight.'
> 'Yes, and the sparks of his father, Balor Béimann.')"

Lugh, then, is Balor all over again—and certainly associated with a technological revolution. In the legend of the Tuatha Dé's victory, Lugh spares the life of Bres, a captured enemy leader, in exchange for advice on ploughing, sowing and reaping. "The story clearly contains a harvest myth in which the secret of agricultural prosperity is wrested from a powerful and reluctant god by Lugh" (MacNeill, *ibid.*, p. 5).

Lugh's superior cleverness and versatility is indicated by his titles *Lugh Lámhfhada* (pronounced 'loo law-*vaw*da') and *Samhioldánach* ('sawvil-*daw*noch', with the 'ch' as in 'loch'), "equally skilled in all the arts". His Welsh equivalent (grandson of Beli and Don) is Llew Llaw Gyffes, variously translated as "the lion with the steady hand" (Graves) and "the shining one with the skilful hand" (Gantz).

Significantly, Lugh is often the patron-deity of a town, such as Carlisle (Luguvalium), Lyon in France, Leyden in Holland and Legnica (German, Liegnitz) in Poland. Towns were alien to the earlier Celts; their first (Continental) towns were for commercial convenience in trading with the Mediterranean civilizations, from which they copied them; for strongpoints in exacting tribute from the trade-routes; or later, as a result of the absorption of Celtic Gaul into the patterns of the Roman Empire. Of the British Celts, a writer as late as Strabo (*c.* 55 BC–AD 25) could still say: "Their cities are the woods. They enclose a large area with felled trees and set up huts to house themselves and their animals, never with the intention of staying very long in these places." So by the time the Celts got around to naming towns, Balor had been outshone by Lugh—apart from the fact that a large proportion of the population of those towns would be craftsmen, naturally devoted to Lugh Samhioldánach.

Talking of take-overs—they happened of course with the arrival of Christianity, too. A prime example is St Michael, who was a later form of the Lucifer he 'defeated'. T. C. Lethbridge, in *Witches: Investigating an Ancient Religion*, has shown how many parish churches of St Michael coincide with places where Lugh, the Celtic Lucifer or 'light-bringer', would have been worshipped (pre-Reformation churches, that is; post-Reformation churchbuilders seem to have lost all sense of place-magic).[1] And Michael, in magical tradition, rules the fire element.

That Lugh is also a type of the god who undergoes death and rebirth in a sacrificial mating with the Goddess, is most clearly seen in the legend of his Welsh manifestation, Llew Llaw Gyffes. This story appears as part of *The Romance of Math the Son of Mathonwy* in the *Mabinogion*; Graves gives Lady Charlotte Guest's translation of it in *The White Goddess*.

Graves also says (*ibid.*, p. 178): "The Anglo-Saxon form of *Lughomass*, mass in honour of the God Lugh or Llew, was *hlaf-mass*, 'loaf-mass', with reference to the corn-harvest and the killing of the Corn-king." The Tailltean Games, held in Ireland at Lughnasadh, were orginally funeral-games, traditionally in honour of Lugh's dead foster-mother Tailte; but as Graves points out (p. 302), this tradition "is late and misleading". The wake-games were clearly to honour the sacrificed Lugh himself. And unless one grasps the meaning of the sacrificial-mating theme, one might be puzzled by the apparent contradiction that an early Irish tradition also refers to the wedding-feats of Lugh at Tailtiu; in a sense, this too is a blurring of a half-remembered story, for he who mates with the Goddess at harvest is already her Waning Year consort. As Máire MacNeill rightly says (*ibid.*, p. 424): "Lughnasa, I would

---

1. On the whole subject of place-magic, not only of places of worship but also (for example) of such things as Bealtaine fires, Tom Graves's *Needles of Stone* is practically essential reading for witches who want not merely to feel but to understand and experiment constructively with their relationship to Earth as a living organism.

suggest, was one episode in the cycle of a divine marriage story but not necessarily the bridal time."

So in Lughnasadh we have the autumn parallel to the Bealtaine sacrificial mating with the God of the Waxing Year. On the human level, it is interesting that the Bealtaine 'greenwood marriages' were paralleled by the Lughnasadh 'Teltown marriages' (i.e., Tailltean), trial marriages which could be dissolved after a year and a day by the couple returning to the place where the union was celebrated and walking away from each other to North and South. (Wiccan handfasting has the same provision: the couple can dissolve it after a year and a day by returning to the High Priestess who handfasted them and informing her.) Teltown (modern Irish Tailteann, old Irish Tailtiu) is a village in County Meath, where tradition remembers a 'Hillock of the Bride-Price" and a 'Marriage Hollow'. The Tailltean Fair seems in later centuries to have become a mere marriage-market, with boys and girls kept apart till contracts were signed; but its origins must have been very different.

It stemmed, in fact, from the *óenach*, or tribal gathering, of pagan times—of which the *óenach* of Tailtiu was the most important, being associated with the High King, whose royal seat of Tara is only 15 miles away. (MacNeill, *ibid.*, pp. 311–338.) These gatherings were a mixture of tribal business, horse-racing, athletic contests and ritual to ensure good fortune; and Lughnasadh was a favourite time for them. The Leinster *óenach* of Carman, the Wexford goddess (MacNeill, *ibid.*, pp. 339–344), for example, was held on the banks of the River Barrow for the week beginning with the Lughnasadh feast, to secure for the tribe "corn and milk, mast and fish, and freedom from aggression by any outsider". (Gearóid Mac Niocaill, *Ireland Before the Vikings*, p. 49.) "Such deep-rooted traditions could not be jettisoned and had perforce to be tolerated and as far as possible Christianized. Thus in 784 the *óenach* of Teltown (*Tailtiu*) was sanctified by the relics of Erc of Slane." Mac Niocaill also says (p. 25) that Columcille—better known outside Ireland as St Columba—is credited with a bid to take over Lughnasadh "by converting it into a 'Feast of the Ploughmen', not apparently with any great success".

The ritual behaviour of the King, as the sacred personification of the tribe, was particularly important. At Lughnasadh, for example, the King of Tara's diet had to include fish from the Boyne, venison from Luibnech, bilberries from Brí Léith near Ardagh, and other obligatory items (Mac Niocaill, p. 47). (The bilberries are significant; see below.)

A formidable list of the taboos surrounding the Roman Sacred King, the Flamen Dialis, is given by Frazer (*The Golden Bough*, p. 230). Graves (*The White Goddess*, p. 130) points out what Frazer omits—that the Flamen, a Hercules-type figure, owed his position to his sacred marriage with the Flamenica; he could not divorce her, and if she died, he had to resign. It is the role of the Sacred King to bow to the Goddess-Queen.

This brings us straight back to Lughnasadh, for Graves goes on: "In Ireland this Hercules was named *Cenn Cruaich*, 'the Lord of the Mound', but after his supersession by a more benignant sacred king was remembered as *Cromm Cruaich* ('The Bowed One of the Mound')."

Crom Cruach (the usual modern spelling), also called Crom Dubh ('The Black Bowed One'), was a sacrificial god particu- larly associated with Lughnasadh; the last Sunday in July is still known as *Domhnach Chrom Dubh* ('Crom Dubh's Sunday') even though it has been Christianized. On that day every year, thousands of pilgrims climb Ireland's holy mountain, whose summit can be seen through our study window—the 2,510-foot Croagh Patrick (*Cruach Phádraig*) in County Mayo, where St Patrick is said to have fasted for forty days and defeated a host of demons.[2] The observance used to be a three-day one, starting on *Aoine Chrom Dubh*, the Friday preceding. It is still Ireland's most spectacular pilgrimage.

---

2. As we were writing this, Ireland's most respected newspaper even suggested that *Domhnach Chrom Dubh* should replace 17th March (the present St Patrick's Day) as Ireland's national day. St Patrick's Day 1979 was celebrated in a blizzard; we watched the Dublin parade and felt desperately sorry for the drenched and frozen majorettes, clad in little more than braided tunics and brave smiles. Two days later *The Irish Times* in a first leader headed "Why March 17?", asked: "Would it not be better for all if the national holiday were celebrated when our weather is more bland? There is one day which is, if not historically, at least in the legendary sense, apposite and from the weather point of view more acceptable. That is the last Sunday in July, Garland Sunday or *Domhnach Chrom Dubh*." Citing Máire MacNeill's *The*

The Sacrifice of Crom himself seems to have been enacted in very ancient times by the sacrifice of human substitutes at a phallic stone surrounded by twelve other stones (the sacrificial hero-king's traditional number of companions). The eleventh-century *Book of Leinster* says, with Christian distaste:

> "In a rank stand
> Twelve idols of stone;
> Bitterly to enchant the people
> The figure of the Cromm was of gold."

This was at Magh Sléacht ('The Plain of Adoration'), generally held to be around Killycluggin in County Cavan, where there is a stone circle and the shattered remains of a phallic stone carved with Iron Age decorations—in keeping with the tradition that St Patrick overthrew the Crom stone.

Later the sacrifice seems to have been that of a bull, of which there are many hints, though only one which can be specifically linked with Crom Dubh. That is from the north shore of Galway Bay. "It tells of the tradition that a beef-animal was skinned and roasted to ashes in honour of Crom Dubh on his festival day, and that this had to be done by every householder." (MacNeill, *ibid.*, p. 407.) Many legends speak of the death and resuscitation of a sacred bull (*ibid.*, p. 410). And, accepting that Croagh Patrick must have been a sacrificial mountain long before St Patrick took it over, we cannot help wondering if there is significance in the fact that Westport, the town that commands its approaches, has for its Gaelic name Cathair na Mart, 'City of the Beeves'.

But underlying all the legends we have mentioned so far is an older fertility theme, which shines through many of the still-remembered festival customs. Balor, Bres and Crom Dubh are all forms of the Elder God, to whom belongs the *power* to produce. Along comes his son/other-self, the bright Young God, Horus to his Osiris—the many-gifted Lugh, who wrests

---

Festival of Lughnasa to support its argument, it ended: "If any interest, therefore, wants to sponsor another date, and a valid one, for remembering our Saint, the folklore files give a ready answer." Ireland's gift for pagan-Christian continuity is clearly indestructible; we are tempted to wonder whether, in this epoch of religious change, it will work both ways!

from him the *fruits* of that power. Even the colourful St Patrick legends echo this victory. "Saint Patrick must be a latecomer to the mythological legends and must have displaced a former actor. If we restore Lugh to the role taken by Saint Patrick, the legends at once acquire new meaning." (MacNeill, *ibid.*, p. 409.)

In the legends of this fertility-victory (and also doubtless, as Máire MacNeill points out, at one time in the enacted Lughnasadh ritual), Crom Dubh is often buried in the ground up to the neck for three days and then released once the harvest-fruits have been guaranteed.

A sign of the success of the rite is given by—of all things—the humble bilberry (whortle-berry, blaeberry). *Domhnach Chrom Dubh* has other names (including Garland Sunday and Garlic Sunday), and one of them is Fraughan Sunday, from the Gaelic *fraochán* or *fraochóg* for bilberry. On that day still, young people go picking bilberries, with various traditional jollifications, though the custom seems unfortunately to be waning. The forms of the tradition make it quite clear that the bilberries were regarded as a reciprocal gift from the God, a sign that the Lughnasadh ritual had succeeded; their plentifulness or otherwise was taken as a forecast of the size of the harvest. The fact that the two rituals are complementary is still underlined in our locality by the fact that, while adults climb Croagh Patrick on *Domhnach Chrom Dubh*, children are climbing the mountains of the Curraun peninsula, just across the bay, to pick bilberries.

Another Fraughan Sunday site is Carrigroe near Ferns in County Wexford, a 771-foot mountain on the flank of which our first Irish home stood. Within living memory, large crowds used to gather there for the picking, and flowers would be placed on the Giant's Bed, a shelf in the rock which forms the summit. (Our Plate 11 was photographed on that rock.) The fertility association is specific in the joke made to us by more than one neighbour—that half the population of Ferns was conceived on the Giant's Bed; though doubtless that particular ritual has become private rather than communal!

(Incidentally, folk-memories of the magical significance of that little mountain are enshrined in an unwritten local saying, passed to us independently by at least two neighbours, both of whom made it clear they were commenting on our presence there as witches: "As long as Carrigroe stands, there will be people who know." We certainly found it magically super-charged.)

Throughout Britain and Ireland, Christianity notwithstanding, the May Eve greenwood lovemaking which so shocked the Puritans found its cheerful echo not only among the bilberries but in the Lammas (Lughnasadh) cornfields; on which theme, if you like songs at your Sabbats, Robert Burns's *It was upon a Lammas Night*—

> "Corn rigs, an' barley rigs,
> An' corn rigs are bonnie;
> I'll ne'er forget that happy night,
> Amang the rigs wi' Annie"

—is both appropriate and delightful.

The Three Machas—the Triple Goddess in her battle aspect—appear as the triune patroness of the Lughnasadh festival, bringing us back to the sacrificial theme. Another hint is that it was at Lammas that King William Rufus fell to Sir Walter Tyrell's 'accidental' arrow in the New Forest in 1100—a death which, as Margaret Murray and others have persuasively argued, was in fact his willing ritual sacrifice at the end of his term as Divine King and was so understood and honoured by his people. (The nursery rhyme 'Who Killed Cock Robin?' is said to commemorate this event.)

But what of the sacrificial mating theme *as a single concept*, instead of as two separate ones of sacrifice and sexuality? Has this vanished altogether in Irish tradition?

Not quite. In the first place, that tradition as it has reached us is mainly a God-and-Hero one, though with the Goddess hovering powerfully in the background; and it has reached us largely through mediaeval Christian monks who wrote down a body of *oral* legend (albeit surprisingly sympathetically)— scribes whose conditioning perhaps made it difficult for them to recognize Goddess clues. But the clues are there—particularly in the recurrent theme of the rivalry of two heroes (gods) over a heroine (goddess). This theme is not confined to the Irish Celts; it appears, for example, in the legend of Jack the Tinkard, who can be regarded as a Cornish Lugh. And significantly—as with the Oak King and Holly King, these heroes are often alternately successful.

And what is Crom Dubh's three-day burial up to the neck in Mother Earth, and his release when her fertility is assured, but a sacrificial mating and rebirth?

So, in our own Lughnasadh ritual, we have kept to that theme. When our coven first tried out the Love-Chase enactment of the Sacrificial Mating, at Bealtaine 1977, we found it very successful; it portrayed the theme vividly but without grimness. We saw no reason why it should not be repeated, with modifications appropriate to the harvest season, at Lughnasadh; and that is what we have done.

Because the High Priestess at Lughnasadh invokes the Goddess into herself and delays this invocation until after the 'death' of the Holly King, we felt it more suitable in the Opening Ritual to have the High Priest deliver the Charge for her; he *quotes* the Goddess, instead of the High Priestess speaking *as* the Goddess.

Normally, we like to give an active role in the ritual to as many people as possible; but it will be noticed that in this Lughnasadh rite, the men (apart from the High Priest) have practically nothing to do between the Love Chase and the final ring dance. This is in keeping with the tradition surrounding the death of the Corn King; in many places it was a mystery between the women of the tribe and their solitary sacred victim, which no other man was allowed to witness. In our Sabbat, the men can always get their own back during the party-stage forfeits!

The High Priest's declamation "*I am a battle-waging spear . . .*" is again from the Song of Amergin—this time according to Graves's allocation for the second half of the year.

The Preparation

A small loaf is placed on the altar; most suitable is a soft roll or 'bap'.

A green scarf or piece of gauze at least a yard square is laid by the altar.

If cassette music is used, the High Priestess may wish to have one piece of music for the main ritual, plus another of an insistent—even primitive—rhythm for her Corn Dance since it, unlike the Midsummer Dance, is not accompanied by chanting.

The High Priest should have a crown of holly combined with ears of a grain crop. The women many wear grain-crop chaplets, perhaps interwoven with red poppies. Grain, poppies and bilberries, if available, are particularly suitable for the altar, with other seasonal flowers.

The cauldron, decorated with stems of grain, is by the East candle, the quarter of rebirth.

The Ritual

In the opening ritual, Drawing Down the Moon is omitted. The High Priest gives the High Priestess the Fivefold Kiss and then immediately himself delivers the Charge, substituting "she, her, hers" for "I, me, my, mine".

After the Witches' Rune, the coven spread themselves around the Circle and start a soft, rhythmic clapping.

The High Priest picks up the green scarf, gathers it lengthwise like a rope and holds it with one end in each hand. He starts to move towards the High Priestess, making as though to throw the scarf over her shoulders and pull her to him; but she backs away from him, tantalizingly.

While the coven continue their rhythmic clapping, the High Priestess continues to elude the pursuing High Priest. She beckons to him and teases him but always steps back before he can capture her with the scarf. She weaves in and out of the coven, and the other women step in the High Priest's way to help her elude him.

After a while, say after two or three 'laps' of the Circle, the High Priestess allows the High Priest to capture her by throwing the scarf over her head to behind her shoulders and pulling her to him. They kiss and separate, and the High Priest hands the scarf to another man.

The other man then pursues *his* partner, who eludes him, beckons to him and teases him in exactly the same way; the clapping goes on all the time. (See Plate 12.) After a while she, too, allows herself to be captured and kissed.

The man then hands the scarf to another man, and the pursuit-game continues until every couple in the room has taken part.

The last man hands the scarf back to the High Priest.

Once again the High Priest pursues the High Priestess; but this time the pace is much slower, almost stately, and her eluding and beckoning more solemn, as though she is tempting him into danger; and this time the others do not intervene. The pursuit continues until the High Priestess places herself facing the altar and two or three paces from it; the High Priest halts with his back to the altar and captures her with the scarf.

They embrace solemnly but wholeheartedly; but after a few seconds of the kiss, the High Priest lets the scarf fall from his hands, and the High Priestess releases him and takes a step backwards.

The High Priest drops to his knees, sits back on his heels and lowers his head, chin on chest.

The High Priestess spreads her arms, signalling for the clapping to stop. She then calls forward two women by name and places them one each side of the High Priest, facing inwards, so that the three of them tower over him. The High Priestess picks up the scarf, and the three of them spread it between them over the High Priest. They lower it slowly and then release it, so that it covers his head like a shroud.

The coven now spread themselves around the perimeter of the Circle, facing inwards.

The High Priestess may then, if she wishes, change the music-cassette to her chosen dance theme or signal someone else to do so.

She then picks up the small loaf from the altar and holds it for a moment just above the bowed head of the High Priest. She then goes to the middle of the Circle, holds the loaf up high in the direction of the altar and invokes:

"O Mighty Mother of us all, bringer of all fruitfulness, give us fruit and grain, flocks and herds, and children to the tribe, that we may be mighty. By the rose of thy love,[3] *do thou descend upon the body of thy servant and priestess here."*

---

3. The Book of Shadows says "by thy rosy love". Doreen Valiente queried this "rather meaningless phrase" with Gardner at the time, suggesting it might be a corruption of "by thy rose of love" or "by the rose of thy love"—the rose being a symbol of the Goddess as well as Britain's national flower. We have followed the second of her suggestions.

After a moment's pause, and gently at first, she starts her Corn Dance, all the time carrying the loaf as a sacred and magical object.[1] (See Plate 13.)

She finishes her dance by standing facing the High Priest (who is still motionless and 'dead') with the loaf in her two hands, and saying:

"Gather round, O Children of the Harvest!"

The rest of the coven gather round the High Priestess and the kneeling High Priest. (If the High Priestess and the Maiden do not know their words by heart, the Maiden may bring the script and one altar candle and stand beside the High Priestess where they both can read it, since the High Priestess's hands are both occupied.)

The High Priestess says:

"Behold, the Holly King is dead—he who is also the Corn King. He has embraced the Great Mother, and died of his love; so has it been, year by year, since time began. But if the Holly King is dead—he who is the God of the Waning Year—all is dead; all that sleeps in my womb of Earth would sleep forever. What shall we do, therefore, that the Holly King may live again?"

The Maiden says:

"Give us to eat the bread of Life. Then shall sleep lead on to rebirth."

The High Priestess says:

"So mote it be."

(The Maiden may now replace the script and the altar candle and return to her place beside the High Priestess.)

The High Priestess breaks small pieces from the loaf and gives one piece to each witch, who eats it. She does not yet eat a piece herself but keeps enough in her hands for at least three more portions.

She summons the original two women to stand on either side of the High Priest. When they are in position, she gestures to them to lift the scarf from the High Priest's head; they do so and lay it on the floor.

---

4. Like the Midsummer Dance, the Corn Dance may be delegated by the High Priestess to another woman if she wishes. In this case, she will hand the loaf to the dancer after the invocation and receive it back after the dance, before she takes her place facing the High Priest.

The High Priestess says:
"Come back to us, Holly King, that the land may be fruitful."
The High Priest rises, and says:

> *"I am a battle-waging spear;*
> *I am a salmon in the pool;*
> *I am a hill of poetry;*
> *I am a ruthless boar;*
> *I am a threatening noise of the sea;*
> *I am a wave of the sea;*
> *Who but I knows the secrets of the unhewn dolmen?"*

The High Priestess then gives him a piece of the loaf and takes a piece herself; they both eat, and she replaces the last of the loaf on the altar. High Priestess and High Priest then lead a ring dance, building up the pace so that it becomes more and more joyous, until the High Priestess cries "Down!" and everybody sits.

The Great Rite is then enacted.

The remaining portion of the loaf, after the Circle has been banished, becomes part of the Earth-offering along with the last of the wine and cakes.

IX Autumn Equinox, 21st September

The two Equinoxes are, as we have pointed out, times of equilibrium. Day and night are matched, and the tide of the year flows steadily. But while the Spring Equinox manifests the equilibrium of an athlete poised for action, the Autumn Equinox's theme is that of rest after labour. The Sun is about to enter the sign of Libra, the Balance. In the Stations of the Goddess, the Spring Equinox represents Initiation; the Autumn Equinox, Repose. The harvest has been gathered in, both grain and fruit, yet the Sun—though mellower and less fierce than he was—is still with us. With symbolic aptness, there is still a week to go before Michaelmas, the festival of Michael/Lucifer, Archangel of Fire and Light, at which we must begin to say *au revoir* to his splendour.

Doreen Valiente (*An ABC of Witchcraft*, p. 166) remarks that the most frequent spectral appearances of certain recurrent hauntings are March and September, "the months of the Equinoxes—periods well known to occultists as being times of psychic stress". That would seem to contradict the idea of the Equinoxes being times of balance; yet the paradox is only an apparent one. Times of balance, of suspended activity, are by their nature the times when the veil between the seen and the unseen is thin. They are also the seasons when human beings 'change gear' to a different phase, and therefore times of psychological as well as psychic turbulence. That is all the more reason for us to recognize and understand the significance of those natural phases, so that their turbulence exhilarates instead of distressing us.

If we look at the Tree Calendar which Robert Graves has shown to underlie so much of our Western magical and poetic symbolism, we find that the Autumn Equinox comes just before the end of the Vine month and the beginning of the Ivy month. Vine and Ivy are the only two of the month-trees which grow spirally—and the spiral (particularly the double spiral, winding and returning) is a universal symbol of reincarnation. And the bird of the Autumn Equinox is the Swan, another symbol of the immortality of the soul—as is the wild goose, whose domestic variety is the traditional Michaelmas dish.

Incidentally, blackberry is a frequent substitute for the Vine in the symbolism of northern countries. Folk-tradition in many places, particularly in the West of England, insists that black-berries should not be eaten after the end of September (which is also the end of the Vine-month) because they then become the property of the Devil. Might we guess that this means: "Don't try to cling to the incoming spiral once it is over—look onward to the outgoing"?[1]

Lughnasadh marked the actual gathering of the grain harvest, but in its sacrificial aspect; the Autumn Equinox marks the *completion* of the harvest, and thanksgiving for abundance, with the emphasis on the future return of that abundance. This Equinox was the time of the Eleusinian Mysteries, the greatest

---

1. In Ireland, on the other hand, the last day for gathering blackberries is Samhain Eve. After that, the Pooka (see p. 122) "spits on them", hence one of his names—*Púca na sméar*, 'the blackberry sprite'.

mysteries of ancient Greece; and although all the details are not known (initiates kept the secrets well), the rituals of Eleusis certainly based themselves on corn-harvest symbolism. The climax is said to have been the showing to the initiate of a single ear of grain, with the admonition: "In silence is the seed of wisdom gained."

For our own Autumn Sabbat, then, we take the following interrelated themes: the completion of the harvest; a salute to the waning power of the Sun; and an acknowledgement that Sun and harvest, and men and women also, share in the universal rhythm of rebirth and reincarnation. As the Book of Shadows declamation says: "Therefore the Wise Ones weep not, but rejoice."

In the Book of Shadows ritual for this festival, the only substantial items are the High Priestess's declamation "Farewell, O Sun . . ." and the Candle Game, both of which we have retained.

The Preparation

On the altar is a dish containing a single ear of wheat or other cereal crop, covered by a cloth.

The altar and Circle are decorated with pine-cones, grain, acorns, red poppies (symbol of the Corn-Goddess Demeter) and other autumnal flowers, fruit and leaves.

The Ritual

After the Witches' Rune, the coven arrange themselves round the perimeter of the Circle, facing inwards.

The Maiden fetches the covered dish from the altar, places it in the centre of the Circle (leaving it covered) and returns to her place.

The High Priestess says:

"Now is the time of balance, when Day and Night face each other as equals. Yet at this season the Night is waxing and the Day is waning; for nothing ever remains without change, in the tides of Earth and Sky. Know and remember, that whatsoever rises must also set, and whatsoever sets must also rise. In token of which, let us dance the Dance of Going and Returning!"

With the High Priestess and High Priest leading, the coven dance slowly widdershins, hand in hand but not closing the ring head-to-tail. Gradually, the High Priestess leads inwards in a spiral, until the coven are close to the centre. When she is ready, the High Priestess halts and instructs everyone to sit in a tight ring about the covered dish, facing inwards.

The High Priestess says:

"Behold the mystery: in silence is the seed of wisdom gained."

She then takes the cloth from the dish, revealing the ear of grain. All contemplate the ear of grain for a while in silence. (See Plate 14.)

When she is ready, the High Priestess rises and goes to the East candle. The High Priest rises and goes to the West candle, and they face each other across the seated coven. The High Priestess declaims:[2]

"Farewell, O Sun, ever-returning Light,
The hidden God, who ever yet remains.
He now departs to the Land of Youth
Through the Gates of Death
To dwell enthroned, the judge of Gods and men,
The hornèd leader of the hosts of air.
Yet, as he stands unseen without the Circle,
So dwelleth he within the secret seed—
The seed of new-reaped grain, the seed of flesh;
Hidden in earth, the marvellous seed of the stars.
In him is Life, and Life is the Light of man,
That which was never born, and never dies.
Therefore the Wise Ones weep not, but rejoice."

The High Priestess raises both hands high in blessing to the High Priest, who responds with the same gesture.

High Priestess and High Priest rejoin the coven (who now stand) and lead them in a slow dance deosil, gradually spiralling outwards towards the perimeter of the Circle. When she judges that the spiral movement has been sufficiently emphasized, the High Priestess closes the ring by taking the hand of the last witch in the chain and speeds up the pace till the coven are

---

2. Written by Doreen Valiente. In Ireland, instead of *"to the Land of Youth"*, we say *"to Tír na nÓg"* (pronounced 'teer nuh *noge*') which means literally the same thing but has powerful legendary associations—a Celtic Elysium visualized as a magical island off the West Coast of Ireland, "where happiness can be had for a penny".

circling fast and joyously. After a while she cries "*Down!*" and everybody sits.

The Maiden replaces the dish with the ear of grain on the altar, and the cloth which covered it beside the altar.

The Great Rite is now enacted, followed by the wine and cakes.

After the wine and cakes comes the Candle Game, as described on p. 71 for Imbolg; and that should put everyone in the right frame of mind for the party stage.

X Samhain, 31st October

The eve of 1st November, when the Celtic Winter begins, is the dark counterpart of May Eve which greets the Summer. More than that, 1st November for the Celts was the beginning of the year itself, and the feast of Samhain was their New Year's Eve, the mysterious moment which belonged to neither past nor present, to neither this world nor the Other. Samhain (pronounced '*sow*-in', the 'ow' rhyming with 'cow') is Irish Gaelic for the month of November; Samhuin (pronounced '*sav*-en', with the 'n' like the 'ni' in 'onion') is Scottish Gaelic for All Hallows, 1st November.

For the old pastoralists, whose herd-raising was backed by only primitive agriculture or none at all, keeping whole herds fed through the winter was simply not possible, so the minimum breeding-stock was kept alive, and the rest were

121

slaughtered and salted—the only way, then, of preserving meat (hence, no doubt, the traditional use in magical ritual of salt as a 'disinfectant' against psychic or spiritual evil). Samhain was the time when this killing and preserving was done; and it is not hard to imagine what a nervously critical occasion it was. Had the right—or enough—breeding-stock been selected? Would the coming winter be long and hard? And if so, would the breeding-stock survive it, or the stored meat feed the tribe through it?

Crops, too, had all to be gathered in by 31st October, and anything still unharvested was abandoned—because of the Pooka (*Púca*), a nocturnal, shape-changing hobgoblin who delighted in tormenting humans, was believed to spend Samhain night destroying or contaminating whatever remained unreaped. The Pooka's favourite disguise seems to have been the shape of an ugly black horse.

Thus to economic uncertainty was added a sense of psychic eeriness, for at the turn of the year—the old dying, the new still unborn—the Veil was very thin. The doors of the *sidh*-mounds were open, and on this night neither human nor fairy needed any magical password to come and go. On this night, too, the spirits of dead friends sought the warmth of the Samhain fire and communion with their living kin. This was *Féile na Marbh* (pronounced '*fay*luh nuh *morv*'), the Feast of the Dead, and also *Féile Moingfhinne* (pronounced '*fay*luh *mong*-innuh'), the Feast of the White-Haired One, the Snow Goddess. It was "a partial return to primordial chaos . . . the dissolution of established order as a prelude to its recreation in a new period of time", as Proinsias mac Cana says in *Celtic Mythology*.

So Samhain was on the one hand a time of propitiation, divination and communion with the dead, and on the other, an uninhibited feast of eating, drinking and the defiant affirmation of life and fertility in the very face of the closing dark.

Propitiation, in the old days when survival was felt to depend on it, was a grim and serious affair. There can be little doubt that at one time it involved human sacrifice—of criminals saved up for the purpose or, at the other end of the scale, of an ageing king; little doubt, either, that these ritual deaths were by fire, for in Celtic (and, come to that, Norse) mythology many kings and heroes die at Samhain, often in a burning house, trapped by the wiles of supernatural women. Drowning may follow the burning, as with the sixth-century Kings of Tara, Muirchertach mac Erca and Diarmait mac Cerbaill.[1]

Later, of course, the propitiatory sacrifice became symbolic, and English children still unwittingly enact this symbolism on Guy Fawkes' Night, which has taken over from the Samhain bonfire. It is interesting that, as the failed assassinator of a king, the burned Guy is in a sense the king's substitute.

Echoes of the Samhain royal sacrifice may also have lingered in that of animal substitutes. Our village Garda (policeman), Tom Chambers, a knowledgeable student of County Mayo

---

1. These two are interesting. In *Lebor Gabála Érenn*, Part V (see Bibliography under MacAlister), we find (in translation from Old Irish): "Now the death of Muirchertach was in this manner; he was drowned in a vat of wine, after being burned, on Samain night on the summit of Cletech over the Boyne; whence St Cairnech said:—

'I am afraid of the woman
about whom many blasts shall play;
for the man who shall be burnt in fire,
on the side of Cletech wine shall drown him'."

The woman was Muirchertach's witch mistress Sín (pronounced 'Sheen', and meaning 'storm') on account of whom St Cairnech cursed him; the men of Ireland sided with the king and Sín against the Bishop. The King felt she was "a goddess of great power", but she said that, although she had great magical power, she was of the race of Adam and Eve. Sín is clearly a priestess of the Dark Goddess, presiding over a communally-approved sacrifice in spite of her personal grief. (The version that she brought about the King's doom in revenge for his slaying of her father seems a later rationalization.) Of her own subsequent death the *Lebor* says: "Sín daughter of Sige of the *sídh*-mounds of Breg died, repeating her names—

'Sighing, Moaning, Blast without reproach,
Rough and Wintry Wind,
Groaning, Weeping, a saying without falsehood—
These are my names on any road.' "

The story of Muirchertach and Sín is told in the Reeses' *Celtic Heritage*, p. 338 onwards, and in Markale's *Women of the Celts*, pp. 167–8.

Diarmait mac Cerbaill, according to the *Lebor*, was killed by Black Aed mac Suibne after a reign of twenty-one years (the sacrificed king's traditional multiple of seven?). The *Lebor* says Aed "stopped, vexed, slew, burnt and swiftly drowned him", which again has all the hallmarks of ritual sacrifice; and Gearóid MacNiocaill says Diarmait "was almost certainly a pagan" (*Ireland Before the Vikings*, p. 26).

history and folklore, tells us that within living memory cockerels' blood was sprinkled at the corners of houses, inside and out, on Martinmas Eve as a protective spell. Now Martinmas is 11th November—which is 1st November *according to the old Julian calendar*, a displacement which often points to the survival of a particularly unofficial custom (see footnote on p. 95). So this may well have been originally a Samhain practice.

The ending of the custom of actual royal sacrifice is perhaps commemorated in the legend of the destruction of Aillen mac Midgna, of the Finnachad *sidhe*, who is said to have burned royal Tara every Samhain until Fionn mac Cumhal finally slew him. (Fionn mac Cumhal is a Robin Hood-type hero, whose legends are remembered all over Ireland. The mountains above our village of Ballycroy are called the Nephin Beg range, which Tom Chambers renders from the Old Irish as 'the little resting-place of Finn'.)

Ireland's bonfire-and-firework night is still Hallowe'en, and some of the unconscious survivals are remarkable. When we lived at Ferns in County Wexford, many of the children who ambushed us at Hallowe'en hoping for apples, nuts or "money for the King, money for the Queen" included one who was masked as 'the Man in Black'. He would challenge us with "I am the Man in Black—do you know me?"—to which we had to reply "I know who you are, but you are the Man in Black." We wonder if he realized that one of the significantly recurrent pieces of evidence in the witchcraft trials of the persecution period is that 'the Man in Black' was the coven's High Priest, whose anonymity must be stubbornly protected.

In Scotland and Wales, individual family Samhain fires used to be lit; they were called *Samhnagan* in Scotland and *Coel Coeth* in Wales and were built for days ahead on the highest ground near to the house. This was still a thriving custom in some districts almost within living memory, though by then it had become (like England's bonfire night) mostly a children's celebration. The habit of Hallowe'en fires survived in the Isle of Man, too.

Frazer, in *The Golden Bough* (pp. 831–3), describes several of these Scottish, Welsh and Manx survivals, and it is very interesting that, both in these and in the corresponding Bealtaine fire customs which he records (pp. 808–14), there are many traces of the choosing of a sacrificial victim by lot—sometimes through distributing pieces of a newly baked cake. In Wales, once the last spark of the Hallowe'en fire was extinguished, everyone would "suddenly take to their heels, shouting at the top of their voices 'The cropped black sow seize the hindmost!'" (Frazer might have added that in Welsh mythology the sow represents the Goddess Cerridwen in her dark aspect.) All these victim-choosing rituals long ago mellowed into a mere romp, but Frazer had no doubt of their original grim purpose. What was once a deadly serious ritual at the great tribal fire had become a party game at the family ones.

Talking of which, at Callander (familiar to British television-viewers of a few years ago as the 'Tannochbrae' of *Dr Finlay's Casebook*) a slightly different method prevailed at the Hallowe'en bonfire. "When the fire had died down," Frazer says, "the ashes were carefully collected in the form of a circle, and a stone was put in, near the circumference, for every person of the several families interested in the bonfire. Next morning, if any of these stones was found to be displaced or injured, the people made sure that the person represented by it was *fey*, or devoted, and that he could not live twelve months from that day." Was this a midway stage between the ancient sacrificial-victim rite and today's Hallowe'en party custom of cheerful divination from the way in which fire-roasted nuts jump?

The divination aspect of Samhain is understandable for two reasons. First, the psychic climate of the season favoured it; and second, anxiety about the coming winter demanded it. Originally the Druids were "surfeited with fresh blood and meat until they became entranced and prophesied", reading the omens for the tribe for the coming year (Cottie Burland, *The Magical Arts*); but in folklore survival the divination became more personal. In particular, young women sought to identify the husband-to-be, by the way roasting nuts jumped (see above) or by conjuring up his image in a mirror. In County Donegal, a girl would wash her nightdress three times in running water and hang it in front of the kitchen fire to dry at midnight on Samhain Eve, leaving the door open; her future husband would be drawn to enter and turn it over. An alternative formula said that the washing water should be brought "from a well which brides and burials pass over". Another widespread method was for a girl to lay her table with a tempting meal, to which the 'fetch' of her future husband would come and, having eaten, be bound to her. (The 'fetch' is of course the projected astral body— implying that at Samhain not only was the veil between matter and spirit very thin but also the astral was less firmly bound to the physical.)

Hallowe'en nuts and apples still have their divinatory aspect in popular tradition; but like the nut-gathering of Bealtaine, their original meaning was a fertility one, for Samhain, too, was a time of deliberate (and tribally purposeful) sexual freedom. This fertility-ritual aspect is, as one might expect, reflected in the legends of gods and heroes. The god Angus mac Óg, and the hero Cu Chulainn, both had Samhain affairs with women who could shape-change into birds; and at Samhain the Dagda (the 'Good God') mated with the Morrigan (the dark aspect of the Goddess) as she bestrode the River Unius, and also with Boann, goddess of the River Boyne.

Samhain, like the other pagan festivals, was so deeply rooted in popular tradition that Christianity had to try to take it over. The aspect of communion with the dead, and with other spirits, was Christianized as All Hallows, moved from its original date of 13th May to 1st November, and extended to the whole Church by Pope Gregory IV in 834. But its pagan overtones remained uncomfortably alive, and in England the Reformation abolished All Hallows. It was not formally restored by the Church of England until 1928, "on the assumption that the old pagan associations of Hallowe'en were at last really dead and forgotten; a supposition that was certainly premature" (Doreen Valiente, *An ABC of Witchcraft*).

As for the feast itself—in the banquet sense, the original food was of course a proportion of the newly slaughtered cattle, roasted in the purifying Samhain fire, and doubtless having the nature of ritually offered 'first fruits'; the fact that the priesthood had first call on it for divinatory purposes, and that what they did not use provided a feast for the tribe, points to this.

In later centuries, ritual food known as 'sowens' was consumed. Robert Burns refers to it in his poem *Hallowe'en*:

"Till butter'd sowens, wi' fragrant lunt,
Set a' their gabs a-steerin' . . ."

—and in his own notes to the poem, says "Sowens, with butter
instead of milk to them, is always the Hallowe'en Supper." The
Oxford English Dictionary defines Sowens as 'an article of diet
formerly in common use in Scotland (and in some parts of
Ireland), consisting of farinaceous matter extracted from the
bran or husks of oats by steeping in water, allowed to ferment
slightly and prepared by boiling", and says that it probably
derives from *sugh* or *subh*, 'sap'. Maybe—but it is interesting
that 'sowen' is nearly enough the pronunciation of 'Samhain'.

In Ireland, 'barm brack', a dark brown loaf or cake made with
dried fruit, is as much a feature of Hallowe'en as Christmas
pudding is of Christmas and retains the seasonal divinatory
function by incorporating tokens which the lucky or unlucky
eater finds in his slice. The wrapper of a commercial barm brack
in front of us at the moment bears a witch-and-broomstick
design and the information: "Contains—ring, marriage in
twelve months; pea, poverty; bean, wealth; stick, will beat life
partner; rag, old maid or bachelor." The shops are full of them
from mid-October. For home-made barm brack, the essential
item is the ring. The cake has to be cut and buttered by
a married person, out of sight of those who will be eating
it.

For any dead friends whose spirits might be visiting, Irish
families used to leave some tobacco and a dish of porridge—and
some empty chairs—by the fire.

Paul Huson, in his interesting but magically amoral book
Mastering Witchcraft, says: "The Dumb Supper may be performed in honour of the beloved dead, and wine and bread be
ceremonially offered to them, the latter in the shape of a cake
made in nine segments similar to the square of Earth." He
probably means the Square of Saturn, which has nine segments
like a noughts-and-crosses game (and which Huson himself
gives on p. 140 of his book.) There are magic squares also for
Jupiter (sixteen segments), Mars (twenty-five), Sun (thirty-six),
Venus (forty-nine), Mercury (sixty-four) and Moon (eighty-
one), but none for Earth. In any case, Saturn would be more
seasonally appropriate; he has strong links with both the Holly

King and the Lord of Misrule—in fact the three overlap and merge a good deal.

One thing Samhain has always been, and still is: a lusty and wholehearted feast, a Mischief Night, the start of the reign of that same Lord of Misrule, which traditionally lasts from now till Candlemas—yet with serious undertones. It is not that we surrender to disorder but, as Winter begins, we look 'primordial chaos' in the face so that we may discern in it the seeds of a new order. By challenging it, and even laughing with it, we proclaim our faith that the Goddess and the God cannot, by their very nature, allow it to sweep us away.

How, then, to celebrate Samhain as twentieth-century witches?

One immediate suggestion which has become our habit, and which others may find helpful, is to have *two* celebrations—one the Samhain ritual for the coven itself, and the other the Hallowe'en party for coven, children and friends. Children expect some fun out of Hallowe'en, and so (we have discovered) do friends and neighbours expect something of witches at Hallowe'en. So hold a party and give it to them—pumpkins, masks, fancy-dress, leg-pulls, music, forfeits, local traditions—the lot. And hold your coven Samhain ritual on a separate night.

A general point arises here: how important is it to hold Sabbats on the exact traditional nights? We would say it is preferable, but not vital. The fact must be faced that for Esbats and Sabbats alike, many covens *have* to meet on particular nights—usually at weekends—for reasons of jobs, travel, baby-minding and so on. Even the Charge admits this by saying "*better* it be when the moon is full"—not "it *must* be". And as for Sabbats, most witches feel none the worse for holding them on (say) the nearest Saturday to the true date.

In *Quest* magazine of March 1978, 'Diana Demdike' makes a good point on the subject of celebrating festivals before or after the true date. "It is always better to be late rather than early," she says, "for know it or not, you are working with the powers of magical earth tides, and these begin at the actual solar point in time, so to work before then means you are meeting in the lowest ebb of the previous tide, not very helpful."

At Samhain, to be practical, there is an additional consideration: in many places (including America, Ireland and parts of

Britain) privacy on 31st October cannot be guaranteed. To have your serious Samhain ritual disturbed by children demanding "trick or treat", or "money for the King, money for the Queen", or by neighbours waving lighted pumpkins in your front garden and rightly expecting to be invited in for a drink, is clearly not a good idea. So "better it be" perhaps to displace your Samhain Sabbat by a night or two, and to face Hallowe'en Night itself with the appropriate nuts, apples, small change and bottles ready to hand—or, even better, throw a party. It is not the business of witches to do anything which might seem to discourage, or even to exclude themselves from, such traditional celebrations.

In fact, local tradition should always be respected—all the more so if it is a genuinely living one. That is why, out here in County Mayo, we light our Midsummer bonfire on St John's Eve, 23rd June, when many others dot the landscape far and wide like orange stars in the dusk; we light our Lughnasadh bonfire on *Domhnach Chrom Dubh*, the last Sunday in July, which is still named after one of the old Gods, and to which the many Lughnasadh festival customs that survive in the West of Ireland are attached; and make our Samhain party an outdoor one, weather permitting, for Hallowe'en is family bonfire night throughout Ireland.

But to return to the Samhain ritual itself, which is our concern here. Which of the ancient elements should be included?

Propitiation—no. Propitiation reduces the Gods to a human level of pettiness, in which they have to be bribed and jollied out of their capricious moods of spitefulness and bad temper. It belongs to a very primitive stage of the Old Religion, and survived, we feel, more 'by popular demand' than by priestly wisdom. Modern witches do not *fear* the Gods, the expressions of cosmic power and rhythm; they respect and worship them and work to understand and to put themselves in tune with them. And in rejecting propitiation as a superstition, once understandable but now outgrown, they are not betraying the old wisdom, they are fulfilling it; many of the old priests and priestesses (who had a deeper understanding than some of their more simple followers) would doubtless have smiled approvingly. (Though, in fairness to those 'simple followers', we should add that many rites which to the modern student look like propitiation were in fact nothing of the kind but were sympathetic magic; see *The Golden Bough*, p. 541.)

But the communion with the loved dead, the divination, the feasting, the humour, the affirmation of life—most certainly yes. These are all in accord with the Samhain point in the year's natural, human and psychic rhythms.

On the question of communion with the dead, it should always be remembered that they are *invited*, not summoned. Withdrawal and rest between incarnations is a stage-by-stage process; how long each stage lasts, and what necessary experiences (voluntary or involuntary) are gone through at each stage, is a very individual story, the whole of which can never be known by even the most intimate of the individual's still-incarnated friends. So to force communication with him or her may well be fruitless, or even harmful; and this we feel is the mistake many Spiritualists make, however sincere and genuinely gifted some of their mediums are. So, as Raymond Buckland puts it (*The Tree, The Complete Book of Saxon Witchcraft*, p. 61): "Witches do not 'call Back' the dead. They do not hold *séances*—such belongs to Spiritualism. They do, however, believe that, *if the dead themselves wish it*, they will return at the Sabbat to share in the love and celebration of the occasion."

Any invitation to dead friends, at Samhain or any other time, should be made with this attitude in mind.

As Stewart pointed out in *What Witches Do*: "Of all the eight festivals, this is the one where the Book of Shadows insists most emphatically on the Great Rite. If it is not possible at the time, the Book says the High Priest and High Priestess should celebrate it themselves as soon as convenient, 'in token, or if possible in reality'. The point presumably is that since the Hallowe'en ritual is intimately concerned with death and the dead, it should conclude with a solemn and intense reaffirmation of life."

In the present book, we have assumed that the Great Rite is always possible at the Sabbats, at least in its symbolic form. But we feel that the Book of Shadows' insistence on its particular significance at Samhain is valid, and probably a genuine Craft tradition. So we sought, in our ritual, for a way of giving it that special emphasis—hence the device of the circling coven, which for us achieves the desired effect.

If the 'actual' Great Rite is used, of course, the coven are out of the room, and any means of emphasis must be left to the High Priestess and High Priest enacting it. But the emphasis can still be, so to speak, transmitted to the coven on their return; hence the device of the High Priestess and High Priest blessing the wine and cakes immediately after the return, and the High Priest administering them personally to each woman, and the High Priestess to each man, instead of the usual circulation. We suggest that this personal administering should be carried out also if the Great Rite is symbolic.

The Preparation

The cauldron is placed in the centre of the Circle, with glowing charcoal in a tin lid or other container inside it, and incense to hand. (The usual incense-burner on, or by, the altar can be used at the appropriate moment, but a separate one is better.)

For the High Priestess, make a simple white tabard of chiffon or net (terylene net as sold for curtains will do, though chiffon is prettier). The pattern is easy—two squares or rectangles stitched together along the top and sides, but leaving neck- and arm-slits at the centre of the top, and the tops of the sides. A further refinement can be a third square or rectangle of the same size, with its top edge stitched to the top edge of the other two along the shoulders and the back of the neck-slit; this can hang behind like a cape, or be thrown up and forward over the head and face as a veil. (See diagram and also Plates 7, 11, 16 and 17.)

(Incidentally, we have made a selection of these chiffon tabards, with cape/veils and appropriate braid along the seams and hems, in various colours for various ritual purposes. They can be worn either over robes or over the skyclad body, are cheap and simple to make and are strikingly effective.)

For the Lord of Misrule, make a wand of office, as simple or elaborate as you like. Most elaborate is the traditional court-jester's stick topped by a doll's head and decorated with little bells. Simplest is a plain stick with a rubber balloon (or more traditionally, an inflated pig's bladder) tied to one end. It is laid ready beside the altar.

Circle, altar and cauldron are decorated with seasonal foliage and fruit—among which apples, and if possible nuts on the twig, should feature prominently.

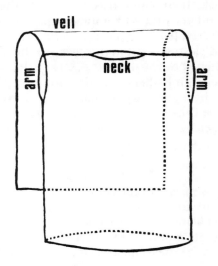

All Sabbats are feasts, but Samhain of course especially so. Food and drink should be ready for the end of the ritual. Nuts should be included, even if you can get only shelled ones at the shop or packets of peanuts from the pub. The tradition of roasting them to read the future from the way they jump (a form of divination best approached in a light-hearted spirit!) is practicable only if you have an open fire in the room.

Personal footnote: we have a tabby cat called Suzie who (alone of our many cats) is our self-appointed familiar. She is very psychic and insists on being present at all rituals; the moment we cast a Circle she bangs on the door to be let in. She behaves very well but has not learned to accept that the feast comes *after* the ritual. So we have to hide the food in a sideboard till the right moment. If you are in the same position, be warned!

The Ritual

The High Priestess wears her white tabard for the opening ritual, with the veil thrown back, if she has one.

After the Witches' Rune, the High Priest and High Priestess

take up their athames. He stands with his back to the altar, she facing him across the cauldron. They then simultaneously draw the Invoking Pentagram of Earth in the air with their athames, towards each other, after which they lay down their athames—he on the altar, she by the cauldron.

The High Priestess scatters incense on the charcoal in the cauldron. When she is satisfied that it is burning, she stands—still facing the High Priest across the cauldron. She summons a male witch to bring one of the altar candles and hold it beside her (so that she can still read her words when, later, she draws her veil over her face). She declaims:[2]

> "*Dread Lord of Shadows, God of Life, and the Giver of Life—*
> *Yet is the knowledge of thee, the knowledge of Death.*
> *Open wide, I pray thee, the Gates through which all must pass.*
> *Let our dear ones who have gone before*
> *Return this night to make merry with us.*
> *And when our time comes, as it must,*
> *O thou the Comforter, the Consoler, the Giver of Peace and Rest,*
> *We will enter thy realms gladly and unafraid;*
> *For we know that when rested and refreshed among our dear ones*
> *We will be reborn again by thy grace, and the grace of the Great Mother.*
> *Let it be in the same place and the same time as our beloved ones,*
> *And may we meet, and know, and remember,*
> *And love them again.*
> *Descend, we pray thee, in thy servant and priest.*"

The High Priestess then walks deosil round the cauldron and gives the High Priest the Fivefold Kiss.

She returns to her place, facing the High Priest across the cauldron, and if her tabard has a veil, she now draws it forward over her face. She then calls on each woman witch in turn, by name, to come forward and also give the High Priest the Fivefold Kiss.

When they have all done so, the High Priestess directs the coven to stand around the edge of the Circle, man and woman alternately, with the Maiden next to the West candle. As soon as they are all in place, the High Priestess says:

"*Behold, the West is Amenti, the Land of the Dead, to which many of our loved ones have gone for rest and renewal. On this night,*

2. Written by Gerald Gardner.

we hold communion with them; and as our Maiden stands in welcome by the Western gate, I call upon all of you, my brothers and sisters of the Craft, to hold the image of these loved ones in your hearts and minds, that our welcome may reach out to them.

"*There is mystery within mystery; for the resting-place between life and life is also Caer Arianrhod, the Castle of the Silver Wheel, at the hub of the turning stars beyond the North Wind. Here reigns Arianrhod, the White Lady, whose name means Silver Wheel. To this, in spirit, we call our loved ones. And let the Maiden lead them, moving widdershins to the centre. For the spiral path inwards to Caer Arianrhod leads to night, and rest, and is against the way of the Sun.*"

The Maiden walks, slowly and with dignity, in a widdershins (anti-clockwise) direction around the Circle, spiralling slowly inwards, taking three or four circuits to reach the centre. During this, the coven maintain absolute silence and concentrate on welcoming their dead friends.

When the Maiden reaches the centre, she faces the High Priestess across the cauldron and halts. The High Priestess holds out her right hand at shoulder level, over the centre of the cauldron, with the palm open and facing to the left. The Maiden places her own right palm flat against that of the High Priestess. The High Priestess says:

"*Those you bring with you are truly welcome to our Festival. May they remain with us in peace. And you, O Maiden, return by the spiral path to stand with our brothers and sisters; but deosil—for the way of rebirth, outwards from Caer Arianrhod, is the way of the Sun.*"

Maiden and High Priestess break their hand-contact, and the Maiden walks slowly and with dignity in a deosil (clockwise) spiral back to her place by the West candle.

The High Priestess waits until the Maiden is in place, and then says:

"*Let all approach the walls of the Castle.*"

The High Priest and the coven move inwards, and everybody (including the High Priestess and the Maiden) sits in a close ring around the cauldron. The High Priestess renews the incense.

Now is the time for communion with dead friends—and for this no set ritual can be laid down, because all covens differ in their approach. Some prefer to sit quietly round the cauldron, gazing into the incense-smoke, talking of what they see and feel. Others prefer to pass round a scrying-mirror or a crystal ball. Other covens may have a talented medium and may use her or him as a channel. Whatever the method, the High Priestess directs it.

When she feels that this part of the Sabbat has fulfilled its purpose, the High Priestess unveils her face and orders the cauldron to be carried and placed beside the East candle, the quarter of rebirth. (It should be put *beside* the candle, not in front of it, to leave room for what follows.)

The High Priest now takes over the explanation. He tells the coven, informally but seriously, that, since Samhain is a festival of the dead, it must include a strong reaffirmation of life—both on behalf of the coven itself and on behalf of the dead friends who are moving towards reincarnation. He and the High Priestess will now, therefore, enact the Great Rite, as is the custom at every Sabbat; but since this is a special occasion, there will be slight differences to emphasize it. He explains these differences, according to the form the Great Rite is going to take.

If the Great Rite is symbolic, the chalice and athame will be placed on the floor, not carried; and the Maiden and the rest of the coven will walk slowly deosil round the perimeter of the Circle during the whole of the Rite. When it is finished, High Priest and High Priestess will first give each other the wine in the usual way; but the High Priest will then personally give the wine to each woman, after which the High Priestess will personally give it to each man. They will then consecrate the cakes and give them out personally in the same way. The purpose of this (the High Priest explains) is to pass on the life-power raised by the Great Rite directly to each member of the coven.

If the Great Rite is 'actual', once the Maiden and coven have returned to the room, High Priest and High Priestess will consecrate the wine and cakes and administer them personally in the same manner.

Explanations over, the Great Rite is enacted.

Afterwards, and before the feast, only one thing remains to be done. The High Priestess fetches the Lord of Misrule's wand of office and presents it to a chosen man witch (preferably one with a sense of humour). She tells him that he is now the Lord of Misrule and for the rest of the Sabbat is privileged to disrupt the proceedings as he sees fit and to 'take the mickey' out of everyone, including herself and the High Priest.

The rest of the programme is given over to the feasting and the games. And if you, like us, are in the habit of putting out a little offering of food and drink afterwards for the *sidhe* or their local equivalent—on this night of all nights, make sure it is particularly tasty and generous!

XI   Yule, 22nd December

At the Winter Solstice, the two God-themes of the year's cycle coincide—even more dramatically than they do at the Summer Solstice. Yule (which, according to the Venerable Bede, comes from the Norse *Iul* meaning 'wheel') marks the death and rebirth of the Sun-God; it also marks the vanquishing of the Holly King, God of the Waning Year, by the Oak King, God of the Waxing Year. The Goddess, who was Death-in-Life at Midsummer, now shows her Life-in-Death aspect; for although at this season she is the "leprous-white lady", Queen of the cold darkness, yet this is her moment for giving birth to the Child of Promise, the Son-Lover who will re-fertilize her and bring back light and warmth to her kingdom.

The Christmas Nativity story is the Christian version of the theme of the Sun's rebirth, for Christ is the Sun-God of the

Piscean Age. The birthday of Jesus is undated in the Gospels, and it was not till AD 273 that the Church took the symbolically sensible step of fixing it officially at midwinter, to bring him in line with the other Sun-Gods (such as the Persian Mithras, also born at the Winter Solstice). As St Chrysostom, Archbishop of Constantinople a century later, explained with commendable frankness, the Nativity of "the Sun of Righteousness" had been so fixed in order that "while the heathen were busied with their profane rites, the Christians might perform their holy ones without disturbance".

"Profane" or "holy" depended on your viewpoint, because basically both were celebrating the same thing—the turning of the year's tide from darkness towards light. St Augustine acknowledged the festival's solar meaning when he urged Christians to celebrate it for him who made the Sun, rather than for the Sun itself.

Mary at Bethlehem is again the Goddess as Life-in-Death. Jerome, the greatest scholar of the Christian Fathers, who lived in Bethlehem from 386 till his death in 420, tells us that there was also a grove of Adonis (Tammuz) there. Now Tammuz, beloved of the Goddess Ishtar, was the supreme model in that part of the world of the Dying and Resurrected God. He was (like most of his type) a vegetation- or corn-god; and Christ absorbed this aspect of the type as well as the solar one, as the Sacrament of the Bread suggests. So as Frazer points out (*The Golden Bough*, p. 455), it is significant that the name Bethlehem means 'the House of Bread'.

The resonance between the corn-cycle and the Sun-cycle is reflected in many customs: for example, the Scottish tradition of keeping the Corn Maiden (the last handful reaped at the harvest) till Yule and then distributing it among the cattle to make them thrive all year; or, in the other direction, the German tradition of scattering the ashes of the Yule Log over the fields, or of keeping its charred remains to bind in the last sheaf of the following harvest.[1] (Here again we meet with the

---

1. Magical transference of fertility from one season to another by a charged physical object—particularly by grain or its products, or by the by-products of fire—is a universal custom. Speaking of the temple of Aphrodite and Eros on the northern slope of the Akropolis, where 'Aphrodite of the Gardens' dwelt,

magical properties of everything about the Sabbat fire, including its ashes; for the Yule Log is, in essence, the Sabbat bonfire driven indoors by the cold of winter.)

But to return to Mary. It was hardly surprising that, for Christianity to remain a viable religion, the Queen of Heaven had to be re-admitted to something like her true status, with a mythology and a popular devotion far outstripping (sometimes even conflicting with) the Biblical data on Mary. She had to be given that status, because she answered what Geoffrey Ashe calls "a Goddess-shaped yearning"—a yearning which four centuries of utterly male-chauvinist Christianity, on both the divine and the human level, had made unbearable. (It should be emphasized that the Church's male chauvinism was *not* inaugurated by Jesus, who treated women as fully human beings, but by the pathologically misogynist and sex-hating St Paul.)

Mary's virtual deification came with startling suddenness, initiated by the Council of Ephesus in 431 "amid great popular rejoicing, due, doubtless, to the hold which the cult of the virgin Artemis still had on the city" (*Encyclopaedia Britannica*, 'Ephesus' entry). Significantly, it coincided closely with the determined suppression of Isis-worship, which had spread throughout the known world. From then on, the theologians strove to discipline Mary, allowing her *hyperdulia* ('super-veneration', a stepped-up version, unique to her, of the *dulia*, veneration, accorded to the saints) but not *latria* (the adoration which was the monopoly of the male God). They managed to create, over the centuries, an official synthesis of the Queen of Heaven, by which they achieved the remarkable double feat of desexualizing the Goddess and dehumanizing Mary. But they could not muffle her power; it is to her that the ordinary worshipper (knowing and caring nothing about the distinction between *hyperdulia* and *latria*) turns, "now and at the hour of our death".

Geoffrey Grigson tells us: "It was to this temple that two girls, two children, paid a ritual visit every spring, bringing with them, from Athene's temple on the summit, loaves shaped like phalluses and snakes. In Aphrodite's temple the loaves acquired the power of fecundity. In autumn they were taken back to the Akropolis, and crumbled into the seed grain, to ensure a good yield after the next sowing." (*The Goddess of Love*, p. 162.)

Protestantism went to the other extreme and in varying degrees tried once again to banish the Goddess altogether. All it achieved was the loss of magic, which Catholicism, in however distorted and crippling a form, retained; for the Goddess cannot be banished.

(For a fuller understanding of the Marian phenomenon, see Ashe's *The Virgin* and Marina Warner's *Alone of All Her Sex*.)

The Goddess at Yule also presides over the other God-theme—that of the Oak King and Holly King, which survived, too, in popular Christmas tradition, however much official theology ignored it. In the Yuletide mumming plays, shining St George slew the dark 'Turkish knight' and then immediately cried out that he had slain his brother. "Darkness and light, winter and summer, are complementary to each other. So on comes the mysterious 'Doctor', with his magical bottle, who revives the slain man, and all ends with music and rejoicing. There are many local variations of this play, but the action is substantially the same throughout." (Doreen Valiente, *An ABC of Witchcraft*, pp. 358–60.) Yuletide mumming still survives locally—for example in Drumquin, County Tyrone, where exotically masked and costumed young farmers go from house to house enacting the age-old theme with words and actions handed down from their ancestors; Radio Telefís Éireann made an excellent film of it as their entry for the 1978 *Golden Harp Festival*.

All too often, of course, the harmonious balance of the dark and light twins, of necessary waxing and waning, has been distorted into a concept of Good-versus-Evil. At Dewsbury in Yorkshire, for nearly seven centuries, church bells have tolled 'the Devil's Knell' or 'the Old Lad's Passing' for the last hour of Christmas Eve, warning the Prince of Evil that the Prince of Peace is coming to destroy him. Then, from midnight on, they peal out a welcome to the Birth. A worthy custom, on the face of it—but in fact it enshrines a sad degradation of the Holly King.

Oddly enough, the popular name 'Old Nick' for the Devil reflects the same demotion. Nik was a name for Woden, who is very much a Holly King figure—as is Santa Claus, otherwise St Nicholas (who in early folklore rode not reindeer but a white horse through the sky—like Woden). So Nik, God of the Waning Year, has been Christianized in two forms: as Satan and as the jolliest of the saints. The Abbot's Bromley Horn Dance (now a September, but once a Yule rite) is based on the parish church of St Nicholas, which suggests a direct continuity from the days when the patron of the locality was not Nicholas but Nik. (On Nik and St Nicholas, see Doreen Valiente's *ABC of Witchcraft*, pp. 258–9.)

Incidentally, in Italy Santa Claus's place is taken by a witch, and a lady witch at that. She is called Befana (Epiphany), and she flies around on Twelfth Night on her broomstick, bringing gifts for children down the chimneys.

An extraordinarily persistent version of the Holly King/Oak King theme at the Winter Solstice is the ritual hunting and killing of the wren—a folklore tradition found as far apart in time and space as ancient Greece and Rome and today's British Isles. The wren, 'little king' of the Waning Year, is killed by his Waxing Year counterpart, the robin redbreast, who finds him hiding in an ivy bush (or sometimes in Ireland in a holly bush, as befits the Holly King). The robin's tree is the birch, which follows the Winter Solstice in the Celtic tree-calendar. In the acted-out ritual, men hunted and killed the wren with birchrods.

In Ireland, the 'Wren Boys'' day is St Stephen's Day, 26th December. In some places (the fishing village of Kilbaha in County Clare on the Shannon estuary, for example), the Wren Boys are groups of adult musicians, singers and dancers in colourful costumes, who go from house to house bearing the tiny effigy of a wren on a bunch of holly. In County Mayo the Wren Boys (and girls) are parties of children, also bearing holly bunches, who knock on our doors and recite their jingle to us:

> "The wren, the wren, the king of the birds,
> On Stephen's Day was caught in the furze;
> Up with the kettle and down with the pan,
> And give us some money to bury the wren."

It used to be 'a penny', but inflation has outstripped tradition. All holly decorations in Ireland must be cleared out of the house after Christmas; it is considered unlucky to let these Waning Year symbols linger.

The apparent absence of a corresponding Midsummer tradition, where one might expect a hunting of the robin, is puzzling.

But there may be a trace of it in the curious Irish belief about a Kinkisha (*Cincíseach*), a child born at Pentecost (*Cincís*), that such a person is doomed either to kill or to be killed—unless the 'cure' is applied. This 'cure' is to catch a bird and squeeze it to death inside the child's hand (while reciting three Hail Marys). In some places at least, the bird has to be a robin, and we feel this is probably the original tradition, for Pentecost is a movable feast, falling anywhere from 10th May to 13th June—i.e., towards the end of the Oak King's reign. It may be that long ago a baby born at this season was in danger of becoming a substitute sacrifice for the Oak King, and what better escape than to find a replacement in the shape of his own bird-substitute, the robin redbreast? And the 'kill or be killed' danger may be a memory of the Oak King's destiny of killing at Midwinter and being killed at Midsummer.[2]

The Waxing Year robin brings us to Robin Hood, cropping up in yet another seasonal festival. "In Cornwall," Robert Graves tells us, "'Robin' means phallus. 'Robin Hood' is a country name for red campion ('campion' means 'champion'), perhaps because its cloven petal suggests a ram's hoof, and because 'Red Champion' was a title of the Witch-god. . . . 'Hood' (or Hod or Hud) meant 'log'—the log put at the back of the fire—and it was in this log, cut from the sacred oak, that Robin had once been believed to reside—hence 'Robin Hood's steed', the wood-louse which ran out when the Yule log was burned. In the popular superstition Robin himself escaped up the chimney in the form of a robin and, when Yule ended, went out as Belin against his rival Bran, or Saturn—who had been 'Lord of Misrule' at the Yule-tide revels. Bran hid from pursuit in the ivy-bush disguised as a Gold Crest Wren; but Robin always caught and hanged him." (*The White Goddess*, p. 397.)

Mention of the Celtic tree-calendar (and of Graves's *White*

---

2. Substitute sacrifice is by no means dead in Ireland. On a County Mayo headland frequently lashed by storms, a few miles from our home, we have seen a celluloid doll nailed to a post at the high-tide mark. It was naked except for a patch of green paint where the nail penetrated. Our local-tradition expert, Tom Chambers, asked questions for us; as we suspected, it turned out to be a propitiatory sacrifice to the sea and is known as a 'Sea Doll' (*bábóg mhara*).

Goddess, its most detailed modern analysis) brings us back to the Goddess and the Sun-God aspect. As will be seen in our diagram on page 26, Graves's "Five Stations of the Goddess" are distributed round the year, but two of them (Death and Birth) are together on consecutive days at the Winter Solstice, 22nd and 23rd December. The latter is the 'extra day' which does not belong in any of the thirteen tree-months. Before it comes Ruis, the elder-tree month, and after it comes Beth, the birch-tree month. The pattern, whose symbolism will repay study (though preferably in the context of the whole year's calendar) is as follows, around the Winter Solstice:

25th November—22nd December: Ruis, the elder-tree; a tree of doom and of the dark aspect of the Goddess, with white flowers and dark fruit ("Elder is the Lady's tree—burn it not, or cursed you'll be"). Bird, the rook (*rócnat*); the rook, raven or crow is the prophetic bird of Bran, the Holly-King deity, who is also linked with the wren in Ireland, while in Devonshire the wren is 'the cuddy vran' or 'Bran's sparrow'. Colour, blood-red (*ruadh*). Line from the Song of Amergin: "I am a wave of the sea" (for weight).

22nd December. Death Station of the Goddess: Tree, the yew (*idho*), and palm. Metal, lead. Bird, eagle (*illait*). Colour, very white (*irfind*).

23rd December The Extra Day; *Birth Station of the Goddess*: Tree, silver fir (*ailm*), the original Christmas Tree; also mistletoe. Metal, silver. Bird, lapwing (*aidhircleóg*), the piebald trickster. Colour, piebald (*alad*). Amergin asks: "Who but I knows the secrets of the unhewn dolmen?"

24th December–20th January: Beth, the birch-tree; a tree of inception and the driving-out of evil spirits. Bird, pheasant (*besan*). Colour, white (*bán*). Amergin proclaims: "I am a stag of seven tines" (for strength).

The Winter Solstice rebirth, and the Goddess's part in it, were portrayed in ancient Egypt by a ritual in which Isis circled the shrine of Osiris seven times, to represent her mourning for him and her wanderings in search of the scattered parts of his body. The text of her dirge for Osiris, in which her sister Nephthys (who is in a sense her own dark aspect) joined her, can be found in two somewhat different versions in *The Golden Bough*, p. 482, and Esther Harding's *Woman's Mysteries*, pp.

188–9. Typhon or Set, the brother/enemy who killed him, was driven away by the shaking of Isis's sistrum, to bring about Osiris's rebirth. Isis herself was represented by the image of a cow with the sun-disc between its horns. For the festival, people decorated the outsides of their houses with oil-lamps which burned all night. At midnight, the priests emerged from an inner shrine crying "The Virgin has brought forth! The light is waxing!" and showing the image of a baby to the worshippers. The final entombment of the dead Osiris was on 21st December, after his long mummification ritual (which began, interestingly enough, on 3rd November—virtually at Samhain); on 23rd December his sister/wife Isis gave birth to his son/other-self Horus. Osiris and Horus represent at the same time the solar and the vegetational God-aspects; Horus is both the reborn Sun (the Greeks identified him with Apollo) and 'Lord of the Crops'. Another name of Horus, 'Bull of Thy Mother', reminds us that the God-child of the Goddess is, at another point in the cycle, her lover and impregnator, father in due course to his own reborn self.

The lamps burning all night on the eve of Midwinter survive, in Ireland and elsewhere, as the single candle burning in the window on Christmas Eve, lit by the youngest in the house—a symbol of microcosmic welcome to the Macrocosm, not unlike the extra place laid at a Jewish family's Pesach table (at which table, incidentally, the youngest son, with his question "Father, why is tonight different from all other nights?", also has a traditional part to play).

The owner of our village pub offers her own microcosmic welcome, following a tradition which she tells us was once widespread among Irish innkeepers. She cleans out a stable stall, spreads fresh straw and leaves there some food, a bottle of wine and a baby's bottle of milk—so that there *shall* be 'room at the inn'. She is shy to talk about it but sorry the custom seems to be dying.

A friend who has lived with the Eskimos in Greenland, where Christianity has bulldozed a formerly well-integrated balance of belief and way of life, tells us how Winter Solstice rituals have died without being meaningfully replaced. The Eskimos can hardly be said to celebrate Christmas at all, in comparison with the festival as it is known in the 'older' Christian countries; yet

11. When privacy permits, outdoor rituals are better

12. Lughnasadh and Bealtaine: The Love Chase
13. (*Facing*) Lughnasadh: The Corn Dance
14. (*Below*) Autumn Equinox: "Behold the mystery"

15. When a High Priestess has two more covens hived off from her own, she is entitled to call herself 'Witch Queen' and to wear the appropriate number of buckles on her witch's garter

16. Yule: The Goddess mourns the death of the Sun God

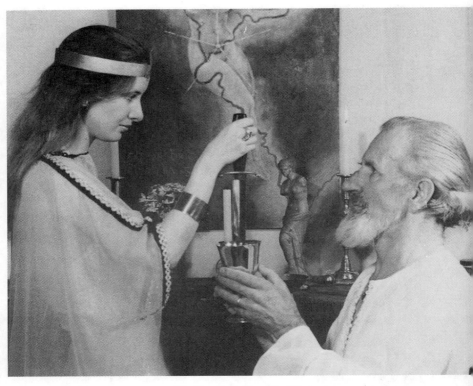

17. Consecrating the Wine

18. Sword and Athame symbolize the Fire element in our tradition. Others attribute them to Air

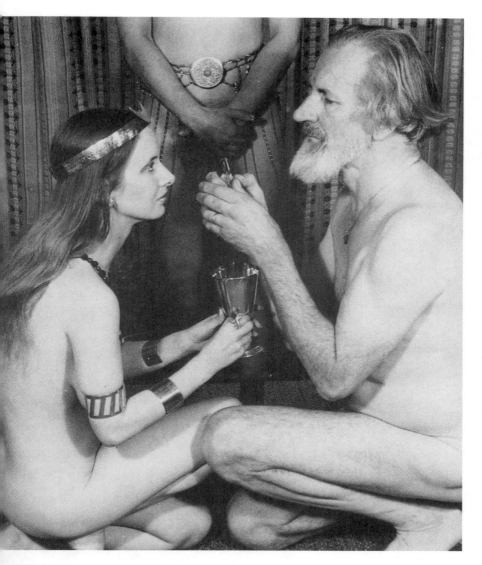

19. The symbolic Great Rite: "Here where the Lance and Grail unite"

the traditional solstice rites (which apparently were memorable occasions) are no longer observed because they depend on exact reckoning of the solstice by stellar observation—a skill which the present generation no longer possesses. So much for the blessings of technological civilization!

In Athens, the Winter Solstice ritual was the Lenaea, the Festival of the Wild Women. Here, the death and rebirth of the harvest-god Dionysos was enacted. In the dim past it had been a god-sacrifice ritual, and the nine Wild Women had torn his human representative to pieces and eaten him. But by classical times the Titans had become the sacrificers, the victim had been replaced by a goat-kid, and the nine Wild Women had become mourners and witnesses of the birth. (See *The White Goddess*, p. 399.) The Wild Women also appear in northern legend; as the Waelcyrges (Valkyries) they rode with Woden on his Wild Hunt.

In the Book of Shadows Yule ritual, only the rebirth of the Sun-God is featured, with the High Priest calling upon the Goddess to "bring to us the Child of Promise". The Holly King/Oak King theme is ignored—a strange omission in view of its persistence in the folklore of the season.

We have combined the two themes in our ritual, choosing the Oak King and Holly King by lot, as at Midsummer, immediately after the opening ritual—but postponing the 'slaying' of the Holly King until after the death and rebirth of the Sun.

A problem arises over the Oak King's crown; while at Midsummer oak and holly leaves are both available, at Yule oak leaves are not. One answer is to gather oak leaves in advance in the Summer or Autumn, press and lacquer them and make a permanent Oak King's crown for Yuletide use. Another, less fragile perhaps, is to make your permanent crown of acorns when they are in season. Or you can use the winter leaves of the Holm or Evergreen Oak (*Quercus ilex*). Failing all these, make the crown of bare oak twigs but brighten it with Christmas tinsel or other suitable decoration.

At Yule, the Goddess is the 'leprous-white lady', the White-Haired One, Life-in-Death; so we suggest the High Priestess should again wear the white chiffon or net tabard we described for Samhain. A dramatically effective addition, if she possesses one or it can be afforded, is a pure white wig, preferably long. If yours is a skyclad coven, she will take off the tabard before the Great Rite but retain the wig if she is wearing one, because it symbolizes her seasonal aspect.

The High Priestess's lament *"Return, oh, return!* . . ." is a slightly adapted form of Isis's lament for Osiris mentioned above.

If, as is more than likely, you have a Christmas tree in the room, any lights on it should be switched off before the Circle is cast. The High Priest can then switch them on immediately after he lights the cauldron candle.

If there is an open fireplace in the room, a Yule Log can be burned during the Sabbat. It should, of course, be of oak.

The Preparation

The cauldron is placed by the South candle, with an unlit candle inside it, and wreathed with holly, ivy and mistletoe.

Crowns for the Oak King and Holly King are ready beside the altar. A number of straws are laid on the altar—as many as there are men at the Sabbat, except for the High Priest. One of them is longer than the rest, and one shorter. (As at Midsummer, if the High Priestess decides to nominate the two Kings instead of drawing lots, the straws are not needed.)

A blindfold is ready by the altar for the Holly King.

A sistrum for the High Priestess is laid on the altar. The High Priestess shall wear a white tabard and, if she so chooses, a white wig.

If there is a Christmas tree in the room with lights, the lights shall be switched off.

If there is an open fireplace in the room, the fire shall be built up till it is red and glowing, and a Yule Log laid on it just before the Circle is cast.

The Ritual

After the Witches' Rune, the Maiden fetches the straws from the altar and holds them in her hand so that all the ends are protruding separately but nobody can see which are the short and long ones. The High Priestess says:

"Let the men draw lots."

Each man (except the High Priest) draws a straw from the Maiden's hand and shows it to the High Priestess. The High

Priestess points to the man who has drawn the short straw, and says:

"Thou art the Holly King, God of the Waning Year. Maiden, bring his crown!"

The Maiden places the holly-leaf crown on the head of the Holly King.

The High Priestess points to the man who has drawn the long straw, and says:

"Thou are the Oak King, God of the Waxing Year. Maiden, bring his crown!"

The Maiden places the oak-leaf crown on the head of the Oak King.

While the crowning is going on, the High Priest lays himself on the floor in the centre of the Circle, curled up in a foetal position. Everyone pretends not to see him doing this.

When the crowning is over, the Oak King says:

"My brother and I have been crowned and prepared for our rivalry. But where is our Lord the Sun?"

The Maiden replies:

"Our Lord the Sun is dead!"

If the High Priestess's tabard has a veil, she drapes it over her face.

The coven arrange themselves around the perimeter of the Circle.

The High Priestess picks up the sistrum, and the Maiden a candle. They walk together slowly round the High Priest, deosil, seven times. The Maiden holds the candle so that the High Priestess can read her script, and counts quietly *"One," "Two,"* and so on up to *"Seven"* as each circuit is completed. As they go, the High Priestess shakes her sistrum and laments:

"Return, oh, return!
God of the Sun, God of the Light, return!
Thine enemies are fled—thou hast no enemies.
O lovely helper, return, return!
Return to thy sister, thy spouse, who loveth thee!
We shall not be put asunder.
O my brother, my consort, return, return!
When I see thee not,
My heart grieveth for thee,
Mine eyes seek for thee,

My feet roam the Earth in search of thee!
Gods and men weep for thee together.
God of the Sun, God of the Light, return!
Return to thy sister, thy spouse, who loveth thee!
Return! Return! Return!"

When the seven circuits are completed, the High Priestess lays the sistrum on the altar and kneels close to the High Priest, with her hands resting on his body and her back towards the altar. (See Plate 16.)

The coven, except for the Maiden, link hands and move slowly deosil round the High Priestess and High Priest.

The Maiden stands by the altar and declaims:[3]

"Queen of the Moon, Queen of the Sun,
Queen of the Heavens, Queen of the Stars,
Queen of the Waters, Queen of the Earth,
Bring to us the Child of Promise!
It is the Great Mother who giveth birth to Him;
It is the Lord of Life who is born again;
Darkness and tears are set aside when the Sun shall come up early!"

The Maiden pauses in her declamation, and the High Priestess rises to her feet, drawing the High Priest to his feet. If she is veiled, she throws the veil back from her face. High Priestess and High Priest face each other, clasping each other's crossed-over hands, and start to spin deosil inside the coven. The coven's circling becomes joyous and faster.

The Maiden continues:

"Golden Sun of hill and mountain,
Illumine the land, illumine the world,
Illumine the seas, illumine the rivers,
Sorrows be laid, joy to the world!
Blessed be the Great Goddess,
Without beginning, without ending,

---

3. Written by Doreen Valiente, with words suggested by a Christmas carol in *Carmina Gadelica*, collected by Alexander Carmichael from Angus Gunn, a cottar of Lewis. (See *Carmina Gadelica*, volume I, page 133, or *The Sun Dances*, page 91.) "It was the first chant or invocation I ever wrote for Gerald," Doreen tells us—at Yule 1953, she thinks. He gave her the task of writing words for the evening ritual without warning, after lunch, "deliberately throwing me in at the deep end to see what I could do".

Everlasting to eternity, Io Evo! He![4] *Blessed be!*
Io Evo! He! Blessed be!
Io Evo! He! Blessed be! . . ."

The coven joins in the chant "*Ivo Evo! He! Blessed be!*", and the Maiden puts down her script and candle and joins the circling ring. The chanting and circling continues until the High Priestess cries "*Down!*"

When all are seated, the High Priest stands up again and goes to the altar to fetch a candle or taper. He carries it to the cauldron and with it lights the candle in the cauldron. He then returns the first candle or taper to the altar. If there is a Christmas tree with lights, he now switches on the lights.

He then takes his place in front of the altar, where the High Priestess joins him, and they stand facing the seated coven.

The High Priestess says:

"*Now, at the depth of winter, is the waning of the year accomplished, and the reign of the Holly King is ended. The Sun is reborn, and the waxing of the year begins. The Oak King must slay his brother the Holly King and rule over my land until the height of summer, when his brother shall rise again.*"

The coven stand and, except for the two Kings, withdraw to the perimeter. In the centre of the Circle, the two Kings stand facing each other, the Oak King with his back to the West and the Holly King with his back to the East.

The Oak King places his hands on the Holly King's shoulders, pressing downwards. The Holly King falls to his knees. Meanwhile the Maiden fetches the scarf, and she and the Oak King blindfold the Holly King. They both now move away from the kneeling Holly King; the High Priestess walks slowly round him deosil, three times. She then rejoins the High Priest in front of the altar.

The High Priest says:

"*The spirit of the Holly King is gone from us, to rest in Caer Arianrhod, the Castle of the Silver Wheel; until, with the turning of the year, the season shall come when he shall return to rule again. The*

---

4. Pronounced 'Yo ayvo, hay' (the 'ay' as in 'day'). A Greek Bacchanalian cry. For some thoughts on its possible sexual significance, see Doreen Valiente's *Natural Magic*, p. 92.

spirit is gone; therefore let the man among us who has stood for that spirit be freed from his task."

The High Priestess and Maiden step forward again and help the Holly King to rise. They lead him to the West candle, where the Maiden removes his blindfold and the High Priestess his crown, laying them beside the candle. The man turns and again becomes an ordinary member of the coven.

The Great Rite is now enacted, the Maiden standing by with the athame and the Oak King with the chalice. (If the Sabbat is skyclad, the Maiden will first help the High Priestess to take off her tabard—which, being white, may then suitably be used as the veil laid over her body for the first part of the Great Rite.)

After the wine and cakes, the cauldron is moved to the centre of the Circle, and everybody jumps over it in the usual manner before the party-stage begins.

Next day, when the fire (if any) is cold, the ashes of the Yule Log should be gathered up and scattered on the fields or garden—or, if you live in town and have not even a window-box, on the nearest park or cultivated ground.

Birth, Marriage & Death

XII *Wiccaning*

This is a book of suggested rituals for those who need to use them and who find them suitable. It is therefore not the place to debate the difficult question of the religious upbringing of children. But we think one point should be made.

Christians, when they have their children christened, do so on the whole with the intention of *committing* them to Christianity, preferably for life—and to the parents' own particular brand of Christianity, at that. The usual hope is that the children will endorse that commitment at confirmation, when they are old enough to acquiesce consciously (though without mature judgement). To be fair, such parents—when they are not merely following social convention—often act in this way because they sincerely believe it is essential for the safety of their children's souls. They have been taught to believe it and often frightened into believing it. (A young Christian friend of ours, heavily pregnant, was warned by the doctor that the child might be born dead; she sobbed in our arms, terrified that her baby would go to Hell if it did not live long enough to be baptized. She was theologically mistaken even in terms of her own creed; but her terror was all too typical. We are glad to say that her baby son, though late, was born fine and healthy.)

This belief, that there is only one kind of ticket to Heaven and that a baby must be given it with all speed for its own safety, is of course alien to Wicca. Witches' belief in reincarnation denies it in any case. But quite apart from that, witches hold the view which was virtually universal before the era of patriarchal monotheism—namely, that all religions are different ways of expressing the same truths and that their validity for any particular individual depends on his nature and needs.

A wiccaning ceremony for the child of a witch family does not, therefore, commit the child to any one path, even a Wiccan one. It is similar to a christening in that it invokes Divine protection for the child and ritually affirms the love and care with which the family and friends wish to surround the newcomer. It differs from a christening in that it specifically acknowledges that, as the child matures into an adult, it will, and indeed must, decide on its own path.

Wicca is above all a natural religion—so witch parents will naturally try to communicate to their children the joy and fulfilment their religion gives them, and the whole family will inevitably share in its way of life. Sharing is one thing; imposing or dictating is another, and, far from ensuring a child's 'salvation', may well retard it—if, as witches do, you regard salvation not as a kind of instant transaction but as a development over many lifetimes.

We have composed our wiccaning ritual in this spirit, and we think that most witches will agree with the attitude.

We knew that the idea of having godparents—adult friends who will take a continuing personal interest in the child's development—was a justifiably popular one; and we felt that a wiccaning ceremony should allow for it too. At first we called these adult friends 'sponsors', to avoid confusion with Christian practice. But on further consideration we saw that 'sponsor' was a cold word and that there was no reason at all why 'godfather' and 'godmother' (if 'god' be taken to include 'goddess') should not serve for witches as well as Christians. After all, given the differences of belief (and Christians differ among themselves, God knows), including the difference of attitude we have already mentioned, the function is the same.

Godparents do not necessarily have to be witches themselves; that is up to the parents. But they must at least be in sympathy with the intent of the rite and have read it through beforehand, to make sure they can make the necessary promises in all sincerity. (The same would apply, after all, to witches who were asked by Christian friends to be godparents at a church baptism.)

If the High Priestess and/or High Priest are themselves standing as godparents, they will make the promises to each other at the appropriate moments in the ritual.

There is a story attached to this ritual of ours which is both funny and sad. We wrote it originally in 1971, and we gave a copy to a High Priest friend who we thought might like to have it. A couple of years later, an American witch friend was visiting us, and we happened to describe our wiccaning to him in conversation. He laughed and said: "But I've read that ritual. Last time I was in London, —— showed it to me. He said he'd got it from a very old traditional source."

By such irresponsibility are apocryphal stories launched; and they do no good to Wicca at all. Besides, we have since amended the ritual slightly in the light of experience—so will people who know of the original now accuse us of 'tampering with tradition'? It could happen!

Following Wiccan patterns, we have suggested that the High Priest should preside at the wiccaning of a girl child, and the High Priestess at that of a boy. To avoid lengthy repetition, we give the ritual for a girl child in full, and then indicate the differences for a boy child.

The Preparation
If the coven normally works skyclad, the decision whether the ritual shall be skyclad or robed shall on this occasion rest with the parents. In either case, the High Priestess shall wear symbols of the Moon, and the High Priest symbols of the Sun.

The Circle is marked with flowers and greenery, and the cauldron placed in the centre, filled with the same, and perhaps with fruit as well.

Consecrating oil is placed ready on the altar.

Only very light incense should be used—preferably joss-sticks.

Gifts for the child are placed beside the altar, and food and drink for a little party in the Circle after the ritual.

The parents should choose beforehand a 'hidden name' for the child. (This is largely for the child's own benefit; growing up in a witch family, he or she will almost certainly like having a private 'witch name' just as Mummy and Daddy do—and if not, it can be quietly forgotten until and unless its owner wants to use it again.)

The Ritual for a Girl Child

The Opening Ritual proceeds as usual up to the end of the "Great God Cernunnos" invocation, except that everyone, including the parents and child, is in the Circle before the casting, seated in a semicircle close to the cauldron and facing towards the altar—leaving room for the High Priestess to cast the Circle around them. Only the High Priestess and High Priest are standing, to conduct the Opening Ritual. To cut down excessive movement which might frighten the child, the High Priestess casts the Circle with her athame, not the sword; and nobody moves with her, or copies her gestures, when she invokes the Lords of the Watchtowers. She and the High Priest carry round the elements.

After the *"Great God Cernunnos"* invocation, the High Priestess and High Priest consecrate the wine. They do not taste it but place the chalice on the altar.

The High Priest then stands before the altar, facing the cauldron. The High Priestess stands ready to hand him the oil, wine and water.

The High Priest says:

"We are met in this Circle to ask the blessing of the mighty God and the gentle Goddess on ——, the daughter of —— and ——, so that she may grow in beauty and strength, in joy and wisdom. There are many paths, and each must find his own; therefore we do not seek to bind —— to any one path while she is still too young to choose.

Rather do we ask the God and the Goddess, who know all paths, and to whom all paths lead, to bless, protect and prepare her through the years of her childhood; so that when at last she is truly grown, she shall know without doubt or fear which path is hers and shall tread it gladly.

"———, *mother of* ———, *bring her forward that she may be blessed.*"

The father helps the mother to rise, and both of them bring the child to the High Priest, who takes her in his arms (firmly, or she will feel insecure—too many clergymen make that mistake!). He asks:

"———, *mother of* ———, *has this your child also a hidden name?*"

The mother replies:

"*Her hidden name is* ———."

The High Priest then anoints the child on the forehead with oil, marking a pentagram and saying:

"*I anoint thee,* ——— (ordinary name), *with oil, and give thee the hidden name of* ———."

He repeats the action with wine, saying:

"*I anoint thee,* ——— (hidden name), *with wine, in the name of the mighty God Cernunnos.*"

He repeats the action with water, saying:

"*I anoint thee,* ——— (hidden name), *with water, in the name of the gentle Goddess Aradia.*"

The High Priest gives the child back to the mother and then leads the parents and child to each of the Watchtowers in turn, saying:

"*Ye Lords of the Watchtowers of the East (South, West, North), we do bring before you* ———, *whose hidden name is* ———, *and who has been duly anointed within the Wiccan Circle. Hear ye, therefore, that she is under the protection of Cernunnos and Aradia.*"

The High Priest and High Priestess take their places facing the altar, with the parents and child between them. They raise their arms and call in turn:

High Priest: "*Mighty Cernunnos, bestow upon this child the gift of strength.*"

High Priestess: "*Gentle Aradia, bestow upon this child the gift of beauty.*"

High Priest: "*Mighty Cernunnos, bestow upon this child the gift of wisdom.*"

High Priestess: *"Gentle Aradia, bestow upon this child the gift of love."*

The High Priest, High Priestess and parents turn to face into the Circle, and the High Priest then asks:

"Are there two in the Circle who would stand as godparents to ——?"

(If he and the High Priestess are standing as godparents, he will ask instead: *"Is there one in the Circle who will stand with me, as godparents to ——?"* and the High Priestess answers: *"I will join with you."* They then face each other and speak the questions and the promises to each other.)

The godparents come forward and stand, the godmother facing the High Priest, and the godfather facing the High Priestess.

The High Priest asks the godmother:

"Do you, ——, promise to be a friend to —— throughout her childhood, to aid and guide her as she shall need; and in concord with her parents, to watch over her and love her as if she were of your own blood, till by the grace of Cernunnos and Aradia she shall be ready to choose her own path?"

The godmother replies:

"I, ——, do so promise."

The High Priestess asks the godfather:

"Do you, ——, promise . . ." etc., as above.

The godfather replies:

"I, ——, do so promise."

The High Priest says:

> *"The God and the Goddess have blessed her;*
> *The Lords of the Watchtowers have acknowledged her;*
> *We her friends have welcomed her;*
> *Therefore, O Circle of Stars,*
> *Shine in peace on——,*
> *Whose hidden name is——.*
> *So mote it be."*

All say:

"So mote it be."

The High Priest says:

"Let all be seated within the Circle."

All sit down, except the High Priest and High Priestess, who

taste and pass round the already-consecrated wine in the usual
way and then consecrate and pass round the cakes in the usual
way.

They then fetch the gifts and the party food and drink and sit
down with the others, and the proceedings become informal.

The Ritual for a Boy Child
The basic difference if the child is a boy is that the High Priest
and High Priestess exchange duties. She makes the opening
statement and performs the anointing, the High Priest handing
her the oil, wine and water. She presents the child to the
Watchtowers.

The call to the God and Goddess for their gifts of strength,
beauty, wisdom and love, however, is made exactly as for a girl
child, and in the same order.

The High Priestess calls forward the godparents and takes the
godfather's promise; the High Priest then takes the godmother's promise.

The High Priestess pronounces the final blessing.

XIII   Handfasting

A handfasting is a witch wedding. Stewart has explained handfasting at some length in Chapter 15 of *What Witches do*, so we will not repeat that explanation here. All the widely differing versions of handfasting ritual which we have come across (including the one outlined in *What Witches Do*) have been devised in recent years and are a mixture of bits of tradition (such as jumping the broomstick) with the devisers' own ideas. So far as we know, no detailed and provably ancient handfasting ritual exists on paper.

So when we were asked to conduct a handfasting for two of our members a few days after their legal marriage, we decided that we too would write our own, since none of the ones we knew of quite satisfied us.

Like many other witches and occultists, we have found Dion

Fortune's unforgettable novel *The Sea Priestess* (Aquarian Press, London, 1957) a goldmine of material for devised rituals and have benefited from the results. So, for our friends' handfasting, we incorporated some of the Priest of the Moon's words to Molly in Chapter XXX of *The Sea Priestess*;[1] we felt they might almost have been written for the purpose. They are the four quotations below from "*Golden Aphrodite cometh not as the virgin . . .*" down to "*they become the substance of the sacrament*". Our only alteration of the original has been to substitute "*bride*" for "*priestess*" at one point; this seemed a legitimate amendment for a handfasting ritual.

These passages are included here by kind permission of the Society of the Inner Light, who hold the copyright of Dion Fortune's works. Responsibility for the context in which they have been used is, of course, entirely ours and not the Society's; but we like to think that, if the late Miss Fortune had been able to be present, we would have had her blessing.

One other point: in the presentation of the symbols of the elements, we attribute the Wand to Air, and the Sword to Fire. (See Plate 18.) This is the tradition which we follow—but others attribute the Wand to Fire and the Sword to Air. The Wand Fire, Sword/Air attribution was a deliberate 'blind' perpetrated by the early Golden Dawn, which has unfortunately not yet died a natural death; it seems to us contrary to the obvious nature of the tools concerned. However, many people have been brought up to believe that the 'blind' was the genuine tradition, so that by now, for them, it feels right. They should of course amend the wording of the presentation accordingly.

The Preparation

The Circle is outlined, and the altar decorated, with flowers; but a gateway is left in the North-East of the Circle, with flowers to hand for closing it.

The broomstick is kept ready beside the altar.

The cauldron, filled with flowers, is placed by the West candle—West representing Water, the element of love.

---

1. Chapter 14 of the paperback edition (Star, London, 1976).

The Ritual

The Opening Ritual is conducted normally, except that (a) the bride and groom remain outside the gateway, which is not closed yet, and (b) the Charge is not given yet.

After the *"Great God Cernunnos"* invocation, the High Priestess brings in the groom, and the High Priest the bride, each with a kiss. The High Priest then closes the gateway with flowers, and the High Priestess closes it ritually with the sword or athame.

The High Priestess and High Priest stand with their backs to the altar. The groom faces the High Priestess, and the bride the High Priest, in the centre of the Circle.

The High Priestess asks:

"Who comes to be joined together in the presence of the Goddess? What is thy name, O Man?"

The groom answers:

"My name is ——."

The High Priest asks:

"Who comes to be joined together in the presence of the God? What is thy name, O Woman?"

The bride answers:

"My name is ——."

The High Priestess says:

"—— and ——, we greet you with joy."

The coven circle round the bride and groom to the Witches' Rune; then all return to their places.

The High Priestess says:

"Unity is balance, and balance is unity. Hear then, and understand."

She picks up the wand and continues:

"The wand that I hold is the symbol of Air. Know and remember that this is the element of Life, of intelligence, of the inspiration which moves us onwards. By this wand of Air, we bring to your handfasting the power of Mind."

She lays down the wand. The High Priest picks up the sword and says:

"The sword that I hold is the symbol of Fire. Know and remember that this is the element of Light, of energy, of the vigour which runs through our veins. By this sword of Fire, we bring to your handfasting the power of Will."

He lays down the sword. The High Priestess picks up the chalice and says:

"The chalice that I hold is the symbol of Water. Know and remember, that this is the element of Love, of growth, of the fruitfulness of the Great Mother. By this chalice of Water, we bring to your handfasting the power of Desire."

She lays down the chalice. The High Priest picks up the pentacle and says:

"The pentacle that I hold is the symbol of Earth. Know and remember, that this is the element of Law, of endurance, of the understanding which cannot be shaken. By this pentacle of Earth, we bring to your handfasting the power of the Steadfast."

He lays down the pentacle, and continues;

"Listen to the words of the Great Mother . . ." etc., to introduce the Charge.

The High Priestess and the High Priest deliver the Charge, in the usual way. When it is finished, the High Priest says:

"Golden Aphrodite cometh not as the virgin, the victim, but as the Awakener, the Desirous One. As outer space she calls, and the All-Father commences the courtship. She awakeneth Him to desire, and the worlds are created. How powerful is she, golden Aphrodite, the awakener of manhood!"

The High Priestess says:

"But all these things are one thing. All the goddesses are one goddess, and we call her Isis, the All-woman, in whose nature all natural things are found; virgin and desirous by turn; giver of life and bringer-in of death. She is the cause of all creation, for she awakeneth the desire of the All-Father, and for her sake He createth. Likewise, the wise call all women Isis."

The High Priest says:

"In the face of every woman, let man look for the features of the Great Goddess, watching her phases through the flow and return of the tides to which his soul answereth; listening for her call."

The High Priestess says:

"O daughter of Isis, adore the Goddess, and in her name give the call that awakens and rejoices. So shalt thou be blessed of the Goddess, and live with the fulness of life. Let the Bride show forth the Goddess to him who loves her. Let her assume the crown of the underworld. Let her arise all glorious and golden from the sea of the primordial and call unto him to come forth, to come to her. Let her do

these things in the name of the Goddess, and she shall be even as the Goddess unto him; for the Goddess will speak through her. All-powerful shall she be on the Inner, as crowned Persephone; and all-powerful on the Outer, as golden Aphrodite.[2] So shall she be a priestess in the eyes of the worshipper of the Goddess, who by his faith and dedication shall find the Goddess in her. For the rite of Isis is life, and that which is done as a rite shall show forth in life. By the rite is the Goddess drawn down to her worshippers; her power enters into them, and they become the substance of the sacrament."

The High Priest says to the bride:

"Say after me: 'By seed and root, by bud and stem, by leaf and flower and fruit, by life and love, in the name of the Goddess, I, ——, take thee, ——, to my hand, my heart and my spirit, at the setting of the sun and the rising of the stars.[3] Nor shall death part us; for in the fulness of time we shall be born again at the same time and in the same place as each other; and we shall meet, and know, and remember, and love again.'"

The bride repeats each phrase after the High Priest, taking the groom's right hand in her own right hand as she speaks.

The High Priestess says to the groom:

"Say after me: 'By seed and root, by bud and stem . . .'" etc., as above.

The groom repeats each phrase after the High Priestess, retaining the bride's right hand in his own.

If the couple wish to exchange rings, this is now done.

The High Priest says:

"Let the sun and the moon and the stars, and these our brothers and sisters, bear witness; that —— and —— have been joined

---

2. We cannot resist noting here a belief that still lingers in the gale-prone West of Ireland—that a newly-wed bride has the power to calm a storm at sea. As a neighbour (living, like ourselves, a mile from the Atlantic) said to us: "I believe there may be some truth in it. A bride has a certain blessing about her."

3. At their own discretion, the couple may end their pledge here, omitting the last sentence from "*Nor shall death part us . . .*" if they do not yet see their way to a soul-mate commitment, which should never be undertaken without careful thought. (See *What Witches Do*, Chapter 15.) The Mormon Church, incidentally, has the same provision; Mormons have two forms of marriage— one for life, and the other (called "Going to the Temple") for eternity. About fifty per cent choose the latter form.

*together in the sight of the God and the Goddess. And may the God
and the Goddess bless them, as we do ourselves."*

All say:

"So mote it be!"

The High Priestess takes the broomstick and lays it down on
the ground before the couple, who jump over it hand in hand.
The High Priestess then picks up the broomstick and ritually
sweeps the Circle clear of all evil influences.

The couple now enact the Great Rite, and it is entirely their
choice whether it should be symbolic or actual. If it is actual, the
High Priestess leads the coven out of the room, instead of the
Maiden as is usual.

After the Great Rite, the couple consecrate the wine and
cakes (or the cakes only if the Great Rite has been symbolic, in
which case the wine will already have been consecrated). The
proceedings then become informal.

If the feast includes a handfasting cake, tradition says that
this is the one occasion when the coven's ritual sword may be
used for actual cutting.

XIV Requiem

The first time we lost a coven-member by death, this is the Requiem we held for her. 'Lost' is an inappropriate word, of course; her contribution to the building of our group mind remained, and in our incarnations to come we may well be drawn together again. But the ending of a chapter needs to be acknowledged and absorbed, and the urge to say *au revoir* with love and dignity has been universal since Neanderthal man laid his dead to rest on a couch of blossom.

Two symbolic themes seemed to us to express what we wanted to say. The first was the spiral, which since the very dawn of ritual has stood for the parallel processes of death-rebirth and initiation-rebirth; winding our way back to the source, the universal womb, the Great Mother, the depths of the collective unconscious—meeting the Dark Mother face to face and knowing that she is also the Bright Mother—and then winding our way outwards from the encounter rejuvenated and transformed. This inward and outward spiral naturally took the form of a dance; and the inward spiral seemed again to call for that rare use of a widdershins movement, employed in Wiccan ritual only when it has a precise symbolic purpose (as in our Autumn Equinox and Samhain rituals). It would be followed naturally by a deosil movement for the outward spiral.

The other theme was that of the silver cord. Time and again, people who have experienced astral projection have spoken of this silver cord, which they have seen weaving, and infinitely extendable, between the astral and the physical bodies. On physical death, all traditions maintain, the cord is severed. This is a natural process, the first stage in the withdrawal of the immortal Individuality from the physical, lower and upper astral, and lower mental bodies of the Personality which has housed it during one incarnation. Any blocking or interruption of this withdrawal is a malfunction, as abnormality; it may be caused by some obsession, and this explains many 'hauntings'. In most cases (certainly, we think, in that of our friend) there is no such undue retardation. But even if no help is needed to smooth the withdrawal, it is fitting that it should be symbolized in the rite.

Tradition also maintains that the beautiful words of Ecclesiastes xii, 6–7, refer to this process; so we used them in our Requiem, substituting 'Goddess' for 'God'—which, in view of our declared philosophy, we hope will offend no one.

The second part of the ritual is the enacting of the Legend of the Descent of the Goddess into the Underworld, which appears in the Book of Shadows as a kind of epilogue to the second-degree initiation ritual. Where Gardner obtained it, not even Doreen Valiente knows. "I had nothing whatever to do with writing this," she tells us. "Whether old Gerald wrote it himself or whether he inherited it, I do not know. I suspect a bit of both, namely that he inherited the rough outlines of it and wrote it down in his own words. It is, as you say, a version of the Ishtar story and similar legends; and it relates to the initiation ritual in obvious ways."

Initiation and rebirth are closely parallel processes, so we found that the Legend enriched our Requiem as it does the second-degree rite. The spoken words of the Legend are given in *What Witches Do* and (in slightly shorter form) in Gardner's *Witchcraft Today*, but we repeat them for completeness, interspersed with the appropriate movements, which the Book of Shadows leaves to the imagination. If the Legend is enacted at all frequently—and there is no need to confine it to the second-degree initiation, we have found that it is easy, and worth while, to learn them. To get the most out of the Legend, it is even better if the three actors learn the dialogue parts of it by heart and speak them themselves, instead of leaving all the speaking to the Narrator as we have done below. But unless they know them by heart, it is better to leave them to the Narrator, because for the three actors to carry books in their hands spoils the whole effect.

Finally, the High Priestess announces the love-feast, with a closing valediction to the dead friend.

We would like to make one comment on the rite as we first experienced it. The moment of the breaking of the bowl had an unexpected impact on all of us; it was as though it echoed on all the planes at once. Our youngest member gasped out loud, and we all felt like it. A sceptic might say that the sharp sound of the breaking, charged with symbolism as it was, provided a psychological shock; but even if this were all, it would still be valid—concentrating our group awareness of the meaning of what we were doing into one intense and simultaneous instant.

When the ritual was over, we felt a calm happiness none of us had known since our friend became ill. Seldom have we been so aware of a ritual's being successful and reverberating majestically far beyond the limits of our Circle.

In the text below, we have used 'she' throughout, for simplicity. If the Requiem is used for a man, it may be felt appropriate to exchange the roles of High Priest and High Priestess for the first part of the ritual, up to the Legend; as always, it is a matter of what feels right to the coven concerned.

The Preparation

The decoration of the Circle and the altar for a Requiem will be a matter of individual taste, depending upon the circumstances, the time of year and the character and associations of the friend being remembered.

A small earthenware bowl (a mug or cup with a handle is suitable) is laid beside the altar, with a silver cord tied to it; also a hammer for breaking the bowl, and a cloth to break it in.

For the Legend of the Descent of the Goddess, jewels and a veil are laid ready by the altar for the Goddess, and a crown for the Lord of the Underworld. A necklace is laid ready on the altar.

The Ritual

The opening ritual proceeds as usual, up to the end of the *"Great God Cernunnos"* invocation. The High Priestess and High Priest then face the coven from in front of the altar.

The High Priestess says:

"We meet today in both sadness and joy. We are sad because a chapter has closed; yet are we joyful, because, by the closing, a new chapter may begin.

"We meet to mark the passing of our beloved sister, ———, for whom this incarnation is ended. We meet to commend her to the care of blessing of the God and the Goddess, that she may rest, free from illusion or regret, until the time shall come for her rebirth to this world. And knowing that this shall be so, we know, too, that the sadness is nothing and that the joy is all."

The High Priest stays in his place, and the High Priestess leads the coven in a spiral dance, slowly inwards in a widdershins direction, but not closing in too tightly.

The High Priest says:

"We call to thee, Ama, dark sterile Mother; thou to whom all manifested life must return, when its time has come; dark Mother of stillness and rest, before whom men tremble because they understand thee not. We call to thee, who art also Hecate of the waning Moon, dark Lady of wisdom, whom men fear because thy wisdom towers above their own. We, the hidden children of the Goddess, know that there is naught to fear in thine embrace, which none escape; that when we step into thy darkness, as all must, it is but to step again into the light. Therefore, in love and without fear, we commend to thee ———, our sister. Take her, guard her, guide her; admit her to the peace of the Summerlands, which stand between life and life. And know, as thou knowest all things, that our love goes with her."

The High Priest fetches the bowl, cord, hammer and cloth. The dance stops, and the coven part to admit the High Priest to the centre of the spiral, where he lays the cloth on the floor and the bowl upon it. He hands the free end of the cord to the Maiden.

The High Priestess says:

"Or ever the silver cord be loosed, or the golden bowl be broken, or the pitcher be broken at the fountain, or the wheel be broken at the cistern; then shall the dust return to the earth as it was; and the spirit shall return to the Goddess who gave it."

The High Priest unties the silver cord, and the Maiden gathers it up. The High Priest then wraps the cloth around the bowl and breaks it with the hammer. He replaces the folded cloth with the pieces of the bowl in it, and the hammer, beside the altar. The coven re-closes.

The Maiden carries the silver cord and, during the following invocation, proceeding deosil round the Circle, offers it first to the Lords of the Watchtowers of the West (the Lords of Death and of Initiation) and then to the Lords of the Watchtowers of the East (the Lords of Rebirth). She then lays the cord on the floor in front of the East candle and joins the High Priest at the altar (proceeding always deosil).

Meanwhile the High Priestess leads the dance again, doubling back deosil to unwind the spiral, until it is once again a full circle, which continues to move deosil.

As soon as he has replaced the cloth and hammer beside the altar, the High Priest faces the coven and says:

"We call to thee, Aima, bright fertile Mother; thou who art the womb of rebirth, from whom all manifested life proceeds, and at whose flowing breast all are nourished. We call to thee, who art also Persephone of the waxing Moon, Lady of Springtime and of all things new. We commend to thee ——, our sister. Take her, guard her, guide her; bring her in the fulness of time to a new birth and a new life. And grant that in that new life she may be loved again, as we her brothers and sisters have loved her."

The High Priest and the Maiden rejoin the circling coven, and the High Priestess starts the Witches' Rune, which the rest join in. When it is over, the High Priestess orders *"Down"*, and the coven sit in a ring facing inwards.

The High Priestess then allots roles for the Legend of the Descent of the Goddess into the Underworld: the Narrator, the Goddess, the Lord of the Underworld and the Guardian of the Portals. The Goddess is adorned with jewellery and veiled and stands at the edge of the Circle in the South-East. The Lord of the Underworld puts on his crown, takes up the sword and stands with his back to the altar. The Guardian of the Portals takes up his athame and the red cord and stands facing the Goddess.

The Narrator says:

"In ancient times, our Lord, the Hornéd One, was (as he still is) the Consoler, the Comforter. But men knew him as the dread Lord of Shadows, lonely, stern and just. But our Lady the Goddess would solve all mysteries, even the mystery of death; and so she journeyed to the Underworld. The Guardian of the Portals challenged her. . . ."

The Guardian of the Portals challenges the Goddess with his athame.

". . . 'Strip off thy garments, lay aside thy jewels; for naught mayest thou bring with thee into this our land.' "[1]

The Goddess takes off her veil and jewellery; nothing must be left on her. (If the Requiem is robed, only her plain robe must be left on her.) He then binds her with the red cord in the manner of the first-degree initiation, with the centre of the cord round the front of her neck, and the ends passed over her shoulders to tie her wrists together behind her waist.

"So she laid down her garments and her jewels and was bound, as all living must be who seek to enter the realms of Death, the Mighty One."

The Guardian of the Portals leads the Goddess to stand facing the Lord of the Underworld. The Guardian then steps aside.

"Such was her beauty that Death himself knelt, and laid his sword and crown at her feet. . . ."

The Lord of the Underworld kneels before the Goddess (see Plate 20), lays his sword and his crown on the ground on each side of her, then kisses her right foot and her left foot.

". . . and kissed her feet, saying: 'Blessed be thy feet, that have brought thee in these ways. Abide with me; but let me place my cold hands on thy heart.' "

The Lord of the Underworld raises his hands, palms forward, and holds them a few inches from the Goddess's heart.

---

1. Since all the words of the Legend are spoken by the Narrator, we have not repeated "The Narrator says" each time. If the three actors can speak their own lines from memory, so much the better.

"And she replied: 'I love thee not. Why dost thou cause all things that I love, and take delight in, to fade and die?'"

The Lord of the Underworld spreads his arms outwards and downwards, with the palms of his hands forward.

"'Lady,' replied Death, 'it is age and fate, against which I am helpless. Age causes all things to wither; but when men die at the end of time, I give them rest and peace and strength, so that they may return. But thou, thou art lovely; return not, abide with me.' But she answered: 'I love thee not.'"

The Lord of the Underworld rises, goes to the altar and picks up the scourge. He turns to face the Goddess.

"Then said Death: 'An thou receivest not my hands on thy heart, thou must kneel to Death's scourge.' 'It is fate—better so,' she said, and she knelt. And Death scourged her tenderly."

The Goddess kneels, facing the altar. The Lord of the Underworld gives her three, seven, nine and twenty-one very gentle strokes of the scourge.

"And she cried: 'I know the pangs of love.'"

The Lord of the Underworld replaces the scourge on the altar, helps the Goddess to rise and kneels facing her.

"And Death raised her, and said: 'Blessed be.' And he gave her the Fivefold Kiss, saying: 'Thus only mayest thou attain to joy and knowledge.'"

The Lord of the Underworld gives the Goddess the Fivefold Kiss (but without the usual spoken words). He then unties her wrists, laying the cord on the ground.

"And he taught her all his mysteries and gave her the necklace which is the circle of rebirth."

The Lord of the Underworld fetches the necklace from the altar and places it round the Goddess's neck. The Goddess then takes up the crown and replaces it on the Lord of the Underworld's head.

"And she taught him the mystery of the sacred cup, which is the cauldron of rebirth."

The Lord of the Underworld moves in front of the altar at its East end, and the Goddess moves in front of the altar at its West end. The Goddess picks up the chalice in both her hands, they face each other, and he places both his hands round hers.

"They loved, and were one; for there be three great mysteries in the life of man, and magic controls them all. To fulfil love, you must

return again at the same time and at the same place as the loved ones; and you must meet, and know, and remember, and love them again."

The Lord of the Underworld releases the Goddess's hands, and she replaces the chalice on the altar. He picks up the scourge in his left hand and the sword in his right and stands in the God Position, forearms crossed on his breast and sword and scourge pointing upwards, with his back to the altar. She stands beside him in the Goddess Position, feet astride and arms outstretched to form the Pentagram.

"But to be reborn, you must die, and be made ready for a new body. And to die, you must be born; and without love, you may not be born. And our Goddess ever inclineth to love, and mirth, and happiness; and she guardeth and cherisheth her hidden children in life, and in death she teacheth the way to her communion; and even in this world she teacheth them the mystery of the Magic Circle, which is placed between the worlds of men and of the Gods."

The Lord of the Underworld replaces the scourge, sword and crown on or by the altar. This completes the Legend, and the actors rejoin the rest of the coven.

The High Priestess says:

"Let us now, as the Goddess hath taught us, share the love-feast of the wine and the cakes; and as we do so, let us remember our sister ——, with whom we have so often shared it.[2] And with this communion, we lovingly place our sister in the hands of the Goddess."

All say:

"So mote it be."

The wine and cakes are consecrated and passed round.

As soon as practicable after the Requiem, the pieces of the bowl are ritually thrown into a running stream or river, with the traditional command: "Return to the elements from which thou camest."[3]

---

2. If the Requiem is for a non-witch friend, or for a witch who was not a member of the coven, the phrase "with whom we have so often shared it" is of course omitted.

3. Any ritually-used object which has served its purpose and will not be needed for further working—especially if, like the Requiem bowl, it has been linked with an individual—must be ritually neutralized and disposed of; it is irresponsible, and may be dangerous, to allow it to linger. The running-water method is a time-honoured and satisfactory ritual of disposal.

Bibliography

It would be impossible to name all the books that have helped us in our study of the Eight Festivals and the concepts that lie behind them; but the following is a list of those we have found particularly informative, illuminating or even provocative. It also includes all books mentioned in the text. The editions named are not always the first ones, but are those we have used or have found to be currently available.

ASHE, GEOFFREY—*The Virgin* (Routledge & Kegan Paul, London, 1976)

BUCKLAND, RAYMOND—*The Tree, the Complete Book of Saxon Witchcraft* (Samuel Weiser, New York, 1974)

BURLAND, C. A.—*The Magical Arts, a Short History* (Arthur Barker, London, 1966)

CARMICHAEL, ALEXANDER—*Carmina Gadelica, Hymns and Incantations, with Illustrative Notes of Words, Rites and Customs Dying and Obsolete* (Oliver & Boyd, Edinburgh); volumes I and II, 1900; 2nd edition, volumes I–VI, 1928 onwards.

CARMICHAEL, ALEXANDER—*The Sun Dances* (Floris Books, Edinburgh, 1977). A paperback selection from the English translations contained in *Carmina Gadelica*.

CLÉBERT, JEAN-PAUL—*The Gypsies* (English translation by Charles Duff, Vista Books, London, 1963)

CROWLEY, ALEISTER—*777 Revised* (Neptune Press, London, 1952)

CROWLEY, ALEISTER—*Magick* (Routledge & Kegan Paul, London, 1973)

CULPEPER, NICHOLAS—*Culpeper's Complete Herbal* (mid-seventeenth century; current edition W. Foulsham & Co., London & New York, undated)

175

DILLON, MYLES & CHADWICK, NORA—*The Celtic Realms* (Weidenfeld & Nicolson, London, 1967)

DINNEEN, REV. PATRICK S.—*Foclóir Gaedhilge agus Béarla—An Irish-English Dictionary* (Irish Texts Society, Dublin, 1927). Note for Irish scholars: the new Niall Ó Dónaill *Foclóir Gaeilge-Béarla* (Oifig an tSoláthair, Dublin, 1977) is admirable for modern Irish usage but less informative than Dinneen on mythological and folk-lore references. (See "MacALPINE, NEIL" for Scottish Gaelic.)

DONOVAN, FRANK—*Never on a Broomstick* (Stackpole Books, Harrisburg, Pa., 1971)

DUFFY, MAUREEN—*The Erotic World of Faery* (Hodder & Stoughton, London, 1972)

DURDIN-ROBERTSON, LAWRENCE—*The Cult of the Goddess* (Cesara Publications, Clonegal, Ireland, 1974)

DURDIN-ROBERTSON, LAWRENCE—*The Goddesses of Chaldaea, Syria and Egypt* (Cesara Publications, 1976)

DURDIN-ROBERTSON, LAWRENCE—*The Symbolism of Temple Architecture* (Cesara Publications, 1978)

Encyclopaedia Britannica, 1957 edition.

FARRAR, STEWART—*What Witches Do* (2nd edition, Capel Books, Dublin, 1983, and Phoenix Publications, Custer, WA., 1983). (Spanish translation *Lo que Hacen las Brujas*, Ediciones Martinez Roca, Barcelona, 1977.)

FORTUNE, DION—*The Mystical Qabala* (Rider, London, 1954)

FORTUNE, DION—*The Sea Priestess* (Aquarian Press, London, 1957)

FORTUNE, DION—*Moon Magic* (Aquarian Press, 1956)

FRAZER, SIR J. G.—*The Golden Bough (Abridged Edition)* (Macmillan, London, paperback 1974). Our page references are to this reprint, which differs from the 1922 original and is more easily obtained.

GANTZ, JEFFREY (translator)—*The Mabinogion* (Penguin, London, 1976). This paperback is now more easily obtained than the well-known Everyman translation by Gwyn and Thomas Jones (J. M. Dent & Sons, London, 1949)

GARDNER, GERALD B.—*Witchcraft Today* (Rider, London 1954)

GARDNER, GERALD B.—*The Meaning of Witchcraft* (Aquarian Press, London, 1959)

GLASS, JUSTINE—*Witchcraft, the Sixth Sense—and Us* (Neville Spearman, London, 1965)

GRAVES, ROBERT—*The White Goddess* (3rd edition, Faber & Faber, London, 1952)

GRAVES, ROBERT—*The Greek Myths*, two volumes, revised edition (Penguin, London, 1960)

GRAVES, TOM—*Needles of Stone* (Turnstone Books, London, 1978)

GRIGSON, GEOFFREY—*The Goddess of Love: The birth, triumph, death and return of Aphrodite* (Constable, London, 1976)

HARDING, M. ESTHER—*Woman's Mysteries* (Rider, London, 1971)

HARRISON, MICHAEL—*The Roots of Witchcraft* (Frederick Muller, London, 1973)

HAWKES, JACQUETTA—*Dawn of the Gods* (Chatto & Windus, London, 1968)

HERM, GERHARD—*The Celts* (Weidenfeld & Nicolson, London, 1976)

HITCHING, FRANCIS—*Earth Magic* (Cassell, London, 1976)

HUSON, PAUL—*Mastering Witchcraft* (Rupert Hart-Davis, London, 1970)

INWARDS, RICHARD—*Weather Lore* (Rider, London, 1950)

JACKSON, KENNETH (translator)—*A Celtic Miscellany* (Penguin, London, 1971)

JUNG, CARL G.—*Collected Works, volume IX; 2nd edition* (Routledge & Kegan Paul, London, 1968)

JUNG, CARL G.—(editor) *Man and His Symbols* (Aldus Books, London, 1964)

KIPLING, RUDYARD—*Puck of Pook's Hill* (Macmillan, London, 1906)

Larousse Encyclopaedia of Mythology (Hatchworth Press, London, 1959)

LELAND, CHARLES G.—*Aradia: the Gospel of the Witches*, introduced by Stewart Farrar (C. W. Daniel Co., London, 1974)

LETHBRIDGE, T. C.—*Witches: Investigating an Ancient Religion* (Routledge & Kegan Paul, London, 1962)

MacALISTER, R. A. STEWART (editor and translator)—*Lebor Gabála Érenn, the Book of the Taking of Ireland*, Parts I–V (Irish

Texts Society, Dublin, 1938–56). Commonly known as *The Book of Invasions*, this is a collection of mediaeval texts in which monks recorded very much older, originally oral, material.

MacALPINE, NEIL—*Pronouncing Gaelic-English Dictionary* (Gairm Publications, Glasgow, 1973). This for Scottish Gaelic; for Irish, see under "DINNEEN, REV. PATRICK S.".

MacCANA, PROINSIAS—*Celtic Mythology* (Hamlyn, London, 1970)

MacNEILL, MÁIRE—*The Festival of Lughnasa* (Oxford University Press, London, 1962)

MacNIOCAILL, GEARÓID—*Ireland Before the Vikings* (Gill & Macmillan, Dublin, 1972)

MARKALE, JEAN—*Women of the Celts* (Gordon Cremonesi, London, 1975)

MARTELLO, Dr LEO LOUIS—*Witchcraft, the Old Religion* (University Press, Secausus N. J., undated)

MATHERS, S. LIDELL MacGREGOR (translator and editor)—*The Key of Solomon the King* (*Clavicula Salomonis*), with foreword by Richard Cavendish (Routledge & Kegan Paul, London, 1972). (The original Mathers edition was published by George Redway in 1888.)

MICHELL, JOHN—*The Earth Spirit, its Ways, Shrines, and Mysteries* (Thames & Hudson, London, and Avon Books, New York, 1975)

MURRAY, MARGARET A.—*The Witch-Cult in Western Europe* (Oxford University Press, London, 1921)

MURRAY, MARGARET A.—*The God of the Witches* (Daimon Press, Castle Hedingham, Essex, 1962)

MURRAY, MARGARET A.—*The Splendour that was Egypt* (revised edition, Sidgwick & Jackson, London, 1964)

NEUMANN, ERICH—*The Great Mother* (2nd edition, Routledge & Kegan Paul, London, 1963)

OVID—*Fasti*, Henry T. Riley's translation (Bell & Daldy, London, 1870)

REES, ALWYN & BRINLEY—*Celtic Heritage* (Thames & Hudson, London, 1961)

REGARDIE, ISRAEL—*The Golden Dawn* (four volumes, 3rd edition, Hazel Hills Corpn., River Falls, Wisconsin, 1970)

ROSS, ANNE—*Pagan Celtic Britain* (Routledge & Kegan Paul, London, 1974)

SEYMOUR, St. JOHN D.—*Irish Witchcraft and Demonology* (1913; reprinted by E. P. Publishing Co, East Ardsley, Yorkshire, 1972)

"SHEBA, LADY", who claims to be America's Witch Queen, is listed here only in order to warn our readers that her 1971 published version of *The Book of Shadows* is garbled, illiterate and better ignored.

STONE, MERLIN—*The Paradise Papers, The Suppression of Women's Rites* (Virago Ltd., in association with Quartet Books, London, 1976)

SYKES, EGERTON (compiler)—*Everyman's Dictionary of Non-Classical Mythology* (J. M. Dent & Sons, London, 1968)

TRYON, THOMAS—*Harvest Home* (Hodder & Stoughton, London, 1974, and Coronet paperback, London, 1975)

VALIENTE, DOREEN—*Where Witchcraft Lives* (Aquarian Press, London, 1962)

VALIENTE, DOREEN—*An ABC of Witchcraft Past and Present* (Robert Hale, London, 1973)

VALIENTE, DOREEN—*Natural Magic* (Robert Hale, 1975)

VALIENTE, DOREEN—*Witchcraft for Tomorrow* (Robert Hale, 1978)

VOGH, JAMES—*The Thirteenth Zodiac; The Sign of Arachne* (Granada, St. Albans, 1979; first published as *Arachne Rising*, Hart-Davis, MacGibbon, London, 1977).

WARNER, MARINA—*Alone of All Her Sex—the Myth and the Cult of the Virgin Mary* (Weidenfeld & Nicolson, London, 1976)

WILDE, LADY—*Ancient Legends, Mystic Charms and Superstitions of Ireland* (Ward & Downey, London, 1888, reprinted in paperback by O'Gorman Ltd., Galway, 1971)

WILSON, ANNIE—*The Wise Virgin, the Missing Link Between Men and Women* (Turnstone Books, London, 1979)

WYATT, ISABEL—*Goddess into Saint; the Foster-Mother of Christ* (article in *The Golden Blade*, 1963, reprinted as booklet by Mitchell & Co., Arundel, Sussex)

Index

Some of these items (such as 'Circle', 'High Priestess', 'Candle') appear on almost every page; for these, we have listed only certain key references.

We have taken some arbitrary decisions whether to list some items under (e.g.) 'Celtic Cross' or 'Cross, Celtic'; if in doubt, look under both.

Individuals are listed generally under surnames (e.g. 'Jung, Carl G.'); but legendary, and some ancient, ones under the first element of their names as usually written (e.g. 'Fionn mac Cumhal', 'Maid Marian').

Sea, 164
—— Doll, 142
Set (Typhon), 144
Sex, 17–21, 48–9, 85–7, 126, 149
Shamrock, 75–6
Shannon, River, 141
Shechem, 81
Sidhe, 56, 77, 122, 136
Sín (Irish witch), 123
Sistrum, 144, 146–8
Skyclad, see Nudity, Ritual
Snake (Serpent), 76
Society of the Inner Light, 161
Solomon, Key of, 37
——, Temple of, 52
Solstices, see Midsummer and Yule
Sorrel, 76
Soul-mates, 164
Sow, 125
Sowens, 127
Sowing, 75, 86
Spain, 66
Sparta, 42
Spear, 101
—— of Lugh, 83
Spiral, 23, 117–19, 166–7, 169–70
Spiritualism, 130
Spring Equinox, 13–14, 23–4, 26, 72–9, 86, 116–17
—— Queen, 77, 79
Squares, Magic, 127
Staffordshire, 62
Stone of Fál, 83
Stone, Merlin, 19, 20, 74
Strabo, 104

Subconscious (Unconscious), 18–20, 74, 166
Sun, 38, 72, 76–8, 81, 86, 96, 116, 118, 119, 127, 134, 144, 155; see also God, Sun
Swan, 117
Sword, 36, 156, 161, 162, 165, 171
—— of Lugh, 83

Tabard, 131–2, 145–6
Tailte, Tailltean Games, 105–6
Tammuz, 23, 138
Tanit, 82
Taper, 36, 66, 78–9, 88, 90–1
Tara, 82–3, 106, 107, 123, 124
Teltown marriages, 106
Temple, 35–7
Thoth, 81
Tiber, River, 82
Tír na nÓg, 119
Titans, 145
Trefoil, 76
Trignetra, 76
Trinity, 75–6
Tuatha Dé Danann, 83, 103–4
Tuaitheal, Tuathal, see Widdershins
'Turkish Knight', 140
Tuscany, 42, 72, 84
Tyrone, County, 140

Uist, North, 78
Ulster, 82
Unconscious, see Subconscious
Underworld, 81, 163, 171–3
——, Lord of the, 169–73
Unius, River, 126

Part 2

Principles, Rituals and Beliefs of Modern Witchcraft

also published separately as The Witches' Way

with line illustrations by Stewart Farrar

Appendix by Doreen Valiente

Contents

Photographs

CREDITS

Stewart Farrar: Plates 1, 9, 10, 12, 13A, 13C, 13D, 17, 19, 20, 21
Janet Farrar: Plate 18
Doreen Valiente: Plates 2, 5
Ron Cooke: Plate 3
Alan Meek: Plates 7, 11
Virginia Russell: Plates 6, 13B
Martin Kane: Plate 22
Bibliothèque Nationale, Paris: Plate 8
Museum der Bildenen Künste, Leipzig: Plate 14
Dorset County Library: Plates 15, 16
Unknown: Plate 4

Figures

Acknowledgements

Our thanks are again due to Doreen Valiente for her help in preparing this book; for making available to us the unpublished authentic texts of Gerald Gardner's Book of Shadows, for amplifying these with her personal knowledge of his views and practices, for writing Appendix A which is a real contribution to Wiccan history – and always for her constructive advice.

We are also grateful to the Society of the Inner Light for permission to use passages from Dion Fortune's *The Sea Priestess* in our Seashore ritual.

We would also like to thank the Dorset County Library for their help in locating and supplying the photographs of the Rosicrucian Theatre from the now-defunct *Christchurch Times*, reproduced here as Plates 15 and 16.

Our thanks also to Penelope Shuttle and Peter Redgrove for permission to quote extensively from their book *The Wise Wound: Menstruation and Everywoman*.

And to Geoffrey Ashe for permission to quote a passage from his book *The Finger and the Moon*, © Geoffrey Ashe 1973.

This book is dedicated to our own coven, to our witch friends in many lands – and in particular to the memory of our dear friend Gwydion Pendderwen, who sang for us all.

Introduction

This book is intended as a companion volume to our earlier one, *Eight Sabbats for Witches*, and it has a double purpose.

When we wrote the earlier book, we were fortunate in being able to enlist the help of Doreen Valiente. She was one of the late Gerald Gardner's High Priestesses, and she was co-author with him of the definitive version of the Book of Shadows, the ritual anthology which is copied out by hand by each new Gardnerian (or Alexandrian) witch when he or she is initiated, and which is by now the accepted liturgy (to borrow a Christian word) of an unknown but certainly large number of covens throughout the world.

The Book of Shadows has never been published; it only exists in handwritten copies, which are in theory only available to initiated witches. But Gardner himself revealed elements of it, disguised in his novel *High Magic's Aid* (1949), and undisguised in his non-fiction books *Witchcraft Today* (1954) and *The Meaning of Witchcraft* (1959).[1] And since Gardner's death in 1964, almost all the remainder has been leaked, plagiarized (usually without acknowledgement) or distorted either deliberately or by careless copying. This produced the unsatisfactory situation where a theoretically secret document was public property, but in a number of versions which varied from reasonably accurate to maliciously or ignorantly garbled.

With Doreen's agreement, therefore, we were glad to be able to begin the task of defining what the Gardner/Valiente Book of Shadows actually said. Also, we were able to identify at least some of the sources from which the Book was compiled. This was not always easy, because Gardner himself (perhaps not foreseeing how widespread and public the revival which he initiated would become) never bothered to identify them, except now and then to Doreen in passing. (See the remarks on Texts A, B and C below.) Apart from the genuinely traditional passages, some elements, such as the Kipling verse in the Bealtaine ritual, or the Crowley passages in the Great Rite declamation, were self-identifying; others, such as the borrowings from Carmichael's *Carmina Gadelica*, were more obscure; and the passages which Doreen herself wrote, such as the bulk of the prose version of the Charge, she could of course tell us about. Some passages' origins remain a mystery. But we were able to clear the air a good deal.

In *Eight Sabbats for Witches*, this defining and clarifying process only covered the rituals relevant to our theme: namely, those for setting up and banishing the Circle, the Great Rite and the fragmentary Book of Shadows rituals for the eight seasonal Festivals which we incorporated in our own expansions. In the present book – again with Doreen's permission and help – we continue the process with the other substantial elements of the Book of Shadows: the first, second and third degree initiation rituals, the consecrations and some miscellaneous items.

There is only one necessary overlap between the two books. In *Eight Sabbats for Witches* we gave the ritual for casting the Circle in Section I and for banishing it in Section III, with explanations and notes. Since the rituals in the present book cannot be worked without casting and banishing the Circle, we have repeated the casting and banishing rituals here (Appendix B), without the explanations and notes and with condensed instructions, to make this book complete in itself.

We would like to make one or two things clear. First, in taking on this task, we are not setting up the definitive Gardnerian Book of Shadows as Holy Writ. Modern witchcraft is a growing and developing thing, and we ourselves have departed from the original when we felt we had a good reason. But where we have done that, we have always said so, and have said as well what the original was – either in a footnote or in the opening explanation. Nor do we suggest that the Gardnerian body of rituals is 'better' than other Wiccan systems. What we do suggest is that, for us and thousands of others, it works; that it is coherent and self-consistent; and that if there is a standard to which the whole movement's rituals can be related, and which is followed by more working covens than any other, this is it. Again, since it is the 'liturgy' which (like it or not – it is too late by many years to argue about that) has become most publicly known, there are more and more self-initiated groups which are basing their working on whatever Gardnerian rituals they can gather – and some of what they are finding is garbled. We discuss the question of self-initiation, and the setting up of covens without outside help, in Section XXIII; but whether one approves or not, it is happening, and it will happen more healthily if they have the genuine material to work with. Finally, the Gardnerian Book of Shadows is one of the key factors in what has become a far bigger and more significant movement than Gardner can have envisaged; so historical interest alone would be enough reason for defining it while first-hand evidence is still available.

In this book, we refer to Texts A, B and C of the Book of Shadows. We attached these labels ourselves to the three versions of the Book of Shadows which are in Doreen Valiente's possession. They are:

Text A Gardner's original rituals as copied down from the New Forest coven which initiated him, and amended, expanded or annotated by himself. His own amendments were very much influenced by the OTO,[2] of which he was at one time a member. His process of making a coherent whole out of the fragmentary traditional material used by the New Forest coven had already begun.

Text B The more developed version which Gardner was using when he initiated Doreen Valiente in 1953.

Text C This was the final version which Gardner and Doreen produced together, and which was (and still is being) passed on to later initiates and covens. It eliminated much of the OTO and Crowley material which Gardner had introduced; Doreen felt, and persuaded Gardner, that in many places 'this was not really suitable for the Old Craft of the Wise, however beautiful the words might be or how much one might agree with what they said'. Substantial passages in it were written by Doreen herself, or adapted by her from sources more appropriate than the OTO or Crowley, such as the *Carmina Gadelica* (see *Eight Sabbats for Witches*, p.78).

The parts of the Book of Shadows which changed least between Texts A, B and C were naturally the three initiation rituals; because these, above all, would be the traditional elements which would have been most carefully preserved, probably for centuries, and for which Gardner would have to find little if any gap-filling material. However, the third-degree rite (see Section III) does include some Crowley material in the declamation, where for once it seems entirely suitable.

A note on the Alexandrian offshoot of the Gardnerian movement. In the 1960s Alex Sanders, having failed to gain admission to any

Gardnerian coven (including Patricia and Arnold Crowther's), somehow obtained a copy of the Gardnerian Book of Shadows and used it to found a coven of his own. He attracted, and welcomed, a lot of publicity and initiated people wholesale. He and his wife Maxine were much criticized by Gardnerian and other witches for showmanship, for his claim to be King of the Witches and for the way he freely added any other occult or magical elements that caught his fancy to the strict Gardnerian canon. He had, like Aleister Crowley, a wicked sense of humour, and no scruples about exercising it, which also did not endear him to the rest of the Craft. But like the Joker in a pack of cards, he had a role to play. He and Maxine initiated hundreds of people who might otherwise not have heard of the Craft until years later; many of them of course drifted off or otherwise fell by the wayside, but a substantial number went on to found their own covens and achieve their own balance and build on it. It has to be said that there are many excellent covens working today which would not exist but for the Sanders.

We ourselves were initiated by Alex and Maxine early in 1970, and founded our own coven at Yule of that year. From that London coven, and from our later Irish one, others have hived off – and others, in turn, from them.

Alex and Maxine separated soon after we left them. Alex is in semi-retirement in Sussex, his headline days behind him. Maxine stayed in London, where she worked more quietly and solidly with her half-brother David Goddard as High Priest. In March 1982 she announced that she had become a Liberal Catholic, but added: 'It would be quite untrue to say that I have given up all my previous activities.' That may well be; we have known other Liberal Catholics who are first-rate occultists.

The Book of Shadows with which we began working was, of course, copied from Alex's. It is basically Text C but, as we suspected at the time and confirmed later, it was incomplete and contained many amendments of Alex's own – and many mistakes, for he was not a careful copyist.

We have pointed out several Alexandrian amendments in this book; and to be fair, one or two of them we have found worth retaining ourselves – though again, where we have done this we have always said so, and footnoted Gardner's original.

The first part of our book, 'Leaves from the Book of Shadows', consists of the Gardnerian rituals we have discussed above (plus, in Section V, some non-ritual material), with commentaries. The second part, 'More Wiccan Rituals', offers some of our own which we hope other witches may find useful (as we did with our Wiccaning, Handfasting and

Requiem rituals in *Eight Sabbats for Witches*) and also a Section on protective rituals and talismans.

The third part, 'The Wiccan Path', fulfils the second purpose of our book – namely to summarize the various aspects of modern witchcraft in what we hope is a concise and helpful form. It includes Sections on the rationale of witchcraft, its ethics, the problems of running a coven, witchcraft and sex, astral projection, spells, clairvoyance and divination, healing, ritual nudity, self-initiation, the role of Wicca in the modern world, and so on.

There seems to be a need for a compendium of this kind, both for the Craft itself and for those who want to know what it is all about. Stewart attempted something of the sort in his 1971 book *What Witches Do*, and many witches have been good enough to commend it. But here we try to go into more of the reasons behind the reasons, and to expand on some of the things we have learned since 1971. *What Witches Do*, we like to think, has a special value in that it records the reactions of a new witch exploring an unfamiliar field, and there is little in it which Stewart would want to change. (After many years out of print, it has been republished at about the same time as this present volume, with a new Foreword to the Second Edition, by Phoenix Publishing Co., PO Box 10, Custer, WA 98240, USA.)

In the third part of this book, we do not claim to speak for the Craft as a whole, nor to propose any final authoritative orthodoxy; finality, authority and the very concept of orthodoxy are foreign to Wicca anyway. We have merely put down things as we see them, as we have experienced them and as we have learned them from witch friends of many paths – as a basis for discussion, agreements and disagreement, and (always) for further study.

We would like to think that these two volumes together, *Eight Sabbats for Witches* and *The Witches' Way*, offer a basic 'liturgy' and working handbook on which any coven can build its own unique philosophy and practice, within the common tradition – and that to interested non-witches they will give an overall picture of what these strange people in their midst are doing and believing, and why; perhaps persuading them that witches are not so bizarre, misguided or dangerous after all.

Finally, we are very happy to include an Appendix by Doreen Valiente herself, entitled 'The Search for Old Dorothy'. Gerald Gardner claimed to have been initiated in 1939 by Old Dorothy Clutterbuck, a New Forest witch. Some of his detractors have suggested that Old Dorothy, and even the New Forest coven, were a fiction invented by Gardner to give plausibility to his 'pretence' to be an initiated witch. Doreen set

herself the task of proving the detractors wrong – and did so. We leave
it to her to describe her search and its fruits, which are a solid
contribution to the history of the Craft revival.

JANET FARRAR
STEWART FARRAR

Note to Fourth Impression
Two years after its publication, we find no need for changes in our text.
But we would make two points: our remarks about the Irish Craft scene
(p. 184) have been overtaken by events. The Craft revival is on the move
in Ireland, and we are certainly no longer the 'only known witches'. A
symptom of this is the lively little pagan magazine *Ancient Ways*,
produced by Dublin initiates of ours who hived off and founded their
own coven. (It can be obtained from The Alchemists' Head, 10 East
Essex Street, Dublin 2.)

The second point is that we make several references to our living in
Co. Louth. We have moved since then, but have allowed the references
to stand.

A point on the Charge (pp. 297–8). This was written before the
current (and justified) sensitivity about the patriarchal slant of the
English language, and uses the words 'man' and 'men' to include men
and women. We have left the printed text as it is, but our own practice is
to amend the Charge in places to correct this, and others may wish to do
the same. For example, we say 'heart of mankind' instead of 'heart of
man', which some may not feel radical enough. But in amending it, care
should be taken not to destroy the rhythm and poetry of this lovely
declamation.

We would like to thank the hundreds of readers all over the world
who have written to us, and still do; and if pressure of work, and the
sheer volume of these letters, has prevented us from answering all of
them promptly, we hope they will understand.

Herne's Cottage,	J.F.
Ethelstown,	S.F.
Kells,	
Co. Meath,	
Ireland.	

Leaves From
The Book of Shadows

I *First Degree Initiation*

In a formal sense, first degree initiation makes you a rank-and-file witch. But of course it is more complicated than that.

As every experienced witch knows, there are some people who are natural witches from birth – often maybe from a past incarnation. A good High Priestess or High Priest is used to spotting them. Initiating one of these is not 'making' a witch; rather it is a two-way gesture of recognition and acknowledgement – and, of course, a ritual of welcome to a valued addition to the coven.

At the other extreme, there are the 'slow starters' – often good, sincere and hard-working people – who the initiator knows very well have a long way to go, and maybe a lot of hang-ups and false conditioning to overcome, before they can be called real witches. But even for these, initiation is no empty formality, if the initiator knows his or her job. It can give them a sense of belonging, a feeling that an important milestone has been passed; and just by giving a sincere postulant, however apparently ungifted, the right to *call* himself or herself a witch, you are encouraging him or her to work hard to live up to the name. And some presumed slow-starters can take you by surprise with a sudden acceleration of development after initiation; then you know that it has 'taken'.

In between are the majority, the postulants of average potential and blossoming awareness, who realize more or less clearly that Wicca is the path they have been looking for, and why, but who are still only beginning to explore its implications. For these, a well-conducted initiation can be a very moving and powerful experience, a genuine dialectical leap in their psychic and emotional growth. A good initiator will do everything to make it so.

After all, the initiator is not alone in his or her efforts (and we are not just referring to the support of his or her working partner and of the coven members). An initiation is a magical rite, invoking cosmic powers, and it should be conducted in the full confidence that the invoked powers will manifest.

Every initiation, in any genuine religion or fraternity, is a symbolic death and rebirth, consciously undergone. In the Wiccan rite, this process is symbolized by the binding and blindfolding, the challenge, the accepted ordeal, the final removal of the bonds and the blindfold, and the anointing for a new life. The initiator should keep this meaning clear in his or her mind and concentrate on it, and the ritual itself should impress the same meaning on the mind of the postulant.

In more primitive centuries, the death-and-rebirth imagery was doubtless even more vivid and explicit, and probably enacted largely without words. Patricia Crowther, the renowned Sheffield witch, tells in her book *Witch Blood* (see Bibliography) how she had an intimation of this during her initiation by Gerald Gardner. The ritual was the normal Gardnerian one, basically the same as we give it in this Section, but before the Oath, Gardner knelt beside her and meditated for a while. Patricia herself, bound and waiting, went suddenly into trance (which she discovered afterwards lasted for some forty minutes) and seems to have experienced an incarnation recall. She found herself being carried, bound and naked, in torchlight procession into a cave by a group of naked women. They withdrew, leaving her terrified in bat-filled pitch darkness. Gradually she conquered her fear and became calm, and in due course the women came back. They stood in line with their legs astride, and she was ordered to struggle, bound as she was, through the vagina-like tunnel of legs, while the women swayed, howled and screamed as though in childbirth. When she was through, she was pulled to her feet and her bonds were cut away. The leader, facing her, 'offered me her breasts to symbolise that she would suckle and protect me as she would her own children. The cutting of my bonds symbolised the cutting of the umbilical cord'. She had to kiss the proffered breasts, and she was then sprinkled with water and told that she had been reborn into the priesthood of the Moon Mysteries.

Gardner's comment, when she regained consciousness: 'For a long time, I had an idea that it used to be performed something like you have described, and now I know I wasn't far wrong. It must have been centuries ago, long before verbal rituals were adopted by the Craft.'

Death and rebirth, with all its terrors and promise, could hardly be more starkly dramatized; and we have a feeling that Patricia's recall was genuine. She is obviously a natural witch from way back.

But to return to the Gardnerian ritual. For this, we had not three Gardner texts, but four; in addition to Texts A, B and C (see page 3), there is Gardner's novel *High Magic's Aid*. This was published in 1949, before the repeal of the Witchcraft Acts in Britain, and before his two non-fiction books *Witchcraft Today* (1954) and *The Meaning of Witchcraft* (1959). In it, Gardner revealed for the first time in print, disguised as fiction, some of the material he had learned from his parent coven. For example, in Chapter XVII the witch Morven puts the hero Jan through his first-degree initiation, and the ritual is given in detail. We found this very useful in clarifying one or two obscure points – for example, the 'Feet neither bond nor free' order, which we knew from our own Alexandrian initiation but suspected was misplaced (see note 5 on page 301).

The first degree rite was perhaps the one that had altered least by the time the Book of Shadows had reached the Text C stage. This is because, among the incomplete material in the possession of the New Forest coven, it would naturally be the part which had survived most completely in its traditional form. Gerald Gardner would therefore have had no need to fill in gaps with Crowleyana or other non-Wiccan material, and Doreen Valiente therefore did not have to suggest the kind of rewriting that was necessary (for example) with the Charge.

In Wiccan practice, a man is always initiated by a woman, and a woman by a man. And only a second- or third-degree witch may conduct an initiation. There is, however, a special exception to each of these rules.

The first exception is that a woman may initiate her daughter, or a man his son, 'because they are part of themselves'. (Alex Sanders taught us that this could only be done 'in an emergency', but Gardner's Book of Shadows makes no such stipulation.)

The other exception concerns the only time when a first-degree witch (and a brand-new one at that) may initiate another. Wicca lays great emphasis on male-female working partnerships, and most covens are delighted when a suitable couple come forward for initiation together. One rather pleasing method of carrying out such a double initiation is exemplified by that of Patricia and Arnold Crowther (who were then still only engaged) by Gerald Gardner.

Gardner initiated Patricia first, while Arnold waited outside the room. Then he put the Book of Shadows into her hand and stood by, prompting her, while she herself initiated Arnold. 'This is the way it is always done,' Gardner told her – but we must admit it was unknown to us until we read Patricia's book. We like it; it creates a special bond, in the Wiccan sense, between the two newcomers from the start of their working in the coven.

Doreen Valiente has confirmed to us that this was Gardner's frequent practice, and adds: 'Otherwise, however, we did keep the rule that only a second-degree or third-degree witch could initiate.'

We would like to mention here a couple of differences (in addition to small points noted in the text) between the Alexandrian initiation rite and the Gardnerian one which we have taken as our standard. We do not mention them in any sectarian spirit – every coven will and should do what feels right to them – but merely to put on record which is which, and to express our own preferences, to which we too are entitled.

First, the method of bringing the Postulant into the Circle. The Gardnerian tradition is to push him into it from behind, as described in the text. The Book of Shadows does not say how it is done; after the Initiator's statement, "*I give thee a third to pass thee through this dread door*", it just adds cryptically 'Gives it'.

High Magic's Aid is more specific: 'Then clasping him from behind with her left arm around his waist, and pulling his right arm around her neck and his lips down to her, said: "I give you the third password: 'A kiss'." So saying she pushed him forward with her body, through the doorway, into the Circle. Once inside she released him, whispering: "This is the way all are first brought into the Circle." ' (*High Magic's Aid*, p.292.)

Pulling the Postulant's right arm round her neck is of course not possible if his wrists are bound together; and pulling his head round with her hand, to kiss him over his shoulder, is almost impossible if he is much taller than she is. That is why we suggest she kisses him *before* going round to his back. It is the pushing-from-behind which is the traditional essential; Doreen says Gardner's coven always did it.

'I think it was originally intended as a sort of test,' she tells us, 'because a questioner could say, as in *High Magic's Aid*, "Who led you into a Circle?" The answer was, "They led me from behind." '

The Alexandrian practice is to grasp the Postulant's shoulders from in front, kiss him and then pull him into the Circle, spinning deosil. This is how both of us were initiated, and we feel none the worse for it. But we see no reason, now, for departing from the original tradition, especially as it has an interesting historical meaning attached to it; so we have reverted to the Gardnerian method.

When Stewart visited the Witches' Museum in the Isle of Man in

1972 (then in the care of Monique Wilson, to whom Gardner had left his irreplaceable collection which she later unforgivably sold to America), Monique told him that, because he had not been pushed into the Circle from behind at his initiation, 'no real witch would touch you with a bargepole'. She then offered to re-initiate him 'properly'. Stewart thanked her politely but declined. The catch-question precaution may have had a valid basis in the persecution days; to insist on it today is mere sectarianism.

The second major Alexandrian departure from tradition is in the taking of the measure. Gardnerian covens retain the measure; Alexandrians give it back to the Postulant.

In the Alexandrian ritual, the measure is taken with red thread, not twine, from crown to heel only, omitting the forehead, heart and hips measurements. The initiator says: 'Now we are going to take your measure, and we measure you from the crown of your head to the soles of your feet. In the old days, when your measure was taken, hair and nail clippings would have been taken at the same time from your body. The coven would have kept the measure and the clippings, and if you had tried to leave the coven, they would have worked on them to bring you back, and you would never have escaped. But because you came into our Circle with two perfect words, perfect love and perfect trust, we give you your measure back, and charge you to wear it on your left arm.' The measure is then tied round the Postulant's left arm until the end of the ritual, after which he can do what he likes with it. Most initiates destroy them, some keep them as mementos, and some put them in lockets and present them to their working partners.

The 'love and trust' symbolism of the Alexandrian custom is clear, and some covens may prefer it. But we feel there is even more to be said for the coven retaining the measure, not as blackmail but as a symbolic reminder of the new initiate's responsibility to the coven. Otherwise there seems to be no point in taking it at all.

Doreen tells us: 'The idea of giving the measure back is definitely, in my opinion, an innovation of Sanders'. In Gerald's tradition, it was always retained by the initiator. *Never*, however, was there any suggestion that this measure was to be used in the blackmailing way described by the Alexandrian ritual. On the contrary, if anyone wanted to leave the coven they were free to do so, provided they respected our confidence and kept the secrets. After all, what is the point of trying to keep someone in a coven against their will? Their bad vibrations would only spoil things. *But* – in the old days the measure *was* used against anyone who deliberately and maliciously betrayed the secrets. Gerald told me that "the measure was then buried in a boggy place, with curses, so that as it rotted so the traitor would rot." Remember, betrayal in those days was a matter of life and death – literally!'

We would emphasize again – views on differences of detail may be strongly held, but in the end it is the coven's own decision which matters in deciding on a particular form, or in devising their own. The validity of an initiation does not depend on the small print, and never has. It depends on the sincerity and psychic effectiveness of the coven, and on the sincerity and psychic potential of the initiate. As the Goddess says in the Charge: 'And thou who thinkest to seek for me, know that thy seeking and yearning shall avail thee not, unless thou knowest the mystery: that if that which thou seekest thou findest not within thee, then thou wilt never find it without thee. For behold, I have been with thee from the beginning; and I am that which is attained at the end of desire.'

Smallprintitis (if we may coin the word) has been the disease, sadly, of all too many Christian liturgies, including those which had their origins in beauty; witches should not fall into the same trap. One is tempted to say that liturgies should be written by poets, not by theologians.

A word on the names Cernunnos and Aradia, the deity-names used in Gardner's Book of Shadows. Aradia was adopted from the witches of Tuscany (see Charles G. Leland's *Aradia: the Gospel of the Witches*); on her possible Celtic links, see our *Eight Sabbats for Witches* p.84. Cernunnos (or, as Jean Markale renders it in *Women of the Celts*, Cerunnos) is the name usually given by archaeologists to the Celtic Horned God, because although many representations of him are found, everywhere from the Gundestrup Cauldron to the Hill of Tara (see Plate 10), only one of these bears an inscribed name – a bas-relief found in 1710 under the choir of Notre-Dame de Paris, and now in the Cluny Museum in Paris. The '-os' ending suggests that it was a Hellenization of a Celtic name; the Druids are known to have been familiar with Greek and to have used the Greek alphabet for their transactions in ordinary matters, though in this case the actual letters are Roman ones. Also the Greek for 'horn' is κέραζ (keras). Doreen Valiente suggests (and we agree with her) that the name which was thus Hellenized was actually Herne (as in Herne the Hunter, of Windsor Great Park). 'Have you ever heard the cry of a fallow deer in rut?' she asks. 'You hear this all the time in the autumnal rut of the deer in the New Forest, and it sounds just like "HERR-NN ... Herr-rr-nn ..." repeated over and over again. It is a most thrilling sound and one never forgotten. Now, from the cave-drawings and statues that we have of him, Cernunnos was pre-eminently a stag-god. So how would mortals have best named him? Surely from the sound that most vividly reminds one of the great stags of the forest.'

To which one might add that the interchangeability of the 'h' and 'k' sounds is suggested by the place-names Cerne Abbas in Dorset, site of the famous hillside Giant. There are quite a number of places called Herne Hill in Britain, as well as two Herne villages, a Herne Bay, a Hern Drove, a Hernebridge, a Herne Common, a Herne Pound, and so on. Herne Hill is sometimes explained as meaning 'heron hill', but, as Doreen points out, herons breed near rivers and lakes, not on hills; 'it seems more likely to me that Herne Hill was sacred to the Old God.'

In the Alexandrian Book of Shadows, the name is 'Karnayna' – but this form appears nowhere else that we or Doreen have found. She thinks 'it is probably – though not certainly – a mishearing of Cernunnos. The actual name may have been omitted in the book Alex copied from, and he had to rely on someone's verbal recollection of it.' (Knowing Alex, we would say 'almost certainly'!)

In the text which follows, the Initiator may be the High Priestess or High Priest, depending upon whether the Postulant is male or female; so we have referred to 'the Initiator' as ' she' for simplicity, and to 'the Postulant' (later 'the Initiate') as 'he', though of course it may be the other way round. The Initiator's working partner, whether High Priest or High Priestess, has certain duties to perform as well, and is referred to as 'the Partner'.

The Preparation

Everything is set up as for a normal Circle, with the following additional items also in readiness:

a blindfold
a length (at least eight feet) of twine or thin string
anointing oil
a small hand bell
three lengths of red cord – one of nine feet, and two of four feet six

It is also usual, though not essential, for the Postulant to bring his own new athame, and red, white and blue cords, to be consecrated immediately after his initiation.[1] He should be told, as soon as he knows that he is to be initiated, to acquire for himself any black-handled knife with which he feels comfortable. Most people seem to buy themselves an ordinary sheath-knife (the sheath is useful anyway, for bringing it to and from the meeting-place) and enamel the hilt black if it is not black already. There may not be time for him to engrave the traditional symbols on the hilt (see Section XXIV) before it is consecrated; this can be done later, at leisure. Some witches never put the symbols on at all, preferring the alternative tradition that one's working tools should be unidentifiable as such to any outsider;[2] or because the hilt-pattern of the chosen knife does not lend itself to engraving. (Stewart's athame, now twelve years old, bears the symbols; Janet's, of the same vintage but with a patterned hilt, does not; and we have another athame, hand-made by a craftsman friend, which has a deer's-foot hilt obviously unsuitable for engraving.) We suggest that athame blades and points should be blunted, since they are never used for cutting but *are* used for ritual gestures in what may be a crowded and skyclad Circle.

The three cords he brings should be nine feet long each. We like to prevent the ends from fraying with Sellotape or by binding ('whipping', in the sailor's term) with thread of the same colour. However, Doreen says, 'we tied knots at the ends to prevent fraying, and the essential measurement was from knot to knot.'

He should also be told to bring his own bottle of red wine – if only to impress on him from the start that the expense of catering for the coven, whether it be the Circle wine or any food taken before or after the Circle, should not fall entirely on the High Priestess and High Priest!

As for the additional items listed above – any scarf will do for the blindfold, but it should be opaque. And the choice of anointing oil is up to the High Priestess; Gardner's coven always used pure olive oil. Alexandrian custom is that it should include a touch of the sweat of the High Priestess and High Priest.

The Ritual

Before the Circle is cast, the Postulant is stood outside the Circle to the North-East, and blindfolded and bound by witches of the opposite sex. The binding is done with the three red[3] cords – one nine feet long, the other pair four and a half feet long. The wrists are tied together behind the back with the middle of the long cord, and the two ends are brought forward over the shoulders and tied in front of the neck, the ends left hanging to form a cable-tow by which the Postulant can be led.[4] One short cord is tied round the right ankle, the other above the left knee – each with the ends tucked in so that they will not trip him up. As the ankle cord is being tied, the Initiator says:

'*Feet neither bond nor free.*'[5]

The Circle is now cast, and the Opening Ritual proceeds as usual, except that the 'gateway' in the North-East is not closed yet, and the Charge is not spoken yet. After Drawing Down the Moon,[6] the Initiator gives the Cabalistic Cross,[7] as follows: '*Ateh*' (touching forehead) '*Malkuth*' (touching breast) '*ve-Geburah*' (touching right shoulder) '*ve-Gedulah*' (touching left shoulder) '*le-olam*' (clasping hands at breast level).

After the Witches' Rune, the Initiator fetches the sword, or her athame, from the altar. She and her Partner face the Postulant.

They then declaim the Charge (see Appendix B, pp. 297-8).

The Initiator then says:

'*O thou who standest on the threshold between the pleasant world of men and the dread domains of the Lords of the Outer Spaces, hast thou the courage to make the assay?*'

She places the point of the sword or athame against the Postulant's heart and continues:

'*For I say verily, it were better to rush on my blade and perish, than make the attempt with fear in thy heart.*'

The Postulant replies:

'*I have two passwords. Perfect love, and perfect trust.*'[8]

The Initiator says:

'*All who have such are doubly welcome. I give thee a third to pass thee through this dread door.*'

She hands the sword or athame to her Partner, kisses the Postulant and goes round behind him. Embracing him from the back, she pushes him forward with her own body into the Circle. Her Partner ritually closes the 'gateway' with the sword or athame, which he then replaces at the altar.

The Initiator leads the Postulant to the cardinal points in turn and says:

'*Take heed, ye Lords of the East [South, West, North] that ———— is properly prepared to be initiated a priest [priestess] and witch.*'[9]

The Initiator then leads the Postulant to the centre of the Circle. She and the coven circle round him deosil, chanting:

'*Eko, Eko, Azarak,*
Eko, Eko, Zomelak,
Eko, Eko, Cernunnos,[10]
Eko, Eko, Aradia,'[10]

repeated over and over, while they push the Postulant back and forth between them, sometimes turning him a little to disorient him, until the Initiator calls a halt. The Partner rings the handbell three times, while the Initiator turns the Postulant (who is still in the centre) to face the altar. She then says:

'*In other religions the postulant kneels, while the priest towers above him. But in the Art Magical we are taught to be humble, and we kneel to welcome him [her] and we say ...*'

The Initiator kneels and gives the Postulant the Fivefold Kiss, as follows:

'Blessed be thy feet, that have brought thee in these ways' (kissing the right foot and then the left foot).

'Blessed be thy knees, that shall kneel at the sacred altar' (kissing the right knee and then the left knee).

'Blessed be they phallus [womb], without which we would not be' (kissing just above the pubic hair).

'Blessed be thy breast, formed in strength [breasts, formed in beauty]' [11] (kissing the right breast and then the left breast).

'Blessed be thy lips, that shall utter the Sacred Names' (embracing him and kissing him on the lips).

The Partner now hands the length of twine to the Initiator, who says:

'Now we are going to take your measure.'

The Initiator, with the help of another witch of the same sex, stretches the twine from the ground at the Postulant's feet to the crown of his head, and cuts this length off with the white-handled knife (which her Partner brings her). She then measures him once round the forehead and tied a knot to mark the measurement; once (from the same end) round the heart, and ties a knot; and once round the hips across the genitals, and ties a knot. She winds up the measure and lays it on the altar.

The Initiator asks the Postulant:

'Before thou art sworn, art thou ready to pass the ordeal and be purified?'

The Postulant replies:

'I am.'

The Initiator and the other witch of the same sex help the Postulant to kneel, and bow his head and shoulders forward. They unwind the loose ends of his ankle and knee cords and bind his two ankles and his two knees together.[12] The Initiator then fetches the scourge from tne altar.

The Partner rings the handbell three times and says *'Three'*.

The Initiator gives the Postulant three light strokes with the scourge.

The Partner says *'Seven.'* (He does not ring the bell again.)

The Initiator gives the Postulant seven light strokes with the scourge.

The Partner says *'Nine.'*

The Initiator gives the Postulant nine light strokes with the scourge.

The Partner says *'Twenty-one.'*

The Initiator gives the Postulant twenty-one light strokes with the scourge. (The twenty-first stroke may be more vigorous, as a reminder that the Initiator has been being deliberately restrained.)

The Initiator says:

'Thou hast bravely passed the test. Art thou ready to swear that thou

wilt always be true to the Art?'

The Postulant replies: '*I am.*'

The Initiator asks:

'*Art thou always ready to help, protect and defend thy brothers and sisters of the Art?* '

The Postulant replies: '*I am.*'

The Initiator says (phrase by phrase):

'*Then say after me: "I, ————, in the presence of the Mighty Ones, do of my own free will and accord most solemnly swear that I will ever keep secret and never reveal the secrets of the Art, except it be to a proper person, properly prepared within a Circle such as I am now in; and that I will never deny the secrets to such a person if he or she be properly vouched for by a brother or sister of the Art. All this I swear by my hopes of a future life, mindful that my measure has been taken; and may my weapons turn against me if I break this my solemn oath."* '

The Postulant repeats each phrase after her.

The Initiator and the other witch of the same sex now help the Postulant to rise to his feet.

The Partner brings forward the anointing oil and the chalice of wine.

The Initiator moistens her fingertip with the oil and says:

'*I hereby sign thee with the Triple Sign. I consecrate thee with oil.*'

She touches the Postulant with the oil just above his pubic hair, on his right breast, on his left breast and above the pubic hair again, completing the inverted triangle of the First Degree.

She moistens her fingertip with wine, says '*I anoint thee with wine*', and touches him in the same place with the wine.

She then says: '*I consecrate thee with my lips*', kisses him in the same places and continues: '*priest[ess] and witch*'.

The Initiator and the other witch of the same sex now remove the Postulant's blindfold and untie his cords.

The Postulant is now an initiated witch, and the ritual is interrupted for each member of the coven to welcome and congratulate him, kissing or shaking hands as appropriate. When this is done, the ritual continues with the presentation of the working tools. As each tool is named, the Initiator takes it from the altar and hands it to the Initiate with a kiss. Another witch of the same sex as the Initiator stands by, and as each tool is finished with, she takes it from the Initiate with a kiss and replaces it on the altar.

The Initiator explains the tools as follows:

'*Now I present to thee the Working Tools. First, the Magic Sword. With this, as with the Athame, thou canst form all Magic Circles, dominate, subdue and punish all rebellious spirits and demons, and even persuade angels and good spirits. With this in thy hand, thou art the ruler of the Circle.*

'*Next I present the Athame. This is the true witch's weapon, and has all the powers of the Magic Sword.*

'*Next I present the White-hilted Knife. Its use is to form all instruments used in the Art. It can only be used in a Magic Circle.*

'*Next I present the Wand. Its use is to call up and control certain angels and genii to whom it would not be meet to use the Magic Sword.*

'*Next I present the Cup. This is the vessel of the Goddess, the Cauldron of Cerridwen, the Holy Grail of Immortality. From this we drink in comradeship, and in honour of the Goddess.*[13]

'*Next I present the Pentacle. This is for the purpose of calling up appropriate spirits.*

'*Next I present the Censer of Incense. This is used to encourage and welcome good spirits and to banish evil spirits.*

'*Next I present the Scourge. This is the sign of power and domination. It is also to cause purification and enlightenment. For it is written, "To learn you must suffer and be purified". Art thou willing to suffer to learn?*'

The Initiate replies: '*I am.*'

The Initiator continues: '*Next and lastly I present the Cords. They are of use to bind the sigils in the Art; also the material basis; also they are necessary in the Oath.*'

The Initiator says: '*I now salute thee in the name of Aradia, newly made priest[ess] and witch,*' and kisses the Initiate.

Finally, she leads him to each of the cardinal points in turn, saying: '*Hear ye Mighty Ones of the East [South, West, North]; ——— has been consecrated priest[ess], witch and hidden child of the Goddess.*'[14]

If the Initiate has brought his own new athame and/or cords, he may now, as his first magical work, consecrate them (see Section IV) – either with the Initiator or with the person who is to be his working partner, if that is already known, or if (as in Patricia and Arnold Crowther's case) they have been initiated on the same occasion.

II   Second Degree Initiation

Second degree initiation promotes a first-degree witch to be a High Priestess or High Priest; not necessarily, of course, as the leader of her or his own coven. If our readers do not mind a military parallel, the distinction is the same as between 'a' Colonel and 'the' Colonel; the former implies that one is speaking of a holder of that particular rank, whatever his actual job; the latter means one is naming the commander of a particular unit.

A second-degree witch may initiate others – only, of course, of the opposite sex, and only to the first or second degree. (The two special exceptions to this rule have already been explained on page 11.) We are speaking here about the normal Gardnerian or Alexandrian tradition. Self-initiation, and the founding of covens where no outside help is available, is another matter, and we shall discuss that fully in Section XXIII; but even then we suggest that, once such a self-created coven is properly established and functioning, it would be well advised to stick to the Gardnerian/Alexandrian rule (or to the equivalent in whatever tradition it has based itself on).

We need hardly emphasize that initiating anybody lays a

responsibility on the initiator, both in deciding whether the postulant is suitable (or, if potentially suitable, ready) for it, and in making sure his or her training will continue. Initiation can have deep psychic and karmic repercussions, and if it is irresponsibly given, the results may become part of the initiator's own karma. Coven leaders should remember this when they are deciding whether somebody is ready for his or her second degree, and ask themselves in particular whether the candidate is mature enough to be entrusted with the right to initiate others; if not, his or her mistakes may well rebound on *their* karma!

If a newly made second-degree witch has been properly instructed and wisely chosen, of course he or she will *not* be eager to rush off and initiate people just because the rules permit it. The practice in our coven (and, we are sure, in most others) has always been that second- or third-degree witches other than the High Priestess and High Priest do not normally conduct initiations except at the request, or with the agreement, of the High Priestess. Very often this will be done if the postulant is a friend introduced by the member concerned, or if they wish to become working partners. Or it may be done to give the member practice and self-confidence in the ritual.

Another implication of being a second-degree witch is that you may, with the agreement of your High Priestess, leave the coven and found your own with your working partner. In that case, you are still under the guidance of the parent coven until its leaders decide you are ready for complete independence; they will then give you your third-degree initiation, after which you are completely autonomous. (We followed this pattern ourselves; Alex and Maxine Sanders gave us our second degree on 17 October 1970; we remained in their coven for another couple of months, and then, with their agreement, took three of their students who had not yet been initiated, and founded our own coven on 22 December 1970, initiating the three ourselves. On 24 April 1971 the Sanders gave us our third degree, and we and our coven became independent. We have reason to believe that Alex, at least, later wished the umbilical cord had not been cut quite so soon. But it had, and – without malice – we are prepared to stand by the result.)

The tradition, in Gardnerian witchcraft at least, is that the new coven's base or 'convenstead' must be at least a league (three miles) from the old one, and that its members must sever all contact with the members of the old. Any necessary contact must only be between the High Priestesses and High Priests of the two covens. This practice is called 'voiding the coven' and obviously has its roots in the persecution centuries. It would be very difficult to observe it to the letter these days, particularly in urban conditions; the league rule, for example, would be quite impracticable in places like London, New York, Sydney or Amsterdam. But there is still a lot to be said for 'voiding the coven' in the sense of deliberately preventing any working overlap between the old coven and the new. If this is not done, the frontiers will be blurred, and the new group will be hampered in its necessary task of establishing its own identity and building up its own group mind. There may even be a tendency, among the weaker members of the new coven, to 'run to Mummy' with criticisms of its leaders – which Mummy, if she is wise, will firmly discourage.

Maxine imposed the coven-voiding rule rigorously on our own infant group; and, in retrospect, we are glad that she did.

Two or more covens (including parent covens and their offspring) can always get together, by invitation or mutual agreement, for one of the seasonal Festival sabbats, and very enjoyable these combined sabbats can be; but they are celebratory rather than working occasions. Combined working esbats, on the other hand, are not generally such a good idea, except for special, and specific, purposes (the classic example perhaps being the famous wartime effort of witches in the South of England to frustrate Hitler's invasion plans – though the 'specific purpose' does not always have to be as momentous as that).

Second- and third-degree witches together form the 'elders' of the coven. Just how, and how often, the elders are called upon as such, rests with the High Priestess. But for example, if a disciplinary issue arises which the High Priestess feels she should not deal with on her personal authority alone, the elders provide a natural 'magistrates' bench'. The High Priestess should be the unquestioned leader of the coven – and within the Circle, absolutely; if anyone has honest doubts about her rulings, the question may be calmly raised *after* the Circle has been banished. But she should not be an autocratic tyrant. If she and her High Priest have had enough respect for, and confidence in, particular members of their coven to make them elders, they should be expected to value their advice on the running of the coven and the work to be done.

All this may seem to be wandering a little from the subject of second-degree initiation into more general topics; but it is highly relevant to the question of deciding who is, and who is not, ready for the second degree.

As to the initiation ritual itself: Texts B and C of Gardner's Book of Shadows are identical. The first part of it follows a similar pattern to that of the first-degree rite (though with appropriate differences): the binding, the presenting to the Watchtowers, the ritual scourging, the consecration with oil, wine and lips, the unbinding, the presentation of the working tools (but this time to be ritually used by the Initiate immediately) and the second presenting to the Watchtowers.

Three elements enter into the second-degree rite which are not part of the first degree.

First, the Initiate is given a witch name, which she or he has chosen beforehand. The choice is entirely personal. It may be a God-name or Goddess-name expressing a quality to which the Initiate aspires, such as Vulcan, Thetis, Thoth, Poseidon or Ma'at. (The very highest names of a particular pantheon, such as Isis or Zeus, should, we suggest, be avoided; they might be interpreted as implying arrogance in the Initiate.) Or it may be the name of a legendary or even historical figure, again implying a particular aspect, such as Amergin the bard, Morgana the sorceress, Orpheus the musician, or Pythia the oracle. It may even be a synthetic name made up of the initial letters of aspects which create a balance desirable to the Initiate (a process drawn from a certain kind of ritual magic). But whatever the choice, it should not be a casual or hurried one; thoughtful consideration before the choice is in itself a magical act.

Second, after the oath the Initiator ritually wills all her or his power into the Initiate. This, too, is not mere ceremony, but an act of deliberate magical concentration, in which the Initiator puts everything possible into maintaining and handing on the continuity of psychic power within the Craft.

And third, the ritual using of the cords and the scourge is the occasion for dramatizing a lesson about what is often called 'the boomerang effect'; namely, that any magical effort, whether beneficent or malicious, is liable to rebound threefold on the person who makes it. The Initiate uses the cords to bind the Initiator in the same way as the Initiate herself or himself was bound earlier, and then delivers to the Initiator a ritual scourging of three times the number of strokes which the Initiator used. As well as being a lesson, this is a test – to see whether the Initiate is mature enough to react to other people's actions with the necessary controlled restraint. A subtler aspect of the lesson is that, although the Initiator is in command, that command is not fixed and eternal but is a trust – the kind of trust which is now being bestowed on the Initiate too; for both Initiator and Initiate have ultimately equal stature in the cosmic plan, and both are channels for the power being invoked, not its source.

The second part of the ritual is the reading, or enactment, of the Legend of the Descent of the Goddess. We have given that in full detail, together with the movements for enacting it, in Section XIV of *Eight Sabbats for Witches*; so all we will do here is to give the text itself, as it appears in Texts B and C of the Book of Shadows. Doreen Valiente comments that our text in *Eight Sabbats for Witches* is a bit fuller than this (and incidentally points out that the word 'Controller' on p. 171, line 7, of the first printing should be 'Consoler'). Gardner gives a slightly different version in Chapter III of *Witchcraft Today*[1]; but here we have kept to the Text C wording (with two small exceptions – see page 303, notes 10 and 11).

Doreen tells us that in Gardner's coven, 'this Legend was read after the Initiation to the Second Degree, when all were sitting quietly in the Circle. If there were sufficient people present, it might also be presented as a dramatic mime, the players performing the actions while one person read the Legend aloud.'

In our coven we always act out the Legend while a narrator reads it – and if possible we have the actors saying their own lines. We find the enacted Legend, with the Initiate playing the Lord of the Underworld if he is a man, or the Goddess if she is a woman, a much more effective climax to the ritual than a mere reading. It is a matter of choice; but those who share our preference for an enactment are referred to *Eight Sabbats for Witches*.

In the ritual below, since the Initiate is already a witch, we refer to 'the Initiate' throughout; and again to the Initiator as 'she', the Initiate as 'he', and the Partner as 'he', for simplicity – although as before, it may be the other way round.

We would point out that American witches now universally use the *upright* pentagram – i.e. with a single point uppermost – as the Second Degree sigil, because the inverted pentagram is associated in the American mind with Satanism. European witches, however, still use the traditional *inverted* pentagram, with two points uppermost, but without any sinister implications. The European symbolism is that although the four elements of Earth, Air, Fire and Water are now in balance, they still dominate the fifth, Spirit. The crowned *upright* pentagram of the Third Degree symbolizes that Spirit now rules the others. Because of the difference between European and American usage, we give two alternative anointing procedures in the ritual which follows.

The Preparation

Everything is set up as for a normal Circle, with the following additional items also in readiness:

a blindfold
three lengths of red cord – one of nine feet, and two of four feet six
anointing oil
a new white unlit candle
a small handbell
items of jewellery
a necklace on the altar ⎱ if the Legend of the Descent of the
a veil ⎰ Goddess is to be enacted and not
a crown ⎰ merely read

The items of jewellery are for the woman enacting the Goddess; so if the ritual is skyclad, they should obviously be such things as bracelets, rings and earrings, and not pin brooches! The crown is for the man enacting the Lord of the Underworld and can be as simple as a circlet of wire if nothing better is available.

The blindfold should be of some opaque material, as for the first degree; but the veil should be gauzy and becoming, and preferably in one of the Goddess colours – blue, green or silver.

The Ritual

The opening ritual proceeds as usual, up to the end of the 'Great God Cernunnos' invocation, with the Initiate taking his normal place in the coven. At the end of the Cernunnos invocation, the Initiate stands in the centre of the Circle and is bound and blindfolded by witches of the opposite sex, exactly as for the first-degree initiation.

The Initiator leads the Initiate to the cardinal points in turn and says:

'*Hear, ye Mighty Ones of the East [South, West, North],* ———— [ordinary name], *a duly consecrated Priest[ess] and Witch, is now properly prepared to be made a High Priest and Magus [High Priestess and Witch Queen]*'[2]

She leads him back to the centre of the Circle and faces him towards the altar. She and the coven now link hands and circle round him three times.[3]

The witches who bound the Initiate now complete the binding by unwinding the loose ends of his knee and ankle cords and tying his knees together and his ankles together. They then help him to kneel facing the altar.

The Initiator says:

'*To attain to this sublime degree, it is necessary to suffer and be purified. Art thou willing to suffer to learn?*'

The Initiate says:

'*I am.*'

The Initiator says:

'*I purify thee to take this great Oath rightly.*'

The Initiator fetches the scourge from the altar, while her Partner rings the bell three times and says: '*Three.*'

The Initiator gives the Initiate three light strokes with the scourge.

The Partner says: '*Seven.*' (He does not ring the bell again.)

The Initiator gives the Initiate seven strokes with the scourge.

The Partner says: '*Nine*'.

The Initiator gives the Initiate nine light strokes with the scourge.

The Partner says: '*Twenty-one.*'

The Initiator gives the Initiate twenty-one light strokes with the scourge. She then hands the scourge to her Partner (who returns it and the bell to the altar) and she says:

'*I now give thee a new name,* ———— [his chosen witch name]. *What is thy name?* ' She gives him a light smack as she asks it.[4]

The Initiate replies:

'*My name is* ————.' (Repeating his new witch name.)

Each member of the coven in turn then gives the Initiate a light smack or push, asking '*What is thy name?* ' and the Initiate replies each time '*My name is* ————.' When the Initiator decides this has continued long enough, she signals the coven to stop, and they resume their places.

The Initiator then says (phrase by phrase):

'*Repeat thy new name after me, saying: "I,* ————, *swear upon my mother's womb, and by mine honour among men and my Brothers and Sisters of the Art, that I will never reveal, to any at all, any of the secrets of the Art, except it be to a worthy person, properly prepared, in the centre of a Magic Circle such as I am now in. This I swear by my hopes of salvation, my past lives, and my hopes of future ones to come; and I devote myself and my measure to utter destruction if I break this my solemn oath." *' The Initiate repeats each phrase after her.

The Initiator kneels beside the Initiate and places her left hand under his knee and her right hand on his head, to form the Magic Link. She says:

'*I will all my power into thee.*'

Keeping her hands in the Magic Link position, she concentrates for as long as she feels necessary on willing all her power into the Initiate.[5] After this, she stands.

The witches who bound the Initiate come forward and untie his knees and ankles and help him to rise. The Partner brings forward the chalice of wine and the anointing oil.

The Initiator moistens her fingertip with the oil and says:

'*I consecrate thee with oil.*'

She touches the Initiate with the oil just above the pubic hair, on his right breast, on his left hip, on his right hip, on his left breast and just above the pubic hair again, completing the inverted pentagram of the Second Degree.[6]

(In the American usage : throat, right hip, left breast, right breast, left hip, and throat again.)

She moistens her fingertip with wine, says '*I anoint thee with wine*', and touches him in the same places with the wine.

She then says '*I consecrate thee with my lips*', kisses him in the same places and continues: '*High Priest and Magus [High Priestess and Witch Queen]*'.

The witches who bound the Initiate now come forward and remove the blindfold and the remaining cord. The ritual is interrupted for each member of the coven to congratulate the Initiate, kissing him or shaking hands as appropriate. When this is done, the ritual continues with the presentation and using of the working tools. As each tool is named, the Initiator takes it from the altar and hands it to the Initiate with a kiss. Another witch of the same sex as the Initiator stands by, and as each tool is finished with, she takes it from the Initiate with a kiss and replaces it on the altar.

To begin, the Initiator says:

'*You will now use the Working Tools in turn. First, the Magic Sword.*'

The Initiate takes the sword and re-casts the Circle, but without speaking.

The Initiator says: '*Second, the Athame.*'

The Initiate takes the athame and again re-casts the Circle without speaking.

The Initiator says: '*Third, the White-hilted Knife.*'

The Initiate takes the white-hilted knife and picks up the new white, unlit candle from the altar. He then uses the knife to inscribe a pentagram on the candle, which he replaces on the altar.[7]

The Initiator says: '*Fourth, the Wand.*'

The Initiate takes the wand and waves it to the four cardinal points in turn.[8]

The Initiator says: '*Fifth, the Cup.*'

Initiate and Initiator together consecrate wine in the cup.[9]

The Initiator says: '*Sixth, the Pentacle.*'

The Initiate takes the pentacle and shows it to the four cardinal points in turn.

The Initiator says: '*Seventh, the Censer of Incense.*'

The Initiate takes the censer and carries it round the perimeter of the Circle.

The Initiator says: '*Eighth, the Cords.*'

The Initiate takes the cords and, with the help of the Partner, binds the Initiator in the same way as he himself was bound. Initiate and Partner then help the Initiator to kneel facing the altar.

The Initiator says:

'*Ninth, the Scourge. For learn, in Witchcraft you must ever give as you receive, but ever triple. So where I gave thee three, return nine; where I gave seven, return twenty-one; where I gave nine, return twenty-seven; where I gave twenty-one, return sixty-three.*'

The witch who is standing by hands the scourge to the Initiate with a kiss.

The Partner says: '*Nine.*'

The Initiate gives the Initiator nine light strokes with the scourge.

The Partner says: '*Twenty-one.*'

The Initiate gives the Initiator twenty-one light strokes with the scourge.

The Partner says: '*Twenty-seven.*'

The Initiate gives the Initiator twenty-seven light strokes with the scourge.

The Partner says: '*Sixty-three.*'

The Initiate gives the Initiator sixty-three light strokes with the scourge.

The Initiator says:

'*Thou hast obeyed the Law. But mark well, when thou receivest good, so equally art thou bound to return good threefold.*'

The Initiate, with the help of the Partner, assists the Initiator to rise and unbinds her.

The Initiator now leads the Initiate to each of the cardinal points in turn, saying: '*Hear, ye Mighty Ones of the East [South, West, North]:* ——— [witch name] *has been duly consecrated High Priest and Magus [High Priestess and Witch Queen].*'

The coven now prepares for the Legend of the Descent of the Goddess. The Initiator names a Narrator to read the Legend, if she is not going to read it herself. If the Legend is also going to be enacted, she will name actors for the Goddess, the Lord of the Underworld, and the Guardian of the Portals. It is usual for the Initiate to act at the Goddess or the Lord of the Underworld, according to sex, and for either the Initiator or the Initiate's working partner (if there is one) to act as the other. In strict mythological tradition, the Guardian should be male, but this is not essential. (In the Gardner texts, 'Guardians' is plural, but this seems to conflict with the mythology.)

The Legend of the Descent of the Goddess [10]

Now our Lady the Goddess had never loved, but she would solve all the Mysteries, even the mystery of Death; and so she journeyed to the Underworld.[11]

The Guardians of the Portals challenged her: 'Strip off thy garments, lay aside thy jewels; for naught mayest thou bring with thee into this our land.'

So she laid down her garments and her jewels, and was bound, as are all who enter the Realms of Death, the Mighty One.[12]

Such was her beauty, that Death himself knelt and kissed her feet, saying: 'Blessed be thy feet, that have brought thee in these ways. Abide with me; but let me place my cold hand on thy heart.'

She replied: 'I love thee not. Why dost thou cause all things that I love and take delight in to fade and die?'

'Lady,' replied Death, ''tis age and fate, against which I am helpless. Age causes all things to wither; but when men die at the end of time, I give them rest and peace, and strength so that they may return. But thou! Thou art lovely. Return not; abide with me!'

But she answered: 'I love thee not.'

Then said Death: 'An thou receivest not my hand on thy heart, thou must receive Death's scourge.'

'It is fate – better so,' she said. And she knelt, and Death scourged her tenderly. And she cried, 'I feel the pangs of love.'

And Death said, 'Blessed be!' and gave her the Fivefold Kiss, saying: 'Thus only mayest thou attain to joy and knowledge.' And he taught her all the Mysteries, and they loved and were one, and he taught her all the Magics.

For there are three great events in the life of man: Love, Death, and Resurrection in the new body; and Magic controls them all. For to fulfil love you must return again at the same time and place as the loved one, and you must remember and love them again. But to be reborn you must die and be ready for a new body; and to die you must be born; and without love you may not be born; and this is all the Magics.

III   Third Degree Initiation

Third degree initiation elevates a witch to the highest of the three grades of the Craft. In a sense, a third-degree witch is fully independent, answerable only to the Gods and his or her own conscience. He or she may initiate others to the first, second or third degree and may found a fully autonomous coven which (unlike one with second-degree leaders) is no longer subject to the guidance of the parent coven. Of course, as long as he or she remains a member of the parent coven, this independence is in abeyance; every coven member, of whatever degree, must willingly accept the authority of the High Priestess and High Priest; if a third-degree member no longer can, it is time to hive off.

As it says in the Law:[1] 'If they will not agree with their Brothers, or if they say, "I will not work under this High Priestess," it hath ever been the Old Law to be convenient to the Brethren and to avoid disputes. Any of the Third may claim to found a new Coven ...'

The initiation ritual of the third degree is that of the Great Rite. We gave a form of this, for use at the Festivals, in Section II of *Eight Sabbats for Witches*. Below, we give Gardner's Text B version, plus the

Text C alternative verse form of the declamation.[2] Each of these three forms can be either 'actual' or in token. All these ways of enacting the Great Rite differ, but their intent and spirit are the same; and we need hardly re-emphasize that any other ritual form which suited a particular coven would be equally valid provided that that intent and spirit were understood and truly expressed.

In its 'actual' form, the Great Rite is a sexual ritual, involving intercourse between the man and woman concerned. In its symbolic or token form, it may be called a ritual of gender, of male-female polarity but not involving intercourse.

We deal in depth with the Wiccan attitude to sex in Section XV below. But to avoid misunderstanding, we should emphasize here that to the witch, sex is holy – an unashamed and beautiful polarity-force which is intrinsic to the nature of the universe. It is to be treated with reverence, but without prudery. The Craft makes no apology for using intercourse between an appropriate man and woman, in private, as a profound ritual sacrament, bringing in all the levels – physical, astral, mental and spiritual. The key to the 'actual' (and indeed to the symbolic) Great Rite is the statement in the declamation: 'For there is no part of us that is not of the Gods.'

In the ritual, the body of the Priestess is regarded as the Altar of the Goddess whom she represents, and for whom she is a channel. Her focal womb is revered as 'the fount of life without which we would not be'; and no apology is needed for this ancient and holy symbolism either.

The question is, of course, who are 'an appropriate man and woman' to enact the 'actual' Great Rite instead of the symbolic one?

We would say categorically (and we think that most of the Craft would agree with us) that it should only be a man and woman between whom intercourse is already a normal and loving part of their relationship; in other words, husband and wife or established lovers. And it should always be enacted in private.[3] Wicca is unashamed, but not promiscuous or voyeuristic. The 'actual' Great Rite should invoke all the levels; and such a total involvement, in the power-raising atmosphere of a solemn ritual, would do violence to any relationship which was not already attuned to it.

That is not to imply that the *symbolic* Great Rite is a mere makeshift, or in any way ineffectual. It can be a powerful and moving rite, when sincerely worked by two harmonious friends who are not lovers. It, too, invokes all the levels, but in a way which a mature Brother and Sister of the Craft are well able to handle.

Why *does* the Craft use a sex-ritual, or a gender-ritual, to mark its highest degree of intiation? Because it expresses three fundamental principles of the Craft. First, that the basis of all magical or creative working is polarity, the interaction of complementary aspects. Second, 'as above, so below'; we are of the nature of the Gods, and a fully realized man or woman is a channel for that divinity, a manifestation of the God or the Goddess (and each in fact manifesting elements of both). And third, that all the levels from physical to spiritual are equally holy.

A man and a woman who are ready for their third degree are witches who have developed to the stage where these three principles are not merely acknowledged in theory but have been integrated into their whole attitude to life and therefore into their Craft working. So the Great Rite, whether 'actual' or symbolic, ritually expresses their stage of development.

How then is the Great Rite applied in practice to third degree initiation?

There are only two active participants in the Rite; the rest of the coven merely support it by their silent presence, whether for the whole of a symbolic Rite or for the first part of an 'actual' one. These two may be either the man (already third degree) initiating the woman; or the woman (again, already third degree) initiating the man; or the man and woman may both be second degree, taking their third degree initiation together under the supervision of the High Priestess and/or High Priest. The last case is of course particularly suitable for a working partnership, especially if they are preparing to set up their own coven or are already running one as second-degree witches under the guidance of the parent coven (we ourselves received our third degree together in such circumstances, as we explained on page 22).

The ritual in each of these cases is the same; so in the text which follows, we refer to the woman and the man simply as 'the Priestess' and 'the Priest'.

Unless the Priest is in fact the High Priest, accustomed to enacting the Great Rite at festivals or on other occasions, it would be asking too much to expect him to know the long declamation by heart. So it is a matter of choice whether he reads it or has the High Priest declaim it while he performs it. (This is the only situation in which a third person takes an active part.) If the Rite is 'actual', he will of course have to read or learn the final passages himself.

Gardner's Great Rite texts include three successive ritual scourging – the man by the woman, the woman by the man, and again the man by the woman. We do not use these ourselves, but we give them below for completeness, as their use is optional. Some witches hold that Gardner was too fond of ritual scourging, and many of his detractors maintain that he had a psychologically unhealthy addiction to flagellation. Quite apart from the fact that such a notoriously gentle person as Gardner is most unlikely to have had any such leanings, all this is based on a complete misunderstanding. The technique of not-too-tight binding and *gentle* monotonous scourging is not even a symbolic 'suffering to learn' as it is in the first- and second-degree rites; it is a deliberate and traditional method, hedged about with precautions, to 'gain the Sight' by influencing the blood circulation. It is described in detail in a non-ritual passage of the Book of Shadows, which we give in full on pp. 58-60, with Doreen Valiente's and our own comments.

The Preparation

Neither Text A, B nor C mentions or describes the point at which the Priestess, after the Fivefold Kiss, lays herself down on or in front of the altar, where she has to be from '*Assist me to erect the ancient altar*' (or its verse equivalent) onwards. But Doreen Valiente tells us that the Priestess 'would have been lying across the Circle, placed thus by the Priest, with her head to the East and her feet to the West. She would be lying either actually upon the altar or upon a suitable couch or pallet laid in front of it, with a cushion beneath her head. The Priest would kneel beside her, facing North'.

So in preparation, either the altar (if it is large enough for the Priestess to lie on it) must be cleared of its normal candles and tools and made suitably comfortable, or the couch or pallet must be ready. Using the altar itself seems to imply the old custom of having the altar in the centre of the Circle instead of at its northern edge (the usual practice nowadays, especially in a small room, to leave room for working) because Doreen goes on to say: 'In this position, the vagina of the Priestess would actually be about the centre of the Circle' – thus symbolizing its focal significance as 'the point within the centre', as the declamation refers to it. If, then, a couch or pallet is used, it should be so placed, along the East-West diameter.

If the ritual scourgings are to be included, a nine-foot red cord must be to hand for the cable-tow binding.

The chalice filled with wine, and the cakes, must be ready as usual. So must the Priestess's athame and the scourge (whether or not the scourging is included, because she has to hold it at two points in the Osiris Position).

If the Priestess will not be sitting on the altar itself at the beginning of the ritual, a suitable throne (a draped chair) should be placed in front of it.

The Ritual

The Priestess seats herself on the altar (or on a throne in front of the altar) with her back to the North, holding the athame in her right hand and the scourge in her left, in the Osiris Position (wrists crossed in front of her chest).

The Priest kneels before her, kisses both her knees and then lays his forearms along her thighs. He bows his head to touch his forehead to her knees, and remains there for a moment.[4]

He then rises and fetches the filled chalice. He kneels again, holding the chalice up to the Priestess.

The Priestess lays down the scourge and, holding the athame hilt between the palms of her hands, she lowers the point into the wine, saying:

'As the athame is to the male, so the cup is to the female;[5] *and conjoined, they bring blessedness.'*

She then lays down the athame, takes the chalice, kisses the Priest and drinks. She kisses the Priest again and gives him the chalice.

The Priest drinks, rises and gives the chalice to another woman with a kiss. The wine is passed woman-to-man, man-to-woman, with a kiss, until all have drunk, and the chalice is then returned to the altar.

The Priest fetches the dish[6] of cakes and kneels again before the Priestess, holding the dish up to her.

The Priestess touches each cake with the moistened tip of her athame, while the Priest says:

'O Queen most secret, bless this food unto our bodies, bestowing health, wealth, strength, joy and peace, and that fulfilment of Will, and Love under Will, which is perpetual happiness.'[7]

The Priestess takes a cake and bites into it, then kisses the Priest, who takes a cake himself. The cakes are then passed round with a kiss in the same way as the chalice, and the dish is then returned to the altar.

The Priest again kisses the Priestess's two knees, lays his forearms along her thighs and touches his forehead to her knees for a moment. Priest and Priestess both rise.

(If the scourgings are to be omitted, proceed directly to the presentation to the Watchtowers, and then to the Priest saying, 'Now I must reveal a great mystery.' If not ...)

The Priest says:

'Ere I dare proceed with this sublime rite, I must beg purification at thy hands.'

The Priestess fetches a red cord and binds the Priest, tying the middle of the cord round his wrists behind his back, bringing the two halves of the cord over his shoulders to tie them in front of his neck, and letting the ends hang down his chest as a cable-tow. She then takes him once round the Circle, deosil, leading him by the cable-tow.

The Priest then kneels facing the altar. The Priestess fetches the scourge and gives him three[8] light strokes with it. She lays the scourge on the altar.

The Priest rises, and the Priestess unties him. He then ties her in the same way and takes her once deosil round the Circle, leading her by the cable-tow. She kneels facing the altar. The Priest fetches the scourge, gives her three light strokes with it and returns it to the altar.

The Priestess rises, and the Priest takes her by the cable-tow to each of the quarters in turn, saying:

'*Hear ye, Mighty Ones of the East [South, West, North]: the twice [thrice]*[9] *consecrated and holy* ———, *High Priestess and Witch Queen, is properly prepared, and will now proceed to erect the Sacred Altar.*'

He then unties her and says:

'*Now again I must beg purification.*'

The Priestess ties him, leads him round and gives him three light strokes with the scourge, as before. He stands, and she unties him, replacing the scourge and cord on the altar.

The Priest says:

'*Now I must reveal a great mystery.*'[10]

The Priestess stands with her back to the altar, in the Osiris Position (again taking up the scourge and athame in her hands). The Priest gives her the Fivefold kiss.[11]

The Priestess puts down the scourge and athame.

The Priestess now lies face upwards, either actually upon the altar or upon the couch or pallet in the centre of the Circle. Her head is to the East and her feet to the West.

The Priest kneels beside her, facing North across her body. (In the following declamation, '[kiss]' means he kisses her just above the pubic hair, except in the two instances where it is otherwise described – namely, the kisses on the breasts and the kisses of the Third-Degree Sigil.)

The Priest says:

'*Assist me to erect the ancient altar, at which in days past all worshipped,*
The Great Altar of all things;
For in old times, Woman was the altar.
Thus was the altar made and placed;
And the sacred point was the point within the centre of the circle.
As we have of old been taught that the point within the centre is the origin
    of all things,
Therefore should we adore it. [Kiss]

Therefore whom we adore we also invoke, by the power of the Lifted Lance.'
(He touches his own phallus and continues:)
'O Circle of Stars [kiss]
Whereof our father is but the younger brother [kiss]
Marvel beyond imagination, soul of infinite space,
Before whom time is bewildered and understanding dark,
Not unto thee may we attain unless thine image be love. [kiss]
Therefore by seed and root, by stem and bud, by leaf and flower and fruit,
Do we invoke thee,
O Queen of Space, O dew of light,
Continuous one of the heavens [kiss],
Let it be ever thus, that men speak not of thee as one, but as none;
And let them not speak of thee at all, since thou art continuous.
For thou art the point within the circle [kiss] *which we adore* [kiss],
The fount of life without which we would not be [kiss],
And in this way are erected the Holy Twin Pillars.'[12]
(He kisses her left breast, and then her right breast.)
'In beauty and in strength were they erected,
To the wonder and glory of all men.'

If the Great Rite is 'actual', all but the Priest and Priestess now leave the room, opening the ritual gateway and then closing it behind them.
The Priest continues:

'O Secret of Secrets,
That art hidden in the being of all lives,
Not thee do we adore,
For that which adoreth is also thou.
Thou art That, and That am I. [Kiss]
I am the flame that burns in the heart of every man,
And in the core of every star.
I am life, and the giver of life.
Yet therefore is the knowledge of me the knowledge of death.
I am alone, the Lord within ourselves,
Whose name is Mystery of Mysteries.'

He then kisses her in the pattern of the Sigil of the Third Degree (the upright triangle above the upright pentagram)[13] as follows: above the pubic hair, on the right foot, on the left knee, on the right knee, on the left foot, and above the pubic hair again; then on the lips, the left breast, the right breast and finally the lips again. (See Figure 1.)

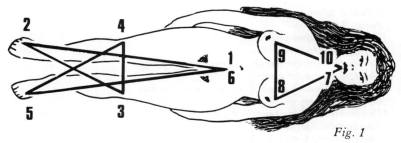

Fig. 1

He lays his body gently over hers[14] and says:

'*Make open the path of intelligence between us;*
For these truly are the Five Points of Fellowship –
Foot to foot,
Knee to knee,
Lance to Grail,[15]
Breast to breast,
Lips to lips.
By the great and holy name Cernunnos;
In the name of Aradia;
Encourage our hearts,
Let the light crystallize itself in our blood,
Fulfilling of us resurrection.
For there is no part of us that is not of the Gods.'

The Priest rises; the Priestess remains where she is. The Priest goes
to each of the cardinal points in turn, saying:
'*Ye Lords of the Watchtowers of the East [South, West, North]; the*
thrice consecrated High Priestess greets you and thanks you.'

Alternative Verse Version

The verse version of the Priest's declamation, which Doreen Valiente
wrote for Text C, is available as an alternative. It replaces the
declamation from '*Assist me to erect the ancient altar*' down to '*Lips to*
lips' (or, if preferred, the whole declamation down to '*not of the Gods*').
The kisses are as in the Text B version, just above the pubic hair –
except in the two places indicated as 'kisses on the breasts' and 'kisses
of the Third Degree Sigil'.

'*Assist me to build,*
As the Mighty Ones willed,
The Altar of Praise
From beginning of days.
Thus doth it lie

'Twixt the points of the sky,
For so it was placed
When the Goddess embraced
The Horn'd One, her lord,
Who taught her the Word
That quickened the womb
And conquered the tomb.
Be this, as of yore,
The shrine we adore, [kiss]
The feast without fail,
The life-giving Grail. [kiss]
Before it uprear
The Miraculous Spear, [touches own phallus]
And invoke in this sign
The Goddess divine! [kiss]
Thou who at noon of night doth reign
Queen of the starry realms above,
Not unto thee may we attain
Unless thine image be of love. [kiss]
By moon-ray's silver shaft of power,
By green leaf breaking from the bud,
By seed that springeth into flower,
By life that courseth in the blood, [kiss]
By rushing wind and leaping fire,
By flowing water and green earth,
Pour us the wine of our desire
From out thy Cauldron of Rebirth. [kiss]
Here may we see in vision clear
Thy secret strange unveiled at length,
Thy wondrous Twin Pillars rear
Erect in beauty and in strength.[16] [kisses on the breasts]
Altar of mysteries manifold,
The Sacred Circle's central point,
Thus do I sign thee as of old,
With kisses of my lips anoint. [kisses of the Third Degree Sigil]
Open for me the secret way,
The pathway of intelligence
Beyond the gates of night and day,
Beyond the bounds of time and sense.
Behold the mystery aright;
The five true points of fellowship,
Here where the Lance and Grail unite,
And feet and knees and breast and lip.'

IV Consecrations

Witches make a practice of consecrating their working tools and ritual substances such as water, wine and cakes or biscuits. Most religions do the same, in one form or another; but in Wicca, there are two notable differences. First, because of Wicca's emphasis on male-female polarity, consecration is normally done by a man and a woman together. And second, in Wicca the right to consecrate is not confined to the priesthood as a separate class, because every witch is regarded as a priest or priestess, and this is stated in each of the three initiation rituals. The power to consecrate is regarded as inherent in every human being, and as being effective if sincerely carried out. In fact, we (and doubtless other covens) often encourage neophytes who have not yet been initiated, but who have been attending Circles long enough to understand what they are doing, to carry out consecrations (except of a sword or athame) in the coven Circle, and we cast no doubt upon their effectiveness.

Consecration has two basic purposes. The first is psychological; to set the tool or substance aside as something special, and thus to modify the user's attitude to it – which in turn strengthens his or her confidence, creative imagination and willpower for any ritual in which it is used.

The second purpose can be called psychic, magical or astral. Witches (and many others) believe that every material object has 'bodies' on the other levels; and that, just as the material object itself can be altered, decorated, carved, moistened, dried, cooked, frozen, given a static electrical charge or what have you – all without robbing it of its identity, sometimes even enhancing it – so also (for example) can its astral 'body' be altered, charged, rendered harmless or actively beneficial, and so on, by human action, whether deliberate or involuntary. Deliberate action of this kind includes consecration, exorcism, the making of talismans, and many other steps – even the conscious love or resentment with which a gift is presented. Involuntary action includes a long (or short but intensive) use by a particular person, the involvement of the object in some emotionally charged situation – or again the spontaneous love or subconscious resentment which may accompany a gift. All of these affect the invisible but often very powerful astral or even spiritual charge carried by a material object.

It is not always easy to separate these two effects – the psychological and the astral – into watertight compartments; indeed, they overlap a good deal, and some people would lay more emphasis on one than on the other, or even deny that the effect is anything but psychological. After all, if a surge of confidence comes from a Catholic grasping a rosary, a Jew touching a mezuzah, or a pilgrim to Mecca circuiting and kissing the Ka'ba – or if an Irish farmer has bad luck when he finds a *piseog*[1] on his land – who is to say how far the effect is psychological, and how much of it is due to the non-material charge which has been put into, or accumulated by, the physical object?

Be that as it may, strong confirmation of the reality of the non-material charge is given by the often startling accuracy with which a skilled psychometrist can tell the history and emotional associations of an object simply by holding and concentrating on it.

Many witches and occultists would admit, if they are honest, that they started off by only being really certain of the psychological effectiveness of consecration, but that experience convinced them of the reality of the psychic-charge effect, which of course also grows stronger as the consecrated object continues in ritual use.[2]

There are three forms of consecration ritual in the Book of Shadows: for water and salt, for a sword or athame, and for other tools. All of them come from *The Greater Key of Solomon*, first published in English by Macgregor Mathers in 1888 (see Bibliography under Mathers) who translated it from mediaeval manuscripts in the British Museum. In Text A (and in Chapter X of *High Magic's Aid*) the strings of Hebrew, Greek or Latin Names of Power were retained as they appear in the *Key of Solomon*; but in Text B these were replaced, in two of the three rituals, by the names Aradia and Cernunnos. Text C is the same as Text B.

Doreen Valiente tells us: 'This shows how old Gerald's mind was working, as he gradually modified the rituals and incantations of the Hebrew *Key of Solomon* into a simpler and more pagan form. This important magical work first became generally available in 1888, so it had been around for quite a while among students of the occult. However, Gerald also told me that when the Jews were forced to go underground in Britain in the Middle Ages, some of them were helped and protected by the witches, who regarded them as companions in misfortune and fellow refugees from a persecuting Christian Church. Consequently, there was a certain amount of Qabalistic[3] lore which found its way into the hands of the witches, who esteemed the Jews as powerful ceremonial magicians. Occultists who were not witches had the same idea, and wanted to study the secret lore of Israel; but they had to be careful, so they pretended to be studying Hebrew in order to convert the Jews to Christianity, and to be studying the Qabalah with the same pious end in view. As you know, a lot of Hebrew Qabalistic lore has found its way into the Western Tradition; so much so that Dion Fortune (*The Magical Qabala*, p.21) says that Hebrew is the sacred language of the West as Sanscrit is of the East. *High Magic's Aid* in fact portrays a working relationship between a Qabalistic magician and a witch, and as we now know,[4] this book was published in Old Dorothy's lifetime; so I think she and Gerald probably used the *Key of Solomon* wording for these consecration rituals, which he later shortened and simplified. But I wish we knew what the older witches used!'

So do we; and it may well be that these old forms, or variations of them, have been preserved by other hereditary covens. For it is time that critics of Gardner who like to maintain that he 'invented' his system faced the fact that the ancient rituals of the Craft have survived piecemeal and unevenly; and that while they may genuinely possess some of them, so undoubtedly did the New Forest coven – and not necessarily the same elements. And that they or their forebears, like the New Forest coven, have doubtless filled in the gaps with material from other occult sources, or of their own devising. This was a perfectly legitimate process – indeed a necessary one if the Craft was to survive, especially during the fragmented and secret years. What matters is *does it work?* – and the Gardnerian system, as well as many others, undoubtedly does. Given the spirit and the understanding of the Old Religion, the forms are secondary. The old forms are to be valued, of course, because they represent our roots and enshrine wisdom which we are all striving to rediscover. If we can abandon sectarianism, and witches of many traditions can get together without bias, honest research and pooling of evidence could give us a far clearer overall picture of what the old forms actually were. Till then, we may all be sitting on different pieces of a rather important jigsaw puzzle.

We give below the Text B/C version of the three consecration rituals, plus an element-based form which we ourselves use for other objects such as personal jewellery. All these rituals should of course be performed within a Magic Circle. Even if the water and salt are being consecrated for a single purpose such as the Openings of the Body ritual (see p. 85), you should at least cast a mental Circle around yourself before you start.

One other point. At the banishing of the Circle, one witch should not join the others in making the Banishing Pentagrams but should carry any objects which have been consecrated during the Circle, and move round to be behind the coven as they face each of the cardinal points. To make a Banishing Pentagram towards a newly consecrated object might have a neutralizing effect.

Consecrating the Water and Salt

Our own usage is for the High Priestess to consecrate the water, and the High Priest the salt; the High Priestess then holds up the bowl of water while the High Priest pours the salt into it. But the whole thing can of course be done by one person.

The Text B/C version given here is a shortened form of that given in the *Key of Solomon*, pp.93-4 (see also *High Magic's Aid* pp.144-5). The list of Hebrew and other Names of Power has also been reduced – with the water from thirty-two to five, and with the salt from nineteen to six. As will be seen, in the other two consecration rituals, Gardner eliminated the Hebrew and other names altogether and substituted those of Aradia and Cernunnos (as we do ourselves), and we are a little puzzled by the fact that he did not do the same here.

The Ritual

Place the bowl of water on the pentacle, hold the tip of your athame in the water, and say:

'*I exorcise thee, O Creature of Water, that thou cast out from thee all the impurities and uncleanness of the spirits of the world of phantasm. Mertalia, Musalia, Dophalia, Onemalia, Zitanseia.*'

Remove the bowl from the pentacle, replace it with the bowl of salt, hold the tip of your athame in the salt, and say:

'*Blessings be upon this Creature of Salt; let all malignity and hindrance be cast forth thencefrom, and let all good enter therein. Wherefore I bless thee and invoke thee, that thou mayest aid me.*'

Changing over the bowls again and pouring the salt into the water, say: '*Yamenton, Yaron, Tatonon, Zarmesiton, Tileion, Tixmion. But ever mind, water purifies the body, but the scourge purifies the soul.*'

Consecrating a Sword or Athame

The Book of Shadows says that this consecration should if possible be done by a man and a woman, 'both as naked as drawn swords'. If a solo witch has no choice but to do it alone, the final embrace could perhaps be replaced by holding up the newly consecrated sword or athame for a moment in silent offering to the God and the Goddess, envisaged as being beyond the altar.

If possible, the weapon should be consecrated in contact with an already-consecrated sword or athame – as *High Magic's Aid* puts it (pp.159-60), 'to communicate increased power'.

The actual words should be spoken by whichever of the couple is the owner of the weapon to be consecrated. If, in the case of the sword, it belongs to both of them or to the coven, either of them may say the words, or both of them together. Where appropriate, '*I*', '*me*', '*my*' are replaced by '*we*', '*us*', '*our*'; or if the weapon is being consecrated for someone else, by the person's name and by '*he*' or '*she*', etc.

The original words of this ritual, as used in Text A, may be found on pp.101 and 118 of the *Key of Solomon*, and on p.160 of *High Magic's Aid*.

We give the Text B/C version below, expanded slightly to make the movements clearer. After the ritual itself, we give verbatim the explanatory passage as it follows the spoken words in Text B/C. It is interesting to note that in this text, 'Witch' means the woman witch and 'Magus' the man witch.

The Ritual

Lay the sword or athame over the pentacle, preferably together with, and touching, another already-consecrated weapon. The man sprinkles them with the salt-and-water mixture. The woman then picks up the weapon to be consecrated, passes it through the smoke of the incense, and replaces it over the pentacle. Man and woman lay their right hands on it and press down. Say:

'*I conjure thee, O Sword [Athame], by these Names, Abrahach, Abrach, Abracadabra, that thou servest me for a strength and defence in all magical operations against all mine enemies, visible and invisible. I conjure thee anew by the Holy Name Aradia and the Holy Name Cernunnos; I conjure thee, O Sword [Athame], that thou servest me for a protection in all adversities; so aid me now.*'

(This is called the First Conjuration.)
Once again, the man witch sprinkles and the woman witch censes, and the weapon is returned to the pentacle. Say:

'I conjure thee, O Sword [Athame] of Steel, by the Great Gods and Gentle Goddesses, by the virtue of the heavens, of the stars and of the spirits who preside over them, that thou mayest receive such virtue that I may obtain the end that I desire in all things wherein I shall use thee, by the power of Aradia and Cernunnos.'

(This is called the Second Conjuration.)
The one who is not the owner then gives the Fivefold Kiss to the owner. (If they own it jointly, or if they are consecrating it for someone else, the man gives the Fivefold Kiss to the woman.) For the final kiss on the mouth, they take the sword or athame and embrace with it flat between their breasts, held there by the pressure of their bodies. After the kiss, they separate (being careful to take hold of the hilt of the sword or athame before releasing the pressure on it, as dropping it may be painful as well as undignified).

The owner, or owners, of the newly consecrated weapon should then immediately use it to re-cast the Circle, but without words.

In Text B/C, the following explanatory paragraph is given after the ritual:

'If possible, lay sword with an already consecrated sword or athame. It should, if possible, be consecrated by both a woman and a man, both of whom are initiated, and both as naked as drawn swords. During consecration, press down on sword hard with consecrated sword or athame. If possible, partake of Wine and Cakes first, then Magus should sprinkle with the water, Witch should cense in first Conjuration, then sprinkle and cense again and conjure again with second Conjuration. If true sword and athame are available, a sword and athame can be consecrated at the same time in which case Magus should press with sword on sword and Witch with athame on athame, and new sword and athame should touch. In any case, when finished the weapon should be handed to new owner with Fivefold Salute, and should be pressed against the body for a time to get the aura; and it should be in as close connection as possible to the naked body for at least a month, i.e. kept under pillow, etc. Do not allow anyone to touch or handle any of your tools until thoroughly impregnated with your aura; say, six months or as near as possible. But a pair working together may own the same tooks, which will be impregnated with the aura of both.'

Consecrating Other Working Tools

This form is used for any ritual tool except a sword or athame. The original words, as used in Text A, may be found on p.102 of the *Key of Solomon* and on p.155 of *High Magic's Aid*. Again, in Text B/C the names of Aradia and Cernunnos have been substituted.

Here, too, we give the Text B/C version, slightly expanded to make the movements clear, followed verbatim by the explanatory paragraph from the Text.

In this paragraph, once again the words 'Witch' and 'Magus' are used – but here, we think, they do *not* mean 'woman' and 'man'. We are told that the Witch may leave and re-enter the Circle freely and safely, but that it is dangerous for the Magus to do so – which would be strange if it were a sexual discrimination! In this particular statement, pretty clearly 'Witch' means Wiccan operator (man or woman), and 'Magus' means ceremonial magician (man or woman), and what the Text is doing is to stress the difference between 'Art Magic' – i.e., a ceremonial magician's Circle (which is purely protective, against spirits being summoned *outside* it) – and the witches' Circle (which is primarily to contain and amplify power which is being raised *inside* it, and only secondarily protective). We discuss this difference more fully on p.83. Such a change in the meaning of words between related passages would not be surprising; as Doreen comments, 'this part of Gerald's book is rather difficult to unravel! He had the endearing habit of copying half of something on to one page and then copying the other half on to another page mixed up with something else – though this may have been deliberate in case the book ever fell into the hands of an uninitiated person, who just wouldn't have been able to make head or tail of it.'

The Ritual

Man and woman place the tool on the pentacle, and lay their two right hands on it. Say:

'*Aradia and Cernunnos, deign to bless and to consecrate this White-hilted Knife* [or whatever it is] *that it may obtain the necessary virtue through you for all acts of love and beauty.*'

The man sprinkles the tool with the salt-and-water mixture, and the woman passes it through the smoke of the incense and replaces it on the pentacle. Say:

'*Aradia and Cernunnos, bless this instrument prepared in your honour.*' In the case of the Scourge or the Cords, add, '*... that it may serve for a good use and end and for your glory.*'

Once again, the man sprinkles and the woman censes.

The one who is not the owner then gives the Fivefold Kiss to the owner. (If they own it jointly, or if they are consecrating it for someone else, the man gives the Fivefold Kiss to the woman.) For the final kiss on the mouth, they take the tool and embrace with it between their breasts, held there by the pressure of their bodies. After the kiss, they separate (again, carefully holding the tool so as not to drop it).

The owner, or owners, of the newly consecrated tool should then immediately use it, in the way suggested in the Text B/C explanatory paragraph which follows:

'All these weapons should be presented to the new owner with Salute. If a Witch Queen: ∇ [as in the first degree initiation – see p.19]. End ceremony with Fivefold Salute. The new owner should immediately use the new instruments, i.e., form Circle with Sword, then Athame, incise something with White-hilted Knife, exhibit Pentacle to Four Quarters, wave Wand to Four Quarters, cense to Four Quarters, use Cords and Scourge; and should continue to use all of them in a Circle as often as possible, for some time. To mark out a new Circle, stick sword or athame in ground, make a loop in cord, and slip over; then, using cord, mark out a circle, and later mark it with point of sword or athame. Always renew the Circle with sword or athame when about to use, but have it marked so that you always retrace it in same place. Remember the Circle is a protection, a guard against evil influences, and to prevent power created from dispersing; but the Witch, not being evil, may enter and leave freely. But in Art Magic, it is a barrier against forces raised, and when once in the Magus may not leave without great danger. If any great danger is manifested it would be advisable to take refuge in the Circle; but ordinarily sword or athame in hand is perfect protection against anything. Those who make these tools must be purified, clean and properly prepared. When not in use, all tools and weapons should be put away in a secret place; and it is good that this should be near your sleeping place, and that you handle them each night before retiring.'

Consecrating Personal Jewellery, Etc.

The Book of Shadows gives no ritual for this. We have found that a satisfactory way is to do it in terms of the four elements – again in the names of Cernunnos and Aradia. We include our ritual here in case other witches find it useful.

Incidentally, it should hardly be necessary to point out that covens should use whatever God- and Goddess-names they are in the habit of using (in this and other rituals). We have used the names Cernunnos and Aradia throughout this Section because these are what the Book of Shadows gives, and what we normally use ourselves. But 'all Gods are one God, and all Goddesses are one Goddess'; and the names one uses are a matter of choice. They may also be varied for the occasion. For example, we might consecrate a Celtic brooch in the names of Lugh and Dana, a dog's collar in the names of Pan and Diana, or an engagement ring in the names of Eros and Aphrodite. Suiting the God and Goddess names to the nature of a rite helps to emphasize its purpose.

An invaluable and encyclopaedic book on the significance of Goddess-names is Lawrence Durdin-Robertson's *Juno Covella, Perpetual Calendar of the Fellowship of Isis.*

The Ritual

Man and woman place the object on the pentacle, and lay both their right hands on it. Say:

   '*We consecrate thee in the element of Earth.*'

They sprinkle the object with the salt-and-water mixture, saying:

   '*We consecrate thee in the element of Water.*'

They pass the object through the smoke of the incense, saying:

   '*We consecrate thee in the element of Air.*'

They pass the object above the flame of the candle (well above, if it is something which flame could damage), saying:

   '*We consecrate thee in the element of Fire, in the names of Cernunnos and Aradia.*'

They then embrace and kiss with the object between their breasts, in the same way as for ritual tools.

Finally, if the object is something which can be worn immediately (obviously not possible for example if it is a brooch and the owner is skyclad!), the one who is not the owner places it round the owner's neck, wrist, finger or wherever.

V The Rest of the Book of Shadows

We have now, in this book and in *Eight Sabbats for Witches*, covered the ritual parts of Gerald Gardner's Book of Shadows (Text B), and of its definitive version as compiled by Gardner and Doreen Valiente together (Text C). Wherever possible, and greatly helped by Doreen's knowledge, we have given the sources of this material.

But there is also much non-ritual material in the Book of Shadows; and some of it has suffered the same fate as the rituals of being misquoted, distorted and plagiarized. Like the rituals, its 'secret' days are long past, whether one regrets the fact or not. So we agree with Doreen that the point has been reached where, in the interests of the Craft and of historical accuracy, the authentic texts of these non-ritual passages should also be published.

The work which Doreen did for Gardner in revising Text B was confined to the rituals; as far as the non-ritual passages are concerned, Texts B and C are identical.

Doreen tells us: 'These passages do not appear in Text A, the oldest book; but you will note a curious point in the passage headed *Of Calls*, indicating that Gerald must have copied it from someone else's book. Old Dorothy's? I don't know. My impression is that people copied from each other's books what appealed to them and what they considered important, adding stuff of their own from time to time (spells, recipes and so on) so that in practice no two Books of Shadows would be exactly the same. Also, in those days when occult books were nothing like so easy of access as they are today, they copied passages from printed books they had been given the loan of, on subjects which interested them. Old Gerald does this extensively in his old book, concerning the Knights Templars, the Qabalah and so on, interspersed with favourite poems.'

It is thus almost always impossible to identify sources as far as these passages are concerned. As Doreen says, they are clearly 'of varying importance and age'. Evidence of the differences in age is the variety of prose styles; some passages seem genuinely old, some comparatively modern (or interspersed with modernisms), while some are frankly pseudo-archaic.

For clarity, we give the Book of Shadows texts in italic type, and any comments (of our own or Doreen's) in roman type. The heading to each passage is as it appears in Text B.

Preface to the Book of Shadows

'Keep a book in your own hand of write. Let brothers and sisters copy what they will; but never let the book out of your hands and never keep the writings of another, for if found in their hand of write they may well be taken and tortured. Each shall guard his own writing and destroy it whenever danger threatens. Learn as much as you may by heart, and when danger is past rewrite your book if it be safe. For this reason, if any die, destroy their book if they have not been able to, for an it be found 'tis clear proof against them, and "Ye may not be a witch alone", so all their friends be in danger of torture. So destroy everything not necessary. If your book be found on you 'tis clear proof against you alone and you may be tortured. Keep all thoughts of the cult from your mind; say you had bad dreams, a devil caused you to write this without your knowledge. Think to yourself, "I know nothing. I remember nothing. I have forgotten all." Drive this into your mind. If the torture be too great to bear, say, "I will confess, I cannot bear this torment. What do you want me to say? Tell me and I will say it." If they try to make you speak of impossibilities, such as flying through the air, consorting with the Devil and sacrificing children and eating man's flesh, to obtain relief from torture say, "I had an evil dream, I was not myself, I was crazed."

'Not all magistrates are bad. If there be an excuse they may show

mercy. If you have confessed aught, deny it afterwards; say you babbled under the torture, you knew not what you did or said. If you be condemned, fear not; the Brotherhood is powerful. They may help you to escape if you are steadfast. IF YOU BETRAY AUGHT THERE IS NO HOPE FOR YOU IN THIS LIFE OR IN THAT WHICH IS TO COME. 'Tis sure, if steadfast you go to the pyre, drugs will help you; they will reach you and you will feel naught. An you go but to death, what lies beyond? The ecstasy of the Goddess.

'*The same of the Working Tools; let them be as ordinary things that any may have in their houses. Let the pentacles be of wax that they may be melted or broken at once. Have no sword unless your rank allows you one, and have no names or signs on anything. Write the names and signs on in ink before consecrating them and wash off immediately after. Never boast, never threaten, never say you would wish ill to anyone. If you speak of the Craft, say, "Speak not to me of such, it frightens me, 'tis evil luck to talk of it".*

Doreen's comment: 'I regard this as being of dubious authenticity, because it talks of going "to the pyre", whereas in England after the Reformation witches did not "go to the pyre" unless they had been adjudged guilty of killing their husbands, which was regarded as petty treason. The punishment for witches in England was hanging; it was only in Scotland that they were burned at the stake. Lots of writers about witchcraft slip up on this detail. So this "Preface" would either have to be pre-Reformation, which I doubt very much, especially with its reference to magistrates, or Scottish, which I see no reason to think it is.'

We, too, have always suspected the Preface. At the time when torture was used, most ordinary witches would be illiterate, and it would certainly not be a rule to 'keep a book in your hand of write'; and even if they had all been literate, learning the Craft would still have been a word-of-mouth process for security reasons. If such books had been kept, during the two or more centuries of persecution some would inevitably have been captured by the authorities and been made much of, and to our knowledge this never happened – which suggests strongly that there were none.

The instructions about how to behave if captured, and on working tools, ring rather more true. It seems to us that the 'Preface' is a late (perhaps nineteenth-century) commitment to paper of a mixture of verbally handed-down lore and contemporary practice. The prose style, which smacks of the pseudo-archaism the Victorians loved and regarded as 'literary', rather supports this view. And 'going to the pyre' would be a confusion with the fate of other martyrs, understandable at a time when most people's historical knowledge was elementary and highly coloured.

The Ways of Making Magic

'*The sign* ✳ *on the Athame is said to represent, among other things, the Eight Paths which all lead to the Centre and the Eight Ways of Making Magic, and these are:*

'*1. Meditation or concentration.*
'*2. Chants, Spells, Invocations. Invoking the Goddess, etc.*
'*3. Projection of the Astral Body, or Trance.*
'*4. Incense, Drugs, Wine, etc. Any potion which aids to release the Spirit.*
'*5. Dancing.*
'*6. Blood control. Use of the Cords.*
'*7. The Scourge.*
'*8. The Great Rite.*

'*You can combine many of these ways to produce more power.*

'*To practise the Art successfully, you need the following five things:*

'*1. Intention. You must have the absolute will to succeed, the firm belief that you can do so and the determination to win through against all obstacles.*
'*2. Preparation. You must be properly prepared.*
'*3. Invocation. The Mighty Ones must be invoked.*
'*4. Consecration. The Circle must be properly cast and consecrated and you must have properly consecrated tools.*
'*5. Purification. You must be purified.*

'*Hence there are 5 things necessary before you can start, and then 8 Paths or Ways leading to the Centre. For instance, you can combine 4, 5, 6, 7, and 8 together in one rite; or 4, 6 and 7 together with 1 and 2, or with 3 perhaps. The more ways you can combine, the more power you produce.*

'*It is not meet to make offering of less than two score lashes to the Goddess, for here be a mystery. The fortunate numbers be 3, 7, 9 and thrice 7 which be 21. And these numbers total two score, so a less perfect or fortunate number would not be a perfect prayer. Also the Fivefold Salute be 5, yet it be 8 kisses; for there be 2 feet, 2 knees and 2 breasts. And 5 times 8 be two score. Also there be 8 Working Tools and the Pentacle be 5; and five eights are two score.*

'*(Note: 8 plus 5 equals 13. 8 multiplied by 5 equals 40.)*'

There is no doubt that from time immemorial both drugs and the scourge have been used (though under carefully controlled conditions, and with knowledge) to 'release the Spirit' – i.e., to expand consciousness. In today's circumstances, we are completely opposed to the use of drugs in the Craft, in any form; for our arguments on this, see pp. 139-40. On the controlled use of the scourge, there are divided opinions. For ourselves, we use it only symbolically; but that is a personal choice. Scourging is dealt with fully in the passage *To Get the Sight*, on pp. 58-9 below, and we have added Doreen's comments on its constructive use to that.

The paragraph on 'fortunate numbers' is interesting and worth study. So is the fact that it is in quite a different, and apparently older, prose style than the foregoing paragraphs.

Power

'*Power is latent in the body and may be drawn out and used in various ways by the skilled. But unless confined in a circle it will be swiftly dissipated. Hence the importance of a properly constructed circle. Power seems to exude from the body via the skin and possibly from the orifices of the body; hence you should be properly prepared. The slightest dirt spoils everything, which shows the importance of thorough cleanliness.*

'*The attitude of mind has great effect, so only work with a spirit of reverence. A little wine taken and repeated during the ceremony, if necessary, helps to produce power. Other strong drinks or drugs may be used, but it is necessary to be very moderate, as if you are confused, even slightly, you cannot control the power you evoke.*

'*The simplest way is by dancing and singing monotonous chants, slowly at first and gradually quickening the tempo until giddiness ensues. Then the calls may be used, or even wild and meaningless shrieking produces power. But this method inflames the mind and renders it difficult to control the power, though control may be gained through practice. The scourge is a far better way, for it stimulates and excites both body and soul, yet one easily retains control.*

'*The Great Rite is far the best. It releases enormous power, but the conditions and circumstances make it difficult for the mind to maintain control at first. It is again a matter of practice and the natural strength of the operator's will and in a less degree of those of his assistants. If, as of old, there were many trained assistants present and all wills properly attuned, wonders occurred.*

'*Sorcerers chiefly used the blood sacrifice; and while we hold this to be evil we cannot deny that this method is very efficient. Power flashes forth from newly shed blood, instead of exuding slowly as by our method. The victim's terror and anguish add keenness and quite a small animal can yield enormous power. The great difficulty is in the human mind controlling the power of the lower animal mind. But sorcerers claim they have methods for effecting this and that the difficulty disappears the higher the animal used and when the victim is human disappears entirely. (The practice is an abomination but it is so.)*

'Priests know this well; and by their auto-da-fés, *with the victims'*
pain and terror (the fires acting much the same as circles), obtained
enormous power.

'Of old the Flagellants certainly evoked power, but through not
being confined by a circle most was lost. The amount of power raised
was so great and continuous that anyone with knowledge could direct
and use it; and it is most probable that the classical and heathen
sacrifices were used in the same way. There are whispers that when the
human victim was a willing sacrifice, with his mind directed on the
Great Work and with highly skilled assistants, wonders ensued – but of
this I would not speak.'

This passage has all the hallmarks of a dictated talk, or an
individual's essay copied down. (Old Dorothy again?) The 'I' in the last
sentence alone indicates this. It is all in modern (nineteenth- or early
twentieth-century, we would say) phraseology, and it strikes us as the
work of a keen brain. It starts off with helpful and practical advice on
Wiccan methods of power-raising, and goes on to a shrewd analysis of
the 'abomination' of sorcerers' blood sacrifices and the Inquisitors'
burnings, and of the wastefulness of the Christian Flagellants'
methods.

The comments on the Great Rite, with its (male) 'operator' and
'trained assistants', seem more in tune with ancient public sex-magic
(such as that performed by a High Priest with a chosen temple virgin at
the annual Festival of Opet at Thebes in ancient Egypt) than with
today's practice. Modern sex-magic calls for balanced male/female
polarity and is conducted by the couple in private; see pp. 170-2,
in Section XV, 'Witchcraft and Sex'. Such privacy was also observed in
Gardner's coven, Doreen tells us.

The remarks on the containing and amplifying effect of the Magic
Circle underline the point we made on this on p. 46. The suggestion
that the fire of an *auto-da-fé* had this same containing effect is
interesting.

Properly Prepared

'Naked, but sandals (not shoes) may be worn. For initiation, tie hands
behind back, pull up to small of back and tie ends in front of throat,
leaving a cable-tow to lead by, hanging down in front. (Arms thus form
a triangle at back.) When initiate is kneeling at altar, the cable-tow is
tied to a ring in the altar. A short cord is tied like a garter round the
initiate's left leg above the knee, with ends tucked in. Another is tied
round right ankle and ends tucked in so as to be out of the way while
moving about. These cords are used to tie feet together while initiate is
kneeling at the altar and must be long enough to do this firmly. Knees

must also be firmly tied. This must be carefully done. If the aspirant complains of pain the bonds must be loosened slightly; always remember the object being to retard the blood flow enough to induce a trance state. This involves slight discomfort; but great discomfort prevents the trance state, so it is best to spend some little time loosening and tightening the bonds until they are just right. The aspirant alone can tell you when this is so. This, of course, does not apply to the initiation, as then no trance is desired; but for the purpose of ritual it is good that the initiates be bound firmly enough to feel they are absolutely helpless but without discomfort.

'*The Measure (in the First Degree) is taken thus:*

'*Height, round neck, across the heart and across the genitals. The old custom is, if anyone were guilty of betraying the secrets, their measure was buried at midnight in a boggy place, with curses that "as the measure rots, so they will rot".*'

These instructions on binding will be seen to refer to two different things: the binding of an initiate, where the sole purpose is a proper feeling of helplessness, and binding to restrict the flow of blood to aid a trance condition. As the text emphasizes, the latter should be done very carefully; unless the instructions are followed meticulously, it could be dangerous.

On the taking of the measure – Doreen tells us that Gardner's practice was to measure round the forehead, not round the neck; see p.18. Today, when security is no longer a life-and-death matter, the measure is kept as a symbol of loyalty to the coven, not as a threat.

The Meeting Dance

'*The Maiden should lead. A man should place both hands on her waist, standing behind her, and alternate men and women do the same, the Maiden leading and they dance following her. She at last leads them into a right-hand spiral. When the centre is reached (and this had better be marked by a stone) she suddenly turns round and dances back, kissing each man as she comes to him. All men and women turn likewise and dance back, men kissing girls and girls kissing men. All in time to music, it is a merry game, but must be practised to be done well. Note, the musician should watch the dancers and make the music fast or slow as is best. For the beginners it should be slow, or there will be confusion. It is most excellent to get people to know each other at big gatherings.*'

A merry game indeed, and comment is hardly necessary – except to say that, while most Circle music these days is (sadly, perhaps) from tape or disc, this is certainly one of the occasions for using a musician if you have one. In our coven, we are lucky in having three members who can play the *bodhrán* (the Irish hand-drum, ideal for this Conga-type dance) and two guitarists. Such people should not be wasted.

Of Calls

'*Of old there were many chants and songs used, especially in the dances. Many of these have been forgotten by us here; but we know they used cries of IAU, HAU, which seems much like the cry of the ancients: EVO or EAVOE. Much dependeth on the pronunciation if this be so. In my youth when I heard the cry IAU it seemed to be AEIOU, or rather HAAEE IOOUU or AA EE IOOOOUU. This may be but the way to prolong it to make it fit for a call; but it suggests that these be the initials of an invocation, as AGLA used to be. And of sooth the whole Hebrew Alphabet is said to be such and for this reason is recited as a most powerful charm. At least this is certain, these cries during the dances do have a powerful effect, as I myself have seen.*

'*Other calls are: IEHOUA and EHEIE. Also: HO HO HO ISE ISE ISE.*

'*IEO VEO VEO VEO VEOV OROV OV OVOVO may be a spell, but is more likely to be a call. 'Tis like the EVOE EVOE of the Greeks and the "Heave ho!" of sailors. "Emen hetan" and "Ab hur, ab hus" seem calls; as "Horse and hattock, horse and go! Horse and pellatis, ho, ho, ho!"*

'"*Thout, tout a tout tout, throughout and about" and "Rentum tormentum" are probably mispronounced attempts at a forgotten formula, though they may have been invented by some unfortunate being tortured, to evade telling the real formula.*'

Doreen tells us: 'I copied this verbatim from Gerald's book, as he in turn seems to have copied at least the first part from someone else's older book, because Gerald could not have talked about being a witch "in my youth".'

As with the passage *Power*, this one suggests an intelligent mind talking or writing about inherited material, and speculating on its sources and meaning. The style is modern with pseudo-archaic intrusions – the latter inserted, we would guess, by a copyist rather than by the original writer or speaker.

The Cone of Power

'*This was the old way. The circle was marked out and people stationed to whip up the dancers. A fire or candle was within it in the direction where the object of the rite was supposed to be. Then all danced round until they felt they had raised enough power. If the rite was to banish they started deosil and finished widdershins, so many rounds of each.*

Then they formed a line with linked hands and rushed towards the fire shouting the thing they wanted. They kept it up till they were exhausted or until someone fell in a faint, when they were said to have taken the spell to its destination.'

Doreen comments: 'Gerald told me that this was the way in which the rites against Hitler's invasion were worked in the New Forest during World War II. He said that there was a tradition that similar rituals had been worked against the Spanish Armada and against Napoleon.'

We would point out that, although this passage is headed *The Cone of Power*, it is only one particular (though certainly very powerful) application of the Cone, which is also envisaged as being raised by the Witches' Rune and by such things as cord magic (pp. 239-40) and linked-hand magic (pp. 239-40).

Of the Ordeal of the Art Magical

'Learn of the spirit that goeth with burdens that have not honour, for 'tis the spirit that stoopeth the shoulders and not the weight. Armour is heavy, yet it is a proud burden and a man standeth upright in it. Limiting and constraining any of the senses serves to increase the concentration of another. Shutting the eyes aids the hearing. So the binding of the initiate's hands increases the mental perception, while the scourge increaseth the inner vision. So the initiate goeth through it proudly, like a princess, knowing it but serves to increase her glory.

'But this can only be done by the aid of another intelligence and in a circle, to prevent the power thus generated being lost. Priests attempt to do the same with their scourgings and mortifications of the flesh. But lacking the aid of bonds and their attention being distracted by their scourging themselves and what little power they do produce being dissipated, as they do not usually work within a circle, it is little wonder that they oft fail. Monks and hermits do better, as they are apt to work in tiny cells and caves, which in some way act as circles. The Knights of the Temple, who used mutually to scourge each other in an octagon, did better still; but they apparently did not know the virtue of bonds and did evil, man to man.

'But perhaps some did know? What of the Church's charge that they wore girdles or cords?'

This looks to us like genuinely old material which has been copied and recopied (note the inconsistent use of the '-eth' ending, a mistake that could easily creep in). The last two sentences look like a later copyist's footnote – perhaps Gardner's own, since Doreen says he was well-read on the subject of the Knights Templar.

To Get the Sight

'*Sight cometh to different people in divers ways; 'tis seldom it cometh naturally, but it can be induced in many ways. Deep and prolonged meditation may do it, but only if you are a natural, and usually prolonged fasting is necessary. Of old the monks and nuns obtained visions by long vigils, combined with fasting and flagellation till blood came; other mortifications of the flesh were practised which resulted in visions.*

'*In the East 'tis tried with various tortures whilst sitting in a cramped position, which retarded the flow of blood; these tortures, long and continued, gave good results.*

'*In the Art, we are taught an easier way, that is, to intensify the imagination, at the same time controlling the blood supply, and this may best be done by using the ritual.*

'*Incense is good to propitiate the spirits, also to induce relaxation to the aspirant and to help build up the atmosphere which is necessary for suggestibility. Myrrh, Gum Mastic, Aromatic Rush Roots, Cinnamon Bark, Musk, Juniper, Sandalwood and Ambergris, in combination, are all good, but the best of all is Patchouli.*

'*The circle being formed, and everything properly prepared, the aspirant should first bind and take his tutor into the circle, invoke suitable spirits for the operation, dance round till giddy, meanwhile invoking and announcing the object of the work, then he should use the flagellum. Then the tutor should in turn bind the aspirant – but very lightly, so as not to cause discomfort – but enough to retard the blood slightly. Again they should dance round, then at the Altar the tutor should use the flagellum with light, steady, slow and monotonous strokes. It is very important that the pupil should see the strokes coming, as this has the effect of passing, and helps greatly to stimulate the imagination. It is important that the strokes be not hard, the object being to do no more than draw the blood to that part and away from the brain; this, with the light binding, slowing down the circulation of the blood, and the passes, soon induces a drowsy stupor. The tutor should watch for this, and as soon as the aspirant speaks or sleeps the flagellum should cease. The tutor should also watch that the pupil become not cold, and if the pupil struggles or seems distressed he should at once be awakened.*

'*Be not discouraged if no results come at the first experiment – results usually occur after two or three attempts. It will be found that after two or three attempts or experiments results will come, and soon more quickly; also soon much of the ritual may be shortened, but never forget to invoke the Goddess or to form the circle, and for good results 'tis ever better to do too much ritual rather than too little at first.*

'*It has been found that this practice doth often cause a fondness between aspirant and tutor, and it is a cause of better results if this be so. If for any reason it is undesirable there be any great fondness between aspirant and tutor this may easily be avoided by both parties from the onset, by firmly resolving in their minds that if any fondness ensues it shall be that of brother and sister, or parent and child, and it is for this reason that a man may only be taught by a woman and a woman by a man, and that man and man or woman and woman should never attempt these practices together, and may all the curses of the Mighty Ones be on any who make such an attempt.*

'Remember, the circle properly constructed is ever necessary to prevent the power released being dissipated; it is also a barrier against any disturbing or mischievous forces; for to obtain good results you must be free from all disturbances.

'Remember, darkness, points of light gleaming amid the surrounding dark, incense, and the steady passes by a white arm, are not as stage effects; they are mechanical instruments which serve to start the suggestion which later unlocks the knowledge that it is possible to obtain the divine ecstasy, and so attain knowledge and communion with the Divine Goddess. When once you have attained this, ritual is needless, as you may attain the state of ecstasy at will, but till then, or if, having obtained or attained it yourself, you wish to bring a companion to that state of joy, ritual is best.'

To Leave the Body

"Tis not wise to strive to get out of your body until you have thoroughly gained the Sight. The same ritual as to gain the Sight may be used, but have a comfortable couch. Kneel so that you have your thigh, belly and chest well supported, the arms strained forward and bound one on each side, so that there is a decided feeling of being pulled forward. As the trance is induced, you should feel a striving to push yourself out of the top of your head. The scourge should be given a dragging action, as if to drive or drag you out. Both wills should be thoroughly in tune, keeping a constant and equal strain. When trance comes, your tutor may help you by softly calling your name. You will probably feel yourself drawn out of your body as if through a narrow opening, and find yourself standing beside your tutor, looking at the body on the couch. Strive to communicate with your tutor first; if they have the Sight they will probably see you. Go not far afield at first, and 'tis better to have one who is used to leaving the body with you.

'A note: When, having succeeded in leaving the body, you desire to return, in order to cause the spirit body and the material body to coincide, THINK OF YOUR FEET. This will cause the return to take place.'

This is the longest non-ritual passage in Gardner's Book of Shadows, and we infer that it describes a practice which was central to the tradition and activities of the New Forest coven which trained him. It is explained carefully, with meticulous emphasis on the tutor-pupil relationship and on the necessary practical, psychic and inter-personal safeguards. The purpose of the not-too-tight binding and the deliberately light scourging is plain: to help to bring about what may variously be called clairvoyance, expansion of consciousness, opening up the levels, opening up the Third Eye, or communion with the Goddess; and, at a more advanced stage, astral projection. (It is interesting that the text uses none of the technical terms of contemporary occultism or psychical research such as 'astral projection' or 'astral body'; this strongly suggests a tradition handed down person-to-person from, at the very least, earlier than the second half of the nineteenth century.) To distort this into an allegation that Gardner himself had an unhealthy urge to flagellation, whether sadistic or masochistic (and the procedure described above is clearly neither), is nonsense.

There may be differences of opinion about whether the procedure described could be dangerous; what cannot be denied is that the text goes to great pains to ensure that it *will* be safe, and to stop it at once if there is any doubt.

Doreen's comment: 'The reason we used the scourge is a very simple one – it works! What old Gerald had described is a very practical way of making magic. I speak from experience when I say that it does what he claimed it to do, and I don't care what anyone says about being "kinky" or whatever. Perhaps it has become associated with kinky sexual matters; but long before that it was part of very ancient mystical and magical practices. You can find mention of it from Ancient Egypt and from Ancient Greece; and no doubt you are familiar with the famous scene from the Villa of the Mysteries in Pompeii which shows a new initiate being scourged – a point which Gerald referred to in *Witchcraft Today*. Although the description in *To Get the Sight* particularly refers to the obtaining of clairvoyance, I have found it very inducive to magical visualisation also.'

What we feel should be emphasized (as the Book of Shadows does) is that when the scourge is used in Wiccan practice, *no pain should be either inflicted or expected*; it is always used gently. Its purpose is *either* symbolic (as for example in the Legend of the Descent of the Goddess) *or* to induce trance by light hypnosis and the redistribution of blood circulation.

The Working Tools

'*There are no magical supply shops, so unless you are lucky enough to be given or sold tools a poor witch must extemporise. But when made you should be able to borrow or obtain an Athame. So having made your circle, erect an altar. Any small table or chest will do. There must be fire on it (a candle will suffice) and your book. For good results incense is best if you can get it, but coals in a chafing dish burning sweet-smelling herbs will do. A cup if you would have cakes and wine and a platter with the signs drawn into the same in ink, showing a pentacle. A scourge is easily made (note, the scourge has eight tails and five knots in each tail). Get a white-hilted knife and a wand (a sword is not necessary). Cut the marks with Athame. Purify everything, then consecrate your tools in proper form and ever be properly prepared. But ever remember, magical operations are useless unless the mind can be brought to the proper attitude, keyed to the utmost pitch.*

'*Affirmations must be made clearly, and the mind should be inflamed with desire. With this frenzy of will you may do as much with simple tools as with the most complete set. But good and especially ancient tools have their own aura. They do help to bring about that reverential spirit, the desire to learn and develop your powers. For this reason witches ever try to obtain tools from sorcerers, who being skilled men make good tools and consecrate them well, giving them mighty power. But a great witch's tools also gain much power; and you should ever strive to make any tools you manufacture of the finest materials you can obtain, to the end that they may absorb your power the more easily. And of course if you may inherit or obtain another witch's tools, power will flow from them.*'

The statement 'there are no magical supply shops' is of course no longer true; and there have been other developments in Wiccan practice since this passage was written. Although a sword is not strictly necessary (the athame serving the same purposes), most covens now like to have one – a symbol of coven identity in contrast to the athames, which are symbols of each individual witch's identity.

Also, for most covens the cup or chalice is one of the more important symbols (representing the female principle and also the element of Water) and not a mere accessory 'if you would have cakes and wine', though the apparent downgrading of the cup in this text may have been a deliberate 'blind', for the reasons which Gardner was given and which we explain on p. 258.

But apart from these minor points, the principles laid down in this passage are as valid as ever.

We find interesting the implication that witches may have been in touch with 'sorcerers' (meaning what we would call today 'ritual magicians').

Making Tools

'*It is an old belief that the best substances for making tools are those that have once had life in them, as opposed to artificial substances. Thus, wood or ivory is better for a wand than metal, which is more appropriate for swords or knives. Virgin parchment is better than manufactured paper for talismans, etc. And things which have been made by hand are good, because there is life in them.*'

Comment would be superfluous.

To Make Anointing Ointment

'*Take a glazed pan half full of grease or olive oil. Put in sweet mint leaves bruised. Place pan in hot water bath. Stir occasionally. After four or five hours pour into linen bag and squeeze grease through into pot again and fill with fresh leaves. Repeat until grease is strongly scented. Do same with marjoram, thyme and pounded dried patchouli leaves, an you may have them (for they be best of all). When strongly scented, mix all the greases together and keep in a well-stoppered jar.*

'*Anoint behind ears, throat, breasts and womb. In rites where "Blessed be …" may be said, anoint knees and feet, as also for rites connected with journeys or war.*'

Our old friend the pseudo-archaic copyist has been at work again here; a couple of his favourite clichés stick out like sore thumbs in this obviously modern text. But the recipe itself is worth trying and is quite possibly much older than the present wording.

'Journeys or war': smelling of mint, marjoram, thyme and patchouli in the London Underground, or in the front rank of No. 4 Platoon, may not be everyone's idea of practical magic. But to be serious – the devising and preparation of body-ointments to suit individual witches' personalities, or the emphasis of particular rites, is well worth pursuing, especially if you have a coven member who is gifted at such things. But their use is best confined to the Magic Circle, and (unless you want to spend half your spare time washing robes) to skyclad practice.

Various Instructions

'*A note upon the ritual of the Wine and Cakes. It is said that in olden days ale or mead was often used instead of wine. It is said that spirits or anything can be used, "so long as it has life" (i.e. has a kick).*'

We question the modern addition in the brackets. 'Has life' seems to us more likely to mean 'is of organic origin'. Mead is a favourite witches' drink and would bear out this point by being both vegetable and animal in origin, since it is based on honey, which bees make from flower nectar. Beer was the ritual drink of the ancient Egyptians.

'*All are brothers and sisters, for this reason; that even the High Priestess must submit to the scourge.*'

When she is giving someone his second degree initiation, for example.

'*The only exception to the rule that a man only be initiated by a woman and a woman by a man, is that a mother may initiate her daughter and a father his son, because they are part of themselves.*'

We were taught that mother-daughter, father-son initiations were permissible 'in an emergency'. It is interesting that Gardner's Book of Shadows makes no such qualification.

'*A woman may impersonate either the God or the Goddess, but a man may only impersonate the God.*'

A woman witch takes on a male role by buckling on the sword; see p. 78.

'*Ever remember, if tempted to admit or boast of belonging to the cult, you be endangering your brothers and sisters. For though now the fires of persecution have died down, who knows when they may be revived? Many priests have knowledge of our secrets and they full well know that much religious bigotry has died down or calmed down, that many people would wish to join our cult if the truth were known of its joys and the churches would lose power. So if we take many recruits we may loose the fires of persecution against us again. So ever keep the secrets.*'

This would appear to be a fair observation and warning from the period after the persecution centuries, but before the twentieth-century occult and witchcraft revival. The situation has changed vastly in recent decades. But every witch should bear in mind that persecution, in one form or another, *could* always rear its ugly head again. And even now, it should be an absolute rule that no witch's membership of the Craft may be revealed except by his or her own free choice.

'*Those taking part in a rite must know exactly what results they wish to attain and must all keep their minds firmly fixed on the desired result, without wavering.*'

Again, no comment is called for.

Doing our best to be impartial – what overall impression do we get from these texts, and indeed from the Book of Shadows as a whole?

We get the firm impression of an old and continuing tradition handed on at first by word of mouth, and later (perhaps some time in the nineteenth century) in writing; gathering interpretations, additions and the occasional misunderstanding as it progressed; in the written stage, sometimes put down by a teacher and sometimes taken down in dictation during training. The variety of styles, the occasional first-person sentence, the odd sentence which has become confused – even our friend the pseudo-archaic copyist – all seem to us to confirm this human picture. But the basic spirit, and the consistent wisdom, of the message seems to shine through it all.

The one impression that it does *not* give, by any stretch of the imagination, is that of a total invention by Gerald Gardner – or, come to that, by Old Dorothy or anybody else.

More Wiccan Rituals

VI   *Drawing Down the Sun*

The ritual of Drawing Down the Moon (see *Eight Sabbats for Witches*, pp. 40-42) is a central element in the holding of a coven Circle. By it, the High Priest invokes the spirit of the Goddess into the High Priestess, using his male polarity to call forth the divine essence in her female polarity. If the ritual is successful, she then becomes truly a channel of the Goddess for the duration of the Circle (and often the effect of the invocation may linger in her after the Circle is banished). Some male witches seem to have a natural gift for Drawing Down the Moon; we have known first-degree witches, called upon to conduct a Circle for their first time, who have induced a surprising air of authority into an equally inexperienced female partner. Other men have to work hard to develop the gift. But given sincerity and an understanding of the meaning of the rite, it is always there to be developed.

That it actually works, no one who has attended more than a few Circles can doubt. Drawing Down the Moon, in the normal Opening Ritual (see Appendix B, pp. 296-7), is followed immediately by the Charge (pp. 297-8); so it is here that the effect first manifests.

The Goddess *does* come through, in the tone and emphasis of the delivery of the Charge – often to the surprise of the priestess delivering it. Janet admits frankly that she 'never knows how it will come out'. Sometimes the wording itself is completely altered, with a spontaneous flow which she listens to with a detached part of her mind. It is as though the Goddess knows better than the priestess just what emphasis, or encouragement, or even warning or reprimand, is called for at that particular Circle, and controls the Charge accordingly.

Since Wicca is a Goddess-oriented religion, laying particular stress on 'the gift of the Goddess' (the intuitive and psychic faculties) because of the nature of its work,[1] the complementary process of invoking the spirit of the God into the High Priest occurs less often. The High Priest does invoke the God aspect on behalf of the whole coven, during the Opening Ritual, by means of the 'Great God Cernunnos' invocation; and in the Imbolg, Spring Equinox, Midsummer, Autumn Equinox, Samhain and Yule Festival rites, the High Priestess invokes the spirit of the God into the High Priest either specifically or by implication. But we have found that there are occasions when it is fitting that this invocation should have a weight and solemnity comparable with Drawing Down the Moon. For example, there are times when the work in hand calls for an emphasis on the balance of polarity between priestess and priest – on the Gift of the Goddess and the Gift of the God in perfect harmony.

For those who have also felt the need for such a rite, we offer the following – for which 'Drawing Down the Sun' would seem the natural title. Doreen Valiente thinks that there may once have been a ritual for this purpose in the Craft, but that it has been lost over the years.

Because the High Priestess, representing the Goddess, is always in charge of the Circle, we suggest that Drawing Down the Moon should always precede Drawing Down the Sun. The High Priestess then invokes the God aspect *in the name* of the Goddess.

The Preparation

No particular preparation is needed for this ritual – except that if the coven possesses a High Priest crown, he should be wearing it.

The Ritual

At the end of Drawing Down the Moon, after the High Priestess's words 'Here I charge you, in this sign', the High Priestess and High Priest change places, moving deosil, so that he stands with his back to the altar and she faces him from the centre of the Circle.

The High Priest picks up his athame from the altar and holds it in his right hand over his left breast, point upwards.

The High Priestess gives him the Fivefold Kiss, as follows:

'*Blessed be thy feet, that have brought thee in these ways*' – kissing his right foot and then his left foot.

'*Blessed be thy knees, that shall kneel at the sacred altar*' – kissing his right knee and then his left knee.

'*Blessed be thy phallus, without which we would not be*' – kissing him just above the pubic hair.

The High Priest spreads his arms to the Blessed Position, still holding his athame in his right hand, point upwards.

The High Priestess continues:

'*Blessed be thy breast, formed in strength*' – kissing his right breast and then his left breast.

'*Blessed be thy lips, that shall utter the sacred names.*' They embrace, length for length and with feet touching, and kiss each other on the mouth.

The High Priestess steps back a pace and kneels. She invokes:

> '*Deep calls on height, the Goddess on the God,*
> *On him who is the flame that quickens her;*
> *That he and she may seize the silver reins*
> *And ride as one the twin-horsed chariot.*
> *Let the hammer strike the anvil,*
> *Let the lightning touch the earth,*
> *Let the Lance ensoul the Grail,*
> *Let the magic come to birth.*'

She touches with her right forefinger his throat, left hip, right breast, left breast, right hip, and throat again (thus forming the Invoking Pentagram of Fire). She then spreads her hands outwards, palms forward. Meanwhile she continues to invoke:

> '*In her name do I invoke thee,*
> *Mighty Father of us all –*
> *Lugh, Pan, Belin, Herne, Cernunnos –*
> *Come in answer to my call!*
> *Descend, I pray thee, in thy servant and priest.*'

The High Priestess stands and takes a step backwards. The High Priest makes the Invoking Pentagram of Fire towards her with his athame[2], saying:

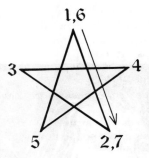

Fig. 2

'*Let there be light!*'

VII   Three Goddesses Ritual

Wiccan rituals may be for worship; for the raising and utilizing of power; or for the dramatization of archetypal concepts. Some (such as initiation, handfasting and other rites of passage) combine more than one of those elements. But here is an example of a ritual whose central intent is dramatization. Such rituals serve a very constructive purpose, because they help those who take part to visualize these archetypes vividly as real, and to build up healthy links between their unconscious awareness of them, and their conscious understanding of them.

The concept of the Triple Goddess is as old as time; it crops up again and again in widely differing mythologies, and its most striking visual symbol is the Moon in her waxing, full and waning phases. The fact that the Moon-cycle is reflected in the menstrual cycle of women touches on deep and mysterious aspects of the feminine principle, and of the Goddess herself. (On this, Shuttle and Redgrove's book *The Wise Wound* – see Section XV and Bibliography – deserves serious study by every male or female witch.) All Goddesses are one Goddess – but she shows herself in many aspects, all of which relate to the three fundamental aspects of the Maid (enchantment, inception, expansion), the Mother (ripeness, fulfilment, stability) and the Crone (wisdom, retrenchment, repose). Every woman, and every Goddess-form, contains all three – both cyclically and simultaneously. No woman who fails to grasp it can understand herself; and without grasping it, no one can understand the Goddess.

We composed this ritual while we were still living in England, and the first time we enacted it was in an ideal setting: a friend's riverside house in secluded country, with a little bridge to a private island which nobody else could reach. On that island, in a clearing screened by thick trees, within sound of the hurrying river, we could light our bonfire and hold our skyclad rituals without fear of interruption. Sadly, house and island have long since been sold to strangers; but we remember the place with affection.

Perhaps because of that memory, we give our Three Goddesses Ritual here as for outdoor observance – flaming torches and all. But although that is ideal, it can be adapted to indoor working.

The Preparation

The Circle is set up in the normal way, but with a bonfire in the centre. (Indoors, the cauldron with a candle in it.) Outside the Circle, preferably in the North-East, is an avenue of three pairs of inflammable torches (candles indoors), ready for the three Goddesses to ignite as they approach between them. Means for igniting them must be available, and also some means for the Crone to extinguish them as she leaves; for flaming torches, we used a can open at one end and nailed across the end of a stick.

A reasonably loud bell, gong or cymbal is ready on or by the altar.

Three women witches are chosen to enact the Maid, the Mother and the Crone. If they are robed, the traditional colours are white for the Maid, red for the Mother, and black for the Crone. Even if the ritual is skyclad, the Crone alone should be robed in black, preferably with a hood or a head-scarf draped like a hood. Imagination should be used in adorning the Maid and the Mother, whether skyclad or robed, to bring out the springtime freshness of the Maid and the summer ripeness of the Mother.

The High Priest conducts the ritual; and since the High Priestess is likely to be one of the Three, we refer to his working partner for the occasion simply as 'the Priestess'.

Suitable Goddess-names should be chosen for the Maid, the Mother and the Crone, according to the coven's own background or tradition. Here we use three Irish ones – Brid (pronounced 'Breed') for the Maid, Dana for the Mother, and Morrigan for the Crone. Brid or Brigid, Goddess of inspiration, is the one most often referred to as triple – 'the

Three Brigids' – in Irish mythology and has a springtime air about her; Dana is the predominant Irish Mother-Goddess name; and the Morrigan, Goddess of battles and of destiny, is the most powerful of the dark Goddess aspects.

The Ritual

The High Priest casts the Circle, with everyone inside it except the Maid and the Mother, who are at the outer end of the avenue (out of sight if possible). The elements are carried round and the Lords of the Watchtowers summoned.

The Priestess stands with her back to the altar. The High Priest and the Crone face each other between the altar and the bonfire, the High Priest carrying the wand. The rest of the coven stand around the perimeter of the Circle facing inwards but leaving the inner end of the avenue free.

The High Priest walks round the Crone once, deosil, faces her again and says:

'*Within each man and each woman lies the mystery of the Dark Mother of all creation, the ruler of the oceans, the still centre to which all must return as their prelude to rebirth. Let her come to us this night, but so as to create no imbalance in this our Priestess* ———— [witch name] *who shall represent her; for no human can bear the undiluted power of the Great Mother in her dark aspect; whereas in the balance of her Three Aspects, all are safe. Do thou,* ————, *therefore represent her dark aspect without fear, knowing that her other aspects are also present within our Circle. With this wand do I protect and fortify thee for thy task.*'

The High Priest then gestures ritually towards each of the thirteen openings of the Crone's body in turn (see page 85) with his wand. He then uses the wand to open a gateway in the Circle in front of the avenue. The Crone leaves the Circle along the avenue to join the Maid and the Mother, and the High Priest closes the gateway with the wand.[1] He replaces the wand on the altar.

The High Priest then gives the Priestess the Fivefold Kiss (but Drawing Down the Moon is not enacted, and the Charge is not given). He then delivers the '*Bagabi laca bachahe*' and '*Great God Cernunnos*' invocations.

High Priest, Priestess and coven circle to the Witches' Rune.

The coven return to the perimeter.

High Priest and Priestess consecrate the wine (with only a little wine in the chalice). The Priestess holds up the chalice and says:

'*Dana, old Earth of untold summers, beloved Earth and womb of the golden corn, warm beating heart of the greenwood, nourishing within us thy warmth and thy love; Lady of the Harvest and Mother of us all*

— hold us now close to thy breast, and fill us with thy bounty, thou who art the source of all life.'

She then empties the chalice on to the ground in front of the altar.

The High Priest refills the chalice and replaces it on the altar.

The High Priest then faces the avenue and invokes in a clear voice:

'Brid of the waxing Moon, daughter of Spring, sweet Goddess of the Flowers, we call to thee. Come to our Circle and bring to us the breath of Spring. Fill us with thy joyful music and laughter. Let blossom rise from beneath thy feet, and the singing of water be thy voice. Come to our Circle, Brid of the waxing Moon.'

The Priestess strikes the bell three times.

The Maid approaches the Circle along the avenue of torches, and lights the pair nearest to the Circle. She then walks deosil outside the Circle and stands behind the East candle.

The High Priest, still facing the avenue, invokes:

'Dana of the full Moon, thou Great Mother, most wonderful Lady of the Lands of Summer; we call to thee. Come on the Summer wind, bringing unto us ripe grain and sweet fruits. Fill us with the joy of maturity; teach us the wisdom of fulfilment; bathe us in the reflected glory of thy consort, the Sun. Come to our Circle, Dana of the full Moon.'

The Priestess strikes the bell seven times.

The Mother approaches the Circle along the avenue of torches, lighting the middle pair. She then walks deosil outside the Circle and stands behind the South candle.

The High Priest, still facing the avenue, invokes:

'Morrigan of the waning Moon, thou most secret face of the Goddess; we call to thee. Bring to us the knowledge of the Wheel of Death and Re-birth; grant us thy power, and the wisdom to use it rightly, for we know that to use it wrongly is to poison the soul. Teach us to use it, not to harm, but to heal. Come to our Circle, Morrigan of the waning Moon.'

The Priestess strikes the bell nine times.

The Crone approaches the Circle along the avenue of torches, lighting the final pair. She then walks deosil round the outside of the Circle and stands behind the West candle.

When the Crone is in place, the High Priest fetches the wand and opens the Circle beside the East candle. He says:

'Brid, Maiden-Goddess of the waxing Moon — be welcomed into our Circle.'

The Maid takes three paces into the Circle, and the High Priest closes the Circle behind her. He then kisses her on the lips, takes her hand and leads her to stand in front of the altar at its Western end.

The High Priest goes to the South, opens the Circle beside the South candle and says:

'*Dana, Mother-Goddess of the full Moon – be welcomed into our Circle.*'

The Mother takes three paces into the Circle, and the High Priest closes the Circle behind her. He then kisses her on the right hand and, still holding her hand, leads her to stand in front of the altar at its centre, beside the Maid.

The High Priest goes to the West, opens the Circle beside the West candle and says:

'*Morrigan, Crone-Goddess of the waning Moon – be welcomed into our Circle.*'

The Crone takes three paces into the Circle, and the High Priest closes the Circle behind her. He then kisses her on the right foot, takes her hand and leads her to stand in front of the altar at its Eastern end, beside the Mother.

The High Priest lays the wand on the altar and takes up the sword. He walks deosil round the bonfire and faces the Triple Goddess across it. He salutes them with the sword (hilt in front of face with point upwards, sweep downwards and outwards to the right front, hilt in front of face again with point upwards). He then reverses the sword so that its point is on the ground just in front of his feet, and rests both his hands on the hilt (or one hand only if he has to read the script). He says:

'*Behold the Three-Formed Goddess;*
She who is ever Three – Maid, Mother, and Crone.
Yet is she ever One;
For without Spring there can be no Summer;
Without Summer, no Winter;
Without Winter, no new Spring.
Without birth, no life;
Without life, no death;
Without death, no rest and no re-birth.
Darkness gives birth to light,
Light to darkness,
Each needing the other as man needs woman, and woman man.
So it is
That were she not Maid, Mother, and Crone,
The Goddess herself could not exist –
And all would be nothingness,
Silence without beginning or end.

Behold the Three-Formed Goddess;
She who is ever Three – Maid, Mother, and Crone.
Yet is she ever One;
She in all women, and they all in her.
Behold her, remember her,
Forget not one of her faces;

With every breath, hold these three in your heart –
Maid, Mother, and Crone;
Look on these Three, who are One, with a fearless love,
That you, too, may be whole.'

The High Priest then walks deosil round the bonfire till he reaches the avenue, where he opens the Circle with his sword. He says to the Three:

'All hail, and blessed be.'

The Maid leaves the Circle along the avenue, followed by the Mother, followed by the Crone. The High Priest bows to each as she passes, and finally closes the Circle behind them.

The Maid and the Mother continue up the avenue, out of sight if possible. The Crone extinguishes the torches as she passes them, and then follows the Maid and the Mother.

Meanwhile High Priest and Priestess have returned to the altar, where the High Priest puts down the sword, and they both stand with their arms raised until the Three have disappeared into the darkness. Then they and the coven link hands and circle deosil round the bonfire in silence.

When the Three are ready, having removed their adornments, they come back down the avenue, in their normal role as witches, and wait on the edge of the Circle. The High Priest breaks away from the circling coven long enough to open and close the Circle to admit them. All rejoin the others, and the circling become joyous.

VIII   *Rite of the Thirteen Megaliths*

Our next ritual, which Janet wrote, also dramatizes archetypal concepts. We hope it is self-explanatory, as every effective ritual should be; but if 'explanation' were all, the printed word would be enough. Ritual effectiveness lies in the awareness engendered, which is always more than the mere words.

In itself it is a simple rite, but it does call for the theoretical ideal coven of six man-woman couples and a leader (the High Priestess) which few covens ever achieve; we certainly never have. It might, however, be an interesting set-piece to stage on one of those occasions when two or more covens get together, by selecting a suitable cast of thirteen from the total gathering while the rest watch.

We ourselves have only been able to perform it a few times, for this very reason. But everybody enjoyed it, and it generated a strange and unexpected power from which we all benefited. One very new member remarked, after taking part in it for the first time, that it was also the first time he had directly *felt* psychic power, as compared with being psychologically aware of it. He thought this was because he had a specified part to play (Sol, as it happened) and was aware that each of us was making a unique contribution to the whole; which made the whole thing more real to him. A shrewd observation – and it taught us one of the benefits of such a ritual, namely that it reminds us that, even in 'ordinary' group power-rising, each individual's contribution is unique, and therefore valuable; and subsequent 'ordinary' working is heightened by the lesson.

Incidentally, this problem of assembling a suitable cast for any given rite raises a point of tradition which is worth mentioning. When it is necessary, a woman witch may act the role of a man. She symbolizes this by buckling on a sword; and she acts as a man, and is regarded and treated as a man, for as long as she wears it. When Joan of Arc put on a sword, it is said that her followers of the Old Religion understood at once the significance on her act as Maiden of the realm. But the tradition insists firmly that in no circumstances may a man enact the role of a woman. See Gerald Gardner's *Witchcraft Today*, pp. 43-4 and 131 – and also remember Carl Jung's dictum: 'A woman can identify directly with the Earth Mother, but a man cannot (except in psychotic cases).' (*Collected Works, Vol. IX, Part 1*, 2nd edition, para. 193.)

The perfect place to enact this ritual would of course be a megalithic circle, with each of the thirteen participants standing in front of one of the stones. But it can be just as well performed in the ordinary indoor nine-foot Circle.

The Preparation

No special preparation is needed for this ritual, apart from those made for a normal Circle; but it may be thought worth while for each of the participants to have his or her words written out on a separate piece of paper. This will save having to pass the script from hand to hand – which would be difficult anyway if the rite is in a large Circle out of doors.

If the rite is being performed on a special occasion, such as a multi-coven Festival, the 'producer' has plenty of scope for equipping each participant with appropriate symbols, and robes if any. But this is not essential. What *is* essential is that each actor speaks slowly and with dignity.

The Ritual

The ritual requires the High Priestess, High Priest, six other women and five other men.

High Priestess and High Priest stand at the altar, and the remainder of the coven arrange themselves around the perimeter, man and woman alternately, deosil in the order of their allotted roles. (There will thus be a woman at each end of this 'horseshoe'.)

The Opening Ritual proceeds as usual, up to and including Drawing Down the Moon. The God- and Goddess-names used will be ones appropriate to the megalithic areas, such as Cernunnos, and Cerridwen, Dana or Anu.

After '*Here I charge you, in this sign*', High Priestess and High Priest stand with their backs to the altar, with him on her left, completing the ring of the coven.

All start circling slowly deosil without speaking, until the High Priestess calls '*Stand.*' She will do this at a moment when she and the High Priest are once again in front of the altar. All then face inwards.

The High Priestess says:

'*I am the first of the Old Ones. I have seen the dawn of time, from the suns beyond our earth. Men call me the Stone Goddess, old, steadfast, and wise.*'

She then moves slowly and with dignity to the centre of the Circle. From there, she faces each person in turn as he or she is speaking.

The High Priest says:

'*I am the second of the Old Ones. I opened my arms to the First One, and cooled her fire with my breath. I was the primordial movement, the first stirring of the winds. Men call me the Father of Chaos.*'

The woman on his left says:

'*I am the third of the Old Ones. I was the waters upon the face of the Two. From my depths all life was formed. My face was softened by the breath of the Second One. Men call me Mara, the Bitter One, the Sea.*'

The man on her left says:

'*I am the fourth of the Old Ones. I gave my warmth to the Three. From my brilliance the Third One was given beauty. Men call me Sol, the Sun.*'

The woman on his left says:

'*I am the fifth of the Old Ones. I gave my light to the darkness. Mine are the tides to rule. Though my brother the Fourth shows greater brilliance, I too have my beauty. Men call me the Virgin; also I am named Luna, the Moon.*'

The man on her left says:

'*I am the sixth of the Old Ones. I ride the Earth on cloven feet, or on wings of air. I am the hunter, and the hunted. Stag and horse, bird and beast are mine; and with the aid of the Fifth, whose call all must answer, I reproduce my kind. Men kill in lust for me. I am named Herne or Pan, Cernunnos or the Hornéd One.*'

The woman on his left says:

'*I am the seventh of the Old Ones. I am the Floral One; all laughter and joy are mine. With the Sixth, I call all living things to join our dance. I am the eternal She who knows not destruction. The silver fish are mine, as are also the spinners of webs, the weavers of dreams. Men know me as the Mother, and call me Great.'*

The man on her left says:

'I am the eighth of the Old Ones. I am a mystery, for I am my own twin. My two faces are Life and Light. Sol and the winds that cool him are both of my essence. Men know me as the Mover and Fertiliser, and call me Air and Fire.'

The woman on his left says:

'I am the ninth of the Old Ones. With the Eighth, I am Wholeness, for I am Love and Law. The Father of Chaos and the Bitter Sea are my parents. Men know me as the Nourisher and Shape-giver, and call me Water and Earth. My brother the Eighth and I are the Quartered Circle of Creation.'

The man on her left says:

'I am the tenth of the Old Ones. I am the pupil of all the others. I begin with Four, and then have Two, and end with Three. From the belly I came, and to the womb I go. I am nothing, and yet I am Lord of All. I shall cease, and yet return. I am good, yet am I more terrible than those who have gone before. I am Man.'

The woman on his left says:

'I am the eleventh of the Old Ones. I too am the pupil. With the Tenth, I seek the Truth. There is no He without She. Mine is the great Cauldron of Creation, yet am I ever Virgin. I am even more terrible than the Tenth, for logic and reason are not mine when my little ones are destroyed by any of the others. I am warm yet cold, gentle yet destructive. I mirror the Stone One and the Floral One. I am Woman.'

The man on her left says:

'I am the twelfth of the Old Ones. Hide from my face if you will, but know that I am the most powerful of all. The Tenth and Eleventh dance with me, and even the Floral One weeps summer tears at my command. For I am an ever-turning Wheel. I am the Spinner and the Weaver, and I also cut the silver cords of Time. Men know me as Fate, and I am the Hermaphrodite.'

The woman on his left says:

'I am the thirteenth of the Old Ones. I am the Shadow of the Sanctuary, and the Silver Wheel of Arianrhod. I am feared, yet loved and often yearned for. I ride my white mare over the battlefields, and in my arms the sick and the tired find rest. We shall be together many times, for though I am the Victor, yet am I also the loneliest of all the Thirteen. To seek the Twelve is to know that I am but an illusion. Woe is to me, the Thirteenth One – and yet all joy is mine also; for from my embrace is renewed life; and to know me is to meet, know, remember, and love again. Men know me as Death – yet I am the Comforter and Renewer, the correcting principle in creation. The scythe and the

victor's crown are mine; for all the Thirteen, I am the only one who is not eternal.'

All the coven (except the High Priestess in the centre), moving forward if necessary, now place their hands on each other's shoulders with their arms straight, as in a Greek dance, and start to circle slowly together deosil, saying in unison:

'We are the henge of Creation, the megaliths of old, the guardians of the path of knowledge, the thirteen keepers of the Sacred Circle.'

As the coven circle deosil, the High Priestess slowly raises her arms, fully outstretched, above her head. When she is ready for the circling to stop, she lowers them again slowly to her sides. The circling then continues till the next time the High Priest is at the altar, when he and the coven halt and lower their arms and stand facing inwards.

The High Priestess rejoins the High Priest at the altar, placing herself on his right. She kisses him, and the kiss is passed man-to-woman, woman-to-man round the entire Circle.

High Priestess and High Priest consecrate the wine, and the chalice is passed round deosil in the usual way till all have partaken. It is then replaced on the altar.

The High Priestess says:

'O Man, O Woman, come forth.'

The Tenth (Man) and the Eleventh (Woman) come forward and stand facing the High Priestess and High Priest. The High Priestess takes up the dish of cakes.

The High Priestess says:

'O Woman, O Man, it is for you to fathom the Mysteries which have here been shown. Thus it has ever been, since first we gave birth to you. Therefore it is to you we give this food, which being of the Earth, is the fruit of us all, that you may bless it for us all. For as you have need of the Gods, so also do the Gods have need of you.'

All say: *'So mote it be.'*

The High Priestess hands the dish of cakes to the Man, and the High Priest hands an athame to the Woman. Man and Woman bless the cakes and they are passed round, in the normal way.

IX   Rituals of Protection

The most basic, and useful, protective ritual of all for witches is the Magic Circle; which is one reason why it is cast at the beginning of every coven meeting, and not banished until the meeting is over. We gave the full procedures for casting and banishing the Circle in *Eight Sabbats for Witches*, and in Appendix B to the present book.

It is worth remarking, though, that for a coven meeting, protection is not the only purpose of the Circle. In fact, it may be argued that it is not even its primary purpose. The main function of a coven Circle is to 'preserve and contain the power that we shall raise within thee' – in other words, to concentrate and amplify the psychic effort of the group. Witches meet for worship and to raise power for useful work; and for these purposes 'a boundary between the world of men and the realms of the Mighty Ones' is set up, an astral capsule intermediate between the levels, in which the Cone of Power can be built and prevented from dispersing until the moment comes to discharge it for the working purpose decided upon beforehand. From this point of view, the Circle is rather like a cylinder in a car engine. A petrol-soaked newspaper, if lit, will merely flare up; but contain the same amount of petrol, as vapour and under control, in the cylinder and ignite it stage by stage, and it will produce enough explosive force to drive the car for a mile or more.

This is a difference of emphasis from the mediaeval magician's Circle; the power he hoped to tap was that of spirits summoned into the Triangle *outside* the Circle, and his Circle was cast purely to protect himself in such a dangerous encounter. Any weakness in it could blast him as surely as a puncture in an astronaut's space-suit.

Witches do not summon the kind of nastiness which mediaeval magicians hoped to control like lion-tamers; they invoke divinity, or sometimes nature-elementals – the latter cautiously but sympathetically, not with chair and whip. And the power is raised *within* the Circle. So containment, rather than exclusion, is the main function of their Circle.

That is why witches at work often become aware of unwanted entities 'taking an interest', but they tend to deal with them confidently as they arise, rather than to alter the emphasis of the Circle so as to make it unapproachable in the first place.

This is not to say that the witches' Circle has no protective function; it is declared, among other things, to be 'a shield against all wickedness and evil'. But we would suggest that for most working meetings the protective function (unlike that of the magician's Circle) is secondary.

However, witches can and do cast purely protective Circles when the need arises; round the house at night when the astral plane is felt to be turbulent, round their beds when a house-guest (often unwittingly) has vampiric tendencies,[1] or even round a desk when there is work to be done requiring undisturbed concentration. And so on.

With this in mind, it is important to have a very clear idea of just what a Magic Circle is, and of what it 'looks and feels like' on the astral plane. (This clear idea is just as important for a normal concentration-and-amplification Circle, of course.)

In the first place, it is in fact not a Circle at all, but a sphere; and it should always be so envisaged. The Circle is merely its equator, the line where the sphere cuts the ground. When one is casting it, one should picture an upright axis in the centre, with a semicircular arc running from its top, through the ground at the edge of the intended Circle, and so on down to its bottom. As one casts the Circle with sword or athame, one should feel one is pulling this semicircular arc round like the edge of a curtain, building up the sphere segment by segment like a reconstructed orange, until one comes back to the starting point and the sphere is complete. That may sound complicated, but Figure 3 should make it clear; and it is a visualization worth practising until it becomes automatic with the casting of every Circle.

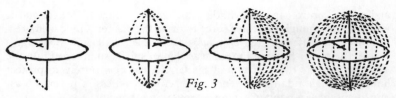

Fig. 3

The sphere itself should be envisaged as a glowing, transparent, electric-blue or violet globe, brightening to a fiery line of the same colour where it cuts the ground.

As for the wording of the casting, if the Circle is to be purely protective, the words *'a rampart and protection that shall preserve and contain the power that we shall raise within thee'* should be omitted, because no power is to be raised; and in summoning the Lords of the Watchtowers, the words *'to witness our rites and'* should be omitted, because no rite is to be performed.

In protective situations (which may often arise, for example, in public or in non-witch company) one may wish to cast a Circle mentally, often without giving any outward sign that one is doing so. This is not difficult, with practice; what is called for, as with the physically enacted rite, is powerfully concentrated imagination and willpower; physical actions certainly make such concentration easier, but they can never make it less necessary, and the occasional purely mental operation is a very good way of developing it. Casting a mental Circle may involve anything from a rapid 'zipping-up' of the electric-blue sphere to a complete visualization of the entire ritual, including the smell of the imagined incense as you carry it round, and the familiar feel of your athame-hilt in your hand; that depends on the circumstances and the time available. In an emergency, the instant 'zip-up', envisaged with a deliberate surge of psychic effort, can be just as effective. But if you have the time, and are undisturbed, visualizing the entire ritual is a good discipline, and avoiding it may betray laziness, which weakens the effect.

One thing to remember in casting a protective Circle: be sure to include everyone nearby who is vulnerable. If you expect a psychic attack from outside, a Circle that merely embraces your bedroom may protect you, but the foiled attack may expend itself on an innocent member of the family in another room. Or if, like us, you have poultry and ponies in the house's outbuildings, they may take the brunt. That may sound paranoid and over-imaginative, but it is sheer practical experience – our own and other people's.

Lighting the West candle: Temple decorations can emphasize the elemental
character of the Watchtowers

Altar with Goddess and God figures by Bel Bucca, and Gerald Gardner's own Book of Shadows open at the First Degree Oath

Doreen Valiente by 'The Naked Man', a traditional witches' meeting place in the New Forest

Gerald Gardner in his home
on the Isle of Man

The house on the edge of the
New Forest where Dorothy
Clutterbuck initiated Gerald
Gardner

Drawing Down the Sun, in our Garden Temple

In blessing the wine, the woman holds the active symbol, the athame, because hers is the positive polarity on the inner planes

The earliest written text of the 'Bagahi' incantation (see Appendix B), from the thirteenth-century French troubadour Rutebeuf's manuscript in the Bibliothèque Nationale, Paris

American witches Oz (left) and Wolf (right) visiting the Lia Fáil (Stone of Destiny), said to be one of the Four Treasures of the Tuatha Dé Danann, on Tara Hill, Co. Meath. With them are Janet and our coven Maiden, Virginia Russell

Stone carving identified by archaeologists as a Cernunnos figure, in the churchyard on Tara Hill

Candle and needle spell (see Section xxii, 'Spells')

The Openings of the Body Ritual

A time-honoured method for the psychic protection of an individual is the Openings of the Body Ritual. In effect, it seals the aura at its most vulnerable points.[2] It can be used by the followers of any tradition, by merely changing the Names of Power; we remember once recommending it to a Christian friend who was sensitive enough to be aware of a psychic danger to herself, and she used it successfully in the name of Christ, and with water from her church font.

We give here, naturally, the Wiccan form.

The Openings of the Body Ritual can be performed either by oneself or by one's working partner. The person to be protected must be skyclad, for obvious practical reasons.

First, consecrate water and salt in the normal manner (see pages 43-4), and pour the salt into the water. The God- and Goddess-names may be those normally used or may be chosen specially for the situation; for example, if we have just written something which may provoke a malevolent reaction, we may invoke the God of Scribes (say the Egyptian Thoth or the Celtic Oghma Grianaineach) with an appropriate Goddess partner (in these cases Isis, or Brid or Dana, respectively).

Moisten the index finger of the right hand with the salt-and-water mixture, and touch each of the openings of the body in turn, saying each time: '*Be thou sealed against all evil.*' Strongly visualize the seals which you are creating. Re-moisten your finger as necessary, so that each opening receives the consecrated mixture.

The openings are as follows:

On a man: Right eye, left eye, right ear, left ear, right nostril, left nostril, mouth, right nipple, left nipple, navel, tip of penis, anus (twelve openings in all).

On a woman: Right eye, left eye, right ear, left ear, right nostril, left nostril, mouth, right nipple, left nipple, navel, urethra, vaginal opening, anus (thirteen openings in all).

Any supernumerary nipple should also be sealed; these are more common than is generally realized, usually being tiny but genuine rudimentary nipples placed on the 'milk line' running downward from the ordinary nipples. If you think you have one, a doctor will confirm whether it is genuine or a mere mole. (They used, of course, to be regarded as unquestionable 'witch marks', and oddly enough Janet, one other of our female witches and one of our male witches all possess one.)

If you have any kind of still-unhealed wound or injury on your body, this too should be sealed.

As with casting the Circle, the Openings of the Body Ritual can, when the situation demands, be performed mentally and astrally, without physical movement. On more than one occasion Stewart, feeling that Janet might be under psychic attack while she was asleep beside him, has gone through the whole process mentally for her, from the consecration of the water and salt onwards – sometimes instead of, and sometimes in addition to, the casting of a mental Circle.

Which raises the question: when should the Openings of the Body Ritual be used instead of (or as well as) the casting of a protective Circle? The answer is: when the individual concerned is *specifically* under attack, or for some reason especially vulnerable (if he or she is ill or tired, for example). It is also useful when the individual is going to be physically on the move, or about to take his or her physical body into a psychically dangerous situation. This again is an aid to imagination and willpower. A cast Circle *can* be carried with you as you move (we have often cast a Circle round a moving car, for instance), but it requires deliberate and continuing visualization. If the ritual protection has been applied to your own body, however, your mind automatically accepts that that protection will accompany your body wherever it goes, like a suit of armour; so greater effect is achieved with less effort.

Talismans

A talisman is not exactly a ritual, though the making and consecration of one is a ritual act, so they may suitably be mentioned here.

A talisman is an object created, or adapted, for a particular magical purpose – a kind of portable physical condensation of a spell, to be worn or carried by the person it is intended to benefit. The purpose may be success in a specified activity, but as often as not it is protection against a specified danger. Popular examples of the two types are a rabbit's foot carried in a gambler's pocket, for success, and a St Christopher medallion on a car dashboard, for protection.

True magical talismans, however, are always more tailor-made, both for the user and for the purpose intended, than the rabbit's foot or the St Christopher badge. A talisman is designed and made to symbolize the purpose and the user precisely, and to link the two together. It is then consecrated, with the intention behind its making firmly in mind, and carried (just like the rabbit's foot!) whenever its effect is needed.

A common form of talisman is made by cutting out two discs of paper or parchment joined together by a hinge. This provides four surfaces on which symbols can be drawn or written, and the whole thing can be closed like a book into a single disc-shape.

Suppose, for example, that Stewart were negotiating with a publisher about one of his manuscripts, and wanted protection against possible sharp practice or hidden traps in the small print of the contract. (A purely hypothetical supposition, we hasten to add, because we have an excellent literary agent, and no misgivings whatever about our present publishers!) He might design a talisman like the one in Figure 4 and carry it in his pocket when he sat down to talk terms.

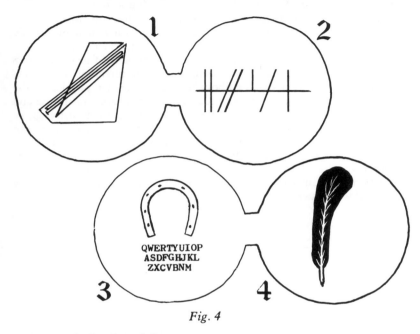

Fig. 4

The symbolism is as follows:

Side 1 Stewart's name plotted out on the magic square of Mercury, who is both the God (and planet) of Communications and the quick-witted one who spots the aces up the sleeves.

Side 2 The name of Oghma, Celtic God of Wisdom and of Scribes, written in the Ogham script which he is credited with having invented.

Side 3 First, the points-down horseshoe, symbol of smiths and farriers – and the name Farrar means 'farrier'. Smiths and farriers were always regarded as natural magicians, and only they were allowed to display the horseshoe points downwards, to pour power onto the forge. (Blacksmiths still nail horseshoes to their smithy doors this way.) Stewart's 'forge' is of course his typewriter, so in this symbol his hereditary horseshoe is pouring power on to the letters of a typewriter keyboard.

Side 4 The red feather of Ma'at, Egyptian Goddess of Justice and Fair Dealing. By a happy double symbolism, it can also be regarded as the quill pen, traditional emblem of the writer.

Our diagram is in black and white, but coloured inks would of course be used to enhance the symbolism further. For instance, Side 1 could be in orange, the Cabalistic colour of Hod/Mercury. Side 2 might be in green, since Oghma Grianaineach is the Irish Celtic aspect of the God of Scribes. Side 3 might be in black, the colour of iron and of typewriter ribbons. And Side 4, of course, in red, the colour of Ma'at's feather.

And in case anyone should complain that this talisman mixes Roman, Celtic, Egyptian, astrological, modern-technological and Cabalistic symbolism, we would answer – so what? We would never so mix symbol-systems in a ritual; but a talisman is a *personal* thing, and in this case, what mattered would be Stewart's own resonance with the symbols he had chosen. If *he* was happy with that particular complex of symbols, that would be all the justification he needed. (As a witch, we might add, he would also be happy that both God and Goddess aspects were invoked.)

The magic squares of the planets are very useful in designing talismans, because, as in the example above, a personal name can be linked directly to any given planetary quality. These squares are made up of smaller squares, like a chessboard, with numbers in the smaller squares. Here are the seven squares:

4	9	2
3	5	7
8	1	6

SATURN

4	14	15	1
9	7	6	12
5	11	10	8
16	2	3	13

JUPITER

11	24	7	20	3
4	12	25	8	16
17	5	13	21	9
10	18	1	14	22
23	6	19	2	15

MARS

6	32	3	34	35	1
7	11	27	28	8	30
19	14	16	15	23	24
18	20	22	21	17	13
25	29	10	9	26	12
36	5	33	4	2	31

SUN

22	47	16	41	10	35	4
5	23	48	17	42	11	29
30	6	24	49	18	36	12
13	31	7	25	43	19	37
38	14	32	1	26	44	20
21	39	8	33	2	27	45
46	15	40	9	34	3	28

VENUS

8	58	59	5	4	62	63	1
49	15	14	52	53	11	10	56
41	23	22	44	45	19	18	48
32	34	35	29	28	38	39	25
40	26	27	37	36	30	31	33
17	47	46	20	21	43	42	24
9	55	54	12	13	51	50	16
64	2	3	61	60	6	7	57

MERCURY

37	78	29	70	21	62	13	54	5
6	38	79	30	71	22	63	14	46
47	7	39	80	31	72	23	55	15
16	48	8	40	81	32	64	24	56
57	17	49	9	41	73	33	65	25
26	58	18	50	1	42	74	34	66
67	27	59	10	51	2	43	75	35
36	68	19	60	11	52	3	44	76
77	28	69	20	61	12	53	4	45

MOON

In each square, the numbers in any one row, horizontal or vertical, add up to the same total. These totals are: for Saturn 15, for Jupiter 34, for Mars 65, for the Sun 111, for Venus 175, for Mercury 260 and for the Moon 369.

Other planetary symbols useful in making talismans are given, along with the squares themselves, in many books; for example in Barrett's *The Magus*, which was published in 1801 and is available in modern reprints. *The Magus*, a fascinating compendium of traditional ceremonial magic, includes a whole section on talismanic magic. But the most easily obtained book on the subject is Israel Regardie's *How to Make and Use Talismans*, one of the little booklets in the *Paths to Inner Power* series.

Incidentally, there is an error in Barrett's version of the Square of Venus, which Regardie has unfortunately repeated. The third number from the left in the second row down should be 48, not 43; you can confirm this by checking the row-totals.

Names are turned into sigils by converting the letters to numbers, and then tracing a continuous line from number to number over the chosen magic square. Here is the conversion table:

1	2	3	4	5	6	7	8	9
A	B	C	D	E	F	G	H	I
J	K	L	M	N	O	P	Q	R
S	T	U	V	W	X	Y	Z	

Taking our example – the name STEWART FARRAR thus converts to 1255192619919.

Another useful book for talisman-makers is Crowley's *777*; his voluminous tables of correspondences can be very helpful in selecting symbols to express the concepts you wish to embody.

You can make a talisman as simple or as complicated as you like; the good old basic rule applies, that the finished object should 'feel right' to you. But in the case of talismans, there is one advantage of complication; the research, thought and design skill involved do help to root the purpose of the talisman firmly in your mind, and to build up the robust thought-form which is the actual 'bit that works'; the physical talisman is, so to speak, a buoy to which the thought-form can moor itself.

Once the talisman is completed, it must be consecrated. We suggest the elemental form of consecration given on pp. 47-8.

Protection of the Home

The best psychic protection of your home is a healthy psychic atmosphere within the home itself, which (apart from being desirable anyway) automatically deals with most undesirable outside influences through the Boomerang Effect. (See p. 24.) You should also remember always the basic occult rule: 'The only thing to fear is fear itself.' Quiet confidence is the finest psychic armour in the world; and a home that is infected by fear, personal tensions or other negative attitudes cannot expect to be invulnerable to outside infection. A man with a cold is more susceptible to pneumonia than a healthy one, and the same principle applies on all the levels.

That having been said – there is no harm in erecting purposeful psychic barriers round your home on principle, or as a specific defence at a time of possible danger; just as a sensible healthy man takes reasonable precautions against catching a cold, without being paranoid about it.

The actual form of the protective ritual you use will depend on several things and should always be tailor-made to your own situation; so we do not propose to offer a detailed one, only to suggest a few basic magical methods which you can adapt, combine or develop to meet your own sense of what 'feels right'.

The simplest method of all is, of course, the Magic Circle around the home. For proper emphasis, it should be cast in actuality, using your physical magical tools, rather than mentally when this is possible. If you are lucky enough to live in a detached house, you can walk round the outside to cast it. If you live in a semi-detached or terrace house, or in a flat, you can walk round the inside perimeter, but mentally projecting the Circle outside the walls.

But the thing to remember about a Magic Circle is that it is a temporary measure unless it is deliberately maintained. A coven Circle is very vigorously maintained by the ritual performed within it, and by the togetherness-sense of the coven's group mind; and it is banished when the meeting disperses, so until then the knowledge that 'we haven't banished yet' has in itself a maintaining effect psychologically. An 'unattended' Circle, however, fades away of its own accord as the hours pass. The general opinion is that its average life is around twenty-four hours.

So for a longer-lasting effect, something else is needed. The difference is basically psychological (and therefore magical); you *know* that you intend the protection to be effective for a week or a month, or whatever – and the mere fact that you are using a technique which has that intent, and is therefore purposely not the same as your usual Magic Circle, helps to establish its desired life-span on the astral plane.

A good start is to consecrate water and salt, mix them and go round the home anointing every windowsill, chimney entrance, ventilator and outer doorstep with it. As you do so, declare: *'No evil can enter here'* – and envisage the astral reality of the spot (its astral molecular structure, so to speak) actually changing to meet the new requirements. Do this with all the willpower you can muster.

Next, go round all these places again with your athame in your hand, and make the Banishing Pentagram of Earth (see Figure 5) towards each. As you do so, declare: *'All evil is turned back.'*[3]

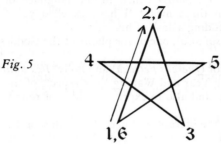

Fig. 5

Physical objects or symbols expressing the idea of guardianship, in appropriate places, may help you to build up an awareness of continuing protection. For example, there is a stainless steel pentagram on our temple door, and a transparent coloured pentagram on its window; they were put there because they are attractive and appropriate, not through anxiety – but they do enhance the temple's atmosphere of security. Again, if you are in tune with Egyptian symbols, a picture of Anubis over a door is dramatically effective. And so on.

But we would emphasize again – what does the work is the thought-form built up on the astral and mental planes; any physical object is just 'a buoy to which the thought-form can moor itself', and you should be aware of this in all your working.

One of the most traditional of these physical mooring-buoys is the witch's bottle buried under the doorstep (not so easy in a town flat or a cemented entrance, but securing it over or beside the door-frame has the same mental and astral effect). Such bottles have been used for many purposes over the ages, and filled with many substances from the exotic to the nauseating. For our present purpose of domestic protection, we would suggest filling the bottle with a small collection of herbs which have traditional protective qualities, and then sealing it firmly. It might, for example, contain the following. (We have given the Latin botanical names as well because these are universal, whereas local names differ; aconite, for instance, is called wolfsbane, monkshood, friar's cap or blue rocket in various places, but *Aconitum napellus* will always identify it.)

Houseleek (*Sempervivum tectorum*) against lightning.

Garlic (*Allium sativum*) against psychic vampirism.

St John's Wort (*Hypericum perforatum*) against 'ghosts, devils, imps and thunderbolts' or demons in general; its old Latin name was *Fuga daemonum* because of this reputation.

Pennyroyal (*Mentha pulegium*) against 'swimming of head' and hysteria – i.e., mental disorientation or 'freaking out'.

Fumitory (*Fumaria officinalis*) which in the language of flowers elaborated in Victorian times meant 'I have expelled you from my thoughts'; no harm in adding a dash of humour.

Blackthorn (*Prunus spinosa*), one of the plants of the Goddess in her dark, protective aspect.

Oak (*Quercus robur* or *Quercus petraea*) and holly (*Ilex aquifolium*), symbolizing the Waxing Year and Waning Year aspects of the God, to balance the blackthorn, and also to express the idea of round-the-year protection.

A little research into the literature of herbalism will soon help you to draw up a list suitable to your own needs. For example, if you are

Celtic-orientated, you might feel suited by a bottle containing the seven sacred herbs of the Druids: mistletoe (*Viscum album*), vervain (*Verbena officinalis*), henbane (*Hyoscyamus niger*), primrose (*Primula vulgaris*), pulsatilla (*Anemone pulsatilla*), clover (*Trifolium pratense*) and aconite (*Aconitum napellus*).

It should be noted that henbane and aconite are both poisonous plants; they are harmless enough in a sealed bottle, but they should not be used medicinally except under expert advice.

From plants to animals: Michael Bentine, that highly intelligent author, comic, psychic and paranormal researcher, in his book *The Door Marked Summer* (p.34), gives a useful tip which our own experience confirms. 'No self-respecting cat or dog, or for that matter any domesticated animal, will remain for more than a few moments where any "Dabbling with the Devil" or other negative practices are being indulged in, and will rapidly leave the scene of the crime. I like to have an animal around me when I am opening up to the paranormal field of force, to give me a corroboratory warning of anything negative being attracted to the focus of power that I am tuned in to. This I learned from my parents, who always welcomed the presence of a dog or cat when conducting their investigations.'

This use of witches' familiars as psychic radar is more important than some of the bizarre functions attributed to them by folklore.

Incidentally, *The Door Marked Summer* should come high on any witch's reading-list; a warm but level-headed book, it is a mine of useful information from first-hand experience in the whole psychic field. Another shrewd quote from it (p.36) on the subject of defence: 'Evil or negative forces abhor the sound of genuine laughter, not snide, sarcastic, sneering laughter, but that marvellous deep belly laughter that shakes the solar plexus and rids the soul of darkness. Hatred, in particular, instantly dissolves in the presence of a good old down-to-earth guffaw.' (Which makes Bentine himself an outstanding crusader against the dark forces.)

All these magical methods of protection are useful tools when they are needed. But no witch should develop a 'belt-and-braces' attitude to psychic defence. Paranoid witches, prone to psychic hypochondria, are of little use to themselves or others. Awareness of possible psychic danger should always be balanced by a calm, even joyful, self-confidence. A suit of armour is very handy on occasion, but worn round the clock it prevents the sun and air getting to your skin.

It cannot be repeated too often: the only thing to fear is fear itself.

And finally – for a deeper study of the whole subject, Dion Fortune's book *Psychic Self-Defence* should be obligatory reading for every witch and occultist.

X   A Seashore Ritual

As we pointed out in *Eight Sabbats for Witches*, Dion Fortune's novel *The Sea Priestess* is a goldmine of material for devised rituals. There, we used a passage from it as part of our Handfasting ritual, and many people have found it moving and very appropriate.

Here is a Seashore Ritual which we have based on several incidents in *The Sea Priestess*. The novel is available in two editions, the full-text hardback and an abridged paperback (see Bibliography for details). The passages we have drawn on for our ritual will be found on pages 189-90, 214, 217-20 and 315 of the hardback, or on pages 102-3, 118, 121-4 and 173 of the paperback. But every witch should study the whole book, which has had a profound effect on many people.

As with our Handfasting ritual, we use this material by kind permission of the Society of the Inner Light, who hold the copyright of Dion Fortune's works – and we repeat what we said there: 'Responsibility for the context in which they have been used is, of course, entirely ours and not the Society's; but we like to think that, if the late Miss Fortune had been able to be present, we would have had her blessing.'

In their letter of permission, the Society asked us to say 'that Dion

Fortune was not a Witch and did not have any connection with a coven, and that this Society is not in any way associated with the Craft of Witches'. We accede to their request; and when this book is published, we shall send them a copy with our compliments, in the hope that it may give them second thoughts about whether Wiccan philosophy is as alien to that of Dion Fortune (whom witches hold in great respect) as they seem to imagine. In all friendliness, we must admit that we sometimes wonder if the Society have not departed farther from the mainstream of Dion Fortune's teaching than the witches have. But that, of course, is their own affair.

Central to this ritual is the Fire of Azrael, which consists of three woods – cedar, sandalwood and juniper. Azrael is the Angel of Death, but in the kindly aspect of 'the Consoler, the Comforter' – the Psychopompos who smoothes the transition from bodily incarnation to the Summerlands. But his Fire is not a funereal one; it is rather a means of clairvoyance into the past, in particular the past of the place in which it is burned. Vivian Le Fay Morgan explains its purpose to Wilfred Maxwell in *The Sea Priestess* (hardback p. 133, paperback p. 66): 'She asked me if one day I would like to look in the coals of the Fire of Azrael, and I asked her what it meant; and she said that one made a fire of certain woods, and gazed into the embers as it died down and saw therein the past that was dead. We would do this, she said, one day, and then we would see all the past of the high sea-down and the hollow land of the marshes reconstructing itself.'

Clairvoyant reaction to the Fire of Azrael depends on the individual, so to discuss it here might put preconceptions into the experimenter's mind. But the Fire can also be used as a focus of invocation, as both Morgan and later Molly used it in *The Sea Priestess*; and it is with this emphasis that we have assembled our ritual.

Incidentally, we have often made an incense based on the Fire of Azrael, by blending sandalwood chips, cedar oil and mashed juniper berries. We have found it very rewarding – but again, we leave experiment to the reader. (See p. 261 for our recipe.)

There is no reason, of course, why this Seashore Ritual should not be enacted with a fire of other woods, if you have difficulty in laying your hands on sufficient quantities of cedar, sandalwood and juniper. The meaning of the invocation is the same, and the setting should have the same effect on the psyche. But there is something special about the Fire of Azrael which is worth discovering for yourself, so we put it forward as the ideal.

Information on the Fire of Azrael, and its materials and use, will be found in *The Sea Priestess* on pages 136-40, 143-7, 154, 185-6, 288-9, 302-3 and 311 of the hardback, and pages 68-70, 75, 99-100 and 155-7 of the paperback.

But to return to 'the meaning of the invocation', with or without the Fire of Azrael. Its purpose is to call on Isis Unveiled by way of Isis Veiled. Isis Veiled is manifested Nature, which is the clothing of the Goddess; Isis Unveiled is the keeper of the Inner Mysteries. In the Tarot, Isis Veiled is the Empress, and Isis Unveiled is the High Priestess. Moon and sea evoke the overlap between the two aspects; in a sense this borderland is symbolized in the Tarot by the Star, who is always shown as being herself unrobed and yet at one with both Nature and Heaven – and, significantly, kneeling upon a shore and pouring her influence on both water and land. So by holding our ritual on a seashore by moonlight we attune ourselves to this same borderland and enter it psychically and reach beyond it.

We would say again: the ritual as we give it is the ideal one, and it will not always be possible to achieve all its elements – a lonely beach with a coincidence of full moon reflected on the water and a rising tide, not to mention a warm night. So we do not insert 'preferably' or 'if possible' in every sentence. The more of the ideal elements that can be achieved, the better; but every witch knows that even a makeshift ritual (if the makeshift is unavoidable and not mere laziness) can have heartening results if undertaken in the right spirit.

One thing can always be done, and it is worth doing: that everyone should learn his or her words by heart – all the more so because reading in the open by moonlight is hardly practicable. To make it easier (and also to give everyone an active part, however small), we have divided up the prose declamations among several coven members.

A slightly cynical note of warning: those witches who have a horror of 'contaminating' themselves with Cabalistic or Egyptian names (see note 3, p. 312) had better skip this ritual, because Dion Fortune uses both! But we find them perfectly in tune with the style of the rite, and with the spirit of the Old Religion.

The Preparation

Find a stretch of beach, as lonely as possible, where the tide comes in steadily and not in a rush. Study the tide tables and observe the tides on the beach, so that you know just when the tide will come up and cover your chosen spot for the fire. This spot may be either on the sand or on a convenient ledge of rock, provided the latter is not too heavily sprayed by the waves.

Choose a night when the tide will be rising at a convenient time, and arrange to start your ritual an hour or more before the tide will reach your fire. The moon should be as close as possible to the full.

It is somewhat unlikely that a skyclad ritual will be possible even with a fire, unless your beach is very private indeed, and the night very

warm. (Swimsuits, swimming-trunks or bikinis may be practicable.) So
the High Priestess, like the others, will probably be robed. Appropriate
colours are a silver robe with a dark blue cloak.

Apart from wood for the fire and means of lighting it, the only
materials or tools required are a chalice for the wine, some 'moon-food',
white in colour, and an athame to consecrate both. Dion Fortune's
moon-food menu was: 'Almond-curd such as the Chinese make; and
scallops in their shells; and little crescent honey-cakes like marzipan for
dessert – all white things. And this curious pallid dinner-table was
relieved by a great pile of pomegranates.' (*The Sea Priestess*, hardback
p. 204, paperback p. 111.) But your own moon-food depends on your
taste, resources and imagination.

Finally – dogs are sacred to the Moon Goddess, so if you have dogs
who can be relied upon to stay close at hand, by all means take them
(and their food). And never demand rigid discipline from animals at a
ritual, because the Goddess certainly will not!

The Ritual

The High Priestess withdraws as far from the coven as she reasonably
can, while still seeing and hearing what is going on. If she can conceal
herself behind a rock or a turn of a cliff or a sand-dune, so much the
better; but in any case the coven ignore her until the time comes for her
to approach them.

The coven prepare the Fire of Azrael at the chosen spot. When all is
ready, the High Priest and the Maiden face each other across the unlit
fire, on a line parallel to the edge of the sea. The rest of the coven
arrange themselves in a semicircle between them, facing the fire and the
sea.

The Maiden says:

'*Be ye far from us, O ye profane, for we are about to invoke the
descent of the power of Isis. Enter her temple with clean hands and a
pure heart, lest we defile the source of life.*'

A male witch says:

'*Learn now the secret of the web that is woven between the light and
the darkness; whose warp is life evolving in time and space, and whose
weft is spun of the lives of men.*'

A female witch says:

'*Behold we arise with the dawn of time from the grey and misty sea,
and with the dusk we sink into the western ocean, and the lives of a
man are strung like pearls on the thread of his spirit; and never in all
his journey goes he alone, for that which is solitary is barren.*'

A male witch says:

'*Learn now the mystery of the ebbing and flowing tides. That which is dynamic in the outer is latent in the inner, for that which is above is as that which is below, but after another manner.'*

A female witch says:

'In the heavens our Lady Isis is the Moon, and the moon-powers are hers. She is also the priestess of the silver star that rises from the twilight sea. Hers are the magnetic moon-tides ruling the hearts of men.'

A male witch says:

'In the inner she is all-potent. She is queen of the kingdom of sleep. All the invisible workings are hers, and she rules all things ere they come to birth.'

A female witch says:

'Even as through Osiris her mate the earth grows green, so the mind of man conceives through her power.'

The High Priest says:

'Let us show forth in a rite the dynamic nature of the Goddess, that the minds of men may be as fertile as their fields.'

The Maiden turns to face the land, and raises her arms high. She says:

'Be ye far from us, O ye profane, for the unveiling of the Goddess is at hand.'

The Maiden then walks deosil round the fire and joins the High Priest. The Fire of Azrael is then lit. When it is burning satisfactorily, the coven and the Maiden sit down in their semicircle. The High Priest remains standing.

'O thou that was before the earth was formed –
  Rhea, Binah, Ge.[1]
O tideless, soundless, boundless, bitter sea,
I am thy priest; O answer unto me.

'O arching sky above and earth beneath,
Giver of life and bringer-in of death,
  Persephone, Astarte, Ashtoreth,
I am thy priest; O answer unto me.

'O golden Aphrodite, come to me!
Flower of the foam, rise from the bitter sea.
The hour of the full moon-tide draws near,
Hear the invoking words, hear and appear –
  Isis Unveiled, and Rhea, Bina, Ge.
I am thy priest; O answer unto me.

'O Isis, veiled on earth, but shining clear
In the high heaven now the full moon draws near,
Hear the invoking words, hear and appear –
  Shaddai el Chai,[2] *and Rhea, Binah, Ge.*

On the last line, the High Priest raises his arms high and wide.

The High Priestess emerges from her hiding-place and walks to the edge of the sea opposite the fire, continuing until the water actually laps her feet.[3] She raises her arms high and wide for a moment as she faces the sea; then she lowers them and turns, and walks in a slow and stately manner up to the fire. When she reaches it, she stands facing the High Priest across it.

The High Priest lowers his arms and bows to her.

The High Priestess raises her arms in a curve like the Horns of Isis (which can also represent the crescent Moon) with the palms of her hand inwards. She holds them like this while she sings:

'I am she who ere the earth was formed
　Was Rhea, Binah, Ge.
I am that soundless, boundless, bitter sea,
Out of whose depths life wells eternally.

'Astarte, Aphrodite, Ashtoreth –
Giver of life and bringer-in of death;
Hera in Heaven, on earth, Persephone;
Levanah of the tides and Hecate –
All these am I, and they are seen in me.

'I am that soundless, boundless, bitter sea.
All tides are mine, and answer unto me.
Tides of the airs, tides of the inner earth,
The secret, silent tides of death and birth.
Tides of men's souls, and dreams, and destiny –
　Isis Veiled, and Rhea, Binah, Ge.

'The hour of the high full moon draws near;
I hear the invoking words, hear and appear –
　Isis Unveiled and Rhea, Binah, Ge.
I come unto the priest that calleth me.'

The song over, without haste the High Priest kneels, and the High Priestess lowers her arms. The seated coven change to a kneeling position. Proceeding deosil, the High Priestess walks round and lays her two hands on each head in turn, starting with that of the High Priest. As she leaves each person, he or she resumes a sitting position. (If there are any dogs with the coven, she blesses them in the same way, but also fondling or patting them to put them at ease.) Finally she sits down facing the High Priest across the fire.

The High Priest says:

'Let us now commune with the secrets of the fire.'

The whole coven, including the High Priestess, now gaze into the fire and speak of what they see. The High Priestess guides this part of the ritual, encouraging and calming as necessary.

When she feels that it has gone on long enough, she calls for the moon-food, which is brought forward and shared, as is the wine – both being consecrated in the normal manner by herself and the High Priest. A little of the food is kept aside.

The coven stay with the fire until the incoming tide quenches it. When the quenching is complete, the High Priestess says:

'*Consummatum est. Those who have received the Touch of Isis have received the opening of the gates of the inner life. For them the tides of the moon shall flow and ebb and flow and never cease in their cosmic rhythm.*'

The High Priest then brings her the food which has been kept aside, and she throws it onto the water as an offering to the sea.

Finally she stretches her arms out over the sea. After a moment she lowers them again and turns, and she and the High Priest lead the coven away.

The Wiccan Path

XI *The Rationale of Witchcraft*

Witches are neither fools, escapist nor superstitious. They are living in
the twentieth century, not the Middle Ages, and they accept the fact
without reservation; if they do tend to have a keener sense of historical
continuity, and a broader time-canvas, than most people, that makes
their awareness of the present more vivid, not less. Many witches are
scientists or technicians, and in our experience often very good ones. If
modern witchcraft did not have a coherent rationale, such people could
only keep going by a kind of deliberate schizophrenia, with neither
watertight compartment of their lives particularly happy – and we have
seen no signs of that.

Modern witchcraft does have a rationale, and a very coherent one.
This may surprise some of our readers, who know only that witchcraft
comes from the gut. So it does, as far as motivation and operation go.
The working power and the appeal of the Craft do arise from the
emotions, the intuition, the 'vasty deep' of the Collective Unconscious.
Its Gods and Goddesses draw their forms from the numinous
Archetypes which are the mighty foundation-stones of the human
racial psyche.

But Consciousness is human, too. The individual conscious mind is a comparative newcomer to the evolutionary scene on this planet, and – at least as far as land animals are concerned[1] – it is the unique gift of *homo sapiens*. No other physically manifested land animal has it, though one or two of the higher mammals seem to possess its first embryonic stirrings. Sentimentalists credit their favourite animals with it to a quasi-human degree, but this is pure projection (and a misunderstanding of the nature of consciousness) given colour by the fact that some of the animals' instinctual patterns, conditioned reflexes and learning ability overlap recognizably with human ones. Pet-owners would understand and learn from the creatures they love much better if they gave up this fantasy and saw (for example) a cat as a cat, with the dignity of its own nature, and not as a furry human.

Consciousness is not only a gift, it is a responsibility. It gives man 'dominion over the fish of the sea, and over the fowl of the air, and over the cattle, and over all the earth, and over every creeping thing that creepeth upon the earth'. Dominion in this sense does not mean the right to exploit them; it means that, since man's growing complexity makes him, for better or worse, the spearpoint of Earth's evolution, he has the greatest responsibility (indeed, his is the only species with *conscious* responsibility) towards the whole of manifested Nature. Witches are specially aware of it; Wicca as such is non-political, embracing voters and activists of many shades; but witches all tend to jump on the same soap-box when it comes to environmental issues.

But consciousness burdens man with a responsibility to himself, to his own race, as well. He must integrate conscious with unconscious, intellect with intuition, head with heart, brain with gut. If he does not, their conflict will paralyse or even destroy him, and possibly the Earth too; he will have betrayed the trust of his 'dominion'.

So it is incumbent upon witches, whose religion and Craft stem from the inner depths, to be truly the Wise People and show that Wicca satisfies the intellect as well. They have to demonstrate to themselves and to the world that their faith accords with reality and therefore does not (however beautiful it appears on the surface) contain the seeds of self-destruction.

The rationale of Wicca is a philosophical framework into which every phenomenon, from chemistry to clairvoyance, from logarithms to love, can be reasonably fitted. And since Wicca is a fast-growing movement, active in a real world, it must (without ever losing or weakening its preoccupation with the psychic depths) constantly explain, examine, develop and improve that philosophy.

The rationale of Wicca, as we see it, rests upon two fundamental principles: the Theory of Levels, and the Theory of Polarity.

The Theory of Levels maintains that reality exists and operates on many planes (physical, etheric, astral, mental, spiritual, to give a simplified but generally accepted list[2]); that each of these levels has its own laws; and that these sets of laws, while special to their own levels, are compatible with each other, their mutual resonance governing the interaction between the levels.

The Theory of Polarity maintains that all activity, all manifestation, arises from (and is inconceivable without) the interaction of pairs and complementary opposites – positive and negative, light and dark, content and form, male and female, and so on; and that this polarity is not a conflict between 'good' and 'evil', but a creative tension like that between the positive and negative terminals of an electric battery. Good and evil only arise with the constructive or destructive *application* of that polarity's output (again, as with the uses to which a battery may be put).

The Theory of Levels describes the *structure* of the universe; the Theory of Polarity describes its *activity*; and structure and activity are inseparable. Together, they *are* the universe.

Let us examine each of them in more detail.

The Theory of Levels (even if over-simplified to matter, mind, spirit and God) was more or less taken for granted until about a couple of centuries ago, when the avalanche of the Scientific Revolution (and its dark offspring the Industrial Revolution) really began to move. The Scientific Revolution, almost exclusively concerned with the physical level of reality, was a necessary if often temporarily disorienting stage in man's development; the time had come for him to understand and conquer matter and its laws.

The trouble was that he did it so brilliantly, with such awe-inspiring and heady success, that he deluded himself into thinking that matter was the *only* level of reality. He came to believe that mind was merely an epiphenomenon, an electro-chemical activity of the physical brain; and that 'spirit' was a fantasy, a symbolic projection of man's mental or even glandular conflicts and uncertainties, or at best of his urge to perfection, the true key to which (it was believed) lay in material progress.

One would have thought that organized religion would have put forward a meaningful corrective to all this; but in fact its voice was barely head crying in the wilderness of triumphant materialism. In all the active arenas of human ideas, religion was relegated to the ethical or charity-doling sidelines, or to moral rationalizations of the social consequences of industrialization. As far as philosophy, the interpretation of cosmic reality, was concerned, it could fight only rearguard actions. Materialism was the actual dynamic force of the epoch.

And yet, for those with eyes to see, the discoveries of science were full of hints of the wider truth. Within its own limits, science reflected the Theory of Levels. The laws of each of its disciplines – mathematics, physics, chemistry, biology and so on – were different, yet compatible. A botanist, analysing the structure and metabolism of a leaf, had to acknowledge and make use of the formulae of chemistry and mathematics and physics as well as his own. Each science's set of laws had its own unique character and relevance; yet they all interacted, and no two sets of laws were in mutual conflict. Where they appeared to contradict each other, the scientists knew it was because they had not yet perfectly understood them, and quite rightly they studied and reassessed them until the apparent conflict was resolved.

It has only been in our lifetime that the wiser scientists have begun, on any significant scale, to have doubts about the neat nineteenth-century vision of a universe as a mere (however complex) physical mechanism.

These doubts, too, are a natural development. If one pushes the investigation of the physical plane to its uttermost frontiers, the very nature of those frontiers brings one face to face with the areas of interaction with other planes; one keeps getting puzzling glimpses over the boundary wall – and it becomes increasingly difficult to ignore what lies beyond.[3]

Einstein's $e = mc^2$ and the transcendental subtleties of subatomic physics (in which scientists find themselves using such words as 'indeterminacy', 'strangeness' and 'charm' as technical terms) are two of the more obvious fields in which the mechanistic view of the universe is wearing very thin.[4]

Until quite recently, it was professional suicide for a respectable scientist to investigate the 'paranormal' (ESP, telepathy, telekinesis, precognition and so on) or even to admit that there might be anything to investigate. But today, even in the dollar-dedicated USA and in the officially materialist USSR, universities and defence departments are allocating good money and first-class brains to such research.[5]

And going even farther in support of the Theory of Levels, Sir Bernard Lovell, the father of radio astronomy, can tell that august body the British Association for the Advancement of Science: 'We have deluded ourselves that through science we can find the only avenue to true understanding about nature and the universe …. The simple belief in automatic progress by means of scientific discovery and application is a tragic myth of our age. Science is a powerful and vital human activity; but this confusion of thought and motive is bewildering.' (*The Times*, 28 August 1975).

Some of Sir Bernard's learned listeners probably took those words to be merely a call to scientists to be aware of their moral and ethical responsibilities to the community – important enough in all conscience. But their philosophical implications are far deeper, which at least a minority must have understood and doubtless agreed with.

Either Sir Bernard's statement means that non-physical levels of reality exist and must be taken into account, or else it is an empty platitude. And we feel that the man who has probably done as much to expand our factual knowledge of the physical universe as any individual since Galileo[6] with his optical telescopes, is not given to empty platitudes.

Granted, as a working hypothesis, that reality is many-levelled – what are the practical implications?

If witches may quote Marxist Scripture for their own purposes (and our desire to see humanity realize its full potential is as strong as the Communists' even though our aims and methods are very different from theirs), we would cite Marx and Engels' statement in *The Communist Manifesto*: 'The philosophers have merely interpreted the world in various ways; the point, however, is to change it', and Lenin's more succinct dictum: 'Theory without practice is sterile; practice without theory is blind.'

Witches are practical people; philosophy to them is not just an intellectual exercise – they have to put it into practice in their everyday lives, and in their working, if philosophy is to have any meaning. Similarly, much as they trust instinct, they do not merely blunder ahead in response to its promptings without any reference to logic – they prefer to understand what they are doing, and why. So on the relationship between theory and practice (if on little else) they agree with Lenin.

Witches know in theory, and have satisfied themselves in practice, that there are points and areas of interaction between the levels; situations in which the mental plane acts powerfully on the astral plane and affects its phenomena – or the spiritual on the physical, and so on. Each plane is affecting the others all the time; but there seem to be what may be called *points of inter-resonance* where this effect is particularly striking and clearly enough defined to be made use of in practice.[7]

It is the discovering and understanding of these points of inter-resonance which constitute a great deal of what witches call 'opening up the levels'; and it is their exploitation, in constructive work, which constitutes the operational side of the Craft.

To make this clear, let us take an example from practical science: namely, television. An event involving movement and sound takes place in the television studio. By suitably designed equipment, this event is transformed into an event on quite a different plane – the plane of electro-magnetic vibrations in what scientists used to call the 'ether'.

(They no longer use the term, because increased knowledge has shown it to be an over-simplification; but it is still a useful bit of shorthand to help the layman to understand what is going on.)

This event in the 'ether', as it stands, is undetectable by the human senses. We cannot see or hear it, in the sky or passing through our walls; but it is there, real and coherent.

In our living-room, another suitably designed equipment takes this 'etheric' event and transforms it, as if by magic, back into a movement-and-sound event. We see and hear a remarkably accurate re-creation of what is happening in the studio.

At the time of writing, this re-creation is merely in two-dimensional light and shade, colour and monaural sound; but there is already no technical reason (merely economic ones) why it should not be in three-dimensional vision and stereophonic sound. And in the future, television scientists may well be able to offer us smell, taste and touch as well.

The scientists here have been doing, between the sub-planes of their own recognized reality, precisely what the witches are doing between the major planes of *their* recognized reality: discovering and understanding the points and techniques of inter-resonance between them, and putting their new knowledge to practical use. In other words, 'opening up the levels'.

In this sense, television *is* magical; for that is exactly what magic is – in Aleister Crowley's words, 'the Science and Art of causing Change to occur in conformity with Will'. He goes on to say: 'Nature is a continuous phenomenon, though we do not know in all cases how these things are connected.' (*Magick in Theory and Practice*, Introduction pp. XII and XV.)

The discovery of those connections is the aim of the scientist (on the physical plane) and of the witch (on all the planes). The use of those discoveries is 'magic'. Magic does not break the laws of Nature; when it appears to do so, that is because it is obeying laws that the observer has not yet understood. A sixteenth-century scientist, for example, however intelligent and well-informed, if he could have seen television might well have branded it as supernatural.

As we have said, many modern scientists are becoming aware of (and some of them are investigating) phenomena which can only be explained on the basis that there are levels of reality other than the physical. Attempts to explain these phenomena in terms of still-undiscovered physical laws keep stumbling over fresh paradoxes. For example, if telepathy exists (and only wilful ignorers of evidence can still deny that it does) and is due to some kind of brain-generated radiation – why does all the evidence show that it is *not* subject to the inverse square law[8] by which every other form of radiation known to physical science is governed?

One could go on at length about recent research into such subjects as telepathy, telekinesis, the influence of thought on growing plants, the statistical analysis of Zodiacal birth-sign types and so on; but this is not the place to do it. For an overall review of the field, we recommend Lyall Watson's *Supernature*; and on telepathy in particular, Targ and Puthoff's *Mind Reach* (both in Bibliography).

We shall have more to say on the Theory of Levels in later Sections. Meanwhile, let us take a closer look at the Theory of Polarity.

This theory is not new, either; it is common to many philosophies, both religious and materialistic.

The trap into which monotheist[9] religions have fallen has been to equate polarity with good-versus-evil. They recognize that the activity of the world around them is engendered by the interaction of opposites; but they see this interaction only as the battle between God and Satan. When this battle ends with God's total victory at the Last Trump, they assume that activity will continue – but on what basis? Apart from mass choirs, and an excessive architectural use of gold, the prognosis is vague. Even the inspired visions of Heaven by gifted poets and seers are really just impassioned descriptions of contemporary evils that will *not* be there.

The most-quoted example, in Revelations xxi and xxii, exults in the New Jerusalem's absence of tears, death, sorrow, crying, pain, fear, unbelief, abomination, murder, whoremongers, sorcerers, idolators, liars, temples, shut gates, night, sea, curses, candles, Sun and Moon. But the *positive* description is purely static: nearly 1,500 miles wide, long and high (!) with walls 216 feet high, and foundations and gates of precious stones. The only mentions of any kind of activity or movement are of the righteous walking in it (xxi:24), the river of life 'proceeding' (xxii:1), the tree of life yielding fruit every month (with no Moon?) (xxii:2), and God's servants serving Him (xxii:3). Verse after verse about excluded evils and about (to be fair, doubtless symbolic) dimensions and materials, but effectively nothing about what *happens* there.

Our point is not to mock at St John's high-rise architecture, nor even to complain at his abolition of Sun, Moon, sea, night and candles, but to suggest that his negative, static description is not just his personal style but intrinsic to the monotheistic, non-polarized viewpoint. Under the unchallenged rule of a non-polarized Creator, nothing *can* happen.

Islam's Heaven is much more interesting, if only because Mohammed was sexually healthy and bequeathed to his followers none of the inhibitions and neuroses which woman-hating Paul of Tarsus imposed on Christianity. So polarity, in its most humanly enjoyable form, brings the Moslem Paradise to life. To the Moslem, woman is inferior but intended by Allah to be the giver and receiver of delight. To Pauline Christianity, woman is not only inferior, she is a temptation to sin, and herself morally weak if not actually wicked (a view of which the Church has never entirely rid itself – though we can find no authority for it in the words or deeds of Jesus). The Moslem view, while of course unacceptably male-chauvinist,[10] does welcome sex into Heaven; so in the presence of at least one aspect of polarity, something actually happens there – and man or woman, one might do a lot worse.

The Buddhist goes to the other extreme; his Nirvana is frankly static, but at least it is consistent. He *aspires* to a pure, polarity-free, activity-free Existence, in the unchanging Eternal Mind; so he does not disguise his aspiration behind gates of pearl, nor plant Nirvana with fruit-bearing trees.

Heaven – whether choral, sexual or motionless – may be a long way ahead for the individual believer; but by studying his vision of it, one can directly assess his attitude to polarity.

The materialist's Heaven on Earth (where else can he put it?) ranges from the capitalist one of individual wealth, fending off death, moth and rust as long as possible, to the Communist one of the classless society. Both recognize polarity at least in the shape of the class war – the latter preaching it, the former vigorously practising it. But it is only the Marxist, on the whole, who has a consistent philosophy of materialist polarity.

Karl Marx did not claim that his Dialectical Materialism was original, at least in its dialectical (polarized-activity) aspect. He acknowledged his debt to the dialectics of Georg Hegel (1770-1831), who had developed an elegant theory of the action of polarity in terms of Thesis-Antithesis-Synthesis and the Interpenetration of Opposites. This system Marx took over in its entirety. But Hegel was an idealist – which in the philosophical sense means not a 'do-gooder' or optimistic dreamer but one who believes that mind or spirit is the basic reality, with matter merely reflecting it; as opposed to the philosophical materialist (such as Marx) who sees matter as the basic reality, with mind and spirit merely reflecting it. By Marx's own metaphor, Hegel's dialectic, in his view, was standing on its head; and he claimed to have set it on its feet. Thus he produced Dialectical Materialism, or Marxism – now the official (and enforced) philosophy of about a third of the world's population.

In strict philosophical terms, witches are idealists; for while they believe that every entity or object on the physical plane has its counterparts on the non-material planes, they also believe that there are real entities on the unseen planes which do *not* have physical forms of their own. To witches, the unseen planes are the fundamental reality, of which material reality is one manifestation.

But to label witches as idealists, while correct, is perhaps misleading; maybe 'pluralists' would be better. For matter is very real to them; they are lovingly rooted in Nature, 'the Veil of Isis', vibrant with overtones of all the other levels. Tangible Nature is holy to them. That is why their Goddess has two main aspects. She is both the Earth Mother, whose fecundity bears and nourishes them during physical incarnation, and the Queen of Night, 'she in the dust of whose feet are the hosts of Heaven, and whose body encircles the Universe', whose most vivid symbol is the Moon. The Earth Mother is the sovereign of physically manifested Nature, Isis Veiled; the Moon Goddess is the ruler of the invisible levels, Isis Unveiled; yet to the witch, the two are one and inseparable. They remain one, even though the complexity of the unseen levels is further symbolized by the Moon Goddess's cyclical aspects of Maid, Mother and Crone – waxing, full and waning. And in her multiformity she is stirred and fertilized by her multiform Consort; for the witches' God, too, is symbolized at the same time by the horned Pan-figure of forest and mountain and by the blazing Sun of the heavens. The witches' vision of their God and Goddess expresses comprehensively their belief in the reality of all the levels, matter included.

So witches see the flaws of the dominant views of the Levels, and of Polarity, as follows:

(1) The materialist (and, in particular, Marxist) view has a basically sound understanding of the actual working of the Theory of Polarity but distorts and impoverishes it by denying the Theory of Levels.

(2) The monotheist-religious view accepts (in one form or another) the Theory of Levels but distorts and impoverishes it by debasing the Theory of Polarity into a mere conflict between Good and Evil.

Pagan, polytheistic religions have always accepted both the Theory of Levels and the Theory of Polarity, without distorting either to fit an inadequate concept (or even denial) of the other. One has only to study the pantheons of Egypt, Greece, Rome and India, with their creator-destroyer Gods and Goddesses, their eternal cycles of becoming and ceasing and re-becoming, their dialectical interplay, to realize how richly these attitudes have been symbolized.

Wiccan philosophy is in this direct tradition.

Every religion is unique, even when it is part of a wider inheritance. Wicca, like every other religion, has its own forms, its own preoccupations, its own atmosphere. And it is a Craft as well; to adopt Margaret Murray's categories, it embraces both Ritual Witchcraft and Operative Witchcraft.

Wicca includes ritual, spell-working, clairvoyance, divination; it is deeply involved in questions of ethics, reincarnation, sex, the relationship with Nature, psychology and attitudes to other religions and occult paths.

In the following Sections, we shall examine these aspects and see how they relate to Wicca's basic rationale.

XII   Reincarnation

Almost all witches believe in reincarnation.[1] It is probably true to say that they share this belief with a majority of the human race (or of those members of it who believe in survival after death in whatever form), because the concept of a single life followed by a one-off, heaven-or-hell judgement is peculiar to the patriarchal monotheist religions of Judaism, Christianity and Islam – though the Jewish belief is perhaps more shadowy than the other two, and reincarnation is certainly implicit in Hebrew Cabalistic thinking.

Belief in reincarnation was widespread among early Christians, and was general among the Gnostics. St Jerome (AD 340-420) says that a form of it was taught to a select few in the early Church.[2] But it was declared anathema by the Second Council of Constantinople in 553, for obvious reasons. The Church had become a State disciplinary machine, with its structure inseparable from that of the Imperial civil service; and the promise of heaven or the threat of hell, as a reward or punishment for behaviour in this immediate life, was therefore an essential Establishment weapon. Gnostic versions of the teachings of Jesus (some of them probably with as much claim to authenticity as the official Gospels) had to be banned, hunted down and destroyed for the same reasons; they saw salvation in terms of individual enlightenment, whereas the official Church saw it in terms of obedience to the bishop.

The theory of reincarnation holds, briefly, that each individual human soul or essence is reborn again and again, in a series of bodily incarnations on this earth, learning its lessons and facing the consequences of its actions, until it is sufficiently advanced to progress to the next stage (whatever that may be). The actual working out of the theory is closely bound up with the Theory of Levels, since it involves the stratification of the human entity into its component planes, which correspond to those of the Cosmos as a whole.

These planes are interpreted in various ways, according to the school of occult thought being followed. But the table of them given on page 117 can be taken as a generally accepted standard. The numbering and definitions are those used by Dion Fortune in *The Esoteric Philosophy of Love and Marriage*, pp. 17-19, and *The Cosmic Doctrine*, p.96. She does not list the Etheric as a separate plane, but this is purely a matter of nomenclature; many other writers (and even Dion Fortune herself elsewhere) often speak of the Etheric Plane, and it is reasonable to do so, because it is of great practical importance in psychic working. It is, for example, the substance of the innermost band of the human aura as seen by sensitives, and there is reason to believe that it is responsible for the phenomena recorded by Kirlian photography.

The seven (or eight, if we include the Etheric) levels or 'bodies' of a human entity are divided into two groups, generally called the Individuality and the Personality. The Individuality (Upper Spiritual,[3] Lower Spiritual and Upper Mental) is the immortal part, which survives from incarnation to incarnation. The Personality (Lower Mental, Upper Astral, Lower Astral, Etheric and Physical) is the transient part, built up during a single incarnation and discarded when it ends.

The Individuality is bisexual – which does not mean sexless but signifies that it contains the creative male and female essences, in dynamic balance. The Personality, on the other hand, is either male or female; each of us has to experience both male and female incarnations, learning the lessons of each polarity, so that the dynamic balance of the Individuality may become fully developed.

The concept is perfectly expressed by the Chinese *Yin-Yang* symbol. (See Figure 6.) The white part represents the male, positive, light, fertilizing *Yang* aspect and can be taken as a symbol of the Personality in a male incarnation; it will be noted that it contains the seed (the black spot) of its complementary opposite, the *Yin* aspect. The black part represents the female, receptive, dark, formative *Yin* aspect and can be taken as a symbol of the Personality in a female incarnation; it

THE COMPONENT LEVELS OF A HUMAN BEING		
Seventh Plane UPPER SPIRITUAL Pure or Abstract Spirit. The 'Divine Spark'. Substance and energy direct from the Great Unmanifest. Astrological symbol: the Sun.	THE INDIVIDUALITY	The Unit of Evolution. Immortal throughout all incarnations.
Sixth Plane LOWER SPIRITUAL Concrete Spirit. Tendency for one of the 'Seven Rays' to predominate and set keynote. Astrological symbol: Jupiter.		
Fifth Plane UPPER MENTAL Abstract Mind. Qualities differentiated into Types. Astrological symbol: Mercury.		
Fourth Plane LOWER MENTAL Concrete Mind. Definiteness, form, memory. Astrological symbol: Saturn.	THE PERSONALITY	The Unit of Incarnation. Lasts for one incarnation only; each incarnation builds up a fresh Personality.
Third Plane UPPER ASTRAL Abstract Emotions. Attraction, desire for union. Astrological symbol: Venus.		
Second Plane LOWER ASTRAL Instincts and Passions. Desire to attract or possess. Astrological symbol: Mars.		
ETHERIC – The tenuous energy-web of near-matter which links the Physical with the subtler planes and maintains it in being. Astrological symbol: the Moon.		
First Plane PHYSICAL Dense matter, the material body. Astrological symbol: the Earth.		

Fig. 6

will be noticed that it, too, contains the seed (the white spot) of its complementary opposite, the *Yang* aspect. The complete *Yin-Yang* symbol represents the immortal Individuality, with both aspects in perfect balance.

Another symbol which represent the process in its serial sense is the Wiccan High Priestess's amber-and-jet 'necklace which is the circle of rebirth' – the amber (solar) beads representing male incarnations, and the jet (lunar) ones female incarnations. (Though such lives do not necessarily alternate.)

However, the 'male-positive, female-negative' formulation is over-simplified – and here again, the levels come into it. The male tends to be positive on the physical and mental planes, and negative on the astral and spiritual; while the female tends to be positive on the astral and spiritual planes, and negative on the physical and mental. Or perhaps it would be better to say 'active-fertilizing' instead of 'positive', and 'receptive-formative' instead of 'negative', in each case. This cross-over pattern of functions between male and female is one of the meanings of the caduceus symbol of snakes intertwined about an upright staff (see Figure 7); it is interesting that it is the badge of Hermes/Mercury, the most bisexual of the Classical gods, whose astrological sign ☿ is itself a combination of male and female symbols.[4]

A familiar example of this change-over of polarity with the different planes is that of the woman-Muse and the man-artist. Beatrice fertilizes Dante, and Dante gives birth to the result; an exact parallel to the impregnation of a man by a woman on the physical plane.[5] As Wilfred says in Dion Fortune's *The Sea Priestess*: 'Then I saw why there must be priestesses as well as priests; for there is a dynamism in a woman that fecundates the emotional nature of a man as surely as he fecundates her physical body; this was a thing forgotten by modern civilisation which stereotypes and conventionalises all things and forgets the Moon, Our Lady of Flux and Reflux.'

But to return to what may be called the mechanics of reincarnation. On physical death, the first of the 'outer shells' is shed: the physical

Fig. 7

body. The etheric body disintegrates, breaking the vital link between the physical body and the astral, mental and spiritual bodies. Cut off from the mains, so to speak, the physical body is no longer a part of the total entity and begins to decay.

The focus of consciousness becomes, in the first place, the astral body. For the time being, one is in a continuous state equivalent to astral projection.

The rate of withdrawal up the planes depends on the person. Some (particularly those with the grosser obsessions, such as alcoholism or an unhealthy sexual libido) resist the process, either taking a long time to understand that they are physically dead, or refusing to come to terms with it; this is the explanation of many 'hauntings' or sensations of psychic vampirism felt by the still-incarnated. Effective exorcism, by a skilled sensitive who knows what he or she is doing, is often a matter of confronting the astral entity and persuading it of the necessity of normal withdrawal. A typical case was recounted to us by our friend the Rev. Christopher Neil-Smith, one of the best exorcists in England; he was called in by a family who could not keep *au pair* girls, because they were all terrified by the bedroom (on the face of it, very pleasant) which they were given. Christopher contacted the cause – a lesbian ghost! He disputed with her, using his own Christian words of power, and persuaded her of the error of her astral molestations. The trouble ceased thereafter.

(On this question of words of power: their effectiveness depends on their reality and significance to the exorcist, and of course to the astral entity. In this case, the Christian ones were obviously the effective ones; a witch, a Hindu or a Jew might use different ones with equal effect – though the beliefs of the 'ghost' are significant too. One is reminded of the story of the vampire challenged with a crucifix, who retorted: 'Oy, oy, oy – have you got the wrong vampire!' – which is not such a joke as it sounds.)

At the other end of the scale, well-integrated and advanced souls may of their own choice delay complete withdrawal in order to help still-incarnated friends. We believe, on good evidence, that Stewart's parents are such a case. His father died physically in 1953, and his mother in 1958; and Stewart and Janet did not meet until 1970. Yet on several key occasions in recent years, Stewart's mother, with his father in the background, seems to have got in touch with us using Janet as a medium, communicating by automatic writing and in other ways, including some startling 'meaningful coincidences', and making use of utterly characteristic phraseology, references and concepts of which Janet could not possibly have known. Leaning over backwards to be sceptical, one might admit unconscious telepathy between Stewart and Janet as an explanation; but in all the circumstances, we can only find direct communication from Agnes Farrar believable.

The intermediate stage between detachment from the physical plane and complete withdrawal of the Individuality seems to be a period of varying duration in what are generally called the Summerlands. The Summerlands have a real existence on the astral plane, and yet are to a certain extent self-created, whether on an individual or a group basis. In other words, the kind of Summerland in which you find yourself, and the company you meet there, depends on your own stage of development and on the strength of your links with the other entities concerned. Parts of the Personality of your last incarnation, on the astral and lower mental levels, are obviously still involved. In general, it seems to be a period of necessary rest and recuperation, and of the absorption (and discussion with friends?) of the lessons of the incarnation just experienced.

In due course, you withdraw from the Summerlands too; all that is left is your Individuality, your immortal self, existing on a level of consciousness about which we, at least, are not prepared to be dogmatic, because its nature can hardly be grasped except perhaps in flashes of intuition, or described in the language of the level on which we find ourselves at the moment. But it can be said that it, too, is a period of absorption of experience, at the fundamental level of the Individual; and perhaps, in proportion to one's degree of development, of consideration and choice of the circumstances of one's coming reincarnation.

As the time for that reincarnation approaches, the Individual starts to gather around itself the raw materials of the 'outer shells' required for a new Personality. They can only be the raw materials, because a fully developed Personality is the gradual creation of the circumstances of the new incarnation, and of one's reaction to it.

The final step is physical reincarnation, when the entity (Individuality plus raw materials of the new Personality) ensouls a foetus at the moment of conception. On the implications of that for the parents, more will be said in Section XV, 'Witchcraft and Sex'.

What does the Individuality accumulate from incarnation to incarnation, apart from 'experience'? It accumulates *karma*. This Hindu term has become the accepted Western word for the concept, because no exact equivalent exists in the European languages. Its original literal meaning is merely 'action', or 'cause-and-effect'.

The simplest way to look at karma is as a kind of spiritual bank-balance of one's good and evil deeds, and of the results of one's wisdom and stupidity, over the totality of one's lives. But to get a clear picture of its meaning, one should not think so much of 'someone up there' totting up the balance and rewarding or punishing us accordingly, as of the root meaning *cause-and-effect*. The concept is that everything we do sets up a chain reaction of effects, as inevitably as a pebble dropped in a pool causes ripples, and that we have to live with the results. A ripple (or tidal wave) which we cause may not bounce back at us till many lives later – but bounce back it will, by the nature of the totally interconnected structure of our universe. This interconnection compels us, sooner or later, to restore equilibrium which we have disturbed, to harvest the crops we have sown (including the good ones), to pay the debts we have incurred and to draw the interest on our wise investments. Creative activity or moral embezzlement alike come home to roost. To return to the bank-balance analogy – the karmic bank's computer is foolproof, inexorable and equipped with infinite memory.

The process of repeated reincarnation, therefore, is one of working out the karmic balance until a permanently healthy equilibrium is achieved. (A *dynamic* equilibrium, not a static one, be it noted.)

The immortal Individual, freed by its own efforts from the need for further incarnations on this plane, can then move on to the next stage. The nature of that stage we can only envisage dimly, at our present level of development; if we could grasp its essence and its detail, we should not still be here.

And yet there is an exception to that rule, too: the *bodhisattva*. This is another Hindu word which has entered into Western usage in the absence of a European equivalent. A bodhisattva is a perfected Individuality which no longer needs to reincarnate but chooses to do so of its own free will in order to help and guide less-developed mortals. One may reasonably infer, for example, that Jesus[6] and the Buddha were bodhisattvas; and human nature being what it is, the impact of such entities on the people of their time often led to their deification in later memory. It may well be, for instance, that such God-figures as Isis, Osiris, Zeus, Athene, Dana and Brid were built on the revered memory of human bodhisattvas. The goddess Aradia, inherited by Wicca from Tuscan tradition, seems to us to bear the hallmarks of such a development, and perhaps more clearly than most; the legend describes her as bringing to humans the teachings 'of my mother Diana'; she represents herself as the channel of divine wisdom, not its source, and this would be typical of a bodhisattva. So if we are right, not even witches are immune from the tendency to turn a dimly remembered outstanding teacher into a God or a Goddess. (Not that that should deter anyone from continuing to use Aradia as a Goddess-name if, like ourselves, they are already doing so. The thought-form has been powerfully built up over the generations, so that Aradia has become an effective call-sign for, and channel to, the Goddess Herself. Which is basically what all God-forms and Goddess-forms are; but more on that in Section XIV, 'Myth, Ritual and Symbolism'.)

Not all bodhisattvas have had such a remembered impact as these great figures, of course. It depends on the nature and scale of the task they have incarnated to perform. Many of them will work unobtrusively, deliberately not letting themselves be recognized as anything more than remarkable human beings; and that, of course, is what they are. The divinity which shines through them does not mean a shedding of humanity, but its perfection.

And in reaching forward towards that goal, the steady working out of karma is the conscious task of all initiates, including those whose path is Wicca. This task, and not mere curiosity, is the purpose of deliberate efforts at incarnation recall, which we shall be dealing with in a minute. Once one reaches a certain stage of conscious development, the wider view one has of the meaning of one's own karma, and of the factors which have created it over a series of lives, the more intelligently one can take control of the way ahead.

There are magical techniques for speeding up karma (or, come to that, for slowing it down) but these are not lightly taught until initiates are ready for them. Well-meaning initiates who plunge enthusiastically into such techniques, in the hope of developing themselves as rapidly as possible, all too often find they have bitten off more than they can chew; the pace of events can run ahead of their understanding, leaving them in a worse state than when they started. The mere fact of genuine initiation, or of occult involvement of any kind, including witchcraft, tends to speed up karma in any case, because of the sleeping levels that are being awakened; and that is as much as most of us can cope with.

One more point should be made on karma, before we go on to the question of group reincarnation phenomena. We have spoken of karma as an almost impersonal process, set in train by the inexorable laws of cause and effect. And that *is* its basic principle of action. But that does not mean there is no intervention or that what are sometimes called 'the Lords of Karma' are mere observers. Higher entities of many kinds do exist and function on the non-material planes, intermediate between humankind and the ultimate creative force, as every religion has recognized. We are only a part of a complex, many-levelled, interdependent Cosmos. And these higher entities have their own roles to play in the evolving life of the whole. So it would be arrogant to imagine that their actions do not affect us, or that they never intervene or steer us in a required direction. What is more, they can be appealed to by the self-attuning process known as invocation.

They can be compared, if you like, with farmers. A good farmer does not ignore or try to sabotage the laws of nature; he works with them for maximum yield and a balanced ecology. In the same way, the Lords of Karma do not override the laws of cause and effect; but they can and do, if we are willing, help us not to fall foul of them. They can help us to make use of natural processes instead of battling against them to our own and other people's hurt. Co-operate with them deliberately, try to put ourselves in tune with their purpose, and we will sometimes find ourselves pushed in directions the immediate significance of which we cannot grasp. In our own professional jargon, we sometimes call this 'the Script'; and for us personally, as for many other people, 'the Script' can move in mysterious ways which turn out in the end to be purposeful.

To sum up: the working out of karma, like farming, is a combination of inexorable natural processes, and the intelligent manipulation of those processes by purposeful beings who are aware of the overall programme.

(If you choose to call these entities angels and archangels and so on, why not? Whether you find the words acceptable depends on how loaded with associations they are from your own upbringing. If those associations raise your hackles, use other words. When you get down to it, the concepts are the same. But there is no point in scratching old sores just for the fun of it.)

As soon as one starts investigating reincarnation, and having one's first experiences of recall, one comes up against the phenomenon of group reincarnation; one discovers that one has met, and interacted with, certain people before, in other lives, perhaps in many lives. This knowledge may range from a sudden (and maybe mutual) flash of recognition when meeting a complete stranger (the flash often having positive or negative emotional overtones that seem quite disproportionate in terms of your this-life situation), to the realization that a relationship in this life is merely the continuation, development and working-out of a many-life relationship, maybe involving several people. The cautious researcher into his own history (and one *should* be cautious in such matters) is likely to tell himself that such a flash or realization is probably wishful thinking, the projection of unresolved emotions, or facile rationalization of puzzling elements in a present relationship. He may well be right, in any particular case; every occultist knows how temptingly easy it is to dodge the hard work of analysing a personal situation by shrugging the shoulders and saying 'it's probably karmic'! But however hard he leans over backwards to avoid such pitfalls, as his past-incarnations picture builds up and is confirmed by external evidence, or by the independently noted recall of others, he will find it more and more impossible to escape the fact that certain people he knows today *have* been associated with him in past lives.

And when you think of it, such continuing relationships are logically to be expected, on several grounds.

The most obvious is the karmic one. The karmic debts one owes, or is owed, must sooner or later be *individually paid by the debtor to the creditor*, if that equilibrium towards which all karmic imbalance strives is to be achieved; they cannot be dodged by physical death.[7] If in one life, for example, I have warped your development by my own selfishness, the balance will not be restored until I have positively (either in spite of myself or by my own improved understanding) contributed to conditions for your natural development in a later life. Such debts, of course, may be more complex than a straight 'one-to-one': A, B and C may have created a distorted situation between them in one life which can only be straightened by A, B and C meeting again in the new circumstances of a later life. Or A, B, C, D and E ...

The factors tending to such re-meetings are not always negative ones, of course. Creative teamwork for which one life was not enough naturally gives rise to a *positive* karmic impulse, an urge (both within each of the developing Individualities involved and in wider karmic energy-fields) for the team to re-combine and carry forward what was fruitfully begun.

Such positive and negative 'loose ends' all tend to draw people together in life after life, as naturally as gravity draws separate tributaries through or round all geological obstacles, to seek out a particular valley floor and combine in a river which is not quite like any other river, even though it flows ultimately to the same ocean (of karmic equilibrium, to pursue the metaphor to its end).

Experience and logic both confirm that the *nature* of a relationship may change from life to life; in fact it is to be expected, for imbalances to be resolved or for dynamic development. A and B may be brother and sister in one life, and re-meet in later lives as mother and son, husband and wife, colleagues, rivals, lovers, casual acquaintances or sister and brother the other way round.

Nor need the importance of the relationship be the same (or even arise at all) in any particular subsequent life. That depends on the nature of the lessons to be learned, or the balances to be worked out, in a particular life.

To take a personal example. Janet and Stewart know that they have met in many lives; but two have been especially vividly (and with much confirmation) recalled in this life, presumably because of their relevance to it. The first was in Egypt about the time of Rameses II, and the second in Segovia about the time of Ferdinand and Isabella. In both incarnations, we were associated with people whom we know or have known in our present incarnation. And yet (so far as we have established up to now) only one of those people was involved in both incarnations, the Egyptian and the Spanish; and even that person was known only to Stewart in Egypt, having been born after Janet's Egyptian death, though in Spain he was involved with both of us. The implication, which tallies with what we know of those two lives, is that they involved different lessons and different problems, which would only be relevant to certain of our 'fellow-travellers' in each case.

This, of course, would explain the phenomenon of intense but passing recognition of a stranger. He or she may have been deeply involved in the central 'agenda' of some past incarnation, but in this life you may be working out quite separate agendas, and therefore be irrelevant to each other at the present stage. But the sudden recall of a now-irrelevant emotion (even though, in most cases, it would only be subconsciously remembered) can be sharp and puzzling at the time.

Sudden if unconscious recall of this kind may not always be irrelevant to this life; it may be the start of an important re-meeting. Genuine cases of 'love at first sight' are often to be explained in this way – being, in fact, not 'at first sight' at all, even though the couple think it is.

Which brings us to one of the most powerful of life-after-life reunion drives: love which truly involves the interaction of two immortal Individualities, and not merely of their Personalities in any one incarnation (happy enough though such Personality-love may often be). It is this kind of love which is implied by the term 'soul-mates'. Perhaps 'binary stars' would be an even apter description; two unique entities, each with its own nature, which have formed a complementary whole by revolving in close orbit around a common centre of gravity, in no way isolating themselves from their neighbouring stars – indeed, often affecting them more powerfully than they would as two lone stars, because of the energy generated by their tight, and therefore rapid, mutual orbiting.[8]

Dion Fortune writes in depth on soul-mates (or, as she calls them, 'twin souls') in *The Esoteric Philosophy of Love and Marriage*, Chapters XVII and XVIII.

As she says (*ibid.*, p. 83), it is 'unexhausted emotion which forms the Karmic Tie'; and such ties can be set up on many levels less intense and all-embracing than that which exists between soul-mates. Any love or friendship of which something still remains at the time of physical death leaves a bond, of varying strength, tending to draw people together in later lives so that the emotion may be either 'exhausted' or developed. As the witches' Legend of the Descent of the Goddess (*Eight Sabbats for Witches*, pp. 172-3) puts it: 'To fulfil love, you must return again at the same time and at the same place as the loved ones; and you must meet, and know, and remember, and love them again.' The witches' attitude in this case is a deliberate one; they work to 'know and remember', not merely to react to unconscious memory.

It should be added that *any* unexhausted emotion sets up a karmic tie – and that includes hatred. This, too, can be treated deliberately; just as one can work to perpetuate a bond of love or friendship, so one can (and indeed would be well advised to) work to resolve a hatred-bond, rather than have it crop up again as unfinished business in a later life.

What are the mechanics of the drawing-together of people who have been associated with each other in past lives? After all, one may accept the principle but still find it hard to swallow that 'unexhausted emotion' should arrange a series of apparent coincidences of residence, employment, chance encounters and so on, which bring about such reunions in practice. For example, we took the conscious decision to move from London to Ireland in 1976 for what seemed to us a purely economic reason – that the Republic does not tax writers. And yet on the one hand it was a profound turning-point in our Wiccan development and our work, and on the other it brought us into intimate contact with several people of whose crucial involvement in our past lives we have no doubt whatever. And of all this, as mere tax-refugees, we had not the slightest precognition. Did the Lords of Karma book our boat-tickets? As we have said, they may nudge us in the required direction when necessary; but there would surely be little karmic progress achieved by turning us into mere puppets.

We would suggest that the explanation of most such 'coincidences' is far more natural. Namely, that closely involved souls communicate and call to each other at Individuality level in ways of which their Personalities are quite unaware. At soul-mate level this would be particularly intense, amounting to continuous dialogue; but it could also be expected between all 'fellow-travellers' in varying degrees. So a totally unconscious decision (as far as the Personality is concerned) could prompt one to buy the necessary boat-ticket, or bring about the necessary meeting, through a message from the Individuality to the Personality, which then takes action for what seem to the conscious mind to be quite different practical or temperamental reasons.

One thing that puzzles many people about reincarnation is the population explosion. If reincarnation is a fact, they argue, surely the number of humans incarnated on the Earth at different periods should remain relatively static?

There seems to us to be several possible answers to this. The first is the simple one that, for reasons known only to the Cosmic Planner (however you define It, Him or Her), new souls are being created all the time, and at present faster than ever. Most sensitive people know the feeling that so-and-so is a 'young soul' or an 'old soul', regardless of his or her chronological age in this incarnation; and this feeling may well be a valid one.

But it may not be as simple as plain 'creation'. The essence of consciousness is individualization. Non-human animals in general (again perhaps excluding cetaceans − see note XI,1, p. 307) are not self-conscious; they are only dimly aware, if at all, of their own separate individuality. Psychically, each of them is part of a group soul.[9] One theory (which makes sense − after all, it is difficult to believe in an individually reincarnating gnat, lemming or herring) is that on physical death the non-physical elements in an animal are reabsorbed into the group soul of the species, which 'buds off' new individuals from the common pool for physical manifestation. Only in some of the higher mammals, the theory suggests, do some individuals (with a small 'i') develop a sufficiently strong 'separateness' (the first step towards Individuality with a capital 'I') to persist as such into a later incarnation; and this is said to happen in particular among species which are closely associated with human beings.

Now it is only comparatively recently, in evolutionary terms, that mankind has emerged from a stage where group-awareness dominated life, and self-awareness (except in outstanding members of the tribe) was a very shadowy thing. One might reasonably deduce that at that stage, reincarnation also operated (again, with outstanding exceptions) on the group-soul principle, differentiating at first, as man's evolution progressed, into racial, tribe and clan souls, and only separating out into uniquely reincarnating Individuals gradually, with the increasing development of the conscious mind and personal self-awareness.[10]

On this basis, the sheer number of souls 'queueing up' for individual reincarnation would have increased greatly in recent millennia, and meteorically in the last century or two. And today, when even primitive peoples are being forced (for good or ill) into regular contact with the highly self-aware 'advanced' cultures, the number of Individuals (with a capital 'I', though at various levels of development) must be unprecedented.

Also, of course, we are at a period of very rapid cultural and psychic evolution; everything is accelerating. One decade sees more changes, in almost every sphere, than a century in our grandparents' time, or a thousand years in neolithic times. Life is an interconnected whole, on all the levels; so is it not likely that this same acceleration, this same compressing of the time-scale, should apply to karma, too, and to the frequency of reincarnation? We are an integral part of Gaia, the Earth Organism, on her spiritual, mental, astral, etheric and physical planes of being; and if some of her rhythms are speeding up, we too are effected on all the levels. Especially as we ourselves are largely responsible for the changes and are at last beginning to worry about their outcome. So may not an increased sense of urgency, a compulsion to be 'back on the job', be influencing Individuals who once took their time between incarnations?

The population explosion, of course, has been a world issue for some time now. Responsible thinkers in many lands have been pointing out the ecologically, economically and politically calamitous situation into which it threatens to plunge our planet if it is not checked as a matter of urgency. Some nations are taking practical steps to encourage rational birth control programmes. The biggest single obstacle to such sane policies is unfortunately the Vatican, whose condemnation of contraception seems to us (and indeed to millions of Catholics) to be socially and theologically insupportable, even on Christian grounds; but more about that in Section XV, 'Witchcraft and Sex'.

It may well be that the human race as a whole, by its irresponsible and head-in-the-sand indifference to the population problem, is actually warping the natural rhythm of reincarnation – to put it bluntly, recalling souls to incarnation faster, and in greater numbers, than Mother Earth can care for them or their healthy karmic progress requires. If so, we are adding dangerously to our negative racial karma; and Mother Earth has drastic ways of saying 'Enough!' when such problems get out of hand.

Many of these foregoing ideas are no more than theory and would not necessarily be accepted by everyone who believes in reincarnation. But we hope they are provocative of thought.

How to set about recalling past lives?

Before we discuss techniques, we would like to point out three rules which are absolutely essential to serious work on incarnation recall:

1. Keep written (and where possible taped) records.
2. Keep an open mind, healthily sceptical and yet receptive (provisionally) to all incoming impressions.
3. Check everything possible against known fact (e.g. parish records, history books, period costume, details of everyday life of the supposed time, and so on – particularly on things you could not have known at the time when your impression was recorded).

As Christine Hartley points out (*A Case for Reincarnation*, p.80): 'Make no mistake about it, even if you have the gift for reading the records there are dangers on the path – the danger of wishful thinking is probably the most pronounced; one is so anxious to "see" that one can easily be led into flights of imagination uncontrolled by critical reasoning and discrimination. Since a degree of imagination carefully controlled is necessary on all occasions to lift one's mind from the rooted base in the material world, it is highly important that there should be great discipline in all experiments that the results may be relied upon.'

To consider Rule 1. Whenever you think you may have had a recall experience, write it down (or dictate it onto tape) immediately, *before* discussing it with anyone else and *before* applying Rule 3. Keep the written record and/or the tape; even if you have transcribed a taped impression onto paper, keep the original tape as well, because hesitations, tone of voice and so on may turn out to have significance unrealized at the time. Include sketches, maps, plans or rooms and so on if you can. Keep all these records permanently – do not weed out what seems irrelevant at any stage, because later developments (sometimes years later) may throw new light on it. Taped records are invaluable when it comes to recall under hypnosis or trance; cassette recorders are very cheap these days and are the greatest gift of modern technology to reincarnation (and many other fields of psychic) research.

Rule 2 is the key to the whole approach. Christine Hartley is right: imagination is essential to the process, but uncontrolled imagination can sabotage it. Scepticism must not inhibit imagination at the time, but afterwards it must check dispassionately on what imagination has produced. This is particularly true of spontaneous bits of recall which may or may not be mere daydreams: the trick is to let them flow without censorship, record them, *then* think about them critically, *but* keep the record with an open mind and see if later knowledge confirms or demolishes it.[11] (And even if it seems demolished, do not throw it away; it may still one day have something to teach you.)

Rule 3 is straight detective work. If a name and a place and a date can be tied up with the Registrar-General's records, or a detail of agricultural practice in eighteenth-century East Anglia seems wrong to you but is confirmed in due course by an expert on the subject, you have strong evidence of genuine recall.

Another, less concrete but equally encouraging, form of confirmation is the impression-records kept by friends who may have been involved in the same incarnation. Here again, written records, made before discussion, prove their worth, because they greatly reduce the danger of wishful thinking or unconscious 'alteration to fit'. (Though with friends so likely to be psychically in tune with each other, always bear in mind the possibility of involuntary telepathy. This can usually be diagnosed, or ruled out, by examining the 'feel' of the records, by seeing if the common material is viewed from convincingly personal viewpoints instead of one 'parroting' the other, and by seeing if each contains its own material so that they overlap instead of merely coinciding.)

One of the most unexpected pieces of confirmation in our own experience came from a five-year-old boy, when we met him and his parents for the first time since he was newborn. He looked at Janet and said at once: 'I know you.' Janet replied: 'I saw you when you were a little baby,' but he interrupted impatiently: 'Oh, not *then* – I mean the *other* time – when you used to have those clicky things in your hands' (imitating castanets). 'But your hair ought to be black ... Where's the other man?' 'What other man?' He brushed it aside and went on: 'You were my Mummy. But you weren't Daddy's wife, you were his friend.' Everything he came out with – quite spontaneously, Janet deliberately avoiding prompting – tallied with what we already believed we knew of Janet's incarnation as a courtesan in Segovia around 1500; it also identified one of her 'missing' children. He seemed to take it all quite naturally and went on to talk of other things as though he had already forgotten it; but he stayed very close to Janet until it was time for the family to go. There was no way that he, or even his parents, could have known anything about Janet's conviction that she had had a Segovian incarnation.

The most startlingly impressive material on reincarnation has been obtained by hypnotic regression. In many cases, professional psychiatrists have stumbled upon the phenomenon quite by accident and have then gone on to study it systematically. Regressing a patient under hypnosis, to relive childhood experiences and unearth traumas which can then be appropriately dealt with, is a normal psychiatric

REINCARNATION 131

technique. But many psychiatrists, in regressing patients to an earlier
and earlier stage, have been astonished to find the patients going back
not merely to birth or to uterine impressions but apparently to the
recall of earlier lives. And many of these doctors, examining the
unexpected data with a healthy professional scepticism, have probed
further, finally becoming convinced themselves.

Arthur Guirdham's book *The Cathars and Reincarnation*, Joan
Grant and Denys Kelsey's *Many Lifetimes* and Dr Edith Fiore's *You
Have Been Here Before* are all fascinating descriptions of this process
of professional discovery. The collaboration of Grant and Kelsey has
been particularly fruitful. She was gifted with apparently total recall of
past lives, which she put into book form in such novels (or
autobiographies) as *Winged Pharaoh* and *Life as Carola*; he was a
psychiatrist who happened upon evidence of reincarnation in the way
we have described. They began working together in 1958, and in due
course were married. *Many Lifetimes* is a classic in the field.[12]

Another interesting book on the subject is *Encounters with the Past*,
by Peter Moss with Joe Keeton; it includes two discs recorded during
actual regression sessions. *More Lives than One*, by Jeffrey Iverson,
describes the famous Bloxham Tapes, recorded over two decades of
work by hypnotherapist Arnall Bloxham.

The case which has attracted the most publicity (although many
others are even more convincing) is described in Morey Bernstein's *The
Search for Bridey Murphy*.

Hypnotism, then, is perhaps the most powerful of all methods of
incarnation recall. The snag is that it can also be the most dangerous in
the hands of amateurs. Traumas can surface which the operator does
not have the knowledge or experience to deal with. Post-hypnotic
suggestions can be unwittingly planted which may have damaging
results. These and other risks are the reason why every professional
hypnotherapist we have spoken to strongly disapproves of stage or
television hypnotism; these professionals may often be called upon to
undo the harm which a stage hypnotist has done, and of which he was
doubtless quite unaware.

There is another danger, in the occult field – that of deliberate
manipulation. Janet's first recall of our joint Egyptian life was obtained
under hypnosis by a highly skilled occultist whom we (being then very
inexperienced) both trusted. We later realized that he was
unscrupulously 'black'. The recall was genuine enough, but he warped
the interpretation of it for his own purposes, and the trouble he caused
to both of us took a year or more to clear up. It taught us a bitter
lesson.

Hypnotism – particularly deep hypnosis – should only be used for
recall or any other purpose when the hypnotist is properly experienced,

preferably a professional (though Bloxham, for example, is a skilled amateur), and when his responsibility is beyond question.

A much safer method, which can be very fruitful, for amateur use is what may be called guided meditation. The guide takes an individual or group on a symbolic journey, down a staircase, through a door, onto a high plateau – any calm and conscious exercising of the imagination which stills the linear-logical (left-brain-function) control of the flow of thought and taps the intuitive (right-brain-function) mode of awareness. This may trigger off light, or even deep, trance; if that happens, the guide converses with the person in trance, but merely to elicit information and to reassure – not to implant ideas or suggestions. One of the essential qualities of an experienced High Priestess or High Priest is to know when and how to bring people out of trance gently, at the first sign of distress or exhaustion. (Janet is a trance medium, and Stewart had to learn very early how to watch over her and when to bring her out of it.)

An excellent form for guided meditation of this kind is known as the Christos Experience and is described in *Windows of the Mind* by G.M. Glaskin. We have used it many times, with interesting results, and have found it quite harmless. Similar techniques are described in Marcia Moore's *Hypersentience*.

As an added insurance, it is a good idea to conduct such experiments within a properly cast and strongly envisaged Circle. (See Section XIV for more thoughts on the protective function of the Circle.)

Dreams can be another source of incarnation information. But to make proper and reliable use of it, one should get in the habit of recording dreams – even if only onto tape – immediately on waking, and carefully adhering to Rules 1, 2 and 3 which we have already described. It is also useful to learn something of the basic mechanism of dreams; for example, to learn to distinguish what Freud calls the 'manifest content' (the obvious material of the dream, often drawn from events of the day before)[13] from the 'latent content' (what the dream is really trying to say). But on the understanding of dreams, as of many other things, for witches and occultists it is Carl Jung who towers head and shoulders above all other psychological teachers; and several of his school, such as Esther Harding (*Woman's Mysteries*) and Erich Neumann (*The Great Mother*), have followed nobly in his footsteps. The best introduction to Jungian thinking is *Man and His Symbols*, an anthology edited by Jung himself.

Once you develop the habit of recording dreams, they surface more readily into consciousness, and it is our experience that three kinds of dream soon emerge as being in a class of their own. First, the dream in which you are aware that you are dreaming. Most people know this kind, but few deliberately take charge of them and study them *while they are going on* – which can be a very revealing experiment.

Second, the dream in which you are astrally projecting. With increasing control, this becomes a special case of the first kind. More about it in Section XX.

And third, the incarnation-recall dream. With experience, you come to recognize the special quality of such a dream; but you still would be wise to apply your knowledge of dream-mechanism to its content. (Was such-and-such a person in the dream a genuine character from the past life? Or a personalized archetype? Or my own animus or anima? Or a screen for someone I don't want to recognize? ... and so on.) Even a genuine recall-dream may be contaminated by other elements.

Incarnation recall in dreams (apart from any telepathic dream-contact, on which again more in Section XX) is a solo process; and the highest development of deliberate solo recall is what Christine Hartley calls 'conscious mediumship'. She writes, 'The state is acquired by discipline, silence and perseverance. It is in some aspects the technique applied by various schools of deep meditation, only in this sense one is not retiring from the outward world but in one way reversing the process and going back into it.' She describes the technique in her book *A Case for Reincarnation*, page 85 onwards. And although in its operation it *is* a solo technique, she strongly advises (pp. 87-9) having a second person with you, 'preferably someone also familiar with the technique, though not necessarily a seer', at least 'until you are very fully aware of what you can or cannot or should not do'.

The most famous of all American clairvoyants, the late Edgar Cayce, used a rather different technique – self-imposed hypnotic sleep – to give psychic readings to more than six thousand people over forty-three years. He discovered the gift by accident in 1923, and it was a great shock to him as an orthodox fundamentalist Protestant, but it convinced him of the truth of reincarnation. His achievements are summarized in Hans Stefan Santesson's *Reincarnation*, p. 126 onwards, and described in depth in Noel Langley's *Edgar Cayce on Reincarnation*.

As one becomes more skilled at recall, one finds that one can not only remember one's own past lives; one can 'read the records' for other people as well. The bulk of Edgar Cayce's work was of this kind, and *Many Lifetimes* gives repeated examples of Joan Grant's use of the gift – often successfully called upon by herself and Kelsey in the diagnosis of patients' problems. Janet has this ability too, though it usually arises spontaneously; at the time of writing, she has not yet reached the stage where she can always exercise it at will.

For a compact guide to various methods of incarnation recall, J.H. Brennan's little book *Five Keys to Past Lives* is well worth reading –

though we think he under-emphasizes the dangers of amateur hypnosis. The past few pages may seem overloaded with book references; but the plain fact is that the various techniques of recall are too complex for a single chapter to do more than outline them. To make full use of them, you would be well advised either to find an experienced teacher or to read the specialized books. Or preferably both.

But however you proceed – never forget Rules 1, 2 and 3.

XIII   The Ethics of Witchcraft

'Eight words the Wiccan Rede fulfil: An it harm none, do what you will.'

Wicca is a joyous creed; it is also a socially and ecologically responsible one. Witches delight in the world and their involvement in it, on all the levels. They enjoy their own minds, their own psyches, their own bodies, their senses and their sensitivities; and they delight in relating, on all these planes, with their fellow-creatures (human, animal and vegetable) and with the Earth itself.

Wiccan ethics are positive, rather than prohibitive. The morality of witchcraft is far more concerned with 'blessed is he who' than with 'thou shalt not'.[1] The extremes of masochistic asceticism on the one hand, or of gross materialism on the other, seem to the witch to be two sides of the same coin, because both distort human wholeness by rejecting one or more of its levels. Witches believe in a joyful balance of all human functions.

This outlook is perfectly expressed in the Charge (see pp. 297-8): 'Let my worship be within the heart that rejoiceth; for behold, all acts of love and pleasure are my rituals. And therefore let there be beauty and strength, power and compassion, honour and humility, mirth and reverence within you.' It is worth setting these qualities out in their polarized pairs:

> beauty *and* strength
> power *and* compassion
> honour *and* humility
> mirth *and* reverence

– and meditating on them as a model for a balanced ethic, while remembering that each of the eight qualities is positive, not restrictive. Compassion means empathy, not condescension; humility means a realistic appraisal of your own stage of development, not self-abasement; reverence means a sense of wonder (that essentially Wiccan attribute), not just remembering to take your hat off in a church or put it on in a synagogue. And the witch is always conscious that compassion must be partnered by power, humility by honour, and reverence by mirth.

The Charge continues: 'And thou who thinkest to seek for me [the Goddess] know thy seeking and yearning shall avail thee not, unless thou knowest the mystery; that if that which thou seekest thou findest not within thee, then thou wilt never find it without thee. For behold, I have been with thee from the beginning; and I am that which is attained at the end of desire.'

This, too, is an ethical statement. To the witch, self-development and the full realization of one's unique yet many-aspected potential are a moral duty. That which helps evolution forward is good; that which thwarts it is evil; and each of us is a factor in the cosmic evolutionary process. So one owes it not merely to oneself but to the rest of mankind and the world to look inside oneself and to discover and release that potential.[2]

Evolution, in this sense, does not merely mean Darwinism (though Darwin certainly defined one of the ways, on one of the levels, in which cosmic evolution expresses itself). It is the continuing process by which the ultimate creative force of the universe manifests itself 'downwards' through the levels, with increasing complexity, and is itself enriched by the experience of that complexity. (In Cabalistic terms, the Kether-to-Malkuth-to-Kether cycle.) This is a very deep subject, deserving of a lifetime (or several lifetimes) of study; for a first approach to it we recommend Dion Fortune's book *The Cosmic Doctrine* and *The Mystical Qabala*.[3] But while many witches do study this deeper philosophy, most of them (and all of them most of the time) are more concerned with a literally down-to-Earth guide to their daily activity.

For this living relationship to the cosmic process, on a scale at which it can be readily seen to affect us, witches are dedicated to the concept of the Earth as a living organism. And this attitude – physical, mental, psychic and spiritual – is the heart and soul of the Old Religion.

Mother Earth is thought of as precisely that. She produces us, nourishes us, makes it possible for us to live (at all levels from the simply biological to the breathtakingly creative), rewards us when we understandingly love her, takes revenge when we abuse her, and reabsorbs our material component when we die. She reminds us that all living creatures are our siblings, different but related offspring of the same womb.

The Mother Earth concept can be envisaged in many ways, from the scientifically sophisticated theory of the Gaia Hypothesis[4] to the worship of her as Goddess. And indeed many witches see the Gaia Hypothesis as a further validation of their own immemorial Goddess approach. As we pointed out in Section XI, the intelligent advance-guard of modern science is coming closer and closer to many of the concepts which witches and occultists have always held; and witches watch this process with satisfaction and sympathy, if with an occasional ironic smile.

That God and Goddess concepts are emotionally and psychically necessary to mankind, and a justifiable approach to reality, will be argued in Section XIV, 'Myth, Ritual and Symbolism'. But accepting them for the moment (and few readers would have got this far if they did not), no one can deny that the Earth Mother is the Goddess concept which is most immediately vital to us, most easily understood and most determinative of the rhythm of our lives. She is the background and foreground to our very existence. Even that other great Goddess aspect which is symbolized by the Moon would be difficult to conceive of separately from the Earth Mother whom she orbits, whose tides she controls and whose creatures she affects in everything from menstruation of women to the growth of plants. The Moon Goddess is the Earth Mother's mysterious other self; any Goddess concept which lies outside the domain of that powerful sisterhood is far more subtle and abstract, and of less immediate concern to ordinary mortals.

How, then, do witches express their devotion to the Earth Mother, in ethical terms? The implications are obvious. The moral duty to the evolutionary process which we mentioned earlier is seen, by the witch, as a personal responsibility towards the natural rhythms and needs of the Earth as a living organism, and towards the needs, rhythms and evolutionary development of her constituent creatures. Those creatures – human, animal and vegetable – are the individual cells, the nervous system, the lungs, the sense organs of Mother Earth, just as the mineral kingdom is her living body-tissue and skeleton, the seas and rivers are her bloodstream, and her envelope of atmosphere is the air which she breathes as we do ourselves.

That is why environmental care and action play such an important part in the Wiccan ethic. That is why witches get angry – and active – when oxygen-creating trees are cut down faster than they are planted, when whales and seals are massacred for commercial profit, when chemical fertilizers and pesticides are used regardless of their ecological impact, when indifferent industries pollute the atmosphere and the rivers and seas with their waste products, and when the concrete jungle (often with more concern for commerce than for housing) spreads like a rash over the Earth's complexion.

(Fortunately, it is not only witches who have begun to realize that the rape of the planet is reaching a critical stage; a symptom of this public concern is that many countries now have a Ministry of the Environment. Their effectiveness may be inadequate to the problem, but the term itself would have been meaningless a generation ago.)

Just how the witches' environmental ethic is translated into action is sometimes a complex matter; there are few easy answers, and witches, like everyone else who takes the problem seriously, may come up with different ones. For example, some witches are vegetarians, while others feel that man as an omnivore is part of the balance of nature, and concentrate on humane methods of meat-production. Some witches regard the micro-chip revolution with horror, while others believe that properly handled it can mean de-urbanization, cheap and simple human communication, increased leisure, the elimination of meaningless jobs, and the shifting of man's effort to essentially human creativity. Some withdraw into self-sufficient communes, while others involve themselves deeply in the existing structure in the hope of transforming it. Some delve into the past for inspiration, while others fix their eyes determinedly on the future.

Now all these attitudes, while they may sometimes conflict with each other, may well contribute something constructive. But the point about them is that they are all motivated by the same ethic; love and respect for Mother Earth and all her creatures. Which is why, for example, urban and rural witches alike put a lot of thought and effort into the Eight Festivals, as a deliberate and sustained method of keeping themselves in tune with Mother Earth's natural cycle on a spiritual as well as a psychological level. They know that if the Festivals do not achieve that purpose, they are mere parties.

It is also one of the reasons why herbalism plays such an important part in Wiccan practice. Few witches would deny, or wish to belittle, the genuine achievements of modern medical science; in fact, many witches are themselves doctors or nurses. (Our English coven included three nurses, an operating theatre technician and a dental surgeon's wife.) But quite apart from tradition (witch-herbalists were the village healers when most 'physicians' were ignorant leeches), witches practise herbalism because its study puts them in direct contact with the Earth's natural flora, literally 'at grass roots'. There are few more comprehensive disciplines for observing and understanding one's natural environment than studying, hunting for and using herbs.

We have found, too, that many doctors accept and respect *well-informed* herbalists, providing they are not irresponsibly treating symptoms in ignorance of causes. When anyone comes to us for healing (whether herbal or psychic), our first question is always: 'Have you been to your doctor, and what is he doing?' If the patient has not gone to a doctor, through fear, prejudice or superstition, we urge him to do so at once. And if he has, we would want to know the doctor's treatment, to be sure that any help we gave would not conflict with it. This is a very delicate area, to be approached with wisdom; a witch should be the doctor's ally, not his rival. Most doctors are dedicated healers – and it is worth remembering that many of them, in addition to their acquired knowledge, have an inborn gift which is psychic in nature and which drew them to the profession in the first place; often it operates without their even being aware that they have it, except perhaps intuitively.

As for psychedelic, hallucinogenic and similar drugs – we do not take them ourselves, and we ban them absolutely from our covenstead. This ban includes cannabis, though we realize that differing views are sincerely held on the question of whether it should be legalized.

Drugs do, in a sense, expand consciousness – but in the same way as a non-swimmer jumping into the deep end gets wet and is also liable to drown. The expansion of consciousness is the central aim of psychic development, *but through step-by-step training and under the individual's full control*. Drugs are a highly dangerous short cut, giving you the illusion, if you are lucky, of having the levels under your command. (If you are unlucky, it may land you in anything from trauma to psychosis.) They are *not* under your command, and neither are the entities which inhabit them, to whose activities you are completely vulnerable in the drugged state. You are like an adolescent who plays with a ouija board for kicks – and, like the adolescent, you can frighten yourself silly in the process, or suffer actual harm.

It is true that in the past (and in some cultures still) shamanistic religions have used drugs for divinatory purposes. But that was by trained priests and priestesses, under rigid social and religious sanctions. Such sanctions no longer exist in our culture, nor are they likely ever to be workably re-established. It is true, too, that serious occultists today have experimented with psychedelic drugs under expert observation and in carefully controlled conditions; Lois Bourne in *Witch Amongst Us* (pp. 176-82) recounts such a controlled experiment with mescalin. But quite apart from the fact that such experiments are of necessity illegal, let us be honest and admit that not one in a thousand of the 'occult' enthusiasts who use these drugs does so in such a controlled way.

The fact must also be faced that, if you use these drugs, you are inevitably supporting the powerful crime networks which supply them. These networks (often with friends in high places) grow rich on the ruining of minds and bodies, including, on an ever larger scale, those of schoolchildren. Their activities interlock with every other form of criminal activity, from blackmail to civic corruption, and they are probably the most vicious and anti-social element in the community today. Some of them are actively interested in the occult scene, both as a market and to abuse its power for their own ends. Added to which, by the time their product reaches you, its purity is, to say the least, dubious.

Buy drugs and you maintain such people in being.

Even if you prepare your own hallucinogens, such as *Amanita muscaria*, you are running grave physical and psychological risks – and your psyche is still attempting a dangerous short cut, to give yourself the illusion of control over the levels.

Wise witches will leave drugs strictly alone, and achieve their expansion of consciousness the hard way – which in both the short and the long run is the only way.

It would be a waste of words, here, to reiterate the 'normal' basic ethical codes which are common to every decent Christian, Jew, Moslem, Hindu, Buddhist, pagan, atheist or what have you – the rules of respect for one's neighbour, of civic responsibility, of parental care, of truthfulness and honesty, of concern for the underprivileged, and so on. These are fundamental human standards which the vast majority acknowledge and try with varying success to live up to. It goes without saying that witches do the same.

What we are concerned with here are the rules of conduct which are special to witches, or on which they lay special emphasis, because of the nature of the philosophy and their activities.

Perhaps the most important of these special areas is magic.

If you deliberately set out to develop your psychic abilities you are awakening a faculty by which you can influence other people, with or without their knowledge; a faculty by which you can obtain information in ways that they do not expect or allow for; a faculty by which you can either enhance their life-energy or sap it. By which you can help them or harm them.

Obviously, you are taking a great responsibility on yourself and this responsibility calls for a set of willingly accepted rules. And these rules are all the more important because very often only you know if you are honestly obeying them.

The observance or non-observance of these rules is precisely what distinguishes 'white' from 'black' working.[5]

All these rules are summed up in the phrase: 'An it harm none.' A witch must never use his or her powers in a way which will cause harm to anyone – or even frighten anyone by claiming to. Another Wiccan rule says: 'Never boast, never threaten, never say you would wish ill of anyone.'

There are two situations in which, at first sight, it would seem that to observe the 'no harm' rule would mean to let a wrongdoer go unchecked, or to leave yourself undefended against attack. But there is an acceptable way of dealing with each of these problems.

If somebody is known to be acting evilly and harming others, witches are fully justified in stopping him. The method used is the magical operation known as 'binding', which is described in Section XXII (pp. 235-7). The very specific object of a binding spell is to render the evil actions powerless – not to harm or punish the wrongdoer; punishment can be safely left to the Lords of Karma. The spell is against the deed, not against the doer – and it works.

The second situation is that of defence against deliberate psychic attack. Most white witches or covens are familiar with this. Their activities may arouse the envy or resentment of black operators – particularly when they are called upon to rescue those operators' victims. It can also happen when a member has had to be banished from a white coven for good reasons, which is fortunately rare but sometimes inescapable; the banished witch is all too likely to express his resentment by lashing out psychically. And of course any efficient coven is quickly aware of such aggression on the astral plane.

A binding spell may be used here as well, of course; but sometimes one is conscious of astral attack without being certain of its source; or the source may be a group, the binding of which would be more complicated because effective binding depends on a clear visualization of the person being bound. The most direct and powerful means of defence, when you as an individual or a group are under attack, is to rely on 'the Boomerang Effect'. This is the principle, proved time and again, that psychic attack which comes up against a stronger defence rebounds threefold on the attacker. So your remedy is to set up strong psychic defences (see Section IX) while deliberately *not* counter-attacking yourself. You invoke the God and the Goddess, in the firm knowledge that they are more powerful than any evil which may be directed against you. The 'boomerang' thus returns to its sender, and if he suffers harm, it is entirely his own doing, not yours.

A sharp line must always be drawn between *influencing* other people and *manipulating* them. Healing, or the solving of the personal problems of someone who has asked you for help, is legitimate and indeed necessary influencing. Manipulation, in the sense of interfering with an individual's right of decision and choice, is not.

To make the distinction clearer, let us take the example of love-spells (which are popularly supposed to be a major part of a witch's stock-in-trade). To use magical means to compel A to fall in love with B, regardless of his or her natural inclinations, is wholly wrong, and if it succeeds, it is likely to be ultimately disastrous to both A and B. Such requests may be even more callous than that; one man rang us up out of the blue and offered to pay us to work magic to get a girl he fancied into bed with him 'just for one night'. He rang off angrily when we told him what to do with his money.

On the other hand, when Janet was a very new witch, she knew two people who she could see were strongly attracted to each other but both too inhibited to make a move. Janet watched the situation drag on, and finally (without saying anything to either of them) she worked a spell to overcome their shyness and to bring them together *if* they were right for each other. Next day the man asked the girl for a date. That was twelve years ago; they, plus three delightful children, are now busy living happily ever after.

That 'love-spell' was perfectly legitimate and helpful; not manipulation, but the removal of obstacles which were hindering a development which was natural in itself. And it contained the kind of rider which every principled witch includes in her spells if there is any doubt: 'if they are right for each other', 'provided no one is harmed', or whatever wording is appropriate. Such a rider as part of the wording of a spell (and spells, like divinatory questions, should always be precisely and unambiguously worded) becomes part of its intent, and therefore of its magical effect. But like the spell itself, you must really *mean* it – not just throw it in as a sop to your conscience; otherwise you may well encounter the Boomerang Effect yourself.

All these ethical standards of not harming anybody, and of relying on the Boomerang Effect instead of counter-attacking, may make it sound as though witches were unqualified pacifists. They are not. There are situations in 'ordinary' life when vigorous action is called for with any weapons available. If you come across an old lady being mugged, you do not preach to the mugger – you knock him out if you can. If bomber planes are attacking your city, you try to shoot them down before they can drop their bombs. If you are being raped, you use your knee with all the strength you can muster, without worrying about how long the rapist may spend in hospital.

Turning the other cheek is all very well – but even Jesus used force on one occasion, when he drove the money-changers out of the Temple with a scourge of cords. They asked for it, they got it, and they would have responded to nothing else.

Similar situations do arise in the magical sphere, when you have to act with no holds barred, and you may have to decide very quickly. But as in 'ordinary' life, a well-trained and conscientious witch knows he or she must take responsibility for the decision, and live with the consequences. To live with the consequences of *not* having acted, when action was called for, may be even more serious.

The Law says: 'Never accept money for the use of the art, for money ever smeareth the taker.' It is a universal principle among white witches that no payment may be taken for magical work. The acceptance of fees does 'smear' the taker; with the best will in the world, it encourages a subconscious tendency to 'put on an act' and to produce impressive results by a little quiet string-pulling; to call the customer in for more sessions than are strictly necessary; and before long to accept assignments that are not exactly black, just a little grey. And so on. More than one witch, or spiritualist medium come to that, has found his or her originally genuine powers waning after 'going professional', because both sincerity and judgement have become eroded.

It is generally accepted, however, that fees may be accepted for such things as Tarot readings. These are consultations, not operations, and depend on intuition rather than magic in the strict sense. The temptation to showmanship is slight, and easily resisted by any honest Tarot-reader. And charging a reasonable fee does cut down the number of merely curious visitors, who can become a serious and time-wasting burden once your reputation spreads. Janet has had to give up 'open door' Tarot readings for this very reason.

We know several good and incorruptible Tarot readers who do it for a modest living, and we have unhesitatingly recommended them. But we have never known a witch or magician who charged for magical working and who retained his or her integrity.

Professional craftsmen who cater for witches' and occultists' needs are of course another matter. We know and deal with several whole-time metalworkers, incense-makers, jewellers and so on in that category, and to one at least we keep saying that he charges too little for his lovely products. (And after all, we get paid for our books, though we hardly get rich on them!) Even within the coven, if some skilled enthusiast makes tools for other members for the love of it, we all insist on paying for his raw materials. The essential point is that none of these payments is for *magical* working.

In our view, it would be wrong for any craftsman to claim, and

144 THE WITCHES' WAY

charge for, an alleged magical element in his products, or to sell them as 'magically charged' or 'already consecrated'. It is a matter of opinion perhaps, but we feel strongly that consecration and charging are the responsibility of the user – or, at most, that witches who give tools to other witches as presents may give them an initial charge or consecration as a token of the love with which the gift is made. But consecration should never be for sale.

Incidentally, when we were initiated we were taught that one should never bargain over magical tools; one should pay the price asked or go elsewhere. Dion Fortune (*Moon Magic* p.67) has her reservations: 'There is an old saying that what is wanted for magical purposes must be bought without haggling, but there is a limit to that sort of thing.' Doreen Valiente feels even more strongly. She tells us: 'In various old grimoires also one finds this statement; but I believe it was invented by some clever dealer in magical accessories. We weren't taught anything about this point in Gerald's day, perhaps because he too thought that this supposed magical law was invented by those who had something to sell, and that students of the Art Magical had been falling for it ever since. However, if you were buying from a brother or sister of the Art, and you couldn't meet the price they asked, then I do think you shouldn't try to beat them down. But with dealers, the more power to your elbow when it comes to haggling, I say!' She adds that of course any object should be cleaned both physically and psychically before being put to magical use, and that this is 'more important than haggling or not haggling'.

Tailpiece to these thoughts on ethics: an American Indian prayer (Sioux, we are told) which appeals to us greatly and which we always try to bear in mind. 'O Great Spirit, let me not judge my neighbour till I have walked a mile in his moccasins.'

XIV   Myth, Ritual and Symbolism

Myth, rituals and symbols all play an essential part in Wiccan practice
– particularly in its religious aspect, though the Craft aspect (operative
witchcraft) also is concerned with the last two at least, since every spell
is in effect the ritual manipulation of symbols.

Every religion, of course, is deeply involved in all three, though with
various degrees of awareness. Some religions try to cram myth into the
straitjacket of factual history – such as those fundamentalist
Christians who insist that every word in the Bible is literally true, from
the Garden of Eden onwards. This approach not only seriously
devalues one of the richest anthologies of myth and symbolism that we
possess; it also lands theologians in some absurd red-herring
controversies. (Did Adam and Eve have navels? How did all the
animals get into the Ark? – and so on.) Some debase ritual into a rigid
pattern of orthodoxy which completely loses sight of its inner meaning,
while others react against this by minimizing ritual to a point where
meaning is also lost. Some have lost all sight of the psychological role of
symbols, merely categorizing them into 'ours' (and therefore holy) and
'theirs' (and therefore devilish), and failing to grasp that a symbol may

have different meanings in different contexts.

Every religion, of course, includes individuals who have a genuine understanding of myth, ritual and symbolism, and who are able to use them creatively within the framework of their own faith. But all too often, if they try to express this understanding to others, they are looked at askance as probable heretics by their co-religionists whose 'faith' is a rigid structure of conditioned reflexes.

Wicca, on the other hand, tries to achieve such an understanding deliberately and to develop it among its members. In other words, to understand and be honest about the psychological and psychic functions of myth, ritual and symbolism, and to make use of them in full awareness, according to the needs and the uniqueness of each individual. This is much easier for a non-hierarchical, non-authoritarian religion such as Wicca, which not only can afford to be flexible but actually values flexibility.

Let us try to define each of these three in turn.

'Myth is the facts of the mind made manifest in a fiction of matter.' (Maya Deren, *Divine Horsemen*, p.29). Or more specifically: 'Myths could be defined as extended symbols describing vividly the typical patterns and sequences of the forces of life, at work in the Cosmos, in Society, and in the individual ... Because every myth has arisen straight out of the human psyche, each one is full of wisdom and understanding about the nature and structure of the psyche itself. Mythology is dramatised psychology.' (Tom Chetwynd, *A Dictionary of Symbols*, p.276.)

Now the purpose of Wicca, as a religion, is to integrate conflicting aspects of the human psyche with each other, and the whole with the Cosmic Psyche; and as a Craft, to develop the power and self-knowledge of the individual psyche (and in a coven, the co-operating group of individual psyches) so that it can achieve results which are beyond the scope of an undeveloped, un-self-aware psyche – much as an athlete develops, and learns about, his muscular power and control to achieve feats impossible for the non-athlete.

Myths (and their folklore descendants, fairy-tales) owe their durability, and their powerful effects on men's minds, to the fact that they dramatize psychic truths which the unconscious mind recognizes at once, even while the conscious mind may think that it is merely being entertained by a well-told story. Both levels of the mind are satisfied at the same time, and the knowledge of this fact filters through to the conscious mind in the form of a strangely enhanced sense of pleasure. Merely entertaining fiction, however good, soon dies. Where the work of a story-teller of genius does embody fundamental psychic truths, it survives either (in pre-literate days) by being absorbed into the body of myth and perhaps altering its form though not its content, or (in later times with such story-tellers as Shakespeare or Goethe) by becoming enshrined in a category of its own, midway between acknowledged myth and acknowledged fiction. *Hamlet, The Tempest* and *Faust,* for all their Renaissance or Age-of-Enlightenment sophistication, are fundamentally pure myths, which is what ensures their immortality.

We have spoken of the integration of conflicting aspects of the human psyche. This is the basis of all character development. It is certainly an essential and continuing process for every would-be witch – not only to achieve happiness and balance as a human being but to release and channel those potentially limitless psychic powers which a witch hopes to put to work.

Every witch would be well advised to study the works of Carl Gustav Jung, the great Swiss psychologist who built on the thinking of Freud and transcended it. Jung's ideas strike an immediate chord with almost every witch who turns serious attention to them. (A useful brief summary of them, with a foreword by Jung himself, is Jolande Jacobi's *the Psychology of C.G. Jung.*) His concepts of the Ego, the Shadow (everything in the psyche apart from the conscious Ego), the Anima (a man's buried feminine side), the Animus (a woman's buried masculine side), the Personal Unconscious, the Collective Unconscious, the Persona (the 'cloak around the Ego'), the four functions of Thinking, Intuition, Feeling and Sensation (which in any one individual can be divided into dominant and inferior), the attitude types of Extraversion and Introversion, and the Self ('the centre and ultimate foundation of our psychic being') – all these seem to us indispensable to a creative understanding of ourselves and other people. And on a wider scale, his concept of the Collective Unconscious offers a key to the understanding of telepathy and clairvoyance, and that of Synchronicity (or 'meaningful coincidence') does the same for divination and magic in general.

The central idea to grasp for our present discussion is that the greater part of the psyche is unconscious, out of reach of our conscious Ego, but strongly influencing the Ego's behaviour without our realizing it. The Unconscious is primordial – which does *not* mean that it is inferior or that we should have outgrown it. On the contrary, it is in more direct touch with the fabric of the Cosmos than is the Ego, and it often knows better what are our real needs. It is also part of the Collective Unconscious – an individual outcrop of it, so to speak – so that it is essentially telepathic with other 'individual outcrops', and has an awareness of overall situations beyond the immediate reach of the Ego, in a way that seems to the Ego almost supernaturally clairvoyant.

The Ego, on the other hand, possesses gifts which the Unconscious lacks: the ability to analyse and categorize incoming data, to think by logical steps and to communicate with other Egos by the precise and subtle medium of speech.

The two sets of gifts are complementary, and so Ego and Unconscious need each other, both for everyday living and for the ultimate liberation of the essential, integrated Self. But very few of us have reached the stage where the two work smoothly together.

When communication between the two departments is faulty (as it is to a greater or lesser degree in all of us but the highest adepts), conflicts emerge. Ego and Unconscious striving in opposite directions can give rise (in ascending order of seriousness) to tension, neurosis, psychosis and schizophrenic breakdown. When the Ego issues impossible orders to the Unconscious, conflicts can arise within the Unconscious itself – in the form of Complexes, autonomous centres which act almost like independent entities; and these, in turn, cause disturbances in the functioning of the Ego. Equally, unacceptable urges from the Unconscious may be pushed back by the Ego below the threshold of consciousness, where they fester and eventually erupt in one way or another.

What is needed, obviously, is greatly improved communication between the conscious Ego and the Unconscious. The Ego must develop techniques, first for being aware of the fact that the Unconscious has messages for it, and second for interpreting those messages, which the Unconscious can only express in symbols. The Unconscious is only too eager to communicate. It is an old joke that Freudian patients have Freudian dreams, Jungian patients have Jungian dreams, and Adlerian patients have Adlerian dreams. In fact it is no joke, but proof that, if the Unconscious is presented with a workable code of symbols which the Ego is learning to understand, it will willingly seize on that code to get its messages across.

This improved communication between Unconscious and Ego is a great part of what is meant by 'opening up the levels' or 'expanding consciousness'. The whole content of the Unconscious can never (at least at our present stage of evolution) be made directly available to the Ego; but a great deal of it can, certainly enough to remove all major conflicts and to enrich significantly the Ego's range of effectiveness – both by increasing the amount and variety of incoming data on which it can act, and by teaching it the lesson (which many Egos resist violently) that it is not the only, or even the most important, function of the total psyche. The more the Ego learns this lesson, and acts on it, the closer it comes to activating the central Self and handing over control to it.

Recording your dreams, and learning to interpret them, is one technique for becoming aware of what your Unconscious is trying to tell your Ego. Another is the study of myths, and their enactment.

Because myths, as we have seen, embody universal psychic truths and dramatize them in a way that appeals to the imagination they not only give the Ego a healthier understanding of those truths (even if only subconsciously)– they also open up channels for the Unconscious to transmit the subtler and more personal truths, and put the Ego in a suitable frame of mind to absorb them. This, too, may be subconscious; you may go away from enjoying hearing or enacting a myth, and then act more appropriately in the everyday world – thinking (or not even bothering to think) that it is by the Ego's conscious decision, whereas in fact it is because both the myth's universal message and the personal messages which have flowed along the channels which the myth has opened up, have influenced the criteria on which the Ego acts.

Many myths and fairy-stories dramatize this integration process itself – the confrontation by the hero of the apparent perils of the Unconscious, and the transforming of his relationship with them. For example, the ugly hag who turns into a beautiful princess when the hero persists in his ordained quest. Here, the Ego comes to terms with his Anima, which if unrecognized or rejected will be a source of conflict. The hero's reward is that he marries (i.e., integration with) the princess and becomes heir to her father's kingdom (i.e., to the Ego's ultimate destiny, the reign of the undivided Self). And so on.[1] In one sense, the witches' Legend of the Descent of the Goddess can be seen as the story of a woman's confrontation with her Animus; in this process, initial revulsion is transformed into understanding and integration, from which both emerge enriched.

This brings us naturally to a consideration of the function of ritual.

To quote Tom Chetwynd again: 'Ritual is the dramatic enactment of myth, designed to make a sufficiently deep impression on the individual to reach his unconscious.' (*A Dictionary of Symbols*, p.342.)

This may seem, at first glance, to be rather a narrow definition of ritual; but if we think about it, it remains true of all ritual. The ritual of the Mass is an enactment of the myth of Jesus' symbolic action with the bread and the wine. Whether the Last Supper was an actual historical event or not, or even if there was no historical Jesus at all (as some people rather improbably maintain), does not effect the point. A powerful myth may be an historical fiction expressing a psychic truth – or a psychically significant act in real history may become the seed of a subsequent myth, or of a new version of an old one (just as the powerful myths of *Hamlet* and *Faust* had historically existing authors). Even simple 'superstitious' rituals can be myth-based; for example, does not turning over your money when you see the new Moon through glass (i.e., from inside your home) relate to myths in which the Moon symbolizes the Mother Goddess whose waxing encourages fertility (and thus domestic prosperity)?

Pursuing the myth-origins of a ritual can be interesting, even enlightening; but success or failure in tracking them down does not alter the validity of the definition. A ritual is an enacted psychic truth; a myth is a spoken or written psychic truth; so both are of the same nature – just as the same story can be told in a novel or a film, or in one based on the other.

In fact, a myth can originate in a ritual as well as vice versa. As Chetwynd points out: 'Communal myths were the ritual words of the great cultic festivals of the ancient world, and the typical features of mythology gave symbolic form to man's life, his longings, his needs.' (*A Dictionary of Symbols*, p.276.)

Ritual, then, performs the same psychic function as myth, but with the added impact on the individual of personal participation. Hearing or reading a myth can have a powerful effect; taking part in it yourself, by enacting one of its roles, can be even more powerful.

Take the example of the Legend of the Descent of the Goddess again. The woman witch who enacts the role of the Goddess visiting the Underworld goes through all the process; her Ego is stripped of its Persona, her comforting but inadequate image of herself; naked she confronts the Lord of the Underworld (her own Animus) and accuses him of being destructive; as long as she persists in regarding him as an enemy, she has to suffer at his hands; but because she does not run away from the confrontation, enlightenment dawns, and she understands his true function. 'They loved, and were one.' Integration achieved, they learn from each other, and the Ego returns to the everyday world wiser and more effective, the supposed enemy, the Animus, having been transformed into an ally.

But the Legend has more than one meaning, and the man who enacts the Lord of the Underworld benefits, too. His Anima makes her presence felt, and at first he tries to dodge the issue by simply appealing to her to be nice to him (Oedipus-like, begging his Anima to identify with his mother?). She will not let him get away with this; she replies, 'I love thee not' – until he continues with the painful part of the confrontation. Wisely, he does not attack her; he 'scourges her tenderly' – in other words, he goes on probing to discover what their true relationship should be. His Anima meets him halfway, in spite of the pains of the attempt at integration: 'I know the pangs of love.' Now they begin the constructive interchange which enriches them both.

Each of these lessons concerns the individual psyche of the person who plays the role. But there is an interpersonal lesson, too; each is reminded vividly that the polarity of male and female aspects is the most powerful of all psychic 'batteries'.

Now all these lessons, if they were merely set down in a psychological treatise, would appeal to the conscious Ego alone. If the Ego were convinced, it would then have the task of finding out how to apply them in co-operation with the Unconscious. But when they are enacted in dramatic form, they appeal directly to the Unconscious – and if the actor has grasped the significance of what he or she is doing, to the conscious Ego as well. The task of applying the lessons in practice is thus made very much simpler.

In dreams, the necessary communication between Unconscious and Ego is initiated by the Unconscious. In ritual, it is initiated by the Ego. So do dream and ritual complement each other.

Myth, ritual and dreams all speak in symbols. All three may use words, but symbols are their real vocabulary. The words of myth may describe factually impossible events or creatures; the words of ritual may seem paradoxical; and the words of dreams may be surrealist and apparently unrelated to the action. Yet in each case, the symbols involved speak the truth.

A symbol is the embodiment of a concept, distilled and condensed and stripped of its inessentials. It may be of many kinds. It may be a physical artefact (or its pictorial representation), such as a Calvary cross, an ankh, a pentagram or a national flag. It may be an imaginary creature, such as a mermaid or a centaur. Overlapping with the last, it may be a visual image giving graspable form to a non-physical entity, such as a human-bodied angel with wings or a Horned God. It may be a natural object in our environment whose behaviour evokes the concept it has come to symbolize, such as the Sun as a fertilizing and light-giving God and the Moon as a many-aspected Goddess who illumines the dark side of the psyche; or as the lotus, which symbolizes the integrated psyche by having its roots in the dark mud and its blossom in the bright air. It may be a piece of music, such as a national anthem or a revolutionary song. It may even be a living person, by the process known as 'projection' – either communally, as when a community projects its sense of national identity onto a sovereign or its sense of mission onto a charismatic leader, or individually, as when you project your own self-contempt onto an acquaintance and treat him accordingly with irrational dislike, or when a husband projects his Anima onto his wife (or a wife her Animus onto her husband) and so treats the partner unrealistically. It may be a colour, such as red for blood, danger or life, or black for death, the Unconscious, malicious magic or civil rights in America (colour is perhaps the supreme example of how symbols can be ambivalent, their meaning changing according to context). It may be a simple device like an exclamation mark or a dollar sign, which started off merely as a convenient bit of humanly devised shorthand, but which through long use became 'numinous' – i.e., charged with emotional significance, which is what distinguishes a symbol from a mere sign. It may be a number; in Christian thinking, 3 represents pure abstract spirit, while in all cultures 4 represents psychic wholeness, pure spirit enhanced and fulfilled by manifestation; and significantly, odd numbers appear repeatedly as masculine symbols, and even ones as feminine.

All these, and many more, are symbols – some obvious to the conscious Ego, and some more subtle and hard to interpret; and myth, ritual and dreams, by dramatizing their interaction, can present complex and vitally important messages.

The most powerful symbols of all are those which stand for the Archetypes – another Jungian word. At first Jung called them 'primordial images' or 'dominants of the collective unconscious', but later he adopted the Greek word ἀρχετυπίαι (*arkhetupiai*), equivalent of St Augustine's Latin *ideae principales* or 'principal ideas'. As St Augustine put it in his *Liber de Diversis Quaestionibus*: 'For the *principal ideas* are certain forms, or stable and unchangeable reasons of things, themselves not formed, and so continuing eternal and always after the same manner, which are contained in the divine understanding. And although they themselves do not perish, yet after their pattern everything is said to be formed that is able to come into being and to perish, and everything that does come into being and perish. But it is affirmed that the soul is not able to behold them, save it be the rational soul.' (Alan Glover's translation.)

The Archetypes are elements of the Collective Unconscious – which is that part of the psyche which is universal to all periods and cultures, and common to all individuals. We inherit it from the human race as a whole, and not modified through the filter of our parents. The symbols by which we become aware of the Archetypes may be culturally or individually conditioned to a certain extent, but the Archetypes themselves are not; they 'continue eternal and always after the same manner'. As Jung says, the term Archetype 'is not meant to denote an inherited idea, but rather an inherited mode of psychic functioning, corresponding to that inborn *way* according to which the chick emerges from the egg; the bird builds its nest; a certain kind of wasp stings the motor ganglion of the caterpillar; and eels find their way to the Bahamas. In other words, it is a "pattern of behaviour". This aspect of the archetype is the biological one – it is the concern of scientific psychology. But the picture changes at once when looked at from the inside, that is from within the realm of the subjective psyche. Here the archetype presents itself as numinous, that is, it appears as an experience of fundamental importance. Whenever it clothes itself with adequate symbols, which is not always the case, it takes hold of the individual in a startling way, creating a condition of "being deeply moved" the consequences of which may be immeasurable.[2] It is for this reason that the archetype is so important for the psychology of religion.

All religions and all metaphysical concepts rest upon archetypal foundations and, to the extent that we are able to explore them, we succeed in gaining at least a superficial glance behind the scenes of world history, and can lift a little the veil of mystery which hides the meaning of metaphysical ideas.' (Jung's Introduction to Esther Harding's *Woman's Mysteries*, pp. ix-x.)

A good idea of Jung's thinking on Archetypes may be gained from his book *Four Archetypes – Mother, Rebirth, Spirit, Trickster*. As will be seen from this title, many Archetypes can usefully be given name-labels. And to take just one of these Archetypes, the Mother: you can get a conception of how vast and complex are the ramifications of a single archetype by reading Harding's *Women's Mysteries* and Erich Neumann's *The Great Mother*. Neither of these authors would claim to have exhausted the subject, for by its nature an Archetype can never be completely defined. It is too fundamental for that. It can only be related to consciousness by means of symbols, and even they, as Jung points out, may not always be adequate.

The Major Arcana of the Tarot owe their power, and their effectiveness in sensitive hands, to the fact that each of them is an archetypal symbol. Yet even here, the elusive nature of archetypal definition makes itself felt. To take the four examples in Jung's *Four Archetypes* and try to equate them with Tarot trumps: the *Mother* corresponds most readily to the Empress, though aspects of her shade off into the High Priestess, the Star and others; *Rebirth* suggests Death, the Tower and Judgement for a start; and the *Trickster* is fairly obviously the Magician – but is he not the Devil as well? As an exercise, we leave you to try equating Jung's fourth Archetype, Spirit, to a Tarot trump.

We tried an experiment ourselves. Stewart wrote the above paragraph and, without showing it to Janet, asked her for her own correspondences. She came up with: *Mother*, the Empress and the Star; *Rebirth*, the Star, Death, the Empress, the World, Judgement, the Wheel of Fortune and the Moon; *Trickster*, the Magician, the Moon and the Wheel of Fortune.

As you will see, our responses overlapped but differed, which does not mean that either of us was 'right' or 'wrong'. It simply underlines the fact that, while the Archetypes themselves are unchanging, the symbols by which we approach them (or the order in which we arrange a complex of symbols) may differ according to our personal make-up, sex and experience.

Consideration of the Archetypes brings us to one of the most important problems of all: that of God-forms.

A God-form – the mental image in which a believer clothes, and through which he strives to relate to, a particular God or Goddess – is unquestionably an archetypal symbol; for equally unquestionably, Gods and Goddesses are themselves Archetypes, fundamental to the nature of the Cosmos. They are unknowable directly, like all Archetypes ('Thou canst not see my face: for there shall no man see me, and live' – Exodus xxxiii:20); but when they are approached through adequate and vividly experienced God-forms – in Jung's phrase, the consequences may be immeasurable.

To the age-old question 'Are the Gods real?' (or as a monotheist would put it, 'Is God real?'), the witch answers confidently 'Yes.' To the witch, the Divine Principle of the Cosmos is real, conscious and eternally creative, manifesting through Its creations, including ourselves. This belief is of course shared by the followers of all religions, which differ only in the God-forms (or single God-form) which they build up as a channel of communication with Its aspects. And even these various God-forms differ less than would appear at first sight. For example, the ancient Egyptian's Isis, the witch's Aradia and the Catholic's Virgin Mary are all essentially man-conceived Goddess-forms relating to, and drawing their power from, the same Archetype. We say 'man-conceived', but the building up of a God-form or Goddess-form is of course a two-way process; even a partially adequate man-conceived symbol improves communication with the unknowable Archetype, which in turn feeds back a better understanding of its nature and thus improves the adequacy of the God-form.

A non-religious psychologist would probably answer 'No' to the same question. He would maintain that the Archetypes, though vital to man's psychic health, are merely elements in the human Collective Unconscious and not (in the religious sense) cosmic in nature.

We stick to our own, namely the religious, view of the Cosmos, which is to us the only one which makes ultimate sense. But from the point of view of the psychic value of myth, ritual and symbolism, the somewhat surprising answer to the question is, 'It doesn't matter.' Each man and woman can worry out for himself or herself whether archetypal God-forms were born in the human Collective Unconscious or took up residence there (and elsewhere) as *pieds-à-terre* from their cosmic home – their importance to the human psyche is beyond doubt in either case, and the techniques for coming to healthy and fruitful terms with them can be used by believers and non-believers alike.

Voltaire said: 'If God did not exist, it would be necessary to invent him.' That remark can be taken as cynical; but it can also be rephrased: 'Whether the archetypal God-forms are cosmically divine, or merely the living foundation-stones of the human psyche, we would be wise to seek intercourse with them *as though* they were divine.'

Myth and ritual bring about nourishing communication with the Archetypes, and because of the nature and evolution of the human psyche, the symbolism of myth and ritual – their only effective vocabulary – is basically religious. Dispensing with myth and ritual cuts us off from the Archetypes, which is a dangerous and crippling separation.

As a practical footnote – a small point on which Stewart in particular (as a professional wordmonger) feels strongly; and we find that Doreen Valiente does, too. Rituals are often couched in archaic language, full of 'thou', 'thee', 'ye' and so on. It is a matter of taste whether one uses such language or modernizes it (though for ourselves, we feel that modernization would sacrifice much of the poetry, as the New English Bible does). But if you *are* going to use it, try to get it right.

The rules about 'thou', 'thee' etc., are simple. In the first place, they are always singular, never plural. To say 'Ye Lords of the Watchtowers of the East, we do thank thee ...' is nonsense. (It should be 'Ye Lords ... we do thank you ....')

'Thou' is nominative (the subject of a sentence) or vocative (the person addressed). 'Thee' is accusative (the object of the sentence) or follows a preposition ('to thee', 'of thee' etc.). If that confuses you – just remember that you use 'thou' in the same place where you would use 'I' or 'we', and 'thee' where you would use 'me' or 'us'. Similarly, 'thy' corresponds to 'my', 'our', and 'thine' to 'mine', 'ours'. (Though archaic usage also has the 'mine', 'thine' form instead of 'my', 'thy' before a vowel – for example, 'mine adversary', 'thine answer'.)

To make it easier, remember the first-degree challenge: 'O thou who standest on the threshold ... hast thou the courage to make the assay? For I say unto thee ...' and the acceptance: 'I give thee a third ...'

'Ye' and 'you' are used in the same ways as 'thou' and 'thee' and the sentence for remembering this is the biblical one: 'Ye shall know the truth, and the truth shall make you free.'

Which is not a bad motto for witches, at that.

XV Witchcraft and Sex

It must be clear to the reader by now that sexual polarity and the role which masculine and feminine play within the individual psyche, in interpersonal relationships and in the Cosmos as a whole, are central to Wiccan philosophy and practice. The gutter Press seize on this (and on the fact that many covens work skyclad) to imply that modern witchcraft involves orgies, promiscuity and God knows what, because such salaciousness sells their newspapers. Everyone who has studied the subject without bias, or who has attended a genuine Wiccan meeting, knows that this is simply not true. So let us, here, not waste time being defensive about it, but get on with discussing the actual Wiccan attitude to sex.

Most dissertations on sex are concerned either with the biology and technique of sex (which is fair enough) or else with trying to discipline it through legislation or dogma (which is purely negative, except in such obviously desirable aspects as laws against rape or child abuse). Wicca on the other hand takes a positive approach. It starts off by accepting sexuality as wholly natural and good, and goes on from there to seek a fuller understanding of masculine-feminine polarity and of how to make constructive use of it – both psychologically and magically. Wiccan sexual morality arises from this attitude, instead of (as happens all too often) being imposed on it.

We shall be talking a good deal here about the patriarchal epoch and its attitudes, so let us start by defining it and trying to explain it. It is the period of male domination of human society which established its hold, approximately speaking, during the last couple of millennia BC. That process was piecemeal but inexorable, and gained particular impetus from the arrival and increasing supremacy of the strongly patriarchal Indo-European peoples in and around the Mediterranean basin. Patriarchal rule, both political and psychological, has been pretty well universal in the two millennia AD and is only now being seriously challenged. It has been characterized by the dictatorship of the God, the King, the Priest, the Father, and the total subordination of the Goddess, the Queen, the Priestess, the Mother; even, in the case of the Goddess and the Priestess, to their total banishment from the major Western cultures at least. There have been exceptions to this process, of course, and late pockets of non-conformity; for example, pre-Christian Celtic society gave remarkably complete freedom and equality to women at all levels (on this, read Jean Markale's *Women of the Celts*). But such pockets vanished one by one, mostly under the pressure of Christianity or Islam.

There is much argument among scholars as to whether there actually was a Matriarchal Period in human prehistory. But one thing is certain: the Goddess preceded the God in human worship, which gave its first attention to the Womb and Nourisher of all things, and even after the concept of the God evolved, Goddess and God remained in dynamic partnership until patriarchal monotheism ruthlessly widowed the God.[1] And even politically – Ancient Egypt for example, remained matrilinear at all levels of society right up to the time of the last Pharaoh, Cleopatra; as Margaret Murray said (*the Splendour that was Egypt*, p. 70), 'The queen was queen by right of birth, the king was king by right of marriage' – and this same rule governed noble and peasant inheritance as well.

What brought about this male take-over of human politics, economics, theology and social attitudes? A take-over so complete that for many centuries now it has been accepted (even by most women) as the natural order of things?

It was, we suggest, an evolutionary stage in the relationship between the conscious and unconscious functions of the human mind. The conscious Ego, which distinguishes *homo sapiens* from all the other land animals, has only been with us since its first rudimentary awakening perhaps half a million years ago. For most of that time, it has been growing, learning and making its contribution to human survival and achievement. It had reached a high level of development long before the patriarchal take-over took shape; we are not suggesting that there has been a sudden evolutionary leap in the inborn *quality* of human consciousness in the past four or five thousand years. But there certainly came a stage (comparatively suddenly, in terms of that half-million-year timespan) when the conscious Ego began to flex its muscles and upset the balance.

It may well be that the trigger was technological development. A hunting tribe lived by what Marx and Engels called 'primitive communism'. When the hunting was good, they fed well, and when it was sparse, they went hungry. There was no appropriable surplus, and therefore no class structure. Clan leadership would fall naturally to the cleverest, strongest and most experienced hunter whose co-ordination of the group effort would be as willingly followed (because it meant more food) as is that of a good football team captain today (because it means more goals). Specialists there might be, such as shaman or shamaness whose magic was also looked to for better hunting, or a gifted flint-knapper relieved of other duties to keep the hunters supplied with arrowheads. Division of labour between the sexes would be largely self-determining because of the demands of childbearing and rearing.[2] But these *would* be specialities, not economic classes – much as when a family entrusts the garden to its most green-fingered member, or a football team puts an agile long-armed player in goal.

In this tribal hunting stage, survival (and good or meagre living) would be entirely a communal matter, to which all abilities would be devoted – both conscious planning and action, and unconscious intuition and instinct. Ego and Unconscious would take co-operation for granted, because survival demanded it.

The development of class structures which began after the introduction of agriculture, with its increasing specializations and its appropriable surpluses, has been very thoroughly written about and there is no need to repeat the story here. But it must have had some increasingly significant repercussions on the human psyche. Conflicts must have arisen in the Ego between the demands of tribal survival and those of personal or class advantage. Group consciousness had dominated the hunting tribe, and individual self-awareness would have been comparatively dim. (This phenomenon persists today in the few environments where a hunting tribe culture is still found; an Australian Aborigine subjected to 'pointing the bone' sees it as ritual exclusion from the tribe and quickly dies because he feels that he no longer exists. Other factors enter into it, of course – we do not doubt the genuine psychic powers of Aboriginal witch-doctors – but the 'non-existence' feeling is certainly a significant one.) But with a class structure, individuation would proceed by leaps and bounds. Pawns were being queened in large numbers; the self-conscious Ego was rapidly differentiating from the tribally conscious Ego. (Class-consciousness, involving as it does the rat-race within the class, is often more an extension of self-consciousness than a contraction of tribal-consciousness.)

In the self-conscious individual, encapsulated in an economic class, conflicts between the Ego and the Unconscious were inevitable. For a start, the tribal archetypes of the Collective Unconscious would often pull in opposite directions from the immediate demands of personal advantage, a situation unknown even to an abnormally self-aware genius in a hunting tribe. Again, each act which was tribally anti-social, but personally necessary for gain or survival or a step up in the pecking-order, would leave a guilty scar on the Personal Unconscious which would have to be sealed off in protection of the Ego, which has to be self-approving if it is to keep control.

Thus the Great Split began between the conscious Ego and the Unconscious, both Personal and Collective. And it was self-accelerating. The structures – first local, then national and finally imperial – created the split individuals and absorbed them into its framework and evolved appropriate ideologies. The split individuals, growing in their collective strength, created bigger, better and more victorious structures. And, of course, more monolithic ideologies.

Like all evolutionary phases, the Empire of the Conscious Mind has had its constructive as well as its destructive aspects. It has vastly extended man's factual knowledge, his technical achievements and his command of his environment. Essentially, he has conquered the physical level of reality to the point where he can do almost anything he wants with it – including destroying the Earth we stand on. (Man, as somebody remarked, is the only animal clever enough to build the Empire State Building, and stupid enough to jump off it.)

But the cost has been tremendous – because of the functions which have had to be suppressed. A free hand for the conscious Ego has meant disciplining, containing, distorting and even denying the rest of the human psyche.

Moreover, the situation has now reached a crisis, in that whatever evolutionary purpose the Ego-Empire had has more than fulfilled itself. The knowledge and the techniques which it has won for *homo sapiens* no longer need the Ego-Empire to prop them up; indeed, they could now achieve much more without its dictatorship, which has become entirely restrictive. But like all dictatorships, the Ego-Empire fights to maintain its regime long after it has outlived any possible useful function. The reintegration of the Ego and the Unconscious, on a new and higher level, has become an urgent necessity for the individual and the race. With *that* process begun, we can look forward to a new and unimaginably fruitful evolutionary phase; call it, if you will, the Aquarian Age.

Necessity is not only the mother of invention; she is also the timely provider of potential answers. It is perhaps not surprising that it is within living memory that Freud paved the way for Jung and a clear understanding of the nature and structure of the human psyche – an understanding which poets, artists and story-tellers have always possessed intuitively (while being regarded as mere entertainers) and which orthodox religion has long ago ceased to be able to supply. And perhaps it is not accidental that woman is at last beginning to rebel against her millennia-long subjection – nor that paganism and our own Craft are going through what may seem an out-of-the-blue revival.

You may be wondering what all this history has to do with the subject of Witchcraft and Sex. It has everything, because the Craft is intimately concerned with the very aspects which have been (and still are being) suppressed, and with restoring the balance; and these suppressed aspects are precisely the feminine ones.

The patriarchal regime has never doubted this and has shown in practice that it regards Woman, and all she stands for, as its enemy. It has subjugated her socially, politically and economically. It has banished the Goddess and made priesthood a male monopoly. Ascetic Christianity branded woman as 'the gate of the Devil'. Feminine intuition, instinct and attunement with Nature were the leak in the dam which must be stopped at all costs, lest the dam should burst and the Ego's attempts to stand on its own be swept away by the flood of the released Shadow. The terrible witch persecutions of the sixteenth and seventeenth centuries were directed consciously (as the working handbook of the persecution, Sprenger and Kramer's *Malleus Maleficarum*, allows no doubt) against these feminine functions; of the millions who died, roughly a hundred women were executed for every one man, according to some estimates.

Patriarchy has stereotyped man and woman into patterns which reflect its demands and which have been all too thoroughly accepted by men and women alike: man as strong, logical, rational, reliable and the natural master, both politically and domestically, woman as weak, illogical, irrational, unreliable and the natural subordinate. Man's sexual needs could not be denied even by Pauline Christianity, so she was allowed to be their outlet, as harlot or housewife – the former hypocritically despised, and the latter just as hypocritically idealized. Her own sexual needs hardly mattered; they were either regarded as a Devil-baited snare for the superior male, or even, during the more extreme periods such as Victorian England, supposed to be no part of a 'lady's' make-up. Woman's one inescapable monopoly – the bearing of children – was (and all too often still is) regarded as her main

God-ordained function and her limiting horizon, beyond which it would be presumptuous for her to look.

It says a great deal for the indestructibility of Nature's workings that, in spite of these stereotypes, and even before the present rebellion against them gathered impetus, so many millions of men and women *have* managed to achieve happy sexual partnerships.

It is understandable that the rebellion against the sexual stereotypes of the Ego-Empire has sometimes fallen into the trap of denying that there *is* any difference between man and woman, except for a 'purely biological' one. This is a forgivable reaction to being told that you are 'unsuitable' for some profession (usually one of the influential and well-paid ones) just because you are a woman. It is also forgivable in cases (and we have known several personally) where a woman *is* a sound professional in some predominantly male sphere but has difficulty in being taken seriously because she happens to be sexually attractive. ('I wish to God I were ugly!' one such friend cried to us in a moment of frustration; we knew that she had too much genuine self-respect to wish any such thing really, but we could understand her outburst.) A woman denied equality by patriarchal society is naturally tempted to retort: 'Stop harping on the differences between men and women! There aren't any, except anatomical ones.'

But understandable or not, the unisex stereotype can be just as dangerous and distorting as the patriarchal stereotypes. There *are* basic differences between the male and the female natures – and these differences are as creatively important on all the levels as are the physical differences to sexual intercourse and procreation. *Vive la différence* has wider implications than 'mere' lovemaking.

The other danger (the one which virtually destroyed the American women's liberation movement in America, after its exhilarating start in 1970, and finally caused the loss of the Equal Rights Amendment in 1982) is the extreme radical feminist wing, the 'misandrites' or man-haters, mirror-opposites of the misogynists. Instead of seeing that the patriarchal stereotypes cripple men as well as women, and seeking the support of the millions of men who sympathize with women's liberation, they regard man himself as the enemy. Instead of aiming at a creative balance which would liberate women *and* men, in effect they strive to replace the male Ego-Empire with a female Ego-Empire, which would of course solve nothing. Being strident out of all proportion to their numbers, they succeed in creating a false public image of the whole movement. The ironic result is that, on the lips of women who genuinely are dedicated to women's fulfilment and equality, and to the creative balance, we hear the now-familiar declaration: 'I'm no women's libber.'

All is not lost, though, even in America. In an article headed 'Who killed the Women's Movement?' in *The Irish Times* of 27 August 1982, American-born Mary Maher answers her own question: it was the radical feminists or 'misandrites'. But she also says: 'Something else has been born over the past few years, something that could most accurately be described as an "equality movement", subscribed to by both men and women, and it is small but healthy and growing. There's been no symbolic christening or militant parading, just a lot of shifting and juggling and trying things out. There's a recognition that it will take political change to end the misery so many women still endure, and a growing hope not to take power so much as adjust the axis of power.'

That is very encouraging news. 'Adjusting the axis of power' is another way of saying 'achieving a creative balance'; so the Craft, which seeks this balance on all the levels, not merely the political and economic, is a natural part of this 'equality movement'. And the Craft in America has certainly been paying great attention to the feminist question – also with much healthy 'shifting and juggling and trying things out', fascinating information on which will be found in Margot Adler's excellent book *Drawing Down the Moon*. (Though the Craft in America is developing so fast that Margot tells us wryly that, although it was only published in 1981, 'a lot of it's out of date already' in 1982. She is too modest; it remains the only detailed survey of the Craft and Neo-Pagan scene in America.)

What, then, *are* the essential differences between man and woman that we have been talking about?

The most obvious difference, of course, is that every woman is potentially or actually a child-bearer. This is really the only difference which patriarchy regards as important, because there must be offspring. So the stereotype emphasizes this, while treating the other physically obvious difference – which is menstruation – as a mere nuisance, a 'curse', a regrettably unavoidable concomitant of the ability to bear children. Men and woman alike fall for this; men by resigning themselves to the fact that a woman may become anything from temperamental to downright ill once a month, and women by accepting its pain and mental upset as 'natural' (which they are not necessarily; and if you think this statement is dogmatic, read *The Wise Wound*, Chapter II).

Yet in fact the menstrual cycle is more fundamental to woman's nature – both physical and psychic – than the vast majority of men and women realize. In fact, its true importance has only just begun to be investigated. Jungian psychologists (in particular the women ones) have made a good start; but the only really important book on the subject that we know of is Penelope Shuttle and Peter Redgrove's 1978 work *The Wise Wound: Menstruation and Everywoman*. When Shuttle and Redgrove started working on their book, around 1971, they asked their College Librarian for some books on the psychology of menstruation. 'Greatly to the Librarian's surprise also THERE WERE NO SUCH BOOKS! ... Astonishingly, this remained the situation until 1975, when Paula Weideger's *Menstruation and Menopause* broke new ground in the US' – and even that, though extremely helpful, provided 'little guide to the inward experience and significance of the menstrual cycle'.

The Wise Wound is that rare thing, a truly revolutionary book. Its main theses, we believe, will be so immediately convincing to most women – and to most men who live with a woman – that we are as astonished as the College Librarian that they have never been set down before. It is essential reading for all witches, male or female – and incidentally it has some pertinent things to say about witchcraft, historical and modern. (It is a sad proof of how deep-rooted the stereotyped attitudes are, that the immediate reaction of some of our male witches, when we told them to read it, was 'Ugh!' – but their attitude changed when they did read it.)

Shuttle and Redgrove point out that there are two peaks to the menstrual cycle – ovulation and menstruation, when the womb sheds its wall and renews itself. And these two peaks have quite different implications and are accompanied by quite different psychic states. In one sense, at ovulation the woman's body belongs to the race; she is a carrier and potential passer-on of the racial DNA genetic codes, and DNA molecules are unconcerned with her as an individual once she has ensured their combination with those of a man and ensured that combination's survival. At menstruation, she belongs to herself; she goes through a process of bodily and psychic renewal.

The quality of her sexuality differs also. At ovulation, typically she is receptive, passive, desiring penetration. At menstruation, she is more likely to be active, taking the erotic initiative, desirous of experience for its own sake, independently of her racial reproductive function.

The patriarchal stereotype only recognizes the sexual peak at ovulation, because it is related to reproduction, which is patriarchy's only 'valid' reason for a woman having sexual feelings at all. Even some capable psychologists, conditioned to believe that woman's sexual urge is essentially passive and receptive, have often missed the menstrual peak altogether – because in questioning women about their sexual peaks, they have naturally been looking for the receptive peaks; and the women, similarly conditioned, have answered accordingly.[3] Stereotyped questions have produced stereotyped statistics. The idea of an *active* female sexual peak 'could be disturbing to men reared on the idea that it is the male prerogative to initiate sex. The combination of bleeding and increased sexual capacity is a formidable one to the conventional view.' (*The Wise Wound* p.89.)

Powerful taboos have always surrounded menstruating women. In pre-patriarchal times (and in many 'primitive' cultures still) 'menstrual taboos and seclusions are for the purpose of safeguarding the woman at a receptive time, during which she may indeed go inwards and produce prophetic information or dreams which are useful to the community, or on the contrary have wrong kinds of experience which can affect her badly ever afterwards.' In particular, 'the menarche or first menstruation was regarded as a time of a particular mental opening, as well as a physical one, during which a girl would have those dreams or other experiences that would guide her in later life, and that if she were to be a shaman or witch-doctor, then this was the time at which she came into a special relationship with the powerful spirits of her menstruation.' (*The Wise Wound* p.65.)

But with the patriarchal take-over, menstrual taboos became a protection *against* the woman, against her 'dangerous' magic, against all those faculties which the Ego-Empire strives to banish. Or to adopt and discipline them for its own use, where it could not banish them; for example, awe of the woman's blood-magic, which if given its due respect is wholly beneficent, may well have given rise to the patriarchal cruelties of blood sacrifice (*ibid.* p.61). Men could not menstruate – but there were other ways of producing blood for magical purposes. The rationale would be: 'Blood is obviously magical. But the menstruating shamaness is dangerous. So let us neutralize her with taboos, and kill something – or somebody – instead.' It is significant that cultures with strong male-imposed menstrual taboos (including our own) seem to be the most prone to aggressiveness and anxiety (*ibid.* pp. 98, 185).

Pagan societies, however, understood and took full advantage of the shamanistic powers of menstruating women. The colleges of Hera, for example, and the pythonesses (oracular priestesses) of Delphi, made their pronouncements monthly, and there are strong indications that in such places the women synchronized their menstrual periods by deliberate psychic disciplines. (This is perfectly possible; research has shown that it often happens spontaneously today in such female communities as convents or women's colleges.) Shuttle and Redgrove argue persuasively that Delphi bears all the hallmarks of menstrual shamanism. They suggest that the famous *omphalos* (still to be seen in the museum at Delphi) is not a 'navel' at all, but a cervix or womb-mouth,[4] and that the tripod on which a Delphic shamaness sat was in fact a speculum device for observing the first signs of menstrual onset. (It had always puzzled us why classical writers laid so much stress on the significance of a mere piece of furniture; this interpretation would explain it.) To which may be added that, in the case of Delphi, the patriarchal takeover is recorded in the legend of

Apollo's conquest of the Delphic Serpent (i.e., the pythonesses); but although Apollo's temple took charge of Delphi, the pythonesses themselves were indispensable; for centuries, no decision of importance was taken in Greece without their oracular advice, so they continued in their role – but with male priests to control and administer them and the rich tribute they attracted.

What does all this mean for today – and for witches?

To sum up: woman's nature is cyclic, from the monthly reproductive, outward-sensitive peak of ovulation, to the intervening monthly renewing, inward-sensitive peak of menstruation. The more she accepts and understands this (and ceases to regard it as a 'curse'), the more fulfilled and effective she will be – and the more man accepts and understands it, the better he will respect and complement her.

Both these peaks are equally significant, forming a dynamic whole, a *yin-yang* total, interweaving up the levels. It is the cycle itself which is important, not one or the other pole of it; the cycle makes a woman what she is. The 'values of ovulation' and the 'values of menstruation' should complement each other; but patriarchy only recognizes the 'values of ovulation', and bases its stereotype of Woman upon them.

This cycle of different kinds of awareness means that woman's overall experience is deeper, and 'the events of the cycle are also more deeply-rooted and physically widespread than anything the male normally experiences. Though this means that the female's experience of life is deeper, it means concurrently that she is more vulnerable when she opens herself to these experiences, more vulnerable to aggression, and to derogation. The man who should be the guardian and student of these abilities in the woman, has in our age become the proud and envious aggressor.' (*Ibid.*, p.33.) Also, as Gerald Massey pointed out a century ago in *The Natural Genesis*, 'the female nature has been the primary teacher of periodicity.'

This may be hard for the proud male, reared on patriarchal stereotypes, to swallow; it seems to put *him* in the novel position of being the inferior sex. But this would be a mistaken reaction. Man, too, has a positive contribution to make.

Typically, the male nature is analytical, with concentrated awareness. The female nature is synthesizing, with diffuse awareness. He is linear, moving forward like a car chassis; she is cyclic, moving forward like a point on the rim of a car's tyre (and note that both kinds of movement can get there just as quickly). He takes things to pieces to see what they are made of; she puts them together to see how they relate.

The two functions need each other. Left to themselves, his concentrated awareness can become tunnel vision, and her diffuse awareness can become disorientation. His analysing can become destructive, enthroning facts above feeling; her synthesizing can lose coherence, enthroning feeling above facts. Her sensitivity, unprotected by its brother strength, can become dangerous vulnerability; his single-minded vigour, unguided by its sister intuition, can become blundering aggression.

Working together, on the other hand, they can find their way through the forest. He may identify single trees and help her not to bump into them. She may have a better map of the whole forest and help him not to get lost.

Not only this – but each nature has within itself the seed of the other, like the white spot in the black *yin* and the black spot in the white *yang* (see Figure 6 on p.118). In the woman, this is the Animus, her buried masculine component, integration with which enriches her femininity; it tends to manifest especially at the menstrual peak, as her 'other husband' or Moon-partner, who may be either frightening or vitalizing according to her degree of self-awareness and the balance she has achieved between her two cyclic sets of values. In the man, it is the Anima, his buried feminine component, integration with which correspondingly enriches his masculinity. Since man is linear rather than cyclic, the Anima's impingement upon man's awareness tends to seem spasmodic and unpredictable; she can perhaps best be identified (and fruitfully listened to) as the dream-figure of a woman who is well known to the dreamer but unplaceable in waking life. (When Stewart began recording his dreams, he labelled her 'the X-woman', until he started reading Jung and realized who she was.) She, too, can be frightening or helpful, depending upon whether a man accepts and reaches out to her or resists her. But she is always there, an inalienable part of the total psyche; and as *The Wise Wound* (p.130) vividly puts it: 'This repressed feminine world must include the problem of menstruation, its shape and form, for man as well as woman. What should never have been forgotten is that *the anima menstruates.*'

It is worth pointing out here that the witches' belief in reincarnation not only agrees with the Animus/Anima concept but must inevitably include it. The immortal Individuality, as we have said (p.116), is dynamically hermaphroditic, with both aspects in a balance which is imperfect or perfect according to its stage of karmic progress. But the Personality of any one incarnation is either male or female; so the other, temporarily subordinated, aspect will naturally make its presence felt – as Anima or Animus. So the degree of harmonious integration that a Personality shows with its Anima or Animus is a revealing pointer to the degree of karmic advancement achieved by the incarnating Individuality.

To turn for a moment from individual men and women to human society as a whole – and the perhaps astonishing fact that it was menstruation brought it about. As Shuttle and Redgrove point out (*The Wise Wound* p. 142 – their italics): '*It is received opinion in zoological science that the development of the menstrual cycle was responsible for the evolution of primate and eventually human societies.*' The majority of mammals have an *oestrus* cycle; they come 'on heat' periodically, and at other times they have no interest in mating. Ovulation is their only peak; sex means begetting young and nothing else, as a survival factor for the species. But 'with the Old World Monkeys, the Apes and the human being, an immense evolutionary change occurred. This was the development of the *menstrual cycle*.' The mating-signal of genital blood was wrenched from its former position at ovulation to a new position at menstruation, when it is very unlikely that ovulation can occur or offspring can be conceived. Sexual libido, too, was now spread over most of the cycle. How could this be a survival factor? 'The answer must be that the sexual experience in primates (monkeys and humans) must have become of benefit and importance to the individual (and thence to the race) as well as to the species by breeding.'

'Non-stop libido', or what *The Wise Wound* (p.152) calls 'sexual brightness', was an evolutionary adaptation favouring the development of social and economic co-operation and promoting insight during problem-solving. The patriarchal epoch may have tried to narrow sex down to copulation for breeding; evolution knows better. 'Sexual brightness' is the urge to relatedness, the thing which makes us human, in contrast to those species with whom sex *is* mere copulation for breeding. 'The creation of children is one half of human joy. The other half is the creation of "mental children": seminal ideas and insights' (*ibid.* p.210) – and Shuttle and Redgrove pertinently add: 'It is too much supposed that the creation of "mental children" is the sole province of men, because the creation of physical children is the exclusive ability of women.'

It is ironic that so many Western religions, from Catholicism to Christian Science, forbid the enjoyment of sex independently of reproduction – and thus, in effect, try to regress humanity to a pre-human stage of evolution!

We can thus see the difference between the positive-creative and negative-restrictive approaches to sexual relationships and sexual morality. If all the aspects we have been discussing are genuinely understood and made part of our living attitude to one another, if we stop seeing stereotypes and instead see living human beings, then increasingly we view the other sex with a respect, and our own sex with an empathy, born of that understanding. Increasingly, we discern the essence of the God (and the Goddess-Anima) within every man, and of the Goddess (and the God-Animus) within every woman. Every relationship, from a sexual pair-bond to friendship, can become illumined with a magical sense of wonder. And with genuine love (at whatever appropriate level of intensity or closeness) problems of morality tend to solve themselves. Morality is not determined by a book of rules; it is determined by the actual nature of real relationships.

All that may sound a bit idealistic and too good to be true; yet in practice it is not.

It is our experience that coven work, sincerely carried out, fosters just this process. The coven join together in active worship of the Goddess and God; and on the principle of 'as above, so below', Wicca does not place a gulf between the divine and the human. The Goddess principle is invoked into the High Priestess, and the God principle into the High Priest. Each strives to put herself or himself in tune with the invoked principle and to act as a channel for it, and is so treated by the rest. And it works, as every experienced coven knows; because you are not trying to relate to something imaginary, you are opening yourself up to an essence that is already there. Moreover, in Wicca there is also no gulf between priesthood and congregation; in the normal process of training, every witch is given opportunities to act as High Priestess or High Priest.

The ritual of Drawing Down the Moon demonstrates both the process and the mental attitude that should be taken to it. First the Priest gives the Priestess the Fivefold Kiss – greeting and acknowledging the individual woman herself, his sister witch. The Priestess accepts the salutation, aware of herself as an individual woman and of the Priest as an individual man. Next comes the invocation, in which the Priest brings together his awareness of the woman and his awareness of the Goddess, in the consciousness that they are of the same essence. The Priestess opens herself to this same consciousness. Then the Priest addresses himself to the Goddess directly in the 'Hail Aradia' declamation, and the Priestess hands over the control of her own individuality to the Goddess. Finally, as channel for the Goddess, she feeds back the manifestation of the Goddess to the Priest, in the 'Of the Mother darksome and divine' blessing.

Only those who have worked this ritual in all sincerity know what startling effects it can have.

The purpose of the Drawing Down the Sun ritual (Section VI) is of course the mirror-image of this.

Men and women witches get used to working together in full recognition of their psychic need for each other's complementary essences. The psychic – and practical – results they achieve do build up their respect for each other, and their understanding of the true meaning of the male and female natures.

Every woman, if she can free herself from the conditioning imposed by the patriarchal stereotype, is a natural witch. Most men, unless they have a well-integrated and fully functioning Anima, have to work harder at it. Witches work primarily with the 'gifts of the Goddess' – the intuitive, psychic functions, the direct awareness, by sensitivity at all levels from bodily to spiritual, of the natural order of things. All this is a woman's immediate inheritance; on the whole, a man approaches it best *via* the woman (and via his own Anima, which is the same process). The Lovers card in the Waite (Rider) Tarot deck expresses this perfectly; the man looks across at the woman, who looks up at the angel. As Eden Gray, interpreting this card in *A Complete Guide to the Tarot*, says: 'The truth conveyed is that the conscious mind cannot approach the superconscious unless it passes through the subconscious.'

That is why Wicca is matriarchal, and the High Priestess is the leader of the coven – with the High Priest as her partner. They are essential to each other, and ultimately equal (remembering that the immortal Individuality, the reincarnating monad, is hermaphroditic), but in the context of Wiccan working and of their present incarnation, he is rather like the Prince Consort of a reigning Queen. He is (or should be) a channel for the God aspect, and there is nothing inferior about that; but Wiccan working is primarily concerned with the 'gifts of the Goddess', so the Priestess takes precedence; for woman is the gateway to witchcraft, and man is her 'guardian and student'.

All-woman covens do exist, particularly in the United States, and they can work, the cyclic natures of the members providing the necessary creative polarity. But an all-male coven, in our opinion, would be a mistake. Men wishing to work together in the occult field should stick to ritual magic of some such pattern as that of the Golden Dawn – though even there we feel they would do better with women fellow-workers.

It would be naïve to pretend that the development of the kind of magically and psychologically creative intersexual attitudes which we have been describing always proceeds without a hitch in a working coven. Witches are human beings, and there will be setbacks, immaturities and the old deeply rooted stereotypes to deal with. But that is one of the purposes of group working; to help each other to develop, and to pinpoint weaknesses in a comradely and understanding manner. It is our experience that, given basically sound human material and a genuine common philosophy, the movement is forward overall. And the God and the Goddess do help those who help themselves.

We deliberately refrain from commenting on the 'gay' covens (another particularly American phenomenon) because we feel that we are not equipped to do so, and because anything we could say might be interpreted as anti-homosexual prejudice. We have homosexual friends to whom we related happily *as people* as we do to other friends – namely, on those things which we have in common, our sexual attitudes *not* being one of those things. We have always regarded their sexual attitude as their own business, and defended them against any attempts to make them suffer for it. We have even had one or two homosexual members during our coven's history, when they have been prepared and able to assume the role of their actual gender while in a Wiccan context, and when their personalities have been harmonious with the rest of us.

But we are utterly heterosexual ourselves, and our own concept of Wicca is built around natural maleness and femaleness of mind, body and spirit. We are therefore personally out of tune with the whole idea of a 'gay' coven, and would be very ill at ease if we were guests at one, however much we liked the people involved. So in the interests of pagan harmony, we leave discussion of the question to those who *are* in tune with it.

(Incidentally, we very much regret the adoption of the term 'gay' for homosexual; quite apart from making a happy little word unusable in its original sense, it implies that homosexuals are in a permanently manic mood, and therefore not ordinary human beings – which is the very charge that homosexuals rightly fight against.)

What about 'sex magic' in the literal sense?

As we explained in *Eight Sabbats for Witches*, the use of man/woman polarity in magical working is of two kinds: the 'magic of gender', which is simply a man and a woman each contributing his or her characteristic mental gifts and psychic power to a magical task; and 'sex magic', which uses sexual intercourse between the partners as a psychic dynamo.

'The magic of gender' is the basic pattern of most coven working – as when a man and a woman hold opposite ends of a cord in cord-magic, or men and women sit alternately in a ring for linked-hand magic, or a man and a woman consecrate the wine or a working tool. It is as essentially intersexual, and as completely removed from coitus, as ballroom dancing. Brother and sister, father and daughter, mother and son, can and do work this kind of magic together, just as effectively and just as free from any 'improper' overtones, as they would partner each other on a dance floor.

'Sex magic' is something quite different; it can be very powerful, both in its effect in terms of the intended outcome of the work and in its effect on the couple concerned (even if they have been lovers, or married, for years).

And we would say categorically: *sex magic as such should only be worked by a couple for whom intercourse is a normal part of their relationship* – in other words, husband and wife, or established lovers – and in complete privacy. For them, it is an extension (and may well be an enrichment) of their customary lovemaking. For a couple not so related, it could be very dangerous indeed; if they approached it cold-bloodedly as a 'necessary magical operation', that would be a gross abuse of their sexuality and their supposed respect for each other; if they rushed into it with a sudden and ill-considered warmth, it could have effects on unexpected levels for which they were quite unprepared – worst of all, it could affect them unequally, leaving one emotionally overwhelmed and the other with a burden of guilt.

Sex magic without love is black magic.

That being said – how can a husband and wife (or established lovers) work sex magic in practice?

There are two simple ways: by harnessing the psychic power of intercourse and by post-coital reverie.

Dion Fortune says (*The Esoteric Philosophy of Love and Marriage*, p.114): 'When the act of sexual union takes place the subtle forces of the two natures rush together, and, as in the case of two currents of water in collision, a whirlpool or vortex is set up; this vortex extends up the planes as far as the mating of the bodies takes place' (i.e., as far as the couple's seven component levels – see p.117 – are united with each other – *our note*) 'so that should two people who idealise each other, and whose love has elements of a spiritual nature in its composition, meet in coitus, the vortex so created will extend on to one of the higher planes.' In other words, the more united the couple on all the levels, the higher up those levels will the vortex take effect; when soul-mates make love, the vortex reaches *all* the levels; and at the other extreme, the callous copulation of a pair with no higher-plane contact will produce a vortex that may be very powerful in the murky waters of the lower astral, but quite uncorrected by the balancing influence of the other planes – which underlines our statement that sex magic without love is black magic.

A closely united couple who wish to use sex magic for a worthwhile objective will first discuss that objective and make sure that they have it clearly in their minds. They will then cast a Circle around themselves and make love unhurriedly and tenderly, with the maximum possible awareness of each other and of the magical objective. Once they have joined their bodies in coitus, if they have sufficient control they may even keep quite still for a while, building up the sexual tension-in-unity to the highest possible peak, so that their awareness of each other and of their purpose reaches as great a level of intensity as they can bear. When they are ready, they will aim at simultaneous orgasm, at which point they will hurl the whole power of the vortex into the achievement of the magical objective. Even if their orgasms should not coincide, they should *both* 'hurl the vortex' at the moment of *each* orgasm.

Sex magic of this kind should not be used too often, because it is a memorably heightened experience and is better not devalued by over-familiarity.

One occasion when we used it ourselves is worth recording. We had been in Ireland a few months, having handed over our London coven to other leaders, and we were feeling frustrated because we now had no coven except for one already-initiated witch who had contacted us and who lived a hundred miles away. So we worked by this method to 'set up an astral lighthouse' over our home, which would attract the kind of people we wanted. The very next day, we met the couple who became our first Irish initiates, and from then on our coven grew. The original couple were a great strength to us in this growth and are now running their own group. (It is perhaps significant of the kind of resonance our 'lighthouse' set up, that the very first people it attracted were a married pair.)

That is active sex magic; the second kind is more receptive. The power of the vortex is reabsorbed by the couple for their own benefit.

Again, the couple make love within a Magic Circle – but this time there is no outside objective to bear in mind. All their attention is directed to awareness of themselves and each other, and to activating all their levels in unison with each other. It is *after* orgasm that magic is invoked. As *The Wise Wound* says (p.172): 'Reveries in enhanced body-consciousness after one's sexual intercourse are probably the deepest of all – with second-stage labour possibly the only exception, when the woman is overwhelmingly "suggestible" – and what is called "sexual magic" is often no other than introducing images into such a reverie.'

A couple who are experienced witches or occultists, and who have developed a high degree of intercommunion on all the levels, can use this method to great advantage – and unlike the 'hurled vortex', it can be used as often as they like, and even made their normal post-coital habit. The insights gained in such a reverie, especially if they are shared and interwoven by a harmonious couple, can be of tremendous value. And as for 'introducing images' – post-coital reverie can be a very effective time for building up and energizing active thought-forms, for the magical purposes explained in Section XXII – 'Spells'.

The subtleties and refinements of sex magic are as varied as those of lovemaking – and as unique to the individual couple. But the principles we have outlined should give a firm foundation on which any couple can build, if this is a path they wish to explore.

This Section would not be complete without some reference to two problems which raise much controversy, nowhere more than here in Ireland: abortion and contraception.

We would not go so far as those who assert that abortion is *never* justifiable. It is an evil, but there are sad situations where it is a lesser evil. A living foetus is the initial stage of the reincarnation of a human entity, and to thrust that entity back so that it has to find (or be drawn into) a new foetal vehicle is a violent act, the traumatic effects of which on the entity may be serious, as well as being a load on the karma of the person who does it. But if the mother's life is at risk, or her health is seriously endangered – or if, because of rape-induced pregnancy or other reasons, the circumstances into which the child would have to be born would be so disastrous for it that the trauma of having to re-start the incarnation process genuinely appears to be the lesser evil – then abortion may be the only solution.

Given a choice between the life of the mother (who is halfway through an incarnation and almost always with many responsibilities and relationships) and that of the unborn child (who has barely started on an incarnation, has acquired no responsibilities and has no direct relationship except the foetal one with its mother), then it seems clear to us that it is the mother who must be saved.

But to use abortion as a lazy alternative to contraception is unforgivable. So, too, is the family pressure which often forces a girl into abortion because of what the neighbours may think. Equally unforgivable is the practice (growing in America, we understand) of determining the sex of a foetus and then aborting it if it does not happen to be of the desired sex.

Abortion and contraception (like 'sex-and-violence') are all too often lumped together by propagandists. This is quite illogical and very wrong.

We cannot see any theological, social, psychological or ecological justification for the Vatican ban on contraception. Pope Paul VI's encyclical *Humanae Vitae* was one of the most disastrous pronouncements of this century. Fortunately, 'the arguments used obviously failed to convince the majority, even within the Catholic Church, and in the years which followed the use of the methods referred to increased rather than declined.' (Hans Kung, *Infallible?*, p. 29.)[5] Millions of good Catholic wives are on the Pill; and many good priests know that they are right, and thus suffer painful stresses of conscience and obedience in the confessional box.

The declared intention of the ban on contraception is the defence of the sanctity of marriage. Its actual effect, on those couples who abide by it, is often the destruction of the harmony of marriage, with love at loggerheads with fear of pregnancy. The one permitted method of pregnancy-avoidance, where 'you make love with a calendar in one hand and a thermometer in the other', is hardly more conducive to a happy sex-life; and its reliability is reflected in its nickname, 'Vatican roulette'.

The insistence that deliberately childless couples are 'selfish'[6] and that parenthood is the obligatory purpose of marriage – and the further insistence, by implication, that a couple may not even choose to limit the number of their children, unless it be by abstinence from marital sex (a dogma in which Mary Baker Eddy antedated Paul VI) – is part and parcel of the patriarchal attitude, which basically hates sex as one of God's incomprehensible afflictions, and fears women as dangerous disrupters of the Ego-Empire.

In the present state of the world, this insistence is also blindly anti-social. If the world-wide population explosion is not checked, civilization (whether capitalist, communist or on any other pattern) will become unworkable and the Earth uninhabitable. That is not panic-mongering; it is plain, unavoidable fact. In this situation, a couple who opt for 'mental children' instead of physical ones are anything but selfish; they are making their own small contribution to avoiding world disaster. And a couple who produce only as many physical children as they can conscientiously and lovingly rear, while continuing to benefit from their own sexual harmony, are making *their* contribution to the quality of the next generation.

Sexuality – 'sexual brightness' – freed from the shackles of obligatory breeding is what makes us specifically human. Zoologists, psychologists and witches all agree about this. Sexual relatedness is a great creative force at all levels, not merely the procreative; and when the patriarchal system, particularly in the shape of a celibate hierarchy, tries to deny or distort that truth, it is blinding itself to reality. Celibates dogmatizing about sexuality are like colour-blind men legislating for the composition of artists' palettes.

Discovering and making use of the true natures of men and women, in mutual respect and wonder, means moving with evolution and even helping it forward. It reaches to the heart of white magic. Attempting to imprison those natures in stereotypes, or to regress them to a pre-human stage, is flying in the face of evolution. And whatever works against evolution is – by any occultist's or witch's definition – black.

XVI   *Many Mansions*

Witches vary a good deal in their attitudes to other religious and occult paths, and even to Wiccan traditions other than their own. Some, regrettably, confuse juvenile rebellion with genuine judgement, and consequently damn everything and everybody Christian (or whatever the parental religion happened to be) indiscriminately. Others insist that *theirs* is the only true Wiccan path and that Gardnerians, Alexandrians, Seax-Wica or whatever are heretics.

But most are more constructive and accept the old occult maxim that all genuine religions (leaving aside the definition of 'genuine' for the moment) are different paths to the same truths, and that the choice of path should depend on the individual's needs, stage of development, cultural environment and so on.

This maxim was universally accepted in the ancient world, before the onset of patriarchal monotheism. A priest of Poseidon visiting a temple of Amun-Ra, or a priestess of Isis visiting a temple of Juno, would be recognized as a colleague, serving the same ultimate Divinity through different symbols. Even the Roman Empire's persecution of Jews and later of Christians was political, not theological; it would have tolerated these exotic religions quite happily, as it had dozens of others, if they had not rejected the mutual-tolerance system and claimed a rigid monopoly of truth, and based their violent or passive resistance to the Empire on that claim. Ruthless conqueror of peoples the Empire might be, but it did not attack alien gods or wage genocide against heretics, as the Jews had and the Christians (and the Empire when it became officially Christian) were later to do.

Paganism is essentially tolerant, and so are wise witches. They will fight bigotry or intolerance or religious persecution; they will criticize what they regard as warped applications of the religious spirit; they will certainly attack the hypocritical use of religious excuses to rationalize cruelty or greed, such as a dictator who wages war in the name of God, a terrorist who blows up religious opponents, or a guru who grows rich on his 'spiritual' charisma. But they will not attack a religion, or its followers, as such. If they do, they are no better than the witch-hunters.

Which brings us back to the question: what is a 'genuine' religion?

A genuine religion is one which uses its own set of symbols, its own mythology (whether recognized as mythology or not) and its own personal disciplines, to develop the individual mentally, spiritually and emotionally, and to put him or her in harmony with Divinity and its manifestations (mankind, Nature and the Cosmos as a whole). To which should be added that it must be followed willingly by the individual of his or her own free choice, and not forced upon anyone.

As *organizations*, it must be admitted that not all religions meet that definition adequately; some have offended grossly against it. But as *symbolic systems*, almost any of them can and do serve to achieve the aims of that definition for a sincere individual who feels in tune with its particular symbols.

In this time of spiritual revolution, it is vital for witches to recognize and act on this distinction, if they are to play a constructive part in that revolution.

For example, we can and do strongly criticize the Catholic hierarchy's attitude to contraception, divorce, the ordination of women, Papal infallibility and many other subjects. On the other hand, we have found that many ordinary Catholics (including quite a few priests and nuns of our acquaintance) agree with us in private that in their approach to the Virgin Mary they are acknowledging the female aspect of divinity – i.e., the Goddess – however carefully official dogma tries to circumscribe and subordinate her; many of them have an innate magical sense and an intuitive understanding of the workings of psychic power; and Catholic folklore (whether in Celtic Ireland or Latin Spain) is inextricably bound up with pagan attitudes. When we first came to Holy Ireland, in 1976, we frankly expected to have a hard time as known witches; to our surprise, we were almost universally accepted and befriended as a natural part of the scenery. Catholic neighbours were apt to react vigorously if anyone from outside made derogatory remarks about 'their' witches. (Once Stewart was even asked to stand godfather to a Catholic friend's new baby; while the compliment was properly appreciated, we and the priest together managed to persuade her that it might not be altogether diplomatic.) Yet we have never played down our own beliefs, our respect for our Catholic friends' faith (even our admiration of some aspects of it) or our criticism of many of the Church's official rulings and attitudes.

Similarly, while we deplore Islam's male chauvinism, its proneness to sudden waves of dangerous fanaticism, and other shortcomings, travelling in Moslem countries has taught us respect for the average Moslem's simple blend of earthiness and spirituality, and for the everyday practicality of much of Mohammed's teaching; moreover, there is much in the thinking of such philosophers as the Sufis with which any Western occultist would feel in tune. As for the Jews, their intellectual and artistic contribution to the best of Western culture has been out of all proportion to their numbers; their non-proselytizing co-existence with other religions, and often that same earthy-spiritual balance, contrasts favourably with some of the less admirable features of Christendom; and they have bequeathed to us the goldmine of the Cabala.

But for most witches, their attitude to Christianity is the main problem, because it is in a Christian environment that most of the Craft as we know it, and as it is at present expanding, has to live and operate.

One of the stumbling-blocks, of course, is the Christians' insistence that Jesus was God Incarnate; that the carpenter of Nazareth, the man who wavered over his destiny in the Garden of Gethsemane, was in fact the creator of the Cosmos. Even accepting the Gospels as a reasonably accurate account of his sayings, we cannot find that he ever claimed to be God. The claim seems to us to have been imposed on him later, and to be a distortion of his actual message (with which any witch or occultist would agree) that divinity resides in all of us. If it shone through him more brightly than through most other people in history, that is another matter.

The character of Jesus is such a loaded concept in the West, so charged with centuries of love, fanaticism, psychological projection, politics and distortion, that it is hard to discuss him dispassionately; but his bodhisattva nature (see pp. 121-2) must surely be beyond doubt. He even seems to hint at it himself in the Gospels as we have them ('Before Abraham was, I am'), and his disciples reported the popular belief ('Some say, Elias; and other say, that one of the old prophets is risen again').

As for his teachings, even the Gospels make it clear that he distinguished sharply between his exoteric preaching to the masses and his inner teaching to his chosen disciples. One interesting occult theory (see Dion Fortune, *Aspects of Occultism*, Chapter III) is that he left reincarnation out of his public teaching, because his message to the masses concentrated on the transformation of the Personality as the immediate step towards perfection, and the most they could grasp at the time; but that to his disciples he taught the inner truths of the reincarnating Individuality (as St Jerome implies – see p.115).

What would be very fruitful would be for some well-informed occultist who is also a Biblical scholar to take all the available Gospels, official, apocryphal and Gnostic, without preconceptions and in the light of modern knowledge, to reassess their relative authenticity; to correct where possible, with an understanding of the politico-theological manoeuvrings of the Byzantine Empire, any early editing and censoring of the original texts; to correct mistranslations which were made in ignorance of the technical terms used by the Hebrew mystery schools, and thus by Jesus himself; and in this way to compile an anthology of the totality of Jesus' probable actual teachings, both exoteric and esoteric.[1] A task for a scholarly genius, or team of geniuses. But the overall picture which emerged might be startlingly different from the one on which official Christianity has been built.

It might even lend force to the feeling of many witches that a first-century Christian meeting must have had a family likeness to a twentieth-century witches' esbat – love-feast, healing work, psychic training and all.

In trying to reach understanding with Christians who criticize the kind of work we set out to do, it is worth pointing out that Jesus told his followers to go forth and do just that: 'Heal the sick, cleanse the lepers, raise the dead, cast out devils' (Matthew x:8). Raising the dead may be beyond the capacity of most of us, but at least witches work hard at the other three (which may be summed up in modern terms as 'Heal the physically and mentally ill'), while with a few honourable exceptions Christians seem to have abandoned psychic healing altogether and to have confined 'casting out devils' to a handful of licensed exorcists. (Casting out devils can mean actual exorcism or psychiatric work, which is mostly left to lay experts; witches and occultists are almost the only people who distinguish between entities attacking the psyche from outside, and disorders within the psyche itself, and try to tackle both – with specialized help if necessary.) We have found that quite a lot of sensible Christians pause and think again when we talk to them on these lines.

Like it or not, the Craft has a contribution to make in today's world which often transcends the primary task of looking after its own; on this subject, more in Section XXVI – 'In Tune with the Times'. And it will make it better if we do not treat as automatic enemies those whose paths are different but whose ultimate aims may be more like our own than we sometimes think. We do better by trying to understand them and by helping them to understand us.

We once took into our coven a young Christian who had been active as a lay missionary but who had lost heart and a great deal of his faith. We initiated him and trained him as a witch, and a very good witch he made. After a year, he told us that he wanted to go back to the Church; he said that our training had helped him to understand his own Christianity and cleared up the conflicts which had been paralysing him. We sent him on his way with our blessing, a transformed man, and he remained our friend.

Whenever we are tempted to react aggressively to someone who is on a different path from our own, we remember that young man – and remind ourselves that, although another path may be illumined by different symbols, it may be aligned on the same distant peak.

XVII   On Running a Coven

A coven is an organized group of witches, and it is pronounced 'kuvv'n' (not 'koe-v'n'). Its original meaning was simply a meeting or gathering; its root was the Latin *convenire*, 'to come together' (from which we also get convene, convention and convent).

The traditional full membership of a coven is thirteen, but in fact an effective working coven can consist of anything from three members upwards, though four is a more practicable minimum. The leader-plus-twelve unit is a very old tradition found in many other magical or religious fields beside witchcraft; Jesus, Arthur, Robin Hood, Ireland's Crom Cruach and others often follow this pattern. It is probably Zodiacal in origin, suggesting an ideal balanced unity of aspects encircling a central leader. It is interesting that the lunar complement is often to be found, too, in single or multiple form: Virgin/Magdalene, Guinevere/Morgana, Marian and so on.

Most covens today regard thirteen as the workable maximum, for two reasons. First, it is about the most that the traditional nine-foot-diameter Circle can comfortably contain. Second and more important, a larger group than that tends to become depersonalized. The essence of coven working is the building up of a group mind, a

Gestalt to which each member makes his or her own unique contribution, and in which each is continuously aware of the individuality and unique contribution of every other member. Few people could build or maintain that kind of interpersonal awareness in a group larger than a dozen or so.

A fair parallel is a good jazz combo, which depends on a delicate balance of individual spontaneity, mutual awareness and a shared feeling about the kind of music they want to produce. It can only work with a few instrumentalists; if there are too many, the group enters the big-band category, which is something quite different. Mutually aware, and mutually supportive, spontaneity is replaced by the prepared score and individually focused attention on a single conductor.

A coven which grows too large tends to alter its nature in the same way.

The normal process when a coven becomes (or is about to become) too large is for a suitable couple to 'hive off', taking with them any members of the parent coven who wish to join with them, and to form a new coven under their leadership as High Priestess and High Priest. As we explained on page 22, any second-degree couple may do this with the agreement of the parent coven's High Priestess and High Priest (strictly speaking with that of the High Priestess alone, but any coven whose leading partnership could not agree on such an issue would be in sore straits anyway). In that case, the infant coven, though working separately, remains under the guidance of the original High Priestess and High Priest until they judge its leaders ready for their third degree, after which it becomes autonomous.

Strictly speaking again – any third-degree couple could hive off *without* the High Priestess's permission, but one hopes that such a situation would seldom arise. It is obviously better for the Craft, and for the friendship and understanding which ought to exist between witches, for hiving-off always to be by mutual agreement. This may sometimes mean acknowledging the existence of differences; but a divergent view which causes friction within a coven may turn out to be constructive when it is away 'doing its own thing' with others of like mind.

A third-degree hive-off is autonomous from the start. (When we say 'second-degree couple' or 'third-degree couple', this may of course also mean a partnership in which only one holds that degree, because he or she is entitled to give it to the other.)

Once a new coven has hived off, it is advisable to observe the rule of 'voiding the coven' which we explained on pp. 22-3.

Back to the coven itself, and a summary of its structure.

The High Priestess is the leader, with the High Priest as her partner; he acknowledges her primacy and supports and complements her leadership with the qualities of his own polarity. Leadership is required from him, too, in his own way; and in the kind of harmonious partnership that is needed to run a good coven, they will find their own natural balance. The one thing he should not do is to assume the primacy himself. This is not a dogma imposed to put shackles on natural gifts; it is observed experience. We have known at least three covens – two English and one Irish – which were dominated by the High Priest, with his partner staying quietly in the background. Two of them were well-intentioned and hard-working, though we had our doubts about the third; but in due course all three of them disintegrated. Two of them sank without trace, and in the other one the High Priestess picked up the pieces and began again successfully with a new High Priest. However much drive and enthusiasm a High Priest has, he *must* channel it through the leadership of his High Priestess.

A third function in most covens is that of the Maiden. She is a kind of assistant High Priestess, but mostly for ritual purposes; she may or may not be the High Priestess's and High Priest's lieutenant in leadership. Whether she is will depend on the personalities involved and on the needs of the coven. Often it is her job to allot coven chores such as cleaning the Temple, polishing candlesticks or preparing food, or to summon everyone to the Temple when the High Priestess is ready. This is not because the High Priestess and High Priest are too lofty to do this allotting and summoning themselves; in our experience, on coven nights, there are always several members who want a quiet word with either or both of the leaders outside the Circle, and they are usually too busy with these to run around like sheepdogs seeing that everything is in order.

Talking of summoning, there is one other functionary who was very important during the undercover centuries, and is sometimes still needed today. He is the Fetch (sometimes called the Summoner or Officer) and he is usually a man. His job is to act as a courier, and sometimes an escort, between covens or between a coven and somebody who for one reason or another must remain 'unlisted'. He is a High Priestess's confidential messenger, used particularly on formal occasions or where discretion is called for. (This use of the word 'Fetch' must not be confused with its other meaning – that of a projected astral body or thought-form deliberately sent out to make its presence known to a particular person; or with its dictionary definition, 'the apparition, double, or wraith of a living person'.)

Ideally, a coven consists of equal numbers of men and women in working partnerships, though of course this ideal is seldom achieved. Even when it is not, as far as possible the man-woman polarity should be observed in coven working. For example, when the coven is circling with linked hands in the Witches' Rune, they will arrange themselves alternately, man and woman, without being told; or if for example there are more men than women, the women will so place themselves that if possible each man at least has a woman on one side of him. Again, in cord magic (see p.239), each cord should have a man holding one end and a woman the other; or if the numbers are uneven, then (say) a man may hold two cord-ends, with two women holding the other single ends. And so on. This may sound over-fussy; but the point is to make the principle of male-female polarity in magical working second nature – almost a conditioned reflex – in every member.

Although in a coven where the sex-numbers are uneven (or, as often happens, where not every member can attend every Circle) members get used to working with a variety of members of the opposite sex, established working partnerships are to be encouraged where they arise naturally, because they usually develop greater effectiveness (just as established dancing-partners do). Husband and wife are an obvious example, because their polarity is already mutually attuned; and if it is inadequate, then working magic together is a very healthy way of improving it.

(A word of warning here: if a husband and wife are members of the same coven, it is asking for trouble to allow one of them to form a magical working partnership with someone else. We once had a male witch who worked particularly well with one of our female members, and continued to do so as a regular working partnership after his wife joined the coven, claiming that there need be no conflict. We, being then very inexperienced, allowed this to continue. Witches are human, and before long came the explosion we should obviously have foreseen. That was a long time ago, and we are happy to say that the married couple are now running their own coven and the other lady is running hers.)

We are sometimes tempted to think that the almost-perfect working coven consists of three married couples[1] who are all closely in tune; a self-contained hexagram, combining the essence of even and odd numbers, and the two bonds of sexual love and friendship; a unit small enough for each member to be fully aware of all the others, on several levels, throughout the working ... So almost-perfect as to be almost-selfish; Wicca lives in a real world where the honest seeker may not be turned away just to preserve some self-contained ideal.

Which brings us to the next problem, often an acute one in this time of Craft expansion and growing interest: how to achieve a balance between the working effectiveness of a coven of trained witches and the training of newcomers.

The problem will vary with the nature of the coven. Many covens – perhaps most – are quiet and even secret, often for necessary reasons such as job protection. When such covens take on new members, it is likely to be one or perhaps two at a time. The balance is not upset, nor the coven effectiveness weakened, because the newcomers are a small minority, in some ways more easily trained and absorbed into the whole.

But some covens are publicly known – not necessarily because they are publicity-seekers. Writers on Wicca, for example, can hardly hide themselves. Their books are reviewed, newspapers interview them, they are invited to take part in television and radio programmes. They sometimes (and you can believe us on this!) wearily wish it were not so; but that's how it is, and they have to make the best of it.

We have been in Ireland ourselves for six and a half years; in that time we have been featured (often more than once) in every national daily, three Sunday papers and two local papers, have appeared three times on television, including the Saturday-night *Late Late Show* and have been on radio more times than we can remember. *Not one of these interviews or appearances was sought by us – it is always the media who approach us.* Fortunately, with the exception of one single article, we have always been treated remarkably sympathetically. We are now, quite simply, 'Ireland's witches', recognized wherever we go; not because we are the only ones, or even necessarily the best ones, but because we are the only *known* ones. And Ireland loves eccentrics.

We are not boasting about this – it is simply a by-product of our profession as writers; and we often think how peaceful life would be if it were otherwise. But one inevitable result is that people who are interested in the Craft or in allied subjects (and there are many such people) have no one else to turn to, even if it is only to ask questions and go away again. Among these, there are quite a few who are seriously interested and want to become active, and it is from these that we have built our coven. More than half of them are in their twenties, and more than half of them at this moment have been initiated for less than a year. Average attendance at regular meetings is ten or twelve people, but if everyone was able to be present on the same night it would be about twice that. Although there have been hive-offs, none of the present group feel ready to form their own groups yet, although a handful of them are certainly potential leaders.

Admittedly we are in a strange position, as the only known representatives of the Craft revival in a country where that revival was non-existent, or at least unnoticed, until we came here. But there are many public or semi-public covens in Britain, the United States, Australia and Canada who have similar problems.

One way of dealing with it, of course, is simply to say 'No'; to write, speak, be interviewed, explain yourself – but only very rarely to accept recruits, however promising. You have every right to do that if you wish, but if too many covens react that way, where is the genuine seeker to turn? He may well fall into the hands of one of the less admirable groups on the fringes of occultism whose doors are always open – and we have seen that happen more than once.

Another very practical way is to divide your group into an inner and an outer coven. The inner coven consists of experienced witches, used to working together, with the emphasis on work rather than training (though the latter must never be neglected, however experienced you think you are). The outer coven consists of new initiates and postulants, plus one or two volunteers from the inner coven to help you train them. As the outer coven members advance, they can be admitted to the inner coven; and of course the possibility of hive-offs will be always borne in mind, to keep the overall numbers reasonably stable. Typically, the inner and outer covens might meet on alternate weeks.

The other solution (which is the one we are following at the moment) is to accept the situation and keep everyone together – again, with one eye open for suitable hive-offs. This is a livelier and in many ways a more productive system, especially in places where the Craft revival is new on the ground.

But one trap to be avoided, either with an outer coven or with a mixed and relatively fluid one, is that of thinking that it is 'only' a training group, from which not much effective magical work can yet be expected. It must learn by doing, and in the confidence that what it is doing will produce results. This attitude must be instilled from the start. Every coven, however raw, is a working one.

One way of maintaining the emphasis on working is to keep a coven record. This helps you to judge honestly how successful your healing and other work is, and even to check for yourself such things as the traditional preferability of certain phases of the moon for certain kinds of working, and the helpfulness of certain incenses or music.

You can also note any interesting phenomena, such as when two or three people have the strong feeling that 'someone in *that* direction is very curious about what we're up to', or are aware of a perfume which cannot be explained by anything which is physically in the room. Such experiences are always cropping up, and if they *are* noted, very often they tie in with something which you discover later; if they are *not* noted, they are apt to slip by without anything having been learned from them.

As an example, let us look at one night's coven record of the (fictitious but typical) coven of Mary and John Smith. It might run something like this:

Saturday 5 June 1982   At Mary and John's house.
Present: Mary, John, Susan, Andrew, Bridget, Harry, Brian.
  Drawing Down the Moon *was* performed.

Cord magic was worked for the following purposes:

Mary and John   For Mary's brother Phil, depressed by a threat of redundancy. (Not told.)

Susan   For a neighbour, Mrs White, suffering from rheumatism. (Request.)

Andrew   For his forthcoming exam.

Bridget and Harry   To find a missing document.

Brian   For a friend Anne, who suffers from migraine. (Not told.)

John gave a talk on the meanings of Tarot Major Arcana O and I-IV. Bridget and Brian made some interesting points.

Bridget and Harry consecrated a necklace of Bridget's, and Susan and Brian a pentacle which Brian had made for himself.

Mary reported that the South Side coven had invited us to hold a joint Midsummer Sabbat with them, and everyone agreed to accept.

Music: Sinfonia Antarctica.

Incense: Silver Lady.

Moon: 4 days before full.

P: 27/2 (PM).

Over the following days or weeks, notes would be added on the success or failure of the five objectives for which cord magic was worked.

One or two explanations. 'Drawing Down the Moon *was* performed' (or 'was *not* performed') is noted because many experienced High Priestesses maintain that to do it at every Circle can be very draining on the woman concerned, and recommend a safe maximum of once a month. This does seem to be a matter for personal experience to confirm or refute, so Mary and John are experimenting to see how its frequency affects her, if at all.[2]

'Not told' or 'Request' after the various cord-magic entries indicates whether or not the person worked for *knew* that he or she was being worked for. This is a help in adjudging the real effectiveness of the work, because if it succeeds without the person knowing it was done, there is no question of a 'placebo effect'. (The placebo effect occurs in witchcraft as well as in medicine. In both cases, it is a matter of 'thy faith hath made thee whole'. More than once, when we have been asked for help and have promised to get the coven to work on the problem at our next Circle, we have been profusely thanked for the success of our work before the coven has even met!)

'*P*:   27/2 (PM)' is a private experiment of Mary's. She is interested in the phenomenon which we explained in Section XV, of the different psychic quality of the ovulation and menstrual peaks. So every time she presides over a Circle as High Priestess, she notes her point in the cycle.

'27/2' means that she is in the twenty-seventh day of her menstrual period, and two days before the onset of her next (the second figure of course being added later). The paramenstruum – from two days before onset to two days after – is considered to be the most clairvoyantly sensitive time; so if the first figure is 1, 2 or 3, or the second figure 1 or 2, she adds '(PM)', for paramenstruum. She has been making this note for five or six months now, and the results so far do seem to indicate that her paramenstruum is indeed a peak of her psychic power.

A good High Priest will keep an eye on his partner for signs of overstrain, because the High Priestess's job is a very demanding one, particularly in a growing coven. She is expected to be a combination of teacher, psychiatrist, nurse, mother-confessor, referee, scapegoat and reference librarian. She is expected to be omniscient and tireless. New young witches especially tend to put her on a pedestal, and to over-react when they discover that she is human after all. She is sometimes tempted to cry, with Hamlet:

The time is out of joint; O cursed spite,
That ever I was born to set it right!

Her High Priest should never allow all this to get out of hand. If she is over-tired before a Circle, he might suggest that tonight would be a good night to let Bridget and Harry preside while she relaxes. He will also be wise to have one or two training talks, or group exercises, up his sleeve which he can conduct himself at short notice or no notice at all, to shift the burden off her for a while. He should never neglect her psychic defence, remembering that all the sensitivity and psychic openness that are required of her make her especially vulnerable. An important part of his job is to be her psychic bodyguard and always to be ready with the Circle-round-the-bed, the appropriate Banishing Pentagram, the Openings of the Body ritual or whatever is called for. If he is not married to or living with her, he must achieve an even more delicate balance – being as alive to her situation as circumstances permit, but without invading her privacy or breathing down her neck. (Even a husband should remember that one; his High Priestess-wife should feel protected but not stifled or coddled.)

A publicly known High Priestess – particularly if she has a vivid and outgoing personality – is likely to arouse a certain amount of jealousy, with its resulting malicious rumours. Among the ones which have come back to us are, that Janet has a string of lovers, some of them named and some of whom she has never even met, and/or that Stewart has a small harem (in fact we have been completely faithful to each other from the start, and have no intention or wish to be anything else, ever); that Janet entertained some of these alleged lovers in our castle in the middle of a lake in Co. Mayo (in fact our Mayo home was a two-bedroomed cottage on a bog); that Janet's figure is largely silicone (in fact it is entirely as Nature made it); that we are rich (in fact, like most freelance writers, we live hand-to-mouth); that Janet has had a sex-change (!); that we are not legally married (in fact we were married at Woking Register Office, Surrey, on 19 July 1975, as anyone may check); and so on and so on.

Doreen Valiente has her own list of stories she has heard about herself. 'The one I like best,' she tells us, 'is that I'm the illegitimate daughter of Aleister Crowley. My mother is supposed to have been a dashing 1920's deb of high family, and I am said to have been farmed out to foster parents who brought me up as their own because their own child had died. Unfortunately, it clashes with the other story that I am a Polish Jewess who came here in wartime as a refugee, having been initiated into the darker secrets of the Qabalah in my own country. The New Forest gypsies took me in, and that is where Gerald Gardner found me. (I've had this one told to me in total solemnity by someone who didn't know whom he was talking to – and I didn't let on!) Moreover, I am supposed to be a secret agent for Scientology, of all things – someone was quite actively spreading this one around Brighton a few years ago. And there was another one about my having organised a Black Mass or a Sabbat orgy or something in Chislehurst Caves – I've never been there in my life! The really funny one is fairly recent. It confuses me with Doreen Irvine, and says that I've become a Christian convert and gone over to the United States, where I am making pots of money lecturing against witchcraft. I hope she won't sue!'

Such gossip would be funny if it were not sometimes distressing. The consolation is that it comes from a small minority of warped minds, and that most people are civilized and friendly if one is civilized and friendly to them. A chip on the shoulder is the very last thing a publicly known witch should carry.

Tradition has it that an expectant mother is Queen of the Circle, and she is especially honoured whatever her degree. But she will find that she cannot *run* the Circle, or lead the work, as effectively as before. A pregnant woman's psychic antennae are withdrawn to concentrate on the new life within her. If she is normally gifted in astral projection, she will almost certainly find that she cannot do it at all while she is expecting a baby (and Nature's reasons for withdrawing the gift at this time are pretty obvious). Her psyche consolidates itself around her pregnancy, so that she is not really equipped to lead, and be the focus for, the coven's psychic work. A pregnant High Priestess would be well advised to appoint a suitable deputy to act for her until after the baby is born – or more probably a working partnership to act together, since it is likely that her own High Priest will wish to withdraw with her. During those months they can of course still take part in Circles, but as elder statesmen rather than as active leaders. The only exception might well be the festival Sabbats, which are celebratory rather than working occasions; for example, a pregnant High Priestess is ideally suited to enact the Mother at the Imbolg Sabbat (see *Eight Sabbats for Witches*, Section IV).   'Every man and woman is a Star', and every woman, like every man, is unique; so there may well be women witches with a special quality of power which, mysteriously, enables them to continue as active High Priestess through part or all of a pregnancy. But any woman who feels so able must be very honest with herself, and be sure that she is not merely rationalizing a desire to keep the reins in her own hands.

Banishment from the coven should be a very rare necessity, and in many covens it may happily never arise at all. But there are times when it is the only course. If a member has deliberately betrayed the confidence of the coven, or lied to its leaders, or carried on hidden activities which he or she knows to be incompatible with the trust which the coven places in him or her, or flagrantly broken a fundamental law of Wiccan ethics, or is causing continuous dissension within the coven, then action has to be taken.

Mere disagreement is not enough reason for banishment. Opinions honestly held and expressed must be thrashed out; the coven and its leaders may even learn from them, or the holder be persuaded of error. What is not acceptable is underhand sabotage or devious lobbying.

Unless the offence is obviously so gross that immediate banishment is imperative, the first step should be confrontation of the culprit, first by the High Priestess and High Priest, and then if necessary by the whole Council of Elders. If the culprit genuinely sees the point, and the matter can be resolved at this stage, so much the better. One possibility to be borne in mind is to tell him or her to stay away from coven Circles, say for a month, for some personal heart-searching and reappraisal, or for private study to correct whatever was the weakness. This can often work wonders.

But if the culprit is stubborn and unrepentant, and banishment becomes the only answer, then it must be done formally and properly and the culprit must know his or her rights. In the time-honoured formula of democracy – not only must justice be done, it must be seen to be done.

The actual banishment may be pronounced either by the High Priestess or by the High Priest. The culprit must be told at the same time that he or she may ask for readmission after a year and a day –

and also told that he or she remains a witch even though banished, because that is something which can never be taken away.

If (as we have known to happen) a culprit refuses to face the High Priestess or High Priest and accept banishment, then it may be done by letter; but personal confrontation should be managed if possible.

In very special circumstances, the High Priestess may decide to readmit the culprit before the year and a day is up, but this should not be done lightly, as it weakens the respect in which banishment is held. If the culprit does apply for readmission at the proper time, it must only be granted if he or she has genuinely understood and regretted the offence and made any practical amends that are necessary.

It goes without saying that a banished witch may not try to join another coven while the banishment is in effect, and that any High Priestess who knowingly accepted such a witch would be breaking the Craft code, unless of course she were satisfied that the banishing coven was corrupt, irresponsible or black – and her conviction would have to be very well founded. Mere belief that the banishment was unfair would not be enough.

A place of occult working, it need hardly be said, acquires a psychic charge; and if the workers move elsewhere without thinking about what they are leaving behind, it may well become 'haunted'. Later users of such a place for ordinary purposes may encounter phenomena which puzzle or alarm them, particularly if they are psychically sensitive and at all nervous – even if the activities of which those phenomena are after-echoes were benign ones.

So when we leave a covenstead, our last Circle is entirely devoted to 'closing the Temple' and to working to ensure that no one who lives in the house after us will receive anything but helpful 'vibes' from our having been there, or will experience any phenomena which might puzzle or distress them.

That, we feel, is only good manners and good discipline, and just as important as leaving the house physically clean and tidy for the next occupants.

There are other arguments in favour of it. If you leave astral loose ends in an abandoned covenstead, you are also leaving open astral links to yourselves, and may thus be affected by any negative emotional or psychic factors which later occupiers may bring into your old home. Having no personal involvement with them, you may not even realize where these negative influences are coming from.

For these and other reasons, we strongly recommend a deliberate closing-down ritual when you leave an old covenstead. The form of the ritual should be a matter of your own devising; what matters is the strongly envisaged intent. But it is a good idea psychologically, and it emphasizes that intent, if the whole coven sets to and strips the Temple entirely and packs its contents ready for moving, immediately the ritual is over and the Circle banished.

It is hardly possible to leave *no* influence behind – or even no manifestations; but if you have done your closing-down properly, such manifestations will be defused, so to speak. For example, we have had the strange experience of becoming 'ghosts' ourselves. We had left a covenstead where we had built up a strong coven and had done a lot of psychic work, much of it relating to our immediate natural surroundings. Much later, we learned that neighbours were quite convinced they had seen us visiting the house, though in fact we had not been within miles of it since we left. We are an easily recognizable couple, and country people have sharp eyes; so we are satisfied that their belief was genuine. But if we had neglected the closing-down ritual, our after-echoes might have been disturbingly 'supernatural', instead of being mistaken for natural happenings.

This Section has naturally talked a lot about structure, leadership, generally accepted rules and so on; just as the first part of this book has dealt with detailed rituals and (largely for reasons of historical interest and putting the record straight) has delved into sources, textual variations and so on.

But we would not want anyone to misunderstand this and get the impression that Wicca is a formalized religion. Rituals which are widely accepted as norms, and rules which have been found to work, are a useful basis of operation – but a *basis*, not a straitjacket. Wicca, being a growing and creative religion drawing on ancient roots, embraces a wide spectrum from time-honoured forms to complete spontaneity. Our own practice (which we think is fairly typical) ranges from the precise observation of loved rituals to the unpredictable inspiration of the moment – often within one evening's Circle. And that is how it should be. Similarly, covens vary greatly in which part of the spectrum they tend to emphasize.

For an intelligent and articulate exposition of the spontaneous (one might almost say Charismatic) end of the Wiccan spectrum we recommend the American witch Starhawk's two books *The Spiral Dance* and *Dreaming the Dark*. Some of the things that she and her friends get up to would make a traditionalist's (with a small 't') hair stand on end; but they are a healthy corrective to over-formalism.

And for a breath of the poetry of witchcraft, the light-dark mystery of it, read Erica Jong's *Witches*, with its haunting paintings by Joseph A. Smith. (It is the kind of book of which you may well want to buy two copies, so that you can cut one of them up and frame the pictures.)

Every coven must find its own character and its own area of

emphasis within the spectrum. But it should be wary of missing out altogether on any of the spectrum's wavelengths. If pure white light symbolizes the fulfilment and the psychic integration which we all seek, it should be remembered that light is never white unless it includes every colour there is – including some which are invisible to the ordinary sight.

XVIII Naked in Your Rites

Ritual nudity is a general practice in Gardnerian and Alexandrian witchcraft and is to be found in other Wiccan paths as well. To those who, like ourselves, have been practising it for many years, nudity seems perfectly normal and acceptable – as it does to the thirty thousand or so naturists in the British Isles, and to anything up to two million on the Continent. We have to remind ourselves that other people find it strange.

By 'strange', of course, the objectors mean 'sexually provocative' or even 'orgiastic'. Nobody who has attended a well-run naturist camp, with its relaxed family membership, or a genuine Wiccan Circle, with its equally relaxed group identity, can really believe that. Familiarity with nakedness very quickly teaches one the actual truth: that the naked body in itself is no more, and no less, sexually arousing than the clothed one – and that even an attractive naked body may be less disturbing than the same body in deliberately provocative clothing. Sexiness is a matter of behaviour, of attitude, of 'vibes' – not of the presence or absence of clothing.

Patriarchal conditioning over the past couple of thousand years or so has ingrained the ideas that nakedness equals sex, and that sex equals danger. Sexuality – and in particular female sexuality – to the patriarchal mind stands for the Shadow, for all the unmanageable depths of the psyche which cannot be disciplined, ordered and contained by the rigid administration of the Ego-Empire. Commercialized nudity (the pin-up, the flesh that sells soft drinks or shampoos or automobiles) is something different; the Ego-Empire must make its profit to survive, and anyway debasing sexuality is one way of containing it. But relaxed, non-commercial nudity, whether social or ritual, is alarming. It is the Shadow refusing to play the patriarchal game.

Witches, too, refuse to play the patriarchal game. And taking off their clothes for their rituals is one sign of that refusal.

As the Charge puts it: 'And ye shall be free from slavery; and as a sign that ye be really free, ye shall be naked in your rites.' This is no Gardnerian innovation, by the way;[1] it is an inheritance from the Tuscan witches (*Aradia: the Gospel of the Witches*, p.6 – see Bibliography under Leland):

> *Sarete liberi dalla schiavitù!*
> *E cosi diverrete tutti liberi!*
> *Pero uomini e donne*
> *Sarete tutti nudi, per fino.*
> (Ye shall be free from slavery!
> And thus shall ye all become free!
> Therefore, men and women,
> Ye too shall all be naked.)

Ritual nakedness, particularly for shamanistic purposes, is an old pagan practice, certainly not confined to the witches of Tuscany. It was even a habit of the old Hebrew prophets: 'And he stripped off his clothes also, and prophesied before Samuel in like manner, and lay down naked all that day and all that night. Wherefore they say, Is Saul also among the prophets?' (I Samuel xix, 24). Even St Francis, that splendidly undevious saint, preached one of his first radical sermons stark naked in the Cathedral of San Ruffino in Assisi, to a large congregation of men and women. Shuttle and Redgrove (*The Wise Wound*, p.227) quote E.A.S. Butterworth as saying that nakedness and prophecy go together: 'We see that the offence of Adam and Eve was, in all likelihood, that they had cultivated a practice, at least akin to shamanism, in which they had attained a condition of ecstatic vision or consciousness, called eating of the tree of life, or of the tree of the knowledge of good and evil. When their eyes were opened and they knew that they were naked, Adam and Eve knew that they were seers

NAKED IN YOUR RITES   195

and persons of power and sacred quality in their own right.' Shuttle
and Redgrove comment that, 'this must have exasperated any Deity
dedicated to any authoritarian or hierarchical rule, or any church
derived from a repressive interpretation of the legend, like the
mediaeval Christian Church.'

There is much argument about whether witches in the British Isles
regularly worked naked – though since in the climate of these islands it
would mostly be indoors and certainly secret, evidence on the subject
would be scanty. But, for example, naked dances for the fertility of
crops unquestionably did take place (we quoted a living-memory
instance of this from Co. Longford on p.86 of *Eight Sabbats for
Witches*). And many experts have written about the witches' 'flying
ointments'[2] which were rubbed all over the body and produced a feeling
of levitation; the users of these powerful and dangerous substances
would hardly have reclothed themselves while the ointment was still
active on their skins.

Continental paintings and drawings of witches often showed them
naked (see Plate 14 for a charming Flemish example), which suggests
that the practice was known about.

But whether or not the widespread Wiccan habit of 'working
skyclad' is mainly a phenomenon of the twentieth-century revival (in
the British Isles at least) or the continuation of a secret custom of the
underground days, is hardly important. Ritual nudity has always been
a feature of pagan shamanistic practice, and even (as we have seen) of
ancient Judaic; and its geographical distribution at any one period is
secondary to the principle. What matters is its validity for witches
today.

There are several good reasons for witches to work skyclad.

The first is that it is a deliberate antidote to the cardinal sin of the
patriarchal period: the split between body and spirit. 'In the split world,
spirit wars with flesh, culture with nature, the sacred with the profane,
the light with the dark' (Starhawk, *Dreaming the Dark*, p.20). This is
patriarchalism's debasement of the creative principle of polarity into a
false dualism of good-versus-evil which we discussed in Section XI,
'The Rationale of Witchcraft'. Witches deny this attitude. They
maintain, with the Cabalists, that 'all the Sephiroth are equally holy';
they insist that good is in fact the macrocosmic and microcosmic
working of polarity, and that evil is its imbalance or denial. The
Christian Church in particular (unlike Jesus who spoke of the 'temple'
of his body) has been responsible for identifying the body with evil and
the spirit with good, and putting them at war with one another, instead
of seeing the body as the incarnated manifestation of the inner levels,
through which those levels enrich and extend their experience.

Shame at nudity is one expression of this false dualism. It pretends that John Smith and Mary Brown are 'really' just spiritual and mental beings (with all their potential or actual good centred upon those levels) trapped in gross physical bodies (which are essentially evil, even though Christian dogma paradoxically maintains that they will ultimately be resurrected in 'purified' form – how clothed, one wonders?). Hiding the body is therefore seen as a spiritually virtuous act.

To the witch, on the other hand, John Smith and Mary Brown, as at present incarnated, are multi-level beings of spirit, mind, astral body and flesh; and each of those levels should shine forth with equal confidence and self-respect (not to mention mutual respect, between levels and between individuals) if integration and fulfilment are to be achieved. When John Smith and Mary Brown, as witches, take off their clothes to work their magic and worship the Goddess and the God, they are openly affirming that principle and striving to make it part of their everyday awareness.

A good reason for skyclad working – and the one most quoted – is a very practical one: experienced opinion holds that it is easier to raise psychic power with an uncovered body than with a covered one. Remembering that psychic power-raising is a two-sided process of input and output (increased awareness and increased psychic energy amplifying each other by mutual feedback) this may well be the original reason for shamanistic nudity – that the naked body is more responsive not only to sensory impressions (which is obvious) but also to psychic ones. And on the parallel process of output – sensitives who can see the human aura find that they can do so more clearly around bare flesh; and those few doctors who use auric examination diagnostically, including those who do not claim clairvoyance, examine their patients unclothed for this purpose (see Kilner's *The Human Aura*, for example).

A witch at work brings *all* his or her levels into operation – spiritual, mental, astral, etheric and physical. Their interrelationships may vary according to the particular level on which the work is intended to take effect, which may be any one of them. But they must all be fully functional; so it may be that trying to work with one of them partly screened is like trying to play the piano in gloves, or to paint a picture in dark glasses. It can be done if circumstances demand it – but if they do not, why add to your difficulties?

There is an interesting biological footnote to this aspect. Everybody knows about hormones, the internal chemical messengers which carry information and instructions around in our bloodstream and regulate the balance of our bodies' functions. But not many laymen have heard of their counterparts the 'pheromones' or *external* chemical messengers. Our bodies give these pheromones off in minute but very powerful quantities; so powerful that (to take a startling example from another genus) a single molecule of the appropriate pheromone enables a male moth to detect a female moth from nearly seven miles away. (Maurice Burton, *The Sixth Sense of Animals*, pp. 104-5.) So the air around us is full of important information which we emit and which we receive from others; much of it unconsciously, but we react to it all the same.

Obviously, the naked body gives off pheromones far more quickly and efficiently than a clothed one. So it may well be that in group working, a skyclad coven is exchanging unconscious information more effectively than a robed one; and this information may be highly relevant to the psychic *Gestalt* which they are trying to build up. Pheromones have been extensively researched by scientists, but so far as we know, no scientist with occult or psychic interests has looked into that possible aspect of their effects. There is room for investigation here.

A third reason for skyclad working is a psychological one. To be an effective witch you must above all be *yourself*; most of the work of self-integration is concerned with finding out who 'yourself' is, with seeing past the Persona, the Ego's comforting mask, the image which the Ego presents to the world and to itself. And there is nothing more image-forming than clothes, which are a precious prop to the Persona. Consciously and unconsciously, how we dress is how we say to the world, 'This is myself as I want you to see me' before we even open our mouths. Taking off our clothes is a psychologically powerful gesture of image-shedding, a symbolic milestone on the road to self-realization. In group working, it not only means that John Smith finds it psychologically harder to project a false image of himself to Mary Brown; it also means he starts seeing past Mary's Persona and relating to her as she really is; while at the same time Mary is going through the same revolution, with the two revolutions feeding each other.

It is interesting to watch, incidentally, how a developing witch may even unconsciously acquire a more pleasing dress-sense in ordinary, clothed life. The reason is plain: his or her Persona is adjusting itself, with improved understanding, closer to the truth of the Self, and this in turn is instinctively reflected in the choice of clothes.

A fourth reason carries more weight with some people than with others: nudity is completely democratic. A few very new witches in a coven whose members come from mixed backgrounds may be a little self-conscious about differences at first. Years ago we had in our coven, at the same time, an Indian princess and a building worker. She was only a jeans-and-sweater law student, and he was a many-skilled and articulate young man; but he admitted to us, months after their first meeting, that for the first weeks he had only been able to feel completely at ease with her when we were all skyclad in the Circle

together, because 'then we were all just people.' (Ironically, that girl
was more 'decent' in the Circle than out; she was tiny, with long thick
hair, and when she sat in the Circle with it spread around her like a
tent, we used to tease her that we could only see her knees and her
nose!) It goes without saying that, once the freemasonry of Wicca starts
working, such differences soon become meaningless. But our
building-worker friend's initial reaction does bear out what we said
about the image-forming function of clothes; he knew what she was,
and they were very *expensive* jeans and sweaters.

Some people, while accepting the idea of ritual nudity without too
much horror, qualify their acceptance by saying, 'Of course, it's all
very well if you're young and good-looking.' We find in fact that this
does not arise. We have had skyclad witches from eighteen to their
sixties; men, women, tall, short, fat, thin, plain, stunning, raven, golden
and grey; and nobody seems to mind. If anything, the less handsome
ones seem reassured by the emphasis on our common humanity which
skyclad practice brings; finding themselves treated as equals, they may
even achieve a new poise and thus start making more of themselves,
discovering attractive potentialities which they did not know they
possessed.

A final advantage of skyclad working is particularly important with
some personalities; the ones who have genuine occult potential but are
glamorized by the appeal of splendid robes and trappings (a
by-product, of course, of the Persona problem). To these, working
naked brings home the lesson that psychic effectiveness comes from
within; it is hard and dedicated work, and no romantic dressing-up will
provide a short cut. We have had one or two of these people, and each
of them had to learn the lesson the hard way.

All this does not mean, of course, that skyclad covens never work
robed. There are occasions when robes are called for: when you are
working ceremonial magic, for instance, as we and many other covens
sometimes do. It is a different technique from normal Wiccan working,
and should be recognized as such. It involves the extensive use of
symbols, colours, perfumes, music and so on, to put yourself in tune
with a particular and precisely defined aspect. It is not witchcraft, but
there is no reason why witches should never work it – any more than
classical musicians should never play jazz, or rock musicians chamber
music, if they feel like it.

Obviously, too, there are occasions when a coven is working out of
doors where they may be observed, or when the weather is unsuitable
for bare skin; there is no occult virtue in goose-pimples or pneumonia.

But in general, when covering *is* called for, special robes are
preferable to ordinary clothes if possible. We have a suitcase full of
plain overall gowns with loose sleeves, suitable for men and women

alike, which may be worn by themselves or over other clothes. The point is to emphasize the Circle as something special, 'a boundary between the world of men and the realm of the Mighty Ones' – just as a Christian will put on his Sunday best to go to church, or a Jew his Sabbath best to go to synagogue. For skyclad covens, 'skin is the livery of the Goddess'; it is *their* Sunday or Sabbath best. But even if that livery must be covered, they still like the Circle to be seen as special, as well as being felt to be special.

To help newcomers over their first shyness, we always offer them a robe for their initial Circle. Some accept it and some do not; but we often find that even those who do, take it off halfway through because their feeling of shyness has transferred its focus to embarrassment at being odd man or woman out.

Most skyclad covens have one other exception to the rule: a menstruating woman may wear panties or a robe as she wishes.

The skyclad rule does not bar the use of particular robes for a symbolic reason in a particular ritual. An example of this is the High Priestess's white tabard in our Yule ritual in *Eight Sabbats for Witches*: but even then she would take it off when the ritual was finished and the Sabbat party began.

We have given here the reasons why many covens work skyclad. They are good reasons, but in cold print, to someone who has never experienced skyclad working, they may appear a little intellectualized. Nothing could be farther from the truth. Witches who are used to working skyclad know how relaxing, natural, psychically powerful and utterly unembarrassing it is.

Skin is indeed the livery of the Goddess.

XIX   Clairvoyance and Divination

Clairvoyance is the art and science of being aware of facts, objects or situations by psychic means when they are not available to 'ordinary' awareness. The word is generally used to cover all such psychic awareness; but strictly speaking, *clairvoyance* means experiencing such awareness in the form of visual images, *clairsentience* means experiencing it in the form of bodily sensations, and *clairaudience* means experiencing it in the form of heard sounds.

Take the example of what is known as a 'crisis apparition' – when a person undergoing a sudden emotional trauma (such as death or a violent accident) manifests in another place to someone who is emotionally in tune with him or her. (There have been many confirmed cases of this in wartime, when a woman has 'seen' a husband or son at the moment when he is killed in action.) In the strict sense, a clairvoyant might see the person standing in the room; a clairsentient might feel a familiar hand on the shoulder; and a clairaudient might hear the familiar voice.

In this book we use the word clairvoyance to cover all these forms, unless we specifically say otherwise.

Precognition is also a form of clairvoyance, when the event perceived lies in the future.

Divination is 'clairvoyance using tools' – that is, with the aid of Tarot cards, a pendulum, the yarrow sticks or coins of the I Ching, rune stones, molten lead poured into water, tea-leaves or any other physical accessory.

Scrying is the use of a crystal ball, a pool of ink, a concave black mirror or any other device for defocusing normal vision, to aid clairvoyance in the strict sense.

To a certain extent, the physical aids used in divination work as triggers to the intuition. The person using them makes contact with intuitive awareness which is hidden in the Unconscious by offering it something onto which it can project that awareness in the form of images or symbols, which an experienced diviner can then interpret; much as a psychiatric patient projects elements of his Unconscious onto the ink-blots of a Rorschach test card, for interpretation by the analyst. Such triggers are useful devices for bypassing the censor which stands on the threshold between Unconscious and the Ego. This censor is a necessary element in the psyche, because without it the Ego-consciousness would be overwhelmed by a flood of incoming data; it enables the Ego to focus attention selectively, which is the essence of consciousness. But in the unintegrated psyche, the censor is a rather rough-and-ready mechanism. With expanded awareness, and improved communication between Unconscious and Ego, the censor becomes more helpfully selective; and what the experienced diviner is doing (whether consciously or not) is instructing the censor to let through intuitive data relevant to the problem in hand.

This triggering process is the main feature of such divinatory methods as gazing at tea-leaves or at molten lead which has solidified in water, or the ancient Roman method of examining the entrails of a sacrificed bird or animal. Scrying, too, is a triggering process; the scryer's defocused eyes and light-trance mind are in a suitable state for visualizing what the censor is letting through. The physical action or ritual involved – whether it is the swirling and draining of a teacup or the arranging of a crystal ball in suitable light – also becomes, with use, a triggering-signal, inducing the right state of mind and inviting the Unconscious to communicate.

The unconscious resources which the diviner or clairvoyant is tapping are far wider, in the occult view, than those of the individual Unconscious as envisaged by Freudian psychology. Jung came much closer to the occult concept with his teachings on the Collective Unconscious, though he carefully limited those teachings to deductions from his experience as a clinical psychologist. But unlike Freud, Jung was a man with a very open mind, and one senses that he knew perfectly well that there were vast fields yet to be explored. His writings on synchronicity (see Bibliography) in particular reveal this.

Occultists and witches see the Unconscious itself as clairvoyant and telepathic. The Personal Unconscious, for a start, contains the buried memories of all the individual's past incarnations. And as a unique outcrop of the Collective Unconscious, it has potential or actual communication with other outcrops, with the Personal Unconscious of other human beings – and also potential access to the Akashic Records, the astral 'recordings' of everything that has ever happened. 'Reading the Akashic Records' is an advanced technique, of which only adepts have real mastery; but every clairvoyant does it in flashes (as we probably all do without realizing it, from time to time).

So the clairvoyant or diviner is not just asking his or her Unconscious: 'Tell me the things which I have forgotten or only subliminally noticed.' He or she is asking: 'Lift the veil on the things I need to know – whether they are buried in my own subliminal awareness, in my or other people's incarnation memories, in or via the Collective Unconscious or in the Akashic Records.'

And the more skilled and confident one becomes, the more clearly the Unconscious answers.

The Ego and the Unconscious can be likened to a farmer and his dog. The dog, like the Ego, is far more acutely aware of his immediate surroundings than the farmer. His physical senses are much sharper, and he is primarily absorbed in what those senses have to tell him. The farmer, on the other hand, has sources of information which are incomprehensible to the dog. He knows that more sheep will be arriving tomorrow because he has arranged it by telephone. He knows that his neighbour has put up an electric fence, which the dog has to learn about by painful experience. He knows that the dog must have an injection because the vet has warned him that there is parvovirus in the area. He knows that his sheep must be moved off a particular piece of rough grazing because work is due to start there on a new bypass. All these things affect the orders he must give to his dog, and some of those orders may puzzle the dog, because the data on which they are based are outside his awareness-capacity. The farmer knows friends from enemies; but all the dog can do is bark at strangers till the farmer has categorized them for him.

If the dog fears and resents the farmer, their co-operation will be forced and minimal. But if there is love and trust between them, so that each can contribute his own special kind of awareness, their co-operation can be almost magical – as anyone who has watched shepherds and sheepdogs working together knows.

Similarly, the Unconscious has sources of information of which the Ego knows nothing. And the sooner the Ego realizes this, and co-operates with that which it cannot directly apprehend, the better the team (which is the total psyche) will work.

This communication of the Ego with the Unconscious is what alchemists and occultists have called the Great Work. Aleister Crowley at first called its aim 'the knowledge and conversation of one's holy guardian angel', and later 'the knowledge of the nature and powers of one's own being'. Geoffrey Ashe, in his stimulating novel *The Finger and the Moon*, speaks of 'the idea that a guardian angel, a spirit-watcher, a higher self as it were, does hover near each one of us' and 'is linked with the conscious mind through the Unconscious'. But he suggests a simpler hypothesis: '*The Unconscious, so-called, and that other self are the same.* Or rather: what Freud and Jung found in each person's psyche, beyond the reach of waking awareness — what they therefore called "subconscious" or "unconscious" — is really an aspect of the life of another being within him, another self from which the ego has split off, but which is still there, still active, still thinking, still in its own way conscious. Viewed under a different aspect, that inner being is also the guardian angel. Scientists may be right when they contend that you and I (meaning what those words commonly mean) have no preternormal powers. But we each carry within us an allied being who has. That is why occult phenomena continue to happen .... The first step is to think of your mighty invisible companion as present, inside you. And the first commandment which follows is: LISTEN, LISTEN TO THAT COMPANION.'

This commandment (capitals and all!) is the secret of clairvoyance and divination.

For most people, the best way of learning the art is to start with divination of some kind. The presence of the 'tools' (Tarot layout or whatever) helps to give one confidence; it offers one something concrete to interpret, and thus primes the pump of the intuition. One tries an interpretation, and with increasing practice one begins to realize that genuine information *is* coming through, and confidence is further reinforced.

The rules are very similar to those we gave on pp.129-30 about judging apparent incarnation recall: namely, let it all flow with an open mind, and keep records — certainly in the early stages and for what you feel to be important readings, particularly those where precognition seems to be involved. Do *not* try to pass judgement on the material as it is coming through. There is nothing so inhibiting to clairvoyance as asking yourself step by step, 'Is this purely subjective, wishful thinking or genuine?' That is an important question, but it is one to ask afterwards, when the session is over.

That divination works in ways which transcend mere 'triggering', no one with experience of it can doubt; and the discovery of this fact is very encouraging to the beginner who perseveres. One becomes impressed by the active co-operation (one can call it no less) which a

Tarot layout or an I Ching reading, for example, can give. The cards or hexagram texts will use everything from puns to startlingly direct references to point in the necessary direction. We have even known more than one case (and we swear that this is true) when a puzzling Tarot layout has prompted us to pick it up, reshuffle the pack thoroughly and deal a new layout – *which turned out to be exactly the same as the first one.* The chances against this are astronomical, but the Tarot seemed determined to reemphasize its point. On other occasions we have done the same thing, and the second layout has been *almost* the same, but with differences which clarified our questions about the first one.

Again, we have found that 'nagging' the I Ching over a single problem frequently produces Hexagram 4, Youthful Folly:

> *At the first oracle I inform him.*
> *If he asks two or three times, it is importunity.*
> *If he importunes, I give him no information.*

which needs no interpretation – and we have never known Hexagram 4 to turn up inappropriately.

By far the best version of the I Ching is the Richard Wilhelm translation, rendered into English by Cary F. Baynes (see Bibliography under Wilhelm). It has the added advantage of a Foreword by Carl Jung, who was profoundly impressed by the system and had some illuminating things to say about the way it works. (Francis King once described the I Ching to us as 'the only cook-book method of divination which does work', and we know what he meant. All divinatory systems require some intuitive interpetation, and so, when it is used properly, does the I Ching; but no other system gives such precise and detailed answers.)

But it is the Tarot which is the witches' most widely used method of divination, and the one most deeply involved in the whole Western occult tradition. The archetypal symbols of the Major Arcana, and the elemental progressions of the Minor Arcana, are endlessly rich, both in their individual significance and in their limitless combinations. Every witch should be familiar with them, and they are the ideal starting-point for a beginner in divination; they produce results from the very start.

With the renewed fashion for things occult, more and more Tarot packs have appeared on the market. (We ourselves have a collection of over thirty.) Some are good, some are atrocious. The generally accepted standard is the Rider (or Waite) pack, designed by Pamela Colman Smith for A.E. Waite early in this century. The artwork looks a little dated now, but the symbolism is excellent. An attractive pack of basically the same symbolism is that designed by David Sheridan, with instructions by Alfred Douglas, and published by Mandragora Press, London, in 1972; so if you like the Rider pack's symbolism but prefer a contemporary design, try this one. Perhaps the most beautiful pack is the one designed by Frieda Harris for Aleister Crowley and published years after his death by Llewellyn Publications, St Paul, Minnesota, as the Thoth Tarot Cards; but the symbolism is very much Crowley's own and would confuse anyone trying to learn the mainstream tradition.

As for books on the subject – the classic work, which is naturally based on the Rider pack, is A.E. Waite's *The Pictorial Key to the Tarot*. Waite is sound but can be annoyingly pompous. An excellent modern authority is *A Complete Guide to the Tarot* by Eden Gray; it, too, is based on the Rider pack.

For those who want to compare the various designs and interpretations of the Tarot, a very useful book is Bill Butler's *The Definitive Tarot*. For each card, Butler describes the symbolism of up to nine different packs (including the three we have mentioned) and summarizes the interpretations given by a dozen or so different authorities.

For the symbolism of the Crowley pack, read Crowley's own work *The Book of Thoth*.

To start your study of the Tarot, we recommend the Rider pack and the Eden Gray book. They will give you a reliable norm by which you can judge the others.

But any Tarot pack will very soon develop meanings which are personal to you. There is no cast-iron, orthodox, 'right' interpretation of any card – but once you have built up your own set of meanings, the cards will speak to you in the language of those meanings. It is a good idea to keep a notebook of the meanings which appeal to you; we have a loose-leaf one, each page of which is headed by miniature colour photographs of the relevant Rider and Sheridan card (because Janet prefers the Rider and Stewart the Sheridan – the choice is always personal). The photographs were easy; we simply laid the packs out in blocks of thirty, photographed them and cut the resulting prints up into miniatures. Underneath we note the meanings that have crystallized for us out of years of use; some of the cards have even acquired nicknames, such as 'Busy-Busy' for the Eight of Wands and 'The Sad Lady' for the Queen of Swords. We are still adding notes to it.

Sometimes a concept from another discipline will throw new light on a Tarot card. For example, we now relate the Chariot card to 'the parallelogram of forces'; look it up in an elementary textbook of dynamics and you will soon see why. The charioteer has harnessed and understood apparently divergent polarized forces, and their resultant takes him where he wants to go.

Each page (like most books on the subject) also gives a meaning for the card when it appears *reversed*. But we find that most books on the Tarot fail to point out a possible source of error here. We would say that a reversed card can have one of two meanings, according to its context: *either* the opposite (or negative aspect) of the card's upright meaning, *or* the upright meaning still in a state of unrealized potential. The rest of the layout, and your own intuition, will usually tell you which of these two interpretations should be given to it.

Layouts are many and various, and again the choice is personal. The Celtic Cross layout (given in most of the books, including Eden Gray) is perhaps the most popular, and it is very straightforward and clear. We tend to use it when we are delving into the past, present and likely future of a problem. If you make use of the Cabala, you may find, like us, that a Tree of Life layout is very helpful for some problems – particularly for analysing an individual's personal make-up and the factors affecting him or her. For those who are not familiar with the Cabala, the layout of the ten Sephiroth of the Tree of Life, with their Hebrew names, is like this:

	1. KETHER	
3. BINAH		2. CHOKMAH
5. GEBURAH		4. CHESED
	6. TIPHARETH	
8. HOD		7. NETZACH
	9. YESOD	
	10. MALKUTH	

If ten cards are laid out in this pattern, for just such a personal-analysis reading, the very much simplified interpretation from their placings would be:

Kether The Self; the person's quintessence – or perhaps present stage of karmic development.

Chokmah The person's present driving force or dominant motivation – whether conscious or unconscious.

Binah The formative aspect; that which is giving shape and effectiveness to the energy of Chokmah.

Chesed The organizing, administering aspect; the person's ability to cope with practical situations.

Geburah The energetic aspect; the person's capacity for positive action.

Tiphareth The key factor which interrelates all the others – whether effectively (co-ordination) or ineffectively (disruption).

Netzach The emotional aspect; instincts and feelings.

Hod The intellectual aspect; mental categories and concepts.

Yesod The astral sphere; the creative imagination; intuition; the bridge between Malkuth and the other planes.

Malkuth Everyday consciousness; physical factors; the person's practical situation as it now stands.

Even a passing knowledge of the Cabala will of course enrich these aspects or their interrelationships; but the above is a basic guide on which to experiment.

We usually follow a Tree of Life layout with three Qualifying Cards – the next three dealt off the top of the pack. These give a guide to future developments and the possible course of action.

Layouts apart – the drawing of single cards to answer single questions can often be helpful. The pack is shuffled and spread face downwards, and a card drawn by the diviner, or by the querent (the person for whom the reading is being made) if there is one.

(As an experiment, having written thus far, we drew a card to ask 'What shall we explain next?' The card was the Four of Swords, upright – our notebook interpretation of which is 'Rest from strife or labour; prudent truce.' In other words – time for a break – and it *is* five to eight in the evening!)

... And the clear light of morning is a good time to discuss scrying, even though one needs dim light actually to do it.

The best-known method is of course the crystal ball. It can be bought from any occult supplier, and the larger it is, the better – but also the more expensive. A home-made alternative which many people have found satisfactory requires a spherical flask from a laboratory supplier, filled with a copper sulphate solution (dissolve the crystals in water till the blue-green colour pleases you). Get rid of all bubbles (careful boiling helps, but let it cool before sealing) and then cork it firmly, wiring the cork in place, making sure that no air is inside.

A still cheaper scrying device is the black mirror, and some people find this easier to work with than the crystal. For this you need a clock glass – the convex disc of glass (plain, not a lens) which protects the face of a mantelpiece clock. Again, the bigger the better – but five inches in diameter is a good working size. Any shop which repairs clocks should be able to sell you one. Clean it thoroughly, and then paint the outside (the convex side) with *matt* black paint – several coats, drying of course in between coats. Aerosol spray paint is the handiest for this. The concave side will now be a shiny black mirror.

The method of using crystal ball, flask or black mirror is the same. Seat yourself comfortably, preferably inside a Magic Circle, with your scrying device cupped in a black velvet cloth in your hands or on a suitable stand. The room should be dark and candlelit, with the candle or candles so arranged that no reflections are seen in the ball or mirror. All you should see to begin with is an empty, featureless pool in space. Relax, empty your mind, allow your eyes to defocus naturally but keep watching that pool. After a while you may find the pool going milky and then clearing, before presenting you with images. But do not be impatient; it may not happen in your first session, or even your fifth or sixth. Perseverance will bring the break-through.

Once the images start coming, they should be recorded. Notes made immediately afterwards are better than nothing, but the ideal is either a patient working partner or a cassette recorder, receiving your running commentary. In this, as in many magical practices, a sympathetic but constructively critical working partner is a great asset; you take it in turns to support each other; and when it comes to interpretation, two minds in tune with each other can often achieve what may be called a stereoscopic vision of the symbols which come to the surface.

(We would remind you again that, in Wicca, a working partnership means a man and a woman, for all the reasons of psychic polarity which we explained in Section XV, 'Witchcraft and Sex'. Even for assistance in scrying, this is desirable, if only because the 'stereoscopic vision' is likely to be much deeper. But a helper of the same sex is better than none.)

When it is not in use, the crystal, flask or mirror should be kept wrapped in its black velvet, which should not be used for anything else. Tradition and our experience both say that a scrying device should be protected from bright light; if it has been so exposed (or when it is first acquired in any case), it should be recharged by bathing it in the light of the full moon.

Many people have their own very personal scrying devices. One of our witches has a $2\frac{1}{2}$ pound lump of reject Waterford glass which she was given when she lived near the factory at Kilbarry; it is beautifully clear but rough and shapeless, and most of us could get nothing from it – but for her it almost talks. Janet has a rock crystal pendant no bigger than a fingernail which would be much too tiny for most scryers; but again, it works for her.

Two of our women witches make a regular practice of using wild plants as clairvoyant triggers. These plants, understandably, put them in touch with the nature spirits concerned, from whom they get information on the processes, and the needs, of the local environment of the plant being handled. (This information is sometimes clairaudient). That may sound over-imaginative, but living as we do in close contact with the area where these two work their plant-scrying, we can confirm that the information they gather in this way proves to be highly relevant.

One woman witch who keeps a couple of ponies finds that some of her sharpest clairvoyance arises spontaneously when she is mucking out the stable of one of them, a twenty-four-year-old dun gelding called Oakie who has been with her since she was a teenager. Unlike the plant-scrying, this clairvoyance usually relates to human and family affairs, presumably because of Oakie's lifelong involvement with her.

Talking of Nature – dowsing is a highly specialized form of psychic awareness which really comes into the clairsentient category and is, we would suggest, particularly concerned with the sensitivity of the etheric body. It would take a whole Section even to summarize it, and for those who want to experiment with it we cannot do better than to recommend Tom Graves' excellent handbook *Dowsing: Techniques and Applications* – and, for its relevance to the earth mysteries, ley lines and megalithic lore, his later book *Needles of Stone*.

Psychometry is the obtaining of psychic impressions from a material object by handling it. A good psychometrist can tell you a great deal about the history and associations of an object in this way. The etheric and astral bodies of the object are brought into contact with those of the psychometrist; for every physically manifested phenomenon, whether it is a human being or a lump of rock, has its corresponding existence on the other levels of reality. As a Persian poet wrote a long time ago, Life is 'sleeping in the mineral, dreaming in the plant, awakening in the animal, and becoming conscious of itself in man'. Or to put it another way – everything is alive, but over a vast range of frequencies. The life-frequency of a mountain is infinitely slower than that of a mouse. Even within the animal kingdom, this can be observed; the life-frequencies of a sloth or a tortoise and of a squirrel or a humming-bird are near the two extreme ends of the animal spectrum, just as red and violet light are at opposite ends of the spectrum of visible light. Radio waves and X-rays are of the same nature as light, but because they are outside the frequency-range of our eyes, we cannot see them.

Similarly, 'normal' human life-awareness is limited to the animal and plant spectrum of frequencies. Anything outside of that, most people regard as being lifeless. But occultists and witches realize that this is not so and work to extend their spectrum of awareness – either directly, by picking up the higher harmonics of the slower frequencies, or indirectly, by observing the effects of low-frequency life on high-frequency life.

An example of the second approach is astrology, which studies the life-frequency of the solar system by observing its effects on the human life-frequency.

In a sense, psychometry is concerned with the first, direct, approach. A diamond ring, for example, is alive on the frequencies of its gem and its gold, which are both far slower than that of the woman who wears it. But there are harmonic frequencies between the two, just as striking top C on a piano with the pedal down will cause the bottom C string to hum (and all the intervening Cs, plus related notes to a lesser degree). If the ring is on her finger for years, all the events on her non-physical levels will cause a harmonic response in the corresponding levels of the ring, and the ring will 'remember' them. A sensitive psychometrist, handling the ring, will pick up these 'memories' by the same harmonic resonance. (This is why it is very difficult to psychometrize plastic objects; being neither organic nor a natural mineral, plastic has virtually no life-frequency of its own.)

All this talk of life-frequencies may seem an unnecessarily technical digression, but it is important for two reasons. With regard to psychometry, it helps to remove the psychological block created by the Ego's whisper: 'How can a dead piece of jewellery tell me anything of the history of a living woman?' And on a wider scale, it helps the Ego to accept consciously the idea that the whole universe *is* alive, without which awareness little psychic development is possible.

But to get back to the actual practice of psychometry. Some people merely hold the object in one hand and close their eyes. Others prefer to hold it against the 'third eye', which occult tradition locates in the pineal body, in the centre of the forehead just above eyebrow-level.[1] Those who hold it in one hand often prefer the left hand, because it is linked, physically and etherically, with the right-brain intuitive function. Only experience will reveal which method works best for you.

Apart from that, the rule is the same as for scrying: let the impressions flow, and voice them without inhibition, leaving analysis till afterwards.

Psychometry is particularly suited for developing by means of coven co-operation. Members can give each other objects to 'read' and tell them immediately afterwards how accurate they were. This process will not only reveal naturally gifted psychometrists; it will help the ones who have to work harder at it (which means most of us) in the key problem of distinguishing between subjective and objective impressions, thus improving their overall clairvoyant ability. The advantage of psychometric exercises between friends is that it trains this discerning function much faster.

Reading the human aura is a special case of clairvoyance in the strict sense of the word; but as that is particularly relevant to healing, we will leave discussion of it till Section XXI.

Divination – 'clairvoyance with tools' – is, we would emphasize again, the very best way of training yourself in 'clairvoyance without tools'. It builds up your confidence; it teaches you to trust your intuition, while at the same time teaching you to distinguish between the genuine and the self-deceptive; it provides a format within which a coven or group of friends can practise together; it gradually convinces you of the synchronicity (or meaningful coincidence) of which the 'tools' are capable, and thus helps you to understand the principle of synchronicity in general; and it teaches you to interpret symbols.

Even for those who have an obvious clairvoyant gift already, divination is a healthy exercise; because such spontaneous gifts (especially in today's world where they are not recognized or intelligently encouraged) are often undisciplined and erratic and may actually be frightening. The discipline of divinatory practice brings the gift under control and makes it discriminating and serviceable.

One of our witches, when she first came to us, was clairvoyant to a degree which overwhelmed her, taking on neurotic proportions. She had no idea how to control it or how to switch it off when necessary. For her, divinatory training turned what had been a burden into a useful talent. She is now an excellent Tarot reader, an often surprising telepath and helpful at alerting us, by her precognitive ability, to developments which might otherwise take us by surprise. Her gift is as powerful as ever, but it is now under her control.

Clairvoyance is a natural attribute of every human being. Like every other human attribute, it can be developed and trained. If we deny or repress it, we distort our own psyche. And if we allow it to run to waste, we are incomplete.

But a note of warning should be added: clairvoyant activity should never be allowed to dominate one's life, twenty-four hours a day, however well developed one has made it. It is only one of our awareness-faculties, and it should be kept in balance with the others. Round-the-clock clairvoyance, or running to the Tarot every five minutes for decisions which only call for common sense, can drain the energies, often weaken the gift and warp the Personality on which the immortal Individuality depends for experience and self-expression.

Over-indulged, psychic awareness can make us neglect our other senses when they are most needed. A close friend of Stewart's parents, before the war, was a Christian Science practitioner of considerable psychic power and healing ability. She died in the prime of life by crashing her car with no apparent cause when she was driving alone. Those who knew her intimately (including her husband and Stewart's parents) were convinced that she had been concentrating her thoughts and her psychic effort on a healing case when she should have been watching the road. An extreme situation – but most psychics have had experience of the same risk at a less alarming level.

An integrated psyche means a balanced one. So sharpen your clairvoyant faculty to a keen edge – but never allow your other tools to deteriorate.

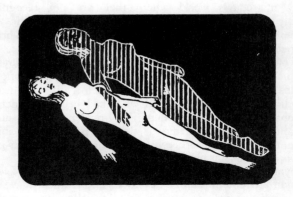

XX   Astral Projection

Normal, everyday, waking consciousness is anchored to the physical brain and nervous system. In this state, the body is thought of as 'I' – an 'I' which can only be aware of the world through its physical senses and can only think about it from inside its own head. It is the only state of which most people are aware, and in practice the only one in which they believe. Even those who believe in an immortal soul usually accept that, for the duration of their earthly lives, their consciousness is inseparable from the body. Dreams are envisaged as the brain's functioning when the flow of sense-data is cut off, and the imagination fills the resulting vacuum with fantasies; these fantasies may be conceded to be psychologically meaningful and of therapeutic value, but they are still regarded as activities of the physical brain, from which 'I' cannot escape.

Witches, occultists and serious students of the paranormal look at the situation rather differently, and their attitude is borne out by formidable evidence.

If one regards a human being as the multi-level entity which we described in Section XII, 'Reincarnation', then one sees the brain

Men and women are the central nervous system of Gaia, the Earth Organism, through which she becomes conscious of herself

The cervix motif (see note to Section xv, 'Witchcraft and Sex'): (A) the Omphalos at Delphi; (B) bullawn stone in Kells Churchyard, Co. Meath; (C) bullawn stone at Clonegal Castle, Co. Wexford; (D) disc and horns of Isis, Abydos, Egypt; and (E) typical form of the Assyrian Sacred Moon Tree

Skyclad working seems to have been common among European witches. 'Love's Enchantment', Flemish school, *c.*1670–80

Above: In this cottage in Co. Clare lived Biddy Early, the famous nineteenth-century Irish witch

Opposite above: A pre-war picture of the Christchurch Theatre, Hampshire, 'the first Rosicrucian Theatre in England', which opened on 16 June, 1938. Membership of this brought Gerald Gardner into contact with the New Forest witches

Opposite: A 1938 or 1939 performance of *Pythagoras*, by Alex Matthews, at the Christchurch Rosicrucian Theatre. Doreen Valiente thinks the man on the extreme left of picture 'just might be' Gerald Gardner

Right: Janet's painting of the group thought-form Mara (see Section xxii, 'Spells')

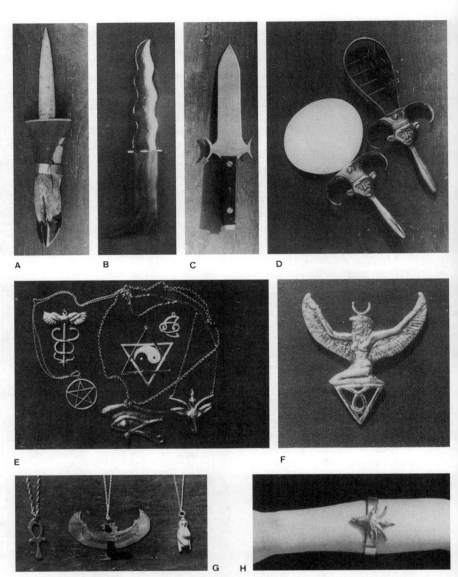

Occult craftsmanship: (A) deer's-foot athame, maker unknown; (B) bronze athame by Peter Clark, Ireland; (C) copper athame by Michael Hinch, Ireland; (D) Hathor mirror and sistrum by George Alexander, England; (E) pendants by George Alexander; (F) Isis brooch by Muriel Chastenet, USA; (G) ankh by Peter Clark, Isis by Christopher Bailey, Horned God Salute by Knut Klimmek, all Ireland; and (H) bracelet by George Alexander

Large jewelled and small plain zodiacal pentacles photo-etched by Michael Hinch from the same design by Stewart (see Section xxiv, 'Witches' Tools')

The restored entrance to Newgrange, the 3000 BC neolithic mound in Co. Meath (see Section xxv, 'In Tune with the Land'). The winter solstice sunrise shines through the 'roof box' (upper opening) to illumine the central chamber 79 feet away inside

The High Priestess, as representative of the Goddess, may on occasion use the
altar as a throne

(complex and marvellous though it is) as merely one mechanism of the multi-level phenomenon of awareness (both conscious and unconscious). It is the mechanism by which, via the etheric body, the physical body interacts with the other levels, and also the mechanism by which the physical body regulates and balances its own functions. It is like a very modern house's wiring, radio, television, telephone and central-heating thermostats. But the occupant of the house is not a prisoner; he can walk out of the front door, meet people instead of phoning them, attend concerts or football matches instead of watching them on television, and know that, although the house is temporarily unanimated by his presence, when he does return it will have kept itself at the right temperature, the television will be waiting to be switched on, his self-timing oven will have his dinner ready, and anyone who phones him will get an answer.

It is the same with human consciousness; while it is reasonable and convenient to spend most of one's time 'at home', centred on the physical body and brain, and communicating with the world through its wiring, its aerials and its windows, one does not have to limit oneself to staying there *all* the time. The front door is not locked.

The technique of shifting consciousness from the physical body and plane to the astral body and plane is known as astral projection. It can be learned, or it can happen involuntarily.

Involuntary astral projection – usually described as an 'out-of-the-body experience' – is more frequent and widespread than is generally realized, partly because those who experience it are either frightened by it or reluctant to talk about it in case their sanity or truthfulness is questioned. Typically, the person suddenly finds himself or herself seeming to stand or hover in a corner of the room, looking down on his or her physical body from several feet away, with complete visual (and often auditory) awareness. The immediate reaction may be curiosity or panic; if it is the latter, consciousness will usually return to the physical body with an unpleasant jerk.

Such projection can happen when the physical body is very relaxed – particularly in the bath, where it is halfway to weightlessness. It can happen, too, when the physical body is weakened by illness; Carrington and Muldoon's classic book on the subject, *The Projection of the Astral Body*, deals with such a case, the physically frail Sylvan Muldoon himself.

Some of the best recorded instances of involuntary projection have been recounted by patients who have recovered from clinical death. Often, 'standing' to one side in the operating theatre or hospital ward, they have watched and listened while doctors and nurses fought to revive their bodies – and after their recovery described the actions and speech (of which their 'dead' physical sense could not possibly have been aware) to an astonished staff. Dr Raymond Moody gives many such cases, with direct quotes from the patients, in his book *Life After Life*.

Descriptions of what the projected state feels like are in general agreement. The astral body feels weightless. Sight and hearing are greatly sharpened. Dr Moody says, 'No one among all of my cases has reported any odours or tastes while out of their physical bodies', but that may be because all of his were in clinical or accident situations, where sight and sound would be of prime importance. Janet has frequently experienced significant odours during astral projection, though she cannot remember having tasted anything – again, presumably because there is no cause to eat or drink in that state; if there were (if she felt impelled to do so as a ritual act, for instance), she thinks it likely that she would be aware of the significant taste.

Which brings us to another point. If Janet, say, were to drink ritual wine during astral projection, it would be *astral* wine, manifested on the astral plane by her own willpower – and the significant taste would manifest, too. All subjects agree that, during projection, the astral body cannot mechanically manipulate the physical plane. If Janet tried to pick up a physical chalice, her astral hand would pass through it. The astral body can *observe* the physical plane, with great acuity, but cannot normally affect it – or be affected by it. The astral body can pass through physical walls, and it need not get out of the way of moving physical bodies, because they will pass through it.

And yet even this is not one hundred per cent true. Very great charges of energy on the astral plane can and do produce effects on the physical – witness poltergeist and telekinetic[1] phenomena. But 'normal' astral projection does not involve such interaction, except sometimes by highly concentrated willpower.

All subjects agree that movement is unrestricted, and thought processes clearer and faster.

One matter on which there does not appear to be general agreement is the 'silver cord'. Many people, over the centuries, have insisted that a silver cord is seen, infinitely extendable, between the astral and physical bodies during projection, and that this cord is only severed on physical death. (Ecclesiastes xii, 6-7, is said to refer to this: 'Or ever the silver cord be loosed, or the golden bowl be broken, or the pitcher be broken at the fountain, or the wheel be broken at the cistern; then shall the dust return to the earth as it was; and the spirit shall return to God who gave it.') If such a cord does exist – and some experienced projectors have never seen it – it would presumably be the vital etheric link between the physical and the astral; and whether one sees it or not would depend on which 'wavelength' of the broad astral spectrum one's projection faculty naturally utilized.

We have very briefly outlined the nature of the experience. How does one learn to bring it about deliberately, and under one's own control?

First, we would emphasize again what we have just said – that the astral spectrum is very broad; some occult traditions divide the astral plane into seven sub-planes, but even these must be regarded as merging into each other. At one end of the spectrum, the phenomena of the astral plane correspond very closely to those of the physical plane. As Doreen Valiente says (*An ABC of Witchcraft Past and Present*, p.18), 'everything in the visible world of matter is surrounded and permeated by its astral counterpart.' It is this world of 'astral counterparts' that Dr Moody's patients were projecting into, for example, when they could see and hear exactly what was happening on the physical plane. This world, this end of the astral spectrum, is the one to be mastered if one wishes to observe events on the physical plane which are not directly available to one's physical senses.

Dion Fortune gives an example of this kind of projection in her novel *Moon Magic* (hardback, p.91). Lilith Le Fay, in London, needs to observe Rupert Malcolm as he visits a house in a seaside resort. 'I made the astral projection by the usual method; that is to say, I pictured myself as standing six feet in front of myself and then transferred my consciousness to the simulacrum thus created by my imagination and looked at the room through its eyes. Then I visualised the face of the man with the greying red hair, and imagined myself speaking to him. The magic worked. I had the sensation of the descent of a swift lift, which always characterises the change of the level of consciousness; all awareness of my physical surroundings faded, and I seemed to be in a strange room ...' which she proceeds to describe in detail.

Put like that, it sounds easy; but Lilith Le Fay (like Dion Fortune herself) was a high adept, whose imagination and willpower were powerful tools perfected by long training. And yet it does sum up the basic technique to be followed for projecting consciousness into this 'astral counterpart' level of the astral plane. You visualize, with all the vividness you can muster, a 'simulacrum' of your physical body; and then, with all the determination you can muster, you will your consciousness to transfer to it. Your astral body, thus encouraged, integrates with the simulacrum.

For most people, acquiring the technique is a long, hard process, requiring great perseverance and a refusal to be discouraged. At the other extreme, there are people who have what is generally called 'a loose astral body' who acquire it all too easily and may have to develop control to prevent it happening spontaneously at the wrong moment.

How best to approach the problem may vary from person to person. A favourite method is the use of a full-length mirror; you relax in a chair facing the mirror, in such a way that your physical body would remain in position and come to no harm if it lost consciousness (which after all is the object of the exercise), and use your mirror-image as the simulacrum, willing your consciousness to enter into it.

Sylvan Muldoon used the mirror method and recommended four stages. First, to build into the subconscious a strong desire to transfer consciousness to the astral body. Second, to concentrate on the mirror image. Third, to make yourself clearly aware of your own heartbeat, first in the heart itself and then in different points of your body, one by one. And fourth, to try to slow down the heartbeat by mental suggestion. (No one with a weak or irregular heart should try this fourth stage, of course.)

Another method is to walk round your room learning its visual details by heart. Then you relax in your chair (or lying down) with your eyes shut, and make a mental tour of the room, visualizing and describing it to yourself as accurately as you can – coupled with a strong desire to transfer consciousness to the simulacrum which is making the tour.

A friend of ours who was a hi-fi enthusiast proposed to try a development of this: to set up two microphones on opposite sides of the room, connected to a stereo tape-recorder. He would then walk round the room from viewpoint to viewpoint, describing what he saw in detail. Finally, in his relaxed sitting or lying position, with his eyes shut and earphones on his head, he would listen to the playback, the stereo effect helping him to identify with the touring simulacrum and, aided by his visual memory, to see what it saw. In this way he hoped to make it easier to achieve projection of consciousness into the simulacrum. Unfortunately we lost touch with him before he tried the experiment, so we do not know whether it succeeded or not. But others may like to follow up his suggestion.

Helpful books on developing the faculty of projection on this level are Carrington and Muldoon, referred to above; Ophiel's *The Art and Practice of Astral Projection*; and Dr Douglas M. Baker's *The Techniques of Astral Projection*.

So far we have concentrated on the 'astral counterpart' level of the astral plane – the level which corresponds most closely to the physical, and through which we can expand our awareness and understanding of the physical. During projection into this level, our consciousness is mainly directed towards the physical world's astral double, and we are unlikely to be aware, except dimly or in flashes, of the discarnate entities and phenomena which throng what may be called the middle and upper reaches of the astral.

But when we explore the astral plane as a whole, we discover that it has two characteristics. First, it *is* populated by the entities and phenomena we have mentioned – and these may be helpful, hostile or neutral. And second, it is extremely malleable – in other words, it can be reshaped and otherwise affected by emotion, imagination and willpower.

This does not mean that what we encounter on the astral plane is illusory; quite the contrary. Just as on the physical plane we may be aware of objects in different ways (a townsman may see a patch of cow-dung as a smelly mess, a farmer see it as valuable manure, and an artist see it as an interesting visual counterpoint to the green of the field – and each one is right), and we can manipulate and reshape our environment physically; so on the astral plane, real entities may clothe themselves in different shapes according to our type of awareness, and we can reshape our astral environment by a different kind of effort.

When we become conscious on the astral plane, we find that in a sense we have more freedom of action on its 'middle reaches' than we do at either the lowest of the highest level of the spectrum. On the lowest plane, as we have seen, the astral is very closely matched to the physical, and while projection can make our awareness of it more acute, and vastly increase our freedom of *movement* within it, our freedom of *action* – our ability to manipulate the 'astral counterparts' by which we are surrounded – is very limited indeed, because of their tight integration with their *physical* counterparts.

The highest astral level, on the other hand, has close links with the mental and spiritual levels. The entities which people it tend to be of a higher order of being than ourselves. Conscious experience on that level, once we achieve it, is therefore likely to be receptive rather than active, and the environment to be awe-inspiring rather than malleable. We may, however, be *internally* active, within the bounds of our own total psyche, because at that level the Personality will be more consciously in communication with the immortal Individuality, to the potential enrichment of the former and the karmic advancement of the latter.

The 'middle reaches' of the astral plane are much more of a free-for-all than either of these extremes. Experience here can be very rewarding – and it can also be dangerous. We are not mere observers; we are participants, responsible for our own actions and their results.

Astral projection onto these middle levels, from a state of normal waking consciousness, can be learned as a development of the lower-level projection we have already described; but it is more likely to be achieved as a natural consequence of one's overall psychic development as an advancing witch or occultist than by any drill-book techniques.

We say 'from a state of normal waking consciousness' because there is one way in which *everybody* projects onto the middle astral levels: in dreaming. Not in all dreams, because most dreams are an internal dialogue between different elements of the personal psyche. But there are some dreams (and one soon learns to recognize them once the usefulness of recognizing them is realized) in which awareness ventures outside the frontiers of the personal psyche into the busy concourse of the middle astral.

One characteristic of the astral-projection dream is that you *know* that you are dreaming. You are asleep, but fully conscious. You can examine your dream, experiment with it and manipulate it. Another very convincing bit of confirmation is when you meet friends in your dream and are able to discover later that they shared the experience; though for this you have to be very honest with yourself, and only compare notes with friends you know to be equally honest and free from wishful thinking. (The women of our coven are particularly good at this; when the morning phone-calls start, Stewart is apt to joke: 'Hullo, the girls were out on the astral again last night.')

Too much of this can be exhausting, and one must have the sense and the willpower to withdraw from it when necessary. A High Priestess in particular, being psychically involved with and concerned for the whole coven, may if she is not careful find her sleep invaded too often for comfort – often involuntarily, where the less experienced members are concerned. In the Sanders' coven, Maxine often used to tell us new initiates: 'Remember, I'm keeping my beady astral eye on you!' It was not till much later, when we were running our own coven, that we realized how little of a joke this could be.

Any responsible sensitive who is involved in occult activity is liable to find herself having to take firm action on the astral plane to deal with a crisis. Such confrontations may be expected to take the forms typical of the middle astral – symbolism and shape-changing mixed with actual awareness of physical objects and locations.

An example from our own experience. We knew that X was bitterly jealous of Y, and also that X had considerable raw psychic power, very little psychic or personal responsibility and marked vampiric tendencies; and we were correspondingly worried, since Y was a close friend. Asleep one night, Janet suddenly found herself astrally projecting and knew that X was on the astral war-path. She saw him as a huge green slug-like creature, and she pursued his green slimy trail all over Dublin. The final confrontation was in Y's flat, where Y was asleep and X attacked him. Janet seized the coven sword and struck at X with it. The green slug disintegrated, the projection ended, and Janet woke up in her physical body.

Now any psychiatrist could diagnose this, on the face of it, as a straightforward anxiety dream triggered off by Janet's concern over the situation – but for two things. Next morning we found that the coven sword (which had been thoroughly cleaned the day before) was coated in a strange green deposit for which we could find no 'natural' explanation, though we tried hard enough, as we always do with such phenomena. And on Y's throat, when we saw him soon after, were two equally inexplicable puncture-marks.

It will be seen from all this that guidelines for conduct on the astral plane can be deduced from what we have said earlier in this book on the theory of levels, on Wiccan ethics and on psychic defence. If all these are constantly borne in mind, astral projection can be an enriching and safe experience, and a great expansion of the human psychic faculties.

A final footnote on one phenomenon which is closely linked to astral projection – bilocation, or the gift of being able to be in two places at once. There are many well-attested cases of people being seen and spoken with, in a thoroughly solid and non-ghostly form, simultaneously in widely separated places. It appears in particular to be a faculty associated with people of outstanding spiritual power, such as the late Padre Pio. If such reports are true (and many of them do seem to be beyond question), one can only infer that the subject has both a perfected gift of astral projection and so much power and motivation that he can make his projected astral body manifest visibility and audibly – and convincingly – to achieve the purpose which he finds important.

Yet there is evidence that it can also happen spontaneously and for no obvious purpose. The French doctor Francis Lefébure, in the Second World War, is a well-known example; and it is interesting that Lefébure was a skilled Yoga practitioner.

And although we do not expect to be believed – we have evidence, which, for all our efforts, we can find no way of breaking, that one or two of our cats have the gift. But then animals are not inhibited by preconceptions. Is there a lesson there for would-be witches?

XXI Healing

Healing has been a central part of witches' activities from time immemorial, and it remains so today. It used to be an accepted function of priesthood, from the healer-priests of Ancient Egypt to the Druids[1] and the first Christians. The Church soon forgot Jesus's command: 'Heal the sick, cleanse the lepers, raise the dead, cast out devils' – at least as far as psychic or spiritual healing goes, though many monks and nuns became gifted herbalists, and no one doubts the dedication of medical missionaries. But the psychic-healing vacuum was filled by the village wise-woman or cunning-man; and it was no accident that many of these were followers of the Old Religion, because such people understood psychic power and were uninhibited by the dogma of a church which regarded it with active suspicion.

Today's witch has (or at least is striving to develop) the same understanding and naturally inherits the same healing tradition. Many witches, as we have pointed out, are professional doctors or nurses, combining psychic understanding with modern medical knowledge; a combination which can be remarkably powerful – and which can also avoid a lot of the blunders of which well-meant but tunnel-vision technology is often guilty.

However, most witches are not professionally trained in medicine or psychiatry. How can they, safely and effectively, exercise their healing function?

A single Section (or even a whole library) cannot teach you to be a healer. But we hope it can point to the ways in which you can *learn* to be a healer.

Healing in the Craft can be divided roughly into four headings, though these overlap, and two or more of them can be (and usually will be) combined. These headings are: herbalism, spells, direct work on the aura, and straight psychology.

Herbalism

As we pointed out on p.138, witches are naturally drawn to herbalism because the Craft is a Nature-based religion, and the study of herbs is a very fruitful way of sharpening their attunement to Gaia, the Earth-organism, on all the levels.

To use herbs for healing, you must (1) know where to find them, (2) be able to identify them infallibly and (3) be very well-informed on the effect and properties of any herb you are using. All that may sound obvious; but there are people around who combine a mystical enthusiasm for 'natural' cures with a slapdash approach to their use, and this is simply not good enough.

Fortunately, one can learn and practise herbalism one herb at a time, and this (short of taking a professional course on the subject) is really the best way to go about it, by extending your repertoire gradually. You can start by choosing herbs which are well-known cures for straightforward ailments and which are unlikely to clash with any treatment a doctor is giving (though you should *always* check up on this too).

Let us take two examples. An elderflower infusion is a very soothing treatment for sunburn. The elder tree, helpfully, is in flower just at the time when sunburn is likely to arise, and is very easy to identify. You can safely use this infusion on the sunburn of yourself or a friend, and you will gain confidence (and enhance your reputation) when it is seen to work. Anyone who can make a pot of tea can make an infusion; the next stage is to learn the rather less easy technique of making an ointment; then you will be prepared to treat sunburn later in the season when the flower has gone. (Or you can infuse the dried flowers.)

The second example is the lesser celandine, or pilewort, (*Ranunculus ficaria*), an early spring flower; it is, as its popular name indicates, an excellent treatment for piles. The whole herb is collected while it is in flower, and dried. This, too, can be used either as an infusion or as an ointment. It is less easy to identify (you must not confuse it with the greater celandine, *Chelidonium majus*, for instance, which has quite different uses) but once it has been pointed out to you you will never forget it. It certainly works and, in view of the distressing nature of the complaint it treats, may land you with some embarrassingly grateful patients.

The point about these two is that you cannot do any harm with either of them through faulty diagnosis; and you will almost certainly do good.

Next, in your herb-by-herb progress, you might turn your attention to eyebright (*Euphrasia officinalis*) for inflamed eyes – again making sure that the patient sees a doctor if the inflammation persists and may be a symptom of something more serious; or the common marigold (*Calendula officinalis*) which is a stimulant useful for local treatment of various kinds – but avoid the marsh marigold (*Caltha palustris*), which is strongly irritant and can produce serious side-effects when used without exact knowledge.

The principle to follow is, not to run before you can walk. Build up your repertoire with safe herbs, one by one, and never outstrip your own knowledge.

If you can do this under the guidance of an experienced herbalist, so much the better. Otherwise you must study, and constantly refer back to, reliable books.

The classic is *Culpeper's Complete Herbal*, written by the seventeenth-century astrologer-physician Nicholas Culpeper, reprinted continuously since, and still in publication. His soundness is shown by the fact that modern books on the subject repeatedly quote him.

Of the modern herbals, *Potter's New Cyclopaedia* by R.C. Wren is very clear and concise; but the most useful work we have found is Mrs M. Grieve's *A Modern Herbal*, first published in 1931. Short of professional training, a would-be herbalist could not do better than to rely entirely on Mrs Grieve.

For the identification of herbs, again the ideal thing is to be shown them, in their natural habitat, by somebody who really knows them. But even that (since you cannot take such a friend round on a lead wherever you go) will have to be supplemented by book knowledge. For Britain and Ireland, the most comprehensive and practical work is W. Keble Martin's *The Concise British Flora in Colour*, with accurate drawings of 1,486 species and descriptions of many more; it has become our botanical Bible wherever we go. As a complement to this, we much appreciate Roger Phillips' *Wild Flowers of Britain*, which is entirely illustrated by colour photographs.

Learn all you can from local lore, particularly if you live in the country; but remember that there may be some chaff among the wheat, so it will do no harm to cross-check it with Culpeper, Potter or Mrs Grieve (discreetly, or your source may take offence and dry up).

Talking of local lore, and slightly off the subject of herbs – it was in Co. Mayo that we realized the origin of the phrase 'the hair of the dog that bit you'. It meant literally that. We saw a neighbour who had been bitten (more or less unintentionally) by a dog, take a hair from the culprit's coat and bandage it in place over the graze. Coincidence or not, it had healed completely by the next day.

Spells

The principles and techniques of spell-working are discussed fully in the next Section. All the methods described (image spells, candle spells, cord magic, linked-hand magic, the creation of thought-forms) can be used for healing purposes; and all the reinforcements suggested (such as the use of appropriate colours and the appropriate God- and Goddess-names) are helpful for healing spells too.

Each method has its advantages. With the image spell, it is easier to concentrate the willpower and imagination on a particular area of the body. Cord or linked-hand magic fits well into the pattern of a normal coven esbat. A candle spell, we have found, is very suitable for a solo witch or a partnership who are asked for immediate healing help but cannot entirely escape from their everyday chores; it is also appropriate when help is particularly needed over a specified few hours, such as the time of an operation, childbirth or the critical phase of an illness.

Thought-form working is very effective when a major effort is required from a group or a partnership, and especially when several factors are involved in the situation; for example, if the behaviour of the patient's family, the weather or the risk of infectious contact with children has to be taken into consideration. The thought-form can be 'tailor-made' to keep watch on all these factors more easily, for instance, than would be possible with an image spell.

One form of spell is exclusive to healing work: the use of a stand-in. A member of the coven, of the same sex as the patient and as far as possible of similar age and bodily characteristics, is chosen as the stand-in – for example, a man in his middle thirties, with dark hair, of sturdy build and medium height. The coven envisage him as a temporary replica of the patient, a kind of two-way TV monitor; and the stand-in so envisages himself, concentrating on forming a strong astral link with the physically absent patient. The healing work is then performed, using the stand-in as a channel. Some covens find this very effective, but it has its dangers – that of psychic infection of the stand-in by the patient being the most obvious. Great care must be taken to protect him, and the coven must be confident of their capacity to do this. It is advisable to have one person, of known healing power and psychic sensitivity, very much in charge of the operation. On the whole, this method is better used only by very experienced covens.

(On the problem of psychic or etheric infection of the healer, see p. 231.)

When the patient is a member of the coven, and present to be worked on, one method of channelling power into him or her can be dramatically successful. We learned it (as one so often does) the hard way, through a magical accident. We were still in the Sanders' coven, and Alex was staging rituals for a visiting German film unit. For one sequence we were demonstrating cord magic, with a radiating wheel of cords having a man and a woman at each end of each cord (see p.239). With his unerring eye for visual effect, Alex had one of our women witches, Wendy, lying face upwards under the centre of the wheel 'as a focus for the power', while we cord-holders moved deosil faster and faster. The cameramen were delighted with the image of the circling figures and the spinning wheel of cords; and as we all entered into the spirit of the thing, we could feel that tremendous power *was* being built up. After a while the director called 'Cut!' and we set up for the next sequence.

We drove home that night in the same car as Wendy – and the poor girl was in agonies from a blinding headache. Unfortunately nobody had thought of choosing a useful objective for the power which had been almost inadvertently raised, or of 'earthing' Wendy immediately afterwards.[2] So Wendy remained bursting with undischarged power, for which she should have been a channel and not a cul-de-sac. And although we realized what had happened, neither we nor Wendy were then experienced enough to put things right.

But we did learn from Wendy's headache that the technique could be usefully and safely applied. We also learned a lesson which every coven involved with the media should remember – that even a staged ritual raises power, and that indeed in the keyed-up atmosphere of a film location or a TV studio it may raise a great deal; so one should always provide it with a constructive outlet, even if it is only to cure a continuity-girl's cold. A useful objective can always be found.

On that subject – performers who stage evocations of sinister entities as a dramatic gimmick are asking for trouble. We recall a well-known rock group in London, some years ago, who put on a stage act in which a magician used such evocations to bring his dead lady-love back to life. A mere dramatic performance on the face of it, and suitably spectacular; but one girl performer had a fit, another was painfully burned and nearly suffered a sword-cut, and several other things went dangerously wrong.

Some performers are admittedly more careful. We were once asked to advise an amateur company on psychic self-defence for the actors and actresses involved in the witch scenes of their production of *Macbeth*. We took the request seriously and made some interesting friends.

These incidents were part of the wave of interest in the occult of the early 1970s – which on the professional showbiz side tended to be mere 'cashing-in', resulting in some casualties. One famous pop personality, now dead, was believed by many to have died as a result of a black-magic attack from someone he had offended; but Janet, who knew him well, believes that it was because he had been dabbling musically with the Enochian Calls, with insufficient knowledge, and 'trying to work the Abramelin on stage'. He got disastrously out of his depth.

Such ill-informed dabbling is dynamite – and there are signs that a new wave of showbiz 'cashing-in' may be on the way. Serious occultists anu witches who have friends in the profession should be ready with first aid – and also with advice; and the advice should be that, if these performers really want to be in tune with the spirit of the times, they should look towards 'clean' paganism and mankind's relationship with Gaia, rather than to a superficial toying with the more convoluted and awesome symbols of an occultism torn out of context. There are many excellent performers who are genuine witches or pagans; but they mean, feel and understand what they are putting across. They are not dabblers cashing in.

This may seem a digression from the subject of healing; but it is a field in which much healing work may be called for.

Auric Healing

The important part of the human aura, from the healing point of view, is the inner band which immediately surrounds (and of course also permeates) the physical body. It is, in fact, the etheric body, the energy-network which links the physical with the astral, mental and spiritual bodies and thus maintains it in being. Its substance is more tenuous than matter (and will contain molecules of matter at least in the form of pheromones – see p.196) but less tenuous than the astral; and at least some frequencies of its energy are discernible by physical instruments, as the achievements of Kirlian photography show.

Like the astral body, though in different ways because of its close links with the physical, it can be strongly affected by emotion, willpower and psychic influences; hence its importance in psychic healing, both diagnostically and therapeutically.

The effect of emotion on the aura has also been recorded by Kirlian photography. In *The Body Electric* (pp. 164-9) Thelma Moss of UCLA

describes experiments in which Kirlian photographs were taken of
adjacent fingers of people who felt antipathy or attraction towards each
other. The antipathy photographs showed a 'haircut effect' with the
two auras rejecting each other; the attraction photographs showed the
auras reaching out to each other and merging (ibid. Figure 5-1). Dr
Moss was startled to find that similar 'electric photographs', showing
the same effect, had been taken in the nineteenth century by a Polish
doctor, Iodko-Narkovitz (ibid. p.151 and Figure 4-1), long before the
Soviet inventor Semyon Kirlian gave his name to the process. *The
Body Electric* gives fascinating information on the healing implications
of the phenomena which Dr Moss and her colleagues were
investigating.

The first doctor to study the human aura as a natural phenomenon
useful in diagnosis was Walter J. Kilner of St Thomas's Hospital,
London, at the beginning of this century. His approach was
deliberately non-occult, though he accepted that clairvoyants could see
the aura; taking this fact as a stimulus, he set out to discover if it could
be seen 'normally'. He found that it could – and made the
breakthrough discovery that one's sensitivity to the frequencies
involved could be improved by the use of optical filters treated with the
dye dicyanin. These filters became known as 'Kilner screens'.
Experimenting further, he found that different characteristics of the
aura could be examined by the use of other filters of various colours.
(Kilner goggles and sets of colour filters can be obtained from
Occultique, 73 Kettering Road, Northampton NN1 ·4AW.) Kilner
published his findings, and many case-histories describing auric
diagnosis, in his book *The Human Atmosphere* in 1911; it was
republished as a paperback in 1973 under the more appropriate title
The Aura.

Kilner distinguished three parts to the aura. First, a narrow band
next to the skin, not more than a quarter of an inch wide, transparent
and appearing as a dark space, which he named 'the Etheric Double' –
confusingly, in view of the general occult use of the term to mean the
whole etheric body. His eyesight, whether wholly 'natural' or (as some
suspect) partly and unknowingly psychic, must have been unusually
sharp, because many sensitives admit they cannot make out such a
band. Kilner's second band he called 'the Inner Aura', the densest and
most easily visible portion, an inch to three or more wide and following
the contours of the body. His third band he called 'the Outer Aura',
extending beyond the Inner Aura and with a smoother outline. Round
the head in particular, the Outer Aura is normally a lot wider than the
Inner Aura. Most sensitives seem to agree with him on the Inner and
Outer Auras, and also on his finding that the Inner Aura is generally
the most useful one to concentrate on for the diagnosis of ailments.

Beyond diagnosis, Kilner found two significant things: first, that rays were often visible between a nearby hand and the aura of the patient; and second, that willpower could affect the aura. The relevance to psychic healing is plain, though Kilner does not pursue it in his book – understandably perhaps, in view of its non-occult approach and his obvious hope that his orthodox colleagues would view his discoveries favourably – a hope that was not fulfilled.

A useful modern (1970) book which follows up and adds to Kilner's findings is *The Origin and Properties of the Human Aura* by Oscar Bagnall.

As to the colour of the aura, both Kilner and Bagnall find that it ranges from blue to grey. Both writers are agreed that highly intelligent subjects have noticeably bluer auras, while mentally dull subjects have noticeably greyer ones.

Many sensitives see more colours than this – everything from gold to red to violet to brown; but this would seem to be a clairvoyant perception rather than an optical one. The sensitive is psychically aware of character qualities, or emotional or spiritual states, in the subject, and this awareness presents itself to him or her as visual phenomena; in other words, there is a scrying element in the sensitive's observation of the aura. This is perfectly valid, of course, and indeed a gift to be worked for and developed; but as with all scrying, in order that one may fully understand and control the gift, it is as well to keep clearly in mind the distinction between clairvoyant and strictly optical vision.

How to develop the ability to see auras?

For most of us, the best approach is to start with the purely optical ability; and once this is established, to strive to build the clairvoyant ability on this foundation.

Conditions for optical viewing of the aura must be right. As we have said, the subject should be skyclad; apart from any effect clothes may have on the characteristics of the aura, their very thickness will obscure at least part of the Inner Aura. Dim daylight or candlelight is needed, as even moderately bright light swamps those cells in the retina which pick up the auric frequencies. The subject should stand against a very dark background; most experimenters prefer black or red. (As Bagnall points out – p.58 – one advantage of a red background is that it gives a guide to the amount of light required; if you can *see* that it is red, the light is too bright and must be dimmed, because it is the red end of the spectrum which is the 'swamping' one.) Only trial and error will find the ideal conditions for you.

Kilner goggles are by no means essential, but most people find that they do help. But read the instructions carefully; remember that their main function is to adjust the sensitivity of the eyes *before* attempting to see the aura, and that any advantage from looking at the aura *through* the goggles is only secondary to this. Bagnall, pp. 62-4, gives detailed advice on their use.

Your first view of the aura will be of the Inner Aura, as a faint greyish or bluish mist surrounding the body. As your sensitivity to it develops, you should begin to discern structure in it. The Inner Aura is normally striated – i.e., it is made up of fine lines or rays very close together, at right angles to the surface of the body. Sometimes brighter rays extend in places beyond the Inner Aura; these will be particularly observed if one part of the body is near another – for example, if a hand is held near the head, when the rays will be seen bridging the gap.

As soon as you have reached this stage, you can start using your auric vision diagnostically. Two phenomena in particular indicate a malfunction and its location; a coarsening of the aura, with the striations becoming markedly granular, and actual gaps in the aura.

Another phenomenon is asymmetry – where the Inner Aura is a different width in corresponding places on the left and right of the body. This is only a significant clue when the subject is viewed from the front or the back, because then the healthy aura should be symmetrical. If the subject is viewed from the side, asymmetry tells you nothing, because the front and back auras differ naturally just as the front and back of the physical body do.

Anyone learning to read the aura diagnostically should study Kilner's book from cover to cover. His case-histories are a goldmine of information. Starting from scratch, and investigating hundreds of patients (and healthy people too), he discovered many useful auric symptoms which he admitted he could not explain but whose diagnostic meanings were confirmed again and again. For example, he found that hysterical patients always had an abnormal bulge in the aura behind the small of the back; and that epileptics always had an asymmetrical head aura, being much wider on the right of the head than on the left. (Why always that way round, Kilner wondered? Possibly because of an imbalance between the left-brain and right-brain functions, which only became understood long after his day.)[3] He also had consistent success in the prediction of early or delayed menstruation, and in the diagnosis of pregnancy.

Janet has found that subjects who have been subjected to ECT (electro-convulsive therapy) have obvious gaps in the aura of the head – often persisting for many years after the treatment. Meeting one of our friends for the first time, she told her at once that she had had ECT, though her medical history had not even been mentioned. Our friend confirmed that she had had it ten years earlier. Auric symptoms often fade slowly after a physical cure, but such a long persistence cannot be healthy – further support for the growing number of doctors and psychiatrists who have serious doubt about the wisdom of ECT.

So far we have discussed the aura as seen, whether optically or clairvoyantly. But the aura (or, at the very least, the inner aura) is a visible manifestation of the etheric body; and for healing work, one will prefer to know more about the structure of the etheric body itself than one's eyes reveal. This brings us on to such concepts as the chakras and their functions, which are beyond the scope of summary such as this. The classic book on the subject is *The Etheric Double* by Arthur E. Powell. It was published in 1925, and, as the Foreword to the 1969 reprint points out, there are aspects of it which might be updated 'in the light of understanding accumulated during the intervening forty-odd years'; but it remains an excellent basis for study, and since much of its contents (to quote the 1969 Foreword again) 'is derived from the exercise of clairsentience', it is a useful complement to Kilner (whom Powell also cites). 'Clairsentience' here is used to mean extra-sensory perception in general, not the stricter definition we gave on p.200.

Auric healing is based on the manipulation of what the Hindus call *prâna* – A Sanskrit word which (like *karma*) has come to be used by Western occultists because it has no exact equivalent in any Western language.[4] 'Prâna, or Vitality, is a vital force, the existence of which is not yet formally recognised by Western scientists, though probably a few of them suspect it.' (Powell, p.8.) It is *the* vital force of the Cosmos as it operates on the etheric level; it permeates our solar system (and certainly all others), and every living organism is charged with a concentration of it; without it we would not *be* living organisms. Each of us can be supercharged with it or suffer from an insufficiency of it – or, through vampirism, steal it from each other. The successful healer learns to draw on the surrounding 'free' prâna and to recharge the patient with it. This is the opposite process to vampirism, and at the end of it, if it has been done properly, the healer is not depleted, because he or she has drawn in at least as much prâna as has been passed on to the patient.

Before doing this, the healer draws off any negative or harmful charge from the patient and disperses it harmlessly.

This is the essence of what has long been known as 'the laying on of hands'. And note that it is not the physical body on which the hands need to be laid; the influence is from the aura of the healer's hands to the aura of the patient's body – an influence which can be seen optically in the form of rays once one's eyes are sensitized to the aura, and which can be recorded by Kirlian photography. Most experienced auric healers will not normally touch the patient's body during the 'laying on of hands'; they will hold them an inch or two away, in contact with the inner aura.

Normally, one of the two hands will be found to be the dominant 'healing hand'. Which of the two hands it is can be detected in any one person by getting him or her to hold them both palm upwards; you then hold your own hand palm downwards an inch or two above each of them in turn, without touching them, several times alternately. Almost certainly one of them will give you a stronger sensation of heat or tingling; that is the healing hand. In healing work, the *other* hand should be used for drawing away negative influences, and then the healing hand for recharging with prâna.

The basis of auric healing is clairvoyance and willpower.

Optical and clairvoyant vision of the aura (in that order) can be built up gradually, but willpower should be at your command from the start, and there is no reason why you should not begin to try auric healing on that basis alone. Say a friend has a headache, and you want to help even though you are not yet at the stage where you can see the aura. Knowing (from Kilner and Kirlian if from no one else!) that influence passes between your hand and your friend's head if they are close together, you hold your less dominant hand an inch or two away from the place where your friend is feeling the pain and, by concentrated willpower, draw out the tension and strain. Every five or ten seconds, *withdraw your hand and shake it to one side as though you were shaking off drops of water* – at the same time vividly envisaging the negative influences falling away from your hand, and willing them to disperse harmlessly. Be careful, of course, that you do not shake your hand towards any other person or living creature. (You may find that even this first part of the process will bring about a marked easing of the headache.)

Now sit back and relax, breathing steadily and slowly – say six seconds in, two seconds hold, six seconds out and two seconds hold, breathing always with your diaphragm (i.e., by pushing your stomach in and out) and not by expanding and contracting your rib cage. As you breathe in, envisage not only your lungs but every pore of your body, drawing in prâna from the surrounding atmosphere. As you hold your full breath, envisage your body (both physical and etheric) absorbing the prâna you have drawn in. As you breathe out, envisage any negative influence in yourself (including any residue of what you have drawn off the patient) leaving your body and dispersing. As you hold your lungs empty, prepare your mind for the next drawing-in of prâna.

When you feel you are sufficiently charged, *will* the newly accumulated prâna into the arm of your healing hand till you feel that it is tingling with it. Then hold your healing hand an inch or two from your friend's head and *will* the accumulated prâna into his or her aura, to do its healing work and restore normality.

You may find it helps if you visualize prâna as a mist of tiny golden specks permeating the atmosphere; and as you draw it into concentration, visualize the concentration area as glowing because of the denser population of these golden specks. (Some sensitives say that, if you look into the clear blue sky of a sunlit day, you can actually see prâna in this form; but we think that this is clairvoyant, a retinal effect, or psychological projection, and not optical, since prâna is surely a homogeneous force rather than separate particles. The 'golden specks' trick is merely a visualization aid, though very useful as such.)

Such non-clairvoyant healing work helps to give you confidence, and in practice it speeds up the development of clairvoyance. As optical vision of the aura, and then clairvoyant vision of it, grows clearer, your diagnostic ability will increase accordingly, because you will have more exact information to go on.

The process we have described emphasizes a vital point – the need for protection of the healer. When our young coven first tried healing work, we were encouraged by some success – but puzzled by the fact that we often felt the very effects of which we had relieved the patient. We would cure Charlie's backache right enough – and end up with backache ourselves.

As we began to realize what was happening, we paid attention to our own psychic protection whenever we undertook healing work. And in particular, with auric healing, we never skipped the hand-shaking drill and its accompanying visualization and willpower. From then on, we stopped collecting Charlie's backache, or whatever.

Remember, also, that when you pass prâna into the patient, you must be sure that you draw a corresponding amount (or more) into yourself from your surroundings, or you will leave yourself depleted. Thelma Moss and her team investigated several healers, including ones who worked by the laying on of hands, by Kirlian photography; and she tells in *The Body Electric* how time and again they found the photographs showed that the patient's Kirlian corona had brightened, while the healer's had become less bright. Some of these healers had discovered their gift by accident and admitted that they did not understand it; one hopes that, with improved understanding, they also acquired the gift of recharging themselves.

A final tip on auric vision: we find its development is greatly helped by studying the auras of animals. Some of them are particularly vivid and easy to see. They are also very sensitive; many animals react positively to the usual two-inches-away handling of their auras. (But with a long-haired animal such as a Persian cat, try to distinguish between genuine auric influence and the coat's reaction to the static electricity of your hand.) We often think that vets could usefully study auric diagnosis. Maybe some of them do so instinctively.

Psychology

A good witch has to be a psychologist, both to enable him or her to understand the reasons underlying Wiccan practices and the ways in which these practices work, and also for the understanding and effective handling of other people. This is especially true where healing is concerned. Unless one is awake to the psychology of the patient, one may miss the key to the case altogether – or, even if one has correctly guessed it, fail to encourage the required attitude of mind in the patient.

Few witches are, or can become, trained psychiatrists; but a certain amount of selected reading can give any sensible witch a helpful grounding in the subject. We firmly believe that the works of Jung and his followers are the very best means to this. Freud opened vast new horizons in human understanding, but his shortcomings are perhaps best summed up in Shuttle and Redgrove's shrewd remark (*The Wise Wound*, p.177): 'Freud was a great man. He was a great *man*, however.' Jung first learned from Freud and then in due course clashed with him over those very shortcomings and went his own way. It is a way which we find remarkably in tune with Wiccan philosophy. He was singularly unhampered by patriarchal stereotypes, which had remained a millstone around Freud's neck; and any small gaps in his awareness which his own maleness may have caused were rapidly compensated for by women Jungians such as Esther Harding, Jolande Jacobi and Aniela Jaffé.

Freud and Jung gave mankind a whole new insight into the structure of its own psyche. It is not too much to say that Jung above all gave Wicca a new understanding of itself – if only by making fully conscious (and providing language for) a range of concepts which most witches had hitherto only grasped intuitively.

We gave on pp. 132 and 147 some of the books which may be read as a short course on the basics of Jung's thinking; and we strongly recommend them. Even if witches find aspects to disagree with, the study should greatly clarify their own ideas.

Our own book is certainly no place to give a basic course in psychology; but we would like to add a thought or two on the psychological aspects of Wiccan healing.

A musician friend of ours once sang: 'The road to her door is washed out with tears.' The road to the healer's door is all too often so washed – by the tears of loss of hope, of guilt, of family brainwashing or of unconscious fears. The witch must be a mental healer as well as a physical one, otherwise the symptom may be dealt with instead of the cause. And as every good doctor knows, you must not allow yourself to become emotionally involved in the patient's suffering. This does not mean that you should remain unmoved or uncompassionate; but if you allow yourself to weep for the patient's pain, you soon lose your own psychic strength – without which, remember, you cannot help the patient.

We once knew a very beautiful and psychically dynamic young witch who had a great compassion for the animal kingdom, but little or none for the human. One night Janet had to point out some of the facts she was refusing to acknowledge, and the resulting show of temper was exhausting for all concerned. One effect was that her psychic healing powers, which had been very vibrant, waned considerably for a while, until she had come to terms with herself. She had, in effect, brought her frustrations to the surface in the same way as a skin throws up a boil. Janet had sensed that her apparent callousness was in fact a fear that, if she opened the floodgates, she would be swamped. Until she faced up to this, she had no way of achieving a *balanced* compassion – which is essential to the successful healer.

Professional psychiatry knows this, which is why every school of training provides for the psychiatrist himself or herself to be analysed. A psychiatric healer who is not as clear of personal hang-ups as is humanly possible will project those hang-ups onto the patient. Amateur psychologists such as witches must, for this reason apart from any other, eliminate their own hang-ups as honestly as they can. So a basic understanding of *their own* psychology is just as important as understanding the psychology of the patient.

A word about the 'placebo effect'. A placebo is a treatment (whether it is a medicine, a pill or a course of action) which a doctor knows has no effect in itself (the pill may be chalk, for example) but which he prescribes because the patient *believes* it will do him good. This is not necessarily cheating; a patient who is almost superstitiously convinced that 'a pill from the doctor' is essential to his recovery will not respond to the real treatment unless he gets it; so the doctor wisely provides it, alongside the real treatment.

Witches, as we pointed out on p.186, soon become familiar with the placebo effect – the patient who gets better just because he has asked the witches for help, before the witches have even had time to work on his request; or the patient who is greatly encouraged by the mere physical evidence of a spell being worked on his behalf. Like good doctors, wise witches should be aware of the placebo effect, allow their patients to benefit from it – but never cheat; in other words, never rely on it alone, never neglect the real treatment as well, and never put on a show to keep the applicant quiet.

The psychological aspect of Wiccan healing is another proof of the benefits of coven working. The use of psychology demands so much honesty and self-awareness that the mutual observation and openness characteristic of a well-integrated coven are an excellent guarantee against losing your way or deceiving yourself.

Two tailpieces to this Section. Everyone interested in psychic healing should read Dion Fortune's *The Secrets of Dr Taverner*. In fictional form, it gives fascinating case-histories of a high adept who ran an occult nursing home. But 'Dr Taverner' and his nursing home actually existed, and, as Dion Fortune says in her Introduction, all the book's stories are 'founded on fact, and there is not a single incident herein contained which is pure imagination'. We know the daughter of one of the characters described in the book, and a High Priestess friend of ours knows another of the characters; and in both cases, the truthfulness of Dion Fortune's account was confirmed.

Her non-fiction book *Psychic Self-Defence*, as we pointed out in Section IX, should be obligatory reading for every witch; we mention it again here because the principles of psychic defence and psychic healing are inseparable.

And the second tailpiece, highly relevant to the importance of imagination and willpower in healing, comes from the late Pablo Picasso: 'When art is properly understood, we will be able to paint pictures to cure toothache.'

XXII   Spells

A spell is a ritual for raising psychic power and directing it to a specific and practical purpose. It is fuelled by vivid imagination and concentrated willpower; and what sceptics usually describe as the 'mumbo-jumbo' of a spell is in fact a dramatization to activate these two and is thus a perfectly reasonable way of going about it.

To take an example: the famous 'wax image' spell, which is almost the only one that non-witches seem to have heard of. They associate it with sinister activities such as the sticking in of nails, pins or thorns to harm the intended victim; and of course it can be used malevolently in this way. But 'white' witches use it responsibly – which means in practice that they confine it to healing work and where necessary to the 'binding' of someone who is acting malevolently (see p.141).

As is normal in Wiccan practice, the image spell is best worked by a woman-man partnership, though the whole coven may usefully support them in it. The image may be of wax, Plasticene or any convenient material, and the entire object of the exercise is to identify it as closely as possible with the person concerned. It should *look* like him or her (we will stick to 'him' for brevity), but it need not be conventionally artistic; for instance, if visualization is helped by incorporating a photograph of his face in the front of the head, by all means do so. If some of his hair-clippings or nail-clippings can be incorporated, this is both traditional and useful, because it helps to make the mental identification more dramatically vivid, and also provides a psychic link on the resonance principle (see pp. 209-10). The image should be naked and unmistakably male or female.

Some witches pierce the core of the image with a skewer and pack the cavity with cotton wool soaked in Planetary Condenser, a fluid prepared by dunking scraps of metal, to represent the various planetary influences, in water. For ourselves, we do not find this necessary, and the skewering weakens the image structurally. But there is something to be said for incorporating a living substance of some kind, and the traditional, non-sacrificial substance is raw egg, as fresh as possible. (This use of fresh raw egg as a 'non-sacrificial living sacrifice' is worth remembering for other purposes.) A little of this in a small cavity inside the chest, where the heart would be, is preferable to the skewered tunnel.

Both partners, and everyone else who is taking part, should be involved in some way, however small, in the making of the image. It should be made inside a Magic Circle.

When the image is ready, the partners take it to the altar and sprinkle it with consecrated water-and-salt, saying: 'We name thee ————, in the names of Cernunnos and Aradia' (or whatever God- and Goddess-names are being used). The image is left on the pentacle, while everybody involved dances to the Witches' Rune to build up the power.

The woman then lays herself down face upwards in the centre of the Circle in the pentagram position, head to the North. The man takes a red cord and ties the middle of it round the image, one end round his own waist, and the other end round the woman's waist.

Now the couple 'conceive' and 'give birth to' the image. Just how vividly and dramatically this is done depends on the couple's imagination and the nature of their everyday relationship: the enactment can be anything from purely symbolic to wholeheartedly 'actual' (the latter, of course, in private); what matters is that it should be done with concentrated willpower and visualization of the intent. (We have known a woman witch to 'suckle' the image immediately afterwards; dramatically effective, but it might possibly have the psychic side-effect of setting up an unwanted dependence of the 'patient' on the woman, and leading to a form of vampirism, so perhaps it is better avoided.)

Next, the man unties the cord from the woman's waist and carries the image, still attached to himself, to the altar. With his athame, he makes the Invoking Pentagram of Earth in front of the image. He then removes the cord from the image and from his own waist.

The partners, or the group, then sit facing each other, and each in turn (the woman, the man and then any others) holds the image. Each addresses it by name and gives it the appropriate healing words and treatment or, in the case of a binding spell, precise and carefully worded orders. In both cases, the image is treated, spoken to *and thought of* as the living person concerned. It is then given any symbolic treatment necessary, such as sewing up the mouth if the person is to be stopped from spreading malice. Finally, it is bound with cord, and wrapped in cloth, of the appropriate colour (red for organic healing, blue for functional healing, black for a binding spell, and so on – see the table on pp. 263-4).

When the Circle is being banished, the wrapped image will be carried by someone *behind* the banisher, as with newly consecrated objects.

After this the wrapped image is taken away and hidden in a secret place, safe from handling, and kept there for as long as the effect of the spell is needed. At times it may be felt that it needs recharging; you should then unwrap it, draw down the power on it with your athame (repeating the orders or healing words), re-wrap it and return it to its hiding-place. This should be done inside a Circle, mental or actual.

An image which has been identified with a person and used in an image spell should never be left in existence once the aim has been achieved or the term of the spell has ended – even if the spell has failed. The image should be dispersed by taking it to natural running water, unwrapping and unbinding it and breaking it up into small pieces, each of which is thrown into the water with the order: 'Return to the elements from which thou camest.'

This spell includes all the essential elements of spell-working: dramatization, imagination, identification, precise intent, willpower and the disposal of loose ends. More elements can be taken into consideration to enhance the effect. For example, you could work a healing spell if possible during the waxing or full Moon, and in the day and hour of Mercury or Jupiter or a binding spell during the waning or new Moon and in the day and hour of Saturn. You could also choose appropriate incense and music, and so on. (For the planetary days and hours, see *What Witches Do*, Appendix 3, or Barrett's *Magus* Book II, Part IV, p.139.)

But a spell can be very much simpler than this, while still following the same principles. For example, suppose you want to bring together two people who are having difficulty communicating. You might consecrate and name two chess pieces (Kings or Queens according to sex), place them at opposite ends of your mantelpiece and move them a little closer to each other daily until they are in contact – speaking your words of encouragement each time you move them.

Or you might feel that a problem requires continuing psychic pressure over several hours; so you might consecrate a candle, mentally concentrate your purpose into it, light it and leave it to burn out (on your altar if you have a permanent one) after declaring firmly and confidently: 'By the time this candle is completely burned out, Mary will be well again' or 'my choice will be clear' or 'John will phone me' or whatever the objective is. During the hours of burning, your attention may be distracted by other unavoidable matters, but your subconscious knows that the candle is being consumed, and for what purpose; so your own flow of psychic effort continues under the surface. An alternative, with a shorter time-span, is the candle-and-needle spell (see Plate 11), where a needle is pushed through the candle partway up; the spell is willed to take effect when the flame reaches the needle. In either case, choose a candle of a colour appropriate to the work if you can.

Use of suitable God- and Goddess-names is a help. If one of our many cats is ill or missing, we always invoke the Egyptian Cat-Goddess, Bast; and it has worked time and again. For a communications problem, Mercury, Hermes or Thoth, according to the pantheon with which you feel in tune; for a problem relating specifically to the Craft, Aradia; for work for children, a Mother-Goddess name – local, if possible, like the Irish Dana; for a karmic question, Arianrhod; and so on. (Even for blocked drains there is that delightful Roman Goddess of Sewerage, Cloacina!).

In devising spells, there is both psychological and psychic advantage in making use of 'correspondences' – the harmonics which magical experience has shown to link objects or beings in various categories (deities, colours, plant and animal species, Tarot cards, perfumes, minerals, musical frequencies, geometrical figures, Tree of Life paths etc.) and which help one to find those 'points of inter-resonance' between the levels which we spoke of in Section XI. For information on these correspondences, the indispensable handbook is Crowley's 777, which some people regard as the most useful and uncontaminated book he ever wrote. (His magical tutor, Allan Bennett, compiled part of it.)

One could list spells indefinitely, and countless books have done so. Very helpful some of them are. But a good witch, like a good chef, does not rely on the recipe books. The best spells are made by using your own imagination in *devising* them, as well as in working them. Janet invented the chessmen-on-the-mantelpiece spell almost on the spur of the moment, to deal with a particular problem (though it may have occurred to others, too); it met the need simply and vividly, it provided clear symbols for the concentration of willpower – and so it worked.

The thing to remember is that you need imagination and willpower

to open psychic channels and activate psychic resonance; and you take
it from there in your own way.

Spell-working is a regular part of most ordinary coven Circles.
Members come with their own or their friends' problems, and the group
works on them together. For such collective-agenda working, most
covens have a regular drill and keep tailor-made spells for special
objectives, or for partnership or solo working.

In our coven, we tend to use either cord magic or linked-hand magic.
Whichever we are using comes immediately after the Witches' Rune
ring-dance; this limbers the psychic muscles and builds up the cone of
power; which must be exploited before it loses intensity.

For cord magic, the coven sits in a ring facing inwards, with a man
opposite a woman as far as possible. Cords are held diametrically across
the ring, turned over each other at the centre to form a hub of the
wheel of spokes. Each cord is held (again, as far as possible) by a
woman at one end and a man at the other, pulling their cord taut. As
each wish is named, everybody concentrates on it and ties a knot to
symbolize that concentration. When all the wishes have been named,
the High Priestess directs everyone to concentrate on the cone of power
as being charged with the total effect; after a while she orders 'Let go!',
and everybody lets go at once, visualizing the power flying outwards to
achieve the various objectives. The cords are gathered into a loose
bundle and laid on the altar; the knots are not untied until just before
the next Circle.

Sometimes, instead of holding a cord herself, the High Priestess will
lie on her back under the wheel of cords, head to the North, grasping
the hub of the cords together with her athame point upwards, as a
focus for the power and as a kind of lightning-conductor for its
ultimate discharge. We find that when she does this she is particularly
well able to assess the amount of power that has been raised.

In our other method, we again sit in a ring, man and woman
alternately as far as possible, clasping hands with our neighbours (left
palm facing upwards, right palm downwards). The wishes are named in
the same way, deosil in turn, and as we concentrate on them we
envisage the power flowing like a current through our arms, deosil
around the Circle, growing faster and stronger and feeding the cone of
power in a rising spiral. New witches are often surprised to find that
they can actually feel the current.

A development of the linked-hand working was invented by Barbara,
one of our witches, and we found it so effective that for us it is now
tending to replace cord magic altogether. To take an imaginary coven,
naming wishes deosil in turn as usual:

Mary: 'For peace of mind for Bridie, who has a persecution

complex.'
Chris: 'For inspiration in my artistic work.'
Susan: 'For success in an interview for a job I've applied for.'
Peter: 'For Arthur, who has an alcohol problem.'
Kathie: 'For my mother, who suffers from arthritis.'
Jim: 'For my sister's cat, who has been missing for two days.'
Without pausing, and still deosil in rotation, the wishes are repeated in shortened form:
Mary: 'Bridie's paranoia.'
Chris: 'Artistic inspiration.'
Susan: 'Successful interview.'
Peter: 'Arthur's alcoholism.'
Kathie: 'Mother's arthritis.'
Jim: 'Sister's missing cat.'
Then faster and faster, reducing each wish to one key word: 'Paranoia ... Inspiration ... Interview ... Alcohol ... Arthritis ... Cat ... Paranoia ... Inspiration ...' – until the High Priestess calls 'Stop!' and the power is discharged to do its work.

This method has several advantages; building up the power in a steady and accelerating rhythm, pinpointing each wish to a single idea, and impressing all the wishes on each person's mind until the whole group is simultaneously aware of all of them at the moment of discharge.

The deliberate building up of thought-forms is another technique much used in spell-working, and it can be done by one person, a partnership, or the whole coven.

A thought-form is similar in nature to what psychiatrists call a complex. A complex is a constellation of elements within the psyche which has acquired a quasi-independent existence and which often acts in conflict with the conscious will and with the genuine need of the individual. A complex may be set up by trauma or repression and is in general a malfunction; the psychiatrist's job is to uncover the cause and to reintegrate the complex's elements with the total psyche.

But although a thought-form built up by a witch or occultist is also a quasi-independent constellation of psychic elements, it is created deliberately and for a useful purpose, to act *in accordance with* his or her conscious will. And when it has fulfilled its function, it is consciously reabsorbed. Properly created, used and reabsorbed, it has none of the malfunction-effects which a complex has.

Also, when built up by a partnership or a coven, it includes elements from each of their psyches. (For parallels here, one would have to enter the realms of social rather than individual psychology.) When this is done, the thought-form's 'quasi-independence' can become even more striking. So much so that, if it is built up carelessly, it can get out of hand and become difficult to control; but its creators can forestall this by precisely worded and firmly impressed instructions.

The necessary factors are the same as for all spell-working; imagination, clear visualization, exact definition of intent, and concentrated willpower. We will discuss the process as for a group; if a solo witch is doing it, the factors are the same, but it may require extra concentration and self-discipline.

The group first discuss the purpose of the thought-form until it is fully agreed and clear in everyone's mind. It is not a bad idea to write it down (and to note the exact wording in the coven record).

They then agree on a name for the thought-form, expressing its purpose and characteristics, and of a gender appropriate to these. It should obviously not be a known Goddess- or God-name, because it is being envisaged as an entity in its own right and not as the invocation of a particular divine aspect, which is rather a different process. The name can even be synthetic; borrowing a technique from ceremonial magic, one can make up a name from the initials of the desired qualities. For example, a thought-form whose function required it to be reassuring, encouraging, selective, humorous and activating might be named R-E-S-H-A, Resha.

They next agree on its visual appearance; and one member with a strong visual imagination may be asked to envisage and describe this. It will normally be envisaged in human form, as this makes the idea of talking to it easier to accept. The group should have clearly in mind the thought-form's sex, apparent age, build, colouring, kind and amount of hair, expression and so on, and whether it (which by now should be thought of as 'he' or 'she') is naked or clothed, and if clothed, what he/she is wearing. If there is an artist in the group, it is a very good idea for anything from a quick sketch to a full painting to be made, for everybody to study and hold in mind.

In building up a group thought-form, there is a lot to be said for consciously incorporating necessary qualities from individual members who are known to possess them, and stating this verbally: for example, 'Shera shall have Mary's compassion, Peter's determination, Sheila's discernment, Tony's quick-wittedness, Moira's joyfulness,' and so on. Apart from anything else, this helps to strengthen the group's awareness that Shera is a 'complex' including elements from all their psyches.

The final thing to be decided upon is the thought-form's life-span. Normally this will be for a definite term and will be included in the instructions: 'You will complete your work within seven days and will then disperse, your elements returning to us who made you.' (Or whatever time-span is felt to be suitable.) But there may be thought-forms whose life-span has to be left open-ended or even made deliberately permanent (for example, if a guardian is being put on a particular place). In that case, the situation should be re-examined periodically, the thought-form recharged and any unexpected side-effects looked for.

(Incidentally, the guardian thought-form is a good example of the usefulness of a name. Suppose we have put such a guardian called Mogrel on a place – the moment we sense that it is under threat, we simply call 'Mogrel – on guard!' with a deliberate surge of willpower, and the whole psychic defence mechanism is triggered off.)

So now our group has defined, named and visualized its thought form, the next step is to activate it ritually. How this is done is a matter for the group's inventiveness and its usual way of going about things. For example, the High Priestess could address the Goddess and the God on behalf of the group, announcing what is intended and invoking their help in giving life to 'Shera', 'Mogrel' or whoever. Or as with the image-spell, a woman-man partnership could ritually 'give birth' to the thought-form, though in the absence of a material image the focus would be purely mental concentration. What matters is that there should *be* a focus, a moment when the whole group simultaneously envisage the thought-form as starting on its independent existence. (Whatever the ritual used, it is effective to mark this moment by the ringing of a bell.)

Once this is done, the group sit in a circle, and each in turn instructs the thought-form by name – using his or her own words but being careful to express exactly the intended purpose.

Here is an example from our own experience. There is off the coast of Co. Mayo a pair of islands called Inishkea, where grey seals come annually in large numbers to bear and rear their pups. In October 1981 certain elements among the local fishermen landed on Inishkea and conducted a wholesale massacre of the pups. Their excuse was that the seals were doing great harm to the salmon-fishing industry – though informed sources (including some in the fishing industry itself) were quick to point out that the real damage was being done by over-fishing, poaching and the use of nets of illegal dimensions. The massacre itself was illegal, since any necessary seal-culling is supposed to be carried out by Government agents after careful official assessment of the need; but somehow (Mayo being a thinly populated, tightly knit area) nobody got prosecuted.

Public opinion was horrified, and controversy raged in the correspondence columns of the newspapers. The Irish Wildlife Federation announced that it would organize volunteer camps on Inishkea to guard the seals during the 1982 pupping season – and many volunteers did in fact spend weeks on the islands in 1982 and 1983.

Our coven, none of whom could physically join these volunteers, felt that we should make our own contribution in our own way. In November 1981 we created a thought-form which we named Mara (Gaelic for 'of the sea'). Janet painted a picture of her (see Plate 18) – a grey-green watery form emerging from, and of the substance of, the sea; and as we had plenty of time in hand, we made small photographic colour prints of the painting so that all our members could carry one. She was instructed: 'You will manifest visually to, and frighten, anyone who tries to harm the seals on or near Inishkea Islands. You will harm no one unless he persists and there is no other way of stopping him.' We recharged her and reinstructed her at each full Moon throughout the year.

The tragedy of 1981 was not repeated in 1982, 1983 or 1984. We like to think that we helped to prevent it. But in any case, Mara is still in existence.

An interesting footnote to this. After the 1983 pupping season, we were talking to a couple who had been ferrying supplies to the Sea Shepherd volunteers on Inishkea. Before we told them anything about Mara, or about our action, they told us how they had been saved from landing on dangerous rocks in dreadful weather by a woman who waved them urgently away. 'She wore something like an ankle-length grey-green mackintosh,' they said, 'You couldn't see her face, but man! – could you see her eyes!' After they had landed safely further along, they were told there was not, and could not have been, any woman there. They also discovered that several people had seen such a woman walking among the seals, who were surprisingly undisturbed by her. She was known as 'the Ghost'.

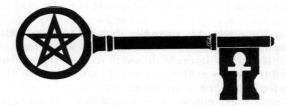

XXIII Self-Initiation

When we were initiated in 1970, we were taught that 'only a witch can make a witch'. In other words, the only way to become a witch was to be initiated by another witch, of the appropriate degree and of the opposite sex to oneself. That was probably the view of the Craft as a whole at the time, and we accepted it ourselves.

We still believe that it is a good rule to follow wherever possible, because it means that a new witch starts his or her training under the guidance of an experienced initiator, and usually as a member of an existing coven. Mistakes are less hazardous, misunderstandings are more quickly cleared up, and the learning process is much quicker. Anything is better learned by apprenticeship than by lone study.

But we no longer believe, at this stage of the Craft's history, that it should be inflexible. Moreover, insistence on it is unrealistic; a large section of today's Craft (and by no means necessarily an inferior section) either is self-initiated or stems from people who were self-initiated.

For example, it is very doubtful whether Alex Sanders was ever 'legitimately' initiated, according to the strict rules which he himself taught us. It is known that he tried very hard to get himself admitted to more than one Gardnerian coven, and failed; it seems that finally he somehow got his hands on a copy of the Gardnerian Book of Shadows and on that basis founded his own. (His story that he copied his Book of Shadows from his grandmother's when he was a boy cannot be true, because that would have been many years before the text, as he had it, was in fact compiled by Gardner and Valiente.) Does that mean that the whole Alexandrian movement (which includes some very fine covens indeed) is 'illegitimate' and that its members are not real witches?

Such a claim belongs in the realm of fantasy. Whatever one thinks of Alex himself, many of the initiates who stemmed from him and Maxine, at first, second or third hand, are real witches by anyone's standards.

Wicca is a way of looking at the world, and of living in it, which has ancient roots but is highly relevant to our own time. As such, it will be practised by those who are naturally drawn to it, and this growth cannot be contained or limited by insistence on any Wiccan Apostolic Succession.[1] If you *are* naturally drawn to it, your best course is to be initiated and trained by existing witches if that is possible. If it is not, you are perfectly justified in setting up shop on your own initiative – preferably with a like-minded working partner and perhaps a small group of friends.

As Doreen Valiente says in *Witchcraft for Tomorrow* (p.22): 'You have a right to be a pagan if you want to be …. So do not let anyone browbeat you out of it' – including, presumably, pedantically minded pagans. She goes on to quote Article 18 of the Universal Declaration of Human Rights, as published by the United Nations. Article 18 is well worth study; and incidentally, as far as our own country is concerned, the same freedom of religious belief and practice is guaranteed by Article 44 of the Constitution of Ireland.

If you want to become a practising witch (in both the religious and the Craft sense) and have no way of joining an existing coven, you should first study the basic philosophy of Wicca and be sure inside yourself that you are in tune with it. Thirty or forty years ago, that would have been very difficult indeed. Today you have the writings of Gerald Gardner, Doreen Valiente, Patricia and Arnold Crowther, Justine Glass, Lois Bourne, ourselves and others, which from their individual but overlapping viewpoints will give you quite complete enough a picture to answer the question 'Is this for me?'

If the answer is a genuine 'Yes', you can do one of two things. The first is to take a very simple system of ritual and practice, and to work with it until you feel thoroughly at home with it. By then you will begin to know intuitively whether, and in what way, you want to complicate it. Needs and responses differ; one Christian may get deep spiritual benefit from a Quaker meeting, another from a High Mass; and the Wiccan spectrum is just as wide.

For this approach, the ideal handbook is Doreen Valiente's *Witchcraft for Tomorrow*, because that is the purpose for which it was written. In it, Doreen sums up the principles and practices of witchcraft and offers a simple but meaningful *Liber Umbrarum* or Book of Shadows which includes casting the Circle, self-initiation, consecration, a full-moon esbat rite, a sabbat rite, initiation into the coven, coven spell-working, invocations, chants and dances. Simple, but certainly not childish; there is no witch, however experienced, who could not benefit from studying it.

The second way is to take the whole structure of an established Wiccan system and to work from that. The Gardnerian structure would seem to be the only one which is comprehensively available; and part of our purpose in writing this book and *Eight Sabbats for Witches* has been to provide the basic material for this second choice, just as Doreen's *Witchcraft for Tomorrow* provided it for the first choice.

(To be quite fair, Raymond Buckland's book *The Tree, the Complete Book of Saxon Witchcraft* also offers an entire system, including self-initiation. It is frankly an 'invented' system, which Dr Buckland synthesized himself out of Saxon mythology and symbology and named 'Seax-Wica'. It is a viable system for those of Saxon background or leanings, and it is none the worse for having been synthesized. Apart from the book itself, more information can be had from Seax-Wica Voys, PO Box 5149, Virginia Beach, Va 23455, USA. But our own books, like Doreen's, are concerned with the Gardnerian tradition, which is basically Celtic; so we will merely set up this Saxon signpost for those who are interested to follow.)

Having decided on your basic pattern, how do you start?

If you are to be a solo witch, even if you intend to follow the full Gardnerian system as far as possible, you could still follow the self-initiation ritual from *Witchcraft for Tomorrow*, because the whole of it was conceived for that purpose. But if you prefer to start with a more typically Gardnerian ritual, then use the form we give at the end of this Section.

Every witch must pay continuous attention to the still small voice within, and give it the time and the conditions in which it can speak; that is what witchcraft is all about. It is the voice of the Unconscious, both Personal and Collective; and the more we perfect our sensitivity to its message, the more clearly it becomes the voice of the Goddess and the God as well (and the better we will understand what those words 'as well' mean). But for the solo witch it is even more important, if that is possible, because he or she is without fellow-workers to check on mistakes or self-deception. For the same reason, the solo witch should be especially meticulous about magical ethics and about psychic self-defence.

The path of a self-initiated solo witch has many possible pitfalls, of which the loneliness of the expanding psyche is not the least. We strongly recommend that the self-initiate should start on the path with a working partner or as one of a small group. The partnership should be a man and a woman, and if it is a group, it should include at least one woman, for the reasons of polarity which we have already discussed in depth. A two-woman initial partnership would be workable, if no suitable man could be found; but a two-man partnership would tend to be magically unfruitful.

Given a partnership, we suggest that the woman should initiate herself first, in her partner's presence, by whichever ritual is chosen, and that she should then initiate the man. In the case of a group, a High Priestess and High Priest should be agreed upon beforehand; the chosen High Priestess should initiate herself in the presence of the others, and then initiate the chosen High Priest. Thereafter she will initiate the men, and he the women. In due course, when they feel they are ready, the High Priest should give the High Priestess her second degree initiation, immediately followed by her giving the second degree to him (in this instance, the Legend of the Descent of the Goddess being performed once only, as a climax to the dual initiation). And when the time comes, they will take their third degree together.

The only self-initiation should be the unavoidable first one. Once that is done, each member should be initiated by an already-initiated witch; and after the High Priestess and High Priest have given each other their higher degrees, the *whole* of the normal rule should be adhered to, that only a third-degree witch may confer the third degree on another. The rule is a good one, with sound reasons behind it, and self-initiation should be seen to be an exceptional procedure to be used only when no other is available.

(The simplified system of *Witchcraft for Tomorrow* does not include the idea of second-or third-degree witches, so if that is being followed, only the first part of the rule arises.)

One tip for all self-made witches, whether solo or group – keep in touch with current thinking, development and controversy within the Craft and the pagan movement in general. Read such Craft newsletters as *The Cauldron* (see p. 277 for the address) – which incidentally contains exchange advertisements for other pagan magazines and newsletters. Involve yourself in any local pagan or occult activities such as symposia, lectures or fairs – but cautiously until you have weighed up their genuineness.

A Self-Initiation Ritual

We have composed this ritual for first degree self-initiation to meet the needs of those who have no alternative to self-initiation but who wish to adhere as closely as possible to a typically Gardnerian pattern.

As elsewhere, we have simplified things by referring to the self-initiate as 'she' throughout (and her partner, if one is present, as 'he'), but the changes for a man are obvious.

The Preparation

The tools on the altar (in addition to candles) should at least be the sword, athame, white-handled knife, wand, pentacle, censer of incense, scourge, cords, chalice of wine, anointing oil, bowl of water, bowl of salt and a necklace or pendant.

The Initiate, and the Partner or anyone else who is present in the Circle, should be skyclad – the Initiate completely so; any jewellery which she normally wears all the time, such as a wedding ring, should be laid on the altar for putting on again after the rite. (Some wedding rings have become irremovable with time, and leaving such a ring in place may be forgiven.)

The Ritual

The initiate consecrates the water and salt, casts the Circle (with anyone else who is present already inside it), carries round the water (sprinkling anyone who is present and finally herself), carries round the censer, carries round the candle and summons the Lords of the Watchtowers – doing all this herself.

If her Partner is present, he gives her the Fivefold Kiss.

She faces the altar and raises her arms high and wide.[2] She says:

'*I invoke thee and call upon thee, Mighty Mother of us all, bringer of all fruitfulness; by seed and root, by stem and bud, by leaf and flower and fruit do I invoke thee to bless this rite, and to admit me to the company of thy hidden children.*'

She then stands with her back to the altar and recites the whole of the Charge, but substituting 'she', 'her', 'hers' for 'I', 'me', 'my', 'mine'.

She then faces the altar again with her arms raised and her hands giving the 'Horned God' salute (forefinger and little finger straight, thumb and middle fingers folded into palm) and delivers the '*Great God Cernunnos*' invocation.

Now she sits or kneels in the centre of the Circle facing the altar. If others are present, they sit or kneel behind her. She pauses to calm herself completely and then says:

'Gentle Goddess, powerful God; I am your child, now and always. Your breath is my life. Your voice, Great Mother, and yours, Great Father, speak within me, as they do in all your creatures, if we will only listen. Therefore here in your Magic Circle, which stand between the world of men and the realm of the Mighty Ones, do I open my heart to your blessing.'

She then meditates in silence on the Goddess and the God, and indeed opens her heart to them. She continues to do this for as long as feels right to her.

If others are present, they will envisage themselves as a protection for her, holding back any influence which might interfere with her communication with the Goddess and the God. Her Partner will be aware of his role as her guardian and student and will dedicate himself to that role. If a group is present, they will be aware that their High Priestess, keystone of their new coven, is being dedicated to that position on behalf of them all.

When she is ready, she will rise (and anyone else present will rise too). She will then go to each of the cardinal points in turn, and say:

'Take heed, ye Lords of the East [South, West, North], that I, ———, am properly prepared to become a priestess and witch.'

Then, standing in front of the altar with her right hand on her heart, she takes the Oath:

'I, ———, in the presence of the Mighty Ones, do of my own free will and accord most solemnly swear that I ever keep secret and never reveal those secrets of the Craft which shall be entrusted to me, except it be to a proper person, properly prepared within a Circle such as I am now in; and that I will never deny the secrets to such a person if he or she be properly vouched for by a brother or sister of the Art. All this I swear by my hopes of a future life; and may my weapons turn against me if I break this my solemn oath.'

She bows to the altar and then fetches the anointing oil. She moistens her fingertip with the oil and says:

'I hereby sign myself with the Triple Sign. I consecrate myself with oil.'

She touches herself with oil just above the pubic hair, on her right breast, on her left breast, and above the pubic hair again, completing the inverted triangle of the First Degree.

She moistens her fingertip with wine, says *'I anoint myself with wine'* and touches herself in the same places with the wine.

She then kisses her fingertip, says *'I consecrate myself with my lips'*, touches herself in the same three places (kissing the fingertip again before each touch) and continues: *'priestess and witch'*.

If others are present, the ritual is interrupted for congratulations to the newly self-initiated witch.

When this has been done, the ritual continues with the new witch taking up each of the working tools in turn from the altar and giving the following explanations. (She kisses each tool before replacing it.)

'*Now I take up the Working Tools. First, the Magic Sword. With this, as with the Athame, I can form all magic circles, dominate, subdue and punish all rebellious spirits and demons, and even persuade angels and good spirits. With this in my hand, I am the ruler of the Circle.*

'*Next I take up the Athame. This is the true witch's weapon, and has all the power of the Magic Sword.*

'*Next I take up the White-Hilted Knife. Its use is to form all instruments used in the Art. It can only be used in a Magic Circle.*

'*Next I take up the Wand. Its use is to call up and control certain angels and genii to whom it would not be meet to use the Magic Sword.*

'*Next I take up the Cup. This is the vessel of the Goddess, the Cauldron of Cerridwen, the Holy Grail of Immortality. From this, brothers and sisters of the Art drink in comradeship, and in honour of the Goddess.*[3]

'*Next I take up the Pentacle. This is for the purpose of calling up appropriate spirits.*

'*Next I take up the Censer of Incense. This is to encourage and welcome good spirits and to banish evil spirits.*

'*Next I take up the Scourge. This is the sign of power and domination. It is also used to cause purification and enlightenment. For it is written, "To learn you must suffer and be purified.".*

'*Next and lastly I take up the Cords. They are of use to bind the sigils of the Art, and also the material basis.*'

She then takes up the necklace and puts it round her neck, saying:

'*With the Necklace, which is the Circle of Rebirth, I seal my commitment to the Craft of the Wise.*'

Finally, she goes to each of the cardinal points in turn and, with her arms raised, says:

'*Hear ye, Mighty Ones of the East [South, West, North]; I, ———, have been duly consecrated priestess, witch, and hidden child of the Goddess.*'

XXIV   The Witches' Tools

We have said enough already in Section IX on the charging of such things as talismans, in Section XIV on the ritual use of symbols, and in Section XIX on the life-frequencies of 'inanimate' objects, for it to be needless here to go into great detail about why witches use magical tools. We will just sum it up by saying that a ritual tool is a psychological aid to concentration and to synchronizing the psychic effort of a group working together; its symbolism is archetypal in nature and therefore activates the Unconscious in partnership with the purposeful Ego; and through consecration and constant use, it acquires a helpful psychic charge of its own.

Most tools belong either to an individual witch or to the coven. The sole exception is the athame or black-handled knife, which is always a personal tool belonging to one witch only. So we will start with that.

The Athame

Any knife which suits the owner can be chosen as his or her athame. Ours are both plain sheath-knives bought in shops; Janet's had a black hilt already, and Stewart's was brown but he enamelled it black. Obviously one should avoid knives which have evil associations, such as the Nazi daggers which are often to be found in antique shops, or ones with an unpleasant history (which a good psychometrist will be able to diagnose).

An athame is normally of steel, but we have seen beautiful bronze ones made by our craftsman friend Peter Clark (of Tintine, The Rower, Co. Kilkenny), and one of our witches uses a copper one which he made himself, with the symbols attractively etched on the blade instead of on the hilt as is usual. (See Plate 19 for both of these.)

Traditionally the hilt is black, but some witches feel the magical symbolism of horn or a deer's foot, in its natural colour, is an acceptable alternative. Back to Rule One – 'what feels right to you'. But if the hilt *can* be blackened without spoiling some other natural characteristic, do not leave it through laziness. Your athame is your personal symbol of witchhood and deserves careful choice and treatment.

An athame is a purely ritual tool and should never be used for actual cutting. It is our practice, therefore, to blunt the blade and its tip, to avoid mishaps with ritual gestures in crowded Circles, especially skyclad ones. (There is a puzzling sentence in the Book of Shadows – see p. 61 above – which suggests that the marks on some tools should be cut with the athame; yet no marks are given. The athame might also share with the sword the traditional privilege of cutting a handfasting cake.)

The athame is interchangeable with the sword for all ritual purposes, such as casting or banishing Circles. It is essentially a masculine symbol, as is seen in the Consecration of the Wine (p.35); so in the hands of a woman witch it may be said to represent her active Animus. In our usage, it and the sword both represent the element of Fire (the wand representing Air). Some traditions attribute sword and athame to Air, and the wand to Fire; but as we explained in *Eight Sabbats for Witches* (p.161), this attribution 'was a deliberate "blind" perpetrated by the early Golden Dawn, which has unfortunately not yet died a natural death; it seems to us contrary to the obvious nature of the tools concerned'. Our authority for this statement about the Golden Dawn blind was *Techniques of High Magic* by Francis King and Stephen Skinner, p. 60. Now King and Skinner are conscientious occult historians, probably the best in print today, so they must have been convinced by their evidence and their sources. Yet a puzzle remains. As Doreen Valiente points out, the earliest Golden Dawn documents which have been published, those owned by R.G. Torrens, dated 1899, give the sword/Air, wand/Fire attributions, and in 1899 'these documents were given out to initiates under the seal of the utmost secrecy. The

very existence of the Order was not permitted to be publicly known.' So
if there was a 'blind', at whom was it directed? Doreen also points out
that the booklet *Yeats, the Tarot and the Golden Dawn* by Kathleen
Raine contains photographs of W.B. Yeats' ritual tools which he made
himself and which follow the same attributions; and Yeats joined the
Order in March 1890.

Doreen herself prefers wand/Fire, sword/Air. However, there is one
thing on which Doreen, King and Skinner and we ourselves are all
agreed: you should stick to the attributions which feel right to *you*.

The markings on the athame hilt vary a good deal, even in
Gardnerian usage. The earliest known design is to be found in *The Key
of Solomon* (see Bibliography under Mathers), of which in turn the
oldest known manuscript is sixteenth century. This does not mention
the word 'athame' but merely calls it 'the Knife with the Black Hilt'
which is 'for making the Circle'. The hilt markings are given as follows:

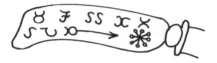

Figure 8

The end-papers of Gardner's *High Magic's Aid* show a drawing of
the athame (named as such) with hilt markings as follows:

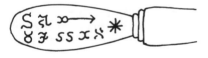

Figure 9

As Doreen Valiente observes, these 'certainly derive from *The Key of
Solomon* (indeed, *The Key of Solomon* is mentioned in the book). This
has led to the conventional explanation that Gerald merely copied them
from *The Key of Solomon*, most probably from its modern edition
translated and edited by S.L. MacGregor Mathers. I find this
explanation inadequate. Because from where did *The Key of Solomon*
derive them?'

In Text B of Gardner's Book of Shadows, the symbols are divided
into two sequences, one on each side of the hilt, as follows:

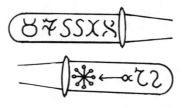

Figure 10

Gardner annotates these symbols with the following interpretations (top diagram, left to right): 'Horned God; Initial of his name; Kiss and Scourge; Waxing and Waning Moon; Initial of many of her names in Hebrew script'; (bottom diagram, left to right) 'Eight Ritual Occasions, Eight Weapons, etc.; the Power flowing from the Horned God; the Sickle, symbol of Death; the Serpent, symbol of Life and Rebirth.'

(On the two 'initials': that given for the God is like the letter F in the magicians' Theban Alphabet, though it might also be a corruption of the H or the C; and that given for the Goddess is the Hebrew Aleph or A.)

Doreen Valiente finds some of these accepted explanations, too, inadequate. She writes to us that, by comparing the various magical weapons in *The Key of Solomon* and their markings, she has arrived at the following conclusions, which she stresses are simply her personal suggestions.

'The markings show some variation from one weapon to another, the most notable of which is the appearance quite unmistakably of the Ankh Cross as the second sigil after the symbol of the Horned God (which is also the astrological sigil of Taurus). Also, there appears the astrological sigil of Scorpio instead of the supposed "first letter" of the Goddess's name in Hebrew.

'Now, Taurus and Scorpio are opposites in the Zodiac. When the Sun is in Taurus, May Eve occurs, the commencement of the summer half of the year; and when the Sun is in Scorpio, Hallowe'en occurs, the commencement of the winter half of the year, according to our Celtic ancestors. I would therefore like to suggest this version of the signs on the athame as being possibly the original and correct one:

'*First Side*: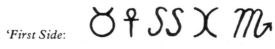

Figure 11(a)

'*Second Side*: ꓩ ꓶ ꭜ⟶ ❋

Figure 11(b)

'Their meanings, briefly, are as follows:

☿ 'The Horned God. Also the powers of fertility, May Eve, the "light" half of the year.

♀ 'The Ankh Cross, a very ancient symbol of life.

♒♒ 'The Salute and the Scourge – probably shown in this plain form (i.e., not as ♒♩ as we sometimes depict it) so as not to be too revealing of a magical secret.

☾ 'The Goddess as the waxing and waning Moon.

♏ 'Scorpio, sign of Death and the Beyond, the "other side" of the God as Lord of the Underworld. Hallowe'en and the "dark" half of the year.

ꓩ ꓶ 'The perfect couple.

ꭜ⟶ 'Power going forth, either from the Horned God or from the "conjunction of the Sun and Moon", i.e., male and female.

❋ 'The Eight Ritual Occasions, Eight Ways of Making Magic, etc.

'I suggest that this interpretation contains more meaning than the one generally given. Moreover, *the meaning is specifically significant to witches*, although it derives from *The Key of Solomon* in MacGregor Mathers' version. Mathers tells us in his preface that he worked from seven manuscripts in the British Museum, the oldest of which dated from "about the end of the sixteenth century". Unfortunately, he does not say if the illustrations of the sigils come from this MS or a later one. So the question of the age and ultimate derivation of these sigils remains; but I hope these notes may shed some light on it.'

We feel that they do, and we are glad to pass them on to our readers.

We would add one little footnote of our own, which may be an Alexandrian innovation, but we find it a pleasant custom. We were taught that after one's third degree initiation with one's working partner, the 'perfect couple' sigil (or, as it was described to us, the 'kneeling man and woman') should be joined together on one's athame hilt, thus:

Figure 12

First and
Second Degree   *Third Degree*

Two final notes on the athame as a personal tool. It is considered good manners *not* to handle another witch's athame without the owner's permission, unless it is your working partner's. And since a normal-sized athame is, to all appearances, a weapon, it may not always be convenient or discreet to carry it about with you – indeed, there may be times and places when it would bring you under reasonable suspicion. So a miniature second athame, which is unlikely to be regarded as more than a gadget, is a useful spare; in fact, we can see no magical objection to a black-handled folding penknife – so long as it has been duly consecrated and you resist the temptation to use it for anything else.

The Sword

As we have said, the sword is ritually exchangeable with the athame. We attribute it therefore to the element of Fire; and it, too, is essentially masculine. Hence the tradition which we mentioned on p.78 – that when a woman witch buckles on a sword, she is ritually assuming a male role and must be regarded and treated as masculine until she takes it off again.

The difference between the two weapons is that the sword is more formally authoritative than the athame. We normally, for example, use the sword to cast a coven Circle, to underline the group significance of the act – whereas a private Circle would be cast with one's own athame. When Joan of Arc took the sword, it was on behalf of France, not just for her personal defence. The sword's presence adds weight to a solemn occasion; when the High Priestess or High Priest has a particularly momentous announcement to make to the coven, she or he might well deliver it in front of the altar with the sword's point on the ground and both hands resting on the hilt. 'With this in thy hand,' says the Book of Shadows, 'thou art the ruler of the Circle.'

Like the athame, the sword is never used for actual cutting – with the happy exception of a handfasting cake.

The design of the sword is entirely a matter of choice; but a reasonably small and light one is more manageable in the Circle. We possess two – one a fairly heavy Toledo weapon with a bowl guard, and the other a gentleman's dress sword, slim and light. Each has its suitable occasions, but it is the light one which we use for normal coven purposes.

The Key of Solomon gives markings for the blade and hilt which are entirely Hebrew lettering. *High Magic's Aid* repeats these and adds two pentagrams. But Hebrew lettering is ceremonial magic rather than witchcraft, and most coven swords are unmarked.

The Wand

The Wand in our tradition represents the element of Air. Its gender is not particularly stressed, though if anything we would regard it as masculine, both because its shape is phallic (in some wands, specifically so – see below) and because Air is the element of the left-brain, linear-logical faculty.

It is a 'quieter' tool than the sword or athame. As the Book of Shadows says: 'Its use is to call up and control certain angels and genii to whom it would not be meet to use the Magic Sword.' It communicates by invitation, not by command. When it and the scourge are held in the Osiris Position (see *Eight Sabbats for Witches*, Plate 10), the scourge represents Severity and the wand Mercy.

The Key of Solomon says that the wand should be 'of hazel or nut tree, in all cases the wood being virgin, that is of one year's growth only', and should 'be cut from the tree at a single stroke, on the day of Mercury, at sunrise' – the day of Mercury being Wednesday. This is the universal magical tradition, and witches follow it too. (One tradition insists that the 'single stroke' should be made with a golden sickle, but we hardly think that is obligatory!)

The Key of Solomon gives markings for the wand which appear to be in one of the many magical alphabets (a selection of which will be found opposite p.64 of Barrett's *The Magus*, Book II). *High Magic's Aid* offers none. Markings, if any, would again seem to be a matter of personal choice. We have given our own wand a male/solar and a female/lunar end, so that it may be held either way round according to the emphasis required, and marked the shaft with the planetary symbols, thus:

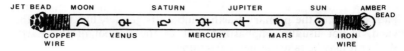

Figure 13

For certain rituals (such as the 'Brid is welcome' ceremony at Imbolg – *Eight Sabbats for Witches*, Section IV) a phallic wand is used. Ours is the usual nutwood shaft tipped with a pine-cone and bound with black and white ribbons interweaving like the snakes of a caduceus (*ibid.*, Plate 6).

The traditional length of a wand is from elbow to fingertip of the owner. For a coven wand, eighteen inches is a handy average.

The Cup or Chalice

The cup represents the element of Water and is the feminine symbol *par excellence*. Its chief use in the Circle is to hold the wine, in which it is consecrated and passed round. It is also used to represent the woman in the symbolic Great Rite (*Eight Sabbats for Witches*, Section II).

Many people have been puzzled by the fact that the cup is not mentioned or presented along with the other magical tools in the first-and second-degree initiation rites. Gerald Gardner was puzzled, too, and explains in *Witchcraft Today* (p.126): 'The answer I get is: In the burning time this was done deliberately. Any mention of the Cup led to an orgy of torture, their persecutors saying that it was a parody of the Mass; also the riding or dancing pole ("broomstick") was cut out. Censer and pentacle were substituted and explanations made to fit what their persecutors expected.'

The witches' ritual use of the wine-cup is of course not a parody of the Mass. The religious blessing and sharing of food and drink is far older than Christianity, and in any case Wicca is a positive religion in its own right and has no need to parody or invert anyone else's.

In these days when the witches' use of the cup is no longer secret (and if persecution were to come, that point would be a drop in the ocean) there would seem to be no reason why the cup, which is just as important as the other tools, should not be reintroduced into the initiatory presentations; so we have done this in Section I, II and XXIII.

The Pentacle

The pentacle is the primary Earth symbol. Its gender, like that of the wand, is not usually emphasized, but as the symbol of the Earth Mother it may be taken as being feminine.

It is the centrepiece of the altar, on which objects are consecrated; the water and salt bowls, too, are placed on it for blessing – indeed, some covens do not use a salt bowl but place the salt directly on the pentacle from which, after blessing, it is tipped into the water.

In persecution days the pentacle used to be inscribed on wax for each Circle, so that it could be destroyed afterwards as a dangerous piece of evidence. Today it is a disc of metal, usually copper, and it is normally five or six inches in diameter. Its markings are as follows:

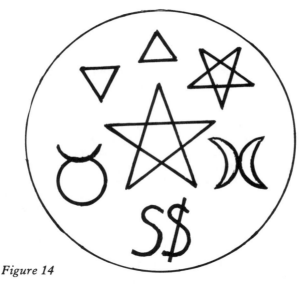

Figure 14

The central upright pentagram is the primary symbol of the Craft. Together with the upright triangle above it, it forms the symbol of third-degree initiation. The inverted pentagram, top right, is that of the second degree, and the inverted triangle, top left, that of the first degree. The Horned God symbol is bottom left, and bottom right are the waxing and waning Moon-crescents of the Goddess (also sometimes described as the breasts of the Goddess). The two SSs at the bottom represent the polarity of Mercy and Severity, in the form of the kiss (plain S) and the scourge (S with a stroke).

Being a centrepiece for the altar, the pentacle lends itself to special aesthetic treatment. We wanted a large pentacle, personal to ourselves, for particular occasions, so Stewart drew a design ringed by the signs of the Zodiac and with points for Zodiacal gems. Since we are both Cancerians, he put Cancer at the top, flanked by our initials. One of our witches is a process-engraver on a newspaper, and he took Stewart's design and photo-etched it onto an $11\frac{1}{2}$-inch heavy copper disc which we provided. We mounted the gems in their appropriate places, and we were very pleased with the result; see Plate 20.

For good measure (since in photo-etching a design can be projected to any size) our friend also made us a $5\frac{1}{2}$-inch version. And because other members wanted one, he then rotated the rim of Stewart's design to put Aries in its conventional position on top, whited out our initials and made $5\frac{1}{2}$-inch 'normal' Zodiacal pentacles for them.

Photo-engraving is a technique well worth investigating; it should not be beyond the powers of any handy witch who owns a photographic enlarger.

Since many witches may wish to embellish tools with their Zodiacal gems, this may be a good place to discuss the subject. For our jewelled pentacle, we consulted ten different lists, ranging from Aleister Crowley to the Jewellery Advisory Centre. The variety of recommendations was bewildering; we give the voting totals below. (Some add up to more than 10, because some lists gave alternatives.)

Aries Diamond 5, sard 2, ruby 1, bloodstone 1, sapphire 1.

Taurus Emerald 6, carnelian 2, topaz 1, chrysoprase 1, sapphire 1..

Gemini Pearl 3, agate 3, topaz 2, alexandrite 1, tourmaline 1, Iceland spar 1, chrysoprase 1.

Cancer Ruby 6, chalcedony 2, carnelian 2, amber 1, emerald 1.

Leo Sardonyx 4, peridot 3, jasper 2, cat's eye 1, onyx 1.

Virgo Sapphire 6, peridot 2, emerald 1, olivine 1, lapis lazuli 1, carnelian 1.

Libra Opal 6, tourmaline 2, emerald 1, beryl 1, jade 1, chrysolite 1, aquamarine 1.

Scorpio Topaz 5, citrine 2, snakestone 1, turquoise 1, amethyst 1, red tourmaline 1, aquamarine 1, cat's eye 1.

Sagittarius Turquoise 6, hyacinth 2, jacinth 1, zircon 1, topaz 1, malachite 1.

Capricorn Garnet 6, black diamond 1, chrysoprase 1, jet 1, ruby 1, jacinth 1.

Aquarius Amethyst 6, rock crystal 2, artificial glass 1, chalcedony 1, jacinth 1, garnet 1.

Pisces Bloodstone 6, aquamarine 3, pearl 1, sapphire 1, amethyst 1.

So we were back to Rule One, 'what feels right'. For example, we could not understand why no list gave moonstone for Cancer, which seemed to us the obvious correspondence. And, of course, we were influenced by particular stones which we had available and which meant something to us. These included an alexandrite which we brought home from Egypt, and a jet left over from the necklace which Stewart dismantled back in 1970 to make Janet's amber-and-jet necklace.

Our set for the pentacle, then, finished up as follows: *Aries*, bloodstone; *Taurus*, carnelian; *Gemini*, alexandrite; *Cancer*, moonstone; *Leo*, tiger's eye; *Virgo*, sapphire; *Libra*, opal; *Scorpio*, lapis lazuli; *Sagittarius*, topaz; *Capricorn*, jet; *Aquarius*, amethyst; and *Pisces*, pearl.

Special note on pentacles: all coven tools should of course be cleaned and, if metal, polished, regularly. But it is as well at least to *wash* the pentacle immediately after the Circle, because it has almost certainly caught drips of the salt-and-water mixture, which corrodes metal (and especially copper) very easily; one minute's washing tonight may save ten minutes' polishing tomorrow. The same post-Circle attention should naturally be given to the cup which has held wine, and to the salt and water bowls if they are of metal; and athame-points which have consecrated wine, water or salt should be wiped clean and dry.

The Censer

Incense belongs to the element of Air. It can be bought at any church suppliers'; plain frankincense is a good general-purpose incense; but since the aroma is intended to help create an atmosphere suited to the particular occasion or work in hand, most covens also like to have a selection of incenses. Occult suppliers are the best source for these, because their incenses are deliberately blended for such needs, and their very titles usually indicate their nature. For example, John Lovett's excellent shop and mail-order business Occultique (73 Kettering Road, Northampton NN1 4AW) lists about seventy varieties, including Zodiacal, elemental, seasonal, Sephirothic and Celtic tree-alphabet ranges.

Experimenting with making your own can be interesting. As an example, you might like to try our Fire of Azrael incense (see p. 96) which is very simple. You need

Sandalwood chips, $\frac{1}{2}$ oz
Juniper berries, $\frac{1}{2}$ oz
Cedarwood oil, $\frac{1}{2}$ oz

Chop and mash the juniper berries, add them to the sandalwood chips, and mix thoroughly. Add the cedarwood oil to this mixture, and again mix thoroughly. Keep in a small screw-top jar, firmly closed.

You can extend your experiments by adding single ingredients to plain frankincense – a few drops of some oil essence, perhaps, or some chopped dried herb. When you are familiar with the results, try mixing ingredients, such as an oil and a herb, with or without the frankincense. Remember that dried herbs alone will burn away much too quickly.

Incense is burned by putting it on a charcoal ring which is already burning. These 'rings' are actually discs with dished tops, of charcoal impregnated with saltpetre to make them easy to ignite. They, too, can be brought in boxes from church or occult suppliers. They should be kept in a dry place, because they absorb moisture like blotting-paper. If a ring will not light easily (you know when it is lit because a row of sparks moves across it steadily), dry it for a minute or two near a fire or other source of heat – but do not pick it up with your bare fingers, because, if it has been very near a fire, for instance, it may self-ignite and already be burning merrily though it still looks black.

The censer itself may be anything from a little metal bowl on legs to a splendid ecclesiastical object hanging from chains. But if it is small or chainless, be careful again when it comes to carrying it round; they can get unexpectedly hot.

One or two drops of (say) rose oil on the burning charcoal before the Circle starts, and before you put on the incense of the evening, can create a pleasing preliminary atmosphere.

Joss-sticks are a very simple and fairly cheap alternative to incense in a censer. Such shops as Indiacraft sell little brass joss-stick holders, or they can be stuck in an eggcup full of sand or soil, a blob of plasticene or even a cut apple or potato. But to get to know your brands of joss-stick before you try them in the Circle; some of them can be cloyingly sweet. Sandalwood is always a safe bet.

The White-Handled Knife

This is literally a working tool, for any actual cutting (for example, the Measure – see p. 18) or inscribing (as the second-degree candle – see p. 28) which has to be done in the Circle; and it may only be used inside the Circle.

Both *The Key of Solomon* and *High Magic's Aid* give markings for the hilt and blade; whether one copies them or not is again a matter of choice.

The white-handled knife, unlike the athame, should obviously be sharp, and kept so. Attractive and efficient ones can be found in kitchen hardware shops. On the other hand, the idea of a matching pair of athame and white-handled knife may appeal to you, and that would involve rather more searching.

The Scourge

The scourge has two uses: (1) purely symbolic and (2) for *gentle*, monotonous, semi-hypnotic application to affect the blood circulation as an aid to 'gaining the Sight'. Use (2) is described in detail, with all the precautions, in a passage in the Book of Shadows which we gave in full, with comments, on pp. 58-60. The Book also says (p. 61 above) that it should have eight tails with five knots in each tail, presumably for the numerological reasons given elsewhere (p. 52). We still have our original one, with a nutwood handle and cords of embroidery silk. But we are even fonder of one which we made when we were living in Co. Mayo; the 'cords' are of black horse-tail hair, collected during the grooming of one of our ponies, and the handle is a piece of bog deal – the perfectly preserved wood, thousands of years old, which is uncovered a few feet down when a peat-bog is cut for fuel.

Neither *The Key of Solomon* nor *High Magic's Aid* gives markings for the scourge.

The Cords

Every witch should have his or her own set of at least three different-coloured cords (red, blue and white seem to be the usual), and most covens have a communal set as well. Each cord should be nine feet long, with the ends either knotted or bound with thread to prevent fraying. The only exceptions to the nine-foot standard are the two four foot six inch cords for the initiation binding (see p.15).

The most practical cords are about as thick as a pencil; they are sold in most fabric shops for such purposes as upholstery trimming. Silk is ideal because it is a natural organic substance – but man-made fibres are easier to find, and since the cords are mainly used as aids to dramatization and concentration, the disadvantage is slight.

Colour symbolism is very complex and will vary according to the context of the work being done. But here is a summary of some of the main colour associations (the Tree of Life ones given being those of the Queen Scale):

White Purity; innocence; work for small children; Kether on the Tree of Life.

Black Restriction; limitation; binding; Saturn; Binah on the Tree.

Gold, Yellow Solar magic; the Sun God; Tiphareth on the Tree. In some systems, the Earth colour.

Silver Moon magic; the Moon Goddess; the Goddess in her winter, Life-in-Death aspect.

Red Life; Fire; vigour; organic healing; Mars; Geburah on the Tree; the male, electric principle.

Orange Intellect; communication; travel; Mercury; Hod on the Tree.

Green Nature; the Goddess in her summer, Death-in-Life aspect; Water; emotion, instinct, intuition; Venus/Aphrodite; Netzach on the Tree.

Blue The Sky Goddess; Air; functional healing; Jupiter; justice; organization, administration; Chesed on the Tree; the female, magnetic principle.

Violet The Akashic Principle; the astral plane; Yesod on the Tree. In some systems, the Spirit colour.

Brown Preferred by some to yellow as the Earth colour.

The Broomstick

This is the only witch's tool, except perhaps for the cauldron, which is identified with the popular image of the witch; so quite apart from its ritual uses, many witches regard it affectionately as a symbol of the Craft and keep one even if it is never used.

It was originally a riding- and dancing-pole, disguised as an ordinary household besom for security reasons. Stories about witches riding through the air on broomsticks doubtless arose from their use in crop fertility rites. Women would ride them around the fields, leaping as high as they could. This was sympathetic magic in two ways. The higher the leap, the higher the crop would grow. And the fertility theme would be dramatized, in those less prudish days, by the way in which the women used their phallic poles during their 'riding'.

After which it is hardly necessary to add that the broomstick is a masculine symbol.

Its chief ritual uses today are for jumping over (as in the handfasting rite – *Eight Sabbats for Witches*, p. 165) and for symbolically sweeping the Circle clean of all evil influence (same page, and also the Imbolg ritual on p. 70).

The Cauldron

This would originally have been identified with the witch because of her mysterious brewing of potions and herbal remedies, though for untold centuries it was simply the family cooking-pot, as it remained in Ireland (where it is called a skillet) until fairly recently. (We have seen the traditional skilletful of potatoes simmering away over an Irish farmworker's fire, a few feet away from his colour television.) Its association with witches in the popular mind probably arose from pictures of witches at work, which would be about the only situation which would prompt an artist to dramatize the use of a rural cooking-pot, and of course from the witch scenes in Shakespeare's *Macbeth*.

Like the cup, of which it is a larger version, the cauldron is a feminine symbol – 'the cauldron of Cerridwen, which is the Holy Grail of immortality'. Even when it is associated with a God (as for example the Cauldron of the Dagda, one of the Four Treasures of the Tuatha Dé Danann in Irish mythology), it always remains a symbol of renewal, rebirth and inexhaustible plenty.

Its ritual use in Wicca also relates to these concepts. It is more adaptable than the cup, since it may contain water, fire, incense or flowers as occasion demands. Leaping over the cauldron, like leaping over the broomstick or the bonfire, is a fertility rite.

Cauldrons or skillets, usually of cast iron, may be found in antique or junk shops with a little searching; and the old three-legged household cooking-pot is the most satisfactory. But a similarly shaped brass or copper coal-scuttle is a suitable alternative, and probably more easily acquired.

The Necklace

It is customary for women witches always to wear necklaces of some kind in the Circle. In our coven the men, too, wear talismans or pendants round their necks. These represent 'the circle of rebirth'.

The traditional priestess's necklace in the Craft is made of alternate beads of amber and jet. These symbolize the solar/lunar, light/dark, male/female polarity in perfect balance. They have to be made up, of course, by buying an amber necklace and a jet one, dismantling them and carefully grading and threading a new necklace from the alternate beads. You may well find that you have enough beads for two necklaces – unless the beads of the two originals vary considerably in size, in which case you may need the largest from one and the smallest from the other to make a satisfactory finished necklace.

Both antique and modern amber necklaces can be bought, but jet necklaces, which were very popular in Victorian times, are usually more easily found in antique jewellers' shops.

A woman witch's amber-and-jet necklace is a very appropriate present from her working partner. He should of course assemble it for her himself. (A tip here: a sheet of paper, pleated concertinawise and laid on the table, makes the grading of beads in order of size very much easier.)

Apart from the amber-and-jet, the necklace or pendant can be anything that is felt to be suitable; for a woman, any favourite necklace, particularly if it is of a colour fitting to the work in hand, or perhaps a Moon-pendant or other Goddess symbol; for a man, a solar or Horned God symbol; and for man or woman, a pentagram, ankh, Eye of Horus, birth-sign pendant, yin-yang symbol and so on. As always – 'what feels right'.

The Garter

The magical significance of the garter seems to go back to Palaeolithic times; one cave-painting shows a male figure in the centre of a ritual dance wearing a garter on each leg. Margaret Murray (*The God of the Witches*, pp. 52-3) says: 'The garter has long been credited with magical properties, especially when belonging to a woman. The bride's garters were fought for at a wedding, and the Mettye Belt was always a man-witch's belt or a woman-witch's garter. The Mettye Belt was the recognised magical means of ascertaining whether a sick person would recover or not' – and Murray cites other magical uses. She also makes out a very convincing case for the Order of the Garter having witchcraft origins (*ibid*. pp. 53-4). She suggests that the garter which the Countess of Salisbury dropped was no ordinary garter (which would not have embarrassed a fourteenth-century lady in the least) but her badge of rank as a High Priestess; and that in putting it on his own leg, Edward III was putting her under his protection. It is significant that the Order he immediately founded consisted of twenty-six knights – i.e., a double coven, one for the Sovereign and one for the Prince of Wales.

The garter, then, is both a magical object and a badge of rank – and both usages are to be found in the modern Craft. In some covens, all the women members wear one; in others, only the High Priestess. Erica Jong (*Witches*, p. 98) says: 'Some writers on witchcraft specify that the garter be green leather, buckled in silver, and lined with blue silk.' We have also met the tradition that it should be of snakeskin. The oldest ritual garter which either of us has seen (which was very old indeed, in the possession of a hereditary family) was of blue velvet, with an intricate silver buckle based on a horseshoe design.

When a High Priestess has had another coven hive off from her original one, she is entitled to add a second buckle to her garter – and an additional buckle for each new hiving-off coven. When her garter has at least three buckles, she is a Witch Queen.

A final note on magical tools. Make them yourself if you possibly can. It should not be necessary, at this stage of our book, to explain why.

Of course, personal craftsmanship can and should extend beyond the tools themselves. Embroidered altarcloths, ritual jewellery, ritual robes, candlesticks, altarpiece paintings, elemental paintings for the Watchtower quarters, and so on, all offer plenty of scope for individual skills. We are not suggesting that your Temple ought to look like an overcrowded museum; how much, or how little, embellishment you are happy with depends on Rule One. But the more that is made by the hands of the witches who work and worship there, the more you will find that the requirements of Rule One are satisfied.

XXV   In Tune with the Land

Wicca is a natural religion, in every sense. Witches know that, as men and women, they are part of the central nervous system of Gaia, the Earth-organism, and that this involvement extends to all the levels. They know that the more they can put themselves in tune with the environment in which they live and work – physically, etherically, astrally, mentally and spiritually – the more meaningful will their religion become, the more effective will their psychic working be, the greater will their contribution to Gaia's health and well-being be, and the more fulfilled and integrated will they be themselves, as human beings.

Many of the things which this implies we have already pointed out: putting yourself in tune with Nature as locally manifested, even if you live in the middle of a city; celebrating the eight Festivals for a living awareness of the annual rhythms; taking an active and informed interest in environmental issues; respecting and understanding the true nature and needs of other species, and of the plant kingdom, and constantly enriching your relationship to them; and so on.

But legend, mythology and cultural tradition are also a vital part of the spirit of the land. They are the roots along which flow the sap of our relationship to the particular part of Gaia in which we happen to live. So wise witches draw heavily on these local roots – in their ritual forms, in the Goddess- and God-names they use, in their astral experiments and even in the places they make a point of familiarizing themselves with.

This is one of the advantages of the flexibility of Wicca. No Wiccan ritual form is Holy Writ. Here we can learn from the mistakes of Christian missionaries, who have taken a symbolic system born in the Middle East and ossified over centuries of European feudalism and capitalism, and imposed it chapter and verse on alien environments which have their own rich roots. (To be fair, some missionaries are wiser than this, but not many – and certainly very few in past centuries.)

Wicca has, or should have, no such inhibitions. It should be attuned, and adapted, to the spirit of its actual environment.

To take one concrete example: Australia. We are in touch with several Australian witches, both directly and through Catherine and Kent Forrest's lively magazine *The Australian Wiccan* (PO Box 80, Lane Cove, NSW 2066). Most of them are of European background, and many of them practise a Gardnerian system or one akin to it. It is interesting to see how they cope with the fact that the Sun in their land travels anti-clockwise and that Midsummer is in December. They seem to use a variety of methods, both in the direction of casting the Circle and in the placing of the elements, and also in their arrangement of the Sabbats.

In the Northern Hemisphere, where both the Western occult tradition and Wicca as we know it took shape, the pattern of a witches' Circle is as shown in Figure 15(a). It would seem to us that in the Southern Hemisphere the pattern should be as in Figure 15(b) – so that in both cases the Sun rises in the Air element, reaches its zenith in the Fire element, sinks in the Water element and at night hides behind the Earth element, where the altar stands; and the Circle is cast in the same direction as the Sun moves. Similarly, in the Southern Hemisphere the eight Festival Sabbats should each be moved six months away from the European and US pattern. The Lesser Sabbats of solstices and equinoxes look after themselves in that they would be appropriately named locally in any case – the rebirth of the Sun would be greeted around 21 or 22 June, and so on. But the Greater Sabbats of Imbolg, Bealtaine, Lughnasadh and Samhain could perhaps be more flexibly moved; a strict six-month shift, for example, would bring Imbolg to 2 August, but perhaps the 'first stirrings in the womb of Mother Earth' should be more realistically celebrated earlier or later, in tune with the reality of Gaia's local activity. Again, there may be local folk festivals to which the witches' Sabbats may fittingly be equated; just as when we lived in Co. Mayo we celebrated our Midsummer Sabbat on 23 June because that – St John's Eve – was the night when other Midsummer fires could be seen from horizon to horizon, with all their frankly pagan overtones, and why should the witches be the odd ones out just because the Book of Shadows says 22 June?

Figure 15(a)   *Figure (15b)*

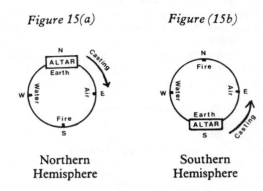

Northern   Southern
Hemisphere   Hemisphere

Australians who are genuinely in touch with Aborigine lore, which has been attuned to Gaia Australis since time immemorial, doubtless integrate elements from that lore into their own ritual forms and into their awareness of the environment.

From twelve thousand miles away, these comments may sound presumptuous; but we are not trying to teach our Australian brothers and sisters to suck eggs – just pointing out, to provoke thought among European witches, the *kind* of approach that witches have to take this problem of fitting their practice and their thinking to their actual surroundings. It may well be that Australian witches will come up with different answers from the ones we have suggested, because of local factors which we know nothing about. That is their business – as long as these answers are based not on some Holy Writ imported from a different environment but on their true relationship to Gaia, as she is where they are.

The Northern origin of most of the existing literature creates a problem, as our friend Robyn Moon of Modbury in South Australia points out. She tells us that the Australian covens she knows of place Earth and the altar in the South, and Fire in the North, and cast the

Circle widdershins. But she finds that 'it feels wrong to us to work anti-clockwise when for so long all our books and references have stressed deosil. What to do?' Refuse to be intimidated by the laws of another hemisphere, of course!

As an example of the kind of attempt Australian witches are making to devise a ritual pattern which stems naturally from their own environment, Robyn sent us this cycle-of-the-year diagram which appeared in the now-defunct occult magazine *Whazoo Weakly* and which she understands was drawn up by Nick Howard of Adelaide. In the accompanying text, he maintained that in the temperate zone of Australia there are not four seasons but either three (as in Egypt) or six, according to the locality; three in the areas approaching the desert, and six in the coastal areas. He cited both desert (Pitjanjara) and coastal (Western Australian) Aborigine seasonal concepts in support of this.

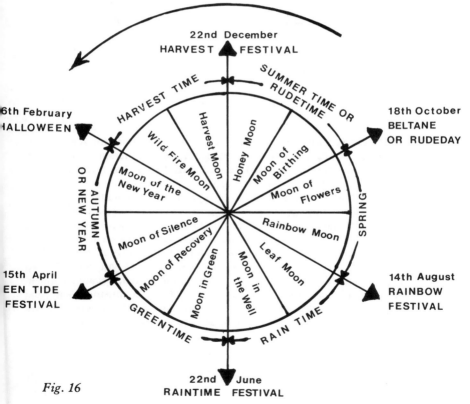

Fig. 16

We leave it to our Australian friends to judge the validity of his calendar. But his *attitude* is certainly right: Mother Earth as she is where we are, and never mind what the existing literature says.

(Talking of existing literature: Nevill Drury and Gregory Tillett's handsomely produced book *Other Temples Other Gods* is a fascinating review of the occult scene in Australia.)

Even the placing of the elements on the simple Solar pattern we have described may differ in some countries. For example, if we lived in Egypt, we might well adopt the ancient Egyptian placings, because they are firmly rooted in the 'feel' of the Nile valley – and even have their own Lords of the Watchtowers, the Four Sons of Horus. The placings are as follows. East, where the blazing Sun of Egypt rises – Fire, under the patronage of Duamutef. South, from whence the life-giving Nile flows – Water, presided over by Imset. West, under the vast skies of the desert – Air, presided over by Qebehsenuf. North, towards which the southern waters bring their blessing – Earth, presided over by Hapy. Anyone who has been to Egypt knows that these are as they should be. (Egypt's three seasons were: Inundation 19 July to 15 November, Winter 16 November to 15 March, and Summer 16 March to 18 July.)

Witches in the United States have their own special problems, similar to but perhaps more complex than those in Australia. Apart from the American Indians (whose pagan roots are as deeply indigenous as those of the Australian Aborigines), they come from a wide spectrum of foreign ancestral backgrounds – Saxon, Celtic, Nordic, Jewish, Slav, African and so on – and many of them live in communities where those traditions are still very much alive, even if they have been subtly altered by importation into the New World and by interaction with each other. So American witches may be torn between basing themselves wholeheartedly on (say) the Celtic ritual and mythological inheritance of their mothers' milk, and rejecting it equally wholesale because the soil on which they stand is not that in which those roots grew. We know some personally who are fortunate enough to have a real contact and understanding with American Indian neighbours in a natural environment, and are enriching their own practice thereby. But for others the problem is a very real one; Margot Adler's *Drawing Down the Moon* gives pointers to how some of them are tackling it. European witches, often perhaps only half-aware of their own good fortune in having little conflict between tradition and environment, are often unfairly critical of American witches for being too experimental. We should be sympathetic rather, because it is a problem which only they can solve, on their own ground – and maybe they can teach us not to take our own ground so easily for granted.

The British Craft – certainly in its Gardnerian stream – is strongly Celtic-orientated; so when we came to Ireland we had a flying start, apart from being predominantly Celtic ourselves. But we, too, have made our adaptations, because the land simply invites them. For example, we usually replace the 'Great God Cernunnos' invocation (see Appendix B, p. 298.) with this, which we composed ourselves:

> *Great God of Erin, Lugh of many arts,*
> *Enter our Circle and inspire our hearts!*
> *Open our eyes – uncover to our sight*
> *The Tuatha's Treasures: Sword and Spear and Light,*
> *The Dagda's Cauldron, and the Stone of Fál.*
> *Great Mother's consort, Father of us all,*
> *Hear this my invocation, grant our wish –*
> *A Lugh Lámhfhada, bí anseo anois!'*

Lugh is the brightest of the Irish Gods; he is sometimes referred to as a Sun God, but this cannot be right – *grian* (Sun) is a feminine noun in both Irish and Scottish Gaelic, just as *Sonne* is in German; to Celts and Teutons the Sun was a Goddess, whereas to Egyptians, Greeks and Romans he was a God. Lugh should rather be called a God of light and fire, a pre-Christian St Michael. Two of his titles were *Samhioldánach* ('equally skilled in all the arts') and *Lámhfhada* ('of the long arm or hand'). The last line in our invocation means 'O Lugh Long-Hand, be here now!' (Our own Co. Louth is named after Lugh.)

The Tuatha Dé Danann (Peoples of the Goddess Dana) in Irish legend, and probably with some factual basis, were the last inhabitants of Ireland before the Celts (the Gaels or Sons of Mil) came here. They were regarded as a magical people, and Lugh was one of their leaders. After the Sons of Mil defeated them in battle, the Tuatha retired by agreement into the hollow hills or *sidh*-mounds of Ireland, where they became the aristocracy of the *sidhe* or fairy folk. As such, in the tolerant atmosphere of Celtic Christianity, they became the acceptable form of the old pagan Gods and Goddesses – and so they have remained. In the tales and beliefs of ordinary country folk (and certainly of witches) the Tuatha Dé Danann are still very much alive and well and living in Ireland.

Their Four Treasures, which are clearly elemental ones,[1] play an important part in Irish mythology. One of them, the *Lia Fáil* or Stone of Destiny, which cried aloud when the true High King of Ireland mounted it (the Earth acknowledging him?), may probably still be seen: many archaeologists maintain that the upright stone on Tara Hill in Co. Meath (see Plate 9) is the true *Lia Fáil*, though a rival claimant is the Coronation Stone in Westminster Abbey.

Like many covens, we save a little of the consecrated wine and cakes of each Circle as an offering – but in accordance with Irish tradition, we place it on a Westward-facing windowsill for the *sidhe*. We accompany this gift with the invocation: '*A Shidhe; a Thuatha Dé Danann: beannacht Bhandé Danann libh agus linn*' ('O Sidhe; O Tuatha Dé Danann; the blessing of the Goddess Dana on you and on us').

The list of Goddess-names at the beginning of the Charge (see Appendix B, p.297) already includes two Irish ones, Dana and Bride (Brid or Brigid); but we like to add a local one. When we lived in Co. Wexford we added Carman, the Wexford Goddess. Now that we live in Co. Louth at the mouth of the River Boyne, we add Boann, the Goddess of that river, whose local mythology is particularly rich.

In the Charge itself, we sometimes change 'the Land of Youth' (also p. 297), to 'Tír na nÓg', which means literally the same thing but has much more significance in Irish legend; and we make the same change in the Autumn Equinox declamation.

Every land has its magical places, its ancient and continuing focal concentrations of power. English witches, and many non-witches also, rightly recognize Glastonbury as such. Stonehenge and Avebury are power foci too (for ourselves, we are more drawn to Avebury, finding it more alive and less psychically overlaid than Stonehenge). Local witches all over the British Isles could add to the list.

Ireland is especially rich in such places; for us Newgrange, ten miles up the Boyne from our home, is the Glastonbury of Ireland. Lovingly and accurately restored by the brilliant archaeological team of Professor M.J. O'Kelly since 1962, it now once again receives the winter solstice sunrise along its seventy-nine-foot passage as it did five thousand years ago, to its central chamber under the oldest roof in Ireland. The great mound of Newgrange, *Brugh na Bóinne* or 'the palace of the Boyne', with its nearby sister mounds of Dowth and Knowth (the latter at present under excavation), was the spiritual and cultural centre of a remarkable neolithic community long before Stonehenge was begun, and it is linked in folk-memory with the great names of the Tuatha Dé Danann. It is officially known as 'passage grave', but its significance was obviously much greater than that – just as a cathedral means much more than the tombs it happens to contain. The power of the place has to be felt to be appreciated.

To be in tune with the land, witches should pay special attention to such places as Glastonbury and Newgrange or their equivalents in their own countries, both in the sense of acquiring archaeological and other academic knowledge about them, and in the sense of using their psychic awareness on them. The power of these places is there to be experienced and tapped.

We keep a personal dossier on Newgrange and add to it regularly. It includes academic information, photographs, recorded dreams, a note of every visit, and the shared experiences of ourselves and of visiting witches from other lands. We find the exercise very rewarding, and we recommend it to other witches for trying with their own places.

Every witch must relate to his or her own environment on all the levels. How he or she does it is a personal and local matter; the first step is to realize that it is important to try – and we hope this Section has given food for thought.

XXVI In Tune with the Times

For many centuries, Wicca has been a personal or small-group religion; and until our lifetime, it has survived those centuries by secrecy. The degree of secrecy has varied a little with time and place. During the terrors of the 'burning time', the persecution which reached its peak in the sixteenth and seventeenth centuries, it had to be absolute. In the slightly less fanatical nineteenth century, a *bean fheasa* (wise-woman) like Biddy Early of Co. Clare, or a cunning-man like 'Old George' Pickingill of Canewdon, Essex, could practise their Craft more or less openly in the turbulent waters between clerical harassment and popular support. But even Biddy and Old George, one feels, would have been in far more serious trouble if they had openly led ritual covens. Individual psychic ability (which could not be denied in those and similar cases) was one thing – a thorn in the Establishment flesh which could be lived with. The Old Religion practised unashamedly in organized congregations would have been quite another. (Biddy Early seems to have been purely a solo worker; George Pickingill – see Doreen Valiente's *Witchcraft for Tomorrow*, pp. 15-20 – is said by Craft sources to have had nine covens, though they were certainly secret at the time.)

It would be unrealistic to deny that the position has changed radically in the past thirty years.

In 1951 Britain's archaic and unworkable Witchcraft Laws were repealed and replaced by the carefully worded Fraudulent Mediums Act, of which any serious witch or occultist can only approve. In 1949 Gerald Gardner had published his guardedly informative novel *High Magic's Aid*; in 1954 and 1959 respectively he published his frank non-fiction books *Witchcraft Today* and *The Meaning of Witchcraft*. Since then, in Britain alone, Doreen Valiente, Patricia and Arnold Crowther, Justine Glass, Lois Bourne and other practising witches, including ourselves, have published books on the Craft. (See Bibliography under all these names.) Witches appear regularly on television and radio, almost entirely replacing the non-witch 'experts' who used to pontificate on the subject. Newspapers and magazines interview them and, apart from the incorrigible sensationalist Press, treat these interviews with increasing seriousness. The current issue (November 1982) of the magazine *19*, for example, contains a four-page article on the witchcraft boom by Barbara Rowlands. In it she interviews English witches of not always identical views, including Seldiy Bate and her husband Nigel, Celia Gough, Alex Sanders, Zachary Cox and others. The article is well balanced, interesting and informative – and would have been unthinkable in a popular women's magazine as little as twenty years ago. We could cite a long list of other examples.

Even the *News of the World*, stuck fast in its rigid and highly profitable formula, has progressed to the stage of admitting in print that white witches and sensible occultists do exist, and that they condemn the sick fringe on whose unhealthy activities the *News of the World* thrives.

All this is not to say, of course, that misrepresentation, bigotry and victimization have entirely died. Examples continue to abound; Mike Howard's *The Cauldron*, the best Wiccan newsletter in these islands (Myrddin, c/o Groesffordd Llwyndrain, Llanfyrnach, Dyfed SA35 0AS) is particularly keen-eyed in pouncing on them. But a generation ago, these would have been the whole picture. That is no longer the case.

The Craft has come into the open (even if many individual witches and covens, for their own understandable reasons, have to stay quiet). The public image of the witch is at last changing and escaping from the stereotype which has lingered on since the persecution days. More and more ordinary people are becoming aware that modern witches exist, that they try to do good and that they too are 'ordinary' even if somewhat bizarre. They have read about them, seen them on television, heard them on radio – and may actually know them to say hullo to. They may even feel that it adds to the richness and variety of life to have one living round the corner.

It is a slow process, but it is happening; and witches who refuse to recognize this are themselves falling into a stereotyped attitude. It would be naïve to think it could not be reversed; engineered hysteria, or an authoritarian regime, in any one country could always turn the emerging witch back into a scapegoat; but in today's unstable world, any minority is vulnerable that way. And the more that witches can speed up the process of correcting the stereotyped image – a process which, we repeat, is already happening – the more difficult and unlikely will such a reversal become.

Just why is this process happening – the emergence of the Craft into the daylight, its increasing acceptance (whether friendly or grudging) as an existing part of the general scene, and above all its accelerating growth?

We believe that it is because a revival of the pagan outlook is an inevitable, and instinctively sought-after, aspect of this point in mankind's evolution. It coincides naturally with the impending end of the patriarchal epoch; with the growing public anxiety over environmental and ecological issues; with the growing abhorrence of nuclear brinkmanship; with the urgent necessity of a shift (enforced willy-nilly by economic and technological developments) from a work-ethic to a personal-fulfilment-ethic as the basis of everything from education to morality; with the increasing independence of the young; with the increasing impossibility (thanks to satellite television and the general communications breakthrough) of keeping any country, from Holy Ireland to Communist Russia, as a mentally and culturally watertight compartment; and a host of other related factors.

A century ago, men and women died in more or less the same kind of world as they had been born into. Today, brothers and sisters born ten years apart in the same family may have to make a real effort to understand each other's worlds. Such a rate of change is not conducive to the unthinking acceptance of established philosophies or conventions, or to the persistence of outworn stereotypes.

Both established religion and tunnel-vision materialism have failed to provide answers to the challenge. Any given religious symbolism may give personal fulfilment, just as determined materialism may make an individual rich; but religion as a bureaucratic structure, or materialism as the driving-force of political and economic planning, lags increasingly behind the real needs of the community.

Thousands know this, instinctively or consciously; and the thousands are rapidly becoming millions.

How any existing religion will react to this evolutionary

turning-point is the affair of its followers. We would dare a prediction; that within the foreseeable future, Christianity as a hierarchic and dogmatic machine will collapse, but that it will be reborn in a flexible and human form very much closer to the outlook of its founder. And the same sort of thing may well happen to other too-long-ossified religions.

That, as we have said, is their affair, to be observed sympathetically but without interference. But the role of the Craft, both present and future, *is* the witches' affair.

Wicca is not a proselytizing religion and is unlikely to become one. In any case, the seeking of converts implies that there is only one true Path and that all else is heresy – an idea which caused untold human suffering, particularly in the past two thousand years, and which should be abandoned once and for all.

But thousands *are* turning to paganism, in one form or another, as a viable philosophy with which to meet the spiritual, ecological and evolutionary crisis. They are looking for existing forms, and already-active comrades, so that they can not merely hold such a philosophy but live it.

The Craft is one such form; and in its flexibility, its sense of wonder, its earthiness, its adaptability to local roots and its emphasis on female-male polarity, it has a lot to offer to such seekers. It should therefore be rendered available to them, by making its image clear but undogmatic. It should not try to recruit them, but it should be there for those to whom it is suited; they will seek it out, but it must be ready to receive them.

There is another reason why the Craft is peculiarly in tune with the times; of all the pagan (as distinct from merely occult) paths, it lays perhaps the greatest emphasis on the development of psychic abilities. Mankind's understanding of the nature of the human psyche, particularly through Jung and his successors, has made great strides in this century; and science itself, at its most creative frontiers, is revolutionizing our ideas on the nature of cosmic reality. We would make another prediction (not an original one; for it is shared by many who are pondering on the Aquarian Age): that *homo sapiens* is on the threshold of an evolutionary leap in his psychic functioning, comparable with the leap that came about with the development of Ego-consciousness. This leap will be more compressed in time, and even more far-reaching in its consequences, than the earlier leap. The time always produces the thinkers necessary for its consummation; and it may be that Gardner, when he pushed the Craft into the daylight, was in his own way arriving as punctually on the evolutionary scene as Freud, Jung, Copernicus and Einstein did in theirs.

We are not suggesting a crusade; religious crusades tend to acquire a momentum of their own which distorts their nature and destroys their original intent. The nature of Wicca is that of small-group, autonomous flexibility and the developments of individual psyches by co-operation among friends. May it always remain so.

But Wicca and its covens exist in a real and changing world. What we are suggesting is that witches should persistently expand their consciousness of that changing world and their role in it – and remember always that the function of tradition is to provide nourishing roots, not to impose blinkers or shackles.

The Craft has come a long way; and it has still a long and exciting way to go.

Merry meet – merry part – and merry meet again.

Appendixes

Appendix A   *The Search for Old Dorothy*

by Doreen Valiente

I really ought to dedicate this essay to Professor Jeffrey B. Russell, whose book *A History of Witchcraft: Sorcerers, Heretics and Pagans* (Thames & Hudson, London, 1980) inspired me to undertake the search I write of. In Chapter 9 of that book, Professor Russell describes how the followers of Gerald Gardner 'tell the story that he was initiated into witchcraft in 1939 by Old Dorothy Clutterbuck, a witch of the New Forest'. He adds the remark, 'In fact there is no evidence that Old Dorothy ever existed,' the implication being that Gerald simply invented her, together with the rest of the alleged tradition of the Craft of the Wise.

Now, I was initiated as a witch by Gerald Gardner in 1953, and he often used to talk to me about Old Dorothy. By the way he spoke of her, she certainly sounded like a real person. I therefore found myself unable to agree with Professor Russell. But was there in fact any evidence of Old Dorothy's existence? And if so, how could I prove it?

I set out to see what I could discover and, being a witch, I started around Hallowe'en, 1980. I knew that, however private a person may be, there are two marks that he or she has to make upon public records, namely a birth certificate and a death certificate. If I could secure these documents relating to Old Dorothy, they would constitute proof that at least she was not a figment of anyone's imagination. So I called at the local Register Office and obtained the address of the Registrar for the New Forest Registration District, which proved to be at Lymington.

I sent off a hopeful letter asking if a death certificate could be traced. Gerald had never told me exactly where Old Dorothy lived or exactly when she died. However, I took my clue from the statement in his biography that he had not been allowed to write and publish anything about the survival of the witch cult 'until Dorothy died'. (See *Gerald Gardner: Witch*, J.L. Bracelin, The Octagon Press, London, 1960). Even then, it was only presented in a fictional setting, in his novel *High Magic's Aid*, which was published by Michael Houghton, London, in 1949. I therefore assumed that by 1949 Old Dorothy had passed on.

I realized that my request to the Registrar at Lymington was vague, so I decided also to try back numbers of Kelly's Directory for the New Forest area, in an attempt to find out where she had actually lived. *The Writers' and Artists' Year Book* provided the address of the publishers of Kelly's Directories and a hopeful letter was sent to them too.

On the actual night of Hallowe'en, 1980, three witches, of whom I was one, met in a wood in southern England. Hallowe'en is the old Celtic festival of *Samhain*, or summer's end, one of the Great Sabbats of the witches' year. It is the old festival of the dead, which the Christian Church adapted as the Eve of All Hallows or All Saints. To witches and pagans, it was and still is the time when the gates of the other world open and our friends and relatives who have passed through those gates into the Land of Faerie, the pagan paradise, can return if they wish and communicate with us. At this time, we always commemorate those who have gone before, both those who are known to us and our predecessors whose names are unknown but who may have been victims of the great witch-hunts of the past, or perhaps managed to live and die without their secret adherence to witchcraft ever being discovered. (There was a very good reason for Old Dorothy to fall into this final category. Witchcraft was actually still illegal in this country up until 1951. Moreover, social attitudes towards the study and practice of the occult in any form are very different today from what they were in the 1930s and 1940s. It may well have been Old Dorothy herself who pointed out to Gerald that 'witchcraft doesn't pay for broken windows,' when he wanted to write about the surviving traditions.)

I had made up my mind to try to contact Old Dorothy on this night of Hallowe'en. The weather was cold and the night dark, with the moon waning in her last quarter. Most of our friends were having merry Sabbat gatherings within their homes. To pagans, the night of the dead is not a dismal occasion, but rather a happy reunion. I knew that the candles and the pumpkin lanterns were glowing, the naked dancers were treading the circle and the cakes and wine were being passed around. But I longed for the dark wood, with the autumn leaves beneath my feet and the stars peeping through the topmost branches of the trees.

I had two companions, whom I will call by their witch-names, Fiona and Dusio. Dusio and I had arrived at the wood as dusk was falling, in order to have enough light to gather fallen branches for a small bonfire. It was quite dark by the time our preparations were made. Then he saw a light approaching through the trees, and Fiona joined us.

We formed our circle and proceeded with our Hallowe'en rites of invoking the Old Gods. The bonfire blazed and mingled its scent of woodsmoke with the incense that burned in the censer. At the four quarters, east, south, west and north, stood lanterns containing candles which made the little clearing a place of glowing light within the surrounding darkness of the trees.

There was no question of working skyclad on this chill October night. We wore robes or hooded cloaks and stout footwear. After we had warmed our blood by dancing round the circle, I told the others what I wanted to do, namely to call upon Old Dorothy's spirit. They agreed and I made a short invocation to her, asking her in particular to show me in some way if she wished me to succeed in my quest.

I hardly expected an immediate physical phenomenon, but we got one. Shortly after I had called upon Old Dorothy, the lantern which was standing at the south quarter suddenly turned right over with such force that it broke the glass.

I thought perhaps the edge of my cloak had caught it; but Fiona who was watching said this was not so, and neither Fiona nor Dusio was wearing a cloak long enough to have done it. Dusio advanced the suggestion that some small animal had run out of the wood and tipped the lantern over; but we saw no such animal. We were compelled to consider at least the strong possibility that this was a supernormal occurrence. I myself believe that it was, because I also heard a voice outside the circle, seeming to come from the southern quarter. It called my name, 'Doreen!' The others did not hear this; but I heard it plainly, and it sounded like Gerald Gardner's voice.

Our friends who have gone before often manage to make their presence felt in some way on this ritual occasion. On a previous night of Hallowe'en, I was working somewhere in the Sussex countryside with Dusio when we saw a beautiful blue light, like a star, appear outside the circle. We both saw this clearly, and there was no natural explanation for it.

I was therefore heartened in my resolve to search for Old Dorothy, even though both my hopeful letters produced no results. The Registrar of Lymington could trace no death certificate and suggested I should try the central registry in London where the national records of births, marriages and deaths are kept. The parent company of Kelly's Directories proved to be in the process of moving their archives from central London to Surrey, so these were temporarily unavailable for research. My only hope in this direction was some big library which had old copies in its stores.

But what big library? There were no big libraries in the New Forest area itself. But how about large neighbouring towns? Winchester? Bournemouth?

The only rough guide I had was the passages relating to Old Dorothy in Jack Bracelin's biography previously referred to, *Gerald Gardner: Witch*. According to these, Gerald Gardner had been resident somewhere in the vicinity of Christchurch, Hampshire, when he discovered the Rosicrucian Theatre 'on one of his long cycle rambles' and became acquainted with the group that ran it. (See Plates 15 and 16.) It was through this group that he eventually met Old Dorothy. So there seemed a chance, just a guess, that, as Bournemouth was much closer to Christchurch than Winchester is it might be more productive of results.

I obtained from my local reference library the correct address of Bournemouth County Library (which is now in Dorset, though the county boundaries included it in Hampshire in old Gerald's time). With no great optimism, I wrote to this library, explaining that I was trying to trace a Miss Dorothy Clutterbuck, resident somewhere in the general area of the New Forest in the 1930s and early 1940s. Could they help?

They could and they did. In fact, this excellent library provided me with my first real breakthrough. In the middle of January 1981, the Reference Librarian wrote to me as follows:

'The Reference Library staff have searched the local directories for Miss Dorothy Clutterbuck and have found the following:

'Street Directory of the Extended Borough of Christchurch, 1933.

'Clutterbuck, Dorothy, Mill House, Lymington Road, Highcliffe.

'Fordham, Rupert, Mill House.'

The letter went on to say that Kelly's Directory of Bournemouth, Poole and Christchurch showed Rupert Fordham at the Mill House in its issue for 1936, but no Clutterbuck. The same directory for 1940 showed Mrs Fordham at that address. So even if I had found the big volumes of Kelly's, they would not have helped me. But that obscure little local directory had produced my first proof that at least a Dorothy Clutterbuck existed. Moreover, as I hastily looked up Highcliffe on the map, I saw that it was closely adjacent to Christchurch. It was in fact the place where I had first met Gerald Gardner, at the house of a friend back in 1952.

The librarian's letter continued:

'The Registrar of Electors at Christchurch Town Hall has through the Hampshire Record Office consulted the Electoral Lists and has found out that Miss Clutterbuck became Mrs Fordham in the 1937/38 list. Unfortunately during the war years the lists were not compiled and Mrs Fordham disappears afterwards. Whether or not this is the lady you are looking for, I cannot say.'

Neither could I for certain. But inwardly I felt sure. The place was right and so was the time. And how fortunate that Old Dorothy had an unusual name like Clutterbuck! If she had been Dorothy Smith or Dorothy Jones, my search would have been hopeless.

But now I had to prove it. I had to get something more substantial than a line in an old street directory. I now had the approximate date of a possible marriage, for which a public record would exist. So if I could find this, it would give her age at the time, which would be a guide to a search for a birth certificate. I wrote off another hopeful letter, this time to the Register Office at Bournemouth, asking for any record of such a marriage or for a record of a death certificate, under the name of either Miss Clutterbuck or Mrs Fordham.

In due course the Superintendent Registrar very kindly replied. His staff had searched the indexes extensively; but there was no record of either marriage or death. The search for a record of a marriage had been from the dates of 1936 to 1940 inclusive. The record of a death had been searched for from the dates of 1943 to 1948 inclusive. As before, he suggested that I make a visit to London and search the national index at the General Register Office.

This was an unexpected setback. However, perhaps Old Dorothy had got married somewhere else. Perhaps she had got married abroad. Perhaps she had even died abroad. Or perhaps her marriage had been a witch handfasting, rather than a legally recognized ceremony. Obviously, I would have to go to London to continue the search; but I had very little to go on, as I had no precise information about either birth, marriage or death. And there might be dozens of Dorothy Clutterbucks among the millions of names in those national indexes.

It sounded like a daunting task and it was. I decided, for luck, to go up to town on May Eve, 1981. I found that the records of births and marriages are held in St Catherine's House, Kingsway, and the records of deaths are in Alexandra House nearby. They are contained in massive volumes, of which there are usually four to a year, covering each quarter. After heaving these on and off the shelves for several hours, one feels as if one has been heaving sacks of coal.

I tried the marriage records first, as being the nearest thing for which I had an approximate date. There was nothing. Then I went across to

Alexandra House and made an even longer search for a death certificate. I knew that Old Dorothy had presided over the rites against Hitler in the New Forest, which had commenced at Lammas, 1940, so she was alive and well then. And Gerald had published *High Magic's Aid* in 1949. That gave me the years 1941–8 inclusive. I went through them all. The only Dorothy Clutterbuck recorded during that period was a girl of fourteen who died in Manchester. The name of Fordham yielded no likely possibilities either.

A thought struck me. Had she ever changed her name by deed-poll? I gladly sought fresh air as I tramped round to the public Records Office. They were kind and helpful; but there was nothing there. There was nothing left to do but get the train home. I needed some vital detail and I had to keep looking for it.

The County Library at Bournemouth had been most helpful in sending me photocopies of the relevant entries from old directories. These had helped further by establishing that Gerald Gardner and his wife Donna had been living in Highcliffe at the time when his biography records that he was initiated by Old Dorothy, namely 'a few days after the war had started' in September 1939. According to *Gerald Gardner: Witch*, this initiation took place in Old Dorothy's home, 'a big house in the neighbourhood'. The same book describes Old Dorothy as 'a lady of note in the district, "county" and very well-to-do. She invariably wore a pearl necklace, worth some £5,000 at the time.' This book was published during Gerald's lifetime, so these details must have been obtained from him.

The reference in it to the Rosicrucian Theatre checked out, too. This was at Somerford and was opened in June 1938. The ever-helpful Bournemouth Central Library provided me with photocopies of Press cuttings about it. As Gerald had said, Mrs Mabel Besant-Scott, the daughter of Annie Besant, lived nearby and was associated with the project. All very interesting; but it did not have a direct bearing on what I wanted to know.

For the time being, I was at a standstill and turned to other work, among which was collaborating with Janet and Stewart Farrar in the first part of this book. Hallowe'en came round again and was merrily celebrated, but indoors this time with a crowd of friends. I often thought about Old Dorothy and remembered that night in the wood the year before. Somehow I felt sure this was not going to be the end of the story.

However, I did not get another breakthrough until 1 March 1982. Then I was dusting some books in a bookcase and rearranging them, when down the back of these books I found a little pamphlet. It was entitled *The Museum of Magic and Witchcraft: the Story of the Famous Witches' Mill at Castletown, Isle of Man*. It was written and published by Gerald Gardner to serve as a guide-book to his witchcraft museum. I thumbed through it, remembering the old days – and saw a paragraph in the book which seemed to leap at me out of the page!

'*Case No. 1*. A large number of objects belonging to a witch who died in 1951, lent by her relatives, who wish to remain anonymous.'

A witch who died in 1951! Could this possibly be Old Dorothy? I knew that it was not the lady who had lent some other objects to the museum, because she was very much alive in 1951. Had the date I had been looking for been hidden in my bookcase all the time?

As soon as I could, I went up to London again to find out. This time, I found the record at Alexandra House almost immediately. In the first quarter of 1951, a Dorothy St Q. Fordham died in the Christchurch area, aged 70. I applied for a copy of the death certificate to be sent to me by post.

Then, elated by success at last, I decided to try for a birth certificate also. Doing a little sum with the figure given for Old Dorothy's age at her passing, it seemed she must have been born about 1881. The indexes for 1880 and 1881 had no record of the birth of a Dorothy Clutterbuck; but the index for 1882 did. Had I really found what I was looking for? I ordered a copy of this certificate also and went off in triumph to celebrate with tea, buttered scones and jam at a nice little café nearby. Then I went home and settled down to wait for the copies of the certificates to arrive.

The death certificate arrived first and told me a great deal. Dorothy St Quintin Fordham had died at Highcliffe in the registration district of Christchurch on 12 January 1951. The gentleman who had supplied the particulars for the registration of her death (whom I later discovered from her will to have been her solicitor) described her as 'Spinster of independent means, daughter of Thomas St Quintin Clutterbuck, Lieutenant-Colonel, Indian Army (deceased)'. The primary cause of death was given as cerebral thrombosis, or in other words a stroke. This was borne out by the death notice which I found in the local reference library's microfilmed records of *The Times* newspaper, which said that she had died 'after a short illness'.

However, when the copy of the birth certificate arrived a few days later, I only had to take one look at it to know that this was not the Dorothy Clutterbuck I was searching for. I had been rather suspicious of the district given in the index, namely Stow in Suffolk. I now saw that the father's name was different also, Alexander Clutterbuck instead of Thomas St Quintin. I still had only half the answer. And I had searched those indexes laboriously in all senses of the word.

Had I come to another standstill? No, because I now had concrete fact to go on, however little: the particulars on the death certificate. I decided to look up Thomas St Quintin Clutterbuck in old Army Lists if

I could find any. Fortunately, my local reference library actually had in its stores the Army List for 1881. I looked through its yellowed pages at the long lists of names. Here were the gallant soldiers of the Queen when Victoria was on the throne and the British Empire reigned pre-eminent and apparently immutable. In my imagination, I saw their scarlet uniforms splendid with gold braid and medals and heard the clatter of their well-groomed chargers' hoofs and the clink of their spurs and swords. And there was Thomas St Q. Clutterbuck, listed as a Major in the Indian Local Forces, Bengal, as of 14 July 1880.

Now, this must have been around the time when Dorothy was born. Had she been born in India? It seemed a distinct possibility. But if so, would any record of such a birth be traceable?

Well, I would go up to town again and try. I had acquired a little book called *Discovering Your Family Tree*, by David Iredale (Shire Publications, Aylesbury, Bucks., 1977). This told me that the General Registry (formerly at Somerset House but now at St Catherine's House) held returns relating to army families which went back to 1761. So there was some hope. In the meantime, it seemed probable that a lady of independent means such as Dorothy would have left a will. As I now had the correct particulars of her death, I wrote to Somerset House and set the formalities in motion to obtain a copy of the will.

It duly arrived. I had a strange sensation as I slit open the long manila envelope and realized that I was about to see the photocopy of Old Dorothy's signature. It was an unusual signature, artistic but very clear; the most personal link that I had yet been able to find with her.

The will ran to several pages and made it abundantly clear that Old Dorothy had indeed been as Gerald described her, 'a lady of note in the district' and 'very well-to-do'. The gross value of her estate had been well over £60,000, which was a lot of money in 1951. Moreover, she had owned some valuable pearls; these were mentioned in the will.

What, then, had I proved so far? A Dorothy Clutterbuck had certainly existed, and her age and background answered to Gerald's description. She had lived at Highcliffe at the same time that Gerald did. She had died in 1951, the date given in Gerald's little book. Also, the Rosicrucian Theatre had certainly existed, under the patronage of Mabel Besant-Scott and a group called the Rosicrucian Order, Crotona Fellowship. This group was headed by Dr G.A. Sullivan, who according to the Press cuttings had been a well-known Shakespearean actor under the stage name of Alex Mathews. He died in 1942.

What had misled me in the early part of my search had been my assumption that, by the time *High Magic's Aid* was published, Old Dorothy had already passed on. I now knew that this was not so, and it cast a new light on the witchcraft rituals described in that book. They had been published in Old Dorothy's lifetime, but under the guise of fiction. *High Magic's Aid* is an historical novel and in my opinion a very good one. On carefully re-reading it, moreover, I found that its setting, called 'St Clare-in-Walden' in the book, corresponds quite well to Christchurch, the oldest town in that area (both Bournemouth and Highcliffe are comparatively modern developments). The action of the book takes place on the edge of a great forest, again corresponding with the location of Christchurch on the borders of the New Forest. Actual local place-names are mentioned: St Catherine's Hill, the River Stour, 'the mill at Walkford'.

We may recall what Gerald Gardner said in his later book, *Witchcraft Today* (Rider, London, 1954): 'I met some people who claimed to have known me in a past life … I soon found myself in the circle and took the usual oaths of secrecy which bound me not to reveal any secrets of the cult. But, as it is a dying cult, I thought it was a pity that all the knowledge should be lost, so in the end I was permitted to write, as fiction, something of what a witch believes in the novel *High Magic's Aid*.'

So the person who gave this permission would actually have been Old Dorothy herself. This seems good presumptive evidence for the authenticity of these rituals, although in later years, when Gerald was being bullied and abused by the sensational Press, he found it expedient to say that the book was merely fiction. And thanks mainly to Gerald Gardner, the Old Religion is no longer a dying cult but one that is alive not only in the British Isles but in the United States of America, Canada, Australia and Holland, all of these countries having their own witchcraft magazines and newsletters at the present time.

But what of Old Dorothy's own origins? I still knew nothing of her mother's family and only the discovery of her birth certificate would tell me. I took another trip to London, this time to enquire after the records of army families mentioned previously. Yes, St Catherine's House did have them. I searched the indexes – 1879, 1880, 1881, 1882. Nothing. I searched the consular records of the births of British subjects abroad. Nothing. I even searched the records of births at sea. Nothing. In sheer desperation, I again searched those ponderous volumes of indexes for the ordinary registrations of births in England and Wales. Had I missed something? Apart from two entries which merely referred to 'Clutterbuck, female', I had not. Neither of the places looked likely, nor did I think that the daughter of Major Thomas St Quintin Clutterbuck would have been humbly registered as 'Clutterbuck, female'.

Well, Old Dorothy had certainly lived and died; but apparently she had never been born! I asked one of the assistants for help. Were there any more army records that were not on display on the shelves? He made a house telephone call to some inner sanctum and put me in touch with the official who was in charge of it. This gentleman went to look and then returned to the telephone. He was very sorry but there was nothing there either.

Then I remembered something that Ginny, the Maiden of Janet and Stewart's coven, had said in conversation when she had visited me recently and I told her about the possibility of Dorothy having been born in India. Something about a friend of hers who had been seeking her birth certificate and 'the Indian authorities had been very helpful.' Could the Indian authorities be helpful about a birth that had taken place back in the far-off days of the British Raj?

I suggested this to the gentleman on the telephone. He sounded doubtful; but I had to persist. (It was all I had left, unless Dorothy had been born in Scotland, in which case the records were in Edinburgh.) Yes, I *could* go to the Indian authorities. Where would I find them? At India House. Was that far? Oh no, just across the way.

India House proved to be a very splendid building, with beautiful paintings on the walls illustrating scenes of Hindu life. Two charming ladies in saris willingly offered assistance and directed me to the India Office Library in Blackfriars Road. I found a taxi and set off there forthwith. I had a feeling that this time I was on the right track.

The security officer in the hall gave me a pass to enter and directed me upstairs to the library itself. There a librarian explained to me that in the days I was enquiring about it had been the parents' responsibility to record a child's birth and there was no birth certificates as such. However, they had ecclesiastical records of marriages and baptisms carried out by Christian chaplains in India. The baptismal certificates usually also recorded the date of birth. He would find me the index of baptisms for the relevant years in Bengal.

Almost as soon as I opened the book, I saw the name 'Clutterbuck, Dorothy'. I filled out the form for the larger book containing the actual ecclesiastical record. It proved to be an even more enormous volume than any I had handled yet, and all its entries were in beautiful copperplate handwriting. Dorothy Clutterbuck had been born on 19 January 1880 and baptized in St Paul's Church, Umbala, on 21 February 1880. Her parents were Thomas St Q. Clutterbuck, Captain in the 14th Sikhs and Ellen Anne Clutterbuck. I had found her.

I sat back and looked around the hushed library, with its venetian blinds drawn to protect the books and the readers from the bright spring sunshine. I could hardly believe that I had finally succeeded. I was sorry that the entry did not give the maiden name of Dorothy's mother; but I had succeeded.

I went back to the librarian's office to enquire about obtaining a copy of the record. Yes, I was told, this could be done and sent to me on payment of the usual fee. An assistant telephoned for the official in charge of this service, then told me, 'I'm sorry about this, but he's engaged at the moment. I'm afraid he might be about twenty minutes or so, if you don't mind waiting.'

I said I would wait and went to look for somewhere to sit. And now ensued a curious incident. There were several chairs nearby for visitors, but they were all occupied. So I wandered into a further part of the library, just looking for somewhere to rest. I had had a long and tiring day. I found myself standing in front of a bookcase full of neat volumes of indexes entitled 'Marriages. Bengal.'

Suppose Dorothy's parents had been married in India? If I could find the entry, that would give me her mother's maiden name. I took out a volume. It *immediately* fell open in my hands and I saw the name 'Clutterbuck, Thomas St Q.'. I admit that I was both tired and excited; but I will swear that that book opened itself.

I returned to the desk and applied for another huge volume of ecclesiastical records. When it arrived in the reading room, I learned from it that Thomas St Quintin Clutterbuck had married Ellen Anne Morgan at Lahore in 1877. He had been 38 years of age and his bride 20.

Somehow I could picture it. The brilliant sunshine of India. An officer in full dress uniform. His young bride in a Victorian wedding dress, all frills and lace. The traditional regimental arch of swords held by his white-gloved brother officers for the couple to walk beneath. A smiling chaplain in his white surplice. A carriage drawn by magnificently groomed horses. Iced champagne in silver buckets. Big green palm trees waving above. Handfuls of money thrown to the natives. Was it really like that? I don't know; but as I sat in that silent library, this is the picture that seemed to pass before me.

I brought my mind back to the present day and went to request a copy of this entry also. It interested me because Ellen Morgan was a Welsh name. So it would seem that Old Dorothy's ancestry on her mother's side was Welsh, that Celtic strain in our national blood which predates the Anglo-Saxon and often carries a psychic heritage with it.

Having ordered the copies of the certificates, I returned home to await their arrival. I expected them to take a few days; and as it worked out, they arrived on the most appropriate day possible. They dropped through my letterbox on the morning of 30 April 1982 – the Sabbat of Beltane. For the time being, my search was ended.

Appendix B
Casting and Banishing the Circle

As we explained in the Introduction, p. 2, the rituals for casting and banishing the Circle are included here for completeness, as the rituals in Sections I-X and XXIII cannot be performed without them. We gave them in full, with explanations and notes, in our *Eight Sabbats for Witches*, Sections I and III, but not all our readers may have this. Here, we have cut out the explanations and notes, and condensed the instructions, but the rituals themselves are nevertheless complete.

Strictly speaking, the Circle is fully cast, and work may be done, after the summoning of the Watchtowers. But the rest of the normal opening ritual (Drawing Down the Moon, the Charge etc.) is necessary to the initiations and other rites in this book, so this too is included.

There are one or two small changes from the *Eight Sabbats for Witches* version. A few words in the Witches' Rune have been altered to bring it in line with Doreen Valiente's Text C version. The *Bagahi* incantation has also been amended slightly, because Doreen has recently obtained the original wording as it appears (see Plate 8) in the thirteenth-century troubadour Rutebeuf's manuscript now in the Bibliothèque Nationale in Paris (their MS No.837 (Ancien 7218), listed as a '*manuscrit célèbre*'). The text we give here is that original.

Three things in this ritual are Alexandrian innovations: the invocation to Boreas, and the copying of the High Priestess's Invoking and Banishing Pentagrams by the whole coven, both of which we include because we like them; and the placing of the altar in the North instead of in the centre as was Gardner's practice. Like many covens, we find the Northern altar more satisfactory, especially in a small indoor Circle, and its symbolism is perfectly acceptable in an Earth religion.

Casting the Circle

The tools are on the altar in the North, with the sword laid on the ground before it. At least one candle (preferably three) is lit on the altar, and one each at the East, South and West points of the perimeter. Incense is burning in the censer on the altar. A bowl of water, and one of salt, are also on the altar. (If the broomstick and cauldron are needed, they can be placed on either side of the altar.)

High Priestess and High Priest kneel before the altar. The rest of the coven stand outside the North-East of the Circle.

High Priestess puts the bowl of water on the pentacle, and the tip of her athame in it, and says:

'*I exorcise thee, O Creature of Water, that thou cast out from thee all the impurities and uncleanness of the spirits of the world of phantasm, in the names of Cernunnos and Aradia.*'

She then holds the bowl of water up before her. High Priest puts the bowl of salt on the pentacle, and the tip of his athame in it, and says:

'*Blessings be upon this creature of salt; let all malignity and hindrance be cast forth thencefrom, and let all good enter therein. Wherefore I bless thee and invoke thee, that thou mayest aid me, in the names of Cernunnos and Aradia.*'

He pours the salt into the High Priestess's bowl of water, and they replace both bowls on the altar. High Priest leaves the Circle to join the coven in the North-East.

High Priestess casts the Circle with the sword, pointing it at the perimeter and proceeding deosil from North to North. As she passes the North-East, she raises the sword higher than the heads of the coven to leave a gateway. As she casts the Circle, she says:

'*I conjure thee, O Circle of Power, that thou beest a meeting-place of love and joy and truth; a shield against all wickedness and evil; a boundary between the world of men and the realms of the Mighty Ones; a rampart and protection that shall preserve and contain the power that we shall raise within thee. Wherefore I bless thee and consecrate thee, in the names of Cernunnos and Aradia.*'

She lays down the sword and admits the High Priest to the Circle with a kiss, spinning with him deosil. High Priest admits a woman in the same way; the woman admits a man; and so on till all are inside. High Priestess picks up the sword and closes the gateway with a deosil sweep of it.

High Priestess names three witches. The first carries the bowl of water deosil round the Circle from North to North, sprinkling the perimeter. He/she then sprinkles each person in turn. If he is a man, he ends by sprinkling the High Priestess, who sprinkles him; if she is a woman, she ends by sprinkling the High Priest, who sprinkles her. The bowl is returned to the altar.

The second named witch carries the smoking incense-burner deosil round the Circle from North to North and replaces it on the altar. The third named witch carries an altar candle round in the same way and replaces it.

All take their athames and face East, with the High Priestess in front. High Priestess draws the Invoking Pentagram of Earth (apex, bottom left, far right, far left, bottom right and apex again) in the air before her, saying:

'*Ye Lords of the Watchtowers of the East, ye Lords of Air; I do summon, stir and call you up, to witness our rites and to guard the Circle.*'

The rest of the coven copy her gestures with their athames.

She faces South with the coven behind her, and again making the Invoking Pentagram of Earth, she says:

'*Ye Lords of the Watchtowers of the South, ye Lords of Fire. I do summon ...*' etc.

To the West, in the same way, she says:

'*Ye Lords of the Watchtowers of the West, ye Lords of Water; Lords of Death and of Initiation; I do summon ...*' etc.

To the North, in the same way, she says:

'*Ye Lords of the Watchtowers of the North, ye Lords of Earth; Boreas, thou guardian of the Northern portals; thou powerful God, thou gentle Goddess; I do summon ...*' etc.

Throughout, the coven copy her gestures with their own athames. All now replace their athames on the altar and kneel in the South of the Circle facing North – except the High Priestess, who stands with her back to the altar with the wand in her right and the scourge in her left, crossed over her breasts; and the High Priest, who kneels before her.

High Priest now 'Draws Down the Moon' on the High Priestess. First he gives her the Fivefold Kiss (see p. 18), and then, kneeling again, he touches her with his right forefinger on her right breast, left breast and womb; the same three points again; and finally the right breast. (During all this, High Priestess spreads her arms outwards as necessary.) As he touches her, he says:

'I invoke thee and call upon thee, Mighty Mother of us all, bringer of all fruitfulness; by seed and root, by stem and bud, by leaf and flower and fruit do I invoke thee to descend upon the body of this thy servant and priestess.'

He spreads his arms outwards and downwards with the palms forward (he is still kneeling) and says:

'Hail, Aradia! From the Amalthean Horn
Pour forth thy store of love; I lowly bend
Before thee, I adore thee to the end,
With loving sacrifice thy shrine adorn.
Thy foot is to my lip [kissing it] my prayer upborne
Upon the rising incense-smoke; then spend
Thine ancient love, O Mighty One, descend
To aid me, who without thee am forlorn.'

He stands up and takes a pace backwards. High Priestess draws the Invoking Pentagram of Earth in the air in front of him with the wand, saying:

'Of the Mother darksome and divine
Mine the scourge, and mine the kiss;
The five-point star of love and bliss –
Here I charge you, in this sign.'

This completes Drawing Down the Moon. High Priestess and High Priest now face the coven and deliver the Charge, as follows.

High Priest: *'Listen to the words of the Great Mother; she who of old was also called among men Artemis, Astarte, Athene, Dione, Melusine, Aphrodite, Cerridwen, Dana, Arianrhod, Isis, Bride, and by many other names.'*

High Priestess: *'Whenever ye have need of any thing, once in the month, and better it be when the moon is full, then shall ye assemble in some secret place and adore the spirit of me, who am Queen of all witches. There shall ye assemble, ye who are fain to learn all sorcery, yet have not won its deepest secrets; to these will I teach things that are yet unknown. And ye shall be free from slavery; and as a sign that ye be really free, ye shall be naked in your rites; and ye shall dance, sing, feast, make music and love, all in my praise. For mine is the ecstasy of the spirit, and mine also is joy on earth; for my law is love unto all beings. Keep pure your highest ideal; strive ever towards it; let naught stop you or turn you aside. For mine is the secret door which opens upon the Land of Youth and mine is the cup of the wine of life, and the Cauldron of Cerridwen, which is the Holy Grail of immortality. I am the gracious Goddess, who gives the gift of joy unto the heart of man. Upon earth, I give the knowledge of the spirit eternal; and beyond death, I give peace and freedom, and reunion with those who have gone before. Nor do I demand sacrifice, for behold, I am the Mother of all living, and my love is poured out upon the earth.'*

High Priest: '*Hear ye the words of the Star Goddess; she in the dust of whose feet are the hosts of heaven, and whose body encircles the universe.'*

High Priestess: '*I who am the beauty of the green earth, and the white Moon among the stars, and the mystery of the waters, and the desire of the heart of man, call unto thy soul. Arise, and come unto me. For I am the soul of nature, who gives life to the universe. From me all things proceed, and unto me all things must return; and before my face, beloved of Gods and of men, let thine innermost divine self be enfolded in the rapture of the infinite. Let my worship be within the heart that rejoiceth; for behold, all acts of love and pleasure are my rituals. And therefore let there be beauty and strength, power and compassion, honour and humility, mirth and reverence within you. And thou who thinkest to seek for me, know thy seeking and yearning shall avail thee not unless thou knowest the mystery; that if that which thou seekest thou findest not within thee, then thou wilt never find it without thee. For behold, I have been with thee from the beginning; and I am that which is attained at the end of desire.'*

All stand up. High Priest raises his arms wide and says:

'Bagahi laca bachahé
Lamac cahi achabahé
Karrelyos
Lamac lamec bachalyos
Cabahagi sabalyos
Baryolas
Lagozatha cabyolas
Samahac et famyolas
Harrahya!'

High Priestess and coven repeat: '*Harrahya!'*

High Priestess and High Priest face the altar with their arms raised in the Horned God salute (fists clenched, palms forward, first and little fingers pointing upwards). High Priest says:

'Great God Cernunnos, return to earth again!
Come at my call and show thyself to men.
Shepherd of Goats, upon the wild hill's way,
Lead thy lost flock from darkness unto day.
Forgotten are the ways of sleep and night —

Men seek for them, whose eyes have lost the light.
Open the door, the door that hath no key,
The door of dreams, whereby men come to thee.
Shepherd of Goats, O answer unto me!'

High Priestess and High Priest together say: *'Akhera goiti'*, lower their hand and say: *'Akhera beiti!'*
High Priestess, High Priest and coven now form a ring facing inwards, man and woman alternately as far as possible, and link hands. They circle deosil chanting the Witches' Rune::

'Eko, Eko, Azarak,
Eko, Eko, Zomelak,   }   [repeated three times]
Eko, Eko, Cernunnos,
Eko, Eko, Aradia!

Darksome night and shining moon,
East, then South, then West, then North,
Hearken to the Witches' Rune –
Here we come to call ye forth!
Earth and water, air and fire,
Wand and pentacle and sword,
Work ye unto our desire,
Hearken ye unto our word!
Cords and censer, scourge and knife,
Powers of the witch's blade –
Waken all ye unto life,
Come ye as the charm is made!
Queen of heaven, Queen of hell,
Hornèd hunter of the night –
Lend your power unto the spell,
And work our will by magic rite!
In the earth and air and sea,
By the light of moon or sun,
As we will, so mote it be.
Chant the spell and be it done!
Eko, Eko, Azarak,
Eko, Eko, Zomelak,   }   [repeated till ready]
Eko, Eko, Cernunnos,
Eko, Eko, Aradia!'

When the High Priestess decides it is time, she orders: *'Down!'* and all sit, still in a ring facing inwards.

Banishing the Circle

All take their athames and face East, with the High Priestess in front. High Priestess draws the Banishing Pentagram of Earth (bottom left, apex, bottom right, far left, far right, bottom left again) in the air before her, saying:

'*Ye Lords of the Watchtowers of the East, ye Lords of Air; we do thank you for attending our rites; and ere ye depart to your pleasant and lovely realms, we bid you hail and farewell ... Hail and farewell.*'

The rest of the coven copy her gestures with their own athames, and say the second '*Hail and farewell*' with her. (They do the same, ranging themselves behind her, at each of the other three Watchtowers.)

To the South, again of course with the Banishing Pentagram, she says: '*Ye Lords of the Watchtowers of the South, ye Lords of Fire; we do thank you ...*' etc.

To the West: '*Ye Lords of the Watchtowers of the West, ye Lords of Water; ye Lords of Death and of Initiation; we do thank you ...*' etc.

And to the North: '*Ye Lords of the Watchtowers of the North, ye Lords of Earth; Boreas, thou guardian of the Northern portals; thou powerful God, thou gentle Goddess; we do thank you ...*' etc.

This completes the banishing of the Circle.

Notes

Introduction

1. Every book mentioned in the text will be found in the Bibliography with publishing details.
2. The Ordo Templi Orientis (Order of the Temple of the East) is a ritual magic order of uncertain age. It was first mentioned in print in 1904; Aleister Crowley (according to his own version) became head of the British section in 1912; and in 1917 Theodor Reuss issued a Manifesto in Switzerland publicizing the Order. (See Francis King, *The Secret Rituals of the O.T.O.*)

I First Degree Initiation

1. These cords are for working 'cord magic', and each witch should have his or her own personal set. (They should not be confused with the one long and two short cords mentioned in the list above, which are used for binding the Postulant; we suggest that the coven should keep a separate set of these, to be used only at initiations.) One traditional use of a nine-foot cord was to tie it in a loop, put it over the athame stuck in the middle of the floor, pull the loop to its full (four feet six inches) length, and use it like a compass to draw the Magic Circle. Doreen says: 'This of course would be in the old days when people had cottage floors of rammed earth. I suppose they could have used the white-handled knife or a piece of chalk to draw the actual circle, depending on the surface they were working on.'
2. One of our witches, a housewife who had to keep her Craft practice secret for a while, had as her athame and white-handled knife two knives among her kitchen equipment, identifiable only by herself; her pentacle was a particular silver dish in her display-cabinet; and so on. Such necessary secrecy, in persecution days, was of course the origin of the traditional witch's broomstick – a magic riding-pole disguised as an ordinary household besom.
3. The Alexandrian practice is to use two cords only – a red cord for the neck and wrists and a white cord for the ankle. But Doreen tells us: 'Our cords were usually red, the colour of life, but sometimes other colours were used, green, blue or black. No particular significance was attached to this, except that we preferred red if we could get it, but it was not so easy then to get good suitable silk cord.'
4. This resembles a feature of the Masonic initiation, as does the presenting of a point to the Postulant's breast.
5. Of Gardner's texts, this only appears in *High Magic's Aid*. The Alexandrian ritual uses it, but as an order later when the two ankles are bound together – clearly the wrong place.
6. If the Initiator is the High Priest, this may be felt a suitable occasion to add Drawing Down the Sun (see Section VI) to the traditional ritual.
7. The Cabalistic Cross is pure Golden Dawn (see Israel Regardie, *The Golden*

302 THE WITCHES' WAY

Dawn, 3rd edition, Vol. 1, p. 106). It appears in Gardner's text, 'but in practice I do not remember us ever doing this', Doreen tells us. We include it here for completeness, but we do not use it at initiations either; like many witches, we often use Cabalistic magic, but feel it is out of context in something as traditionally Wiccan as an initiation rite. Malkuth, Geburah, and Gedulah (otherwise Chesed) are of course sephorith of the Tree of Life, and the Hebrew declamation means literally, 'For thine is the kingdom, and the power, and the glory, for ever' – an interesting hint that Jesus knew his Cabala. Some Cabalists believe that it was this knowledge, even when he was a boy, that astonished the doctors in the Temple (Luke ii, 46-7).

8. *High Magic's Aid* gives this form; Text B gives *'Perfect love for the Goddess, perfect trust in the Goddess'.* We prefer the shorter form, because it also implies love and trust within the coven, and can be quoted and held up as a standard to be maintained.

9. *High Magic's Aid* gives this form; Text B gives *'Ye dread lords and gentle goddesses'.* Since the Lords of the Watchtowers are the recognized guardians of the cardinal points and have been summoned in the Circle-casting ritual, we prefer the *High Magic's Aid* form. The Postulant's ordinary name is used here; a witch name is not taken until the second degree.

10. Or whatever God- and Goddess-names the coven uses. (See our comments on the names Cernunnos and Aradia on p.14).

11. The Gardner texts are the same for both sexes: *'breasts, formed* [or *erected*] *in beauty and strength.'* Doreen explains: 'This was an allusion to the human body as a form of the Tree of Life, with Gedulah on one side and Geburah on the other.' We prefer *'breasts, formed in beauty'* for a woman and *'breast, formed in strength'* for a man; these are more in keeping with the Fivefold Kiss as a salute of male/female polarity, and with the essentially Wiccan (rather than Cabalistic) tone of the other four statements.

12. Elsewhere (see p.54) the Book of Shadows says that while he is kneeling the Initiate's cable-tow should be tied to a ring on the altar.

13. This is our own addition to the Book of Shadows list of presentations: we make it for the reasons we give on p. 258.

14. *High Magic's Aid* merely says 'priest and witch', and Text B 'priest[ess] and witch of the Great Goddess'. For once, we rather prefer the Alexandrian form.

II   Second Degree Initiation

1. Gardner says it is possible that the stories of Ishtar and of Siva may have influenced the myth, 'but the point of the story is different …. I think that its origin is most likely Celtic.' (*Witchcraft Today*, pp. 41-2.)

2. This is the traditional wording of the presentation to the Watchtowers; but a High Priestess is not otherwise referred to as a 'Witch Queen' until she has a coven of her own plus at least two others hived off from it. (See *Eight Sabbats for Witches*, Plate 15.)

3. Text C merely says: 'Circle three times. Secure.' But if the High Priestess prefers, there is no reason why the Witches' Rune should not be chanted during the circling, which in that case continues until the Rune is finished.

4. This questioning and spanking, by the Initiator and then the coven, is an Alexandrian addition. We include it here because we use it ourselves. We find it introduces a stimulating change of pace between the two solemnities of the ritual scourging and the Oath, and also ensures that the entire coven will remember the

new name. But it is a matter of choice. Text C runs without interruption: '*I give thee a new name, ———. Repeat thy new name after me, saying ...*' Doreen Valiente comments on our custom: 'This is just like the old custom of the Beating of the Bounds, when children were given a light blow or a smack to show them where the parish boundaries were; an old folk custom which I believe is still kept up in some places.'

5. It is sometimes our practice for Janet to call Stewart (or vice versa) to kneel on the other side of the Initiate to form the Magic Link as well, so that we can both will power into him or her together. On other occasions, whichever of us is the Partner will just reinforce the Initiator's effort mentally, without moving. It is one of those cases in which a good working partnership will know intuitively what is right at the time.

6. Gardner did not describe these five points in words in his ritual; he showed them by a sketch.

7. Text C merely says 'Use. S.' ('S is the Book of Shadows shorthand for the kiss.) The candle-inscribing is our way of using it. The Initiate keeps the candle in a safe place, and when he founds his own coven, he lights it on the altar for the new coven's first Circle and leaves it to burn out completely. Even if he never founds a coven of his own, he still keeps the candle as a token of his right to do so.

8. The Alexandrian practice is to carry the wand three times round the Circle, thus waving it to the cardinal points twelve times in all. The other tools are only carried round once. We do not know the reason for this.

9. We have added the Cup to the Book of Shadows list of presentations, as we did in the first-degree rite, for the reasons we give on p. 258.

10. Text C is headed '*The Magical Legend of A.*' and begins: '*Now A. had never loved, but she ...*'. The *Witchcraft Today* version is headed '*The Myth of the Goddess*' and begins: '*Now G. had never loved, but she ...*'. '*A.*' is the initial of the Goddess-name used by Gardner, and '*G.*' merely stands for Goddess. There are many Goddess myths, and '*The Legend of the Descent of the Goddess*' seems better as an identifying title. Covens may of course use their own Goddess-name instead of '*our Lady the Goddess*' if they prefer.

11. The Gardner texts say '*to the nether lands*' – one of Gardner's rare bloomers, because it always comes out, comically, as '*to the Netherlands*' – i.e., to Holland. We really do suggest that '*to the Underworld*' is better, for this one reason.

12. Gardner added his own footnote here in the Book of Shadows: 'There was a Celtic custom of binding corpses. The cord which had bound a corpse was useful in learning second sight.' He repeated and amplified this statement in *Witchcraft Today*, p. 159, Note 2.

III   Third Degree Initiation

1. The only published version of the Wiccan Law we know of appears as Appendix A to Alex Sanders' biography *King of the Witches* (see Bibliography under Johns). There, it is quite wrongly entitled 'The Book of Shadows'; but this is typical of the book as a whole, which is more interesting as a case-history than as a factual document. This version of the Law purports to date from the persecution days, but its antiquity and authenticity are highly dubious. It may, however, enshrine fragments of traditional material, and provided that the obviously out-of-date elements are ignored, many of its clauses offer a good working guide to coven procedure. Doreen shares our doubts; she says: 'For one

thing there is a distinct whiff of male chauvinism about it; and for another, it is rather fond of threatening and cursing people who disagree with it, like a preacher in a back-street tin chapel! The verses 51-80 inclusive used to be in old Gerald's book, but not the rest.' She also points out that it implies that witches were burned in England, whereas in fact they were hanged – 'a little point that has tripped up many. I have never regarded this document as being authentic, personally; although as you say, it may enshrine fragments of traditional material handed down orally.'

2. The Text A version is very cryptic, Text B only slightly less so, and Text C merely appends the verse alternative. Most of the details were handed on by word of mouth. Gardner's *High Magic's Aid* (p. 300) alludes to the third-degree rite briefly, when the witch Morven tells the hero Jan: 'When you are past the Pentacle [i.e., the second degree] 'twill be my duty to tell you further mysteries, the Mystery of Mysteries, when you know what it consists of, we will speak further. 'Tis not a thing to be lightly done.' Doreen comments: 'Anything further, and the publisher in those days [1949] might well have refused it!' Leland's *Aradia* (p.14) states plainly that Tuscan witches used to 'love in the darkness' in honour of Diana, though this seems to have been celebratory rather than magical.

3. Referring to Gardner's custom, Doreen Valiente tells us: 'Although in theory the Great Rite could be performed and consummated before the assembled coven, in *practice* I do not remember ever being present when this was done. If others were present, then the Great Rite was done only in token ... If the Great Rite was to be used actually to make magic, then it was always performed in private.'

4. The text simply says, 'kisses both knees, extends arms along thighs and adores'.

5. The text says 'is the male' and 'is the female'; but, for the reasons we give in note 4 on p.310, we feel the correspondence is more complex than this, so we prefer to say 'is to the male' and 'is to the female'. In blessing the wine, normally the Priest speaks the words; but for the Great Rite, Text B allots them to the Priestess, though for the blessing of the cakes it leaves the words to the Priest as usual.

6. The text says 'Paten (Pentacle)'; some covens do serve the cakes on the pentacle, while others keep a special dish for the purpose.

7. In our normal blessing of the cakes, we use the shorter ending, 'that fulfilment of love which is perfect happiness'; and this seems to have become a common form. The whole blessing (with the substitution of 'Queen' for 'Lord') was taken from Crowley's Gnostic Mass, which uses the longer ending as given here. It may be felt that the longer form is appropriate to the special occasion of a Great Rite.

8. The text merely says 'Scourge', without specifying the number of strokes; probably the traditional 3, 7, 9, 21 is intended. We feel that, if the scourging is used at all, three strokes are quite enough.

9. We suggest 'twice' if the Priestess is second degree, now taking her third; 'thrice' if she is already third. Text B says 'twice', but Doreen Valiente thinks this refers to the number of scourgings undergone.

10. The text says after this: 'Only said if Priestess has not prepared the rite before.' We see no reason why it should not be used on every occasion.

11. Doreen's note: 'As the Fivefold Kiss was given, after the first kiss upon the feet, the Priestess opened her arms and stood with feet apart in the Pentacle or Goddess Position, holding the scourge and the athame. She thus impersonated both the God and the Goddess for a brief moment.'

12. Text A says, 'Holy Twin Pillars, B. and J.' This stands for Boaz and Jachin, the Masonic names for the twin pillars of Solomon's Temple, representing the complementary principles of Severity and Mercy. The 'B. and J.' was dropped

from Texts B and C. In this ritual, the 'Holy Twin Pillars' are the Priestess's breasts, which are kissed at this point. (In the alternative form of the Great Rite which we gave in *Eight Sabbats for Witches*, pp. 51-4, because of the different positioning of the Priestess and the Priest, the Pillars are taken to be the Priestess's legs.)

13. This sigil is known as the Crowned Pentagram. The pentagram itself is kissed in the order of the Invoking Pentagram of Earth, and the upright triangle is kissed deosil. Recalling the First Degree Sigil (the inverted triangle) and the Second Degree Sigil (the inverted pentagram), Doreen notes that they are combined in the Third Degree Sigil, 'but no longer inverted; they are now both upright, in their true position. Also, it is a figure which has eight points and thirteen sides, both numbers important in the Craft. It could also be interpreted as "Two joined in One, upon the Five Points of Fellowship". Or as the human being (the Pentagram) crowned with the Cone of Power.' (Incidentally, Stewart would like to point out that the third-degree pentagram in Figure 7(c) of the first edition of *What Witches Do* was unfortunately printed the wrong way up.)

14. When the Great Rite is symbolic, some may prefer the alternative we gave in *Eight Sabbats for Witches*: namely that, instead of the Priest laying his body over the Priestess, a woman witch hands the Priest his athame, and a man witch hands the Priestess the chalice at this point in the declamation. The Priestess holds up the chalice, and the Priest holds the athame point downwards above it; on the words *'Lance to Grail'*, he lowers the point into the wine. After the declamation, he kisses her and she sips; she kisses him and he sips; and the wine is then passed round man-to-woman, woman-to-man, in the usual way. The Priest then addresses the Watchtowers as in the text.

15. Text B says *'Genitals to genitals'*; we find this somewhat clinical in the poetic context of the rest, and prefer Text C's Lance-and-Grail metaphor. If the Great Rite is 'actual', this is obviously the intended moment of union; but equally obvious, one cannot dogmatize about so private a rite.

16. If the rite is 'actual', this is where the rest of the coven leave the room.

IV   Consecrations

1. A *piseog* (pronounced 'pish-*oge*') is a deliberately malevolent charm, kind of debased rural voodoo, of which several cases have come to our attention when farmers have asked us to counteract their influence. It may be anything from an aborted calf foetus to a symbolic arrangement of feathers.

2. It must be remembered that a charged object may also maintain astral links with (for example) a previous owner – a principle made use of in the exchanging of linked talismans or, come to that, of wedding rings. One should also guard against such a link doing unintended harm. For instance, in a recent Circle Janet was wearing a lovely robe made for her as a present by an English witch friend. We were having to work psychically, and very intensively, for the neutralization and capture of a psychotic double murderer who was on the loose and causing great public alarm; and we took special care (since psychotics are astral dynamite) to protect ourselves against any backlash. Just before we began, Janet realized that the robe might form a link with our friend in England, who was unwarned and could be vulnerable. She immediately took the robe off and put it outside the Circle. (We had put a seven-day limit for our working to take effect; and coincidence or not, it was satisfactory that the man was found and arrested six days later, having done no further harm.)

3. The word Qabalah is variously transliterated from the Hebrew as Kabalah or Cabalah, all with or without a double 'b' or the final 'h'. We have settled for Cabala; but where we are quoting someone else, as here, we respect their own choice.
4. See Appendix A on p.283 for Doreen Valiente's research into the facts about Dorothy Clutterbuck, the New Forest witch who initiated Gerald Gardner.

VI   Drawing Down the Sun

1. We would point out again that this does not mean that in Wiccan eyes the Goddess is 'more important' than the God; the two aspects are eternally equal and complementary. For a fuller explanation of Wicca's matriarchal structure and its emphasis on the Goddess aspect, see *Eight Sabbats for Witches*, pp. 17-21, and also Section XV in the present book.
2. When making Invoking or Banishing Pentagrams, some covens include the sixth or 'sealing stroke', as shown here; others merely return to the starting point, omitting the sealing stroke, as was the Golden Dawn custom (see *Eight Sabbats for Witches*, pp. 39-40, footnote).

VII   Three Goddesses Ritual

1. As we explained in *Eight Sabbats for Witches*, whenever anyone has to enter or leave a Circle, a 'gateway' must be ritually opened with a widdershins gesture, and re-closed after use with a deosil gesture. Normally this is done with a sword or athame, but on this occasion the wand may be suitably used.

IX   Rituals of Protection

1. By 'vampiric tendencies' we do not of course mean that your guest is likely to leap on you during the night and sink his Hammer Film teeth into your jugular. Witches and occultists use the term 'vampire' to describe a person who drains energy from those around him or her. Vampirism is not necessarily deliberate, or even conscious; and it may be a temporary condition. For example, elderly invalids are very prone to vampirize young children, and it is inadvisable to have both sleeping in the same house if it can be avoided. If it cannot, wise witch or occultist parents will take steps to protect the child psychically – by a Circle round the child's bed, for example. Vampirism is one of the first phenomena one learns to detect as one trains one's psychic abilities, we have found.
2. On this question of sealing the aura, a tip from Dion Fortune. Her heroine in *Moon Magic* (p.84) tells how after a psychic attack she got out of bed and went to where the remains of supper lay on the table, 'drank what was left of the milk and ate a sandwich, for there is nothing like food to close the psychic centres'. The converse of this, of course, is that positive psychic work may be less effective on a full stomach.
3. It is worth remembering that a mental Banishing Pentagram of Earth, strongly envisaged and coupled with the equally vigorous mental command '*Go away!*', is one of the simplest and most effective ripostes to a psychic threat or an unwanted astral entity. We recommend our own witches to practise it so that it becomes

almost a conditioned reflex to such situations. The first time that one of them made use of it in action was when he was dreaming so vividly and consciously that he knew he was astrally projecting; he found himself being approached by what he described as 'various nasties' of unpleasant appearance. He flung his Banishing Pentagram at them and ordered them to go away (with a rather pithier phrase than that). They all vanished into an image of a bank's night safe and gave him no further trouble. He is still wondering about that unexpected symbolism! These simple responses are often more powerful than complicated ones. A favourite of Janet's, when she is faced by an urgent problem to which she cannot see the answer, is to envisage the Goddess and cry *'Help!'* It has worked time and again.

X   A Seashore Ritual

1. Pronounced 'Reeah, Beenah, Gee' (with a hard 'g' as in 'gate'). Rhea was the primordial Greek Goddess who was the mother of Zeus; it was a pre-Classical, Cretan name, and the deep cave where she is said to have borne Zeus and hidden him from his jealous father Cronos may still be visited high in the Cretan mountains. Binah is the Supernatural Mother sephira on the Tree of Life, which receives the pure directionless energy of Chokmah, the Supernal Father, and gives it form; the Hebrew word means 'Understanding'. Ge is the Greek word for Earth, and also for the Earth-Goddess herself. *The Sea Priestess* gives 'Ea' instead of 'Rhea' throughout; Ea was the Assyro-Babylonian God of the Water element and of supreme wisdom. Dion Fortune may have decided later that a male God-name, however elementally appropriate, was not quite right for this essentially Goddess poem, because in the sequel *Moon Magic* (in which various verses of the poem also appear) she replaced it with 'Rhea'; and for our Goddess ritual we have followed her example.
2. Pronounced 'Shadd-eye el Ch'eye' – both words rhyming with 'high', and the 'ch' guttural as in the Scottish 'loch'. Shaddai el Chai, or Shaddai el Chaiim ('Supreme Lord of Life' or 'of Lives'), is the God-Aspect of the sephira Yesod on the Tree of Life in the World of Atziluth; or, in simple terms, the Moon function of the ultimate Life Principle.
3. If she is skyclad, or in a swimsuit or bikini, she may of course go in farther and actually wade out of the sea; this is naturally more dramatic.

XI   The Rationale of Witchcraft

1. We say 'as far as land animals are concerned' because modern research produces increasing evidence that cetaceans (whales, including the dolphin, which is a small whale) have a level of consciousness which may be comparable to our own, but which has so far gone unrecognized because it has developed a very different 'shape' from ours, thanks to their different environment, different reaction-to-danger problems and different (and in some ways superior) sensory awareness. They have a sophisticated method of communication which many researchers believe has the complexity of a true 'language'. They look after their sick, teach their young manners and have a marked sense of humour. Some whales even produce 'songs' lasting as long as half an hour which they repeat almost exactly on later occasions, of a complexity in terms of 'informational bits' which Carl Sagan has compared to that of *The Odyssey* or the Icelandic *Eddas*.

For an absorbing survey of the field, read *Mind in the Waters* (see Bibliography under McIntyre). But even assuming that whales have consciousness comparable to that of man, our point about *homo sapiens* being the spearpoint of Earth's evolution remains. Whales as we know them have been around for twenty-five million years or so, and in their simpler environment seem to have achieved a balanced and integrated consciousness which minds its own business, so to speak, without crucially affecting the rest of Nature. *Homo sapiens*, on the other hand, has been around for only half a million years and is at a revolutionary stage in his mental (and psychic) development. Because of this, and of his unparalleled ability to manipulate his environment, he has an almost limitless effect, for good or ill, on every other species and on the planet itself. (In this context, it is shaming to realize that man has killed two million whales in the last fifty years, and that some cetacean species are rapidly nearing extinction. Cruel enough by any standards; but if whales do turn out – as seems likely – to be as conscious in their way as we are in ours, this is not even 'hunting'; it is genocide, comparable to Hitler's programme for wiping out the Jews.)

2. The various planes as they apply particularly to the make-up of a human being are discussed in more detail in Section XII, 'Reincarnation'; see especially the table on p. 117.

3. As Thelma Moss vividly describes it: 'The awakening of science from its long sleep in the bed of matter.' (*The Body Electric*, p.253.) And as Gerald Durrell said in his TV series on animals, *Ark on the Move*: 'I think the ideal scientist should be half poet, half lunatic and half artist – that's three halves, which make a whole.'

4. 'To put it in simple, nonscientific terms, nuclear physics has robbed the basic units of matter of their absolute concreteness. Paradoxically, mass and energy, wave and particle, have proved to be interchangeable. The laws of cause and effect have become valid only up to a certain point. It does not matter at all that these relativities, discontinuities, and paradoxes hold good only on the margins of our world – only for the infinitely small (the atom) and the infinitely great (the cosmos). They have caused a revolutionary change in the concept of reality, and irrational reality has dawned behind the reality of our "natural" world, which is ruled by the laws of classical physics. Corresponding relativities and paradoxes were discovered in the domain of the psyche. Here, too, another world dawned on the margin of the world of consciousness, governed by new and hitherto unknown laws that are strangely akin to the laws of nuclear physics.' Aniela Jaffé's section in *Man and His Symbols*, p. 261 (see Bibliography under 'Jung, Carl G').

5. A fascinating example of this changing attitude is the subject of *The Secret Vaults of Time* by Stephan A. Schwartz (see Bibliography), which describes how an increasing number of archaeologists, including J. Norman Emerson, the most respected figure of Canadian archaeology, have made consistent use of psychic sensitives in their work, with demonstrable (and sometimes startling) success.

6. The story that Galileo (1564-1642), after the Inquisition had forced him to recant the Copernican theory that the Earth moved round the Sun, muttered '*Eppur si muove*' ('All the same, it does move'), is probably apocryphal, but it is true in spirit and worth recalling here; for witches and others who know from their own experience the reality of the Inner Planes, but are bombarded with the 'proof' of sceptics that it cannot be so, are familiar with this same reaction: '*Eppur si muove*.'

7. Haitian Voodoo has the same concept. 'The idea of psychic force is sometimes described in the word "poin" (point) which would seem to be a reference to the point of intersection at which the psychic energy from the world of the invisible is

transmitted to the visible, material world.' (Maya Deren, *Divine Horsemen*, chapter 2, note 29.)

8. The law that the strength of any radiation decreases in inverse proportion to the square of the distance from its source. For example, if a lamp sheds x amount of light on an object 1 metre away, it will shed $x/4$ amount of light on an object of the same size 2 metres away, $x/9$ at 3 metres, $x/16$ at 4 metres, and so on. This does not apply to beamed radiations, such as a searchlight or parabolic radar – but telepathy is not like this either; it may be picked up in several directions at once, and the strength of reception seems quite independent of distance.

9. By definition, monotheism believes in one God only, and polytheism in many gods. But we should be clear about this. Most polytheists, from the priests of ancient Egypt to modern witches, know perfectly well that there can only be one ultimate Creative Force; they merely personify 'It' symbolically in a number of different aspects, such as Isis, Osiris, Ma'at, Thoth, Aradia, Cernunnos, Aphrodite, Mars and so on, so as to be able to relate to the many 'wavelengths' on which the Creator manifests Itself. Monotheists, on the other hand, personify It as one (these days exclusively male) figure; Christianity acknowledges something of the aspect-principle by the device of the Trinity, and Catholicism in particular admits the Goddess-aspect through the back door in the carefully subordinated form of the Virgin Mary, and approaches more specialized aspects through the mediation of individual Saints. What it boils down to is that monotheism cannot admit creative polarization at Divine level, whereas polytheism wholeheartedly accepts it.

Polytheism is also by nature tolerant; if a stranger's God seems to have valuable attributes, you can happily add him to your pantheon of God-aspects. (Hindus have often horrified Chistian missionaries in this way; impressed by Christ's teachings, they hang his picture up beside Shiva, Kali and the rest, and wonder why the missionaries object.) Monotheists, on the other hand, inevitably see other people's Gods as devils. 'Quite apart from the genuine insight into the wholeness of existence, the single essence without seam, psychologically there is a tendency for the monotheistic idea to harden intellectually into the monolithic, the uniform, the one-tracked. This is to over-emphasise the One at the expense of the many .... And may lead to intolerance of the variety of life.' (*Tom Chetwynd, A Dictionary of Symbols*, p. 176.)

10. Though in fairness to Mohammed, his Koran gave women certain clearly defined rights which were unheard-of in that time and culture. For seventh-century Arab women, it was a revolutionary document. But it has suffered the fate of all patriarchal dogma; even when it is progressive at the time, it becomes ossified into Divine Law for centuries after changing conditions have made it reactionary.

XII Reincarnation

1. We must emphasize again that it can never be said that *all* witches believe in any particular theory, because dogma is alien to Wicca; each witch believes what he or she finds acceptable or significant. On reincarnation, some witches explain the recall phenomenon in terms of racial or genetic memory, the influence of the Collective Unconscious, or in some other way. For ourselves, we find these other explanations inadequate; but that is only *our* view, even if among witches it is a majority one.

2. A contemporary of Jerome's, St Gregory, wrote: 'It is absolutely necessary that the soul shall be healed and purified, and if it does not take place in one life on

earth, it must be accomplished in future earthly lives.' And Gregory, regarded as one of the four great fathers of the Eastern Church, was famous for his strict orthodoxy.

3. 'Spiritual' is a loaded word for some people, particularly those with a puritanical upbringing. These may prefer the term 'causal body', which is often used as an alternative.

4. The change-over principle provides an answer to a question we are often asked: 'In blessing the wine, why does the woman hold the athame and the man the chalice? – you'd expect it to be the other way round.' The blessing of the wine involves *all* the planes. On the material plane, the couple symbolize male-active, female-receptive by their bodily presence. Again on the mental plane, the man takes the active role by speaking the necessary words. But the blessing is meant to take effect on the astral and spiritual planes; and to express this, the woman holds the *active* symbol (athame) and the man the *receptive* one (chalice). The ritual thus perfectly symbolizes the interweaving of male and female functions on the various planes. All this reminds us that to call the athame 'male' and the chalice 'female' can be misleading in some contexts, but to call them 'active' and 'receptive' respectively is accurate in all contexts and on all the planes.

5. This is not to imply, of course, that only men make proper artists or poets. But it does seem true that the Muse function is typically a female one. Maybe the woman artist or poet does not need a Muse; it is difficult to envisage a female Robert Graves writing a book called *The White God!* Tom Chetwynd suggests that the Eros side of life (the principle of attraction and involvement) is always represented by a male god 'presumably as the more suitable object of pursuit for women' (or for the anima in man), whereas the Muse (of ideas) and Wisdom 'are both feminine for contrary reasons' – as the treasure sought by man or by the animus in woman. (*A Dictionary of Symbols*, p. 143.) The dark aspect of the Muse is the Siren (*ibid.*, p. 274) – in personal relationships, the woman whose influence on the man's psyche is destructive rather than creative.

6. For some thoughts about the role of Jesus, see pp. 177-8.

7. The Druids seem to have been very pragmatic about this. It is said that they sometimes made actual loans to each other, against IOUs repayable in their next common incarnation.

8. Since all relationships are dynamic, we suppose even soul-mates must have their crises. One of our members has threatened to write an occult novel entitled *The Thousand-Year Itch!*

9. A classic example of the animal group soul, on a small scale, is the beehive. In the case of bees, the 'individual' *is* the hive; the separate insects are differentiated for function much like the cells in a mammal body – queens and workers even starting off as identical eggs. The purposeful behaviour of the hive is entirely a collective one, with its separate component insects being as expendable in the interest of the whole as are outworn cells in the human body. It is much easier to understand bees if you regard the swarm as one complex and very well-adapted organism.

10. Racial, tribal etc. group souls may be said to continue to exist as collective influences even with the accelerating individualization of their members; and these influences may be for good or ill. One of the less admirable features of European occult thinking in the nineteenth and early twentieth centuries was a widespread assumption of the superiority of the European (i.e., white Caucasian) racial soul; many writers and fraternities seemed to take it for granted that it represented the peak of human spiritual evolution so far reached, instead of one contribution among many to that evolution – which is the kindest thing one can truthfully say about any racial soul.

11. An example from our own experience: in October 1972, by which time we felt we had the main outlines of our joint Egyptian incarnation clear, but neither of us had been to Egypt in this life, Stewart had a 'waking dream' about the Egyptian life but was uncertain whether it was genuine. He began to tell Janet, who interrupted and said: 'I've seen that room. Don't describe it – draw a plan of it without showing it to me, then I'll draw a plan, and we'll show them to each other.' The two plans were clearly of the same room, even down to a square pillar in the middle of the same wall having no apparent purpose and no relevance to the story. We realized that telepathy was a possible explanation. But a year later we went to Egypt, and when we visited Luxor temple we were convinced that this was where the incident had happened; and Stewart insisted that the room no longer existed but had been in a set of rooms beyond the temple's surviving rear edge and forming three sides of a rectangle. So we checked with our friend Ahmed Abdel Radi of the Department of Antiquities, who confirmed that the rooms had existed, with the layout Stewart described, but their foundations were now covered by the village streets and houses. This was only one of several confirmations which our Egyptian visit produced.

12. *Many Lifetimes* does, however, put forward one concept not found in the classical theory: namely that the immortal Individuality accumulates a 'wardrobe' (the authors' own simile) of 'supra-physical bodies' from life to life, which seem to correspond to the usual idea of the etheric. The suggestion is that the supra-physical body which shapes and sustains your physical body in this incarnation may be a reactivated one from an earlier incarnation (and not necessarily the immediately preceding one). It may even be one appropriate to an earlier stage in *this* incarnation, unhealthily retained beyond its proper term, and thus giving rise to illness because physical and supra-physical are unmatched. The authors seem to have based successful healing on this theory. It is not necessarily incompatible with the classical theory; the Individuality could carry with it remembered 'blueprints' of earlier etheric bodies, and naturally tend to re-use them – much as a liquid solution of a crystalline substance carries the 'blueprint' from which it rebuilds crystals of characteristic shape and structure. This 'wardrobe' theory would certainly explain the fact that 'fellow-travellers' as remembered from past common incarnations are sometimes (though not always) recalled as visually similar to their present appearance, though it must be admitted that, even when the recall is genuine, this apparent similarity may be psychological projection.

13. Or even from the day after; dreams may often use precognitive material, not necessarily significant in itself, but as the simple 'bricks and mortar' of the manifest content. The classic book on this aspect is J.W. Dunne's *An Experiment with Time*. Our own dream recordings confirm Dunne's assertions about precognitive material in dreams, though we keep an open mind on his theoretical interpretation of the phenomenon.

XIII   The Ethics of Witchcraft

1. So was the teaching of Jesus. What started out as a religion of love and positive behaviour has all too often been transformed, by a monstrous growth of official dogma, into a creaking structure of sectarian bitterness and life-denying prohibitions.

2. Jesus again; he made exactly the same point in his too-little-remembered statement, 'The Kingdom of heaven is within you', and in the parable of the talents.

3. Some witches argue endlessly about whether or not the Cabala should be allowed to 'contaminate' Wicca. A review of our *Eight Sabbats for Witches* in *The Cauldron* said: 'At least it is one book on witchcraft you can tell people to buy without first warning them to ignore the Quabalistic bits!' Some feel the Cabala is too steeped in Judaeo-Christian thinking. Others see it as a useful filing-system for concepts, which can be adapted to Wiccan philosophy as it can to many others; and certainly many witches whose outlook is anything but Judaeo-Christian have so found it. For ourselves, we find it a profound and flexible system which helps us to categorize ideas and their inter-relationships in our own minds, and have no difficulty in relating it to the 'pure' Old Religion. We agree, however, that one should not confuse the two symbol-systems, and we prefer therefore to keep Cabalistic symbolism out of our Wiccan ritual practice. On the other hand (for example) we frequently use the Tree of Life layout in Tarot divination, because it is the most fruitful method we know of pin-pointing the key factors in a complex situation. (See Section XIX.)

4. The Gaia Hypothesis was propounded by two distinguished scientists, Dr James Lovelock FRS and Dr Sidney Epton, in an article in *The New Scientist* of 6 February 1975. They put forward the unconventional proposition that 'Life defines the material conditions needed for its survival and makes sure that they stay there.' They point out that for over 3,500 million years on Earth, 'If the temperature or humidity or salinity or acidity or any one of a number of other variables had strayed outside a narrow range of values for any length of time, life would have been annihilated.' The fact that all these variables *have* stayed within the safe limits (often, as Lovelock and Epton show, against all apparent likelihood) led them to the proposition 'that living matter, the air, the oceans, the land surface were parts of a giant system which was able to control temperature, the composition of the air and sea, the pH of the soil and so on so as to be optimum for the survival of the biosphere. The system seemed to exhibit the behaviour of a single organism, even a living creature. One having such formidable powers deserved a name to match it; William Golding, the novelist, suggested Gaia – the name given by the ancient Greeks to their Earth goddess.' They add that 'In man, Gaia has the equivalent of a central nervous system and an awareness of herself and the rest of the Universe' – and they have some sobering and scientifically backed things to say about the responsibility this places on humanity.

5. The use of the terms 'white', for beneficent, and 'black', for malevolent, magic is traditional, but unfortunate nowadays because of its possible racist misinterpretation. Having had coloured witches in our coven, we hope we are absolved from any such misunderstanding. We use the terms in their accepted magical sense merely because they are immediately understood when talking to non-witches. Some occultists use the terms 'right-hand path' and 'left-hand path' instead; but (a) these are not always understood by the layman, and (b) in Tantra they are used respectively to mean the *Dakshina Marg*, or solar-masculine, and *Vama Marg*, or lunar-feminine, magical principles, and their implications of 'good' or 'bad' seem to be a male-chauvinist corruption of these original meanings. (See Kenneth Grant, *Cults of the Shadow*.)

XIV Myth, Ritual and Symbolism

1. 'Prometheus the stealer of fire, Heracles the dragon slayer, the countless creation myths, the fall from paradise, the mysteries of creation, the virgin birth, the treacherous betrayal of the hero, the dismembering of Osiris, and many other

myths and fairy tales represent psychic processes in symbolic images. Similarly, the figures of the snake, the fish, the sphinx, the helpful animals, the Tree of the World, the Great Mother, the enchanted prince, the *puer aeternus*, the Mage, the Wise Man, Paradise, etc., stand for certain motifs and contents of the collective unconscious.' (Jolande Jacobi, *The Psychology of C.G. Jung*, p. 47.) Just after we wrote this Section, Princess Grace of Monaco died tragically after a car crash. World reaction (especially here in her ancestral Ireland) was understandable; she was a much-loved lady, and rightly so. But its intensity was significant. Grace was, literally, a living legend; she lived out a classic myth for all to see – the peasant's granddaughter who became the modern equivalent of a strolling player and was snatched away by her Prince Charming to be his Princess and rule beside him over their fairytale principality. Her story was archetypal right through – so it hit everyone right there in the Unconscious.

2. That this was the explanation for the phenomenal success of that immortal radio series *The Goon Show* was fully understood by one of its creators, Michael Bentine, himself a very gifted psychic. In his book *The Door Marked Summer* (pp. 197-8) he says: 'To me, it is fascinating that there, for anyone to listen to and think about, is a definitive example of the effect of the simple magical principles of repeated ritualization and its proven ability to evoke instant and potent archetypal images in the minds of the participants in its rites. The Golden Dawn, Stella Matutina (another significant magical group), Royal-Arch Freemasonry, the dark rituals of the Nazis or, for that matter, the beautiful rites of the Tridentine Mass – *all* of them use the same basic principles of mind entrainment by ritualized symbols and deliberately evoked imagery by sound that we (unconsciously) used in the construction of *The Goon Show*.'

XV Witchcraft and Sex

1. The American witch Starhawk, who emphasizes the vital distinction between 'power-over' and 'power-from-within', says: 'I use the word *matristic* ("mother-oriented") rather than "matriarchal" because for many people matriarchy implies a reverse image of patriarchy. Academics debate endlessly about whether cultures ever existed in which women exercised power over men. But the point I am trying to make about Goddess-centred culture is that power was based on a principle different from that under patriarchy.' (*Dreaming the Dark*, p. 229.) She defines magic as 'the art of evoking power-from-within and using it to transform ourselves, our community, our culture, using it to resist the destruction that those who wield power-over are bringing upon the world.' (*Ibid.*, p. xi.)
2. Also perhaps by the women's generally greater shamanistic ability; see pp. 164-5.
3. Among those authorities who did *not* overlook the menstrual sexual peak were Jung himself, C.D. Daly, Mary Jane Sherfey, Alex Comfort, Paula Weideger, William Masters and Virginia Johnson.
4. Shuttle and Redgrove suggest that the symbol of the cervix – the cone with the central depression, or more fully (as it is seen in the speculum) as the round swelling nestling in a crescent – appears more widely than has been recognized. The omphalos is one example; the Assyrian moon-tree, one of the oldest symbols of the Goddess, is another. We know of revered omphaloi in Ireland – from a churchyard one at Kells, Co. Meath, to the many apparently natural 'bullawn stones', boulders with a depression on top where rainwater gathers and is considered to have magical healing properties. We wonder, too, if the disc and

horns of Isis, usually interpreted as being a solar disc within cow's horns, were originally a nestling cervix? (See Plate 13 for all these examples.)
5. 'Only a minority of Irish Catholics fully accept the Church's prohibition on divorce and contraception, according to an article by the Rev. Liam Ryan, professor of sociology at Maynooth, in the monthly review, *The Furrow* .... Only 53 per cent of those with third level education fully accepted papal infallibility' (*The Irish Times*, 6 January 1983). Father Ryan wrote of 'a new type of Catholic, as yet in a minority' which is 'characterised by an informed appreciation of the value of the supernatural and sacramental life of the Church but retains an independence of mind largely on moral matters'. He also found that, although women Catholics reflected more orthodox attitudes than men, 'there was evidence of a closing of the gap among the younger age group.'

A report published on 13 January 1983 by the Laity Commission of England and Wales found that Catholic women there agreed that abortion was wrong in general, but not necessarily in all circumstances. Contraception 'was virtually taken for granted and seen as a matter for individual conscience', and there was a feeling that the Church should recognize that valid marriages sometimes broke down and that it should allow the parties to remarry if they so wished. The report, *Why Can't a Woman be More Like a Man?*, was based on discussions by groups of women specially convened for the purpose in 1976 and 1977, but its publication seems to have been delayed because of misgivings among certain members of the Lay Commission. The women in the groups resented being treated as second-or third-class citizens in the Church, and the report itself called on the Church to 'put its own house in order and undertake a rigorous and thorough examination of its own attitudes towards women. At present these still tend towards the mediaeval.'
6. Even Dion Fortune was not entirely free from this prejudice. Her book *The Esoteric Philosophy of Love and Marriage* is mostly excellent and full of occult wisdom; but she wrote it between the wars, and parts of it reflect the attitudes of the time. And to be fair, the implications of the population explosion were unrealized half a century ago.

XVI   Many Mansions

1. The Sufis maintain that Mohammed also gave an inner teaching ('the Wisdom') to a select few, distinct from the outer teaching transmitted in the Koran ('the Book').

XVII   On Running a Coven

1. There is no need for us to keep repeating 'or established lovers' every time. By 'married couple' we mean a man and woman with a continuing and exclusive sexual relationship, whatever their personal or legal arrangement may be.
2. It is our practice, when Drawing Down the Moon is *not* performed, for the High Priestess to deliver the Charge in its 'she, her, hers' form, instead of the 'I, me, mine' form. This emphasizes the difference and gives special meaning to the first-person form when Drawing Down the Moon *is* performed.

XVII   Naked in Your Rites

1. Gerald Gardner's own attitude to naturism had its roots in the 1920s, long before he became a witch. He was in a Malayan hospital, crippled by synovitis in the knee. Medical treatment dragged on, until he persuaded the ward sister to wheel his bed outdoors where he exposed his leg to the sunshine. His bent leg straightened the same day. 'This near-miracle had far-reaching effects on Gardner's opinions. It made sunshine and fresh air suddenly appear to him as the positive forces they are, instead of the taken-for-granted elements they seem to most of the world. It led him, much later, to accept medical advice and take up nudism seriously. It helped to break down the last vestiges of that late-Victorian stuffiness which had surrounded his childhood. Gardner is an empiricist; sun-heat had worked, and later in his career in Malaya and after he had returned to England, he was often to use its healing and stimulating powers to good effect.' (J.L. Bracelin, *Gerald Gardner: Witch*, p. 67.)
2. For some recipes (and warnings) see Erica Jong's *Witches*, pp. 152-4.

XIX   Clairvoyance and Divination

1. There is some physiological support for this tradition. *Black's Medical Dictionary* (see Bibliography under Thomson) says the pineal body 'is of unknown function, although a body resembling an imperfect third eye is found in its position in some of the lower vertebrate animals, as for example in the lizard Hatteria'.

XX   Astral Projection

1. It may be argued, of course, that telekinesis is etheric rather than astral in nature. Perhaps Kirlian photography can throw light on this?

XXI   Healing

1. The Druids may be credited with the invention of the aspirin, since it was they who discovered the pain-killing properties of salicin, the willow-bark extract which is its ancestor.
2. Whenever a High Priestess (or come to that, a solo worker) senses that superfluous power has been left undischarged, she should make sure that it is 'earthed' before the group disperses or the work is put aside. Nonsense games involving physical movement, in clear contrast with the serious work just completed, are one effective way of doing this. Another simple one is for everybody to go out of doors in bare feet, or to press bare hands against the earth, and to envisage the excess charge leaking away into the ground. A more drastic method is to send the coven on a mile run cross-country in the dark!
3. Another strange phenomenon with epilepsy. Once, when Janet was demonstrating clairvoyant diagnosis to a group, a stranger challenged her to say what was wrong with him. She could pick up nothing. He then removed a silver pendant from his neck and said he was an epileptic; he had found that no psychic could diagnose it when he was wearing silver. With the silver gone, Janet could sense the difference at once. We have had no opportunity to test this on other subjects, but other

sensitives may like to experiment further.

4. The same force is called *chi* in China and *mana* in Hawaii; and growing Western interest in such things has produced other names – *od* (Reichenbach, Germany), *animal magnetism* (Mesmer, Austria), *orgone* (Reich, USA), *bioplasma* (Inyushin, USSR) and *bioenergy* (Thelma Moss and others, USA).

XXIII Self-Initiation

1. In passing, we would suggest that the Christian Apostolic Succession was not thought up by Jesus himself, because it seems alien to the spirit of his teaching, but was an invention of the Pauline establishment for its own hierarchical reasons.
2. If she can learn this and the Cernunnos invocation by heart, so much the better; otherwise she will need one hand to hold the text.
3. See p. 258 in the next section on this addition to the traditional list.

XXV In Tune with the Land

1. See W.B. Crow's *The Arcana of Symbolism*, p. 60, for details of the Four Treasures. They were said to have come from four islands in the ocean, the remains of Atlantis; and it is interesting that the legendary East/South/West/North placings of their origins are the same as those of the elements in the witches' Magic Circle.

Glossary

Akasha, Akashic Principle The all-pervading spiritual 'ether', usually envisaged as violet in colour.

Akashic Records The 'recordings' left in the Akasha by every event. Advanced occultists develop the gift of retrieving past events by 'reading the Akashic Records'.

Alexandrians Witches initiated by (or stemming from those initiated by) Alex and Maxine Sanders. An offshoot of Gardnerian witchcraft, though founded independently.

Amulet An object worn as a protective charm against evil. (See also *Talisman*.)

Anima The buried feminine elements in a man's psyche.

Animus The buried masculine elements in a woman's psyche.

Ankh The *crux ansata* or looped cross, Egyptian hieroglyph for 'life'. Widely used as an occult symbol of the Life Principle.

Aradia Widely used Wiccan name for the Goddess, derived from the Tuscan witches' usage as recorded in C.G. Leland's *Aradia: the Gospel of the Witches* (see Bibliography).

Arcana, Major and Minor The seventy-eight cards of the Tarot (*q.v.*) deck. The Major Arcana are the twenty-two 'trumps'; the Minor Arcana are the fourteen cards of each of the four suits. The word Arcana means 'mysteries' (literally 'closed things').

Archetypes Fundamental elements of the Collective Unconscious which determine our patterns of thinking and behaviour, but which can never be directly defined – only approximately, through symbols.

Arianrhod A Welsh Goddess-name much used by witches. The name means 'Silver Wheel', referring to the circumpolar stars – also known as Caer Arianrhod (the Castle of Arianrhod), symbolic of the resting-place of souls between incarnations.

Astral Body The psychic 'double' of the physical body, consisting of substance more tenuous than matter, but grosser than mind or spirit. (See also *Etheric*.)

Astral Plane The level of reality intermediate between the physical and the mental. It is the level of the emotions and instincts.

Astral Projection The transferring of consciousness from the physical to the astral body, so that one perceives and moves about on the astral plane while the physical body remains inert. It may be involuntary or deliberate.

Athame The witch's black-handled knife. Its use is purely ritual (for which purposes it is interchangeable with the Sword) and it is never used for actual cutting (cf. *White-handled Knife*). It is always a personal tool, belonging to one witch.

Aura The force-field which surrounds the human body, the inner bands at least of which are Etheric (q.v.) in substance. The aura is visible to sensitives, who can learn from its colour, size and structure much about the person's health, emotional state and spiritual development.

Banishing (1) Repelling an unwelcome psychic entity. (2) Short for 'banishing the Circle', dispelling a Magic Circle after it has served its purpose. (3) Expelling a witch from a coven for an offence; he or she may apply for readmission after a year and a day.

Bealtaine, Bealtuinn, Beltane The May Eve/May Day Great Sabbat, normally celebrated on the night of 30 April. The original meaning is 'Bel-fire', after the Celtic or proto-Celtic God variously known as Bel, Beli, Balar, Balor or Belenus. Bealtaine is the Irish Gaelic form, Bealtuinn the Scottish Gaelic, and Beltane the usual anglicized form. In Irish it also means the month of May, and in Scottish, May Day.

Black Mass A deliberate and obscene travesty of the Christian Mass for black magic purposes, which strictly speaking can only be performed by an unfrocked or corrupt priest. It has never been a part of genuine witchcraft.

Boaz The left pillar of Solomon's Temple (I Kings vii:21 and II Chronicles iii:17), making a pair with the right pillar, Jachin. Together they represent the polarized forces of strength and mercy, active and receptive, etc. Boaz and Jachin appear repeatedly in Masonic, Cabalistic and Tarot symbolism.

Bodhisattva A human entity so highly developed that it no longer needs to reincarnate on Earth but chooses to do so in order to help mankind.

Book of Shadows A traditional book of rituals and instructions, copied by hand by each new witch from that of his initiator. Different forms are passed on by the various Wiccan traditions; the Gardnerian Book of Shadows has been mostly widely and publicly quoted and misquoted.

Boomerang Effect A popular name for the well-known occult principle that a psychic attack which comes up against a stronger defence rebounds threefold on the attacker.

'Burning Time' A term used by some witches for the period of persecution of witches (actual or alleged) which reached its height in the sixteenth and seventeenth centuries. Used in reference to England, it is in fact a misnomer; English witches were customarily hanged, not burned, though they were burned in Scotland and on the Continent.

Cabala, Qabala, Kabala The ancient Hebrew system of esoteric philosophy centring upon the Tree of Life (q.v.). Probably the biggest single influence on the Western occult tradition. Modern occult Cabalism is not identical with that of the old Rabbis, but its principles 'are the legitimate descendants thereof and the natural development therefrom' (Dion Fortune).

Candlemas– see *Imbolg.*

Cernunnos, Cerunnos The only known name of the Celtic Horned God; it is much used by witches, in the Cernunnos form.

Cerridwen A Welsh Goddess-name, much used to represent the Mother or Crone aspects.

Chalice– see *Cup.*

Charge, The In Gardnerian/Alexandrian witchcraft and some others the traditional address of the Goddess to her followers, delivered by the High Priestess. The definitive Gardnerian form was written for Gerald Gardner by Doreen Valiente, incorporating his inherited material but replacing some which he had adapted from Aleister Crowley's writings.

Clairaudience, Clairsentience, Clairvoyance The ability to be aware of events, facts or phenomena by psychic means. The term 'clairvoyance' is loosely used to cover all forms of this; but strictly speaking it is clairvoyance when the impressions are received as visual images, clairsentience when they are felt as bodily sensations, and clairaudience when they are heard as words, music or other sounds.

Cone of Power The collective psychic charge built up by a coven at work, visualized as a cone whose base is the circle of witches and whose apex is above the centre of that circle.

Coven An organized group of witches, meeting and working regularly together.

Covenstead A coven's normal place of meeting.

Craft, The The witches' name for the religion and practice of witchcraft, and its followers.

Cup, Chalice One of the four elemental tools, representing the Water element.

Deosil In a clockwise or sunwise direction. (Cf. *Widdershins*.)

Divination The art of obtaining psychic information with the help of physical accessories such as Tarot cards, a crystal ball or a pendulum. It might be called 'clairvoyance using tools'.

Drawing Down the Moon Invocation of the Goddess aspect into the High Priestess by the High Priest.

Drawing Down the Sun Invocation of the God aspect into the High Priest by the High Priestess.

Ego The conscious part of the human psyche.

Elders The third-degree and second-degree members of a coven.

Elemental A primitive non-human and non-material entity, of the nature of one of the four Elements (q.v.). The term is also used for a human thought-form which, spontaneously by strong emotion or deliberately by mental effort, is split off from its human originator and acquires temporary quasi-independent existence. 'Created elementals' of the latter kind can be given healing work to do; they are also sometimes used maliciously for psychic persecution.

Elements Earth, air, fire and water – plus spirit which includes and integrates them all. These are regarded as realms or categories of Nature – the basic modes of existence and action. They are not to be confused with the physicist's table of elements, which the witch of course accepts in their relevant context.

Equinoxes– see *Sabbats*.

Esbat A coven meeting other than one of the eight seasonal festivals or Sabbats (q.v.).

Etheric Body A structure intermediate between the Astral Body (q.v.) and the physical body. It is an energy-network which links the physical body to the corresponding astral, mental and spiritual bodies, and thus literally keeps it alive.

Etheric Plane The energy-level, intermediate between the astral and physical, on which the Etheric Body (q.v.) functions.

Evocation The summoning of a non-material entity of a lower order of being than oneself. (Cf. *Invocation*.)

Exorcism The expulsion, by psychic means, of an unwelcome entity from a person or place which it is influencing or possessing.

Familiar An animal kept by a witch for the psychic help it can give; cats, dogs and horses in particular react very sensitively to negative influences, supplying early warning or corroborative evidence. Their human 'owners' (or rather, partners) are careful to give them psychic protection in return. Certain kinds of deliberately created and maintained thought-forms may also be called familiars.

Festival One of the eight seasonal Sabbats (q.v.).

Fetch (1) 'The apparition, double, or wraith of a living person' (*Oxford English Dictionary*). (2) A projected astral body or thought-form deliberately sent out to make its presence known to a particular person. (3) A witch (usually male) sent out by a High Priestess as a confidential messenger or escort; sometimes called the Summoner or the Officer.

Fivefold Kiss, Fivefold Salute The witches' ritual salute, man-to-woman or woman-to-man, with kisses (1) on each foot, (2) on each knee, (3) on the lower belly, (4) on each breast and (5) on the lips – really eight kisses in all. It is only used within the Circle.

Gardnerians Witches initiated by (or stemming from those initiated by) Gerald Gardner or one of his High Priestesses. There are also many witches today who practise the Gardnerian system but whose initiation does not ultimately derive from Gardner's coven, and it would be sectarian not to call them Gardnerians.

Gnome The traditional name for an Elemental (q.v.) spirit of the nature of the Earth element.

Golden Dawn An occult Order founded in London in 1887 by three Rosicrucians, which became a major influence in Western ritual magic. Its rituals (partly written by the poet W.B. Yeats, who was a prominent member) are basically Cabalistic, with elements of the Chaldean Oracles, the Egyptian Book of the Dead and Blake's Prophetic Books. They were later published in full, under the title *The Golden Dawn*, by Israel Regardie (see Bibliography).

Great Rite In Wicca, the major ritual of male-female polarity, which is also the third-degree initiation rite. It can be either symbolic, in the presence of the coven, or 'actual' – i.e., involving intercourse – in which case it is always conducted in private. In our tradition, only a married couple or established lovers may perform the 'actual' Great Rite together.

Greater Sabbat– see *Sabbats*.

Grimoire A (usually mediaeval) book or 'grammar' of magical procedures. The most famous is *The Greater Key of Solomon the King*, generally known as *The Key of Solomon* (see Bibliography under Mathers).

Hallowe'en – see *Samhain*.

Handfasting A Wiccan wedding ritual. (See *Eight Sabbats for Witches*, Section XIII.)

Hereditaries Witches who claim a continuous family tradition and practice of the Craft, from long before the current revival.

Herne A British God-name, the best-known manifestation of whom is Herne the Hunter, leader of the legendary Wild Hunt in Windsor Great Park. The name may derive from the same original as Cernunnos (q.v.).

Hexagram (1) A six-pointed star, formed by two interlaced equilateral triangles. It is generally called the Star of David in non-occult circles, but its use as an occult symbol is far older than its use as a badge of Judaism. It signifies the Hermetic principle of 'as above, so below'. (See *Macrocosm*.) (2) Any one of the six-line figures of the I Ching (q.v.).

High Priest (1) The male leader of a coven, partner of the High Priestess who is the overall leader. (2) Any second-degree or third-degree male witch. (The distinction is between a coven *function* and a personal *rank*.)

High Priestess (1) The female leader (and overall leader) of a coven. (2) Any second-degree or third-degree female witch. (The distinction is between a coven *function* and a personal *rank*.)

Hiving Off The process whereby two or more members leave their parent coven to form their own coven.

Holly King In the folklore of many parts of Europe, including the British Isles, the God of the Waning Year. At the Summer Solstice he 'slays' his twin, the Oak King, God of the Waxing Year; and at the Winter Solstice the Oak King is revived to 'slay' the Holly King in turn. Oak King and Holly King are each other's 'other self', in an eternal cycle of death and rebirth.

I Ching A Chinese system of divination involving sixty-four 'hexagrams' or six-line combinations of unbroken (*yang*) and broken (*yin*) lines. It is one of the few categories of Eastern esoteric learning which transfer wholly satisfactorily to the West, without risk of cross-cultural confusion, and it is widely used here.

Imbolg, Imbolc, Oimelc The early Spring Great Sabbat, celebrated on 2 February. It is often known by the name of its Christian equivalent, Candlemas. The name in Gaelic means 'in the belly' – the first stirrings in the womb of Mother Earth.

Incarnation The manifestations of a living entity into physical form; specifically, any one of the earthly lives of an immortal human Individuality (q.v.) in the continuing Reincarnation (q.v.) process.

Individuality The immortal, reincarnating part of a human being, consisting of the Upper Spiritual, Lower Spiritual and Upper Mental levels; contrasted with the Personality, which consists of the Lower Mental, Upper Astral, Lower Astral, Etheric and Physical levels, and which only persists for one Incarnation (q.v.), a new Personality being built up around the immortal Individuality for each Incarnation. (See also *Reincarnation*.)

Inner Planes Other levels of being and consciousness than the physical or the 'normal' Ego-consciousness.

Invocation The summoning (or more properly, invitation) of a non-material entity of a higher order of being than oneself. (Cf. *Evocation*.)

Jachin —see *Boaz*.

Kabala —see *Cabala*.

Karma The 'spiritual bank balance' carried by the Individuality (q.v.) from one Incarnation (q.v.) to the next. The literal meaning of the word is 'action' or 'cause-and-effect'.

Karnayna Alexandrian (q.v.) form of the God-name Cernunnos (q.v.).

Keridwen − see *Ceridwen*.

Kernunnos − see *Cernunnos*.

Lammas − see *Lughnasadh*.

Left-Brain Function The linear-logical, word-and-number-using, analysing, basically masculine function of the left hemisphere of the brain, which also controls the right side of the body; balanced by the right-brain function, the intuitive, image-forming, synthesizing, basically feminine function of the right hemisphere of the brain, which also controls the left side of the body.

Left-Hand Path Generally used to mean black-magic working, but this is really a corruption of its original Tantric meaning (see note 5 on p. 312).

Lesser Sabbats − see *Sabbats*.

Lughnasadh The August-Eve Great Sabbat, normally celebrated on 31 July. Its name means 'festival of Lugh', the Celtic God of Light. It is also sometimes called Lammas after its Christian equivalent, and it is associated with the harvest. Lúnasa is the Irish Gaelic name for the month of August, and Lunasda or Lunasdal the Scottish Gaelic name for Lammas, 1 August. The Manx for Lammas Day is Laa Luanys or Laa Lunys.

Macrocosm The Cosmos as a whole, in relation to the Microcosm, its detailed manifestation (the human being in particular). In accordance with the Hermetic principle 'as above, so below', the Microcosm is of the same essence as the Macrocosm and reflects its nature.

Magic(k) 'The Science and Art of causing Change to occur in conformity with Will' (Aleister Crowley). Crowley added the 'k' to distinguish true magic from the debased, escape-from-reality concept of magic, and many occultists have adopted this usage.

Magus In general, a male occult adept. In Wiccan usage, a second-degree or third-degree male witch.

Maiden In a coven, the Assistant High Priestess for ritual purposes, who may or may not be the High Priestess's deputy in leadership. In earlier times, the title of Maiden was sometimes applied to the leader whom we would now call the High Priestess.

Manifestation The product on one level of being of a phenomenon or entity already existing on a higher level. Thus physical Nature is a manifestation of creative Divinity; the Earth itself may be regarded as a manifestation of the Mother Goddess principle; and on a much lower level, a seen ghost, or a poltergeist phenomenon, is a visual or physical manifestation of an entity or activity on the astral plane.

Measure In Wicca, the thread with which a first-degree initiate's bodily dimensions are ritually recorded as a symbol of his or her loyalty to the coven.

Microcosm – see *Macrocosm.*

Neophyte, Postulant A newcomer to the coven, awaiting initiation.

Oak King – see *Holly King.*

Officer – see *Fetch.*

Oimelc – see *Imbolg.*

Pentacle One of the four elemental tools; an engraved disc representing the Earth's element. It is normally the centrepiece of a Wiccan altar.

Pentagram A five-pointed star. An upright pentagram (i.e., with a single point uppermost) represents (1) a human being (astride with arms outstretched) or (2) the four Elements (q.v.) governed by the fifth, Spirit. An inverted pentagram (i.e., with a single point downwards) represents Spirit still subservient to the four Elements; it is generally seen as a black magic symbol, except when it is used as the symbol of a second-degree initiate, the implication there being that he or she is still on the way to full development.

Persona The 'comforting cloak' of the Ego (q.v.); the self-image which the Ego builds up to reassure itself and to present to the world.

Personality – see *Individuality.*

Planes The various levels of being and activity – Spiritual, Mental, Astral, Etheric and Physical.

Postulant – see *Neophyte.*

Prâna The vital force of the Cosmos as it operates on the Etheric level; it permeates this and other solar systems, and every living organism is charged with a concentration of it.

Precognition Psychic awareness of future events.

Priest, Priestess Every initiated witch is regarded as a priest or priestess, the priest-function being seen as inherent in every human being who is prepared to activate it.

Projection The psychological mechanism of subconsciously crediting (or discrediting) another person with qualities or shortcomings which are in fact elements of one's own psyche, so that one can confront them while avoiding the truth that one is really confronting oneself. (See also *Astral Projection*).

Psyche The total non-physical make-up of a human being.

Psychometry The psychic 'reading' of a material object, and its associations and history, by handling it.

Qabala – see *Cabala.*

Reincarnation The process, generally believed in by witches and many others, whereby each immortal human Individuality (q.v.) is reborn to life after life on Earth until all of its Karma (q.v.) is worked out and balanced, and it is sufficiently highly developed to progress to a higher stage. (See also *Incarnation, Bodhisattva*.)

Right-Brain Function – see *Left-Brain Function.*

Right-Hand Path Generally used to mean white-magic working, as opposed to the Left-Hand Path of black-magic working; but these are really corruptions of the original Tantric meanings (see note 5, p.312).

Rune (1) A letter or character of the earliest Teutonic alphabet traditionally regarded as being magical. (2) A magical song or chant, as the Witches' Rune (q.v.). The word *rún* in Old Norse and Old English meant 'whisper, secret counsel, mystery', in Irish and Scottish Gaelic it still means 'secret, mystery;.

Sabbats The eight seasonal festivals celebrated by witches and by many others. In order through the calendar year, they are: Imbolg (q.v.) 2 February; Spring Equinox 21 March; Bealtaine (q.v.) 30 April; Midsummer Solstice 22 June; Lughnasadh (q.v.) 31 July; Autumn Equinox 21 September; Samhain (q.v.) 31 October; and the Winter Solstice or Yule (q.v.) 22 December. Imbolg, Bealtaine, Lughnasadh and Samhain are known as the Greater Sabbats, and the Solstices and

Equinoxes as the Lesser Sabbats. The dates for observing the Lesser Sabbats may vary slightly in different traditions, and the actual dates of the Equinoxes and Solstices do vary, by a day at most, from year to year in astronomical fact.

Salamander The traditional name for an Elemental (q.v.) spirit of the nature of the Fire element.

Salt Used in many magical procedures, including Wiccan, as a kind of spiritual antiseptic, or purifying symbol.

Samhain The Hallowe'en Great Sabbat, celebrated on 31 October. In Celtic tradition, it is the start of the new year, and also of winter – Bealtaine (q.v.) being the beginning of summer; the pastoral Celts only recognized two seasons. Samhain is particularly associated with the contacting of dead friends. The origin of the words seem uncertain, though it may relate to the Gaelic verb *sámhaim*, 'to quiet down, become silent'.

Scrying Any form of divination which involves gazing at or into something (crystal ball, black mirror, pool of ink etc.) to induce psychically perceived visual images.

Self The true essence of the human psyche; the integrated individuality towards which all constructive psychic development strives.

Sephira (plural Sephiroth) Any one of the ten spheres on the Tree of Life (q.v.), the central concept of the Cabala (q.v.).

Shadow The buried, unconscious elements of the human psyche; everything except the Ego (q.v.) and the Persona (q.v.).

Shaman, shamaness A priest or priestess who communicates with the inner planes by self-induced trance. Originally a North Asiatic tribal word, it has come to be used to describe such functionaries in other cultures.

Sigil An occult seal or sign. It should be pronounced to rhyme with 'vigil'.

Skyclad The witches' word for 'ritually naked'.

Solstices – see *Sabbats*, also *Yule*.

Soul-mates Individuals (q.v.) who are continuously involved with each other in successive Incarnations (q.v.), becoming rather like a pair of binary stars. Also known as twin souls.

Summerlands A spiritualist word for the Heaven which souls enter after death. Often used by believers in Reincarnation (q.v.) to denote the astral stage of rest after physical death, before the Individuality (q.v.) withdraws from all the lower levels to prepare for its next Incarnation (q.v.).

Summoner – see *Fetch*

Sword One of the four elemental tools, representing the Fire element – or in some traditions, the Air element.

Sylph The traditional name for an Elemental (q.v.) spirit of the nature of the Air element.

Synchronicity Jung's term for 'meaningful coincidence', an acausal connecting principle for which he brought forward much evidence. His discussion of the subject (see Bibliography) is of great interest to all occultists.

Talisman An object, similar to an Amulet (q.v.) but more specific and often constructive and not merely protective. It is designed for a particular individual and purpose, making the maximum use of appropriate symbols.

Tarot A pack of cards, the earliest known examples of which are about thirteenth century, used for divination and meditation. It consists of twenty-two Major Arcana or Trumps, each symbolizing an archetypal concept, and fifty-six Minor Arcana, divided into four suits of fourteen cards each – Cups, Wands, Pentacles and Swords, representing the four elements. Many designs are available nowadays, the most widely accepted standard pack being the Rider (or Waite) Deck. The modern pack of ordinary playing cards descended from the Tarot, all the Major Arcana having disappeared from it except the Fool, who survives as the Joker; and one court card (the Knight) having disappeared from each suit of the Minor Arcana; Cups have become Hearts, Wands Clubs, Pentacles Diamonds and Swords Spades.

Telekinesis The power of moving physical objects by purely psychic effort.

Temple A coven's ritual meeting-place which is used for no other purpose; a desirable asset but not indispensable, since a Magic Circle may be cast anywhere.

Traditionals Witches who follow traditions which they (or their predecessors) were keeping in being before the Gardnerian (q.v.) revival. They overlap with the Hereditaries (q.v.).

Tree of Life The central glyph or diagram of the Cabala (q.v.). It consists of ten interconnected spheres of Sephiroth (singular Sephira), each representing a category of cosmic being and activity, from Kether (the Crown, pure existence) down to Malkuth (the Kingdom, physical manifestation). It also represents the involution from the ultimate Divine principle of Kether into material manifestation, and the evolution from Malkuth back to the source, enriched by the experience of the whole cycle. Any macrocosmic or microcosmic phenomenon or condition can be related to one of the Sephiroth, and the Tree is of great help in understanding their interactions.

Tuathal – see *Widdershins*.

Twin Souls – see *Soul-Mates*.

Unconscious That part of the human psyche not directly available to the conscious Ego (q.v.). It comprises the Collective Unconscious, which is common to the whole human race and which is the home of the Archetypes (q.v.), and the Personal Unconscious, which is all the buried elements of the individual's experience. Constant improvement of communication between the Ego and the Unconscious is the aim of all psychic development, and the basis of all magical work.

Undine The traditional name for an Elemental (q.v.) spirit of the nature of the Water element.

Vampirism The draining of psychic energy from one individual by another.

Voiding the Coven The stage where a new coven refrains from working magically with the coven from which it hived off, until its own identity is firmly established.

Walpurgis Night – see *Bealtaine*.

Wand One of the four elemental tools, representing the Air element – or, in some traditions, the Fire element.

Watchtowers The four cardinal points, regarded as guardians of the Magic Circle.

White-handled Knife A ritual knife for use within the Magic Circle whenever actual cutting or inscribing is called for – this being forbidden for the Athame (q.v.).

Wicca The usual witches' name for the Craft (q.v.). It derives from the Old English *wiccian*, 'to practise witchcraft'. It is a slight mis-derivation, since *wicca* in Old English meant 'a male witch' (and *wicce* 'a female witch'). The actual Old English for witchcraft was *wiccacræft*. But the present usage is now long-established and there is every reason why it should continue.

Wiccaning In Wicca, the ritual blessing of a newly born baby; it is the witches' equivalent of a christening, except that it is not intended to commit the child permanently to any one path, since that should be the individual's adult decision. (See *Eight Sabbats for Witches*, Section XII.)

Widdershins In an anti-clockwise direction, against the sun (cf. *Deosil*). This is a Teutonic word (Middle High German *Widersinnes*); the Gaelic equivalent is Tuathal.

Witch Queen A High Priestess from whose coven at least two other covens have hived off.

Witch's Ladder A string of forty beads, or a cord with forty knots, used (like a rosary) as an aid to concentrated repetition without the need for actual counting.

Witches' Rune A power-raising chant accompanied by a ring dance. The words used by Gardnerians and Alexandrians will be found on p. 299 of Appendix B; they were composed by Doreen Valiente and Gerald Gardner together.

Yule The Winter Solstice Sabbat, celebrated on 22 December. Its central theme is a welcome to the reborn Sun.

Bibliography

Adler, Margot – *Drawing Down the Moon* (Beacon Press, Boston, 1981).

Ashe, Geoffrey – *The Finger and the Moon* (Heinemann, London, 1973; paperback Panther Books, St Albans, 1975).

Bagnall, Oscar – *The Origin and Properties of the Human Aura* (University Books, New York, 1970).

Baker, Douglas M. – *The Techniques of Astral Projection* (Douglas Baker, Essendon, Herts., undated).

Barrett, Francis – *The Magus* (originally published 1801; facsimile reprint Vance Harvey Publishing, Leicester, 1970).

Bentine, Michael – *The Door Marked Summer* (Granada, St Albans, 1981).

Bernstein, Morey – *The Search for Bridey Murphy* (Doubleday, New York, 1956).

Bourne, Lois – *Witch Amongst Us* (Satellite Books, London, 1979).

Bracelin, J.L. – *Gerald Gardner: Witch* (Octagon Press, London, 1960).

Brennan, J.H. – *Reincarnation: Five Keys to Past Lives* (Aquarian Press, London, 1971).

Buckland, Raymond – *The Tree, the Complete Book of Saxon Witchcraft* (Weiser, New York, 1974).

Burton, Maurice – *The Sixth Sense of Animals* (J.M. Dent, London, 1973).

Butler, Bill – *The Definitive Tarot* (Rider, London, 1975).

Carrington, Hereward & Muldoon, Sylvan – *The Projection of the Astral Body* (Rider, London, 1929).

Chetwynd, Tom – *A Dictionary of Symbols* (Granada, St Albans, 1982).

Crow, W.B. – *The Arcana of Symbolism* (Aquarian Press, London, 1970).

Crowley, Aleister – *777 Revised* (Neptune Press, London, 1952). *Magick* (Routledge & Kegan Paul, London, 1973). *The Book of Thoth* (Shambala Publications, Berkely, Calif., 1969).

Crowther, Patricia – *Witch Blood* (House of Collectibles, New York, 1974). *Lid Off the Cauldron* (Muller, London, 1981). *Witchcraft in*

Yorkshire (Dalesman Books, York, 1973).

Crowther, Patricia & Arnold – *The Witches Speak* (Athol Publications, Douglas, IOM, 1965; Weiser, New York, 1976). *The Secrets of Ancient Witchcraft* (University Books, Secausus NJ, 1974).

Culpeper, Nicholas – *Culpeper's Complete Herbal* (seventeenth century; current reprint W. Foulsham, London).

Deren, Maya – *Divine Horsemen* (Thames & Hudson, London, 1953; reprinted in paperback as *The Voodoo Gods*, Paladin, St Albans, 1975).

Dunne, J.W. – *An Experiment with Time* (Faber, London, 1939; paperback Hillary, New York, 1958).

Durdin-Robertson, Lawrence – *Juno Covella, Perpetual Calendar of the Fellowship of Isis* (Cesara Publications, Enniscorthy, Co. Wexford, 1982).

Drury, Nevill & Tillett, Gregory – *Other Temples Other Gods – the Occult in Australia* (Methuen Australia, Sydney, 1980).

Eliot, Roger – *Who Were You?* (Granada, St Albans, 1981).

Farrar, Janet & Stewart – *Eight Sabbats for Witches* (Robert Hale, London, 1981).

Farrar, Stewart – *What Witches Do* (originally published 1971; 2nd edition, Phoenix Publishing, Custer, Wa. 1983. Spanish edition *Lo que Hacen las Brujas*, Ediciones Martinez Roca, Barcelona, 1977).

Fiore, Dr Edith – *You Have Been Here Before* (Coward, McCann & Geoghegan, New York, 1978).

Fortune, Dion– *The Sea Priestess* (Aquarian Press, London, 1957; paperback Wyndham Publications, London, 1976). *Moon Magic* (Aquarian Press, London, 1956; paperback Wyndham Publications, London 1976). *The Cosmic Doctrine* (Helios Book Service, Toddington, Glos., 1966). *The Esoteric Philosophy of Love and Marriage* (4th edition, Aquarian Press, London, 1967). *The Mystical Qabala* (Benn, London, 1935). *Aspects of Occultism* (Aquarian Press, London, 1930). *The Secrets of Dr Taverner* (3rd enlarged edition, Llewellyn Publications, St Paul, Minn., 1979).

Gardner, Gerald B. – *High Magic's Aid* (Houghton, London, 1949). *Witchcraft Today* (Rider, London, 1954). *The Meaning of Witchcraft* (Aquarian Press, London, 1959).

Glaskin, G.M. – *Windows of the Mind* (Wildwood House, London, 1974; paperback Arrow, London, 1975).

Glass, Justine – *Witchcraft, the Sixth Sense – and Us* (Spearman, London, 1965).

Grant, Joan – *Winged Pharaoh* (Methuen, London, 1937; paperback Sphere Books, London 1981). *Life as Carola* (Methuen, London, 1939: paperback Corgi, London, 1976).

Grant, Joan & Kelsey, Denys – *Many Lifetimes* (Gollancz, London, *1969; paperback Corgi, London, 1976).*

Grant, Kenneth – *Cults of the Shadow* (Muller, London, 1975).

Graves, Robert – *The White Goddess* (3rd edition, Faber, London, hardback 1952, paperback 1961).

Graves, Tom – *Dowsing: Techniques and Applications* (Turnstone, London, 1976). *Needles of Stone* (Turnstone, London, 1978).

Gray, Eden – *A Complete Guide to the Tarot* (Studio Vista, London, 1970).

Grieve, Mrs M. – *A Modern Herbal* (Cape, London, 1931; paperback Peregrine, Harmondsworth, Middx., 1976).

Guirdham, Arthur – *The Cathars and Reincarnation* (Spearman, London, 1970).

Harding, M. Esther – *Woman's Mysteries* (Rider, London, 1971).

Hartley, Christine – *A Case for Reincarnation* (Robert Hale, London, 1972).

Iredale, David – *Discovering Your Family Tree* (Shire Publications, Aylesbury, Bucks., 1977).

Iverson, Jeffrey – *More Lives than One* (Souvenir Press, London, 1976; paperback Pan, London, 1977).

Jacobi, Jolande – *The Psychology of C.G. Jung* (7th edition, Routledge & Kegan Paul, London, 1968).

Johns, June – *King of the Witches: the World of Alex Sanders* (Peter Davies, London, 1969).

Jong, Erica – *Witches*, illustrated by Joseph A. Smith (Granada, London, 1981).

Jung, Carl G. – *Collected Works*, vol. 9, 2nd edition (Routledge & Kegan Paul, London, 1968). *Four Archetypes – Mother, Rebirth, Spirit, Trickster* (Routledge & Kegan Paul, London, 1972). *Synchronicity, an Acausal Connecting Principle* (Routledge & Kegan Paul, London, 1955). – (editor) *Man and His Symbols* (Aldus, London, 1969).

Kilner, W.J. – *The Aura* (paperback Weiser, New York, 1973; originally published 1911 as *The Human Atmosphere*).

King, Francis – *The Secret Rituals of the O.T.O.* (C.W. Daniel, London, 1973).

King, Francis & Skinner, Stephen – *Techniques of High Magic* (C.W. Daniel, London, undated).

Kung, Hans – *Infallible?* (Collins, London; Fontana hardback, 1972; Fount paperback, 1977).

Langley, Noel – *Edgar Cayce on Reincarnation* (Paperback Library, New York, 1968).

Leland, Charles G. – *Aradia: the Gospel of the Witches*, introduced by Stewart Farrar (C.W. Daniel, London, 1974).

McIntyre, Joan (assembled by) – *Mind in the Waters, A Book to Celebrate the Consciousness of Whales and Dolphins* (Scribner, New York, and Sierra Club Books, San Francisco, 1974).

Markdale, Jean – *Women of the Celts (Cremonesi, London, 1975).*

Martin, W. Keble – *The Concise British Flora in Colour* (3rd edition, Ebury Press and Michael Joseph, London, 1974).

Massey, Gerald – *The Natural Genesis* (first published 1883, 2 vols.; Weiser, New York, 1974).

Mathers, S. Lidell MacGregor (translator and editor) – *The Key of Solomon the King (Clavicula Solomonis)* (Originally published 1888; Routledge & Kegan Paul, London, 1972).

Moody, Raymond A. – *Life After Life* (Mockingbird Book, Covington, Ga., 1975).

Moore, Marcia – *Hypersentience* (Crown, New York, 1976).

Moss, Peter with Keeton, Joe – *Encounters with the Past* (Sidgwick & Jackson, London, 1979).

Moss, Thelma – *The Body Electric* (Granada, St Albans, 1981).

Murray, Margaret A. – *The God of the Witches* (first published 1931; paperback Daimon Press, Castle Hedingham, Essex, 1962).

Neumann, Erich – *The Great Mother* (2nd edition, Routledge & Kegan Paul, London, 1963).

Ophiel – *The Art and Practice of Astral Projection* (Peach Publishing, San Francisco, 1961).

Phillips, Roger – *Wild Flowers of Britain* (Pan, London, 1977).

Powell, Arthur E. – *The Etheric Double* (Theosophical Publishing House, London, 1925; reprint with Foreword, 1969).

Raine, Kathleen – *Yeats, the Tarot and the Golden Dawn* (Dolmen, Dublin, 1972).

Regardie, Israel – *The Golden Dawn* (4 vols., 3rd edition, Hazel Hills Corpn., River Falls, Wis., 1970.) *How to Make and Use Talismans* 2nd edition (Paths to Inner Power series, Aquarian Press, London, 1981).

Russell, Jeffrey B. – *A History of Witchcraft, Sorcery, Heretics and Pagans* (Thames & Hudson, London, 1980).

Santesson, Hans Stefan – *Reincarnation* (Universal Publishing & Distributing Corpn., New York, 1969, and Universal-Tandem Publishing, London, 1970).

Schulman, Martin – *Karmic Astrology*, Vols. I-IV (Aquarian Press, Wellingborough, Northants, 1975 onwards).

Schwartz, Stephan A. – *The Secret Vaults of Time* (Grosset & Dunlap, New York, 1978).

Shuttle, Penelope & Redgrove, Peter – *The Wise Wound: Menstruation and Everywoman* (Gollancz, London, 1978; 2nd edition, Paladin, London, 1986).

Sprenger, Jakob & Kramer, Heinrich – *Malleus Maleficarum* (first printed 1486; paperback Arrow, London, 1971).

Starhawk – *The Spiral Dance* (Harper & Row, New York, 1979). *Dreaming the Dark* (Beacon Press, Boston, Mass., 1982).

Targ, Russell & Puthoff, Harold – *Mind Reach* (Cape, London, 1977; paperback Granada, St Albans, 1978).

Thomson, William A.R. – *Black's Medical Dictionary* (A. & C. Black, London, 1948; updated every two or three years since).

Valiente, Doreen – *Where Witchcraft Lives* (Aquarian Press, London, 1962). *An ABC of Witchcraft Past and Present* (Robert Hale, London, 1973). *Natural Magic* (Robert Hale, London, 1975). *Witchcraft for Tomorrow* (Robert Hale, London, 1978).

Waite, Arthur E. – *The Pictorial Key to the Tarot* (University Books, New York, 1960).

Watson, Lyall – *Supernature* (Hodder & Stoughton, London, 1973; paperback Coronet, Aylesbury, Bucks., 1974).

Weideger, Paula – *Menstruation and Menopause* (Knopf, New York, 1975).

Wilhelm, Richard (translator) – *The I Ching or Book of Changes*, rendered into English by Caryl F. Baynes, with Foreword by C.G. Jung (3rd edition, Routledge & Kegan Paul, London, 1968).

Wren, R.W. – *Potter's New Cyclopaedia of Botanical Drugs and Preparations* (7th edition, Health Science Press, Rustington, Sussex, 1956).

Index